Date: 6/5/19

BIO REAGAN
Schweikart, Larry,
Reagan : the American
president /

D1410487

REAGAN

THE AMERICAN PRESIDENT

REAGAN

THE AMERICAN PRESIDENT

LARRY SCHWEIKART

Post Hill
PRESS

A POST HILL PRESS BOOK

Reagan:
The American President
© 2019 by Larry Schweikart
All Rights Reserved

ISBN: 978-1-64293-082-5
ISBN (eBook): 978-1-64293-083-2

Cover art by Cody Corcoran
Book design and production by Greg Johnson, Textbook Perfect

Post Hill Press
New York • Nashville
posthillpress.com

Published in the United States of America

Contents

Introduction

No angelic choirs sang; no star in the East seduced curious magi to snowy Tampico, Illinois, the night Ronald Wilson Reagan was born, contrary to the mythology of some biographers. His father only differentiated that night from the birth of his other son, Neil, by blurting out that the newborn had a face as red as a Dutchman's, bequeathing a nickname that stuck with Ronald his entire life. Dutch's entrance into this world was not charged by supernatural signs, nor, as he grew up, was his life characterized by the typical trappings of one destined for the list of history's greatest names. His family lacked wealth, connections, or prestige. As a young man he didn't attend Harvard or Yale, and he was not a lawyer—often seen as the defining profession for a politician.

It was, in fact, precisely the absence of these elements that provided young Ronald Reagan with the most normal of lives, and even when his career elevated him to movie star status, his position as the head of a major American labor union once again placed him closer to the experiences of ordinary people than the vast majority of the politicians with whom he soon circulated. By a sequence of life steps, Reagan embodied almost every touchstone of a typical American: he worked at low-level jobs like lifeguard and radio announcer; he went to an unknown school and had marginal grades; he experienced a failed marriage; when forced out of one career path, he reinvented himself in another and then another; he served in the military; he was a born-again Christian when it was common; he was a member of a labor union. These remarkable twists and turns made Reagan unique among all American presidents, for he was the first to ever lead a student strike, the first to be divorced, the first to be in a union, and the first actor-president. And these characteristics combined with a natural talent for remembering lines, for geniality, for genuine Christian charity and concern, for self-deprecation, for personal heroism, and, yes, for some necessary self-promotion to magnify and then reflect his lifetime back on ordinary American voters. Why did Reagan "connect?" How could he not?

In 2016, when pundits and experts were dumbfounded at the success of a new, very different version of Reagan—Donald Trump—the perceptive among them would admit there were very many similarities, especially when speaking to, and for, the common man. In his speeches, Reagan often referred to "Joe America," and in his inaugural address, Trump said to the Republican convention and all ordinary, forgotten Americans, "I am your voice." Their backgrounds were hardly identical, but the appeal was very much the same: Trump, the glamorous billionaire; Reagan the glamorous movie star. Critics would claim Trump was brash and reckless, forgetting that Reagan, while using a self-effacing humor as a sword ("Well, there you go again!"), was often attacked as even more reckless. One biographer claimed Reagan was "sleepwalking through history."

Occasionally in American history, an "insider" with the proper credentials, with wealth, and with all the chips on his side can leap the chasm to the average person. Teddy Roosevelt did it, his cousin Franklin did it, and John Kennedy did it. Far more often, the gap remains, bridged by respect, but seldom love. Ronald Reagan elicited the affection that was seen in the lives of the presidents who were viewed as men of the people: Andrew Jackson; Abraham Lincoln; and Harry Truman. America's love and respect was on full display upon Reagan's death when his viewing produced endless lines, and the procession to his final resting place along California highways saw crowds with signs standing as adoring sentinels, mile after mile; then again in Washington, DC, when the lines of mourners shocked the journalists who thought Reagan incompetent or even dangerous.

Of course, when it comes to the need for a new Reagan biography, the question is "Why? Who needs one?" Despite some excellent work during

Reagan's life and after his passing, no biography has yet captured the man and his ideas. Indeed, with once-in-a-lifetime access to the Gipper and his family, British author Edmund Morris so utterly failed to understand Reagan that he concluded he was impenetrable. Existing biographies not only lacked the paper support in some cases (relying heavily on interviews with Reagan staff, friends, and family) but usually failed to grasp Reagan's key intellectual secret, which was his holistic view of the world. To the Gipper, there was not "domestic policy" and "foreign policy," nor was there a separation of energy, commerce, civil rights, or defense. It was *all* part of a tightly woven worldview that demanded a resurgence of American power while at the same time fostering a massive recovery in the American economy. As an example: the 1981 sale of AWACS aircraft to Saudi Arabia was not merely a negotiation to ensure some sort of balanced approach in the Middle East. It was a clear quid pro quo for the Saudis to cut prices and increase oil production as soon as possible. And Reagan viewed that, in turn, as a triple set of policy objectives: lowering prices for Americans and thereby increasing economic productivity; reducing inflation and thereby strengthening American family purchasing power; and driving down the price of Russian oil, which in turn meant depriving the USSR of a major source of hard currency at the most critical time.

One could take almost any policy of Reagan's and see a rich tapestry of layers, threading through every department in the US government and, at the same time, many nations. Like the doctor of osteopathy who treats the "whole person," Reagan envisioned all his actions as achieving multiple aims simultaneously. This element of Reagan's vision also explains why in the case of critical mistakes like the insertion of Marines into Lebanon or his dogged commitment to the Iran Contras—even to the point of misleading himself on the nature of the operation—he was always looking at multiple policy objectives.

Other than perhaps Calvin Coolidge and Franklin D. Roosevelt, no other American president in the twentieth century had such scope to his thinking—but in Coolidge's case it's hard to tell where his policies started and his predecessor's (Warren G. Harding's) left off. Roosevelt, while overseeing a vast shift in power and resources from the local and state level to the federal government, was by all accounts given to sudden and significant policy swings depending on which advisor had his ear. Historians were subsequently stuck with insisting there were "two New Deals" to rationalize the shifts in policy. No one ever accused Reagan of needing "two Reagan Revolutions"! FDR bounced from budget balancer to big spender, from partisan subsidizer-in-chief to ideological redistributionist. Until World War II forced on him a unifying discipline, Roosevelt was, within a general range of leftist politics, "all over the map," generally bound by the ignoble partisan objective of institutionalizing the Democratic Party into the dominant political force of the American twentieth century. As historian Burton W. Folsom Jr. would show, political considerations guided virtually every policy enacted under Roosevelt. But there was never a "deeper" FDR: he never seemed the slightest bit concerned with celestial order or heavenly morality. Reagan was.

From the 1960s on—if not earlier—Reagan had a broad vision of what needed to be done to right the USS *America* as well as the world. He possessed the unique perception of how to subjugate every speech, act, and intention to that vision. His understanding placed the evil of "godless" communism (a phrase Reagan well appreciated) and American domestic policies in the same box, addressed by the same solutions. And it ultimately came down to this: America needed to increase, while the USSR needed to decrease and ultimately disappear. Virtually everything the Reagan administration undertook from 1981 to 1989 could be contained in that single line. For Reagan, however, that concept itself was based on scripture (Matthew 5:15: "Neither do people light a lamp and put it under a bowl. Instead they put it on its stand, and it gives light to everyone in the house"). The Gipper saw the light of American freedom expanding, driving out the darkness of Soviet godlessness. To Reagan, America *was* exceptional, and if he never truly outlined the core elements of that exceptionalism beyond the oft-uttered word "freedom," he understood them intimately.

Of course earlier, as governor, and before that, as head of the Screen Actors Guild, Dutch could only address elements of that vision that fell within his power. Yet even then, even in the 1940s, Reagan's speech and actions reflected a constant, repetitive theme: America is great; communism is evil; and for America to remain great, communism must be defeated. But just because Reagan's worldview was opaque and often called simplistic (which it was not) did not make the man himself uncomplicated. Dutch's critics have struggled trying to leverage one part of Reagan at the expense of another, failing to understand his contradictions constituted his strength, not a weakness.

Born of Irish ancestry, his closest political ally and friend was the prime minister of England. Descended from a line of Catholics—then traditional, formal Christians—his most vocal religious supporters were evangelical fundamentalists. A labor union leader, he was vociferously opposed by organized labor. An actor, where by trade he had to always assume a false persona, he was (along with Harry Truman) one of the most transparent and genuine chief executives in American history. Charged by his enemies with lacking compassion, he singlehandedly saved more lives as a lifeguard than any other president in a personal capacity. Though a strong critic of student activism while serving as governor of California in the 1960s, he led a student strike at Eureka and marched labor picket lines as a boy. As a speaker to thousands of General Electric employees and to countless civic groups, Reagan reached more people with substantial political ideas than he ever could have as an A-list actor—something he aspired to but never achieved. As president, Reagan was simultaneously accused of being a poor actor and of performing so well that he was able to "fool" the American public.

For conservatives, the contrasts in his life were as sharp. The only president to be divorced, Reagan was adored by the so-called "Religious Right," despite having signed California's abortion bill into law. Having encountered virtually no Jews until he went to Hollywood, where he worked for the powerful Jack Warner, Reagan became the best friend of Israel since its creation. Long a champion of small government and lower deficits, Reagan had to agree to a tax increase as Governor of California and, later, as President, and had to subordinate those components of his agenda to the greater quest of defeating the Soviet Union. He left office with extremely high (but falling) deficits. A critic of expanding bureaucracies, Reagan was unable to reduce the size and scope of government in a substantial way. Easily the most popular Republican since Teddy Roosevelt, the Gipper was unable to truly ignite a "Reagan Revolution" with a permanent Republican majority as William McKinley did. Yet he was able to capture one of the most decisive Electoral College votes in American history and personally was exceptionally popular.

He did, however, redefine the Republican brand. The Gipper became the new archetype of a Republican as someone who embraced increasingly popular free trade, overseas military involvement, and internationalism—despite the Reagan Doctrine. His two Republican successors, George H. W. Bush and George W. Bush, fit into that mold. But free trade was a relatively new Republican principle, adopted first by Dwight D. Eisenhower more out of necessity than strategy. When Ike surveyed the economic scene in 1953, America was blessed by the "golden accident" in which all our former allies and trading partners, as well as our enemies, were either devastated by war or oppressed by growth-killing communism. The result was that from 1946 to 1959, America stood in the rarest position in all of history, being at the same time the leading producer and leading consumer in the world. America accounted, by some analysis, for 40 percent of world manufacturing and 15 percent of world trade. This not only enabled so-called "free trade," but demanded it. There was no one else to trade with, and the United States had the upper hand in virtually every negotiation.

This was free trade by accident as it were, and while Reagan largely subscribed to it, he still was worried by threats to defense-related industries. By 1981, although most of our allies had rebounded and were already surpassing American manufacturers in electronics, autos, textiles, and steel, the damage of unfettered free trade with partners who were already imposing their own restrictions was not evident. Dutch conceived of the early version of the North American Free Trade Agreement (NAFTA), called the Canada-U.S. Free Trade Agreement (CUSFTA), in order to obtain energy independence and further weaken the USSR. But his embrace of free trade was not unequivocal, especially in those sectors that affected national defense, and he brought tariffs and trade sanctions in some areas. Reagan's cautions were later overlooked by supporters who cited his conservatism as including full-throttle free trade. He accepted the system as he received it, expanded free trade where it could be used as a weapon against the

USSR—especially energy—but sought to mitigate its effects in steel and defense-related industries.

. Dutch, likewise, has been mis-portrayed as a dupe who was bamboozled into signing the Simpson-Mazzoli immigration act that gave amnesty to around three million illegal aliens. From the earliest days of his administration, Reagan addressed many of Jimmy Carter's immigration mistakes, but he always believed that "comprehensive immigration reform"—a twenty-first-century code term for amnesty—would be necessary. While his immigration ideas first and foremost focused on problems involving Haitians and Cubans who had arrived under Carter, Reagan nevertheless *from his earliest* days in the White House had outlined policies that would give amnesty to the over three million Mexican illegal immigrants already here. Reagan supporters would point to his subsequent regret that the Democrats did not live up to their promise of securing the border, but that excuse for the Gipper fails on two fronts. First, he, above all, should have known better in dealing with the Democrats. Second, he—not the Democrats—pushed to provide amnesty since 1981, and the guts of the Simpson-Mazzoli bill was designed in the White House. This aspect of Reaganism would become a point of contention for the "globalist" Republicans who claimed Reagan's mantle in the twenty-first century and the Donald Trump supporters who nevertheless still idolized Reagan as a case of Trump having learned Reagan's lesson.

It is time, then, to reassess Reagan in a number of fundamental ways.

We just don't know the "real" Reagan.

To read Reagan biographers and historians, the personal Reagan mystifies them. Edmund Morris fumed that he couldn't get through to the inner Reagan, a message reiterated by Lou Cannon. Dinesh D'Souza claimed the Gipper was "a mystery personally and politically."[1] Reagan's kids, according to D'Souza, found him "enigmatic and impenetrable," without realizing that, as part of the "GI Generation," Reagan fit right in with his contemporaries John Wayne, Gene Autry, Bob Hope, Tyrone Power, Gerald Ford, and George H. W. Bush, not to mention my own father and, later, stepfather.[2] My encounters with most men of that period were that they were very much like Dutch: unwilling to talk of their "feelings" and finding constant contemplation of their "innermost being" a waste of time. Perhaps for that reason, Reagan's most recent biographer, H. W. Brands, steers clear of psychoanalysis and focuses more on action—a prudent course and one this volume seeks to take.[3] After all, having proclaimed Reagan a "mystery," D'Souza rightly noted that "the American electorate did not regard Reagan as an enigma."[4]

Men of Reagan's generation did not obsess about their emotions and rarely cried in public. Instead they sought solutions to problems. Indeed, Reagan's biographers collectively have only identified a handful of times Reagan cried in public or even teared up—once was when his old high school marching band came by in the inaugural parade.[5] Reagan repeatedly told us who he was: he never told interviewers about personal introspections or how incidents moved him. He used humor as a deflection tool—a common tactic. Talk show host Dr. Laura Schlessinger used to tell her listeners, "Believe someone when they tell you who they are." Yet biographers have simply refused to take Reagan at his word or, more appropriately, at his deeds. There must, they think, "be something deeper," as if action itself wasn't deep enough. In Morris's case, as Reagan close aides Lyn Nofziger and Peter Hannaford observed, Morris "got on Reagan's nerves and he clammed up. That was how Reagan dealt with people who bugged him. He wouldn't talk."[6] Morris's failure to grasp Reagan after being granted such unprecedented access remains one of the greatest historical losses of the Reagan years.

Others who were close to Reagan, however, painted a picture of a tough, energetic, charming man: one who could climb up on the roof of his ranch house while in his sixties and make repairs; one who would ride whenever he could, clear brush on his ranch, or cut down trees. He had a story for every occasion, not because he didn't have anything else to say but because a story told it better than he ever could. He cherished his privacy because the public loved him so much and everyone wanted a piece of Ronald Reagan.

The knock that he had "no real friends" was borne of a relationship in Washington wherein he saw everyone there as employees of the same boss—the American people—not as his peers. He left his friends in California, including William Holden and his wife; Dick Powell; Robert Taylor (who died in 1969); and, after a short time in Washington, Judge William Clark. As Peggy Noonan points out, many of these friends from Hollywood had died, and Reagan would outlive all those listed to be his pallbearers. To Reagan, men such as Edwin Meese, James Baker, Michael Deaver, and others were associates and subordinates, and he had to maintain that professional distance if he was to do the best job for the citizens of the United States. Indeed, foreign leaders such as Margaret Thatcher and Mikhail Gorbachev came to know Dutch fairly quickly and become closer than some of his Washington compatriots, for they were equals.

Reagan was not an intellectual.

We must finally put to rest the notion that Reagan was not an intellectual. The very definition of an intellectual is "a person who places a high value on ideas" or who relies on reason over emotions or feelings. From an early age—certainly after he took an interest in ideas and literature—Reagan was absorbed by ideas. In 1942 he wrote an essay for *Photoplay* magazine in which he listed his favorite books: *Turnabout* by Thorne Smith, *Babbitt* by Sinclair Lewis, *The Adventures of Tom Sawyer* by Mark Twain, and the works of H. G. Wells, Damon Runyon, Pearl Buck, and Erich Maria Remarque.[7] He gravitated toward economics in college, where Dutch carried on a stimulating intellectual life. It greatly accelerated, though, in the 1930s with the New Deal and with his interest in domestic (and localized) economics and attained orbital velocity when he encountered communists in Hollywood. Indeed, his first wife, Jane Wyman, left him largely because he wouldn't stop talking about…ideas. Thinking it a slight, the biographers of his Hollywood years likewise noted that other actors often stayed away from Dutch on their breaks, lest he engage them in a—dare we say it?—intellectual conversation.

The notion that Reagan was no intellectual stems largely from the fallacious comparison with other (supposedly smarter) presidents. Yet in many cases those are fantasies. John F. Kennedy did none of the research for his

Pulitzer Prize-winning book, *Profiles in Courage*. While certainly Reagan had none of the pedigree of writing on serious topics that, say, Woodrow Wilson or Theodore Roosevelt possessed, one could point to Reagan's hundreds of General Electric speeches or his dozens of personally researched and hand-written radio addresses on a vast array of topics to see an active mind. Like Kennedy, he wrote a book (*Abortion and the Conscience of the Nation*, while president), but unlike Kennedy, he authored most of it himself.[8] Another part of what feeds the "no intellectual" meme is that Reagan as an executive required his staff to prepare briefs on all sides of an issue, studied them, then made a decision. But he wanted these stripped of the cover-all-contingencies language so common to academics. (Reagan once quipped he wished he could meet a one-armed economist so he wouldn't have to hear, "on the other hand.") Armed with evidence on both sides, Reagan would agree on a direction. Since he almost never would revisit his decision, historians have concluded he wasn't a deep thinker.

For example, Dinesh D'Souza said "it is hard to think of a single major point on which [Reagan] changed his mind." In fact, Reagan changed his mind on at least *six* major points in his life:

1. Originally, he thought the New Deal was good. Although he never criticized FDR personally, Reagan clearly opposed the basics of most New Deal programs by the early 1960s.
2. He signed the Therapeutic Abortion Act as governor, convinced it would lower the number of abortions. Later, he viewed this as a terrible mistake and wrote about it.
3. After he sent Marines into Lebanon, following the bombing, he agreed he had made a mistake and withdrew, establishing the "Reagan Doctrine."
4. In one of his most crucial and least-reported shifts, Reagan began his responses to Islamic radicals by viewing them as traditional state actors, but after 1986 Reagan—*the first of any president to do so*—began to describe them as "Islamic radicals" or "Islamic fundamentalists." The emphasis was to a shift in understanding that was wholly new to American politics.

5. On two occasions, Reagan changed his mind on tax increases, once in Sacramento and once in Washington.
6. When the Democrats failed to enforce border security, Reagan came to regret his own immigration policy.

Here was a man who could certainly assess a policy after the fact and admit he made a mistake. His campaign manager for much of his 1980 presidential run, John Sears, thought Reagan "willing to listen to others [and] to change his mind in the presence of new facts."[9]

Reagan was not in control but was a figurehead.

A favored interpretation of Lou Cannon, this view held that a disengaged Reagan was a pawn of his subordinates.[10] There is no question that the Gipper's management style was to assemble a team—usually with two or three key subordinates, such as William Clark and Michael Deaver in Sacramento, or the "troika" of Deaver, Ed Meese, and Jim Baker in DC—and to delegate. This has led to former chief of staff Donald Regan and others claiming they ran the show and that all mistakes made in Reagan's administration (especially Iran-Contra) occurred because Reagan was oblivious to what was going on.

To the extent this is true at all, it is a weakness derived from Reagan's core belief that people are mostly good, loyal, and upright. In Sacramento, his first chief of staff was missing work constantly to engage in homosexual trysts, something that just wouldn't have crossed Reagan's mind. He *was* highly averse to personally firing people, much like the wife who demands the husband pick up the dead mouse. But Reagan expected loyalty and competence, and he laid out his instructions quite clearly most of the time. For example, the National Security Decision Directives (NSDDs) were an ongoing stream of Reagan's strategic vision so clear that one can almost hear his voice emanating from the page. No one fed Reagan these positions, and the extensive use of National Security Planning Group meeting minutes show Reagan on top of all the issues, considering all sides. When George Shultz, his secretary of state who did not share the Gipper's faith in "Star Wars," was preparing for his Moscow negotiations, Reagan made it plain that under no circumstances was Shultz to negotiate away the Strategic Defense Initiative, which Reagan thought key to his entire strategic approach. There is no question these were *his words*:

> The overriding importance of SDI to the US is that it offers the possibility of radically altering…dangerous trends and moving to a more stable basis of deterrence. [However] if the promise of SDI is achieved, the Soviet advantage accumulated over the past twenty years at great cost will be largely neutralized.[11]

The reason it is certain these are Reagan's words is that no one else believed them, aside from possibly presidential science advisor George Keyworth, who would not have written an NSDD. Here was Reagan, explaining to his secretary of state, how a single piece of technology not only would force a "more stable basis of deterrence" but would eventually "largely neutralize" the entire Soviet arsenal!

Star Wars was the most prominent but certainly not the sole example of Reagan overriding his entire staff and even his wife, Nancy. His 1976 presidential run came despite a thumbs-down from his entire family. In the 1981 campaign, the Gipper rejected the advice of his campaign managers not to open the Nashua, New Hampshire, event to all the candidates. And in 1986, Caspar Weinberger, his secretary of defense, strongly opposed his order to send troops into Lebanon. These were not decisions made by a man being "guided" and "handled."

Unlike most other biographers, I have not engaged in extensive interviews with Reagan's family, friends, or administration officials. This is well-plowed ground. Those whom I have spoken with are cited in the acknowledgments, and they proved informative. However, my focus has been to delve into the massive collection at the Reagan Library and to tell the story of his presidency from a perspective scarcely touched in those papers. In the process, I hope to shed new light on his immigration and heretofore ignored pre-NAFTA energy policies, his disaster in Lebanon, and above all, his two foremost accomplishments: reviving the American economy and defeating (godless) communism.

As would often happen later with Donald Trump, Reagan's critics searched for every speck of error while ignoring the mountain of truth. Someone once said of Trump that his critics take him literally but not seriously, and his supporters take him seriously but not literally. The same could be said of Reagan. Even Lou Cannon, who in most cases is a "fair" biographer, lapsed into the "gotcha" criticisms of the Gipper. He ridiculed Reagan's claim in 1981 that there was a liberal news collaboration against him. "What I think we're seeing in what's going on is a little journalistic incest," Dutch observed.[12] Yet years later, radio host Rush Limbaugh would play countless montages of reporters and television pundits not only making the same points as each other but using *entirely and exactly the same words and phrases.* Cannon blamed it on "added scrutiny" when the likelihood of his becoming president sank in (again, the same excuse that was made for "journalists" in the Trump campaign). Added scrutiny? Perhaps. Identical words and phrases in reporting? Doubtful. Reagan was the first president to face the equivalent of "talking points" reporting, reflecting not only how much they hated him but how far journalism had fallen since Watergate.[13]

Too often, Reagan's critics focus on the unimportant (the deficits) or the unproven (Iran-Contra) and miss the very real shortcomings of his two terms, largely because they are all indictments of liberalism that Reagan gleefully embraced. The Gipper's administration was not perfect, and it suffered from its share of human misjudgments from which even Reagan was not exempt. But they pale in comparison to his magnificent, world-changing successes of defeating the Soviet Union, putting communist ideology on the road to extinction, and reviving a moribund American economy. Perhaps most important—and the reason so many ordinary Americans cherished him—is that he re-instilled in the common man that sacred presumption that the United States was, and still remains, an exceptional nation blessed by God. While Brands dismisses this as a convenience ("It helped that his beliefs relentlessly flattered the American people.... His message was an easy sell"), Peggy Noonan captured a truer essence of the Gipper when she wrote that "he loved America not only because he'd been taught to by his family and by the culture of his day to love it [but] because he believed completely in the startling trueness and worth of the assertions of its founding documents [and] the concrete and personal fact [of] the freedom it offered."[14] In his Westminster speech, he would conclude: "So let us ask ourselves, 'What kind of people do we think we are?' And let us answer, 'Free people, worthy of freedom and determined not only to remain so but to help others gain their freedom as well.'" This was anything but an "easy sell," for the cost was high, and the commitment, heavy.

In 2001 a CNN/*USA Today* poll placed Reagan as the greatest president ever—a presentist bias, of course, that reflected the deteriorating state of history.[15] Even on a more sweeping scale, however, there is no question that Ronald Reagan deserves a place in the top four or five American presidents, and in the twentieth century, he stands alone at the top. This is his story.

A Middle American Boy

When the Reagans settled in Tampico, Illinois, in February 1906, they were far from rich but far from struggling. Indeed they seemed to be on their way to the American dream. John Edward "Jack" Reagan had a steady job at H. C. Pitney general merchandise store, the couple had a large five-room flat over the bakery on 111 Main Street (known as the Graham Building), and while Nelle had to haul water and coal up stairs, and while there was no indoor toilet, the family was well within the definition of "average" Americans.[1] Jack came from Irish heritage. His grandfather Michael (born O'Regan) from Doolis in County Tipperary was a soap maker and came to Canada in 1856, before continuing on to Illinois, where he landed in Fair Haven Township. Michael had a farm valued at $1,120 by 1860.[2] John Reagan, his oldest son, was Jack's father. John had settled in Fulton in 1873, working in a grain elevator, but he also had a farm. He and his wife Jennie Cusick had three children, of which Jack (born 1883) was the youngest.

Jack had a hard life: his parents died when he was six, and he and other siblings lived with his aunt and uncle in Iowa. By all accounts, Jack was a handful, and no doubt his foster parents were glad to see him go. In 1899 he returned to Fulton, Illinois, finding work at J. W. Broadhead Dry Goods Store. There he met Nelle Clyde Wilson, a small girl who worked at Broadhead's. Even though Nelle's father disapproved of Jack—her mother died when she was seventeen—Nelle loved Reagan and the two were married in 1904. Two years later, Nelle suggested they move to Tampico where Jack found work with the H. C. Pitney General Store several miles away. Tampico, a railroad town of just over 1,200 people, serviced local farmers and had two of everything—drugstores, lumberyards, grain elevators, hardware stores, barber shops—but did possess three grocery stores.

Peter Hannaford, a chronicler of Reagan's youth, was asked to explain the source of Reagan's character. He replied, "In a word, 'Illinois.'"[3] Virtually all of Reagan's early years, from childhood through college, were spent in a section of northwestern Illinois, almost all of them in small towns such as Tampico, Dixon, Galesburg, Monmouth, and Eureka. Other than briefly living in Chicago, not until age twenty-one, when he got his broadcasting job in Davenport, Iowa, did Dutch leave the Land of Lincoln. By then, the essence of who Ronald Reagan was had been well formed, and the failure to delve deeply into Reagan's formative years has often led those focused on his presidency grasping for more insights into his "character."[4] Reagan's common origins put him far closer to the life experiences of an Abraham Lincoln than either of the Roosevelts or Woodrow Wilson.

Reagan, part of the "GI Generation," was a doer, an achiever, and one to ask "Why not?" rather than "Why?"

Reagan came from the "GI Generation," as generational scholars William Strauss and Neil Howe call it, with its defining comic book character Superman and its all-star who's who of actors like John Wayne, Bob Hope, Bing Crosby, Kirk Douglas, Henry Fonda, and Jimmy Stewart. Reagan's contemporary political figures included John F. Kennedy and Richard Nixon, both born in 1913, and heroes such as Charles Lindbergh, Billy Graham, and Joe DiMaggio. If anything, Dutch came from a cohort of "can-doers" for whom no challenge was too big.[5]

Much of what we know of Reagan's first years come from the recollections of his brother Neil, born on September 16, 1908. Nicknamed "Moon" (as it seemed all children at the time, particularly males, were endowed with a nickname), John Neil was baptized a Catholic. Nelle, who was religious but not yet formally affiliated with the Disciples of Christ Church, protested. The priest said, "Nellie, you promised to bring up the children as Catholic when you married Jack in Fulton." Nelle insisted no such thing had been discussed, whereupon the priest asked Jack why nothing had been said to his wife about bringing up the children as Catholic. Jack snapped his fingers and said, "Father, I completely forgot!" then added that he had told the priest who married them "not to worry about it, that I would tell her."[6] Nelle relented for the time being but persuaded Jack that when Neil and any future siblings were of age, they would be free to choose their religion. This would be no small milestone in Ronald Reagan's life, for Nelle's muscular Protestantism and fervent faith would infuse her younger son in a way that Midwest Catholicism likely would not have.

Nelle affiliated with the Disciples of Christ (known also simply as the "Christian Church" or "Campbellites"), a variation of the Presbyterian Church. Campbellites practiced baptism by immersion and over time had merged with the Mahoning Baptist Association in the 1830s and settled on the name "Disciples of Christ." In 1906 the church split over the use of musical instruments in services (the Disciples favoring) but otherwise maintained many of the common Protestant traditions of each person reading scripture for himself, evangelization, and more of a congregational church governance. Nelle formally joined the Tampico Disciples of Christ on March 27, 1910, and soon became active.

She was also pregnant again. Labor started late on February 5, 1911, during a serious snowstorm that left "10 inches to a foot on the level and [snow] drifting badly."[7] Jack sent Neil to stay with neighbors, then trudged through the snow to the doctor's house. But the doctor was out on another call, so Jack hurried to the home of Roy Rasine, whose wife was a well-known midwife. She and Jack rushed back to the Reagan household, finally joined by the doctor, who had heard of the labor. After a difficult and arduous delivery, in the early morning of February 6, a crying baby was born. Jack, seeing the baby's red cheeks, uttered, "For such a little bit of a Dutchman, he makes a hell of a lot of noise," to which Nelle weakly replied with his name, "Ronald Wilson Reagan."[8] Later, in his autobiography *An American Life*, Reagan added that Nelle had wanted to name her next male child Donald but that a sister had taken the name for her own baby, so Nelle settled on Ronald. "I never thought 'Ronald' was rugged enough for a young red-blooded American boy," he noted, but he approved of the nickname "Dutch."[9] Neil, meanwhile, didn't see his new brother for days and recalled that two days after he was home he still would not go into the room where his brother and mother were. "I didn't want any part of a brother. I had been promised a sister."[10]

Ronald only had four months in the house on Main Street before Jack moved the family to Burden House on 104 Glassburn Street, across from a park with a Civil War cannon.[11] (During Dutch's entire childhood, before he left for college, the family never lived in a house they owned.) The kids played in that park regularly, and it didn't take long for Neil to accept his brother, even to the point of including him in his schemes. When Dutch was only eighteen months old, Neil was playing with him underneath a train across the street from the park when the train suddenly started in motion. Nelle watched "horrified" from the front porch of her house, relieved when she saw the boys emerge from the other side unharmed.[12] She "earlifted" them home to receive "proper punishment."[13]

During this time, Nelle Reagan became a mainstay at the Disciples of Christ Church, attending services on both Sunday mornings and nights, as well as Wednesday prayer meetings. She led a Sunday school group (as Ronald would eventually do) and even was entrusted to lead regular services when the pastor was absent. In particular, she seemed to have a gift for effective prayer and in today's vernacular would be called a "prayer warrior," and many in her church believed she had the spiritual gift of healing. Nelle's faith deeply influenced Dutch, even at a young age. His mother was everywhere, visiting prisoners in local jails, attending the sick, Bible in hand. James 5:16 seemed perfectly appropriate to describe Nelle: "The effectual fervent prayer of a righteous [woman] availeth much." As Neil got older, he became involved as well, writing church notices and reciting poetry in church meetings. Nelle's faith provided a source of stability amidst the family's constant moves. Where Dutch would describe Jack in terms of energy, ambition, and hard work, he used terms such as "sweetness" and "kindness" to describe his mother.

When Ronald was four, Jack lost his job when Pitney sold the store. Jack moved the family to Chicago (832 E 57th Street), close to the University of

Chicago, where Jack landed a job at the Fair Department Store. It proved a difficult experience. At Pitney, Jack was used to being captain of his own (shoe) ship but now found himself amidst a crew of salesmen. As Reagan noted in his first autobiography, *Where's the Rest of Me?*, his father loved to sell shoes and studied it like an art. Jack took correspondence courses on how to sell more effectively and "spent hours analyzing the bones of the foot."[14] One of his closing sales lines was "Jesus walked barefoot, but then He didn't have to deal with our Illinois winters."[15]

Despite his father's hard work, Dutch recalled this period as one of extreme need. The flat was "lighted by a single gas jet brought to life by the deposit of a quarter in a slot down the hall," and Nelle learned to make "a soup bone last several days."[16] She sent Neil to the local butcher to request liver, which was unpopular then, for the "family cat," but, of course, the Reagans had no cat. "The liver," Reagan recalled, "became our Sunday dinner."[17] Then there was the staple of oat-burgers, concocted by adding oatmeal to a minimal amount of beef. Yet in many ways the Reagans were hardly worse off than their neighbors. Jack fit in to the profile of the average retail worker in America in 1910, who earned $630 a year and spent about $250 a year on food, $150 on rent, and $50 a year on clothing.[18] A Coca-Cola in Reagan's childhood cost a nickel; a shovel, 48 cents; and a bicycle, $15.95; and diners charged 15 cents for a ham and egg breakfast or a steak dinner.[19] That year Detroit Tigers baseball star Ty Cobb made $9,000, an Atlanta doctor would make over $1,200, and a traveling salesman made about $200 a year.[20] The vast majority of Americans baked their own bread, and most families still handed down clothes from one child to the next, a practice that extended to the Reagans, where Dutch wore Neil's shoes. It ironically spoke to the difficulty Jack occasionally had selling new shoes. Neil recalled that "shoes got handed down from one child to another, and folks seldom had more than two pairs."[21]

Ronald Reagan grew up in an age when a full breakfast cost fifteen cents and the biggest star in baseball, Ty Cobb, made $9,000 a year.

Neither child received much physical affection from their father, but both remembered plenty of spankings, which Reagan described as "whippings" or a "licking." On one occasion while in Chicago, Nelle had gone out on one of her church visits to neighbors, leaving the boys home alone. She seemed to be gone longer than normal, so they blew out the small gas lamp and set out to find their mother, instead encountering a drunk who admonished them to go home. Nelle, returning to an empty house with the smell of gas, was frantic and finally found them. When their father got home, Reagan recalled, "Jack clobbered us."[22] None of these incidents of corporal punishment seem to have damaged the boys' psyche in any way. They spoke of their father—calling both parents by their first names—in a somewhat distant tone, but not without respect or affection.[23]

Indeed, the "lickings" didn't stay in Dutch's mind nearly as much as his "worst experience ever as a boy," when his father bought a railroad car full of potatoes for speculation.[24] Jack ordered the boys to sort good potatoes from the bad. Reagan recalled sitting "in a stinking boxcar during [that] hot summer…gingerly gripping tubers that dissolve[d] in the fingers with a dripping squish."[25] The incident left Ronald with a permanent dislike of potatoes and made Jack little money since the queasy boys "simply lied about [finishing sorting] the rest and dumped them all, good or bad."[26]

In December 1916 Jack lost his job and moved the family again, this time to Galesburg, where he had relatives. He took a position as a manager of the shoe department at the O. T. Johnson Department Store. Galesburg, forty miles west of Peoria, was hardly Chicago, but it was ten times larger than Tampico. It was also home to the Davis family, one of whom—young Loyal Davis—would someday become Reagan's father-in-law when he married Nancy Davis. Settling in at 1219 North Kellogg Street, the Reagans resumed their normal activities, Jack at the local pub, Nelle at church, and reading sessions in the evening. It was at one of these Galesburg sessions where Dutch realized the joy of reading. As he put it, "One evening all the funny black marks on paper clicked into place."[27] No one knew he was nearsighted yet—an ailment which explained why he had to read so close to the paper. One evening, Jack saw Dutch lying on the floor looking at a newspaper and asked him what he was doing. "Reading," came the reply.

"Read me something," Jack said. Reagan proceeded to read him the latest news, and Nelle would from that point proudly invite neighbors to come in while her son read events from the papers.

Dutch knew how to read before he entered school—he called it "osmosis"—but nighttime stories at the dinner table or before bed were a central part of the Reagan household. Whether it was adventure stories of the Knights of the Round Table or tales of Americana, Nelle traced the words with her finger for the boys. Modern research has shown bedtime reading to have a major positive intellectual impact on children.[28] Nelle nightly was turning Dutch into a reader with an active imagination.

At the Galesburg house, Reagan also encountered something else that expanded his horizons: the previous occupant of the house had left an attic with a collection of butterflies and birds' eggs. The five-year-old Ronald would sit for hours examining the glass-encased collections, but, more than that, he allowed his imagination to soar. In his first autobiography, *Where's the Rest of Me?*, Reagan recalled, "Here, in the musty attic dust, I got my first scent of wind on peaks, pine needles in the rain, and visions of sunrise in the desert."[29] Later, in *An American Life*, his recollection reflected his spiritual growth by adding, "I escaped for hours...marveling at the rich colors of the eggs and the intricate and fragile wings of the butterflies. The experience left me with a reverence for the handiwork of God that never left me."[30]

It was also at Galesburg, though, that Reagan first sensed an uncomfortable tension between Jack and Nelle, noting that his father would disappear for days. Dutch and Neil heard arguments through the thin walls, and if one of the boys entered the room while an argument was going on, Nelle and Jack would "look at each other pointedly and start talking about something else."[31] The boys got used to unexpected and sudden trips to one of their aunt's houses, thinking they were adventures and not associating the "vacations," as Reagan called them, with Jack's drinking. It wasn't until the family returned to Tampico that Reagan fully understood his father's alcoholism, and contrary to Bill Clinton, whose family dysfunction drove him to gregariousness, Dutch never tried to be the family peacemaker. With Jack, who was a happy drunk (in contrast to his brother William), that was not a problem. Jack told stories and bought rounds but still ended up passed out or missing. Even after Dutch understood his father's alcoholism, he never spoke to others about it.[32]

Both Neil and Dutch cherished fonder memories of their father, whom Dutch called "the best raconteur I ever heard."[33] Jack had "a wry, mordant humor," Reagan recalled, and while he knew how to tell "the smoking-car sort of stories," his father always drew the line at "lusty vulgar humor and filth."[34] Jack had his softer side, too, displayed in particular one Tampico Christmas when Neil had lobbied for an electric train. Nelle, thinking the family had no money, endeavored to let him down gently. But on Christmas Eve, after the boys had supposedly gone to bed, they heard "*whees* and laughing" coming from downstairs where the tree was. Quietly sneaking down the stairs, they saw the Christmas tree with an electric train set up around it, and Jack was acting like a kid with the toy.[35] And, on occasion, Nelle too could still elicit a softer side from Jack, convincing him to appear with her in a church play, *The Dust of the Earth*. Neil also had participated in dramatic readings at the "Opera House" above the bank, meaning that at one time or another, Dutch saw his entire family on a stage.

Dutch was enrolled in first grade at Silas Willard School in Galesburg in the fall of 1916.[36] The following April, the United States declared war on Germany and Jack reported for enlistment but was turned down on the grounds that he had two children. That fall, Dutch was tested in Galesburg schools and was moved ahead to third grade. He got through half the year before Jack lost his job yet again and the family had to relocate. Already, however, Ronald had begun to identify with small-town Middle America. Chicago had its excitements, with its congested streets and occasional automobiles, but the return to rural Galesburg reminded him of its joys—"meadows and caves, trees and streams"—and left him with a lifelong affection for small towns.[37] Walt Disney, ten years Reagan's senior, had a remarkably similar recollection of his youth in Marceline, Missouri, and would "always speak of [his times there] as his halcyon days."[38] He said he felt sorry "for people who live in cities all their lives and…don't have a little hometown" and would later, when creating his magical theme park Disneyland, seek to re-create the Marceline experience on Main Street, USA.[39] In retrospect, it seems fitting that Ronald Reagan was born on a Main Street like the ones Disney re-created at parks around the world.

Reagan shared with Walt Disney a deep affection for small towns and "Main Street."

Jack took his new position as a clerk at E. B. Colwell Department Store, in Monmouth, ten miles away. While his family rented a home at 218 Seventh Avenue, Ronald was enrolled in the second term of third grade where, for the first time, he fully tasted what it was like to be the "new kid." A group of boys and girls chased young Dutch all the way to his home, where he ran up on the front porch. One of the bullies, Gertrude Crockett, recalled that Nelle came out on the porch and "gave us a red hot lecture."[40] But the incident really stuck with Reagan, and in 1976 when he returned to Monmouth as part of his campaign for the Republican nomination for president, he reminisced with Crockett and told her it was the only time in his life he'd been "truly terrified, scared to death."[41] Monmouth involved the typical amount of dues-paying that children go through in any new circumstance. He went through normal doses of self-discovery, a process, according to one classmate, that led him to experiment with different pronunciations of his name, switching between "Ree-gan" and "Ray-gan." But to most of the local girls it didn't matter what he called himself. Already he was displaying rare qualities of class, good humor, and charisma. And it didn't hurt that he had inherited Jack's looks (even to the point of parting his hair the same way well into his teenage years).

By that time, Dutch could be viewed as an introvert. Paul Kengor wrote that due to the frequent moves, "Ronald Reagan came to see a danger in making friends—the risk that any new friend would sooner or later disappear from his life forever."[42] Reagan later admitted that he was "a little slow" in making friends, a "reluctance to get close to people [that] never left me entirely."[43] Yet how much of this was Reagan's own preference for a life in books and stories and the ability to entertain himself and like being with himself? Kengor attributes Reagan's eventual religious attitudes as stemming from his time alone—and with God. Dutch's frequent moves did not appear to damage his self-esteem or confidence, as his lifeguard activities would soon reveal. On the other hand, his imagination could make him the subject of ridicule. Reagan recalled living "in a world of pretend" as a child, although by age eight or nine he began to feel self-conscious about it and would be careful about exposing his imaginary side. "I used to love to make up plays and act in them myself," he noted, "but I soon got self-conscious."[44] Yet in just six years he would be playing the lead in church plays.

While the Reagans lived in Monmouth, a flu epidemic struck in 1918, forcing the school to close down ("everyone wore masks," Dutch recalled). It is estimated that over 650,000 Americans died, and Nelle Reagan nearly became one of them.[45] She took extremely sick, so much so that her sons waiting anxiously as the doctor took Jack outside and spoke with him quietly. Finally, Jack returned with a somber look, saying she would be fine. His face, however, did not reflect his assurances. Nelle's treatment was a regimen of moldy cheese—"the moldier, the better."[46] After a few more days passed, with more cheese, and with another visit from the doctor, Jack informed the boys, "She's going to be all right," but this time his face seemed to confirm the prognosis.[47]

After that, Nelle resumed her prayer leader position with even greater fervor, directing her efforts at Jack's drinking, then expanding them to other church ladies who had similar concerns about their husbands. She had a reputation for success with her spiritual interventions, and her prayers for the sick seemed to bear fruit. None were needed more than when Dutch, who had avoided the flu but contracted pneumonia later that year. Having nearly lost Nelle, the family expended no small degree of attention on Dutch. Even the neighborhood boys that had once chased him down the street brought him lead soldiers to play with—perhaps out of guilt.[48]

Like clockwork, Jack announced the family had to move again. For the first time recently, though, it was not due to him getting fired but out of a real opportunity. H. G. Pitney, who had been Jack's former employer in Tampico, was getting old and blind, and he needed a partner to run the store. If Jack returned, Pitney told him, he would have a stake in ownership as well as better pay. Jack returned in August 1919 but failed to address the details of the deal, which required his stake in ownership to come from his commissions, leaving the Reagans to get by on Jack's salary. Suddenly the more lucrative pay evaporated, and to make matters worse, Jack chafed at the small-town nature of Tampico after he had been in Chicago and even Galesburg. The World War I song "How Ya Gonna Keep 'Em Down on the Farm (After They've Seen Paree?)" released earlier that year captured Jack's reaction to being consigned back to a little town. But Nelle and Dutch loved it—Nelle back with her church group and Dutch with his open streets and freedom.

That school year he entered fifth grade, and with his excellent memory he excelled in history, checking out books from the little bookcase at the front of the class. He and his "West Side Alley Gang" battled Harold "Monkey" Winchell and his "East Side Alley Gang," often engaging in food fights from garbage cans or playing a game of tag that involved racing through the town's stockyards and swinging gates. Rarely did Dutch get in serious trouble, except when he and Winchell got ahold of a pump shotgun in Harold's house. Standing the gun on end, they clicked the trigger and nothing happened. Reagan suggested they pump it, then they pulled the trigger a second time and it shot a hole in the ceiling. Immediately they heard footfalls on the stairs and screaming as Jack and Nelle entered the room, only to find Monkey and Dutch innocently sitting on the couch amidst a cloud of smoke, reading their Sunday school quarterly. This incident resulted in an ever-too-familiar "licking" from Jack. More often, however, life in Tampico involved Saturday afternoon movies, where he and his friend Vernon "Newt" Dennison got free admission (plus ten cents a week) for hauling coal to the Opera House and straightening chairs before the shows. Vernon recalled Dutch as "just a regular boy....He'd forget his mittens and overshoes. He was just like the rest of us."[49] Dutch's partner-in-crime Monkey said, "We were poor folks, but [Dutch] and Neil were always dressed clean, not raggedy."[50]

The Reagan boys had a secondhand bicycle—a rarity in town—which they shared with all. Dutch especially relished the times Jack would come home for lunch and push him around. And while ball playing was always popular, the kids developed another game on the train that ran the thirteen-mile route between Tampico and Yorktown and Hooppole called "the Dummy." There was no turnaround, so the train ran forward one direction and backwards going the other at the blazing speed of five miles per hour. In what would make twenty-first-century safety-obsessed helicopter parents apoplectic, Dutch and his friends would play train robbers on the moving train, unsupervised. During these carefree summers—what Reagan later referred to as his "Huck Finn years," a local group of businessmen took Tampico kids to the Hennepin Canal to teach them to swim.[51] Dutch excelled in the water and soon led others down to the canal. Sundays were spent at church in the morning, where the Dennisons and Reagans alike wore knee pants and black stockings. When a hole wore in one of the stockings, the kids painted their legs with shoe polish to conceal the gap.

Dutch developed a close relationship for Emma and Jim Greenman, who ran the jewelry store next to Pitney's and who became "Aunt Emma" and "Uncle Jim" for Ronald. He was always welcomed with cookies, chocolate, and a ten-cent-a-week allowance (on top of the ten cents a week he got for his coal hauling). The Greenmans had an old rocking chair that invited Ronald to curl up in it, creating what Reagan later recalled as a "mystic atmosphere."[52] He loved the furnishings in their living room, everything from glass globes with birds in them to an array of books, not to mention the intriguing jewelry store they ran, with its numerous clocks. A local taxidermist's collection of stuffed animals also proved captivating. Whether through his egg collection, his books, his plays, or any number of other escapes, Ronald Reagan had an intellectual curiosity that escaped his more hardscrabble brother.

Neil took after his father, whereas Ronald sought to please everyone, especially women. Possessed of a natural politeness (he immediately removed his hat in the presence of women, sitting only after they did), this respect for females would be transferred in his presidency to a reverence for the Oval Office, where he never removed his coat. Yet scrawny as he was, he loved roughhousing and, after his first football game at nine, found a sport he could quite literally hurl himself into. He recalled after a tackle there would ensue a pileup, under which Dutch occasionally found himself. "I got frightened," he recalled, "to the point of hysteria in the darkness under the mass of writing, shouting bodies."[53] Since no one had yet figured out he was nearsighted, Reagan was a poor baseball player and recalled being the last chosen for either side.

Whereas baseballs were small, bodies were large enough he could block and tackle with abandon. Dutch's love of football stayed with him throughout college, although he was never as good a football player as he was a swimmer.

At Christmas, the Reagans visited the Wilsons in Morrison, Illinois, taking the train to a station where the Wilsons would pick them up in a horse-drawn sleigh. Reagan recalled the horse literally dashing through the snow, its bells jingling, as the passengers sat beneath warm buffalo robes with a container of hot bricks at their feet. Once at the Wilsons', the family gathered around a crystal set. Reagan listened with "breathless attention" to KDKA Pittsburgh, until the show ended, whereupon he stood up and imitated the announcer to the delight of the families.[54]

Jack's drinking, a constant source of concern for Nelle, may have cost him at least one of his previous jobs. She prayed for him constantly, with Reagan recalling his mother "on her knees several times a day."[55] And it appeared she might have an ally in the law, for in 1920 the Volstead Act (which Nelle's Disciples of Christ had emphatically supported) went into effect as the authorizing law for the Eighteenth Amendment. Technically the consumption of alcoholic beverages was not prohibited, just the "manufacture, sale, and transportation," but for Jack it was the same thing. Tampico's saloon closed, and with it went one of Jack's main social outlets. Nelle saw Jack's problem as a disease, constantly forgave him, and never lost faith. Her favorite scripture verse, 2 Chronicles 7:14, embodied her approach to Jack, and her hope for his salvation: "If my people who are called by my name and humble themselves and pray and seek my face, and turn from their wicked ways, then I will hear from heaven, and will forgive their sin and heal their land."

That December, Jack suffered another blow. Pitney sold his store and gave Jack another business he owned (instead of a percentage of the sale of the store, which he had been promised). Jack would take over the Fashion Boot Shop in Dixon, some twenty miles away. Dutifully the family packed up once again, posed for a picture with neighborhood friends, and then climbed into their first car. Dutch had a trio of kittens named King Arthur, Sir Galahad, and Buster, which Jack had decreed would stay behind, but Nelle crowded them into a covered basket hidden under the rear seat and with anticipation, they headed off for a "big city" as Jack described it, their possessions stacked and tied on top of the car. They arrived in Dixon on December 6, 1920, and while Reagan is often associated with Dixon, he always had a soft spot in his heart for his birth home, Tampico, returning there three times: 1950 with his mother as grand marshal of a homecoming parade; 1976 while campaigning for president; and 1992 with Nancy.

After driving the family through the Dixon Memorial Arch, Jack planted the family at 816 South Hennepin Avenue, a two-story house the Reagans rented from John and Teresa Donovan for twenty-three dollars a month—pricey for the time, but with an indoor toilet. Dixon had over eight thousand people and a number of larger businesses, including J. J. Case farm implements, Reynolds Wire, and a dozen farms that supplied milk to Borden Milk Company. The boys shared a room as well as a single bed, but the property contained a barn with a loft in it. Dutch collected birds' eggs in a display case Jack supplied, while Neil raised rabbits and pigeons, which he killed, cleaned, and sold to a local market. It was an enterprise too grisly for Dutch. And Neil intimated that while he was a more than casual visitor to the local pool hall, his younger brother "would never do anything like that."[56] Indeed, whether due to Nelle's influence or his own sense of propriety, Dutch was already rounding into an all-American boy. He would recall Dixon with the fondest of memories: "It was a good life. I have never asked for anything more, then or now," he wrote in 1965.[57]

Young Reagan read constantly—prone, the paper or a book directly in front of him—and as a ten-year-old he took out a library card number, reading an average of two books a week, including tales by Edgar Rice Burroughs, the Frank Merriwell series, and almost any adventure story. It wasn't until after he turned thirteen that the family discovered his nearsightedness. They were on a Sunday drive, and Neil was reading each highway billboard they passed, especially the signs for Burma-Shave, which often came in a series of six large red signs posted a distance apart, each carrying a part of the message. (This is common in religious messaging: "Hell is real." "Repent now." "Jesus saves.") When Dutch said he couldn't see them, he took his mother's glasses and was astonished to find that "a glorious, sharply outlined world jump[ed] into focus…houses had a definite texture and hills…made a clear silhouette against the sky."[58] Now reading came alive more than ever, but it was movies where better distance vision made a significant difference. Dutch had always tried to sit in front at the theater. With glasses, he could sit anywhere and see much clearer definition. His favorite movies were westerns with Tom Mix or William S. Hart and a new genre of cliff-hangers that featured sports heroes such as Jack Dempsey and Red Grange. When Jack had enough money, the family went to a Friday night feature, but Dutch lobbied his father for an additional dime to return on Saturday for the matinee. "You think I'm made of money?" he'd ask, then fork over the dime.[59]

Once, however, the film was D. W. Griffith's *Birth of a Nation*. Jack refused Dutch the money and lectured him, saying, "The Klan's the Klan and a sheet's a sheet, and any man who wears a sheet over his head is a bum."[60] From an early age, Ronald learned to abhor racism. One of Neil's friends, Winston "Wink" McReynolds, spent time in the Reagan home, and race consciousness did not surface with the Reagan family, although it clearly was on display at the local hotel or golf club. Irish Catholics were no strangers to prejudice, however, and Jack battled it in his own small way. Years later, during the Depression, Jack had to travel as a shoe salesman and arrived at a small-town hotel to register. When the clerk said, "You'll like it here, Mr. Reagan. We don't permit a Jew in the place," Jack replied, "I'm a Catholic…and if it comes to the point where you won't take Jews, you won't take me either." He spent the night in his car in the snow—which Reagan later blamed for the "near-pneumonia" he contracted.[61]

Whereas Jack continued to mold Dutch's character in terms of an ethic for hard work and color blindness, Nelle worked on the boys' eternal souls. Her efforts paid off when, on June 21, 1922, both her sons were baptized at the Christian Church. Reagan testified that upon his baptism he had "a personal experience when I invited Christ into my life."[62] Nelle had considerable help from a book Reagan later said "made a lasting impression on me…mainly because of the goodness of the principal character."[63] The book, *That Printer of Udell's: A Story of the Middle West*, was written by Harold Bell Wright, a midwesterner and a child of a drunken father. Wright later became a minister for the Disciples of Christ. His book, published in 1903, inspired Reagan to go "to my mother and [tell] her I wanted to declare my faith and be baptized."[64] In *That Printer of Udell's*, a boy named Dick runs away from his home after his dying mother—a committed Christian— expires. Dick lands a job as a printer for George Udell, then rises, Horatio Alger-style, to prominence.[65] Biographer Edmund Morris claimed the book was "a religious experience" for young Reagan and was no unsophisticated denominational tract. Quite the contrary, the messages were that Jesus and His truth are found in the "church" broadly speaking—a "follower of no creed but Christ," although Dick eventually joins the Disciples of Christ before he sets off for Washington, DC.[66]

Those seeking to know Reagan would do well to understand the practical Christian message of *That Printer of Udell's*, particularly its depiction of a fundamental struggle between good and evil. Reagan himself would often refer to Wright's character as a "hero" of his, or a "role model." The born-again Dick Walker seeks to save "Boyd City" with a welfare plan that distinguished between "deserving and undeserving," to "make it possible for those in want to receive aid without compromising their self-respect."[67] It was, as Paul Kengor observed, "a virtual blueprint for [Reagan's] thinking on welfare."[68] *That Printer of Udell's* ends with a newly elected Congressman Walker kneeling in prayer before he leaves for the nation's capital.

Reagan's familiarity with *That Printer of Udell's* came only a short time after another event that strongly shaped his memories. Sometime in 1922, Dutch came home to find Jack passed out drunk on the front porch, "his hair soaked with melting snow, snoring as he breathed."[69] Dutch's first impulse was to just step over his father and "go to bed and pretend he wasn't there." But he came to what he called "that first moment of accepting responsibility," and the boy bent over his father—smelling the whiskey as he grabbed Jack's overcoat—and dragged him inside. Somehow, he put Jack into bed, and in a few days, Jack was back to the "bluff, hearty man I knew and loved."[70] In just a few months, then, Dutch had come face-to-face with some of the most defining characteristics of his mother and father and followed the path of his mother. It came without a conscious decision, provoked by reality to pick a path in life.

Even before he declared his faith, Reagan had been attending Sunday school—the class met in the furnace room of the church—as Nelle required. "Sunday school [on] Sunday mornings," Neil recalled, then "church Sunday morning, Christian Endeavor Sunday evening, church after Christian Endeavor, and prayer meetings on Wednesdays."[71] While it may have been an obligation for the children, or even a burden, in small town America in the early 1900s, church provided the only consistent opportunity for social interaction for much of the population. The furnace room was unfinished and cluttered. Dutch asked his teacher, Lloyd Emmert, for permission to fix up the messy area (recaptured in a painting done in 1999 to re-create the event). Along with his classmates, Reagan plastered and painted the room, and at age fifteen Dutch himself was teaching there. His specialty was stories of sports heroes who applied Christianity to their lives, such as outfielder Billy Sunday, who converted after he and his teammates listened to gospel hymns emanating from the Pacific Garden Mission in Chicago. Even though many of the boys were older than Dutch, they later described him as "their supremely self-assured teacher," remembering his specific lessons decades later.[72] They and others in the church saw him as mature beyond his years. More than a few thought he would become a minister— even after they had seen him act many times.[73]

Nelle held her own study groups, called the "True Blue" class, which moved from home to home among the members. When the group came to the Reagan home, Dutch participated in those as well. Through the True Blue classes and his general attendance at the Disciples of Christ Church, Reagan became friends with Reverend Ben Cleaver, who had only been at the church as associate pastor three weeks before baptizing Dutch. Cleaver became one of his first nonfamily male role models and advisors, teaching him how to drive and helping him apply for college.

It didn't hurt that Ronald had his eye on Cleaver's daughter, Margaret. As it seemed with everyone at the time, Margaret had a nickname— "Mugs"—and Reagan spent countless hours at the Cleaver home in part to be near her. While there, Dutch absorbed both theology and politics from Cleaver, who in turn had developed his worldview from Disciples of Christ leader Alexander Campbell. The messages that Cleaver internalized included what many would later call "American exceptionalism," positing that the United States had a special mission to lift up human liberty against oppression. Kengor, the best historian of Reagan's faith life, showed that Campbell and many other Disciples leaders believed America had a divine mission from the Lord to not only spread the gospel but also the enlightened institutions that God had established in the American Republic.[74]

Nelle had other opportunities for her son to grow in the faith (Neil didn't seem all that enthused). She took Dutch to the local Chautauqua and Rock River Bible conferences, had him perform church readings, and brought him on hospital visits where the mother-son duo performed short programs (Nelle also played the banjo). Reagan recalled leaving the Chautauqua meetings optimistic and energized.

By the time the family moved from the Hennepin Avenue house to a smaller home on 338 West Everett Street, Reagan was enrolled in high school, which meant that he attended North Dixon High School while Moon remained at South Dixon. As with most towns with rival high schools, each took on its own personality: South was tougher, more streetwise, more sports oriented, while North was more directed at academics and arts—for "sissies," according to Neil. The older Reagan boy had already begun hanging out with a tougher crowd at the local pool hall in "Demon Town," a waterfront area known for its speakeasies.

Physically, Dutch had not bloomed yet, and as much as he enjoyed football, he found himself riding the bench for his first two years at North Dixon. Even though he rarely played, he memorized the plays and was always prepared. More importantly, he had honor, reporting to an official during a game that he had held on a block, incurring a fifteen-yard penalty for the team. Reagan remembered the incident forty years later when he wrote to his friend.[75] Due to his size, Dutch found it hard to crack the starting lineup, but the high school conference created a new division for players 135 pounds and under, allowing him to play regularly. Reagan looked back fondly on his times spent on football fields: "I loved playing on the line.... It's as fundamental as anything in life—a collision between two bodies, one determined to advance, the other determined to resist."[76]

By 1925, however, Reagan grew and put on muscle, allowing him to join Moon in a part-time job as roustabouts for the Ringling Brothers Circus when it came to town. Dragging circus wagons around and blocking them so they wouldn't roll away, Dutch earned a respectable twenty-five cents an hour. His day started at 4:00 a.m. to feed the elephants, which were used to pull the ropes that erected the tent. Then he landed his first full-time summer job working for a contractor building St. Anne's Catholic Church at thirty-five cents an hour, ten hours a day, six days a week. He confessed that part of his motivation was "to build up my muscles for the next [football] season" as well as to start a college savings account.[77] Most of the time, he helped dig the foundation, learning how to lay floors, shingle a roof, pour concrete, and in general to work with his hands. Once, when a noon whistle blew, Dutch was in mid-swing. He immediately let the pick drop right behind him, where it narrowly missed his boss's toes. Jack happened to be nearby, picking up his son for lunch, and the foreman shouted, "This kid of yours [is so lazy] he can get less dirt on a shovel than any human," but Reagan kept his job and earned $200 toward college that summer.

Dutch's newly developed physique finally paid off on the football field when one of the regular guards disappointed the coach with his play. The coach shouted, "*Right guard, Reagan.*"[78] He managed to keep his starting position for the rest of the year and his senior year. This new strength and physique also enhanced his ability to swim, which he had come to do through a program sponsored by the YMCA and local businessmen at Lowell Park. The three-hundred-acre reserve was home to the Rock River, which had its treacherous zones, mostly caused by a downstream dam that—when its sluices were opened—created a strong current. Moreover, Reagan recalled that the bottom sloped down at a sharp angle not far from the bank, and that the opposite bank, some six hundred feet in the distance, was no easy swim. As he put it, "Once started you had to go all the way, or else."[79] Dutch had quickly matured into a strong and fast swimmer. After a number of drownings in 1926, he approached the park concessionaires,

Ed and Ruth Graybill, and offered to be a lifeguard. He was hired at the salary of eighteen dollars a week plus all the root beer and hamburgers he could drink and eat, and Dutch earned every penny, reporting for work at ten in the morning and often staying until ten at night. Once again, to Reagan it was fun. He was on stage. He was the "only one up there on the guard stand....Everyone had to look at me."[80] If the river wasn't busy with swimmers, in the mornings Dutch would give children swimming lessons.

Lifeguard Ronald Reagan became lifesaver Ronald Reagan, saving over seventy people from drowning, including one girl whom he saved after becoming governor of California.

It should not be minimized, however, that Reagan treated his position solemnly, as one involving life and death. Ruth Graybill recalled that in Reagan's six years on duty, "we never had a drowning."[81] Even Reagan admitted that people often later insisted they were not in trouble, and critics could claim he inflated his rescue numbers. Graybill doubted that he ever went in after someone who didn't need saving. "Some swimmers," she recalled, "would shrug off his help. 'Oh, I could have made it all right'... [and] I guess they resented being 'saved'...they felt he was showing off. Maybe."[82] Reagan himself, however, dismissed such notions. "I guarantee you they needed saving—no lifeguard gets wet without good reason."[83] He added, "a wet suit was a real hardship and I was too money-conscious to have a spare."[84] Of the seventy-seven people he saved over those six summers, only one ever thanked him. Reagan was somewhat offended but concluded that "they felt insulted," and some even "sought me out and angrily denounced me for dragging them to shore."[85]

In fact, there were news reports substantiating some of the rescues. The August 3, 1928, *Dixon Evening Telegraph* ran the sensationalistic headline "Pulled from the Jaws of Death," with the ensuing article relating the struggling James Raider. After the swimmer went down once, Dutch dove in and, after "quite a struggle," saved Raider, who was in desperate enough straits that he was given artificial respiration.[86] On another occasion, Gertrude Childers, fifteen, was under the slide next to the dock. She pushed out into the water just as a boy shot down the slide and landed on her, sending her to the bottom, unconscious. "I remember going under," she later said, "but that's about all I remember because it knocked me out."[87] When she recovered on the beach, she had a nosebleed and hadn't been aware that Dutch had pulled her out.[88] After his first rescue, Jack told him to keep a record by making a notch on an old log.

When people asked how many people he saved, Reagan pointed to the log: "You count 'em." He also proudly kept an accurate total in his head, and it may have been low.[89] A year after he left the job, he returned to Lowell Park to visit a friend, who coincidentally was also the lifeguard. The friend asked him to watch the beach while he went to the bathroom, and when he came out, Reagan told him, "Would you believe I had to go in and make a rescue while [you] were gone?"[90] A Des Moines newspaper in the 1930s reported that Reagan reportedly saved one or possibly two swimmers at the Camp Dodge pool and another as governor of California, where he hosted a party at the governor's mansion. A little girl sank to the bottom of the swimming pool and Reagan saw her. Fully dressed, he entered the pool and brought her out.[91] Reagan's friend and close advisor, William Clark ("the Judge") later told historian Paul Kengor that "lifeguarding instilled in the young man a basic respect for the dignity and sanctity of human life," not to mention the young man's self-confidence.[92]

Lowell Park and the Rock River eventually became home to a lodge, where Dutch taught summer residents to swim. The river also became the setting for his continuing courtship of Mugs. She and her friend Elizabeth "Bee" Drew frequented the river, Bee with her boyfriend and Mugs alone. Tied to his lifeguard stand, Reagan couldn't flirt with Mugs until he got rid of swimmers, so he skipped rocks into the river and told swimmers they were "river rats." That tended to chase them away quickly, and Dutch could hop in a canoe with Mugs, Bee, and her boyfriend. Dutch, however, had prepared for the moment, bringing a portable Victrola along for what turned out to be a half-hour cruise, playing the only record they had—"Ramona"—over and over until Bee's boyfriend threw it in the Rock River. When he graduated, Reagan wrote an article in the class annual called "Meditations of a Lifeguard." He described a "frail and forty maiden" and a "hippopotamus," before he notices Mugs (though he avoided naming her). She "trips gracefully over to the edge of the crowded pier, and settles like a butterfly. The guard [Reagan] strolls by…[then] assumes a manly worried expression designed to touch the heart of any blonde, brunette or unclassified female."[93]

Of course, Dutch had first noticed Mugs in church—"a sparkling brunette," he called her—and found that their shared denomination gave him an edge over other would-be suitors. Ben Cleaver's mentoring relationship with Dutch gave him still other opportunities to be around Margaret. As with most girls at that age, she was more mature than Reagan and knew the difficulties associated with relationships between teenagers. Even so, before long the two fell in love, and Reagan took her to the senior banquet.

Reagan had made acceptable grades at North Dixon, relying on his memory to overcome his nearsightedness and reading what was on the blackboard. But his English and world history teacher, B. J. Fraser, noticed in Dutch another talent. Fraser advised the Dramatic Club, and he didn't need much to convince Reagan to join: Mugs was already a member. Fraser found his new discovery "possessed a sense of presence on the stage, a sense of reality.… He fit into almost any kind of role you put him into" and was "head and shoulders above the [other actors]."[94] Of course, Dutch had already participated in dozens of plays and readings with Nelle and probably had more experience than most of the others. At Reagan's suggestion, the club opened its presentations to the general public, and in his senior year (1928), Dutch was Dramatic Club president, as well as the president of the senior class. Thus, from an early age, Ronald Reagan had both acting and politics in his blood. To him, they went together.

In a school as small as North Dixon, most students participated in a wide number of activities. Reagan, no exception, oversaw the art editing of the *Dixonian*, played on the varsity basketball team, eventually climbed into the starting right tackle position on the varsity football team, was vice president of another campus club (Hi-Y, which promoted "Clean Speech, Clean Sports, Clean Living and Clean Scholarship"), and wrote a short story called "Gethsemane" for the *Dixonian* about a young football player.

His poem, also in the *Dixonian*, "Life," had overtones of the unbroken spirit in Teddy Roosevelt's "Man in the Arena":

> We hang onto a jaded life,
> A life full of sorrow and pain,
> A life that warps and breaks us,
> And we try to run through it again.[95]

As a writer, actor, storyteller, and student leader, Dutch had already demonstrated his talents repeatedly.

Throughout the spring of 1928, he continued to work when he could, caddying at the Hazelwood Country Club, which had deteriorated for several years before Charles Walgreen, the Chicago entrepreneur whose string of drugstores would dot the land, bought the property. Walgreen personally came to Dixon to oversee rehabilitation of the facility's log cabin and occasionally brought his friends (including Commander—later Admiral— Richard Byrd who would fly to the South Pole in 1929). When Walgreen held a picnic for the caddies at the season's end, Reagan was "stretched out in a hammock and Mrs. Walgreen herself brought me a plate of food. That was my idea of being King," he recalled.[96] By that time he had saved almost $400 for college.

Reagan had achieved almost every type of success one could expect from a young man, although his grades were mediocre. Still, in 1928 he was senior class president and spoke at the Dixon High School graduation, quoting John 10:10: "I have come in order that they have life, and have it more abundantly." While college remained a luxury for most young men, and while Neil thought it "a waste of time," Reagan had already seen plenty of physical labor and "had enough of working."[97]

He had his eye set on Eureka College for a number of reasons, even though it was too expensive. Most important, Mugs was headed there. Eureka was a Disciples of Christ college one hundred miles south of Dixon, and Mugs, following her sister's example, had already enrolled. Reverend Cleaver was appointed head minister of the Eureka Christian Church and would move there in 1931.[98] Dutch accompanied her in September on a trip to the school and met with Dean Samuel Harrod to discuss attending.

In *Where's the Rest of Me?* Reagan said, "I fell head over heels in love with Eureka."[99] Reagan had other incentives for wanting to attend Eureka: Garland Waggoner, a star fullback at Dixon, had gone there and was an inspiration that, perhaps, Dutch too could make the Eureka football team. But the small-town atmosphere, the church affiliation, and the overall comfort level sealed in his mind that somehow he needed to attend Eureka.

To his rescue came the athletic director and football coach Ralph "Mac" McKinzie, to offer Dutch a ninety-dollar athletic scholarship covering half his tuition, and he paid the other half from his savings. Through the Cleavers and one of Mugs's sister's boyfriends, Reagan was admitted to the Tau Kappa Epsilon fraternity and stayed at the Teke house. All those expenses left him with a mere thirty-five dollars to cover all of his other costs for the year. The ever-industrious Dutch landed a dishwashing job at the Teke house that covered his board, then he cleaned tables at the girls dorm, and by his junior year, he was the pool lifeguard during swimming season and became the official swimming coach.

By the time he walked onto the Eureka College campus as a freshman, Dutch was certain he and Margaret would be married. But if Ronald Reagan thought he was following Mugs to Eureka, he was wrong. He was following destiny.

2

Student Activist

Eureka College offered a bucolic nineteenth-century campus life wedded to a religious background. It was the first co-ed college in Illinois (and only the third in the United States) with a church affiliation in which participation in religious activities was expected but not required. Virtually no discrimination existed. With only 250 students—one fifth of them studying for the ministry—Eureka as a college had fewer students than many modern freshman lecture courses, and yet by design it was "the cheapest school in this or any other state" as its 1878 catalog had boasted.[1] Certainly, it was old-fashioned in the extreme, even out of date to some more urbane outsiders. Its small size made it comfortable to all and ensured that a student could become anonymous easily. But even the introverted Ronald Reagan was not looking to disappear into the woodwork. In fact, he had arrived expecting to show the college kids what a real football player looked like.

Dutch officially registered for classes at Eureka on September 18, 1928, signing up for classes in English literature, zoology, history of civilization, phys ed, and coaching fundamentals—and two courses in rhetoric. The next day, he pledged the Tau Kappa Epsilon fraternity.[2] Ruminating on the word "eureka" itself, meaning "I have found it," Reagan later wrote that "it described perfectly the sense of discovery I felt the day I arrived."[3] The fact that Reagan took two classes of rhetoric underscored the fact that, like Abraham Lincoln, he already appreciated and cherished language and its powers of persuasion. Indeed, it is almost humorous that years later, as president, critics would knock Reagan for being an intellectual lightweight. Nothing could be further from the truth: he was *already* an intellectual-in-training before he entered college, as amply demonstrated by his thoughtful poems, stories, one-man scripts, and Sunday school lessons. But as Reagan would demonstrate and repeatedly admit, his grades and study habits often concealed an active mind. When biographer H. W. Brands wrote that Reagan was "insufficiently brilliant to make good grades without effort," one suspects that the emphasis was on "insufficiently brilliant" as opposed to "without effort."[4] Reagan himself seemed to validate that view when he insisted he had come to college primarily for "the chance to play football for four more years," or that at Dixon he had "never bothered to do much more [academically]…than remain eligible [for football]."[5]

Reagan, already with an active imagination, began to shape himself into a genuine intellectual at Eureka College, focusing especially on rhetoric and language.

In "Rudy-esque" fashion, the undersized Dutch always envisioned himself a football star, and in that same manner he impressed coach Ralph McKinzie as tenacious, a "plugger." Reagan "never quit," never whined, kept going when others gave up. But he was shorter and skinnier than the other players. As McKinzie put it, "I had a team to consider. He was nearsighted.… Couldn't see worth a damn."[6] McKinzie "never let him on the field" in his first year, and while Reagan knew the plays intricately, his body simply could not execute them. Like Rudy Ruettiger, Dutch did anything he could to be involved in football, including using an old broom as a microphone and "announcing" the latest Golden Tornado's game. However, unlike Rudy and his quest merely to "run out of that [Notre Dame] tunnel," Reagan was shocked—and bitter—that he wasn't a starter. "I told everyone who would listen that coach didn't like me. I was the victim of unreasoning prejudice."[7] Indeed, when he finally snapped out of it and took responsibility for his own play, it stuck with him as a political lesson for the rest of his life.

Basketball gave Dutch a second shower of reality. He had just assumed he could play and expected to just walk on the team.[8] All it took was one look at a practice in the gym and Reagan's jaw dropped. "I went to the first practice, looked through the door, adjusted my glasses…turned and walked away. I saw fellows doing things with a basketball that I just didn't believe."[9] Even in swimming, where Reagan indeed was a star, it took him time to get acclimated. McKinzie noted that Reagan probably had never swum in a pool before, and it took time to get "the oil off his wings."[10] Once he adjusted to the pool, Reagan became the outstanding athlete he could never be on the gridiron. As a freshman, he won every event he entered—the crawl, backstroke, and 100- and 200-meter relays.

Off the football field and out of the pool, Reagan was most at home on stage. He joined the Dramatic Club, advised by Ellen Johnson, soon after he enrolled. Naturally, Margaret's presence was a motivation, but Reagan deliberately overemphasized the opportunity to see Mugs and escort the leading lady home afterward as a cover for his genuine growing fondness for "communing with the Arts," as he put it.[11] Leading roles came to him effortlessly and were usually accompanied by positive reviews.

Within a month of landing on campus, he was on the football team, in the Dramatic Club, was a reporter for the *Pegasus*, and was swimming, all the while working at least one job and often two. He recalled daily and devoted attention to the Bible.

Although Eureka was a school with a religious affiliation and by all accounts quite conservative (even puritanical, with dancing prohibited), every year the school held a sanctioned event called the "Grind." Boys would assemble in an outside circle, girls in an inside circle, and they would move—one might say, "dance," since it was to music!—in opposite directions. Like musical chairs, when the music stopped, the boy and girl opposite each other would introduce themselves, talk a little, then the music would start again. After a while, in which most people had a chance to interact with everyone else, the circles would break up and students continued their conversations over ice cream and cookies. But the Grind was about to become a political football.

The trouble started with money: Eureka didn't have enough of it. The boom of the 1920s, which benefitted almost every sector of the American economy, missed farming and agriculture.[12] After land values soared 11 percent from 1915 to 1920, farmers "borrowed as never before on land."[13] Added to that, after World War I, thousands of men returned to family farms from military service, pushing production up even further. With wheat prices supported by the government at $2.96 a bushel (compared to Australia's farmers getting ninety-eight cents), the United States was "sitting on a mountain of wheat."[14] When sales of high-priced wheat and other commodities fell, farms failed, and by extension Illinois farming towns— like those in every other agriculturally dominant state—felt the pain. Much of Eureka College's funding depended on generous, believing midwesterners, and it had slumped badly by 1928.

College president Bert Wilson proposed course cutbacks in arts and home economics in 1926, but the board rejected his request. He tried again in 1928, with sports clearly in his crosshairs. Eliminating many of the courses would have affected juniors and seniors, who needed them to graduate, possibly tacking on an additional year to their matriculation. The match that ignited the flame of student unrest, however, came when Wilson banned the Grind in an overt attempt to appeal to the more pious of the donors or even get a direct boost from the Disciples of Christ Church itself. Whether he knew of off-campus dances already going on among Eureka students at the local Legion Hall (nicknamed "Damnation Hall") is unclear, although a spy was dispatched by someone in the administration to take down names. In short, Wilson managed to unite the students over two hot-button issues. Student disaffection soon began to spread to faculty.

Wilson's strategy was to offer his resignation on November 22, 1928, at a public meeting in the chapel, with the tacit understanding that the trustees would not accept it. Speaking to the assembled students, townspeople, and faculty, Wilson blamed the small size of the town of Eureka for the lack of support. He questioned whether the school could survive in the current economic climate, a view that angered alumni and led 145 students to petition to have Wilson removed.

On Tuesday, November 27, the trustees met just as Dutch and the football team took the field for a game against Illinois College, after which all the students were to go home for Thanksgiving break. According to Reagan, "no one saw the game," meaning their minds were on the meeting. The crowd was further distracted by a special edition of the newspaper announcing the student petition to the board had been denied. Reagan recalled looking into the stands and seeing nothing but open newspapers— no faces at all. The board had gone even further than Wilson in its cuts, too, reducing the number of teaching departments to eight instead of the nine Wilson suggested.

Les Pierce, the student president of Tau Kappa Epsilon and a football player, organized a resistance at 11:45 that night. He and his supporters rang the campus bell nonstop as students and townspeople arrived at the chapel and filled it up. Pierce was the ringleader, but he had already decided that a freshman, not a senior (who might be viewed as acting out of self-interest to restore the eliminated classes), should speak. A freshman would be around for four years and have a long-term stake in the outcome. The rebels selected Reagan, already known as a good speaker, to address the crowd, then stationed members of the football team outside the doors to prevent unwanted protestors from interrupting. But what was Dutch to say? Pierce and the others had settled on a strike as the best tactic to force Wilson out. This would be no easy task, as the students would have a full week's break before they would return to implement the strike. In short, it required terrific discipline and, most of all, motivation. Reagan outlined his talk much the way he would in speeches to the American public in the future, beginning with the history of the disagreement, the students' patient and sincere efforts at a reasonable solution with the administration, and the deception with which Wilson and the trustees had responded.

*Freshman Ronald Reagan was the only US president
to lead a student demonstration or strike.*

Dutch was surprised at the immediate grip his words had on the crowd: "In the parlance of the theater, that audience and I were together."[15] Reagan was so good, by the time he actually presented the motion, parliamentary procedure went out the window in a roar of support. Reagan thought "with two more lines I could have had them riding through 'every Middlesex village and farm.'"[16] After the crowd calmed down—and a girl who had fainted was revived—a vote on the strike was taken and carried. The official resolution declared a strike pending the acceptance of Wilson's resignation (and a copy was placed under Wilson's door). It was a risky gamble, especially since the student action relied on everyone coming back from Thanksgiving vacation steeled for a fight.

Reagan, now a student activist, returned to Dixon, and to a tumultuous family situation. Jack had been drinking more than usual, and Moon had lost his accounting job at the Fashion Boot Shop, though he still worked in other tasks there at a lower wage. In another era, where divorce was more acceptable, Nelle likely would have left. Not only did she stay, but when Dutch considered the option of leaving Eureka to help out, she strenuously refused. There were pleasant moments in the return home, however. Margaret Cleaver's family invited Dutch to go with them to Rockford to see a play called *Journey's End*, set in World War I with the hero, Captain Stanhope, captivating Reagan. It was his first exposure to professional theater, leaving Reagan energized. "I wanted to speak his lines," he said of the actor playing Stanhope.[17] Despite his time in high school drama and his brief experience with college productions, for the first time Reagan began to look at acting as a career choice, or, as he put it, "nature was trying to tell me something—namely that my heart is a ham loaf."[18]

When Reagan and the organizers returned to campus, they could not have been more pleased: with the exception of six students—two of them Wilson's own daughters—the strike produced 100 percent compliance. As if to twist the knife a little, the student committee held a dance every afternoon yet at the same time established regular study hours and policed the students so as to not give the impression they were merely interested in a long break. After only a week, Wilson resigned and this time the trustees accepted it. Appropriately, the resignation was celebrated with…a dance!

As the campus quickly returned to normal, Dutch increasingly participated in plays, usually landing the best role. He had a natural stage presence and easy manner that drew attention to him, and he developed many of the movie-star tricks that are necessary to succeed. He learned how to stand, be relaxed while posing for pictures, how to tilt his head and smile. He also persevered in football, occupying his familiar spot on the bench. His exploits in the swimming pool impressed everyone. In the classroom, however, it was a different matter. Reagan liked economics, history, and English, relying on his good memory to get by. In 1939, Reagan joked to an interviewer that he deliberately kept his grades low so that he wouldn't end up a high school athletic teacher. If so, Dutch didn't have to try too hard: classroom work stayed low on his priority list, which included football, drama, politics, and Mugs. As school ended in his freshman year, there was a better-than-average chance that Dutch would not return for a sophomore year, and it had nothing to do with his grades.

Money was tighter than ever. Reagan had his lifeguard job back, allowing Margaret to regularly visit him at the river. When there were no swimmers, the two relaxed in a rowboat, where Dutch spoke to Mugs of his dream of becoming a professional athlete. Yet a second year at Eureka was looking less likely. Dutch's lifeguard savings would amount to $200 at the end of the season, not enough to allow him to return to college. He had, in the meantime, begun working with a land surveyor at the park who tried to recruit him to the University of Wisconsin on a rowing scholarship to take effect in a year. Instead, he announced his intention to return to Eureka.

He had already beaten the odds, though, for less than 10 percent of Dixon High graduates even went to college. Coach McKinzie finagled a deferment of half Reagan's tuition ("my first experience with credit," he noted) and arranged for Dutch to get a job washing dishes in the girls' dormitory.[19] "I was seduced by Eureka all over again," he wrote in *An American Life*, making a call home telling his parents he would return for a second year at college.[20]

Seeing that McKinzie wasn't his enemy emboldened Dutch to ask the coach to try out Neil, who was a better athlete. McKinzie gave Moon a tryout, was impressed, and got him a partial scholarship with the same half-tuition deferment he acquired for Dutch. Moon found life at Eureka an odd inversion, for there Dutch was the veteran. Ronald now seemed "older," and Moon soon became identified frequently as "Dutch Reagan's brother."

Reagan began to see spotty playing time after making an impressive block during a practice and finally found himself in the starting lineup. Football offered one small insight into Reagan's attitude toward race. During one of his away football games, the team had to spend the night in Dixon. There a hotel refused to board the two black players on the team, William "Burgie" Burghardt and Jim Rattan. McKinzie planned to tell them there was no room and that they would have to sleep on the bus. But Reagan convinced the coach to allow Burghardt, Rattan, and himself to stay at his house, showing up on Nelle's doorstep with his teammates in tow.

Other than football, the most constant element in Reagan's life was Margaret. He gave her his fraternity pin early in his sophomore year, when the two dated consistently. One of the preferred hangouts was the local graveyard, which was a favorite "make-out" spot for Eureka students. Increasingly, though, Dutch wanted to talk politics—Hoover versus Roosevelt—while Mugs showed little interest. Dutch had absorbed his father's Democratic Party preferences. To Jack, the Democrats were the party of the "little fella," and especially for Catholics and other minorities. He had brought his son to march on the Galena Street bridge with protest signs during the 1928 elections. Of course, Al Smith needed to do little more than oppose Prohibition to win Jack Reagan over.

With his father, Democrat Ronald Reagan participated in a
protest march during the 1928 elections.

By the late 1920s, Illinois' farm sector struggled, taking banks down with them. Almost half the banks in the western states failed or would fail between 1920 and 1932, especially in those communities that had expanded their acreage during the war.[21] Most of the failed Illinois banks outside Chicago held high levels of commercial loans, keeping their local businesses afloat with credit, as did banks in Dixon and Tampico.[22] The Dixon cement plant had already begun cutting workers, while other familiar stores in Dixon shut their doors. Once the market crashed, hard times descended on almost everyone in Dixon.

It's not surprising that whatever politics Dutch absorbed he got from his father, the ardent anti-Prohibitionist and Catholic. And given Dixon's agricultural character, it's also not surprising that Reagan inherited sympathy for farmers and suspicion over the government's inability to stem the growing recession. Yet it is also likely that he inherited an intuitive understanding that even in his youth the nation was changing rapidly with the spread of consumer items like radios and automobiles. Samuel Insull's Chicago-based utilities had stretched their power lines across the city, electrifying a million homes, while nationally electricity began to stretch its crackling fingers across the land. For much of the 1920s, larger towns nearby like Rockford were bustling. Whatever political speeches Reagan read from the major parties, he was exposed to the openness and tolerance of the Republicans for blacks and the hostility of the Democratic Party to people of color. Representative Leonidas C. Dyer, a Republican from Missouri, had introduced the nation's first anti-lynching law in 1922, filibustered by Democrats. President Calvin Coolidge, in his first State of the Union address, had insisted that the rights of African-Americans were "just as sacred as those of any other citizen," and under his administration the Democrat-originated Ku Klux Klan ceased to have any national influence.[23] In short, while Reagan would start his political life as a Democrat, his transition was more understandable and even predictable than many have heretofore claimed.

In the difficult economy, things were destined to get even worse for Jack and Nelle. On Christmas Eve 1931, a special delivery envelope arrived at the Reagan house. Jack thought it might be a bonus. Instead, it was a layoff notice, and the Reagans had to move yet again, this time into one of the two bedrooms to rent out the other. They lacked a kitchen now and cooked their meals on a hot plate. Before long, the grocer cut off their credit, and Dutch's cash contributions went from being supplemental to lifesaving income. Often, however, Nelle didn't tell Jack about Dutch's money, quietly putting it in the grocery fund. On vacations home—when Dutch slept on a cot in the upstairs landing and Moon slept on the couch—Reagan recalled that despite the poverty, "there was a spirit of warmth and helpfulness and, yes, kindness abroad in the land that was inspiring to me as we all clung to the belief that, sooner or later, things would get better."[24] He described this bouncy optimism and faith in eventual improvement as a "small beacon of light amid the misery."[25]

For Jack, out of a job and the Depression deepening, politics seemed the only way out of the tunnel. He spent his time working for the Democrats, convinced that removing Herbert Hoover would return the country to prosperity. The Depression left a different message with Dutch, attuning him to the importance of money—although not greed of acquisition, but as a fact of life. It led him to add a second major to sociology, a new joint economics/sociology major introduced by Eureka's economics professor, Alexander Charles Gray.

Reagan's study strategy consisted of listening in class and reading a book the night before a test with his near-photographic memory, which drove Neil to distraction ("In about an hour he would thumb through it and 'photograph' those pages and write a good test").[26] Professor Gray complained that he never saw Dutch open a book, yet "when the test comes, I just have to give him his grade.... He has it all cold."[27] Reagan himself consistently joked about his academic performance at Eureka, much the way George W. Bush would joke about his own, years later. Reagan received an honorary degree from Eureka in 1957, and a decade later he returned to dedicate the Melick Library, saying, "Ten years ago I was just across the campus...to receive an honorary degree.... I had always figured the first degree you gave me was honorary."[28] Biographer Lou Cannon could not recall a single anecdote told by the master storyteller Reagan that involved a classroom, and academics are almost entirely missing from the Gipper's biographies. Yet, to the dismay of many career academics and intellectuals, study habits—like any habit—can be learned. No greater example is needed than Abraham Lincoln, who was self-trained in literature, politics, and law.

Professor Gray came from what would today be called a "social justice" Marxist perspective. While he used a traditional textbook, Lewis Haney's *The History of Economic Thought*, he also invited socialist Norman Thomas to speak on campus and suggested that Dutch read Lenin's biography. Gray's economics class reinforced some of the messages Reagan internalized from his father, but the sermons of Reverend Cleaver still remained fresh.

Cleaver taught that "of greater importance than full treasuries and receipted accounts are clean hearts...filled with faith." While members should rejoice over their "record and standing of matters of business," they needed to seek even more a relationship with the Lord.[29]

Throughout the summer, Dutch continued to court Mugs. Her family had lived in Eureka since the fall of 1931, but she visited friends in Dixon frequently. She met Dutch in the evenings at Fluff's Confectionary, which featured phosphate drinks, or for ice cream at Prince Ice Cream Castle. More often than not, they took in a movie at the Dixon Theater, even seeing *Journey's End* on the big screen. A who's who of Hollywood greats came across Reagan's gaze at the Dixon Theater: Frederic March, Greta Garbo, the Marx Brothers, Jean Harlow, Walter Huston, Douglas Fairbanks, and, of course, Tom Mix. At the end of that sophomore summer, though, Reagan was shocked by Margaret's announcement that she would not be attending Eureka that year. She found the academics insufficiently challenging and transferred to the University of Illinois at Champaign. A disappointed Dutch was not mollified when she pointed out that Champaign was closer to Eureka than Dixon. That junior year was Reagan's first year apart from Margaret.

Football, theater, and Margaret absorbed most of Reagan's time and attention as a sophomore at Eureka. He acted in a total of fourteen plays in his four years at Eureka, including Edna St. Vincent Millay's *Aria Da Capo*. Whatever the theme of the play, it had less significance for him than the process of acting and the thrill of the theater audience. He even got to play his ideal role, that of Captain Stanhope in *Journey's End*—the play he had seen with the Cleavers in Rockford on the night when he recalled being "drawn to the stage...as if it were a magnet."[30] Ellen Johnson, the English professor who coached drama, entered Eureka in a one-act play contest at Northwestern University. Eureka by far was the smallest school in the competition and the only one lacking a full-time dramatic arts department. Nonetheless, Eureka managed a second-place showing and Reagan won individual awards, leading the head of the Northwestern speech department to track down Dutch after the event and suggest that he consider a career in acting.

His junior year, Reagan played the lead in four productions, including *The Brat*, in which he had the role of a playboy who saved a young woman from the advances of his brother. In that play, Reagan got his first taste of what he called "leadingladyitis," finding himself attracted to his female lead. His brief fling with his female counterpart in *The Brat* ended, followed by Margaret's announcement that she would return to Eureka for her senior year. That meant Dutch would see a great deal of Mugs. It would have been normal for the couple to consider marriage, but Reagan still didn't have any job prospects and his dream of becoming a football star had faded. Jack's layoff notice in December impressed on Dutch more than ever the value of economic stability, while the number of students in the graduating class continued to shrink. That June 7, 1932, only forty-five graduates of Eureka College took the stage to receive their diplomas. Ronald Reagan spoke as the representative of the senior class, telling them not to let the future "bully you into non-achievement."[31]

Dutch returned to Dixon, resuming his lifeguard job amidst a darkening depression. News of police and soldiers driving the Bonus Marchers from their encampments on Pennsylvania Avenue reached the Reagan household, and both father and son shared the view that the government had gone too far. At the same time, Dutch was alerted to a program run by a Chicago evangelist, Paul Rader, called the "Pantry of Plenty" campaign, to feed the poor in Chicago and other struggling towns. The Disciples of Christ sent 3,800 cans of food for Dixon residents, reminding everyone that the most effective form of "welfare" was on a personal and local level. Reagan also saw the large house of drugstore magnate Charles Walgreen being erected on the Rock River (nicknamed in Dixon the "castle on a hill"). For Dutch, it stood as a reminder that the American dream lived, and that success through good ideas and hard work was still possible.

Reagan did not make the acquaintance of Walgreen himself but did meet a Kansas City businessman named Sid Altschuler at Lowell Park. Altschuler brought his family for a vacation at the lodge there, and the two began discussing business and careers. Altschuler asked Reagan what he wanted to do. Although Dutch strongly wanted to say what he knew to be true—he wanted to be an actor—he thought that might be too far-fetched for Altschuler. Dixon had produced a silent screen star in Douglas MacLean, but the most famous show business personality to come from Dixon was entertainment columnist Louella Parsons. (Reagan, as a young actor, would return with Parsons to Dixon in 1941 for "Louella Parsons Day.") At any rate, Dutch knew that he could not tell Altschuler he wanted to be an actor, and in *Where's the Rest of Me?* Reagan admitted he dodged the question, obliquely referring to the "entertainment" industry until the businessman pressed harder. "You have to tell me what you want to do," Altschuler said. Recalling his mimicking of radio announcers, Dutch replied, "What I'd really like to be is a radio sports announcer."[32] The question finally focused Reagan on a career path. And there were possibilities close to home—in Chicago.

The young announcer-to-be wasted no time. As soon as the summer earning season ended, Dutch hitched a ride to Chicago. Before he left, he met with Margaret for a final time as she prepared to take a teaching job in a nearby town. She was not enthused about Reagan's plans to be an announcer, and Reagan described it as a "sad parting."[33] In Chicago, Reagan roomed with an ex-Eureka student studying medicine. When Dutch hit the broadcast stations, visiting NBC first, he learned quickly that program directors did the interviewing, and in the case of NBC, he arrived on the wrong day. A receptionist changed his life, suggesting that no big station would hire someone with no experience and that he start in some of the smaller markets, or what she called "the sticks."[34] Hitchhiking back to Dixon in the rain, Dutch acquired the family Oldsmobile on loan from Jack as he began plotting a course to towns in a radius around Dixon. Davenport, Iowa, some seventy miles to the west, had a station with the call letters WOC, standing for "World of Chiropractic," since it broadcast from space above the Palmer School of Chiropractic. There, Reagan met Peter MacArthur, a well-known announcer and the station manager, who, by sheer chance, had come into the business because he needed help for back pain.

Once again, Dutch was too late. MacArthur had auditioned ninety-four applicants and selected one. As Reagan turned away, he mumbled, "How does anyone get a chance as a sports announcer if you can't even get a job in a radio station?"[35] The big Scotsman overheard Reagan and caught him at the elevator: "Not so fast, ye big bastard," MacArthur said. "Do ye perhaps know football?"[36] One could almost see Reagan's eyes light up from a century away. MacArthur asked Dutch to describe a game to him "and make me see it." Dutch was ushered into a sound studio, sat before a microphone, and told to talk. When the red light came on, he recalled a Eureka game against Western State University, with Eureka trailing 6-0 at the end of three quarters. Reagan jumped in like a pro. "We are going into the fourth quarter now. A chill wind is blowing in through the end of the stadium."[37] Although he got all the names right, Reagan massaged the actual events, noting in *Where's the Rest of Me?* that in the real game he missed his block (though the running back got through anyway) but in his radio broadcast "I murdered the linebacker with a block that could be felt in the press box."[38] Then, with the flair of a pro, he returned the broadcast to "our main studio." MacArthur came in, beaming, and offered him a live test at the University of Iowa game the following week, for which he'd get bus fare. If Reagan did well, he would be paid to broadcast the final three university games.

In his first job audition in entertainment—
radio broadcasting—Dutch re-created a Eureka College game
from memory, spicing it up with imaginative action.
It would not be the first time in his broadcasting career where
he would have to "imagine" a game while on air!

An anxious Reagan arrived early, ate some hot dogs—which remained "in a lump right in my middle"—and looked in awe at the press box. Paired with a seasoned professional announcer, Reagan would handle play-by-play and what is known today as "color commentary." His partner clearly did not know football, so Dutch jumped in like he was born in the press box, establishing his own vision lines so the listener could picture himself at the game. By his own admission, Dutch played it straight, then dutifully handed it over to the main announcer at the end of each quarter. But at the end of the third quarter, a yellow paper was dropped on the table between the two announcers with MacArthur's scrawl: "Let the kid finish the game." Reagan was elated, and more so, when, after the game, MacArthur said, "Ye'll do the rest of the games." He got an impressive ten dollars a week and bus fare, and, most important to Reagan, he got his first job in show business.[39]

The prospect of hearing his son on the radio so excited Jack that he told everyone he knew to tune in. With no work, Jack had spent his time engaged in Democratic Party politics, helping to get Franklin D. Roosevelt elected. (Dutch cast his first vote for FDR in 1932.) Roosevelt's election also underscored the growing presence of radio in American life, although the 1920 election of Warren Harding had been the first carried on the airwaves, and the 1921 World Series the first sporting event to have radio coverage. Radio Corporation of America (RCA), one of those magic stocks that soared from a few dollars in the early twenties to over $400 a share, had crashed along with the rest of Wall Street in 1929, but by then the radio had a place in many American homes. Radio brought with it a unique business model, for, by itself, a radio was entirely useless: it depended entirely on advertisers to pay for yet a third group—broadcasters, singers, musicians, actors, news announcers—to provide the programming. In short, Reagan had out of passion landed in one of the few growing industries during America's worst depression. Even then, keeping a job as a sports announcer was iffy.

Reagan's first full paid game, a 21-6 beating of Iowa by Minnesota, yielded positive reviews for the young announcer, with a *Chicago Tribune* critic labeling the broadcast a "crisp account of the muddy struggle [that] sounded like a carefully written story."[40] At season's end, and with Christmas looming, Dutch contemplated going back to manual labor when MacArthur offered him a staff announcer's job at $100 a week, 50 percent more than the average radio broadcaster in America made![41] Indeed, the salary was some four times what a traveling salesman like his father made, and more than most except star athletes and top executives. Even then, Dutch's upbringing in thriftiness continued to define him. He paid off some of his college debt and sent money home to Nelle. He also asked a local Disciples of Christ minister if the Lord would consider it a tithe for him to send 10 percent of his salary to Moon each month for college expenses and was assured God would look favorably upon that.[42]

In his new position of full-time announcer, Reagan was a fish out of water. His eyesight was too poor to read the script quickly, even with glasses. Spinning records was a far cry from spinning tales of tailbacks sweeping around the end. Not surprisingly, he was relieved after a mere three weeks, but the station reversed course when his replacement proved worse than Dutch. Given a reprieve, Reagan threw himself into the job and was asked to stay on. It left him with a profound lesson for his acting career, encapsulated in the old saw, "There are no small parts, only small actors." Getting sacked also put him in solid company with other success stories who failed their first time out, including actress Lucille Ball (who was once fired by Flo Ziegfeld), gun maker Sam Colt, radio king Rush Limbaugh (fired seven times), and auto tycoon Henry Ford. The genius of America, Reagan learned, was not in the first chances that people are given but in the second, third, and fourth chances.

Jack had another chance of his own, landing a job with Roosevelt's new Works Progress Administration to manage work and food distribution in Dixon at modest pay. As Reagan recalled, "There was no bureaucracy at Jack's level: he shared an office and secretary with the Country Supervisor of Poor."[43] Jack found every odd job or stray chore he could find, then set up a schedule for the unemployed so that everyone worked for their food. Dutch recalled a common sight of men asking, "When are you going to have another job for me, Jack?"[44] Watching his father—and the other men—at work showed Reagan that there was a dignity to employment and that his neighbors did not want charity. The flexibility Jack enjoyed, and the judgment calls he made—insisting that food be tied to some effort— would become impossible before long by the very New Deal incentives FDR created (and which Lyndon B. Johnson later expanded in his "Great Society" in the 1960s). Both Reagans, though, saw first-hand what damage even a little bureaucracy could do. If a man went off relief for a job, then was laid off, it took three more weeks for him to get back on the dole.

As Reagan's admiration of Franklin Roosevelt developed during this impressionable age, it was not surprising that Dutch tended to recall only the positive elements of FDR—his fireside chats with his "strong, gentle, confident voice resonat[ing] across the nation…[bringing] comfort and resilience…and reassured us that we could lick any problem."[45] Admitting that FDR "set in motion the forces that later sought to create big government and bring a form of veiled socialism to America," Reagan convinced himself of Roosevelt's sincerity in wanting to balance the budget or reduce waste in government. In *An American Life* he would quote FDR as saying that giveaway programs "destroy the human spirit."[46] He generously suggested that "even FDR didn't realize that once you created a bureaucracy, it took on a life of its own."[47] In fact, Roosevelt knew precisely that his massive structures would be almost impossible to kill, his programs nearly immortal. (Reagan in 1964 would quip that "a government bureau is the nearest thing to eternal life we'll ever see on this earth.") The cold-blooded deliberateness with which the New Dealers instituted their programs has been exhaustively exposed by Burton Folsom, who found that not only did most programs rob people of initiative and seek to make them permanent wards of the state, but almost as important they were designed to ensure a permanent Democratic Party majority. Largesse was doled out on the basis of party affiliation and friendship to Roosevelt (Illinois got 20 percent of all federal funds).[48] FDR sicced the Internal Revenue Service on political enemies. He spoke about American businessmen the way Reagan as president would only describe Soviet totalitarians.

During the Great Depression, Reagan came to idolize FDR and separate him from policies that, already, Dutch was seeing as destructive. His affinity for Roosevelt personally never left him, even as he later railed against the New Deal in his political speeches.

Young Dutch would carry into maturity a rosy interpretation of Roosevelt personally, if not the New Deal in its early stages more generally. Slowly, though, he formed some observations based on Jack's difficulties in keeping people working once they got relief. Through Jack, he learned that federal welfare workers actively discouraged able-bodied men from working because they were receiving a handout. "After a while," Reagan wrote, "Jack couldn't get any of his projects going: he couldn't get enough men sprung from the welfare giveaway program."[49]

Called back to the station, Dutch was set to be assigned an on-air assistant who would help him with his delivery, rhythm, flow into and out of commercials, and so on. He quickly mastered the medium and landed his own show, and in early 1933, MacArthur assigned Reagan to Des Moines at WHO, which needed an announcer for the Drake Relays, an annual track and field event held at Drake University. Once again, Dutch was in an element he knew well, and once again, he had that streak of Irish luck: WHO soon received a permit for a 50,000-watt transmitter, and as a result, WOC in Davenport would be closed and everyone transferred to Des Moines at WHO. Reagan had his own shows and time slot, "The World of Sports with Dutch Reagan," wisely insisting on his name in the title and revealing that even at a young age he understood the importance of name recognition. Overnight, Reagan's broadcasts reached thousands of additional people, and his job became permanent.

He also learned in a phone call home that Margaret was leaving for France when she finished her first year of teaching. Dutch was stunned, especially since he just landed a job with enough money to support two. It finalized in his mind that he and Mugs were over, a conclusion cemented in 1936 when she sent him a letter from France with his fraternity pin. She informed him that she had met someone and planned to marry. An anguished Dutch called his mother, who already had learned through the grapevine of Margaret's betrothal. Next, he bought his first car, a Nash convertible. And, before long, he found other girls.

Moon visited Dutch in Des Moines and was invited to the studio to watch the broadcast. Reagan was making game predictions and Moon, outside the booth, was shaking his head. Dutch brought him in and put him on air, which proved so entertaining—an early version of "Mike and Mike"—that it became a regular Friday night feature. Indeed, Moon eventually became an announcer himself, then a program director, then, after that, producer and network executive. Meanwhile, Ronald Reagan covered hundreds of events, including baseball games played far away with the play-by-play sent by Morse code on a telegraph after each pitch. Dutch sat across from a telegrapher who would write out the play (say, "out four to three," meaning a ground ball to second base, who threw the runner out at first base) on a slip of paper and hand it to him through a slot in the glass separating the two men. Even though several stations covered the games, and some live, Reagan and his telegrapher were able to keep up within a half-pitch of the live broadcast. In between plays, Dutch had to fill time, "describing" the field, the weather conditions, the crowd—whatever was entertaining.

In a famous story that Reagan admitted retelling more than any other, Reagan "broadcast" a 1934 game between the Cubs and the St. Louis Cardinals (Reagan claimed it was a "scoreless tie," but it was 3-1 and scoreless over the last three innings). The famous Dizzy Dean was pitching to Augie Galan as Reagan described the action when suddenly the telegrapher began shaking his head.[50] When the note came through the glass, it had no play, just the words "The wire's gone dead." Reagan didn't dare tell listeners that the wire had gone dead or they would switch channels, so he called a foul ball. By then Dutch realized he might have to ad-lib a great deal. He slowed down Dizzy Dean, had him shake off signs, fouled more pitches, missed a home run by inches, had a redheaded kid track down a fouled pitch, and on and on. Reagan's ad-lib narration continued for almost seven minutes, only to learn that Galan popped out on his very first swing!

He also broadcast university football games by wire, including a University of Michigan game featuring a center named Gerald Ford. But he also engaged in general announcing duties, including interviews of celebrities who passed through. Once, evangelist Aimee Semple McPherson came to Des Moines. She had been in the midst of accusations of having an extramarital affair. After interviewing her and touting her revival in town, Reagan found she had mesmerized him and seized control of the program, before suddenly saying, "Good night" and leaving. There was still four minutes remaining in the broadcast, so he twirled his finger to have his engineer spin a record. Unfortunately, a Cab Calloway song, "Minnie the Moocher's Wedding Day," came on.[51] A number of other celebrities came to the station, including actor Leslie Howard and famous boxer Max Baer (whom Reagan described as "a beautiful piece of physical machinery as ever stepped into a fight ring.")[52] Baer, demonstrating a punch, accidentally hit the mailroom clerk in the stomach and put him out for seven minutes.

While in Des Moines, Reagan learned that the 14th US Cavalry regiment was stationed nearby. He had always wanted to ride horses, like his hero in the movies, Tom Mix. Now he saw his opportunity. Through provisions of the National Defense Act of 1916, candidates for officer commissions could actively train with the regiment before receiving the commission in the reserves. For Dutch, this was perfect because at that time the physical examination—which would expose his terrible vision—did not come until *after* the acceptance of a candidate and only immediately before the actual commission. Assuming he would eventually flunk the physical, Reagan rode and trained extensively but cleverly avoided ever completing the coursework that would trigger his physical exam. When he finally had to meet the doctors, he told them, "Fellows, you might as well save some time…[and] take a look at my eyes."[53] Rather than fill out a form, they let Reagan go to a civilian doctor for the exam, at which point he held his hand over his eye, squinted and focused through the hole between his fingers, and managed to pass.

His final test for commission involved leading a platoon through maneuvers with West Point grads riding on each side of him screaming in his ear. It was pouring rain, and his unit had no love for a lieutenant-in-waiting marching them around in a storm ("I could almost feel the hatred," he noted). Finally, his last task was to have his horse jump a hurdle. Sure he would fall off and land in a mudhole, Second Lieutenant Reagan successfully made the leap. His once-a-month training did not interfere with his forays to Hollywood, and when he moved his commission was transferred to the 323rd Cavalry in California.

Already Reagan pondered new career moves, and once again, sports provided his big break. The Chicago Cubs held their spring training camp in California on Santa Catalina Island from February 12 to March 15, which presented an opportunity. He pitched to management an idea to use his vacation time to accompany the Cubs in spring training and file reports. It would provide color for his broadcasts during the season. Taking the train across the American West, Reagan arrived in Los Angeles and grabbed a room at the Hollywood Plaza Hotel near Hollywood and Vine—the place of dreams to many in America. He immediately hopped a taxi to the Republic Pictures studios, where the Oklahoma Outlaws were filming with cowboy star Gene Autry. Dutch met with their representative, who tossed some scripts to Reagan and told him to return in "a week or two" for a read. Excited, Reagan nevertheless had the maturity to see that Republic was a low-budget studio that would never make him a major star.

While in Des Moines, Dutch had interviewed Joy Hodges, a local girl made good as a singer based in Hollywood. After their interview, Dutch invited her to go riding, but she lacked any riding clothes and stood him up (to her great regret). When Reagan went to California, she was singing at the Biltmore Bowl and he looked her up. She met him for dinner between shows, whereupon he told her he wanted to screen-test with a studio. Hodges asked him to stand up and was impressed with his height and good looks…but the horn-rimmed glasses! She said, "Take off your glasses," and he complied. "Better. Don't ever put them on again," she admonished him. Then she said she would arrange for him to meet her agent George Ward. But she didn't give him her phone number, and Reagan thought he had been put off until a waiter arrived with a slip of paper and her contact information. He didn't know that during a break Hodges had already called Ward and pitched him on Dutch.

One of the up-and-coming stars at Warner Brothers (usually referred to as Warner Bros.) was Ross Alexander, whom the studio groomed to replace Dick Powell. But Alexander committed suicide in January 1937, and the studio was anxious to find a replacement in a similar mode. Dutch Reagan fit the mold—especially his voice, which impressed everyone—but time was running out on his vacation. He had to leave by train on March 16, forcing Ward to schedule a pair of tests, one at Warner Bros. and one at Paramount. On Sunday, March 13, Reagan showed up for a morning test at Paramount, knowing he had to be available to remotely cover a Cubs exhibition game back at Wrigley Field at noon. By one o'clock, he still hadn't been called and, when he inquired, was told it might be close to midnight before he got his shot. Reagan was outraged, especially by the dismissive response: "Son, this is Hollywood." Dutch said, "Well, this is Des Moines and you can shove Hollywood." He left, but knew he still had the Warner Bros. test coming up Tuesday. If he had not taken the Paramount test seriously, he most certainly approached the Warner Bros. test with determination and preparation, learning his lines by applying his impressive memory ("I couldn't believe his ability to read a page and practically recite it back," Hodges said).[54]

He was given pages from *The Philadelphia Story*, then rehearsed Sunday with Hodges. At the screen test, he benefitted from a seasoned director and cameraman. More importantly, Reagan's instincts for what grabbed people were on full display. Jack Warner, after seeing the test later, thought Dutch's shoulders were too wide, his head too small, but that he had a quality, a kind of wholesomeness. Ward told him the screen test went well and urged Reagan to stay in California until Warner himself could see the film, but Dutch insisted he had to get back to work in Des Moines. (He told Ward he had "another offer," but of course his other offer was his full-time job.) Although Reagan had unwittingly played "hard to get," jumping on the train with the Cubs, there is no indication that he thought he was leveraging anyone.[55] All the way back to Des Moines, he was convinced he had made a terrible mistake. When he reported to work at WHO on Monday, March 22, he had no sooner regaled the staff with stories of his star-powered screen test when a telegram arrived from Ward:

WARNERS OFFER CONTRACT SEVEN YEARS, ONE YEAR'S OPTION, STARTING AT $200 A WEEK. WHAT SHALL I DO? GEORGE WARD MEIKLEJOHN AGENCY

It only took Reagan as long as it was required to get to Western Union to wire back and (referring to his sudden departure from Hollywood) to admit leaving was a "childish trick:"

SIGN BEFORE THEY CHANGE THEIR MINDS. DUTCH REAGAN[56]

Hodges, who was invested in Reagan as well, fired off her own telegram to the *Des Moines Register* alerting the paper that "you do have a potential star in your midst." Dutch spent the rest of the day walking on air, accepting accolades from friends and coworkers and generally amazed that he had in fact landed his dream job. He called his parents and promised to bring them out as soon as he could manage it.

His contract did not start until June 1, so Reagan arranged to stay at WHO until May 21 to train a replacement. The lifeguard, football player, and student activist had transformed into the movie star.

3

Limelight

The Ronald Reagan who arrived for a second time in Los Angeles knew he was no star—yet. Little did he know he had already been assigned a picture, *Love Is on the Air*.[1] Warner Bros. Studios in the 1930s had developed a system of grooming actors and actresses through lower-budget films called "B" movies or B productions. Whereas some of the A pictures could have a budget of $5 million or more, *Love Is On the Air*, for example, had a budget of $119,000. Reagan and his screen test partner June Travis were the leads. Under the studios' contract systems, a film company would introduce its budding new talent to the public. As employees, they did not have the right to refuse a picture, nor have any say in the director or other cast. Ostensibly, Reagan worked under Hal Wallis, a veteran executive producer who handled the A pictures, although he more directly was assigned to Bryan Foy, who supervised the B productions (and whose nickname was "keeper of the Bs" and who came from the famous "Seven Little Foys" act).

Supposedly it was difficult to move up from the Bs to A-level pictures—the scholar of Reagan's Hollywood years, Marc Eliot, quipped that "getting out of Alcatraz was easier"—but it happened on occasion. Humphrey Bogart had moved up, despite being far from the typical leading man. Republic, almost an exclusive B-movie studio, featured John Wayne, who would become one of the biggest stars ever. Still, far from serving as a "farm team" for the pros, the B companies constituted their own genre and, in some ways, a separate product altogether. The designation "B" referred to the length and budget of films (hence, usually, the expectations associated with them), though not necessarily the quality of acting. Studios packaged B movies in contracts with the A films to movie theaters. When shown in theaters, B movies appeared prior to the lead film in a double feature; hence, they were intended to be shorter. Audiences often missed some or all of the opening feature. On the other hand, poorer theaters often would run nothing but B films, sometimes continuously all night.[2]

Reagan got the makeover treatment, quipping that the in-house studio team apparently found him too big a challenge and subcontracted the work out to the House of Westmore salon ("they circled around me as if I were a racehorse," he recalled).[3] *Love Is On the Air* opened to good reviews, particularly for Reagan, whom reviewers described as warm, likeable, and pleasing. For marquee and publicity purposes, he had agreed to use the name "Ronald Reagan." His debut led the *Hollywood Reporter* to praise him for "giving one of the best first picture performances Hollywood has offered in many a day."[4]

"Leadingladyitis," that disease that Reagan was afflicted with in college, infected him again, leading to a brief affair with his costar June Travis.[5] She certainly seemed a good match. Travis could ride, and her father was the vice president of the Chicago White Sox. As Reagan soon discovered, such leading-lady romances tended to end the moment the director yelled, "That's a wrap."

By then he was "Ron" or "Ronnie" to his coworkers. They not only befriended him but taught him the ropes—cinematographer James Van Trees, in particular, who instructed him on hitting his marks, tilting his head in the right direction, and so on. This began an inner tension that would mark Reagan's entire Hollywood career. At one level, Dutch was self-critical about his shots, calling his first day's rushes (raw footage) a "let down."[6] More than just the shock of seeing oneself on camera, Reagan had placed himself in the role and halfway expected to see his persona on the rushes, not himself. Yet the camera liked him, a point that he also internalized. He was concerned with his appearance on screen and would perfect all the mechanics that affected that element of his acting, but to Reagan it was always just...acting. With only two exceptions—*Knute Rockne,*

All American and *Dark Victory*—Dutch never "became" the character on screen. Later, actors would so immerse themselves so completely in roles that they literally changed, either physically (Robert De Niro in *Raging Bull* or Matthew McConaughey in *Dallas Buyers Club*) or mentally (Heath Ledger, it was rumored, in *The Dark Knight*), but Reagan never would have gone to such lengths. In most cases, he did not want to work that hard at acting, but on a more fundamental level, to Dutch it was just acting, after all, not life.

Indeed, on set, Dutch (though he steadily referred to himself by that nickname less and less) relished the countless hours of downtime waiting for a shot to be set up, cheerfully telling sports stories or dissembling about one of his celebrity interviews. At times, his facility with numbers and his attention to world events proved too taxing for his fellow actors, who developed systems to avoid sitting with him at lunch. He was, one could argue, too intellectual for many of them, always consumed by ideas and events of the day.

True to his promise, after his first paychecks, Reagan sent for his parents and set them up in an apartment near Sunset, containing his shock when he saw Jack's condition. By then totally dependent on Nelle, Jack had a withered arm and could no longer drive. Reagan got Warner to give his father the job of opening and replying to fan mail at a salary of twenty-five dollars a week. Every Sunday night, Reagan took a break from his frequent dates to have dinner with his parents at LaRue's, an Italian restaurant. Having drifted away from regular churchgoing in Des Moines, Reagan began attending services with his mother again and resumed his tithing. He and Jack grew extremely close during these California years, more so as Moon had defected to the Republican Party. And now that Jack had given up the bottle, the two talked regularly (and Jack, more coherently).

When not with his parents or on a date, Reagan hung out with several of his fraternity brothers who had trekked westward hoping their famous friend could line them up a place in pictures. Instead, they spent days touring the stars' homes in Beverly Hills or drank coffee at Barney's Beanery. Those months reinforced the awareness Reagan had that although he made movies, he had few friends *in* movies. And it must always be kept in mind that unlike most of his fellow actors, Reagan had a college degree and generally, in terms of intellectual curiosity, was ahead of them.[7]

Those early Hollywood experiences reinforced Reagan's B casting. Within the industry, B films were made so quickly and the cast and crew moved so rapidly that Reagan had no time to develop lasting bonds. This factor underscored the reality that *very* few B actors ever moved into A roles: there simply was no time to immerse oneself in a role. As Dutch would joke, the studios "don't want it good. They want it Thursday." But, as with all filming, there was extensive downtime, which Reagan used to read, tell stories, and above all talk politics. Ironically, then, the very nature of B movies contributed to Reagan's development as a political force.

When Reagan began work his second film, *Sergeant Murphy*, a horse movie shot in Monterey, he hung out with the troopers from the Eleventh Cavalry. When the movie was finally released in February 1938, Reagan impressed New York *Daily News* critic Dorothy Masters, who cited Dutch as the best thing about the show. Masters wrote that Reagan's "looks and personality scoot out toeholds for a plot that can barely make the grade."[8] Warner Bros. then filmed him in *Hollywood Hotel* and *Swing Your Lady*, using him in minor parts. Reagan described these early roles as follows:

> Remember the guy in the movies who rushes to the phone booth, pushes his hat to the back of his head…drops a nickel in the [phone], dials a few numbers and then says, "Gimme the city desk. I've got a story that'll split this town wide open!" That was me.

In *Hollywood Hotel*, Reagan played alongside Dick Powell (whom Reagan was to eventually replace) and Louella Parsons as herself, who reminisced with the young actor about his years in Dixon, Illinois. *Swing Your Lady* was a Bogart film (which Bogie would later call his worst)—both parts were small, with Reagan playing a sports reporter. He wrapped up his appearances quickly. And, typically, in the midst of filming those two pictures, Reagan was shipped by Warner Bros. to Coronado to film a *third* movie with a minor role in *Submarine D-1*. Reagan's encounter with Parsons provided the shot in the arm his mud-stuck career needed. She began to write favorably about her fellow Dixonite and later would become a champion of sorts. But at that time, things hardly seemed to improve for Dutch. After the forgettable *Accidents Will Happen*, Reagan was called up to the majors again for another movie with Powell, *Cowboy from Brooklyn*—another musical. Alongside Powell was Pat O'Brien, a top star in the Warner Bros. stable. O'Brien grew fond of the youngster and inducted him into the "Irish Mafia" (an unofficial group consisting of himself, Spencer Tracy, Jimmy Cagney, and Frank McHugh), but that didn't stop the wily vet from stealing the scenes. It was a classic difference of perceptions: established actors saw Reagan as a threat, while Dutch fretted that he had been relegated to a permanent also-ran status. Yet Reagan—who worked nonstop—found no time for drama classes or theater groups that might have given him the practice to refine his craft.

Reagan used to quip of his B movie roles that they "didn't want it good. They want it Thursday."

O'Brien's friendship got him a seat at the A tables in the commissary but, more than that, gave him the position of emcee and entertainer. O'Brien loved Dutch's stories, sports tales, jokes, and his Irish roots. Outside the studio, Reagan quickly developed a reputation as a ladies' man, which caused problems for both Jack Warner and Louella Parsons. Warner wanted to avoid any unfavorable publicity—Reagan was dating Lana Turner (the two attended the 1938 opening of *Jezebel* together) and Susan Hayward. Having crafted a persona of all-American boy for her Dixon connection, Parsons grew concerned about Reagan's frequent public appearances with these glamorous women, but she had far less influence over Reagan than did Warner, who signed his paychecks. When he had a fling with Ila Rhodes, another actress in the Warner B-movie company, and got serious to the point of becoming engaged to her, Jack Warner let him know in no uncertain terms that the studio would frown upon it. Rhodes had no place as a major actress in Warner Bros.' future, meaning Jack did not want Reagan tied to her. Warner still hadn't decided if Reagan had potential to become a star, but he wanted to take no chances. The engagement ended.[9] Parsons, however, continued to weave her story of Ronald

Reagan, the well-mannered midwestern churchgoing boy who bought a house for his parents.

Despite his fortunate connections in O'Brien and Parson's efforts, Reagan's career progress was slow. When he did an infrequent A picture, such as *Boy Meets Girl* with O'Brien and Cagney or *Naughty But Nice* with Dick Powell, his parts were so small as to be missed in a popcorn gulp, and when he had a lead role, it came in a B picture such as *Girls on Probation* (another Foy product) opposite Jane Bryan. In 1938, his ninth picture, *Brother Rat*, about Virginia Military Institute cadets, put him with Eddie Albert, Jane Bryan again, and an actress named Jane Wyman.

Another midwestern product (born in Missouri in 1917), Jane Mayfield had come up as a singer, moved to Los Angeles at sixteen, and married Ernest Wyman.[10] Now as Jane Wyman, she had a pretty face and a distinct button nose, allowing her to snag a place in the chorus line known as the Goldwyn Girls, and made several pictures. By the time she met Ronald Reagan, she had long since dumped Ernest Wyman and had married another man who was seldom around, only to separate after only three months and then file for divorce from him. With his churchgoing upbringing, Reagan wanted nothing to do with a woman who was still another man's wife. But the feeling was not mutual: "I was drawn to him at once," she recalled.[11] His personality trait of rolling with the punches, of being slow to anger, impressed her when they had a long wait for a photo shoot. Wyman, ready to blow up and feel victimized, calmed down when Reagan quietly said, "It's just a mistake.... It's no one's fault."[12] Indeed, Reagan's overall good humor and political knowledge "overwhelmed...[and] intimidated" her.[13]

At one time or another, Ronald Reagan dated virtually every glamour girl in Hollywood: Lana Turner, Ann Sothern, Piper Laurie, Patricia Neal, Rhonda Fleming, Doris Day, and, of course, his future wife Jane Wyman.

Wyman, having gone through two husbands, was emotionally unstable at best (one source suggested she had a nervous breakdown prior to meeting Reagan), and writer Marc Eliot described her as "wearing chips on her shoulder[s] like epaulets."[14] She had experienced few of life's leisures, despite having had at least one husband who wanted to pamper her. Reagan was surprised to learn she'd not been swimming or golfing, nor could she ice skate. He quickly fixed that, teaching her to skate until the pair were figure skating as a couple. But *Brother Rat* failed to provide the vehicle for either of them to skate into the next level of stardom, and Jane took to calling herself the "queen of the subplots."[15]

The yo-yo nature of Reagan's movie career continued with an A picture that came out after *Naughty But Nice* but which was filmed beforehand, again with Dick Powell, and again with no noticeable benefit to anyone in the film. Following *Naughty But Nice*, Reagan got demoted to Foy's B unit again for *Secret Service of the Air*, the latest studio attempt to shift audiences from an A-list star (in this case, Errol Flynn) to possibly a new star: Reagan. And, again, Dutch did not seize the day. Warners, having failed to make Dutch the "next" Dick Powell, and now the "next" Errol Flynn, was running out of "nexts."

Nor did it help Reagan that he consistently found himself teamed up with notorious scene-stealers like Wallace Beery, or the improvisational Lionel Barrymore, who managed to run over Reagan's foot with a wheelchair in one scene.[16] On another occasion, Reagan suffered permanent hearing loss when a pistol went off too close to his ear.

Still assigned to Foy for a sequel to *Secret Service of the Air*, Reagan found himself abruptly shifted to *Dark Victory*, an A film (and one of Hollywood's first dark tales) that happened to give Bette Davis a role for which she is forever remembered. Reagan had a small part again, but in an important change in his attitude, he fully embraced his character and found himself fighting with director (Edmund Goulding) over how the lines should be done. He ended up "delivering the line my way."[17] Not surprisingly, Davis never remembered he was in the movie—but even Humphrey Bogart disappeared in the shadows behind her as *Dark Victory* went on to be one of the biggest success stories of 1939.

The impressive list of films that appeared that year was a testament to the golden age of Hollywood. Reagan's new career suddenly hurled him into competition with arguably the best talent ever assembled, including

Jimmy Stewart, Tyrone Power, Henry Fonda, Greta Garbo, Jean Arthur, Claudette Colbert, Clark Gable, Rita Hayworth, James Cagney, Laurence Olivier, Marlene Dietrich, Vivien Leigh, and his costar in *Dark Victory*, Humphrey Bogart. In addition to *Dark Victory*, *Beau Geste*, *Drums Along the Mohawk*, *Destry Rides Again*, *Stagecoach*, *Young Mr. Lincoln*, *Goodbye Mr. Chips*, *Gone with the Wind*, and *The Wizard of Oz* all came out that year—which made *Dark Victory's* Oscar nomination for Best Picture all the more remarkable. Davis received a Best Actress nomination.

Thrown into this competition, Reagan lacked the meanness some of his screen competitors possessed and which was required to steal scenes. Some of his later comments about wanting to be an A-list actor notwithstanding, the choices he made with his time off and his preference for spending time with family and friends suggest that Ronald Reagan enjoyed being a B star. Such roles certainly paid the bills: he earned a very respectable $1,600 a year in 1939 (about $40,000 in 2017 dollars).

In December 1940, Jane Wyman's second divorce became final. Reagan felt free to ask her to marry, which he did while she was in the hospital recuperating from a stomach disorder. Squeezed in between the proposal and the wedding, Louella Parsons pitched Warner Bros. on a national tour with some of their top talent, including the newly engaged couple. With Dutch now on the cusp of being a leading actor, he was sent off along with Susan Hayward, Joy Hodges, and others. A sort of traveling variety show, the format included songs, skits with Reagan, Wyman, and Hayward, and a chorus line. Parsons' brainchild played to full houses and more than a few good reviews.

The Reagan/Wyman wedding, on January 26, 1940, at Hollywood Beverly Christian Church, was followed by a reception at Parsons' home. Of course, she had already touted the pairing of the two clean-cut kids in her columns, pointing out that one of Hollywood's leading bachelors had been scooped up. Wyman had drifted into serious debt and quite heroically had paid off every cent she owed prior to the marriage. She admitted she only had $500 to her name when they tied the knot.[18] Wyman recalled that even when they went to a new restaurant, they received "special treatment" because of Reagan's kind, friendly manner—"as friendly when he spoke to a waiter as it was when he spoke to a friend."[19] The couple had a Palm Springs honeymoon, then returned to Los Angeles and celebrated at the Cocoanut Grove. They both liked golf and applied for membership at the Lakeside Country Club, but once Reagan found out the club wouldn't allow Jack Warner because he was a Jew, he abruptly resigned. He joined the Hillcrest Country Club, which did have Jews as members, instead. Five months after the marriage, Wyman was pregnant (which she hid from the studio for four months). For Reagan, it was all there: a great salary, a beautiful wife, a baby on the way—the nearly perfect life. The only thing still missing was a genuine starring role for the leading man.

Then it appeared. A new Pat O'Brien movie, *Knute Rockne, All American*, popped up on the radar screen of Reagan's new agent, Lew Wasserman, for inside that film was the role of the Notre Dame football player George Gipp. Reagan and his new wife had been cast in a *Brother Rat* sequel that did nothing, as well as a film called *An Angel from Texas*. Another Foy movie playing on the "air" theme—*Murder in the Air*—came Dutch's way before he became aware of the George Gipp role. In both his biographies, Reagan insisted he drove to Hal Wallis's office to plead for the role, unaware that Wallis, through Wasserman, had already rejected him twice. Indeed, Wallis once referred to him as a "hick radio announcer from the Middle West."[20] The truth is that Reagan had already approached his friend and director Foy, but Foy's pull in the A units was minimal. O'Brien, on the other hand, had considerable heft, and the veteran actor saw things in Reagan, including the fact he resembled Gipp and knew football, that he thought would help the film. Once Spencer Tracy lost the starring role of Rockne (because his studio wouldn't lend him out), leaving the role to O'Brien, he wanted his friend Reagan for the role of Gipp. O'Brien even offered to do a screen test with Reagan, an act that convinced Wallis to offer him the role. Like *Rudy* decades later, *Knute Rockne* celebrated tenacity, climbing the American success ladder, and competition, and wielded a powerful Christian (and obviously Catholic) theme, just as Rudy would.

Reagan was well paid for the picture (over $2,000, as Lew Wasserman had tripled his salary through deft negotiations), and, while he only had ten minutes' worth of screen time, he embraced the role that would become for him an alter ego. He captured the athleticism of the Notre Dame half-back naturally because of his football days, but the part required more. In the film, Gipp contracts a rare disease while playing at Notre Dame and as he is dying whispers to Rockne, "Some day when the team's up against it and the breaks are beating the boys, ask them to go in there with all they've got, win just one for the Gipper."[21] It was a line that took its place among other unforgettable movie phrases such as "You can't handle the truth" and "Houston, we have a problem," and, as Eliot observed, "Culturally, he became the poster boy for self-sacrifice, teamwork, humility, and, ultimately, the American Way."[22] Reagan received star-quality reviews for a supporting role and got fawning treatment in the general press, and he and O'Brien were greeted by massive crowds after their train arrived back in Los Angeles from a South Bend premiere. Moreover, the studio rewarded him with another solid part, that of George Armstrong Custer in *Santa Fe Trail*. He took his place amongst an all-star cast that included Errol Flynn, Olivia de Havilland, and Raymond Massey. Reagan delivered, but he was overpowered by Flynn and Massey in a huge hit for Warner Bros. He closed out 1940 as a supporting actor with two major hits, one of which gained him a fan base.

Yet he struggled with parts he could not identify with. In reality, when Reagan couldn't play a hero—or least a red-blooded American male—he didn't do well. It was a weakness in his craft he had not identified. In the end it wouldn't matter because he was slowly drifting into an altogether different world: that of politics.

When first approached about joining the Screen Actors Guild (SAG), Reagan, the rugged individualist, had little use for it. His Democrat/New Deal leanings made him generally sympathetic to unionism, but his hard-scrabble life and self-motivation left him personally uninterested. His wife, however, was an active member of SAG, and he soon accompanied Wyman to SAG meetings and social functions.

As war clouds gathered, Reagan's facility with numbers, statistics, and current events (which at one time had caused crew and cast to steer clear of him on the set) now became the feature that gained him a wider circle of friends. Still a Roosevelt supporter, he had become friends with Justin Dart, a part owner of Walgreens who had married, then divorced, Ruth Walgreen. Reagan met him during filming of *Brother Rat and a Baby* with Jane Bryan, who had become engaged to Dart and introduced him to Reagan. Dart became one of Reagan's closest Republican friends and would later hire Neil Reagan to run ad campaigns for him. Dart opened Dutch's eyes to some of the underhanded tactics FDR routinely used, and while he certainly didn't convert Reagan overnight, Dart had a lasting influence on his political thinking. So did his fellow actor and Republican Dick Powell. For several years, Powell and Dutch had argued politics, each trying to convert the other. Powell already saw in Reagan a political future that would eclipse his acting career. But neither Wyman nor Powell's wife, June Allyson, cared for the political discussions that inevitably ensued at social gatherings.

A new Reagan, their daughter Maureen, arrived on January 4, 1941. Wyman later said she wanted a boy and was "terribly disappointed" for months.[23] Having outgrown their small apartment, the family had to move to a house they built on a lot overlooking Sunset. Wyman's career suffered, predictably, as she focused on Maureen and on furnishing the new home they had built in the Hollywood Hills. They had acquired the $15,000 house with a twenty-year mortgage at $125 a month, which, while nicer than the home of an average American (about $3,000 at the time), was well below Hollywood star standards. The Reagans wisely concluded that the nature of the film industry was fickle, and they should get a house they could acquire even if Ron's acting career dried up.[24] Perhaps the only real extravagance was a pair of bathrooms that also contained dressing rooms— a requirement for two actors who often had different casting schedules. FDR's high tax brackets on the wealthy also chipped away at their income, and the couple lived on less than 30 percent of their earnings. One source claimed they each had a cash allowance of only twenty-five dollars a week (about $440 in 2017 dollars).[25]

It slowly began to eat at Wyman. She was unhappy in the role of homemaker and mother, even when Reagan hired a nursemaid. Rifts began to grow between the couple, especially regarding Reagan's growing interest in world events and politics. Wyman quietly grew to resent his focus on the world outside of Hollywood, made famous in her comment to columnist

Earl Wilson, "You ask what time it is and [Ronnie will] tell you how the watch was made."[26]

When Wyman received a call from John Dales, executive director of SAG, asking her to be an alternate member of the board, she introduced him to her husband and suggested that he would do a better job. Moreover, Reagan fit the need, which was that new policies in SAG required "a broad representation of all segments of the actor's world," Reagan wrote, and "one of the vacancies happened to fit my classification: new, young contract player."[27] Reagan applied himself to the position, studying the issues and the union's history. It could be said he worked harder for his SAG job than he had for any acting part. And he got along well with Dales, although the ultimate trick would be getting along with Jack Warner.

A month after Maureen was born, Reagan received a draft notice. By a single vote, the US Congress had approved the selective service system in light of war clouds in Europe (though few guessed at the time it would be Japan that drew us into the conflict). He still retained his commission in the reserves from the cavalry back in Iowa that was transferred to the 323rd Cavalry in California.[28] Reagan was eligible to be called up, but he knew he had finagled his way into the reserves in the first place and that his eyes would not pass a legitimate test. Jack Warner, unaware of Reagan's eyesight problems, sought a deferment for him, which was granted.

His yo-yo career continued with *Million Dollar Baby*, in which he played a concert pianist—a role for which he toiled diligently to get the moves of a piano player down. It did not work. The director, Curtis Bernhardt, wrote to Warner insisting Reagan was without "any musical feeling or sense" and that he would have to shoot around Reagan's hands, but Reagan remembered it slightly differently: "I became pretty good as long as the piano remained silent."[29] His next film, *Nine Lives Are Not Enough*, however, won him high praise (*Variety* said his character was "hilariously scatterbrained and devilishly resourceful").[30]

Reagan then filmed the first of his war movies, *International Squadron*, about an American flyer who joins the Royal Air Force to fight in the Battle of Britain. He was good enough in *International Squadron* that both Warner and Wallis began to see him in a new light—again thinking he could be star material. Their new vehicle for Reagan: director Sam Wood's *King's Row*. A major costarring role as Drake McHugh offered Reagan a meaty part, a wealthy orphan who loses his fortune and, ultimately, his legs.

The script, in its first iterations, was too racy for Warner Bros. *King's Row* was a story set in a typical American town that quickly pulled the curtain back to reveal Sin City. Five children are followed to young adulthood, where the family secrets are uncovered, threatening to ruin their lives in a web of illicit romances, perverted behaviors, and social pathologies. As a book, *King's Row* had as its main theme incest. This remained taboo under the Production Code in 1942, so the screenwriter changed the subject to insanity with sexual themes. In addition to McHugh, the main characters in *King's Row* were Dr. Parris Mitchell (played by Robert Cummings), childhood friend Randy Monaghan (Ann Sheridan), McHugh's love interest Louise Gordon (Nancy Coleman), and her father Henry Gordon (Charles Coburn), who disapproves of Drake. They all come together in a swirl of madness and deception.

McHugh pursues Louise against her father's wishes. She is driven to madness by her parents' command that she not see the now-broke Drake, who has gone to work for the railroad where his legs are badly injured in an accident. Drake is taken to the sadistic Gordon, where the doctor exacts even more retribution by unnecessarily amputating Drake's legs. No one will tell Drake the truth that his legs are gone. Finally, Parris informs him and, together with Randy, helps him rally as Drake defiantly sets himself to regain his life.

Reagan's key scene in the picture, and the one (other than that of the Gipper) for which he is most remembered, is when he comes out of anesthesia and reaches for his legs—which are no longer there. "Randy," he screams, "where's the rest of me?" He did it with no retakes and when Warner saw the rough cut, in which Reagan stole the picture, he quickly renegotiated his new star's contract into a long-term deal. In fact, for the first time outside of *Knute Rockne*, where Reagan through his own football experience had "done his homework," Reagan threw himself into a part the way many of his A-list colleagues normally did. He talked with doctors, especially psychologists, and met with disabled people, all "brew[ing] in myself the cauldron of emotions a man must feel who wakes up one sunny morning to find half of himself gone."[31]

In *Where's the Rest of Me?* Reagan wrote, "I never did quite as well again in a single shot."[32] One can almost sense in Reagan's analysis of what went into that scene that he could have made himself into a star-quality actor, but the cost was too great. His costar in *King's Row*, Robert Cummings, described Reagan as "a hell of a good actor—a far better actor than most people give him credit for."[33]

Far from being a bad actor, Reagan simply never threw himself fully into acting and never applied himself relentlessly, except in the two films for which he was best known, **Knute Rockne** *and* **King's Row.**

In September 1941, after Reagan's major filming for *King's Row* ended, he joined Louella Parsons and Jerry Colonna on a promotional trip back to Dixon for "Louella Parsons Day." He had brought his family along on the train (the *City of Los Angeles*), but Jane had stayed home, recuperating from an operation. The entourage arrived to banners saying "WELCOME HOME DUTCH." Bob Hope came out of the station house and jumped on the platform to serve as emcee. Despite the fact that the day was to honor Parsons, Dutch Reagan was the real celebrity. He appeared at a red-carpet screening of *International Squadron*, his mother walking with him, arm in arm. She was overcome by the adulation heaped on her son. When Reagan addressed the crowd before the show, he said, "I was born in Tampico, but.... Dixon is my birthplace from now on."[34] The evening wrapped up with a second short Reagan speech after a boisterous applause, then the next day the Reagans took a car to the station, where Dutch boarded last, waving goodbye to his admirers. Once again, Dutch Reagan grabbed the spotlight as the train pulled out of the station.

With *King's Row* still in theaters in 1942, Reagan plunged into another film, *Juke Girl*. A murder film set among fruit workers in Florida, *Juke Girl* again paired Reagan and Ann Sheridan, allowing them a "hot love scene" (according to the Warner Bros.' publicity director). Warner Bros.

continued to give him new contracts and, based on his marketability with *King's* Row, negotiated a massive new deal worth $758,000 over seven years (or $8.5 million in 2017 dollars). It was an enormous leap, but one typical of Hollywood. Reagan actually expected to get his first "million dollar contract." Wyman also received a raise, a whopping $1,450 a week ($848,000 in 2017 dollars). Nevertheless, the studios remained concerned that at any time Reagan might be called up to military service, although he was less eligible than many of the other male leads.

As war clouds in Europe and Asia grew darker, the Army continued to pursue Reagan, but it kept granting him deferments. After Pearl Harbor, pressures mounted anew. Already an even bigger star like Jimmy Stewart had been drafted, though he was at first rejected due to height and weight requirements and then bulked up and managed to enlist in the Army in March 1941. John Wayne, coming off his huge hit *Stagecoach*, was initially classified 3-A ("family deferment") and was thirty-four—too old for service—but did not resist reclassification to 1-A (eligible for the draft).[35] Republic (for Wayne) and Warner Bros. (for Reagan) lobbied the War Department to keep their stars free to make films, and Warners promised regular military pictures for Reagan if Washington complied.

Finally, Lieutenant Reagan was ordered to active duty on April 19, 1942, where the eyesight test classified him for limited service only, meaning he would not be sent into combat. Virtually all of Hollywood's male contingent would serve during the war: a too-young Tony Curtis would end up on a submarine tender, Lee Marvin would fight and be wounded on Tarawa, and even the too-old Bogart tried to enlist. Clark Gable, too old to serve, joined up and eventually was in a training-film unit that flew in eighteen combat missions over Europe. Gable was shot at almost every mission. Walter Matthau, William Holden, Charles Bronson, Gene Roddenberry, Burgess Meredith, Karl Malden, Red Buttons, Robert Taylor, and Martin Balsam all spent time in the Army Air Force, and dozens of others served in the army, navy, and Marine Corps.[36]

Hollywood's studios saw almost every one of their major stars and many future stars enter the military, many of them volunteering.

Reagan, new commission and contract in hand, wrapped up the pro-union movie *Juke Girl* (which had a contentious sub-story brewing over the role of unions). He and director Sam Wood had increasingly talked politics, especially (prior to Pearl Harbor) the wisdom of keeping America out of the war. Also, however, there was a growing concern about the role of communists in the unions and—after June of 1941, when Germany invaded the Soviet Union—their pressure to enter the war to aid Russia.[37]

The invasion of Russia came on the heels of a less bloody conflict going on within Hollywood over the role of the unions. In 1940, Disney, about to release its animated (and revolutionary) feature film *Fantasia*, sought to have a new soundtrack that needed to be carried with a unique stereophonic sound system called "Fantasound." Disney required theaters showing *Fantasia* to install Fantasound, but trouble erupted when two unions fought over who got the largesse from the installation contracts. The International Alliance of Theatrical Stage Employees, or IATSE, and the International Brotherhood of Electrical Workers (IBEW) both sought the installation money. IBEW had already gained Disney's ire by trying to unionize the Disney animators through the independent Screen Cartoonist's Guild. Like Andrew Carnegie and Henry Ford before him, Walt Disney had successfully staved off the unions by paying more than what they could offer. Before either union could win, the US government, in a move reminiscent of the *Gibbons v. Ogden* case in the early 1800s, did not find in favor of either union but rather scotched the rollout of Fantasound altogether on the grounds that wartime demands required conservation of the raw materials needed to make the system.[38] But union turmoil didn't end there: Disney's animators went on strike in 1941, and across the board, studios grew concerned enough that they attempted (often successfully) to place their own sympathetic "leaders" in union hierarchies. Although *Juke Girl*'s pro-union message may have resonated with unionists and the American Left, it went largely ignored by audiences, who just saw another (as Reagan would put it) "good yarn."

Communism, unionism, and the war, however, were all beginning to swirl together even before Pearl Harbor. Sam Wood and Reagan constantly talked politics, with Dutch's admiration of Roosevelt dimming if only slightly under Wood's logical assaults. At times, Wood's assertions seemed far-fetched. Wood, for example, insisted that communists were infiltrating Hollywood and especially the unions. Reagan waved that off, instead relating the position of the employees and their struggles for higher wages and better conditions. He knew through his participation in SAG that genuine grievances existed and that they weren't all part of a "communist plot." These political concerns were also driving Wyman crazy. When Robert Cummings worked with her on *Princess O'Rourke* in 1942, he told her that her husband "amazes me—his grasp of politics," to which Wyman replied, "Ooh, politics. He gives me a pain in the ass. That's all he talks about!"[39] Increasingly, however, Wyman was reported out and about in Hollywood at night while Reagan was at SAG meetings, seen in the company of other leading men, such as Van Johnson. Reagan ignored it, treating it as mere Hollywood gossip.[40]

He plunged into his next film, *Desperate Journey*, a war picture Reagan knew was not very good. He played an American serving in the Royal Air Force who is shot down over Germany. It paired Reagan with Errol Flynn again, and again the two did not mesh. Flynn never even tried to take Reagan under his wing, a slight Reagan didn't forget. Reagan also had received his orders to report for duty in the real war, so Wasserman hastily renegotiated his contract to $3,500 a week (with three added workweeks to the contract), bringing his total to forty-three weeks and matching the highest salary Warner Bros. paid anyone. Reagan signed a blockbuster contract, an astounding feat given that he had yet to play the lead in a top-grossing movie. The deal put new pressure on Warner Bros. to keep him out of the military. This time, it didn't work: Reagan had to report to Fort Mason, San Francisco, leaving on April 19, 1942, trading his greasepaint for khaki.

4

Greasepaint for Khaki

Everyone, including Ronald Reagan himself, knew that his eyesight would keep him out of the war—a fact he wasn't overly proud of. His rank in the cavalry had been second lieutenant, a rank he briefly retained at the Public Relations Division, Fort Mason, where as a liaison officer he spent five weeks loading troops bound for Australia. Since Fort Mason was still a cavalry post, he rode regularly. His duties required him to stage public events, including "I Am An American" day, set for September and later renamed "Citizenship Day." But shortly he received orders to return to the newly formed First Motion Picture Unit (FMPU) in Hollywood under Jack Warner, now also a lieutenant colonel in the United States Army Air Corps.[1] In fact, the movie unit, which was established in Culver City at the Hal Roach Studios, soon renamed "Fort Roach," was Warner's idea. While still officially a military post, it operated on a wholly different level: the "celluloid commandos," as they called themselves, "rarely saluted, and officers and enlisted men called each other by first names."[2] Reagan's new duties came with a promotion to first lieutenant but otherwise were similar to his old: lots of PR, processing applicants for commissions, giving studio tours. He also now got to spend nights at home all the time—and, after 1942, with another officer: his wife. Jane Wyman received a commission as a second lieutenant in the Army Air Corps in 1942, a job that came with no pay and no discernable responsibilities. But it made the trade news and, fortunately, she did not outrank her husband.[3]

Warner and General "Hap" Arnold of the Army Air Corps were sensitive to how effectively the Nazis had used film as propaganda. Already, Leni Riefenstahl's *Triumph of the Will* (1935) was well known and had been quietly shown in numerous venues in the late 1930s, including some German schools. The Museum of Modern Art (MOMA) had acquired a copy in 1936 and showed it in special screenings in its theater.[4] It is not proven if Warner (or Reagan) saw the film, but while it was "never commercially released nor readily accessible in America during the 1930s [it was] well known around Hollywood—mostly by word of mouth, occasionally by sight."[5] Frank Capra, Louis B. Mayer, and possibly Walt Disney all had seen 35mm copies of *Triumph of the Will*. During the war, excerpts were used in some American films, including *Your Job in Germany* (1945).[6] Once war broke out, the Office of Alien Property Custodian working with the Treasury Department confiscated all copies of German films and transferred them to Washington, DC.

With Riefenstahl's work and a new appreciation for the power of cinematic propaganda in mind, Warner Bros. had already made anti-fascist films, such as *Black Legion* (1937). After Pearl Harbor, all the movie studios were anxious to leap into the war effort. Moreover, Hap Arnold told Warner he needed one hundred thousand pilots—and not just pilots, but radiomen and gunners—and therefore part of the FMPU's job would be not only to recruit flyers but to glamorize all the other positions associated with the Army Air Force. At the time, few would guess that for the first year and a half of war, being a B-17 crewman would be the single deadliest combat job, exceeding in terms of percent killed or wounded the casualties incurred by Marines hitting the beaches in the Pacific. Arnold and Warner knew that the early films needed to inspire men with the "full inspirational splendor of roaring engines [and] tight bomber formations."[7] Screenwriter Owen Crump was given command of the FMPU along with a commission.

Reagan, now classified as a personnel officer, or Assistant AAF Public Relations, was assigned the task of recruiting crews who were not eligible for the draft and quickly found himself "offering commissions and ranks as high as major to movie directors, some of whom had previously earned half-million-dollar salaries."[8] At one time or another, other soon-to-be-famous actors such as Burgess Meredith, Arthur Kennedy, Van Johnson, Clark Gable, Alan Ladd, and George Montgomery were also stationed at "Fort Whacky" (as some others called Fort Roach). One of Reagan's still-unit photographers, David Conover, went into the factories photographing women who worked for the war effort. His stop at Radioplane Company and various shots of women on the assembly line produced a blonde with dirt smudges on her face. She struck him as so interesting and photogenic that he asked for permission to take more photos—of Norma Jean Dougherty, later known as Marilyn Monroe.

Despite being commissioned a first lieutenant in the First Motion Picture Unit, Reagan was mostly used by Warner Bros. as an enlisted man in films.

Yet far from being presented by Warner Bros. as an organizer of victory and an officer, Reagan was often cast as an enlisted man in wartime films (although his first part was as an officer). Either way, he "was on the front cover of every magazine, always in full uniform."[9] Likewise, per instructions from Warner, Reagan carefully avoided being seen at nightclubs or "on the town," and whenever he appeared in public, he was in uniform. He continued to appear in films as well, fulfilling Hap Arnold's goal of highlighting the service of non-pilots with 1943's *The Rear Gunner*, the story of a boy (Burgess Meredith) befriended by a lieutenant (Reagan). Its surprising success led the film unit to do several more with Reagan, sometimes playing on screen, sometimes narrating. In *Beyond the Line of Duty* (1942) Reagan's voice was used along with FDR's, and in *For God and Country* (1943) Reagan played a Catholic priest whose friends, a Protestant and a Jew, die trying to save an Indian. These films served as B movies once had—warm-ups for the A picture—but they brought such audience affection for Reagan that his fan mail swelled and Warners hired his mother for seventy-five dollars a week (deducted from her son's pay) to answer the letters. His voice was also in demand, and he narrated numerous documentaries, including a speech by George Patton in Los Angeles during his final US speaking tour.

After the 1939 Oscar nominations left Reagan without a nomination for his role in *King's Row*, he had taken the slight bitterly. James Cagney's *Yankee Doodle Dandy*, another Warner film, received the studios' full support, leaving Reagan—in the best role of his life—without a nomination. Moreover, the role he hoped *King's Row* would land him, that of "Rick" in *Casablanca*, was given to Humphrey Bogart. Now as part of the wartime film machine, Reagan was given a big-budget extravaganza in which he had to sing, a film called *This Is the Army*. Warner needed 350 soldiers for the chorus scene, which he convinced the Army to lend him by donating a large portion of the profits to the relief fund. Reagan's featured song, "Oh, How I Hate to Get Up in the Morning" became a minor classic. A forgetful Irving Berlin, who wrote the numbers for the show, was introduced to Reagan no fewer than five times and "each time he was glad to see me," until finally he cornered Reagan and, still not recognizing him, said, "You really should give this business some consideration when the war is over."[10]

This Is the Army grossed $12 million in its initial release, moving Reagan to the top of the box office popularity polls. Overall, movies remained one of the few entertainments left within the budget of average people and provided a gold mine for the studios. Attendance rose by 50 percent, and theaters around the nation often remained open twenty-four hours a day. With a number of stars too old to serve (such as Bogart) and starlets under contract to Warner Bros., the company churned out films, although given the fact that so many servicemen and factory workers were concentrated in some factory areas or bases, movie houses there could run films for weeks instead of days, or months instead of weeks. Such long shelf life allowed studios to cut their output from about sixty movies a year to thirty, which dried up a source of Wyman's B-movie lead roles. However, when the Hollywood Victory Committee learned that Wyman could sing, it signed her up for camp shows, followed by a bond tour.

The separation didn't help the Reagans' marriage. Even when she returned, however, friction began to emerge. She couldn't stand Neil, and when he came over, the two Reagan brothers would "rather argue than do anything else."[11]

Contrary to claims that Reagan tried to "pad" his military experience or career, he only expressed awe for the men who served in combat. He and his FMPU crew had "an almost reverent feeling for the men who did face the enemy," a feeling that only grew after processing the combat footage that began to return to the United States from Europe and the Pacific.[12] Associating with George Murphy in *This Is the Army* also helped shift Reagan's political convictions (Murphy himself had switched from Democrat to Republican in 1939). With as much free time as he had, Reagan searched for outlets where he could explore his political leanings. He was invited by Sam Wood to join the Motion Picture Alliance for the Preservation of American Ideals (better known as the MPA). Although formed in secret in late 1943, MPA went public in early 1944 with a membership that included Ward Bond, Clark Gable, Ginger Rogers, Robert Taylor, and Wood. Its public announcement made clear the organization was established to address the growing influence of communists in the industry. Reagan was still too much a New Deal Democrat for such a group, so he joined the Hollywood Democratic Committee (or HDC), along with Gene Kelly, Olivia de Havilland, and union boss Herb Sorrell.

Reagan's workload suddenly increased and minimized his time spent with HDC. He became focused on making films to teach survival techniques to pilots shot down while bombing Japan. One fellow soldier at the film unit, W. H. Mooring, recalled that at press showings of propaganda films Reagan would deliver a short official speech before the movie started. Mooring thought even then "in his heart [Reagan] has never really felt like an actor....His real interest might be in public service. Maybe politics."[13] Indeed, politics increasingly became an obsession for Dutch. His Fort Roach commitments stretched through most of 1944 and up to the election, where he again supported FDR (Wyman participated in a national radio broadcast to reelect the president). Roosevelt only lived until April 1945, yet already Reagan started to chafe over the waste and abuse in federal wartime spending. The term "bureaucracy" began to take on a negative connotation for him, whereas just a decade earlier it had meant his own father arranging jobs for out-of-work men. No one doubted his lifelong commitment to racial equality, by 1945 more identified with the Democratic Party, but even there Reagan saw serious contradictions. Democrats had blocked anti-lynching laws, and the southern wing of the Democratic Party (which still was the party of the Ku Klux Klan) remained the worst bastion of racism in the country.

These and other political questions gnawed at him, but as he wrapped up his time in the FMPU, something else troubled him even more deeply. After Germany's surrender in May 1945, Owen Crump, as head of the film unit, was assigned to shoot footage of the impact that bombing had made during the war. On his travels, he filmed both the concentration camps of Ohrdruf and Buchenwald. Upon Crump's return, Reagan was among a handful of people allowed to view the footage. Sergeant Malvin Wald, a screenwriter who also saw the film, recalled that "even though it was a summer day, Reagan came out shivering—we all did.... We'd never seen anything like that."[14] In recent years, left-wing rags such as Salon.com have insisted that Reagan lied, saying *he* had visited the death camps. In fact, biographer Lou Cannon reported the conversation in May 1984 as follows:

> When Israeli Prime Minister Yitzhak Shamir visited the White House last November 29, he was impressed by a previously undisclosed remembrance of President Reagan about the Nazi extermination of Jews during World War II.... Reagan had told him that he had served as a photographer in a U.S. Army unit assigned to film Nazi death camps.[15]

Reagan had not told Shamir that he was at the camps but that he had served as a photographer to a unit that was at the camps. One could quibble that his job was not in photography but in command and oversight, but it was a shorthand way of saying that the photography unit he was in had filmed the death camps. Cannon later claimed (and biographer Morris agreed) that Reagan conflated his watching the film with actually being there. But that's nonsense. No matter how fluent in English Yitzhak Shamir or his staff were, it is a very fine distinction to say that he served as a photographer *in* a unit that was assigned and saying he himself did the filming, which he did not do. Such a distinction was obviously missed. The more obvious discrepancy is that Reagan never actually shot film himself but was an officer in the unit. There seems to be no dispute that he saw the footage, that somehow he acquired a copy (because he showed them to his sons), and that he related this to Shamir, who inferred that Reagan meant he shot the footage.[16]

The Reagan family had also grown during the war with the adoption of a son, Michael, on March 18, 1945. A birth announcement went out:

Heavenly H. Q.

Special Order #2

Par. 2. Michael Edward Reagan is relieved from assignment and duty with present station and is assigned to the Reagan Base Unit, 9137 Cordell Drive, Hollywood, California. Duty assignment, "Son and Brother." Rations and quarters will be provided. Travel by stork authorized. Effective date of change on the Morning Report, 18 March, 1945.[17]

Wyman had wanted a son but did not want to take another year off of her career—which was finally showing life, especially after *The Yearling* (1945). That September, then-Captain Ronald Reagan was mustered out of the Army and returned home. While the paychecks would be bigger, the career trajectory was much different than when he went in.

Possibly the first clue came when Warner Bros. threw a celebration party for those who had returned from the armed services. As Reagan quickly discovered, however, the press attention all went to several actors who had never left but who had exemptions and had started to make their mark, including Cornel Wilde, Van Johnson, Peter Lawford, and Gregory Peck. And soon after that—as always occurs after war—society returned to a peacetime normal and veterans lost their heroic status to become everyday people. Army life had dramatically chopped the Reagans' income, which irritated the free-spending Wyman. Moreover, despite the arrival of Michael, ever-increasing rumors of Jane Wyman's extramarital dalliances swirled, especially rumors involving Van Johnson.

Even before *The Yearling*, Wyman, as part of a two-picture loan-out to Paramount, had made *The Lost Weekend*. It added to her luster and assured her role in *The Yearling* opposite Gregory Peck. When Reagan visited the location filming of *The Yearling* at Lake Arrowhead, he was treated as an outsider, finding himself babysitting most of the time while Wyman "sizzled on-screen opposite one of the postwar's newest and brightest leading men," Peck.[18] Reportedly a set member even addressed him as "Mr. Wyman." A frustrated Gipper retreated to Hollywood, with no current roles coming his way, his wife's star ascending, and his home life deteriorating.

Several factors combined to break up the Reagans' marriage, including Jane Wyman's ascending career and Dutch's growing fascination with politics.

Socially, Reagan was not a wild partier like many of his fellow actors. He had a puritanical side, especially when it came to alcohol (with memories of his father's struggles still fresh). Those attitudes bothered some of his friends, such as Dana Andrews and Robert Mitchum, who commented that when going out on the town with Reagan, it was "always like we were being monitored by an eagle scout."[19] Yet those attitudes didn't seem to interfere with his friendship with other notorious drinkers such as William Holden and John Huston. Rather, something else came between Reagan and Huston: *The Treasure of the Sierra Madre*, which both men knew would be a hit. The hang-up was that the part Reagan wanted was a character role, behind the stars Bogart and John Huston. Jack Warner thought Reagan was crazy to take anything less than a lead, and he insisted he wouldn't let Reagan do the part. Huston never forgave Dutch for turning down a costar role.

Reagan expected that once released from the Army he would spend more time with Jane and Maureen. His daughter remembered him as "the great psychologist:" "When he enrolled me in kindergarten, I threw a fit because I wanted to go to acting school." Reagan insisted that actresses needed to read and write. "Why?" Maureen asked. "So they can read scripts and sign contracts," he replied. That was good enough for her.[20] Those instances, however, were rare. Increasingly, Reagan became distant from his children, in part because politics was his new mistress.

Warner Bros. finally had a new film for him, *Stallion Road*, which came up during an actors' strike; he had to cross the picket lines. Initially, *Stallion Road* looked like a hit, featuring Humphrey Bogart and Lauren Bacall. Then, just as suddenly, both stars pulled out of the project. Some suspected that the couple's differences with Reagan over the statement of repudiation of communists caused their exit (more on this below). Playing second bill to a horse in the picture damaged Reagan's hope for a comeback. It dipped further with *That Hagen Girl*, where Reagan was paired with an "eighteen-year-old" Shirley Temple (she was nineteen at the time) in a mismatched love story that damaged his image a second time. Then, before finishing the picture, he developed viral pneumonia, was hospitalized, and suddenly was fighting for his life. At the same time, Wyman went into labor with what would be their second natural child, only to have the girl die within hours of birth. Wyman spiraled into a state of depression worthy of Drake McHugh, and Reagan, just released from the hospital and weak, could not lead her out of it.

The couple continued to deny trouble, but Reagan's increased interest in politics baffled Wyman. She frequently broke up loud discussions between Neil and Ron in the house, complaining she couldn't get a word in edgewise. Warner Bros. desperately tried to paint the marriage in hues of the perfect Hollywood couple ("those Reagans" as they were often called). Many Americans viewed them as a typical middle-class husband and wife, unlike, say, Robert Taylor and Barbara Stanwyck. Yet one thing seemed clear: Ronnie loved her. When he had gone on a bond sales tour in 1944 and his costars hit the town, Dutch stayed alone in his room reading scripts.[21] Still, he had a detachment neither Wyman nor—later—Patti Davis could entirely penetrate. When Jane bustled in with news of a new part, Reagan treated it as part of the normal workday: "That's great," he would say. "You deserve it!" Then he would move onto world events, reflecting his view that movies were just "work" and the "real world" awaited outside the Warner Bros. gates. The American public, also, started to take a different view of dual-career marriages. Reporters increasingly asked about the dangers of both parents working. Wyman managed satisfactory answers and was named the "Ideal Working Mother" by the North Hollywood Women's Professional Club.[22]

With nothing else to consume his time or energy, Reagan turned almost full-time to politics. Both he and Wyman alluded to unnamed suggestions by industry people that he run for Congress.[23] It isn't clear if Dick Powell pressed him to run on the Republican side or if Democrats approached him. Reagan said only that "politicians" asked him to run.[24] Immediately after the war he joined the American Veterans Committee but quit when he was asked to show up in uniform to a strike that he learned had been called by seventy-three out of 1,300 members. Reagan threatened to pay for his own ads in papers denouncing the strike, and it was called off.[25] For the time being, however, he remained on AVC and attended meetings of the Hollywood Democratic Committee, which by then had renamed itself HICCASP (Hollywood Independent Citizens Committee of the Arts, Sciences, and Professions). Although he had swum in HICCASP circles since the 1944 presidential campaign, he didn't officially associate with the organization until the summer of 1946 when he was asked to take a vacant seat on the executive council. Although he had made one of his first public speeches at the spring HICCASP meeting, at his first council appearance, on July 2, a heated argument ensued over communist influence and a number of members resigned. (Reagan at the time believed such claims were "Republican propaganda.")[26] Three days later, at a policy committee meeting at James Roosevelt's house, Reagan's committee read the draft policy it had assembled, only to have John Howard Lawson point his finger at Reagan's nose and shout, "This organization…will never adopt a statement which endorses free enterprise and repudiates Communism."[27]

Lawson's rant suddenly revealed to Reagan exactly how radicalized HICCASP was. What he heard there was shocking: one member announced that if there was ever a war between the United States and Russia, he would fight for Russia; another said he could recite the constitution of the USSR from memory, as it was more democratic than the US Constitution. Neil, who had joined in order to be an informant for the FBI, warned Ron that HICCASP was full of "people…who can cause you real trouble."[28] Soon, Dutch grew so concerned that he himself became a source for the FBI, code-named "T-10."

Whether HICCASP was truly a communist front organization as the FBI maintained, or whether, as the organization's executive director Hannah Dorner claimed, the similarities between her group's program and that of the Communist Party were "purely coincidental," there was little doubt that a number of full-blown communists were on the executive council.[29] One member said of HICCASP "the Commies are boring in like weevils in a biscuit."[30] On one occasion Reagan recalled being late to a HICCASP meeting. When he finally found the location—an abandoned store—he entered to find a full house, and only one or two empty seats. As he sat down, "every member of the board" who had been sitting on that side of the room got up and moved to the other side of the aisle. It was a planned demonstration, as Reagan noted, signaling to him how infiltrated HICCASP was becoming.[31]

In August 1941, Reagan had attended his first SAG meeting as an alternate for Heather Angel. A year later, Jane Wyman was elected to the board, but her husband was still not active in SAG. This meant that at one time or another, Reagan was involved in three of the primary Hollywood political organizations—SAG, HICCASP, and the increasingly defunct HDC. It was with SAG, not HICCASP, where Reagan made his political breakthrough. Reagan returned as an alternate to the SAG board in February 1946 just as Herb Sorrell, the leader of the stagehand workers, brought an industry-wide stagehand strike. While the details are somewhat intricate and involve numerous acronyms, the outcome makes it worth following the trail of breadcrumbs.

At issue was which union had claims on building stage and exterior sets. Having won the Disney animators' strike in 1940, Herb Sorrell consolidated a number of unions into the Conference of Studio Unions (CSU). This brought him into conflict not only with management but with the rival International Alliance of Theatrical Stage Employees (IATSE) as a single bargaining voice for film workers. In March 1945, the opening skirmishes of a labor unrest that lasted almost two years started when a CSU local representing set decorators went on strike. IATSE insisted that CSU's contract had expired and that IATSE had jurisdiction. The studios refused to give in to either union. In December, both unions agreed to observe a decision reached by arbitrators of the American Federation of Labor (AFL). When the AFL ruled in favor of IATSE, Sorrell's CSU rejected the arbitration. An internecine dispute that began over 350 jobs now threatened to encompass more than 30,000 unionists on both sides and shut down all the studios.

Roy Brewer, IATSE's new leader, invoked the "communist" card to weaken CSU. Anyone who sided with Sorrell or the CSU, Brewer said, was a communist, and CSU itself was a Communist Party organ. Undeterred, in July 1946, Sorrell launched a two-day strike that he hoped, over time, would kill two birds with one stone by breaking both the studios and their favored union, IATSE.[32] This strike lasted almost two years.

Reagan was hurled into this three-way viper pit. In *An American Life* he referred to it as "hand to hand combat"—by virtue of being an appointee from SAG to the emergency committee assigned to resolve the dispute.[33] He organized a strategy session with members of HICCASP to find a way to support Sorrell, CSU, or any other striking union without having to fight charges of communist sympathies on the one hand or go out on strike themselves on the other.

At a July 1946 HICCASP meeting, Reagan, Olivia de Havilland, and James Roosevelt drafted a Statement of Ideals that reaffirmed the organization's support of free enterprise and "repudiate[d] communism as desirable for the United States."[34] When it was presented by Roosevelt, the vitriol against it (and his friends) stunned Reagan. He rose to defend Roosevelt, and as Dutch began to speak, cries of "Fascist" and "Capitalist scum!" permeated the air.[35] For the first time, Reagan personally witnessed the vile reprobation heaped on the enemies of communism. Immediately after the meeting, Reagan was asked to go to Olivia De Havilland's apartment, which he did.

According to *Where's the Rest of Me?* the real purpose of the presentation to HICCASP was to smoke out hard-core communists in the organization. De Havilland had already suspected that the group was being heavily infiltrated, especially after Dalton Trumbo gave her a speech to present in Seattle so "full of Communist-oriented tidbits" that she refused to deliver it.[36] As she related the story, she saw Reagan grinning, and she asked Dutch what he found so amusing. Reagan replied, "Nothing…except I thought you were one [of the communists]." De Havilland responded, "I thought you were one.… Until tonight, that is."[37]

Initially Reagan had been sympathetic to the CSU. Just as he thought the concerns about HICCASP itself were the result of "Republican propaganda," he later said he knew "little and cared less about the rumors of communists [as members of CSU]."[38] As part of an emergency committee for SAG, Reagan helped end the July strike, though Sorrell was hardly through. When HICCASP finally held a vote—at Bogart's insistence—over the repudiation clause, to Reagan's shock, the clause was defeated by a significant margin. De Havilland later said she was the only "aye" vote, although on July 10 the council adopted the statement with some amendments. Reagan and his colleagues de Havilland and Roosevelt, who had drafted the statement, resigned immediately after the vote.[39]

SAG now fell in the no-man's-land between IATSE and CSU, claiming this was a jurisdictional dispute over set building. On September 12, the studios fired 1,200 carpenters and painters associated with the CSU for refusing to work, and Sorrell responded with an industry-wide strike. Picket lines went up everywhere, and violence broke out at several studio gates on September 26.

SAG, stuck between the two, was now in the crosshairs. Its very character was as a guild, not a union, and it was not activist, avoiding "controversial issues except where they directly affected performers."[40] Sorrell, however, was intent on forcing the actors into observing the strike, but according to AFL rules, SAG members should be allowed to cross the picket lines because unlike painters or carpenters, they could not find outside work. Indeed, most SAG members did cross the lines, even some of the more liberal stars, such as Bogart, Lucille Ball, and Judy Garland. The board drafted a new SAG statement of principles, similar to the one Reagan and de Havilland had passed at HICCASP. It condemned communism and fascism, but once again the leftist elements in the guild prevented its passage. Even though the statement couldn't get a majority, Reagan was elected vice president.

In his new position, Reagan met with both Roy Brewer and Sorrell, hoping to negotiate a cease-fire until he could hand the issue off to the AFL, ostensibly the head of all the unions, in its October convention. Neither Brewer nor Sorrell played ball. What followed was a milestone in Reagan's career: on October 2, the SAG Emergency Committee held a membership meeting at Hollywood Legion Stadium. Robert Montgomery was to chair, but he could not make it and Reagan was elected to take his place. In an ensuing contentious meeting, Reagan (according to Hedda Hopper) "was a one-man battalion," keeping the "Red nucleus" from controlling the meeting.[41]

It was a temporary holding action until the AFL national convention could take place six days later in Chicago. Originally, only Montgomery and Pat Somerset, head of SAG's labor relations, were to attend, but after Reagan's performance at the general meeting, the Emergency Committee named a larger delegation that included Dutch. At first, the AFL did not take the actors seriously—until Reagan threatened to have SAG send stars to major cities to denounce labor violence. The AFL quickly came aboard, setting up meetings with the leading officials involved in the fight. Shuttling back and forth between the AFL officials, including president William Green, head of the carpenters union, and Sorrell, the group heard one threat after another hurled by the combatants at each other, with little hope of common ground. Reagan claimed that he met with the "Three Wise Men," the AFL's arbitration committee of vice presidents (postal worker William Doherty, barber Felix Knight, and railway worker William Birthright). They split the baby, giving the trim and millwork to IATSE and set erection to CSU.

SAG's board tried to beef up the neutrality statement, but the union was drifting leftward. At a meeting of SAG members in October at Ida Lupino's house, William Holden and Reagan showed up uninvited to argue for neutrality, only to be shouted down. The following day, at a general SAG meeting, Reagan insisted that the guild discipline the ringleaders— Lupino, Sterling Hayden, John Garfield, and Howard Da Silva. Reagan received a phone call a few days later at a gas station near a set where he was filming *Night Unto Night*. An unknown voice warned he would be "taken care of" by having acid thrown in his face if he spoke against the CSU.[42] He reported the call to Warner Bros., and the police showed up with a .32-caliber pistol and a permit. Reagan said he put the shoulder holster on but still thought the call a prank. Then a uniformed officer showed up outside his house for guard duty. Dutch continued to take the threat lightly until he heard gossip through the unions that someone had ridiculed the notion: "If we had wanted to throw acid in Reagan's face," the source supposedly said, "we would have done it, not talked about it."[43] Suddenly Reagan took the threat extremely seriously because no one other than the police had mentioned acid in the face. He carried his pistol with him, and it would not be the last time Ronald Reagan "packed heat."[44]

On December 9, after violence erupted on the picket lines, SAG members Da Silva, Bert Conway, and others submitted a petition signed by 350 other members, including Orson Welles, Katharine Hepburn, Anthony Quinn, Janet Leigh, Rita Hayworth, and Sterling Hayden, to have a general meeting about the ongoing strike. It was called for December 19, again at Hollywood Legion Stadium. Reagan was among those asked to speak to the full body, the second time he did so.[45] Some three thousand members arrived, crossing the picket lines just to attend the event. When Reagan arrived, he was protected by bodyguards.[46] Standing in the middle of a boxing ring, commanding the stage, he called for the members to cross the lines. He reviewed his talk with the Three Wise Men. When he finished, Alexander Knox laid into him with a "very witty… bitter satire" and Reagan likened feeling the blows like a boxer.[47] Biographer Eliot called it "the best performance Reagan had ever delivered," including his screen roles.[48] Katharine Hepburn and Edward G. Robinson spoke against Reagan, while Frank Sinatra spoke in favor of going across the lines.[49] The final vote was more than five to one in favor of crossing the picket lines. Reagan's second political speech was every bit as effective as his first as a student at Eureka.

By that time, Wyman had made *The Yearling*, generally considered her breakthrough part. The pregnant Wyman attended the 1947 Academy Awards ceremonies at the Shrine Auditorium as a Best Actress nominee, but Olivia de Havilland won the Oscar for *To Each His Own*. Wyman then threw herself into another potentially great role in *Johnny Belinda*, which consumed her time just as Reagan was traveling more than ever for SAG. She denied breakup rumors to Louella Parsons, insisting "Ronnie and I haven't had even a good old-fashioned family argument."[50] In fact, that was a symptom of trouble, for the couple rarely delved into the more serious issues separating them.

One thing the Reagans had that almost no other leading couple could claim was good press: all the gossip columnists were pulling for them. Far from trying to throw gasoline on the Reagans' marital fires, Hedda Hopper and Parsons employed every fire extinguisher they could, to no avail. After filming *Johnny Belinda*, Wyman told her friends she was off for a long rest. Someone asked, "With Ronnie and the kids?" Wyman replied, "No...just me."[51] In October, just before Dutch left for Washington and the upcoming House Un-American Activities Committee testimony, she told him by phone that when *Johnny Belinda* was finished, she needed to think through some things. When Reagan asked which things in particular, she told him their marriage.[52]

She further stunned the gossip writers—and Reagan—when in December 1947 she gave the press a comment that indicated things were so bad between the couple that "I hope and believe that we will solve our problems and avoid a separation."[53] Before Reagan could react, Wyman told yet another reporter "We're through. We're finished. And it's all my fault."[54] Although Reagan, responding to a question by Hopper, said, "We had a tiff," he still hoped "to live with her the rest of my life."[55] What the Gipper refused to admit was that his wife might have been in love with another man, in this case, her costar in *Johnny Belinda*, Lew Ayres. At an October party, she held his hand and blurted out, "Lew is the love of my life."[56] Despite making excuses for Wyman, Reagan admitted there were deeper fissures, noting his "seriousness about public affairs has bored Jane."[57] Less than two weeks after dropping her "separation" bombshell, Wyman announced the separation publicly. The statement shook Parsons, who had fancied herself a magician capable of keeping the couple happy through her printed pixie dust.

For the first time in his life, even more than with the goodbye note from Mugs, Reagan collapsed into a depression. He sometimes sat in his car outside her house. Although the couple still had dinner occasionally for the sake of the kids, legal papers for a property settlement were already drawn up. Despite a very short reconciliation, by May they had split again for good, with the final divorce document filed on May 6, 1948. Maureen, then seven, later recalled "my father trying to explain it to me. He said the same things that parents always do at a time like that."[58] In June 1948, Wyman appeared in court, sans Reagan, to tell the judge she needed a divorce on the grounds of "extreme mental cruelty," the catchphrase of the day that has since been superseded by "irreconcilable differences." In fact, the "mental cruelty" entirely entailed Reagan being consumed with political issues. Wyman received $500 a month child support, no alimony, and an undisclosed property settlement. She and Dutch continued to see each other about the children and spoke regularly after that, but according to Nancy, the shocked Ron was totally unprepared and "spent a week living with the Holdens."[59]

In October 1947, Reagan flew to Washington, DC, to represent SAG in testimony before the House Un-American Activities Committee (HUAC) and was considered a friendly witness along with Jack Warner, Louis Mayer, Walt Disney, and Sam Wood. Each lambasted the communists. When Reagan's turn came, he appeared in a white gabardine suit with his reading glasses, looking both heroic and intellectual, but he knew he would face questioning from Robert Stripling, the lead investigator of the committee. Stripling had, in fact, visited Reagan the night before and suggested that if Reagan would name names, he would be permitted to deliver a statement on behalf of the industry. Reagan, preceded by an ineffective Robert Montgomery, was led through a review of an incident where communists had deceptively lured several stars into supporting an event for a charity hospital. He explained that once everyone discovered the deception, they quickly bailed out of the event. Stripling thought he had Reagan ready to roll over on half of Hollywood.

Instead, Reagan echoed Montgomery and George Murphy's testimony, indicating that "99 percent of us are pretty well aware of what is going on" and "we have done a pretty good job in our business of keeping [the communists'] activities curtailed."[60] He noted that "in the case of the Screen Actors Guild we have been eminently successful in preventing them from [running] a majority of an organization with a well-organized minority."[61] It was a brilliant and succinct put-down of the committee and the wider sentiment that Hollywood was a haven for Reds. More than once, Reagan cited a healthy, functioning democracy as the best means to defend against communist incursions. As if to pour salt in the wound, he added, "I believe that, as Thomas Jefferson put it, if all the American people know all of the facts they will never make a mistake." In SAG, that meant keeping members abreast of all developments and holding regular votes. But then Reagan—later known as a hard-core anti-communist—made an amazing statement (especially in the context of the pressure brought on him by HUAC): "As a citizen I would hesitate, or not like, to see any political party outlawed on the basis of political ideology. We have spent 170 years in this country on the basis that democracy is strong enough to stand up and fight against the inroads of any ideology."[62] Interestingly, committee member Congressman Richard Nixon had no questions for Reagan.

While none of the "unfriendly witnesses" summoned after Reagan gave any names—and were celebrated for doing so—neither did Reagan. Even so, upon his return SAG was sufficiently spooked that it voted that no officer or board member could serve without signing a statement certifying that he or she was not a member of the Communist Party of the United States. For anyone who couldn't sign, Reagan and the board offered them the out of naming someone who had already been identified. However, anyone—right or left—who thought having membership in a union could be confined to simple wages and hours issues (what Samuel Gompers had in mind when he started the AFL) was simply naïve. The very nature of unions, as with management, was at some point political, and Reagan had only gotten a small taste of what, by the time of his presidency, would be an active union money-laundering operation for the Democratic Party.

It is wrong to imply, as Reagan biographer H. W. Brands does, that the movie industry was politically divided between the executives/producers and the artists.[63] The studios hedged on loyalty tests, more because they did not want to deal with lawsuits and the possibility of losing some of their stars. But there was *no* split between the studios and the rank-and-file of SAG on the issue of communists in the union: two overwhelming votes in Reagan's favor had shown that. And increasingly Reagan's union activity had opened up new windows on liberalism for him. Contrary to the notion that Reagan was realizing that "liberalism was becoming a liability," he was for the first time seeing that liberalism was a failure.[64] First and foremost, liberalism as contained in the Democratic Party was slowly becoming home to large numbers of out-and-out communists. The large majority of actors were Democrats, and Reagan found that he was spending an inordinate amount of time defending people who, at best, disliked the American capitalist democratic system and at worst openly called for its replacement with a Soviet-style "peoples' republic," even after they well knew the murderous excesses that had occurred under Joseph Stalin. As he would later learn, the Roosevelt (and later Truman) administration had been thoroughly penetrated by KGB agents—not "fellow travelers" or sympathizers but outright paid agents working for the Soviet spy agency.[65]

Second, Reagan, while personally a well-paid actor in films—an industry that had not suffered the same economic ravages as the rest of the economy—saw that the New Deal really had done little to bring the heartland of America out of the Depression. By 1939 the United States still had 17 percent unemployment, down only slightly from the all-time highs that neared 25 percent under Hoover, and nowhere near the all-time low of 2 percent under Calvin Coolidge. In retrospect, Reagan couldn't help but notice that while it appeared on the surface that Franklin Roosevelt had made an effort at rebuilding the economy, the reality was the New Deal was a raw deal for most people. Reagan's first-hand experiences with those on the "dole" in the early 1930s when his father worked with administration officials in Tampico stayed with him. Indeed, it offended him—a notoriously hard worker as a student (on everything but his grades)—that the "non-needy" poor would eschew work for a handout. And here, the messages of *That Printer of Udell's* again bubbled up, where the hero admonishes that poverty-fighting programs must "make it possible for those in want to receive aid without compromising their self respect."[66] Through Jack's WPA experiences, Reagan saw that holding part-time work was discouraged because of the length of time it took to get back on unemployment when the short-term job ended.[67]

Worse, the economic disaster of the New Deal was beginning to be apparent to anyone who wasn't in full-worship mode toward FDR. Real wages had fallen and taxes had gone up, while the minimum wage law had utterly destroyed all business expectations about new hiring and caused a stagnation in new jobs. The National Recovery Administration, with its 546 new codes, was struck down unanimously by the Supreme Court after it threw a hapless chicken butcher into jail for allowing a customer to choose his own bird.[68] At the same time, the national debt had tripled, with no noticeable impact on employment or living conditions. Farmers struggled more than ever. In short, the carnage of New Deal policies was on full display by 1939. Someone as informed as Reagan would have been assaulted by the reality of liberalism's failures on almost every front, and while he still clung to his high opinion of Roosevelt himself, by 1942 Reagan steadily inched away from liberal Democratic policies.

In his transition he was influenced by his pastor Cleveland Kleihauer at the Hollywood-Beverly Christian Church, which Reagan had joined when he moved to California.[69] At various times, Kleihauer had argued that a "Christian society is under sacred obligation so as to organize itself that everyone willing and able to work may be guaranteed meaningful occupation," but that "bums are social parasites and should not be tolerated or encouraged."[70] He warned against "promiscuous charity," and—in a phrase that would describe many of the secularized "development" arms of churches in the twenty-first century—added that many of the social workers "haven't religion enough to fill a thimble" and were little more than bean counters. Kleihauer had already had a profound impact on Reagan's thinking about communism and fascism as similar totalitarian ideologies, imploring him to include communism in his talks on fascism and its threats to individual liberty. Dutch began to note that "tyranny is tyranny, and whether it comes from right, left, or center it's evil."[71] Thus, at a second pivotal instance in his life, Reagan found a religious mentor who helped shape his views on politics and economics.

Perhaps it was fortunate for Reagan's career that SAG activities immediately consumed him, although he still finished two other movies—*John Loves Mary* and *The Girl from Jones Beach*. But a new battle shaped up between SAG and the producers of the new medium of television. The problem was that movies, intended for screening in theaters, were now being shown on television without additional payment to the actors, while the producers received funds (i.e., "residual payments," or just "residuals").

On behalf of SAG, Reagan insisted that actors "get a reasonable portion of the additional revenue from theater films when used in television."[72] Producers, of course, claimed they had paid for the picture already, and it was their property. Negotiations began in 1948, with Reagan joined by guild counsel Laurence W. Beilenson and Jack Dales, executive director of SAG, not just to discuss the residuals but also overtime pay for other work done by actors after a film was completed. Studios wanted to pay by the hour, but the actors wanted the minimum weekly wage. Producers quickly gave in on the overtime issue but dug in on residuals. By June 1, Reagan went back to SAG with three options: a strike; an extension of the current contract for a year; or no strike but no contract renewal.

Within a week, Reagan's hard-nosed negotiations yielded an ongoing deal in which there would be no strike, no real breakthroughs on either side, and an intent to address it again in the future. If neither the actors nor producers gained much ground, Reagan personally did. He already had prepared for the second round of negotiations, when his next movie role, *The Hasty Heart*, took him to England for filming with Patricia Neal. Some suspected Jack Warner had set him up for the role to get him out of the negotiations. While in England, he received an invitation for the screening of *Scott of the Antarctic*, starring John Mills in the role of the tragic expedition's commander. By the time he returned, Reagan may have wished he had joined the hapless Scott: he lost the lead in a movie he desperately wanted to do, *Ghost Mountain*, while *Night Unto Night*, *John Loves Mary*, and *That Hagan Girl* were all critical or box office flops—all while his ex-wife was up for an Oscar with *Johnny Belinda*. Wyman left with her Academy Award and Lew Ayres. And, to top it off, not long after that Reagan broke his leg in a charity baseball event.

When he finally returned to shooting in 1949, Dutch began to see good reviews again but ultimately failed to rekindle his career. Reelected president of SAG, Reagan confronted the issue of the blacklist, where he promised to find an exemption for anyone who would promise their loyalty to the United States. His phone began to ring off the hook from people seeking to escape the blacklist. One of those calls came from director Mervyn LeRoy, who had an actress in *East Side, West Side* who complained that her name was coming up as a communist. LeRoy wondered if Reagan would investigate. After a call to Louella Parsons (always tuned in to "who was who"), Reagan found no communist connections and through a friend agreed to meet the prim and proper Nancy Davis so she could express her gratitude.

Nancy Davis had come from a broken home, and with a different name: she was born in New York City on July 6, 1921, as Anne Frances Robbins. Nancy's mother Edith Luckett Robbins had abandoned a husband and farm life to move to the big city, but having a child in Flushing was too much for an aspiring actress, so Edith parked her daughter with her sister Virginia and her husband Audley while she was on the road. Nancy stayed with her aunt and uncle for six years, by which time her mother had officially divorced Kenneth Robbins and married Loyal Davis, a neurosurgeon who soon relocated his family to Chicago. Interestingly enough, Nancy's new father, whom she adored, nevertheless suffered from the same reluctance to show affection that Jack Reagan had shown with his boys. Loyal had been an aspiring actor, and he wanted none of that for his stepdaughter, despite her announcement that she wanted a career in the theater. She was packed off to Smith College in 1939, which merely delayed her acting efforts by four years. All the while, the Davises thought they were preparing Nancy for a typical upper-class lifestyle, enrolling her in Junior League and celebrating her engagement to James White Jr.—until she broke it off.

Finally, with her mother's help, she landed a role in a play, *Ramshackle Inn*, with ZaSu Pitts. The play made Broadway—with Nancy—where it closed after a week. Determined, she stayed in New York, snagging a part in *Lute Song* with Yul Brynner and Mary Martin. It was successful enough to allow Nancy to get a Manhattan apartment. She then embarked on a series of relationships (some of them little more than one-night-stands) with a number of actors, including Clark Gable. One of her beaus introduced her to Spencer Tracy, who requested a screen test for her. When he found out that Nancy's stepfather had treated his son for deafness, Tracy was even more determined to get her a screen test—and he made sure legendary director George Cukor handled it. Even then, she still almost blew it. As

Marc Eliot observed, Nancy "didn't have the sophistication of Hepburn, the heat of Ava Gardner or Lauren Bacall.... She didn't pump sex like Dietrich, her body wasn't pin-up material like Betty Grable's, she couldn't sing like Doris Day, and she couldn't dance like Ginger Rogers."[73] She received her first part in *Shadow on the Wall* (1949) and took a back seat to Ann Sothern. Nancy didn't even mention the film in her memoirs. Indeed, she was overshadowed in her next two movies as well, *The Doctor and the Girl* (where she had to compete with Janet Leigh) and *East Side, West Side*, where she was in a cast with Barbara Stanwyck and Ava Gardner.

Miriam Schary, wife of MGM director Dore Schary, and a friend of Nancy's, knew she was anxious to meet several top actors. Miriam arranged for a dinner for them with Nancy and Reagan.[74] After dinner, Dore asked Reagan to discuss the state of the guild, which he gladly did. Nancy immediately was drawn to him, and apparently, he to her, for he asked her out.

Nancy later wrote, "My life didn't really begin until I met Ronnie."[75] At the time, however, Reagan had no such commitment. He was still pining over Jane Wyman and was dating no fewer than *fourteen* other women, a who's who of Hollywood, including Ann Sothern, Piper Laurie, Patricia Neal, Rhonda Fleming, and Doris Day. To put it mildly, Reagan was a handsome young movie star with a healthy appetite for sex and no particular interest in remarriage at the moment. Nancy, after insisting that they dated almost steadily after their first encounter ("we must have gone to every restaurant and nightclub in Los Angeles"), nevertheless admitted that "Ronnie was in no hurry to make a commitment."[76] Indeed, once, while Nancy was eating at the commissary with another woman whom Reagan dated, the other actress began talking about a gift Reagan gave her, reminding Nancy that "I was just one girl among many."[77] There was no doubt she was infatuated early, and there is also little doubt that at some level, Nancy saw in him a potential star approaching greatness. But to overemphasize career and security over love would be a mistake.[78]

Meanwhile, Reagan had demanded that he either get better roles from Warner Bros. or be let out of his new contract. He gave an interview to the *Los Angeles Mirror* that appeared on January 6 that claimed the scripts Warner Bros. sent over were so bad he could "telephone [his] lines in and it wouldn't make any difference."[79] The situation continued to simmer as Reagan read rumors that Errol Flynn was getting the part he felt he was destined for in *Ghost Mountain*. And beneath this conflict was a brewing battle between talent agency Music Corporation of America (MCA), who represented Reagan, and Warner Bros., with Jack Warner claiming MCA was, in effect, imposing forbidden "tying clauses" on the production companies by forcing them to hire additional and/or less desirable talent to land the stars. Reagan was unaware of this struggle when he demanded better roles from the studio. By that time, Warner Bros. simply did not think he was star material on the level of John Wayne or Jimmy Stewart. Opting out, Reagan was presented a five-year, one-picture-per-year nonexclusive deal with Universal from Lew Wasserman. (Universal had just merged with International Films, giving it added heft, but also had an undisclosed alliance with MCA, the powerful talent agency.) Reagan learned that his carping about roles had changed the company's perspective of him and possibly cost him the lead in *Ghost Mountain*. While no doubt a factor, clearly by that time Warner Bros. had given up on Ronald Reagan as an A-list star.[80]

Although the money at Universal was lower by half, Reagan had the freedom to choose roles that he always wanted. Indeed, he was slated for a fine film, *Woman in Hiding*, until he broke his leg.[81] (Not long after that, he came to Schary's dinner party with Nancy, still with a cane.)[82] When the first Universal script after *Woman in Hiding* was given to him, for *Louisa*, he accepted only because of the director Alexander Hall (*Here Comes Mr. Jordan*). Yet whether because of Hall failing to rise to his previous levels or Reagan playing down to his, the show did little for the Gipper's career.

Dutch continued dating other women, including Christine Larson, whom he fell in love with and proposed to. But Larson rejected him in favor of pursuing Gary Cooper.[83] After that, Reagan spent more time with Nancy, with the two dating off and on for two years before getting married. She saw the turning point in February 1950 when he invited her to celebrate his thirty-ninth birthday at a Friars Club dinner (and he told her the next day that he would nominate her for the SAG board). In February 1952, Reagan called Nancy's father, Loyal Davis, in Scottsdale and asked for permission to marry his daughter. The old-fashioned Reagan still sought the father's blessing, and when Nancy spoke with her parents after the call they asked what wedding present the two wanted. "We want a camera that can take moving pictures and a screen we can show them on," Nancy replied.[84] The two married on March 4 in the San Fernando Valley and then went to the home of William Holden for a post-wedding party.

After briefly living at Nancy's apartment in Brentwood, they bought a house on Amalfi Drive in Pacific Palisades for $23,000. They deliberately chose a place well away from Hollywood or Beverly Hills, in part because it was cheaper but also to stay out of the limelight. Nancy could have proved a spendthrift and a "show wife" who demanded high-dollar attention, but she did not. And that was a good thing, as Reagan's film career was stuck. After his honeymoon, Reagan learned from Wasserman that Universal was unhappy with his films' performance and that the weak box office permitted the studio to void the deal for his final two movies. This news came just as the Reagans had purchased a 2,500-acre house and ranch in Malibu Canyon for $85,000. This was money Dutch now did not have. Wasserman had already exercised the nonexclusive clause that allowed Reagan to do a pair of Paramount pictures. *The Last Outpost* (1951) was followed with another weak film, *Hong Kong* (1952), which paid $45,000.

Thus, in the last few years, Reagan had played opposite a chimpanzee, a Chinese boy with minimal English skills, and an Indian chief while working with scripts he had once promised himself he would never do. At the same time, he was "debating technical and controversial issues on which the lives of many thousands of people balanced," giving lectures, and leading SAG through the trickiest of negotiations ever—the new television contracts involving MCA. It was perhaps Reagan's most important role as president of SAG, in that in a moribund industry he gained new employment for thousands of actors.

MCA had represented talent for many years under the leadership of Jules Stein and Reagan's agent, Lew Wasserman. The two embraced the new medium of television in 1948, but that was conditional upon being able to produce their own shows, and that, in turn, was conditional upon getting a waiver from SAG that would allow a talent company to become a production company and hire SAG members. TV in 1952 was still largely live and therefore needed no actors. That was about to change.

Movie studios saw television as the enemy, and most actors saw television as a major step down from the big screen. But the studio heads understood that due to the free nature of television, it could deeply affect motion pictures' bottom line—if the wall of production could be breached. MCA approached Reagan and the SAG board in early 1952, in essence threatening to move all the new television production (and union membership) to New York. According to the director of SAG, Jack Dales, MCA offered a proposition to SAG: MCA would bring television production to Hollywood if SAG would grant a waiver to MCA to become a hiring company. Dales called an emergency board meeting with Reagan and six other members present. After a debate, the board voted to give MCA a waiver allowing it to engage in television production under the name Revue Productions while still representing members, but Revue/MCA could not charge any commissions to any clients that appeared in their television films.

Reagan's role in the MCA and later residuals negotiations exposed him to a number of potential conflict of interest charges. He and most of the board walked a very fine line. For example, an actor might be given a part in *another* television production based on inferences that he or she was up for a role in a Revue show (which might or might not be true). Thus the actor, while without question getting work, would pay a commission based on Revue's ability to fudge the story about other work.

Reagan was also at risk in a second way, because in the meantime he had signed a television series with General Electric called *General Electric Theater*. His initial GE contract posed no conflict of interest, but his renewal contract included a bonus of General Electric shares, making him an owner. Therefore, after the renewal he was both an owner of General Electric and a negotiator for the very labor union negotiating with GE. Reagan argued with some strained credibility that his relationship was with the *sponsor* of GE, the advertising agency Batten, Barton, Durstine & Osborn (BBDO) and that BBDO, not General Electric, was really his employer. Dutch's argument convinced no one; however, the value of the shares he owned was so miniscule that no one objected.

Since the Alliance of Television Film Producers had not been paying actors whenever shows they appeared in were resold in a new market or repeated in an existing one, residuals constituted a significant amount of money for actors who were even briefly popular if their shows had been sold over and over again. Wasserman said he would ensure that the Alliance would pay residuals if SAG would agree to the MCA waiver.

The conflict of interest scenarios are obvious, but they were all overridden by a more significant benefit: Reagan and the SAG board had gotten actors a second life as television stars, and they got the residuals. For less-than-A-list actors such as Reagan, this over the years would prove a godsend.

The Gipper also had a new daughter, Patricia, born October 21, 1952. Nancy worried that Ron would be "disappointed" that their first child was a girl, but he responded, "The wonderful thing about having a girl is you get to see your wife as a little girl growing up," something Nancy found "a very sweet thing to say, but [it] didn't turn out that way."[85] Patti was a difficult baby, had trouble with digestion, and cried constantly.[86] Nancy labeled her as defiant, even angry, from the beginning. After Ron Jr. was born in 1958, Patti resented her baby brother. Later in life, Patti claimed these antics were about getting the attention of her father, claiming, "I never knew who he was."[87] Worse, she claimed Nancy constantly abused her verbally about her weight and other issues and that her father would take no interest in her when he came home. To Patti, her mother was a tyrant. In fact, Patti desperately craved even more attention; as she got older and her parents would go out, she would stand at the window and cry until they returned to soothe her. The housekeeper would later report Patti was hysterical for hours. Reagan would typically apply the same "it's only a phase" reasoning to these outbursts, only perpetuating the problem, but neither Patti nor Ron Jr. recall much "connecting" with their father.

Perhaps that was due, in large part, to the growing financial concerns the Reagans had with the addition of a child. They had a big mortgage, owned a ranch where Reagan bred thoroughbreds, and lived in the outrageous 94 percent tax bracket. From May to December of 1953 he was entirely without a film role until he got *Prisoner of War*—which paid him a third of what he'd been receiving. With parts becoming fewer and fewer, roles becoming worse, and deals less lucrative, Reagan looked for ways to supplement his income, leading to one of his worst entertainment-related decisions ever. Invited to do a Las Vegas nightclub show at the Last Frontier Hotel, Reagan emceed for the Continentals for two weeks. While he claimed in *An American Life* that the audience reaction was good and the pay "terrific," most biographers agree it was the low point of his career. Although Reagan would insist that he quit the job because he and Nancy "missed our life in California" and wanted to go home, later he said, "Never again…will I sell myself so short."[88]

Money worries, however, only explained a small part of Reagan's distance from his children. Much more of it was attributable to the fact that increasingly politics, and political ideas, consumed much of his energy. Even lacking star parts, Reagan was still a celebrity, which interfered with his family relationships. Nancy recalled one time after Ron Jr. was older, the four of them went to Disneyland, a trip she described as a "complete disaster" because people kept asking for autographs and the family never made it to any of the rides.[89] In *An American Life*, Reagan hurried past discussions of family life as though they were inconvenient or, worse, irrelevant.[90] Michael would later ask, "Why don't you look for family photos? Oh, that's right, there aren't many."[91] A child of the Great Depression, Reagan's generation of men still saw their chief purpose as family providers and wage earners, not emotional support. And to that end, Reagan dedicated himself to finding a more secure income stream—one that would prepare him for, as biographer Lou Cannon called it, "the role of a lifetime."

5

Apprenticeship for Public Life

Long overlooked in Reagan's development, his General Electric years have enjoyed renewed attention in the past two decades. In addition to new biographies, which have placed new emphasis on his GE years, author Thomas W. Evans' *The Education of Ronald Reagan:* celebrated his activities as spokesman for GE as a central component of his "conversion from actor to politician," and Reagan himself, in *An American Life*, noted that when speaking to GE employees and management, "I wasn't just making speeches—I was preaching a sermon."[1] What happened to Ronald Reagan between 1954 and 1962 honed, but did not create, his communication skills, and enhanced, but did not give birth to, his political concepts.

The series originated in 1953 as a radio show, a replacement for the Bing Crosby program, with the pilot called "The Token" featuring Dana Andrews. Reagan's participation wasn't automatic; indeed, he was "adamant" against doing television. At the time, far more than today, TV was viewed as Death Valley for actors. If available on the small screen, no theater owner could sell the star to a movie audience that would pay money to see the actor or actress on the big screen. Reagan knew that taking such a step would likely exclude him from feature films—and their more lucrative paydays—forever. On the other hand, television was becoming a powerhouse of its own, with the number of sets in American homes doubling from thirty million in 1955 to sixty million five years later. Movie attendance dropped accordingly. For the actor, work was much steadier, with regular shooting and almost always domestic locations that favored a more stable home life.

Reagan had fought against merging television actors with SAG for years—with good reason. SAG was the elite organization, and its wage scales reflected that. But on another level—and not just his personal circumstances—Reagan appreciated the necessity of change. After all, he was a radio guy who had started on stage then made it in movies. He had seen and participated in the unending evolution of the entertainment industry during his life, so one more change hardly concerned him. When he noted to Hedda Hopper that there were sixty-five million Americans who never went to the movies, it insinuated he knew a major transformation was on the horizon.

Dutch still got a few calls from producers he likened to "buzzards" gathering over a corpse—and following the Las Vegas debacle that nearly left him for one—Reagan got a call from Wasserman about a proposal from General Electric to host a weekly dramatic show, featuring a different cast each episode. The idea originated with the advertising firm Batten, Barton, Durstine & Osborn (famous for Bruce Barton, the 1920s marketing guru who wrote the bestselling book *The Man Nobody Knows* about Jesus as a CEO). BBDO approached MCA, whose format promised that the show could break the barrier between the big screen and television if GE followed the structure MCA submitted. The key to attracting big-screen talent hinged on allowing each week's star to pick his or her own role. Jack Benny, for example, played detective Sam Spade.

Not only would Reagan be the "star" of the new show, appearing on each broadcast, but General Electric wanted to hire him to tour its plants, speaking to the company's workforce. He also would address local Rotary, Kiwanis, and other groups in the company's orbit. It was a strategic move by GE along the lines of Henry Ford lowering the price of his Model Ts so that his workers could each afford one, in that the company workforce would become regular viewers of the show. For Reagan, it all fit: he could continue to preach capitalism; stay in front of the public; and draw uninterrupted regular pay, with the only disadvantage being the extensive travel to the plants involved. He explained that the format would also allow him to avoid the typecasting that he so feared, and the MCA format enticed "virtually every Oscar winner" to show up in one of the episodes.[2] Over the years Jimmy Stewart, Tony Curtis, Alan Ladd, and others appeared, given the flexibility to stretch by the opportunity to play against type. Reagan claimed the series was created with him in mind, but Earl Dunckel, who helped design the show for GE, later said while the company had a model of who they wanted in the host role, "we looked at several people."[3] Both men, in fact, could be correct: shows and films are often created with specific actors in mind but always retain the flexibility to insert others if circumstances change.[4]

Reagan, who had personally moved from stage to radio to the big screen, sensed that a new change was coming from movies to television.

Beyond that, Reagan appreciated the fact that American industry itself was expanding from region-specific to national—that whereas American steel was largely located in Pennsylvania, auto in Michigan, coal in West Virginia—General Electric was (thanks in part to the war) dispersed across the country. Even the structure of the company, with its largely decentralized management and local autonomy, greatly appealed to him. And not only did he get to stay in front of the camera, but the plant visits ensured he met with enthusiastic crowds. It couldn't help but feed his ego, and it also perfectly aligned with almost every core value he saw in America, from strong neighborhoods and local shops to the Schumpeterian replacement of one industry with another. During his tours, Reagan constantly asked questions about production, plant processes, and labor-management relations, feeding his understanding of American enterprise. As the biographer of the Gipper's Hollywood years put it, "he became the physical embodiment of the credo of progressive corporate sponsorship, the notion that a better life was to be had living in America [thanks to] cheap and abundant electricity."[5]

America's progress, of course, now was tied to electricity as it once had been tied to coal. By 1960, 98 percent of Americans had electric power, and electrical use rose at 8 percent per year, delivered by some three hundred electric utilities. There is no question that between 1950 and 1965 domestic life was better in the United States. America, due to its high home ownership rates that led the world, only worked if homes could be heated and cooled, then furnished with appliances. To Reagan, this was merely the birthright of an American citizen. He relished the opportunity to talk about it.

Dutch's contract, the biggest at the time in television, still allowed him to make movies. But he took genuine pride in *General Electric Theater*, boasting of its star-studded casts and deep stories. The show also constituted a new form of public relations, making Reagan the "face" of GE, selling a warm feeling most Americans already had about him. Although the Gipper may not have had leading man appeal anymore, he still had charm and drew nothing but positive emotions from viewers. When he and Earl Dunckel met in August 1954, the GE exec was immediately impressed: "He was the continuity…the element that tied the whole thing together," Dunckel recalled.[6] Reagan became a human version of the late twentieth-century "image" advertising that General Electric would be known for with its later "GE: We bring good things to life" ads. And as much as Reagan worked on screen, it was his visits to GE's 135 plants that told management they had made the right choice.

Dunckel served as Reagan's early GE traveling partner—an advance man of sorts—but the mastermind behind GE's Reagan gambit, Lemuel Boulware, was a communications guru who had studied corporate public relations. Boulware sought to use Reagan as a double-edged sword, obviously to appeal to the television audiences but also to disarm and enlist the support of the workforce.[7] Who better but the former head of one of the most high-profile unions in America? Reagan had already established himself as a top negotiator who had repeatedly fought against the hard-core leftist/socialists in Hollywood. Boulware was visionary. His approach understood the revolution in the chain of communications that had occurred over the past century, where layers of managers passed along information to employees. In addition to transmitting specific work information (corporate goals, targets, etc.), though, managers also spread an understanding of the company's culture. Up until the Great Depression, that had included the notion of employees as "family." Of course, the Depression shattered that concept, leaving companies such as GE in the position of having to rebuild employee trust without encouraging the rise of job-killing unions. In Reagan, Boulware had the perfect vehicle for such a message. After all, what could be better than having a Hollywood star show up on your shop floor and spend time with employees? Better than a Christmas ham!

Reagan appeared in the first *General Electric Theater* on September 26, 1954, alternating between live and recorded film airings. In October, he acted for the first time in one of the episodes, but normally he introduced each show in a two-minute segment. Even before filming for the first episode started, Dutch was already on the "campaign trail" with an appearance at the Schenectady turbine plant that had originally blossomed under Samuel Insull in the 1920s before Insull started his own utility empire.[8] Despite being nearly blind (he was unable to wear his contact lenses due to the smoke) and having a deafening roar of machinery to compete against, Reagan was an instant hit. Workers recognized him as soon as he got down to the floor, and the machines quickly came to a halt as a crowd gathered. After four hours, Reagan finished his first appearance, having won over almost everyone he met. Dunckel accompanied Reagan and marveled at how women came "running up" to get autographs or give him notes while, at first, males huddled at a distance saying things such as "I bet he's a fag," only to have Reagan come over to them and exude manliness. "That's the way, Ron," they would say, slapping him on the back.[9] In Schenectady, there was a nearby meeting of more than three thousand teachers whose featured speaker had just taken ill. When they learned Reagan was close by, they asked if he would be the guest speaker. With no prepared remarks, the Gipper won them over and astounded Dunckel with the depth and breadth of his knowledge, who called it a "tour de force."[10]

Dutch's humor overcame almost any hostile person and opened the door to any audience. He had a repertoire of jokes and funny stories—some of which were "filthy"—which Reagan "could clean up...and make them fit for old nuns." One observer called Reagan the "most inventive man with a dirty joke I've ever seen."[11] During these talks, Dutch developed a technique of using stories to make a point, weaving together the threads of both his mother's morality stories and his father's humor. As Reagan recalled, his mother's stories cemented in him "an abiding belief in the triumph of good over evil."[12] When he found a story that worked, even if taken from true circumstances, he began to reshape it for the audience, acquiring what Dinesh D'Souza called "a bad habit…[of] embroidering new accounts by adding details for effect."[13] Reagan's *near* photographic memory did not help here, for it wasn't quite perfect. Dutch would recall an incident with clarity, but while the incident was true, specifics may have gotten jumbled.[14]

Reagan's famed communication skills were honed on the shop floors of General Electric, where he blended his mother's moralistic stories with Jack Reagan's jokes.

The diversity of people who went out of their way to see Reagan included budding actors and actresses. One woman asked Reagan to sign her breast. In one location, a woman Dunckel described as the "bull of the woods…[a] big woman," said to Dutch, "Buster, I'd like to back you up in a corner sometime." Without missing a beat, Reagan replied, "Well, it would have to be a pretty big corner."[15] At another location, told about a mother who had a seriously depressed young boy, Reagan and his assistant staged a phony survey going house to house until they came to the mother's home and were invited in, whereupon the Gipper inspired the youngster and brightened his spirits.

Simultaneously, Reagan sold America on electricity and Hollywood to the American workforce, epitomizing each as an example of the virtues of capitalism. Though he varied his speech—giving talks to almost any group that would listen, including schoolkids at the Rhode Island statehouse—Dutch began introducing the themes for which he would become famous. Indeed, at the Rhode Island impromptu talk, he used the phrase "you and I…have a rendezvous with destiny" for the first time.[16]

In addition to a new public life and good pay, GE had fully furnished Reagan's new Pacific Palisades home with state-of-the-art appliances, including a built-in garbage disposal that wasn't even available in most locations. He told Louella Parsons that everything in the house was electric…"except the chair."[17] Nancy, however, chaffed at having her home turned into a showroom.

Historian Thomas Evans speculated that while Reagan spoke about the GE products the plants made, his "command of the product line was so extensive, however, that he might go far afield of the local product" and even give hints of GE's prototypes or research and development that wasn't available to the general public yet.[18] The Gipper found that discussions on the shop floors soon allowed him to venture into his SAG leadership and to relate to the employees on the basis of a fellow union member who was held accountable by performance standards. He encountered hecklers who asked how much he made (to which he replied, "They haven't got enough to make me put up with you").[19] He also inevitably encountered the "grandmother of the gang" who hugged him and wanted him to run a machine or demonstrate a movie punch.[20] At one plant where the entire workforce was female, he told the ladies that while he was thrilled to be at a place with five thousand "girls," the next stop was Pittsfield, Massachusetts, with fifteen thousand men. Dunckel was astounded at Reagan's energy—which would become a hallmark of his presidency twenty years later, when he was twenty years older!

His duties allowed him to start up a jet engine, drive a locomotive, and fire a 20mm. cannon so secret at the time that he couldn't even tell Nancy about it. He goofed on the cannon, and in the time it took to remove his thumb from the firing button, he had squeezed off 150 rounds. On other occasions, he handed out 10,000 photos and signed each over a two-day period, shook 2,000 hands, and walked forty-six miles of an assembly line floor—twice. His feet were so swollen Reagan recalled he had to cut off his shoelaces to get his shoes off.[21]

More often than not, though, Reagan was able to keep to general themes about America, freedom, capitalism, and government, calling the tour "a postgraduate course in political science."[22] While he studied, discussed, and thought about policy on the GE tour, Reagan more importantly interacted with *people* and learned their concerns. It was invaluable when he later ran for office. Later, on the campaign trails, Reagan didn't have to ponder the "right line" to use in front of crowds to appeal to them—he already knew from years of hearing the concerns of employees and mid-level managers what was on their mind. Indeed, Reagan's "focus groups" *were* the people he met at GE.

The GE tours handed Reagan a gift few politicians ever received: extensive time, close up, with the voters across America.

He recalled in *Where's the Rest of Me?* that "the trips were murderously difficult," that schedules were tighter than Swiss clocks, and that he rarely slept.[23] Even so, he loved them immensely because they validated him on a daily basis—not just him as a person but America as a nation. Indeed, as Reagan put it, "no barnstorming politician ever met the people on quite such a common footing."[24] That's because at that time, Reagan was not a politician at all. Later, it would become nearly impossible for a public figure to devote such time as to actually listen to large groups of people, and the security issues alone would be nearly insurmountable. Dutch *wasn't* a politician, and therefore there were no paid protestors, no organized opposition (even the unions stood down), and no visible political agenda at all.

Dunckel observed that at first Reagan did not use the infamous 3" × 5" cards for his remarks on "the mashed potato circuit." Every once in a while, he would take out a card and write down a note or question someone had asked him. "Everything that went into his mind stayed there," Dunckel recalled, and Reagan could quote it or cite it at a moment's notice. He certainly never wrote prepared speeches, though, until late in the first year of his GE tour, when he insisted that the audiences wanted to discuss world issues, not just his Hollywood topics.[25] As he developed topics, however, he carried the index cards and wrote down phrases in shorthand—"that" became "tht" or "barren desert" became "barrn dsrt." Jotting down only a few points or specific memory-joggers, Reagan could deliver a speech without reading it, while still maintaining order and discipline to hit the main points.

As he noted, slowly the "Hollywood" portion of his talks grew shorter and his discussion of government longer. Some of what Reagan expounded upon came from Boulware's GE school, but since Reagan could absorb almost anything, he soaked up free market material from such influential sources as Henry Hazlitt's *Economics in One Lesson* (1946), which in turn opened the door to the deeper writings of Ludwig von Mises and Friedrich Hayek. Hazlitt's message emphasized what modern economists call "externalities," or the consequences of a single policy in various areas and on different groups. One of his classic illustrations was the "broken window" example (originated with Frédéric Bastiat)—that while a broken window indeed generates economic activity in that someone must be hired to fix the window, it does not stand to reason that breaking windows is sound policy because *other* activities must be foregone to replace the window. It was a brilliant assault on government spending at any level, for a dollar spent on an activity deemed useful by the government is a dollar that cannot be spent by individuals of their own volition (what economists would call "opportunity costs").

Of course, Reagan never referred to von Mises, Hazlitt, Hayek, or Bastiat or invoked highfalutin phrases like "opportunity costs" or "externalities." He kept the language in the common vernacular, using examples everyone could readily imagine. One of the biggest issues that he returned to from his readings was that of debt, which two wars had caused to skyrocket. It would be ironic that Democrats would carp about President Reagan's deficits and the national debt when real dollar deficits as a share of gross national product (GNP) under the Gipper would be a tiny fraction of what they were under FDR (even before the war), Truman, Eisenhower, and Kennedy.[26] Reagan saw the opportunity costs at work: if government was absorbing so much of individuals' money, they couldn't possibly be spending it and investing it on their own free will in the economy.

Invitations to speak outside of GE grew exponentially as well, to the point that when he finally left GE in 1962, he had a three-year speaking backlog. In 1958, however, management at GE decided Reagan's role was more important than ever right where he was. Dwight D. Eisenhower, who had been reelected in 1956, had, for the first time in a century, failed to bring in a majority of his party in either the House or the Senate. Many attributed this to the rebounding influence of organized labor in the unions' efforts to defeat "right to work" measures. Indeed, the unions succeeded in five of the six states where such legislation was considered, targeting senators who had supported right to work legislation with good results, knocking out nine of them (and two others decided not to run for reelection). Unions pressed for antitrust legislation against General Motors, and GE saw itself as in the crosshairs next. Moreover, the unions had focused heavily on educating employees (i.e., propagandizing them) well before Election Day.

By that time—after sixteen weeks—Earl Dunckel had left the job as Reagan's tour guide and was replaced by a former B-29 pilot named George Dalen. Reagan praised Dalen for preventing the schedule from overwhelming them, mixing the appropriate amount of local hospitality with the required plant visits and speeches.

It was the speeches, however, that showed the most promise. They changed, slowly evolving by paring down Reagan's Hollywood stories and focusing more on policy. Reagan, in *Where's the Rest of Me?* alluded to the fact that he had been caught without documentation for some of his stories and that the bureaucracy fought back against criticism with "a knee to the groin" a time or two.[27] While he remained nonpartisan, referring to "the average guy" or "Joe Taxpayer," increasingly it dawned on him that he had been voting for the very people responsible for the growing government he criticized in his speeches. Reagan maintained that this awareness was in full force in 1958 but that he remained a Democrat on voting rolls until 1960. After each speech, Reagan would hear from audience members who had more stories about government's encroachment on their liberties and businesses. He began taking notes and doing research on what he heard. And while some might be reluctant to hear about economics from an actor, Reagan could fall back on his experience with the hard-core communists in Hollywood, instantly establishing a rapport.

These speeches began to take on the shape of *the* speech, Reagan's "A Time for Choosing" speech on behalf of Barry Goldwater's presidential campaign. He regularly addressed high levels of taxation, regulatory harms done to individual liberty, the threat of communism, and the overall burden of government control. Lem Boulware and lawyer Laurence Beilenson were key influences in shaping "the Speech." Beilenson infused in Reagan a new, robust appreciation of the struggle with communism as one to the death.[28] There could be no permanent, long-term compromise with an ideology that demanded the total enslavement of the individual to the state, or separation from God. Just as the founders in all their rhetoric inexorably tied their own political freedom to the prospect of slavery, with its specific and distinct allusions to European monarchs and peasants, so too did Dutch demand that godless world communism and American Fabian socialism were inseparable in their result. Beilenson only built on foundations others had already laid in Reagan.[29]

Resisting communism was not a compartmentalized "foreign policy" issue but a single granite core, chiseled by Reagan's Hollywood years on which the red wave crashed—and was halted. Many biographers treat "the Speech" and Reagan's views contained therein as almost springing, in this case, from the forehead of William F. Buckley Jr. In fact, as Paul Lettow observed, scholars overlooked "the extent to which he had formed—and espoused, over and over again—deeply held views regarding America's Cold War policy before he entered even state politics."[30] Between 1960 and 1962, the Gipper constantly hammered home the threats of communism abroad and at home. He said "containment won't save freedom on the home front any more than it can stop Russian aggression on the world front. We must roll back the network of encroaching control."[31] American accommodation, he argued, was immoral, essentially saying to "a billion enslaved human beings behind the Iron Curtain—'Give up your hopes of freedom because we've decided to get along with your slave masters.'"[32] These cornerstone principles, in turn, reignited Reagan's temporarily dampened Christian beliefs, for the atheistic element of communism began to emerge as not some dark passenger of Leninism but as its satanic core.

In his GE speeches, Reagan developed the holistic view of freedom tied inseparably both to capitalist success and the defeat of Soviet communism.

Reagan found time for a commencement address at Eureka College in 1957, where he increasingly referred to America's destiny as a charge from

God. American freedom was not just a gift but was an obligation to share with the rest of the world. He likened the clash between communism and American exceptionalism as "the oldest struggle of human kind" between those who believed in the right to shape their own destiny and those who believed in the supremacy of the state.[33]

Reagan and GE had a conflict, though, when it came to the negotiations with the International Union of Electrical Workers (IUE), in that as head of SAG, Reagan was bound to support fellow labor unions, while as spokesman for GE, he had a commitment to management. Nevertheless, there is no evidence that GE ever tried to direct or control his comments about the IUE during this time. Further, Reagan had enhanced his reputation for negotiating in complete objectivity. When the SAG contract for residual payments to actors was finally resolved, Reagan gained nothing personally from the negotiation, compromising on the only clause that would have benefitted him. Now Reagan, as a GE spokesman, was dealing with concerns about fair wages and corporate profits. Reagan's presence on shop floors could have opened the door for unfair labor practice charges with the government, and therefore he had to be taken out of the factories.

Another stress on Reagan's relationship with GE derived from the fact that he was becoming more ideological, and while he remained strictly nonpartisan, it was getting harder for him to conceal his political sympathies. His speeches usually had a section about government growth or overreach, and he used the Tennessee Valley Authority (TVA) as an example. In 1959, Reagan was told by George Dalen that a "government bureaucrat was on the warpath" because GE received $50 million in contracts from the federal government, which Reagan was criticizing. Government pressure mounted for GE to fire Reagan. Prior to a big speech for a convention in Los Angeles, the Gipper asked Dalen to contact Ralph J. Cordiner, the chairman of the board of GE, and ask for his views. Dalen came back with the report from Cordiner that GE stood behind Reagan's right to say what he pleased, and the government could take its business elsewhere. But Dutch was concerned he might be costing his boss a lot of money and spoke directly with Cordiner, who told the Gipper that the government was "my problem and I've taken it on."[34] Reagan offered to take the TVA reference out and use any of a number of other government programs as the example, whereupon Cordiner admitted "it would make my job easier."[35]

The 1958 midterm elections were not kind to Republicans, who lost fifty-eight House seats and thirteen Senate seats. "Mr. Conservative," Robert Taft Jr., had died in 1953 shortly after Eisenhower took office. The McCarthy hearings were over, with Joe McCarthy "condemned" by the US Senate in December of the following year. Ike had not allied with either Taft or McCarthy. His middle ground politics may have benefitted him personally, but he had not had coattails in either 1956 or 1958 and hardly embodied a conservative counterrevolution.

None of this reflected on Reagan's micro-level speaking efforts, even after he moved onto the "mashed potato circuit" and out of the GE factories. He continued to be as popular as ever. Joseph Kennedy called Reagan prior to the 1960 campaign and urged him to support his son, John F. Kennedy, but Reagan had already decided he could—and would—support Richard Nixon. Although never a Nixon enthusiast, Reagan was persuaded, allowing his name to be used as a "Democrat for Nixon."

Reagan suddenly noticed that in "city after city" where he would speak "there'd be a cabinet member or other high official from the Kennedy administration...giving a speech on the same day."[36] He didn't think it was coincidental, but a less modest man might have gone so far as to say that Ronald Reagan had become a threat to the Democratic Party. At roughly the same time, a change in management at General Electric put in new leadership who wanted Reagan to more aggressively "become a pitchman for General Electric products."[37] Having built a successful record of discussing issues, Reagan was offended. He refused to go out and "peddle toasters." He blamed that resistance for GE cancelling *General Electric Theater*, although the program had fallen behind *Bonanza* as the top-rated show. Still itching to do movies, Reagan took a part—for the only time in his career—as a villain in *The Killers* in 1964. It was his last film, and it didn't do well. Reagan himself admitted most of his fans were puzzled by the movie, waiting for him to at some point don the white hat.

From *The Killers*, he took another television series hosting job with *Death Valley Days*. He drove down from his ranch, taped for an hour, and even filmed some of the introductions in his ranch clothes. *Death Valley Days* required a minimum of Reagan's time, leaving him plenty of openings for speeches.

During that time, the Reagans' personal life had involved no small degree of chaos. For many years in the 1950s, Patti was still having emotional fits and experienced regular vomiting, which prompted the family to bring in a nurse. On May 20, 1958, Nancy had her second child, Ronald Prescott Reagan, and despite Reagan's desire not to call him "Ron," he indeed became "Ron Reagan" or "Ron Junior." Two years later, in the heat of the SAG negotiations for residuals, the Reagans had another addition to the family, this one totally unexpected. A child psychologist had ordered Michael, Reagan's adopted son with Jane Wyman (who was then married to Fred Karger), to live with his father. Once again, Wyman had trouble with a marriage and fourteen-year-old Michael, who had already been making regular visits to his dad's house, needed a father figure. Nancy found an already delicate dynamic with her husband made more confusing.[38] A partial solution was arrived at by placing Michael at Loyola High School, a live-in private school, but adding a teenager to the newborn infant and Patti's erratic behavior burdened Nancy further. Michael had to sleep on a sofa until finally Reagan built an additional bedroom for him, a situation the boy resented.

Nancy retreated to a small circle of friends, almost all wealthy Republicans, including Holmes and Virginia Tuttle, Walter and Lee Annenberg, Henry and Grace Salvatori, and Alfred and Betsy Bloomingdale (the only Democrat in the group). Those connections, mostly outside of entertainment (although one of the group, Charles Wick, was an entertainment lawyer), expanded Reagan's web of contacts who would eventually support his political activities.

As the GE project wound down, Reagan remained as active as ever in his SAG work, which was dominated by the renewed discussions of television residuals. Studios were now selling a number of their films a second time, increasing profits but paying the actors in those films nothing. Given that the studios had a massive backlog, containing some of the greatest names in film history, older actors stood to lose a great deal. There was a simple legal reality, namely the films were the property of the studios, and they had no desire to pay for something not covered in the original contracts. However, from purely a good business perspective in keeping existing talent happy and "doing the right thing" for public relations, the studios knew they needed to address the residuals. The second issue, stemming from the first, was SAG's effort to set up a pension and welfare fund.

Jack Dales took the lead in the negotiations, but Reagan has often been credited with a significant role. The studios refused residuals across the board, forcing SAG to walk out on strike for the first time in its history. (Universal was exempted due to a separate Wasserman-negotiated deal with SAG.) When SAG finally settled, the actors got a substantial deal: the studios paid out $2.65 million into a welfare/pension fund and agreed to 6 percent of the gross of all films and TV shows sold to TV after 1960, though not any of the gross of shows *made* after 1960, which would have come under new separate contracts. All in all, it amounted to a modern-day payout of about $2 billion. Dave Robb, a labor reporter for *Hollywood Reporter* described the plan as "huge." The studios, he noted, were never going to renegotiate pre-'48 residuals.[39] Some veterans with plenty of pre-1948 movies, such as Mickey Rooney (who threatened to bring a suit against SAG) and Bob Hope, sharply criticized the deal. Rooney later claimed SAG never did anything for actors except "give them a home to die in."[40] In fact, it was likely all SAG could hope for in all its wildest dreams.

Reagan's role in the negotiations has been overstated both by his admirers and his detractors. But even those who have focused on Reagan's Hollywood career have not explained his influence well. Previously underused SAG minutes provide a much different picture. The negotiating committee in 1960 consisted of nineteen members, including Reagan (Dana Andrews, also a star at the time, was on the committee), plus SAG staff members Jack Dales, Chet Migden, Kenneth Thomson, Pat Somerset, and counsel Bill Berger.[41] SAG archivist Valerie Yaros also pointed out that James Garner and Charlton Heston were later added but that at the January 18, 1960, meeting with the studio presidents, Ward Bond, James Cagney, Jeff Chandler, and Warner Anderson were present. Thus Reagan was a cog in the wheel—an important cog, but just one cog nonetheless.[42]

Moreover, it is a myth that the membership opposed the deal. Quite the contrary, on March 4, just before the strike had started, Reagan and the board received a letter from 154 motion picture workers criticizing the strike, and the vote was overwhelming for accepting the deal. On April 18, 1960, when he presented the package to the SAG membership, he got a standing ovation and the membership approved the package overwhelmingly, 6,399 to 259. In short, Reagan deserves some credit—but only some—for making the deal happen, and SAG got at least half a loaf.[43]

Dutch's role in the Screen Actors Guild negotiations of key residual payments in 1960 has been overblown by both supporters and critics: he was one of nineteen members of a committee.

Residuals negotiations raised another thorny problem for Reagan, however, for by then he was a 25 percent shareholder in *General Electric Theater* shows (and had routinely been making speeches on behalf of GE). In short, he was an owner. SAG members thought Reagan had no conflict of interest, but the government had other ideas. Reagan was called in front of a federal grand jury in February 1962 to testify in the Justice Department's investigation of MCA's practices. John Fricano, a federal attorney, interrogated Reagan on his role in the residuals contract and his deal with General Electric. Marc Eliot, who chronicled Reagan's time in Hollywood, said Reagan's testimony was remarkable for its "evasiveness, charm and self justification."[44]

Yet Reagan's responses were typical of someone remembering back ten years in time when he was going on a honeymoon. Asked if Art Park, an MCA vice president who worked with Reagan on the deal, had attempted to obtain ownership interest for Reagan in *General Electric Theater*, Reagan said no because the show was only done with a few pilots and they didn't know if it would be picked up. Further, Reagan told Fricano that there were no residuals for *General Electric Theater* and he didn't get residuals for the introductions, so whatever ownership sums would have been involved were minuscule. When asked repeatedly if, when signing his GE deal, Reagan ever considered the ownership interest, he again said the show was not the kind to see big residual payments. However, when his five-year deal was up, he started looking for ways to minimize his tax exposure. The idea of taking something besides cash salary—ownership shares—"was my own idea," he noted.[45] Despite Fricano's dogged questioning, it was clear that Reagan at the time never even considered any monetary gain from ownership in his initial *General Electric Theater* work and only sought it later as a tax shelter.

Another issue involved whether Reagan had received bribe money or future roles for the original MCA deal. On the key issue of the blanket waiver, Reagan answered that had other talent agents requested waivers under the same conditions, they would have been granted. There was no question that MCA benefitted disproportionately from the waiver. Anne Edwards concludes that while "no substantiating proof appears in the six-thousand-page transcript" of the Justice Department's hearings, or from the Internal Revenue Service, his $75,000 fee in his next Universal picture, *Law and Order* (1953), was well above what he had previously been earning.[46] On the other hand, he had already decided to retire from SAG—in part, concerned about his own power over the board. He told Jack Dales, "I'm beginning to wonder, is there anything that I can't get out of the board?"[47] What cannot be denied is that whether or not Reagan ever personally benefitted from the MCA waiver, thousands of other actors and actresses did, with their careers extended indefinitely because of Reagan's foresight.[48]

However, previously uncited evidence exists from a 1998 video interview with Chet Migden, who in 1952 was the head of SAG's Agency Division. He recalled that it was "increasingly difficult to get work for talent.... I can still picture in my mind's eye the boardroom and the debate [over the MCA waiver]." The proposal, he said, was "abhorrent to everybody in that boardroom.... [and] was going down to total defeat until one actor beloved by all in that boardroom [spoke]...Walter Pidgeon."

Pidgeon said, "We're dying. What's the alternative? To go to New York [and work in] live television for a couple of hundred dollars?.... What have we got to lose? Let 'em try it."

According to Migden, everyone suddenly changed their position and agreed to let MCA try, and "all of a sudden we had a television industry."[49] As to Reagan's role, Migden noted, "There are a lot of myths told about the debate and the waiver, including Reagan's role at the time. My recollection is he chaired the meeting and didn't say a goddamn word…[He] recognized the speakers and didn't participate in the debate."[50]

Reagan left SAG immediately after the MCA vote (on July 9, 1960), claiming Nancy was having a difficult pregnancy, but he also worried he was no longer looked at primarily as an actor. In the depths of the SAG residuals negotiations, Nancy received a daily call from John Wayne, who told her to stay strong and tell Dutch "not to let those bastards get you down."[51] While the residuals negotiations had not gotten him down, even before then Reagan had come to grips with the fact that, indeed, he was part of ownership via his producing line roles in some of the *General Electric Theater* shows. So once again, the rich tapestry of his life now included both labor and ownership, union negotiator and investor. His appeal to blue-collar workers and white-collar management translated into a potential vote-getting machine, and his actor status, which at the time was evolving into more of a high-class glamour profession than it had been in Reagan's star years, brought him into contact with people who had money and influence.

In 1962, John Kennedy's Justice Department announced a consent decree that would settle the case against MCA. All criminal proceedings were dropped against MCA, and there would be no further need for testimony from Reagan. His association with *General Electric Theater* wrapped up at the same time. Within weeks of the MCA settlement, Nelle Reagan died in a nursing home. In many ways, Reagan's life had changed momentously in less than a year.

Therefore, when the opportunity came to be the cochairman of Barry Goldwater's 1964 presidential run in California, he leaped at the opportunity. Reagan had read *Conscience of a Conservative*, Goldwater's book, and met him at his in-laws' Phoenix home. As cochairman, Reagan left daily management in the hands of someone else while he traveled to fund-raise and make speeches. By that time, Reagan had focused on four essential themes in his speeches: (1) America was inherently good, specially blessed, with a divine purpose or mission; (2) the American people had good sense and would, when given the evidence, make the right choices;

(3) communism was not just bad, it was so evil that it had to be defeated at every level—spiritually, economically, politically, and militarily; and (4) any government's natural inclination was to grow, and would do so without actively being checked by the people. In these speeches, Reagan had meticulously stayed away from party labels or even using "conservative" or "liberal." By so doing, he could frame his talks to the broadest possible audiences.

Of course, his enemies already had perceived the threat Reagan personally posed. Here was a veteran, college educated, labor union leader, and well-liked actor with a national presence. The AFL-CIO put him on a list of "dangerous anti-Communists," calling him a "right-wing zealot."[52] And increasingly he was speaking to political groups, even some far-right functions—as a Democrat.

His party affiliation insulated him from requests that he run for office. For example, in 1962, he was urged to run against Senator Thomas Kuchel for the Republican nomination. While in effect a Republican, he still hadn't changed parties, though in his mind he already had. At a campaign stop for Nixon, who was running for governor of California, a woman in the audience asked if he had changed his registration. Reagan said "I intend to," whereupon the woman said "I'm a registrar," and Reagan signed the form on the spot. He turned to the audience and said, "Now where was I?"[53]

Registering as a Republican constituted only the first step for Reagan becoming a true party activist. In August 1964 at a meeting of the California Citizens for Goldwater-Miller, Reagan found himself being lambasted by Phil Davis, a businessman and party insider who wanted the state chairmanship of the Goldwater campaign. Davis and others saw Reagan as an interloper—much along the lines that party elites rejected Donald Trump in 2015–2016 in his successful run for the presidency. After Davis's tirade, Reagan took the podium to admit that "I'm the new boy on the block" and that they all needed to unify behind Goldwater. His humble plea won over the audience, and he and Davis were immediately named as cochairmen.[54]

At the Cocoanut Grove, Reagan gave what he thought was a typical speech, tweaked a little to include references to Goldwater. After he finished, several of the biggest contributors asked Reagan if he'd repeat the speech he'd just given on national television if they could raise the money. This became known in Reagan hagiography as "the Speech." The group had enough money to buy a half hour on NBC, and the speech would be taped in front of a live audience at the NBC studio, re-creating the set where Reagan had spoken for years before. As Reagan recalled, after he taped it—but just before the speech was scheduled to air—Goldwater called. His advisors had recommended airing a tape of the senator meeting with Eisenhower at Gettysburg instead of Reagan's speech. When the Gipper pressed Goldwater, he said that his advisors were uneasy about the references to Social Security and that he had spent a year denying he was going to eliminate the federal program.

Reagan was somewhat surprised. His speech supported Social Security but argued that it had transformed from a "retirement fund" to a compulsory tax, and that other improvements were needed to ensure it was solvent. Further, Reagan argued, he'd been making the same speech for some time and it was well received. Finally, it wasn't up to him to cancel the speech, since he hadn't paid for it. He convinced Goldwater to actually watch the speech after the senator admitted he hadn't seen it and was later told that Goldwater, upon finishing the tape, asked his advisors, "What the hell's wrong with that?"[55]

Meanwhile, the whole episode had shaken Reagan's confidence, even after Goldwater called him and said to proceed with the airing. He was in the big leagues now, in essence advising a presidential candidate as to strategy. Ultimately, Reagan thought he had done well in the speech, and it aired on October 27, 1964. Once again, the Gipper laid out his fundamental assumptions that government was "beholden to the people" and that the issue of the election was "whether we believe in our capacity for self-government or whether we…confess that a little intellectual elite in a far-distant capital can plan our lives for us better than we can plan them ourselves." Warning against those who "would trade our freedom for the soup kitchen of the welfare state," Reagan insisted that the solutions to dealing with communists were indeed simple, though not easy. Throughout he was stern, lacking the humor that later made him accessible. He concluded with the now-famous words, "You and I have a rendezvous with destiny. We will preserve for our children this, the last best hope of man on earth, or we will sentence them to take the last step into a thousand years of darkness."[56]

In fact, it was Goldwater who was doomed, even with Reagan's speech. He had already been painted as a warmonger wishing to use nuclear weapons against the North Vietnamese with the infamous "Daisy Girl" ad. The senator had spent a year already trying to deny he opposed Social Security, which at the time did not seem on a path to final bankruptcy as it would to younger voters years later. How much John Kennedy's assassination played into the election cannot be measured, but most scholars think it was extremely important and that not enough distance had yet been put between the utopian-sounding Kennedy and the tax-and-spend policies of Lyndon B. Johnson to yet make a difference. Goldwater's perceived opposition to civil rights legislation, which he maintained were necessary protections of states' rights, was the final nail in the coffin. He carried only Arizona and the Deep South as Johnson walloped him.

With "the Speech," Reagan catapulted past the real candidate—Goldwater—as the man who should have been the Republican nominee in the eyes of many party faithful.

Reagan, on the other hand, emerged a political star. Fan mail poured in, almost all positive ("I've never had a mail reaction like this in all my years in show business," he told the *Los Angeles Times*).[57] He, not Goldwater, should have been the nominee, many argued. Before the Arizona senator was even buried, Richard Bergholz, a political handicapper, said Reagan was "the hottest—and the newest—prospect" for the Republicans.[58] Liberal Republicans saw the threat too; they scampered to portray the election as a complete disavowal of conservative positions and an indication that the party had to move to the Left, especially on social issues. Goldwater's crushing defeat empowered the Nelson Rockefeller/George Romney wing of the party to claim validation of their Democrat-lite strategy. Yet Reagan had convinced others, including Holmes Tuttle, a Los Angeles car dealer who had been in the audience at the Cocoanut Grove, that Reagan could win the governor's seat in California. He invited Reagan to a meeting at his home in the spring of 1965, shocking him with his proposal. "I'm an actor, not a politician," Reagan told the group.[59]

If, in fact, Reagan had by some miraculous stroke been the nominee for anything, it would have destroyed his political career. He still wasn't seasoned enough, and with no actual governing experience at all other than SAG. A smaller step was required—one that could give him administrative experience in a setting where he would deal with other elected representatives. The California governorship was a giant-sized challenge, given the intricacies and size of the state, but if Reagan could master that, the presidency would be well within his reach.

6

Golden State Governor

Modern political observers comment frequently on the rapid shift in California politics from a strongly competitive two-party state to one that is currently just as (or more!) dominated by Democrats as any state in the union, including Massachusetts. From the vantage point of the second decade of the twenty-first century, it's remarkable to find that California twice elected Ronald Reagan—who at the time was one of the most conservative candidates on the scene—then twice elected the conservative George Deukmejian, and then twice elected the only somewhat less conservative Pete Wilson. Some assert California's rapid descent into liberalism was directly linked to a law Reagan himself signed into law as president—the Simpson-Mazzoli Act. But that is speculation about a later time.

In 1965, California was fully up for grabs with either party, in part because the issues the state faced only reflected national trends. Its turmoil during the decade served as a grim mirror for the angst and anger that settled in over the entirety of America, leading to subsequent books about the "unraveling" of the nation or the United States "coming apart." Three "streams" had converged that, even without the added pressure of Vietnam and the accelerating civil rights movement that had started in the 1950s, would have produced chaos and conflict. First there were the baby boomers, America's largest generation, who came of college age in the 1960s. Second, Sputnik, the Soviet satellite that portended intercontinental ballistic missiles with nuclear warheads, provoked massive federal spending in education. Federal dollars flowed into mathematics and sciences departments but quickly cascaded down to liberal arts. Third, a backlash to McCarthyism and the ostracizing of communist-leaning faculty now led universities to accept radical professors with open arms. These three streams flowed together in colleges and universities across the land to bring the largest number of college students ever recorded into universities that were being drowned in money to be educated—for the first time—by instructors who genuinely disliked America and who wanted to force radical, often violent, change. The result was entirely predictable: campuses became the center of agitation, riots, and violence. And ground zero was the University of California, Berkeley.[1]

Reagan would find that addressing college violence was an increasingly important topic in his speeches to civic and political groups. But it wasn't immediately apparent, as positive reviews from "the Speech" continued to pour in. National political columnists Rowland Evans and Robert Novak thought Reagan had already supplanted Goldwater after a speech in Cincinnati. They laid out a case that Reagan was the one candidate the Republicans had who could sell a conservative message in a more appetizing fashion.[2] Reagan offered a combination of Goldwater's ideas in a JFK-like package. It didn't hurt that *National Review*'s William F. Buckley Jr. also liked the Gipper.[3]

When, exactly, Reagan made up his mind to run for the governorship is in dispute. Thomas Evans notes that comedian (and friend of Reagan's) Jack Benny was calling him "Governor" for at least three years prior to his announcement.[4] Anne Edwards claimed Reagan had received a phone call in 1964 suggesting he run for governor.[5] Indeed, she implies Reagan at that time really sought to run for the presidency in 1968. But Steven Hayward's extensive *Age of Reagan* cites a meeting between Reagan and Union Oil's Sy Rubel in February 1965 in which he was urged to run for the governorship and refused.[6] In any case, in April 1965 Reagan held the first meeting with Republican campaign advisors Stuart Spencer and Bill Roberts. The two entered the meeting with preconceived notions that Reagan was another Goldwater and told him an "ultraconservative" couldn't win California… and Reagan agreed.

Spencer and Roberts may have provided the political expertise a Reagan gubernatorial campaign needed, but they still harbored concerns that he did not have the backing in California politics to win. Their firm suggested he bring in two academics, professors Kenneth Holden of UCLA and Stanley Plog of San Fernando Valley State, whose company BASICO (Behavioral Science Corporation of Van Nuys) would give Reagan a crash course in state issues. They met in Malibu over a weekend, where they found that their candidate had a "well-developed ideology and a set of fundamental beliefs rooted in the Constitution."[7] Still, the professors also saw that Reagan's grasp of California issues was minimal, given that he had spent his time on the bigger picture. They immersed him in California politics, using his favorite study guide: index cards on every issue relevant to California politics. Typically, they underestimated both his ability to apply large principles to local concerns and his rapid retention of new information. Briefly, they even thought *they* were responsible for suggesting the insertion of historical figures into Reagan's speeches, not realizing he had done it for years. In the end, their candidate was fully prepared on matters of interest to Californians.

Part of Reagan's team was William Clark, whom Reagan had been grooming for over a year for a political position, urging Clark to run for the state assembly. After throwing his hat into the governor's race, the Gipper again contacted Clark to be the campaign chairman of Ventura County. Early on, Clark recalled, state campaign chairman Phil Battaglia had adopted a Southern California strategy, writing off San Francisco and the north. But Clark's friend Tom Reed took over the northern campaign, and with Reed's effort the campaign made a transition to a full statewide effort.

The most overlooked person in all of Reagan's biographies is his brother, Neil, whose connections in advertising enabled Dutch to have access to top-level California executives and their financing for his governor's run.

No one was more influential or important in winning the governorship for Dutch than his brother Neil. As vice president of McCann Erickson,

Moon handled accounts for a number of wealthy Californians, including Holmes Tuttle and Justin Dart, both of whom would prove critical in Reagan's run for office. According to Michael Reagan, Neil has been overlooked by almost all biographers when it came to his role in the campaign. Moon arranged a luncheon for Dutch in Los Angeles at a country club with Tuttle, Dart, and several others. There was only one problem: Dutch would have to fly, and he hated flying. Neil outlined the meeting for him by phone. "Do you want to be governor?" he asked. Reagan replied he did. "Well, you need to attend this luncheon tomorrow." "Fine," Dutch said. "Where is it?" Moon replied, "Los Angeles." Dutch was hesitant. "That means I'd have to fly to get there in time." He hesitated again. A miffed Neil repeated his question: "Do you want to be governor?" and hung up. Reagan took a flight the next morning and made the meeting.[8]

Of course, Tuttle, Dart, and the rest didn't just happen to coalesce around Reagan: Neil had organized everything. Dutch promised himself he would make it up to his brother one day. That "one day" came in 1976, when Maureen Reagan—Reagan's first child with Jane Wyman, who had developed an interest in politics—asked if she could be one of the delegates from California that, as candidate, Reagan could name himself. He replied, "Your uncle may not make it to another convention. Can I name him?" Maureen agreed, but was extremely disappointed, because, as Michael said, "none of us thought [Dad] would get another chance."[9]

On January 4, 1966, the Gipper delivered a statewide television address, which he had written personally, and officially announced that he was a candidate for governor of the state of California. As with his national Goldwater speech, Reagan addressed the unraveling of America in the form of rising crime and collapsing universities. But Dutch offered solutions, including cracking down on rebellious students and tough enforcement of existing laws, leading the liberal media to (as it always did) call his proposals "dark" and "divisive." Fortunately, Reagan's opponents always underestimated him: the actor, the novice—but most of all, the *radical*—who wanted the governor's seat was treated as a joke. And, as they would do with Donald Trump half a century later, opponents presumed Reagan was an intellectual lightweight who couldn't escape a 3" × 5" card. The Gipper's strategy was to go on offense: he suggested to his managers that he say "a few words to whatever group I'm with…then just open it up to questions and answers?"[10] Such an approach would not work today: the Left's destruction of all political civility and polite behavior, constant demonstrations and disruptions, with chanting and violence, would preclude anyone from such an approach in a general meeting. At the time, however, Reagan could still count on basic manners from audiences, and his disarming style combined with his self-deprecation worked. His managers, who were concerned at first and only agreed to a few trial runs, were shocked at its success.

Issues were drifting in Reagan's favor too. Campus protests, inner-city riots, soaring crime rates, and family breakdowns seemed to validate every one of Reagan's core beliefs. His outsider status helped as well, and in the primary against former San Francisco mayor George Christopher, Dutch grabbed 77 percent of the vote. Pollster Lou Harris found that California on the whole had moved to the right on many issues, with Southern California 50 percent conservative.[11] Now Reagan faced Edmund "Pat" Brown, a lifelong pol who perpetually ran for office. He was far to the Left of Sam Yorty, the more conservative Los Angeles mayor. In other words, Reagan had the perfect foil to differentiate himself from the ideology behind the rioters and protesters.

This separation was key to Reagan's success—and failure—all his political life. When arrayed against die-hard liberals like Brown, Jimmy Carter, and Walter Mondale, Reagan's more conservative ideas seemed like common sense, but when pitted against a "moderate," such as Gerald Ford, it was much harder for Reagan to look less doctrinaire.[12] It didn't help Brown that he was traveling abroad when the riots started, nor did it hurt Reagan that Christopher had spent most of his failed primary campaign attacking Brown, not his Republican opponent. It was a classic case of underestimating a competitor.

Reagan continued to give versions of the Goldwater speech around California, meeting with increasingly more sympathetic audiences. Riots and civil disruption, predictable side effects of the family breakdown already started under welfare and the economy's struggles, reinforced the Gipper's message—but this was only the earliest phase of America's "coming apart."

He led the polls from June forward, and in November he beat Brown by a million votes, carrying fifty-five of California's fifty-eight counties. Thanks to Reed, Reagan won every county in Northern California—which the team had all but written off earlier—except for San Francisco. Republicans also nearly swept the state offices and nationally picked up three Senate seats and forty-seven House seats.

Biographers attribute Reagan's victory to his "winning personality."[13] It continues the underestimation of Reagan's genuine political instincts and political abilities. Moreover, it downplayed the issues that confronted California at the time.

It is worthwhile to take a moment to examine Reagan's America in 1966. John F. Kennedy's assassination in 1963 had, according to some, constituted a landmark change in America's political climate. James Piereson noted that Kennedy's death pushed the Democratic Party to the Left and away from his anti-communism. It created a conspiratorial mindset that blamed "right-wingers" for the actions of an avowed communist.[14] Of course, in life Kennedy was a hard-liner against the Soviets and communism, and while he was not above lying about the "missile gap" to get elected, he was hated by the socialist wing of the Democratic Party. He had entered office essentially running to the right of Dwight Eisenhower on national security. The nation had drifted into a post-"golden accident" malaise following that time in which, due to the circumstances of victory following World War II, America dominated the global economy in both production *and* consumption.[15] With a 1953 GNP almost three times what it was in 1940, America accounted for 15 percent of all world trade and 45 percent of world manufacturing production after the war.[16]

Under such circumstances, it was inevitable that an uncompetitive American industry got lazy: Detroit could continue to pump out cars with almost no significant changes; steel ruled the world and steelworkers could demand whatever wages they wanted; and textiles drifted into uncompetitive routines. The United States was only in a position of growing dominance in the computer and aircraft industries, where companies like IBM, Hewlett-Packard, Boeing, Lockheed, and McDonnell Douglas were introducing breakthrough after breakthrough. By the time Lyndon

B. Johnson took office, the nation appeared to be prosperous, but it was an illusory prosperity already being eaten away by ever-increasing wage demands and corporate paralysis. David Halberstam's *The Reckoning* tells the parallel tale of Ford and Nissan, one tailing downward, one rising rapidly, as they followed different corporate paths.[17]

Under Lyndon B. Johnson, the weaknesses and fissures in the American economy were not yet apparent, while the burdens of a vastly larger government and a foreign war had not yet been added to the weight. Johnson's "Great Society" would heap billions onto the national debt and expand government in nearly as large a leap as FDR had thirty years earlier. Kennedy's quiet but significant insertion of over sixteen thousand advisors into South Vietnam had failed to deter North Vietnam's aggression. Without distracting from his War on Poverty, Johnson would tell his generals, in essence, "Win the war, but don't make a big deal of it." When he met with his Joint Chiefs of Staff in 1965, he asked if the war could be won, and the JCS replied it could, if the administration immediately took steps to do so. Those steps included placing a million men in South Vietnam that year, unrelenting bombing of the North, mining Haiphong Harbor, and cutting the Ho Chi Minh Trail. Those things either never occurred at all or took place too late in the war to make a difference. By 1969, the United States had incrementally bumped the troop levels up to only 549,500. The cost of the war steadily helped grind down the economy as well—but this only began as Reagan moved into the governor's office in Sacramento.

Then there were the cities aflame. Race riots struck Newark, Los Angeles, Detroit, New York, and a half-dozen other cities in the early 1960s.[18] As Mike Allen and I wrote in *A Patriot's History of the United States*, "white liberals responded to the wave of looting by producing reports."[19] Johnson's War on Poverty supposedly would address the causes of that rage, but in fact black activists saw it as too little, too late, and white conservatives saw it as an out-and-out bribe. Even Democrat hard-liners such as Daniel Patrick Moynihan were pointing to the real issue: the destruction of the black family, which was traced to the legacy of slavery, but which welfare only exacerbated. Changes to the Aid to Families with Dependent Children program rewarded single motherhood and almost guaranteed both perpetuating poverty and the rise of gangs by removing the father from the home. Meanwhile, the Great Society advanced notions of "affirmative action," namely that blacks could not make it on their own and needed a head start from government in the form of college acceptance quotas. Steven Hayward, one of Reagan's better biographers, noted that the civil rights movement had already crossed a Rubicon of sorts by shifting focus from equal opportunity to equality of outcome.[20]

On top of race riots, campuses were descending into constant chaos of protests and sit-ins. These irked Reagan, who saw the protests as a breakdown of law and order. All the moorings upon which American society rested were coming apart (leading to the title of a popular book about the decade). As Hayward put it, "with every passing day in the…1960s each of the main troubled currents in American public life—Vietnam, civil rights and race relations, the welfare state, and the student movement—gained momentum."[21]

All of these changes, which had started while Reagan was hosting *General Electric Theater*, had heated up for a decade before boiling over just as the Gipper was about to enter the governor's office. Almost immediately a symbolic controversy presented itself when Governor Reagan, with the support of the University of California board of regents, fired the University of California chancellor Clark Kerr. Over the years, Kerr, known for his condescension and arrogance, had meekly accepted the Free Speech Movement and campus chaos. Technically, while the governor had a seat on the board of regents, few ever attended meetings. But Reagan voted with the majority (his critics of course thought it was his idea) and despite the discomfort of having to confront the matter immediately, Reagan certainly thought Kerr needed to go. Symbolically Reagan had struck instantly at one of the perceived sources of campus disruptions, then heaped salt into the wound by calling for the UC system to charge tuition in his first budget. California falsely claimed to have "free" education while silently loading hundreds of dollars in fees on students that easily equaled tuition. Reagan found that dishonest. Call it what it was, he argued.

Protestors found a day on Reagan's calendar when he was scheduled to be out of state to call a rally. When the Gipper learned of the planned protests, he canceled his trip and strode out to meet the demonstrators. A shocked rabble-rousing leader, who didn't see Reagan come up behind him, meekly handed over his microphone to the governor. Although Dutch tried to have a conversation and explain the changes, the group had no interest in talking and shouted and booed until Reagan told them "nothing I can say would create an open mind in some of you." He concluded by saying that as the representative of the people of the state—who had paid "willingly and happily" for the state's universities—he had an obligation to speak for them.[22] "Lawlessness by the mob," Reagan had said in his inaugural address, "will not be tolerated."[23]

Kerr's firing occurred early in Reagan's tenure, but one of the underlying problems—the need to institute tuition in lieu of fees—dragged on throughout the summer. Charging tuition would have ended a California tradition, and despite their appreciation for the need of such new money, most of the regents did not want to be seen as the ones changing the system. At an August 1967 meeting at UCLA, Reagan proposed a $250-a-year tuition. The plan earmarked half for scholarship and grants, a fourth for new faculty hires, and a fourth for new construction. Democrat Jesse Unruh warned that Reagan's tuition approach would most harm the middle class, already on the hook for much of the state's tax increase.

By the time the regents' vote finally came, Reagan lost 2:1, whereupon he proposed a luncheon recess. Ever the negotiator, the Gipper had no intention of giving up. "You never leave the stadium at the half," he muttered to Lyn Nofziger.[24] In the cafeteria, Reagan buttonholed several regents, who personally supported him. He refused to back down on tuition. "What's the alternative?" he asked. The regents came up with a new draft concept using the term "charge" paid by all students, and the regents adopted the resolution with a voice vote, with Unruh and a few allies voting no. Like Napoleon at Marengo, Reagan had lost the battle at eleven o'clock and won it back by lunch. California retained the facade of "free tuition" (and even that finally vanished), while Reagan had the cash he needed and emerged again as a skilled negotiator.[25]

The university chaos paled in comparison to the state of California's budget. Brown had cheated in numerous ways, such as counting three months of as-yet uncollected revenue as already in and accelerating tax collections.[26] This reality would foreshadow what Reagan would experience in his presidency, namely that he ran on the principle of balanced budgets but inherited a disastrous situation—for which the standard liberal solution was always to raise taxes. Revenues were projected to be 20 percent short of expenses. Reagan described it as follows: "I didn't know if I was elected governor or appointed receiver."[27] Indeed, he was surprised by the depth of the shortfall. Immediately after the election he had asked his Ventura County campaign chairman (and soon to be right-hand man), William Clark, to take two other men to Sacramento and give him a report on the most significant problems he'd encounter as the new governor. When Clark returned with a dim fiscal picture—the state was losing $1 million a day—Reagan asked, "Do you think we can ask for a recount?"[28]

Although Reagan said any "major business" could tighten its belt by 10 percent, he was facing a shortfall double that. Nevertheless, Reagan proposed an immediate 10 percent across-the-board cut as a starting point. He also asked state and local workers to volunteer to work on Washington's birthday, sold the state's airplane, reduced out-of-state travel by state officials, canceled some building plans, and took other measures that still fell short of reducing the budget by the necessary amount.

Biographers have criticized the across-the-board cut as amateurish and naive, though Brands admits it "had the merit of simplicity."[29] Like everything Reagan did, it sought to balance out burdens evenly, without selecting out one group or another. Of course it raised howls of protest from people getting various forms of government assistance or goodies. Assembly Speaker Jesse Unruh, anticipating so many future Democrat Congresses, declared Reagan's budget dead on arrival.

Dealing with this kind of obstructionism might have flummoxed the Gipper had he not already fought hardened communists in SAG. In addition, Reagan had a skilled team in place to assist him. After the election, Reagan asked Clark to remain on, initially as a cabinet secretary on communications and later as chief of staff. (Among others in Sacramento who would later accompany Reagan to Washington were Caspar Weinberger, his budget director, and press secretary Lyn Nofziger.) A California lawyer who had been attracted to Reagan's national vision, not just his plans for the Golden State, Clark worked with Reagan in nearly a symbiotic mode. He understood what the Gipper needed even without directions. They were both westerners, both big men, and both loved horses. Unlike some of Reagan's later advisors, Clark didn't try to talk his boss to death, giving him space.

Clark devised a briefing method for Dutch called the "mini-memo." He would meet every Monday through Friday with the four executive directors of the state agencies or departments to outline the issues of the week. The five also met each morning to prepare issue briefs for Reagan, which all followed an identical form: a one-paragraph statement of the issue, the facts of the case, a pro and con discussion, and a recommendation ("ISSUE, FACT, DISCUSSION, RECOMMENDATION.")[30] If Reagan agreed with the conclusion, he'd initial, "OK, RR." Clark made sure the mini-memos worked because he kept the arguments honest and presented the best points of both sides rather than slanting them toward his favored position. Biographer Steven Hayward notes that Reagan made up to eight decisions an hour following this system.[31]

Typically, the press viewed the mini-memos with disdain, thinking them simple-minded (or "mini-minded," as one reporter described them).[32] Clark defended the process by saying, "The only way the governor can operate efficiently is to ration his time."[33] Throughout his presidency, Reagan would later be portrayed as lacking the energy, and especially the attentiveness, to truly process details. The reality was that he embodied the essential characteristics of a good leader from his first days in Sacramento, understanding that details could always be dealt with at a lower level; understanding the big picture, and how everything fit together, was a genuine gift. While Reagan was too modest to say so, he possessed a trait few other people had. Clark observed that Reagan was "a good listener and a decisive executive" and that he did not shy away from making tough choices—except when it came to firing people.[34] Even the *New York Times* figured that out by the end of the Gipper's first year in Sacramento, admitting "he has turned out to be a man of some strength who likes to make decisions and makes them easily."[35]

Through use of the "mini-memos" in Sacramento,
Reagan constantly fooled people into thinking he was not "deep,"
when in fact he had arguments distilled to their strongest points
on both sides in order to be more decisive.

A "tough choice" arose almost immediately in the form of the Therapeutic Abortion Act. Reagan's aides were divided on the subject, and Reagan admitted he hadn't given the issue much thought. His father-in-law advised him to sign the bill. When the governor asked Clark for background information, Clark provided more than needed. Reagan spent a whole weekend reading and came out quoting St. Thomas Aquinas—but in the end he signed the bill, arguing that he was persuaded by the "mental health" considerations of victims of rape or incest.[36] He knew the perils of the slippery slope: "You can't allow an abortion on the grounds the child won't be born perfect. Where do you stop?"[37] But he was misled into thinking that abortions under the act would be reduced, perhaps even rare. Unfortunately, from Reagan's first year in office, when there were 514 abortions, the number skyrocketed to 100,000 from 1968 to 1974.[38] The consequences bothered Reagan profoundly, leaving him, as Clark said, with a sense of guilt. Reagan would later admit he made a serious mistake, forever changing his approach to abortion and leading him to become the "father of the pro-life movement."[39] According to Clark, Reagan told him "when this subject arises again, we shall be prepared."[40]

An equally tough choice involved an emerging homosexual scandal between two of Reagan's aides, one of them his executive secretary Phil Battaglia. Reagan had not noticed his right-hand man's repeated absences and was oblivious to Battaglia's sexual preferences—at the time, a major scandal. But Reagan's aides and supporters, including Lyn Nofziger, Holmes Tuttle, and Tom Reed were horrified. Many were already envisioning a Reagan presidential run that would be derailed if the episode became public. Others, including Clark, were more concerned with the inefficiency resulting from Battaglia's disappearances, noting, "The sexual issue was the trip wire [but] wasn't the reason we needed to make a change."[41] On August

25, 1967, Reagan met with a group of his aides and supporters at the Hotel del Coronado in San Diego, where the governor was handed a report outlining Battaglia's absences and deficiencies. It took only moments for Reagan to realize the import of the document. Although he said, "I want to sleep on this," there was no doubt among any of the group that he would act on their recommendations to dismiss Battaglia—or, more accurately, to have someone else dismiss him.

It was decided that Holmes Tuttle, not Reagan, would ask Battaglia to resign, and Tuttle flew to Los Angeles the following day to preside over the execution. Tuttle and Henry Salvatori both feared news of the affair would damage Reagan's presidential chances, and Battaglia's exit was swift and quiet. Still, before long the newspapers and especially columnist Drew Pearson began to run stories. In October, Drew Pearson asked if the governor could survive "the discovery that a homosexual ring has been operating in his office."[42] With Battaglia gone, Clark was elevated to chief of staff, wherein the *New York Times* described him as "another of the political amateurs" Reagan brought into government.[43]

Battaglia continued to engage in business and political deals in Sacramento, often referring to his (now defunct) Reagan connection. Reporters soon sniffed out the story and the governor was asked in a November news conference about Pearson's column on his former aide. Reagan defiantly insisted there was no report, when of course there was and almost all the reporters knew it. The scandal resurfaced in the 1976, then again in the 1980 presidential campaigns. It is to the Gipper's credit that he absolutely refused to make Battaglia's sexual preferences a public issue. But, as Cannon points out, Reagan's practice of delegation had ill served him. His lack of oversight and follow-up over those in whom he had entrusted authority had caused a problem. The episode revealed one of Reagan's greatest weaknesses: in his heart, Reagan liked and trusted people, a trait he would see frequently used against his best interests.[44]

But Battaglia's removal did change practices in the governor's office. Clark ended Battaglia's practice of insisting that the chief of staff always be present when other cabinet officers were meeting with Reagan and is largely credited with the phrase "Let Reagan be Reagan," meaning that Clark did not want the Gipper stage-managed. That made Clark truly the first Reagan insider to fully trust the governor to handle himself. Above all, Clark knew Reagan was more intellectually powerful and serious than he let on, and he noticed that in briefings during a key point, while Dutch would say nothing, he'd look at Clark with a wink or a small smile, indicating he got precisely the key points.[45] Moreover, Clark knew that like Lincoln, Reagan often had a purpose with his folksy stories, and that, far from meandering, they encapsulated exactly the issue at hand.

Another matter was more delicate. Nancy called Clark daily, sometimes hourly, to express concerns over articles she had read or news stories she'd seen on television, wanting to make sure "her Ronnie" was fairly treated and his positions accurately reported. It was a symptom of a larger problem that would afflict the Reagan White House. Of course, Clark had no control over what others wrote or said. While he thought Nancy had a good eye for trouble and solid analysis, he couldn't possibly do his job and also interact with her on a minute-by-minute basis. Reagan knew her calls were coming in, often getting off the elevator and saying to Clark, "Well, she called again, didn't she?"[46] Nancy by nature was a "dis-truster," according to Ron, their son, while Reagan by nature trusted everyone until crossed.[47] Eventually, Clark tasked Michael Deaver to interact with Nancy, making Deaver in essence Clark's second in command and creating a relationship that would work well into Reagan's presidency.

Although Reagan asked Clark to become his lieutenant governor when the current occupant of that seat, Robert Finch, joined the Nixon administration, Clark refused. He did not like being out front and certainly didn't want to be governor in the future. Instead, in November 1968 Reagan accepted Clark's resignation as well, conditional upon Clark accepting an appointment to the Superior Court of San Obispo County. Clark left Sacramento having provided his boss with a foundation of success and a record of victories that would prepare him for the presidency.[48] The Gipper replaced Clark with another future key advisor, Edwin Meese III, at that time Reagan's legal affairs secretary.

Lou Cannon maintains that the last months of 1967 were a type of "receivership" in which Reagan cut himself off from his staff, leaving the office to be run by Clark. Others, including Caspar Weinberger, noted only that Clark handled the Battaglia episode "skillfully and very fairly" and that Clark had done such a good job of keeping "things straight and clean in the Governor's house" that Reagan was "laid out on a bed of linen from the governor's house to the presidency."[49] Once again, however, even Reagan's close associates failed to appreciate the Gipper's gifts, making it appear that his success was always the result of those closest to him.

Ultimately, the budget issues that plagued Reagan initially were solved (as are most things in government) by compromise—though Reagan got most of what he wanted. Unruh sought a tax increase, but with taxes withheld from paychecks. Reagan resisted, knowing that an unseen tax is a tax impossible to repeal. His carrot to Unruh was property tax relief in the future—which the Gipper also wanted. On July 28, the legislature passed a $1 billion tax increase without withholding. Reagan signed it, causing conservatives to moan. A month later, however, he won the tuition fight. Together, the pair of bookends that established his administration solidly before summer beach season was over. "Reagan was not about to 'grow in office'" (a favorite phrase of liberals for conservatives who lose their principles); he adopted the tax increase under duress and insisted it "does not represent my philosophy of government."[50]

Lingering problems of student protests did not yield so quickly. Indeed, this was an international development, not merely an American disease. Germany, with "Hitler's children," as historian Tony Judt called them, "resembled their protesting American counterparts, embracing a radical theology of free love, Spock-influenced child rearing, and nudity."[51] In June 1967, one hundred thousand people, mostly students, turned out to demonstrate in Berlin, and riots ensued, killing four hundred. That same year, twenty-five thousand—again, mostly students—turned out to march in Washington, DC. Universities had, of course, grown at exponential rates. Arizona State University, Ohio State University, the University of Michigan, and the University of Wisconsin soon all had student populations of more than forty thousand each. But the "Cal" system was already radicalizing faster than many others. This, too, was predictable, the natural merging of the baby boom, the Sputnik-era funding for higher education, and the radicalization of faculties in the backlash against McCarthyism.[52] The resulting explosive mixture was guaranteed to be set off by any match. Vietnam provided the most convenient excuse, but any other would have done just as well.

Despite having been an average student in college and diverting his attention from studies to football and theater, Reagan was much like the character "Rudy" in the film of the same name, who wept when he finally was accepted into Notre Dame. For Dutch, a college education was a mark of prestige and accomplishment, something that very few of his father's generation had. It was to be treated with respect. Now, confronting campus radicals, Dutch felt on the one hand they were not representative of the majority (which was true) and on the other that as long as they complied with basic rules and propriety, they could demonstrate all they wanted. He also was unafraid to engage them with humor and even ridicule. On one occasion, while meeting with the board of regents at UC Santa Barbara, the Gipper found the sidewalk to the meeting room lined on both sides with students standing in silent protest. As he got to the door, he turned, put his fingers to his lips, and said, "Shhh." The students laughed.[53] At Santa Cruz, students surrounded his limousine, which crawled along. A bearded demonstrator shouted at Reagan, "We are the future!" to which Reagan quickly grabbed a piece of paper, holding it up to the window for the student to see. It said, "I'll sell my bonds."[54] He entertained conservative audiences with his anti-hippie rhetoric ("For those of you who don't know what a hippie is, he's a fellow who dresses like Tarzan, has hair like Jane, and smells like Cheetah," and "Their signs said, 'make love, not war,' but it didn't look like they could do either.")[55] The Gipper had variations on these for a variety of occasions, and while some of the more moderate members of his staff cringed, thinking it made him a target of the "pointy-headed intellectuals" (as George Wallace used to call them), the quips endeared him to the majority of California Republicans and many independent Democrats. It had to pain the radicals, therefore, that in November 1967 in the middle of the California campus turmoil, Reagan traveled to Yale where he was named a Chubb Fellow, leading him to joke "I am not a Yale man [but] the Yale hippies are just as dirty and unshaven as the ones we have in California."

And just as radicalized. The California state college system, which was bidding for university status, had spun out of control, especially at San Francisco State, a campus of 18,000 where in 1965 students had organized to send student teachers into poor neighborhoods. Some 1,500 students took classes in black culture, guerrilla warfare, and other nonacademic topics, putting on anti-white plays and holding seminars on dodging the draft. Particularly active was the Black Student Union (BSU), which became a magnet for radicals from all over the country. While Reagan was at Yale, conservative students won elections and cut funds for the nonsense "classes," whereupon the BSU broke into the student newspaper's office, hospitalized the editor, then subsequently invaded the administration building, "looted the college bookstore, and attacked bystanders."[56] Reagan phoned his staff, then demanded the state colleges maintain law and order on their campuses—a sentiment supported by Jesse Unruh, giving Reagan the Democrat backing he needed to restore order. Under fire, San Francisco State president John Summerskill resigned in February 1968 and was replaced by Robert Smith, who closed the college when renewed violence broke out.

Reagan did not support what he called an "act of capitulation" but waited two days before reopening the college via the trustees. Smith then resigned, replaced by Reagan's pick, semanticist S. I. Hayakawa, a well-known defender of civil rights. Known for his tam o' shanter, the flamboyant polymath Hayakawa provided the perfect intermediary between Reagan and the students. He tried to impose order, while at the same time offering sops such as a black studies department to the militants. (Typically, the media lied about this: Chet Huntley, on his January 17, 1969, news program, said Reagan only supported the move because the chairman of the department was white, when in fact the very proposal required hiring a black person to head the department. Huntley learned of his error and sent an apology but did not retract the statement on air.)[57] Increasingly, Reagan was determined to keep San Francisco State open, allowing people who wanted an education to get one "at the point of bayonet if necessary."[58]

When it came to campus protests, the governor who had once been a student protester himself insisted on law and order and peaceful demonstrations—whatever the cost.

In fact, the violence was just starting. On January 22, a left-wing coalition struck at UC Berkeley with bomb threats and actual fire bombings. After law-abiding students were assaulted by "strikers" on February 5, police moved in to protect them, only to come under attack from rocks and cans, leaving three officers hospitalized. A furious Reagan declared a state of emergency, called out the California Highway Patrol to guard students, and promised to end the reign of "off-campus revolutionaries."[59] After issuing the proclamation, he confided in Paul Beck, his press secretary, "I'll sleep well tonight." Certainly he should have, for even Democrats praised his handling of the issue. Still, the radicals had only started.

When a new round of Berkeley violence erupted over the occupation of a "people's park" by the radicals on May 15, 1969, police moved in again. This time, they were heavily outnumbered and one deputy fired a shotgun into the air, killing a student standing on a nearby roof. Reagan placed the blame squarely on the rioters and, at the request of law enforcement officials, called out the National Guard to enforce a curfew and virtual martial law at the university for another two weeks. Lou Cannon observed, "The deployment of the Guard broke the back of the rebellion at Berkeley and enabled students to attend classes."[60]

All along, Reagan explained to the voters of California that what was occurring at the universities was not a few college pranks gone bad but a dangerous trend in the making. In a televised speech before the Commonwealth Club of San Francisco, Reagan laid out the toll of eleven months of violence: eight major bombings or attempted bombings, the confiscation of explosives and hundreds of weapons, "dozens" of arson attempts, and shots fired at police. In May 1969, the riot showed that stockpiles of rocks had been assembled on rooftops. Police, he said, were "literally fighting for their lives."[61]

Tensions eventually eased at most other campuses that experienced similar strikes, but the University of California, Santa Barbara (UCSB) soon found itself immersed in the worst violence of all. On February 24, 1970, a riot broke out on UCSB campus following the attempted arrest of two agitators. A violent crowd gathered, overturned and burned a police car, marched to the Isla Vista branch of the Bank of America, and set fires to protest the bank's refusal to withdraw its "support" of the Vietnam War and grape growers in the San Joaquin Valley.[62] Anti-war attorney William Kunstler gave a frenzied speech ("the shadow of the swastika is on every courthouse, on universities"), and further chaos erupted after police beat a student returning to his apartment. More mobs appeared, with rioting carrying on into the night. The Bank of America was again torched—this time to the ground.

On February 26, Governor Reagan arrived in Santa Barbara. He labeled the protestors "cowardly little bums," but before the National Guard could arrive, more mobs pushed the police completely out of Isla Vista. Finally the Guard restored order, but not before more rioting and more fires left another bystander dead from a ricochet. Reagan told the press it was irrelevant where the bullet came from: it was "sent on its way several years ago when a certain element in this society decided they could take the law into their own hands."[63] Attacks on the Bank of America spread, but Santa Barbara, after one more spate of violence in June, finally settled down. Many students dropped out, unwilling to put up with the radicals' lunacy. Still others reverted to more traditional "protest" in the form of liberal classes and public service.

By 1970, tolerating no lawlessness, Reagan had brought the vast California university and college system to heel to some degree and established himself as the law and order governor. As was typical for him, Reagan was generous in victory: after restoring order so the universities could function, he supported the re-designation of the college system as universities and hiked professors' salaries at the college system. While some voters deserted him over the deaths that had occurred, most deemed it a sad and necessary corollary of the riots.

Reagan campaigned for Nixon in 1968, when Nixon carried California and the Republicans controlled the California state legislature for the first time in ten years. Yet, already national figures increasingly mentioned the name Ronald Reagan for the presidency. Tom Wicker of the *New York Times* thought 1968 was Reagan's last chance to run! "For one reason or another, chiefly age, it's 1968 or never."[64] Dutch also held a reverence for the mystical notion that the office sought the man and that certainly after only one year of being a governor, it was not seeking him at that point. Still, he expressed a willingness to entertain offers, saying, "If the Republican Party comes knocking at my door, I won't say, 'Get lost, fellows.'"[65]

George Romney, touted by the mainstream Republicans as a front-runner, suffered from a charisma gap, something that clearly did not afflict the Gipper. Reagan's "weaknesses" were precisely his strengths—his ability to speak plainly and in language average people understood, as opposed to carefully scripted "politicizese." Reagan's "conservatism" was supposed to be a "liability," while Romney's moderation was seen (by the liberal journalists) as an asset. Of course, in both cases, it was exactly the opposite. Reagan's attraction *was* his conservatism, his plain talk. Even so, there was Nixon, who could claim the conservative wing almost as well as Reagan could. Nixon was viewed as a "law and order" candidate and a strong anti-communist.

Seeing Nixon, not Reagan, as the greatest threat to a Democratic ticket, magazines and the print media began urging a Romney/Reagan ticket in October 1967—of course, with Reagan in the vice presidential slot. Romney was open to the idea because it removed a potentially powerful opponent. For his part, Reagan wasn't sure he wanted to run, but wouldn't rule it out either. But by then, Reagan had developed a reputation as a "responsible" conservative. Joseph Kraft of the *Washington Post* labeled Dutch a "dekooking agent" for the right wing and said he had demonstrated that it was indeed possible for a "straightforward citizen leader" to govern without decades of political practice.[66] In his televised debate with Robert F. Kennedy in May 1967, which was taped in front of an international audience with questions from eighteen students in London, Reagan looked sober and bright. He appealed to idealism and repeatedly pointed out the greatness of America while Kennedy got into the mud of criticism. *Newsweek* admitted that the "rookie Reagan…left old campaigner Kennedy blinking when the session ended,"[67] and even the liberal writer David

Halberstam said "Reagan...destroyed him."[68] Reagan, the entertainer, wisely spoke to the television audience, while Kennedy directed his remarks to the students. Kennedy would later fume at aides, asking who "got me into this?" Kennedy biographers such as Arthur Schlesinger quickly edited out any references to a debate in which their candidate was embarrassed.

Of course, liberal Republicans warned that Reagan would consign the party to "permanent minority status."[69] Romney, the icon of the liberal wing, immolated himself with his comment that after returning from a trip to Vietnam to see the war up close, he "had the greatest brainwashing that anyone can get...not only by the generals but also by the diplomatic corps."[70] In every campaign, there is a phrase or a comment that either makes or breaks a candidate. Romney's son, Mitt, running for president in 2012, privately told a group that 47 percent of Americans were dependent on government, a comment that was used to destroy him. In 2012, Hillary Clinton described supporters of Donald Trump as a "basket of deplorables." But one has to look long and hard to find a single word like "brainwashing" that so undid a major candidate. Senator Eugene McCarthy quipped, "There was no need to brainwash the governor. All he required was a light rinse."[71] Nelson Rockefeller bowed out, and that really left only Nixon as Reagan's top competitor. Nixon knew it, and bested Reagan when the two showed up at the Bohemian Grove in California, where Nixon—fresh off his world travels—delivered a well-conceived analysis of the world's hot spots, while Reagan was seen as coming up short.[72] Still, the American public was at that point more focused on rioting and crime, giving the Gipper a fighting chance based on his record at the California campuses.

Nixon knew Reagan was his chief foe, calling him "a real contender" in 1967 and noting that his "strength is vastly underrated by the Eastern press."[73] Of course, Nixon more than anyone understood the press and its significant handicaps when it came to assessing conservatism or conservatives. He would soon become the most hated target of the media, but already Nixon had discerned what it took other Republicans decades to figure out—that reporters were overwhelmingly liberals and had no difficulty stretching the truth to prevent conservative policies from triumphing. On the other hand, Reagan thought it too soon to seek the presidency directly himself. But the siren calls from the grassroots were alluring, so he approached the campaign with a strategy of attempting to delay Nixon's acquisition of enough delegates long enough for a tidal wave of support to sweep him in. It was a risky strategy, but the Gipper's supporters had put up $500,000 to hire F. Clifton White to quietly woo delegates, especially in the South. There, according to one reporter in a typically demeaning comment, Reagan was "the greatest thing to come along since corn pone and hog jowls."[74] The southern strategy also was necessitated in part by the fact that Reagan had yet to win a primary, but in the South the party bosses still controlled the delegations. He was a huge hit, especially at a Columbia, South Carolina, appearance that was telecast throughout Dixie.

Nixon, though, was a pro. He had suffered his losses, taken his beatings, and learned. He courted Strom Thurmond (the butt of a joke by Beatle John Lennon—"It sounds like a disease. I've got Strom Thurmond in me arm!"). Thurmond favored Dutch but figured Nixon would be the winner, and he extracted a promise by Nixon to deploy the anti-ballistic missile system then being tested and a pledge to name a staunch conservative as his running mate. At almost that very time, Governor Spiro Agnew of Maryland announced his support for Nixon.

As the race ebbed and flowed, Nixon quickly lost the advantage he had gained over Reagan. In early August, the California delegation publicly declared Reagan a candidate and virtually secured the Golden State for their golden boy. Suddenly Nixon seemed in trouble, even more so after a Miami radio station sponsored a poll about Reagan for president and got responses in the 70 percent "yes" range.

As quickly as the Reagan wave rose, however, it receded. Not a single southern state delegation abandoned Nixon. Ultimately, the Gipper came in third, with 182 delegates to Rockefeller's 277 and Nixon's winning total of 697 (barely more than needed). Steven Hayward maintains that had the vote gone to a second ballot, Reagan may have stolen a significant number of delegates, especially from the South. Perhaps that's true, but a gap of 510 was hardly likely to be bridged by defectors.

In the end, Reagan knew he wasn't ready, and his late start in the campaign admitted as much. He had a "sense of relief" that he hadn't won and confided in Deaver that he was not yet prepared for the White House.[75] At two in the morning on August 8, Reagan appeared before the convention and urged a unanimous vote for Nixon.

It puzzled conservatives such as William F. Buckley that hard-core rightists such as Strom Thurmond and John Tower of Texas had fallen in behind Nixon. Those southern politicians, however, knew Reagan was not quite seasoned, especially when it came to a national campaign. The 1967–1968 campaign provided excellent training for Reagan's next two runs at the White House.

Back in California, between the budget battles and campus conflicts, Reagan had marched to several successes, even if some were mitigated by compromise. Those stood him in good stead as he ran for reelection in 1970. He could rightly run on his balanced budget record and was seen as a practical governor who found a way to get his agenda through, even if he had to compromise from time to time. Mainstream publications developed the proverbial "strange new respect" for Reagan as an administrator. Despite renewed campus violence stemming from Richard Nixon's bombing of Cambodia, Reagan still won reelection with 53 percent of the vote, down just 5 percent from his 58 percent four years earlier.

He now had to confront California's burgeoning welfare problem, which by itself posed a threat to the state's balanced budget. "Unless and until we face up to…complete reform of welfare," he said in his second inaugural address, "we will face a tax increase next year."[76] What had happened to the nation's poor constituted nothing less than a massive attack on fathers. Lyndon B. Johnson's changes in the Aid to Families with Dependent Children (AFDC) program placed significant barriers to marriage. As Charles Murray pointed out in his seminal book *Losing Ground*, the policies penalized married couples and rewarded single mothers. Once the incentives kicked in, generations of fatherless families appeared, spawning gangs and street crime and a complete breakdown of traditional family life in what were then called "ghettos."[77] The programs had been in place for over three years, and already California was feeling their effects. On top of that, the national economy under Nixon—weighted down by the ongoing effects of the Johnson administration's tax-and-spend policies and the costs of the Vietnam War—sagged. Reagan's approach was to cut back on those who were not deserving and to increase aid for those who were truly needy. Nixon's national Family Assistance Plan was instead offering a guaranteed income. Reagan rejected that, noting that "the government is supposed to promote the general welfare.... I don't believe it is supposed to *provide* it."[78]

Contrary to the legislature's approach to the welfare explosion—which was entirely cost-based—Reagan sought to strike at the theoretical grounding of policies that incentivized people to stay unemployed and to have as many children as possible. In August 1970, Meese drafted a memo for the cabinet and staff that returned emphasis to the "tax-payer as opposed to the tax-taker; on the truly needy as opposed to the lazy unemployable...[and on] the basic needs as opposed to unmanageable enrichment programs."[79] Key to that effort was fixing AFDC.

Although AFDC grants had not increased at all during Pat Brown's tenure, neither had Reagan raised them; and AFDC recipients had far less real support than they had twelve years earlier. Reagan knew he had to address the support shortfall while cutting back on the number of recipients, which had ballooned to 1.15 million from 769,000 when the Gipper took office. Reagan conveniently blamed the deepening recession, but he privately understood that it was the nature of the program that spawned an almost automatic increase in clients. A task force devised the California Welfare Reform Act for the governor, which Reagan intended to unveil to the legislature in a speech. However, he found resistance from both the new president pro tempore of the Senate, James Mills, and the new Speaker of the Assembly, Robert Moretti, both Democrats. They hoped to deprive a Republican governor of positive television coverage, but the move backfired when Reagan gave a televised March 3 town hall address in Los Angeles. Reagan adroitly labeled it the "speech the Legislature didn't want to hear."[80] He called for seventy specific changes to "prevent an uncontrolled upward spiraling of the welfare caseload."[81] While Reagan wanted to actually increase help to the "truly needy," he intended to make those who were able to work have to find a job and to "strengthen family responsibility." However—as Charles Murray showed in *Losing Ground*—putting *single mothers* to work undercut the need to encourage marriage.[82] As studies in Wisconsin showed, encouraging single welfare mothers to work indeed could get them to a certain level of self-sufficiency, but it tended to discourage marriage and leave them locked in at that low level. No men, no marriage, no real wealth.[83] As the nation would soon learn, female-headed households were disproportionately likely to be poorer, and as George Gilder later argued, the quickest way out of poverty was marriage.[84] But the quantitative proof of these lessons was not so obvious to Reagan or his generation, who still looked to employment as the main solution to poverty.

In September 1970, California suffered a ruling from a federal judge that required it to increase its welfare payouts or lose federal Health, Education, and Welfare (HEW) funds. Reagan appealed to Vice President Spiro Agnew, and HEW allowed California more time, which Reagan used to meet with Nixon and work out a compromise whereby the state would increase its payments but would also be allowed a test program in which able-bodied AFDC recipients were required to work. In July, the state raised its welfare payments, but Reagan found himself bound by the new Democratic legislature. In turn, the Democrats couldn't pass a bill over his veto. However, in California, the governor had a line-item veto, something President Reagan would later beg for, so Democrats would see much of any budget they passed eviscerated by the governor unless they played ball. When the Democratic Speaker Robert Moretti arranged a one-on-one meeting with Reagan, they agreed to find common ground to get the welfare deal done. The final bill, known as the California Welfare Reform Act of 1971, was, as Cannon called it, "a seminal achievement of the Reagan governorship."[85] It increased aid but at the same time restricted eligibility, included incentives for counties to recover child support payments, and included some work requirements.

The state's welfare caseload dropped by almost 300,000 in three years. Reagan boasted that his policies had reduced a monthly increase of 40,000 to a monthly decrease of 8,000.[86] His "workfare" program was less stellar, putting slightly under ten thousand to work during the program's four years. It's also likely that increased abortions, now allowed by Reagan, reduced the numbers of those in poverty. Regardless, Reagan and the Democrats had

139

both achieved a tangible result, and the public largely credited Reagan for the success.[87]

When a court order in August 1971 (*Serano v. Priest*) ruled the state's system of funding schools through property taxes was inequitable and unconstitutional, the legislature brought on a fiscal crisis, yet adjourned. The Gipper summoned them back in special session and demanded a solution, which, more or less, he got. With a few tweaks—and income tax withholding (which Reagan originally opposed but which was beneficial to state coffers)—enough was raised to avoid running out of money. However, the issue of escalating property taxes remained, resulting in Los Angeles County assessor Philip Watson qualifying a ballot initiative called "Proposition 14" for the ballot. Prop 14, as it was called, raised sales taxes and increased corporate and oil taxes but limited property taxes. Reagan thought the measure went too far and would burden the state with more welfare costs. After more failed attempts at a solution with the legislature, Reagan campaigned against the measure and it was soundly defeated. Part of Reagan's opposition involved a promise that he would propose property tax relief in the next legislative term. He did. It passed, after massive lobbying by both Reagan and Moretti, by a single vote in the senate as Senate Bill 90. It exempted from taxes an additional $1,000 worth of property and increased school funding, but it did nothing about inflation adjustments that would soon bring Prop 14 back.

What then followed was an opportunity for Reagan and the legislature to return to the taxpayers some of the budget surpluses that had accrued since the first Reagan budgets set the state on the road to solvency. Reagan argued for a proposition that would return tax money, while making it extremely difficult to raise taxes in the future. But the legislature created a byzantine bill—Proposition 1—that no one understood, with layers of reductions in different taxes staggered at different times. The governor backed Prop 1 because, after all, it was a tax cut and as a fundamental principle, Reagan always supported tax cuts. But it was so convoluted that it was not clear who got the cuts, how much, or when. When the signature drive stalled, Reagan had to throw his weight behind the proposition earlier than he had expected or wanted. Prop 1 was so poorly written that even Dutch couldn't save it.

Indeed, he may have accidentally delivered the death blow when, asked on a television show if the ordinary voter understood Prop 1, Reagan replied, "No. He shouldn't try. I don't, either."[88] He was joking, but it became a major factor of opposition advertising. Prop 1 lost 54-46. Governor Reagan was damaged, and his inner circle realized that not even the Great Communicator could sell a dead horse to a cowboy. Later, Reagan told *National Review* that Prop 1 was a "daring idea" and the campaign served "a positive purpose."[89] That "positive purpose" was to shine a national light on taxes—a growing issue to many Americans. Within three years, another major tax reform proposition, Prop 13, much simpler in its design, would pass in California and would be said to "set the stage" for the Age of Reagan.[90] Reagan may have prepared the way for his own presidency even in defeat by becoming associated with the "antitax craze."[91] Regardless, the episode cemented in the Gipper his commitment not to run for a third term.

By then he had racked up a stunning record of having 797 vetoes sustained out of 798, but the override was ominous—the first time in twenty-eight years a California governor lost an override vote. Clearly at the sunset of his governorship, Reagan had begun to plan for life after Sacramento. But he was torn as to whether to press on for the presidency or return to the "mashed potato circuit" making well-paying speeches. Ironically, one reporter claimed Reagan's footprints in the California governor's office "can be swept away as easily as if he had walked on sand;" in reality, Reagan had fundamentally transformed California government. As Lou Cannon assessed it in 2003, "Reagan set a tone of skepticism about liberal, expansionist government that persists to this day."[92] Yet that was not exactly Reagan's legacy in California, where, under the Gipper, education spending rose significantly over his predecessor, and spending on higher education shot up 136 percent. Even the Left-leaning State Superintendent of Public Instruction, Wilson Riles, admitted, "We went forward [under Reagan]."[93] Taxes had also gone up, and although later Dutch campaigned on property tax relief, that relief came only on the back of the largest tax increase in history in any state (in inflated dollars). Thus it was a mixed record, captured by a paper somewhat removed from California, the *Baltimore Sun*, which observed that the "Reagan years represent the first attempt by any large government in this country…to do less for people, not more."[94]

In Sacramento, Reagan had managed to control the growth of government by halving the rate of increase of his predecessor, avoided major scandal, enforced some of the toughest air pollution laws in the country, and overall was hailed as a capable administrator. Even his critics at the *San Francisco Examiner*, the *San Francisco Chronicle*, and the *Sacramento Bee* had to admit to his successes. When he left office, a Field Poll showed his approval at over 60 percent.

But in Washington, forces no one could imagine were in motion that would greatly assist Reagan in gaining the presidency. Richard Nixon, who had won a close race in 1968 on a law-and-order/anti-communist platform, skyrocketed to an astounding landslide over the über-liberal George McGovern. Nixon may have governed like a moderate—or even a liberal, creating the Environmental Protection Agency and expanding welfare through the Family Assistance Plan—but he still maintained the aura of a conservative and hard-line anti-communist. That was all he needed against the loopy McGovern, who ran on an immediate withdrawal from Vietnam and legalized marijuana (an extreme position in 1972). In one of the largest electoral victories of all time, Nixon looked secure.

Achieving that victory, however, had led the paranoid Nixon to empower his "plumbers" unit to engage in dirty tricks against the Democrats. Contrary to the self-assurance of some historians, the exact instigator of the Watergate break-in remains in question. Len Colodny and Robert Gettlin's *Silent Coup*, after years of lawsuits, has held up well in pointing the finger at Nixon's White House counsel, John Dean, as the source of the orders to the plumbers.[95] Clearly it was not Nixon himself, who nevertheless fell prey to Dean's machinations to help cover up the break-in. By committing obstruction of justice, Nixon opened the door to impeachment. A failing economy doomed him. Pundits later noted that Bill Clinton, facing similar charges, escaped conviction because his solid economy (for which he owed much to Reagan's foundation) insulated him and maintained his public approval. Nixon had neither the public approval by 1974 nor the support in Congress or the Senate (which Clinton had). Rather than be impeached and convicted, Nixon resigned in August 1974, opening the door once again for a true conservative in Reagan.

Even before Nixon resigned, Reagan had a meeting with a number of his strongest supporters—Tuttle, Dart, Meese, Nofziger, Deaver, and Hannaford, among others. A newcomer, John Sears, had run Nixon's campaign in 1967 and offered a stunning suggestion: no matter what happened to the president, Reagan should run in 1976. Political advisor John Sears claimed Nixon wouldn't survive the Watergate crisis and that Ford would be weak. Sears's message fell on welcome ears.

Part of Reagan's problem was that Nixon left an heir in Gerald Ford, who may not have been the strongest person to serve in the Oval Office, but…he was *there*. The hard-line Spiro Agnew had already been removed, leaving the more moderate Ford to step in. Nor did Nixon leave a particularly strong party. A poll by Robert Teeter in January 1975 showed that only 18 percent of Americans identified as Republicans and that most Americans thought that the Republicans were untrustworthy and incompetent—a crushing fall for the party that throughout the 1960s had been seen as possessing higher integrity than the Democrats. Republicans wallowed in blame, doubt, and—above all—in the second-guessing that perhaps they weren't meant to lead after all. That was not a vision Ronald Reagan could accept.

Not in the least.

7

Interregnum

A window to the presidency opened with Nixon's resignation. Ford pardoned the ex-president, creating a firestorm of charges about a "corrupt bargain." His Boy Scout reputation made such a claim unlikely—impossible to disprove, but a charge that could only erode his credibility for the next two years. Reagan knew Ford was damaged goods. But just how damaged?

Preparing for a presidential run required maintaining a presence in the national media and especially keeping California in his column. Offered a twice-weekly five-minute spot on CBS from Walter Cronkite, the Gipper opted instead for a daily five-minute radio show that reached thirty million people a day (14 percent of the entire US population). He insisted that people would tire of him on television, but "they won't tire of me on the radio."[1] Thus, some fourteen years ahead of Rush Limbaugh, who debuted in 1988, Reagan realized the power of "talk radio." His appealing voice coupled with his powerful ideas—all written by Reagan himself—captured the largely untapped market of political ideology over the radio airwaves. As Limbaugh often explained, radio, as opposed to television, demanded a commitment on the part of the listener to envision the ideas and to participate. It was, Limbaugh maintained, a much more intellectual medium than television. The Gipper intuitively knew that.

Reagan extensively researched his own radio addresses and wrote them all longhand.

When Reagan ran for president in 1980, liberals frequently claimed he had not written the radio addresses. But in 2001, Kiron Skinner, Annelise Anderson, and Martin Anderson published *Reagan, In His Own Hand*, a collection that included his radio addresses among other writings, confirming that Reagan was indeed an "intellectual," that is, someone who makes his living by the power of ideas.[2] The radio addresses in written form display a depth of knowledge about a wide range of topics, everything from specific weapons systems such as the B-1 bomber to strategic locations such as Hong Kong to nations around the world (Chile, Cuba). His commentaries covered foreign aid, public broadcasting, the press, jobs and the economy, the environment and endangered species, food stamps, welfare, and crime. Nor did Reagan "farm out" the research to lackeys. For a single short article on oil in 1977, Reagan noted the following as his sources:

1. U.S. Bur. of Mines Report 1914
2. Dept. of Interior 1939 & 1949
3. Herman Kahn—Book "The Next 200 Years"
4. Council on International Ec. Policy
5. Exec. Office of the Pres. Special Report, Critical Imported Materials, Wash. D.C. U.S. Government Printing Office, Dec. 1974.
6. Prof. Neil Jacoby U.S. L.A.—"Multinational Oil" (Macmillan)
7. Pro's. Phillip Gramm GRAMM [sic] & Richard Davison Wall St. Journal[3]

It should be noted that Reagan, in a short one-page article, had more listed sources than the infamous bestselling book by Howard Zinn, *A People's History of the United States*!

The radio addresses contained the key concepts that would be a hallmark of his philosophy as president, most notably his views on communism. In May 1975, long before he shocked the world with the "Evil Empire" speech, Reagan spoke of "Communism, the Disease." He ascribed communism's ability to survive for so long as an indicator of "just how vicious it really is." Through "doubletalk," Reagan feared "we've lost some of our fear of the disease." Communism, he insisted, was "a form of insanity—[a] temporary aberration which will one day disappear from the earth because it is contrary to human nature."[4] In 1978, he contrasted the words on the Statue of Liberty as symbolic of America's love of humanity with Vladimir Lenin's view of people: "It would not matter if ¾ of the human race perished, the important thing is that the remaining ¼ be communist."[5] One could turn to almost any writing by Reagan on the subject and find similar comments, meaning the "Evil Empire" was nothing new. Of course, such a view influenced the Gipper's approach to the Cold War and national defense. Even when it came to selling grain to the USSR, Reagan wondered, "Are we not helping a Godless tyranny maintain its hold on millions of helpless people? Wouldn't those victims have a better chance of becoming free if their slave masters' regime collapsed economically?"[6]

One could pick any topic at random and find a commonsense argument by Reagan in his radios shows, whether for defense, energy, or economics. For example, one of his many addresses on welfare, in January 1978, noted that in California

> [W]e directed our effort to salvaging human beings & making them self supporting. The proposal for welfare reform in Wash. will *put additional* people...on the dole.... Even that doesn't tell the whole story....[T]here are about 73 mil. people in the country working & earning in the private sector. They are the only source govt. has for tax revenue. Their taxes are supporting 81 mil. *other* Americans who are totally dependent on tax dollars for their year round living. That should be a convincing argument against making govt. the employer of last resort.[7]

Regardless of when the addresses occurred from 1974 on, they seldom changed in their philosophical underpinnings. Government could not make people more prosperous—it could only provide a framework whereby they made themselves better off. Communism was evil and, if unchecked, would conquer whatever it could. The environment was worth protecting, but every single tree and every strip of unsettled land did not constitute a national prize or park to be sealed off from human development. America should not side with Marxist forces of revolution trying to impose communist governments abroad. And so on.

During this time Reagan also served intermittently on the Rockefeller Commission, headed by Vice President Nelson Rockefeller, which was to investigate charges that the Central Intelligence Agency had engaged in American spying and otherwise gone rogue from time to time. It's a near certainty in Washington that any time the president or Congress wishes to avoid dealing with an issue, they create a special commission or panel. These bodies almost never get to the heart of the issue, instead deflecting or ignoring key pieces of evidence or witnesses to protect political insiders (see, for example, the 9/11 Commission, which concealed more than twenty pages of evidence related to Saudi Arabia and which had Jamie Gorelick, a Clinton appointee seen by many as the person responsible for creating the "Wall" memo that hamstrung the intelligence agencies, to serve on the commission). In the case of the Rockefeller Commission, Reagan already had commitments that prevented him from attending many of the meetings. He so informed Rockefeller and attended fewer than half. Ultimately the CIA received a slap on the wrist for certain activities but dodged the serious concerns until the Church Committee in Congress, organized by Frank Church of Idaho, unveiled the Agency's role in the overthrow of the Iranian and Guatemalan governments and in various attempted political assassinations. It's entirely likely that even if he had been able to maneuver out of his previous commitments, Reagan wanted to stay as far away from the CIA's dirt as possible so that later as a candidate he could claim plausible deniability. However, in his radio addresses, Reagan gave the CIA a pass and said, "We are being spied upon beyond anything that the American people can possibly conceive, not internally, not by our own people, but by potential enemies."[8]

With these comments, Reagan displayed a less-appealing trait, namely his idealistic view that the US government itself was more or less pristine but that "there are going to be individuals who make mistakes and do things they shouldn't do."[9] This unwillingness to distrust the motives of people within the government—almost always instead blaming a faceless "bureaucracy" or the size of the system itself—allowed the Gipper to simultaneously criticize "big government" for its incompetence and waste at every opportunity without ever including the very real elements of human corruption, lust for power, and petty jealousy. The agencies entrusted by government over the years to look out for America's safety and security, especially the FBI and the CIA, were largely above reproach to Reagan. Yet the idiosyncrasies of FBI director J. Edgar Hoover, who had stayed as director of the FBI until his death, had distorted and weakened the Bureau's law enforcement mandate by his own refusal to admit to the power of the Mafia. At the CIA, Allen Dulles had a reputation for swashbuckling policies well beyond the Agency's mandate. After the Church Committee, in theory the Agency was reined in some. But Reagan would never be one to demand specific evidence from his director or to insist on knowing exactly how a recommendation for action was decided.

In other words: Reagan loved America, Reagan trusted America, and he largely trusted all the people employed in the service of America. Just as the faithful husband Reagan failed to understand in Sacramento that many of the politicians there saw themselves on a type of party cruise away from their wives and families, so too—as he began to consider Washington— he never imagined that there were those *within* the agencies and bureaus themselves who would put their own lust for power, protection of their turf, or even their access to ready sex from pages and assistants ahead of the national interest. Such deep corruption was beyond him, even with his intellectual appreciation for the wickedness of the Soviet communist regime, which he saw as a manifestation of those vices operating outside of American checks and balances. It was a dangerous mindset for anyone seeking to do business with "the Swamp" (as it would later be called).

But Nixon's resignation shook his faith some, and Ford's initial choice of liberal Nelson Rockefeller as his vice president reaffirmed that Ford was not conservative and didn't care about conservative values.[10] A quiet campaign run by Gordon Luce, who contacted all state chairmen other than California, lobbied them to have Ford name Reagan as his vice president. This of course went nowhere, and Ford didn't even have the Gipper on a five-name list. Publicly, Reagan declared he wasn't campaigning for the office. When he learned that Ford hadn't even considered him, he was all the more piqued. Fortunately, he had not learned of Ford's private impressions of him. In his memoirs, Ford said Reagan was "one of the few political leaders I have ever met whose public speeches revealed more than his private conversations" and complained that Reagan had "simplistic solutions to hideously complex problems."[11] Ford later admitted that he ignored his advisors' warnings that Reagan would be a formidable opponent, saying, "I hadn't taken those warnings seriously because I didn't take Reagan seriously."[12] Denigrating Reagan's "nine-to-five" work habits, Ford was put off by the Gipper's belief that he was "always right." Of course, critics of Ford would say that he didn't know what he was right about most of the time, that activity did not equal accomplishment, and that in fact even the most complex problems have simple answers—*if* one is willing to pay the price for the solution.

Ford no doubt was also miffed that Reagan as governor had sent him a telegram lecturing him on his proposed tax increases. "I am concerned," Reagan wrote, "that press reports indicate you will propose tax increases...in an effort to cure inflation. The 1972 election mandate was clear: no new taxes for four years and reduce the size and cost of the federal government."[13] "Bloated government," Reagan continued, "is the real cause [of inflation].... You have called for an 'inflation-proof' Congress. There is one sure test of Congress' ability to be inflation proof: propose to it immediate cuts in federal spending."[14]

Ford had little ammunition to fight back with: inflation reached 3.7 percent in just the month of July 1974, unemployment neared 7 percent (quite high for the post-World War II boom), and the federal deficit—at the time a scandal—reached almost $52 billion. The weight of Lyndon B. Johnson's Great Society, the economic and human drag of the Vietnam War, and the two decades' worth of protection against foreign competition provided by the "golden accident" of America's postwar dominance had combined to form a perfect storm of stagnation. Traditional Keynesians, and Republicans like Nixon and Ford who quietly bought into Keynesian doctrines, had for years thought the only way to fight such conditions was through government spending. But now deficits were preventing that and causing problems of their own. *Productivity* was the problem—there was not enough of it, and it was being taxed and sapped at every turn by government. Moreover, lack of foreign competition had also stultified innovation since 1950. Occasionally an IBM or a Pan Am would bring radical changes to an industry, but those remained the exceptions, not the rule. Instead, in auto, steel, shipbuilding, robotics, electronics, and textiles, foreign competitors had finally gotten their feet and were plunging into the US market with lower prices as they sought market share. Automakers and steel manufacturers in particular seemed hypnotized, unable to move. As David Halberstam recorded in his dual history of Ford and Nissan, American automakers not only continued in their unproductive ways but didn't even seriously attempt to discern what their problems were.[15] Given who Ford was, he didn't have a chance of really combating these problems. He was a methodical plodder. The times demanded a revolutionary.

Worse still, he was a conciliator when Nixon's strategy of "détente" had started to crack. Largely conceived by Secretary of State Henry Kissinger, a thickly accented academic who oozed imperiousness, détente was the notion that the Cold War was "unwinnable" and that the communists realized that. Ultimately, they would come around through trade and mutual exchanges of ideas. It was the same fatally flawed naiveté that would afflict subsequent presidents in their dealings with radical Islam, and in both cases it led to near-lunatic views that murderous enemies could be defeated by good will, hashtags, and emojis. In a smoking battlefield of defeat, Reagan looked clearly into the future and was disturbed by what it revealed.

When leadership lacks will, it trickles down to the public. By the mid-1970s, as Vietnam predictably fell to the communists and the war's legacy drifted like a dark cloud over America's self-image, polls showed that barely one-third favored American intervention if the Soviets took Berlin, and just over a quarter favored aiding Israel if it were about to be defeated by Arab armies.[16] Nature abhors a vacuum, and not just the Soviets but tyrants everywhere pounced on the hole left by American moral and military withdrawal. The Freedom House's index of free nations was cut almost in half *just in a one-year period* from 1974 to 1975, when almost 45 percent of the world's countries were labeled "unfree." Cambodia, which had fallen to the communists under Pol Pot, seized an American merchant ship, the *Mayaguez.* Ford responded with a poorly planned "Keystone Cops" rescue effort that resulted in sixty-eight men killed or wounded and twelve of the thirteen helicopters used in the mission destroyed—all after the hostages had already been released. Though the rescue was a debacle, Ford's approval rose as Americans gave him credit for firmness—a clear sign of the public's view of what was lacking in US foreign policy.

Ford not only suffered from Kissinger's poor advice—based on his view that the United States was a power in decline—but also from continued ineptness at the Central Intelligence Agency. For years, the CIA had blown call after call, continuously underestimating Soviet military production and prowess while overestimating the USSR's economic strength. For example, in its projections of Soviet missile numbers, the CIA's upper-bound estimate in the National Intelligence Estimate was always lower than the number the Soviets actually deployed. In its primary role of providing intelligence to the executive branch, the CIA had failed repeatedly. One of the worst lapses came when the Agency completely failed to detect the Yom Kippur attack by the Soviet-armed Egypt on Israel. Israel suffered heavy losses, forcing Nixon, in one of his last acts, to send an emergency shipment of arms to Israel.

Reagan was horrified the US was not doing enough. "Why don't you say you will replace all the aircraft the Arabs claim they have shot down?" he asked Kissinger in one of his regular briefings.[17] American emergency arms and Israeli grit staved off the attack, but when Israel took the offensive, the Soviets threatened to directly intervene. A weakened America could not counter and pressured Israel to curtail further actions against Syria. Even when America did attempt to aid our allies, other supposed allied nations (including Greece, Turkey, Italy, and Spain) refused to allow overflight or landing rights when Israel was involved.

Admiral Elmo Zumwalt, later assessing the situation in the Mediterranean, glumly concluded that if war had come, the Soviets would have won. Instead of achieving its goal of marginalizing the Soviets in the region, the Nixon/Kissinger strategy left the US with no land bases and little ability to affect anything on the ground. Other analysis of war in Europe, sparked by a Soviet invasion, led to a similar conclusion: the United States and its allies couldn't stop the Soviets anywhere. NATO commander (and future Reagan secretary of state) Alexander Haig grimly reported, "We are getting to the fine edge of disaster."[18] Soviet leaders celebrated. Premier Leonid Brezhnev said in 1973, "We are achieving with détente what our predecessors have been unable to achieve using the mailed fist." Brezhnev further predicted that by 1985 "we will be able to extend our will wherever we need to."[19]

The CIA's estimate that the USSR was spending 6 percent of its GDP on defense was ludicrous and should have been laughed out of any briefing. Angelo Codevilla asked bluntly, "How could the Soviets, on about half the money spent by the US [according to the CIA's estimate] maintain five times as many tanks...2.5 times the manpower, twice as many submarines...an air defense with 10,000 radars, [and] 12,000 surface-to-air missile launchers?"[20] A defector brought news that the USSR was in fact spending 15 percent of its GDP on the military, though later it was learned this was low *by half*, meaning the CIA was routinely off by several hundred percent, and some estimates put the number at a mind-boggling 70 percent of GDP. Worse, inside the Agency, from 1973 to 1976 there was an unwillingness to admit the obvious: that the USSR was actually planning to fight a war, and to deliver three nuclear warheads to every American missile silo. In these views they were egged on by Kissinger, who asked, "What in the name of God is strategic superiority?"[21] Sanity prevailed when George H. W. Bush was tabbed by Ford to head the CIA and he agreed (possibly at the urging of William Colby) to have a "B team" provide a second, alternative estimate for every major piece of analysis. Later, Reagan would side with the B team repeatedly...and correctly.

Even without knowing all the numbers and specifics, Reagan and other insightful Americans could sense the balance of power shifting to the totalitarians. When American planes can't overfly "allies" to respond to threats and when American ships are taken without concern for retaliation, something is wrong. Ford's support of the Helsinki Accords, which had a clause on the inviolability of national frontiers (a code phrase for consolidating permanently the USSR's grip on its captured nations), prompted Reagan to flatly state, "I am against it."[22] Kissinger's deputy, Hal Sonnenfeldt, made matters worse when he issued comments that US policy should strive to make "the relationship between the Eastern Europeans and the Soviet Union an organic one."[23] Slaves, in other words, should accept their chains. Ford, in Reagan's mind, went from bad to worse, when he refused to meet with Soviet dissident writer Aleksandr Solzhenitsyn, with Ford privately calling him a "goddamned horse's ass."

As Reagan pondered his next political steps, his age began to increasingly weigh on him. At sixty-five, he was already older than any president in history other than William Henry Harrison—who died a month after he took office. When considering Ford's position, Reagan looked at the possibility that a Ford reelection could conceivably last until 1984 (as Ford had not served a full term and was constitutionally eligible for two full terms—as had been Lyndon B. Johnson, who voluntarily declined to run in 1968). If the Democrats nominated another McGovern-type liberal, conservatives might be stuck with Ford for a decade.

Dutch had remained loyal to Nixon, refusing to denigrate the president during Watergate. Even with Nixon's resignation impending, Reagan still held back, insisting only that Nixon go before Congress and give a full account. After Nixon stepped down and Ford pardoned him, Dutch thought that "the punishment of resignation certainly is more than adequate for the crime."[24] Typically, the Gipper referred to Watergate as a "tragedy" that obscured the massive victory Republicans won in 1972. And Reagan's poll numbers increased during the Watergate episode, showing people that he was loyal on the one hand, yet distant from the activities on the other. One insider observed that Reagan lacked "that burning, that gut desire to be president that Jimmy Carter and Richard Nixon have," thinking it a slight. Instead, it was a trait most Americans applauded.[25]

Still, in public Reagan deflected talk about another run, saying he would prefer the Ford administration be successful and that he would be happy to be a "voice" in the Republican Party. He declined Ford's offer to be the ambassador to England and likewise refused to consider a Senate run. Ford continued to try to buy Dutch off, next offering him the Commerce Department, to which Reagan observed, "They're working their way down the scale." At the same time, Ford laid the groundwork to stop Reagan. In April 1975, Ron Nessen, Ford's press secretary, received a request from journalist Marquis Childs for an interview based on Reagan's candidacy, which Childs saw as a "sure way to destroy the Republican Party."[26] Nessen urged Ford to do the interview. By November of 1975, both Nessen and

Dick Cheney were sending press clippings of Reagan's speeches to Ford. When Stuart Spencer joined Ford's team, he warned "he's not thinking about running, I know this man. *Ronald Reagan is running*" (emphasis in original).[27]

But Reagan did not want a repeat of 1968. Instead, he planned to continue with speaking and radio commentary, partnering with Mike Deaver's company, which served as his booking agent. By 1975, these speaking engagements were bringing $800,000 a year and could not be maintained if he were a candidate.

Gerald Ford's weakness and Russia's growing strength convinced Reagan he had to run in 1976.

Finally Reagan concluded he had to run, as a Republican, against Ford in 1976. It was a risky proposition, as no party abandons a sitting president for an outsider except under the most extreme circumstances. Moreover, it would put Reagan in the awkward position of having to criticize his own party during the primaries, then pivot to attack Democrat policies in the general election. As he discussed it with his kitchen cabinet, he lost Henry Salvatori (one of his earliest and most loyal allies), who feared a split party. He also lost David Packard, who actually took the position of national finance chairman for Ford, and even Barry Goldwater, who sided with the president. And while John Sears and Lyn Nofziger pressed Dutch to run, his California advisors Tom Reed and Stuart Spencer also bolted for positions in the Ford administration. Filling the gap was Nevada senator Paul Laxalt, who met with Reagan and was one of the first high-profile Republicans to publicly support him.

Since he couldn't run without obliquely criticizing Ford, and since he had to attack Democrats, Reagan essentially adopted a time-tested strategy of running against Washington. That, in turn, forced Ford into blaming government's "overblown promises and overbearing controls." Reagan, of course, decried the "permanency of Civil Service jobs," which were responsible for most of American policies. He often quoted Franklin Roosevelt himself on the "dole" as a "narcotic, a subtle destroyer of the human spirit."

It was a line he straddled most of his career, whereby he refused to criticize FDR himself while bashing the New Deal when possible.

One of the first challenges candidate Reagan faced—one which today would be entirely inconsequential—was that Reagan had been divorced. In the mid-1970s, there were still a number of religious denominations that frowned on divorce, and for someone running on "traditional" American values, this proved an issue. Reagan's children from Jane—Maureen and the adopted Michael—had maintained an arm's-length relationship with their father due to Jane's influence. By 1976, however, both Michael, who looked for any excuse to spend time with his father, and Maureen, who more than any of the other children had grown interested in politics, wanted to work on the campaign. But Reagan's aides had already had a talk with Maureen when Dutch first ran for governor (and attitudes were even more disapproving) and made it clear Maureen was to stay away from the campaign lest the divorce be raised as an issue. In 1975, once again hoping to be involved in Reagan's political life, Maureen and Michael were again informed that they "made Dad look too old," according to Michael, and that the visuals were better when Reagan posed with Patti (twenty-three) and Ron Jr. (seventeen). While it did make the candidate appear younger, and Nancy approved, the choice was foolish: Michael would later go on to become a major political radio commentator, and Maureen would run for the US Senate in 1982 and for the House in 1992 before dying of cancer in 2001. Ron and Patti, on the other hand, were devout leftists. It was one of the ironies of Reagan's life that he pushed away the two children who most reflected his views and was instead saddled with the two who most detested his policies.

Needless to say, being shunned in favor of Nancy's children hurt both the earlier Reagan siblings. Much of the pain they endured could be laid at Nancy's feet: their presence reminded her of Jane Wyman. Still, the Gipper was hardly the model father, and he let Nancy have her way on this rather than fight to maintain a stronger relationship with his children. In 1971, when Michael got married in Hawaii, his father and Nancy instead attended Tricia Nixon's wedding at the same time. However, Dutch sent Michael a long letter about love and being a husband, urging his son to put into the marriage more than he took out, and to remain faithful. In apparent regret over his own failed marriage, Reagan wrote, "Mike, you know better than many what an unhappy home is.... Now you have a chance to make it come out the way it should." He added, "You'll never get in trouble if you say 'I love you' at least once a day."[28]

When Reagan finally announced his candidacy on November 19, 1975, in Washington, the media predictably depicted him as "an unconvincing candy man," as "a shame and an embarrassment for the country," as "a divisive factor in his party" (as though big-city liberal writers ever cared about the health of the Republican Party), as holding policies that were "cunningly phrased nonsense—irrationally conceived and hair-raising in their potential mischief," or as "just another Barry Goldwater."[29] Liberal Republicans chimed in: Nelson Rockefeller called Reagan a "minority of a minority"; Jacob Javits railed that Reagan's positions were "so extreme" they would "alter our country's very economic and social structure"; Charles Percy called Reagan "foolhardy" and prophesied that his nomination would lead to a "crushing defeat" for Republicans (the same warnings they posed about Donald Trump in 2016).[30]

Some of Ford's staff dismissed any real threat he might pose. Jim Shuman told Ron Nessen that in fact Reagan's candidacy would "prove to be a boon to us," by forcing the team to "tighten [our] staff work." Reagan would be a "stalking horse, criticizing the Democrats and the operation of government [more] than we are able to."[31] Other Ford staffers were dismissive of Reagan: "His general ignorance of national affairs...will make Ford look better and better every day."[32] In January 1976, the Ford team began compiling daily press material on Reagan, highlighting contradictions.

Others in the Ford campaign took Reagan *very* seriously. Some staffers were genuinely concerned about Reagan's effectiveness over the radio: "These spots are well produced.... [and] the thrust of the spots is the leadership issue, which plays to our weakness if you believe what the polls are saying."[33] In August 1975, Ford's team produced its campaign plan for Reagan, stating that Ford needed to "get assurances from delegates," although it instructed the delegates not to "take on" state organizations outside Ford's camp.[34] For a team that dismissed the Gipper as an intellectual lightweight, the campaign urged Ford to make "every effort" to keep from becoming a campaign of "ideological debate." In fact, based on reports that his friends and family opposed Reagan seeking the nomination, Ford's campaign should "without appearing blatant, [make] every effort...to stay in touch with these individuals on a personal basis in order to support the no-win attitude."[35] Concerned word of this would leak; a Robert Visser memo insisted "this is a legitimate activity" and admitted "Reagan's candidacy *will, in fact, make winning the election...considerably more difficult*" (emphasis mine).[36] Ford's own campaign team assured the president that he was "known by too many individuals in the Party to be a solid conservative midwesterner for them to be sold on the idea that suddenly...he has become a wild-eyed liberal." Instead, the campaign needed to portray both Ford and Reagan as conservatives, and "why trade one conservative for another?"[37]

Yet Ford continued to distance himself from conservatism: "The facts of life are that satisfying the extreme right wing dooms any Republican in a Presidential election."[38] Unfortunately, one of Ford's own campaign documents showed "there seems to remain a sense that people do not know where the P[resident] stands on a broad number of issues."[39] And Ford had provided Reagan exactly the answer he needed to counter any notion he was an extremist: If Reagan was so extreme, why did Ford offer him two cabinet positions and an ambassadorship?

Designing a strategy for the primary, Robert Visser and his team played up Ford's strength in midwestern areas, expecting him to win "all" the delegates from Ohio, Indiana, Michigan, Illinois, Wisconsin, Minnesota, Iowa, Missouri, Kansas, Nebraska, and Oklahoma—over half of the ticket. But the key to winning quickly was to take New Hampshire, Florida, and Georgia, "thereby forcing Reagan to quit the race." Visser called this knockout approach the "Early Primary Strategy." Above all, Ford needed to stay away from California, where Reagan had a large share of the delegates and money.[40]

Reagan's September speech to the Executive Club of Chicago called "Let the People Rule" had proposed a sweeping reintroduction of federalism, moving "authority and resources" to the states that could result in a savings to the federal government of $90 billion a year. Ford's advisor (and former Reagan advisor) Stuart Spencer immediately saw a way for his boss to leverage the federal savings into state and local burdens—someone had to pick up the difference—especially in an early primary state such as New Hampshire with its low taxes. Cleverly fanned by the anti-Reagan media, the "ill-conceived plan" was "unworkable" and could be "an albatross."[41] Typically, instead of cowering, Reagan punched back, once again asking if these weren't choices that should be left to the people of a state. More important, he cited his own success in California with welfare reform and noted that since the federal government took tax money, it could earmark it and keep it in each state instead of shipping it to DC with its "freight charge." He cited both FDR and John F. Kennedy as supporters of devolving money, authority, and responsibility to the states, then noted that Ford himself had suggested returning Medicaid and education to the state level before throwing in with Washington. Once again, the Gipper ran against the Swamp. Conversely Reagan's plans for reforming the Social Security system were ahead of their time, and far too scary in 1976 for most voters. Ford claimed that Reagan's solution to let government control privately owned stock portfolios amounted to socialism. (It was an odd claim because Democrats who opposed privatization did so on precisely the *opposite* grounds, namely that it would lead to the "evil" bankers and Wall Street wolves taking over peoples' retirement savings.) And as always, the press tried to make Reagan look bad whenever possible.[42]

Initially, it looked like Ford's strategy worked, aided by a Reagan miscalculation. When polling came in showing Reagan leading in New Hampshire, the campaign decided they had the Granite State won and moved on. But there were still large numbers of undecided voters there and they broke for Ford, who took New Hampshire, narrowly. (In fact, due to quirky rules that provided two different Reagan delegate slates, Reagan likely won more votes in New Hampshire but split among two slates.) The president then won four states in a row, prompting *National Review* to fret "the whole Reagan game plan is now in doubt."[43] Before long, Reagan found he was on defense, and the only way to go on offense was to break the so-called "Eleventh Commandment" not to attack another Republican (i.e., Ford).

The area Reagan chose to target Ford on was foreign policy: "Ford and Kissinger ask us to trust their leadership. Well, I find that more and more difficult to do," Reagan said in Orlando.[44] Ford responded by labeling Reagan a warmonger. But the Gipper found a new issue—retaining the Panama Canal—that produced massive favorable responses. Speaking to a crowd at Sun City, Arizona, Reagan's line "we are going to keep it" produced such loud and sustained applause that he lost his place.[45] The Gipper closed a 17-point gap in the polls to a mere 6 points in Florida before losing, whereupon he suffered a barrage of "are you going to quit" questions from the press. But Reagan staged a comeback in North Carolina. Ford had responded in other states by giving away government contracts (such as a $33 million Air Force contract to Martin Marietta in Florida). Reagan used this against Ford. In North Carolina he said, "I understand Mr. Ford has arrived in the state.... If he comes here with the same list of goodies as he did in Florida, the band won't know whether to play 'Hail to the Chief' or 'Santa Claus Is Coming to Town.'"[46]

Dutch followed with victories in Alabama, Georgia, Texas, Nebraska, and Indiana (the latter two in Visser's "sure" midwestern states) and California (meaning the president, so far, had lost the two largest delegate states). Going to the convention, it looked as though Ford would have 965 delegates to Reagan's 826 but would be short by about 30 delegates of securing the nomination. Pennsylvania would be a key delegation.

At that point, Reagan made two crucial errors. First, hoping to woo the Pennsylvania delegates, Reagan named liberal Richard Schweiker from the Keystone State as his vice president. To say that this was a strange choice is an understatement, but like many decisions Reagan made, it had a strong personal element. When he met with Schweiker, Reagan told him, "I have a strong feeling that I'm looking at myself some years ago," projecting onto the younger man his own conservative conversion—though such a prospect was not at all apparent in Schweiker. "I'm not a knee-jerk liberal," Schweiker said. "And I'm not a knee-jerk conservative," replied Reagan.[47] Many of Reagan's supporters were appalled, and the pick alienated conservative voters in the South—indeed, it outraged some. Schweiker had a voting record from the liberal Americans for Democratic Action identical to that of Senator George McGovern (89 percent) and had voted against two of Nixon's Supreme Court nominees. Even Reagan couldn't put lipstick on Schweiker's pig of a voting record, especially after Jimmy Carter called Schweiker "a good man" and the *Washington Post* praised the choice as "dazzling" and "wise."[48] Schweiker tried to withdraw his nomination, but Reagan turned him down: "I'm not going to leave this convention with my tail between my legs, and neither are you."[49]

Then Reagan compounded his error by trying to change Rule 16-C, requiring *Ford* to name his vice presidential choice, making his campaign appear desperate. While Dutch carried much of the platform, including a plank called "Morality in Foreign Policy" as a critique of the Ford/Kissinger diplomacy, it still lacked some of the key hot-button issues such as the Panama Canal. Ford ultimately supported the platform with the Reagan elements, suggesting he would listen closely to the Right and winning him some fence-sitters. Reagan lost the delegate count 1,187 to 1,070, while winning 1.4 percent more popular votes. He told his delegates he would not take the vice presidential slot if offered.[50] Many of the delegates preferred Reagan but felt honor-bound to support the incumbent. Ford's campaign manager, Stuart Spencer, was terrified that John Sears, Reagan's manager, would "get a policy issue on the floor" that would "bust it wide open."[51] Spencer thought that an emotional policy debate might swing the wavering delegates. In the end, none of the Gipper's advisors wanted to mortally wound Ford coming out of the convention, if, in fact, Reagan still lost the delegate battle.

As Hayward observed, Reagan "failed to capture the nomination, but his capture of the party's soul was nearly complete."[52] After the vote, Ford waved the Gipper over to join him on stage, and Reagan delivered prepared remarks without mentioning Ford. According to a 1998 PBS show, Edmund Morris said that the sense in the hall was "we've nominated the wrong man." Reagan told the delegates a story of a letter in a time capsule to be opened a hundred years from 1976. He ended by turning to Ford and saying, "We must go forth...united [and remember] what a great general said a few years ago is true, 'There's no substitute for victory,' Mr.

President."[53] Everyone watching knew that Ford had been supplanted by the losing candidate.

After Reagan addressed his staff, with tears rolling down Nancy's cheeks, he left the room. Clarke Reed, the chairman of the Mississippi delegation that had given Ford the winning margin, had watched the Gipper's speech and was heard to mutter, "I've made the worst mistake of my life."[54] Indeed, Ford left the Kansas City convention hall down substantially in the polls to Jimmy Carter, while Reagan ironically was criticized by *National Review* for not running harder as a conservative.[55] Ford harbored bitterness against Reagan for even running, the following year asking, "How can you challenge an incumbent president of your own party and *not* be divisive?"[56]

Subsequent polls showed Reagan may have lost the national election and was already slipping against Carter—but over the years polls have been shown to be egregiously wrong, especially when involving hypotheticals. Pollsters then, and now, routinely under-poll conservative voters and their positions, mostly through sampling error.[57] And, to some, it appeared Reagan had missed his opportunity. Many thought the Gipper's age prevented him from another run and he had shot his last bullet As Hayward wrote, "This had been his moment, and the moment had slipped away."[58]

Of course, Reagan's moment had not yet begun.

8

The Worst President Ever*

Historians are quick to write "the first this" or "the first that" when it comes to presidents, but Jimmy Carter was a "first" in a profound way. And it requires a bit of background to appreciate the significance of his victory in 1976.

In the early 1820s, New Yorker Martin Van Buren—from whom we get our modern phrase "OK" (for "Old Kinderhook")—was terrified by passage of the Missouri Compromise. What concerned Van Buren (and Thomas Jefferson, who said the news of passage had awakened him like a "firebell in the night!") was that an invisible line was drawn across the Missouri Compromise territories at the bottom of Missouri (the famous "36 degree 30 minute parallel"): below the line, territories could choose to be slave states or free, but above the line, only free states were permitted. This would, he thought, result in an inevitable majority in Congress that, sooner or later, would vote to abolish slavery. In turn, it would spark a civil war.[1]

The Little Magician, as Van Buren was called, had a brilliant (but, for Americans, ultimately disastrous) solution: create a new political party that could supersede sectional differences over slavery by appealing to the pocketbook. Van Buren's new party would reward supporters through the "spoils system" ("to the victor belong the spoils") in government, doling out government or party jobs to the faithful. He calculated that people would ignore or even abandon their personal views of slavery for money and power. His new party was named the Democrats.

* Prior to 2009

162

The presidency was a key to this system, because Van Buren surmised the nation would never again elect a president from the slaveholding Deep South. Therefore only candidates from the "West" (Tennessee, Indiana, and Ohio, for example), including his own patron Andrew Jackson from Tennessee, could win the office. But another alternative, a "northern man of southern principles" (i.e., northerners who would refuse to act on the issue of slavery) could be elected. Anyone else—a northern man of northern, anti-slave proclivities—would spark a civil war. From 1828 to 1860, Van Buren's system worked like a charm. Only northerners unwilling to address slavery or westerners such as Jackson, William Henry Harrison, and James K. Polk, got elected. What Van Buren failed to predict was that the federal government would continue to grow dramatically in size and power and in the hands of the wrong man would provide the perfect instrument to destroy the institution of slavery. And that's precisely what it got in the first Republican president, Abraham Lincoln.

The Democratic Party was founded in the 1820s to protect and preserve slavery. Martin Van Buren created the "spoils system" to ensure only Democrat loyalists got elected.

And here's where Carter's "first" comes in. Since the Civil War, Van Buren's maxim that no one from a Deep South state could become president held true. Texas, like Tennessee, despite having slaves, had been considered as much "western" as "southern" and thus Lyndon B. Johnson, John Kennedy's vice president, won the election on his own in 1964 against Barry Goldwater. But it took a businessman and Navy vet from Georgia to finally break through the Van Buren "wall" in 1976 as the first true southerner to win election since 1848, ending a shutout of almost 130 years. It is worth spending some time on the rise and collapse of Jimmy Carter because the period from 1976 to 1981 marked a tectonic shift in the American political culture and the first glimpses of the war between the "Establishment" in Washington, DC, and Middle America. Reagan's challenge to the Georgian marked the first successful uprising of "the people," really, since Andrew Jackson in 1828.[2]

In 1976 Jimmy Carter still rode a Watergate wave. The Republicans only controlled four state legislatures and thirteen governorships. Kansas was the singular state with both a Republican governor and legislative majority. As a brand, the Republicans were toxic. Countless editorials gleefully predicted that the GOP "is perhaps closer to extinction than ever before."[3] Carter's margin of victory against Gerald Ford was deceiving (a popular vote advantage of just 50.1 percent to 48 percent, with a 297 to 240 electoral vote margin). Ford's pardon of Nixon had not helped him, and while people viewed the president as honest, that was about all.

Meanwhile, Carter emerged from a Democratic slate as an unexpected winner. One biographer noted that he benefitted "immeasurably from the unique circumstances" in 1976 and "it is unlikely that he could have succeeded in any other year."[4] Even then, it still took rock and roll to save him. Phil Walden, president of Georgia-based Capricorn Records, had to hustle up a series of rock concerts with the Amazing Rhythm Aces, Marshall Tucker Band, Charlie Daniels, the Outlaws, and The Allman Brothers Band to rack up instant money for the cash-strapped campaign.

The Georgian piously played up his Southern Baptist credentials, even to the extent that Carter gave an interview to *Playboy* magazine in which he admitted to lusting in his heart after other women.[5] To those concerned he'd be a wild-eyed redistributionist, he played up his business success. To those worried about another dovish McGovern, Carter touted his experience on board a nuclear submarine in Admiral Hyman Rickover's fleet. A notoriously weak campaigner, Carter's efforts were made worse by his continued vagueness on issues. A workaholic who read three hundred pages of briefs a night and was caught up in assigning tennis court times, Carter touted managerial efficiency, yet his chaotic management style doomed his relations with Congress.[6] Above all, Carter was tone deaf to the American people.

He came out of the gate insisting on a balanced budget and looking like a Republican. Even Reagan wrote a column urging Americans, "Let's Give Carter a Chance."[7] Quickly, however, Carter fell back on liberal spending policies. Inflation—Ford's nemesis—had marched up again, from 7 percent in 1977 to 9 percent a year later, with the prime rate approaching 20 percent. When it came to energy, Carter's views were equally disastrous.

"We must face the fact that the energy shortage is permanent," he told Americans, labeling his energy policy the "moral equivalent of war" (the acronym was MEOW). As Steven Hayward noted, to Carter "the American people were the enemy, because of our profligate, energy-wasting lifestyle."[8]

Indeed, Carter was another "first": he was the first president in American history to blame the American people themselves for whatever problems they faced. Franklin Roosevelt had said we had nothing to fear but fear itself, and John Kennedy inspired Americans to put a man on the moon in a decade, but Carter had nothing to offer but negativity. It was ever present in his language. Whereas Vladimir Lenin's speech was peppered with violent activist verbs such as "shoot," "goad," "exterminate," and "force," Carter's utterances were laden with helplessness, hopelessness, and futility: "unpleasant," "overwhelmed," "sacrifice," "selfish," "shrinking," and "catastrophe."[9] Long before Barack Obama circled the globe apologizing for America's past, Carter was apologizing for America's present. Instead of being free of "fear itself," Carter in his inaugural address had claimed that Americans were now free of an "inordinate fear of communism"—at the very time the Soviet empire was expanding and growing. Instead, he insisted, his new policy "rooted in our moral values" constituted a "new era." To the Georgian, previous eras were *not* rooted in our moral values, which would have come as a surprise to George Washington, Abraham Lincoln, or Teddy Roosevelt.

And he was flat wrong in his assessments. In 1977 Carter said that "oil and natural gas.... [were] running out," a statement proven wrong consistently over the next forty years.[10] His obsession with human rights abroad, which included a new position in the State Department for monitoring abuses, led to grave misjudgments about who our allies and enemies were. When he told a group of two hundred religious and civil rights leaders "human rights is the soul of our foreign policy," he had accidentally revealed that the safety and security of American citizens was not.[11] Above all, these blinders meant that Carter placed the treatment of some of those abroad—for he always selectively enforced his doctrine—above the safety and security of all Americans. It was a recipe for disaster, and one that Reagan diametrically opposed.

For Reagan, there could *be* no rights abroad for anyone if the American vision and its values, first and foremost, were not paramount. Indeed, every one of Carter's foreign policy failures would in time become a Reagan success. They constituted the essence of Reagan's convention night acceptance speech, where he said, "The major issue of this campaign is the direct, political, personal, and moral responsibility of Democratic Party leadership... for this unprecedented calamity which has befallen us."[12]

In historical hindsight, Carter's missteps were stupefyingly obvious. An emphasis on human rights led Carter to straddle the fence on two fronts. In Central America, Nicaragua's dictator Anastasio Somoza, the very definition of a *cadillo*, nevertheless was enmeshed in a death struggle against communist Sandinista revolutionaries backed by Cuba. Carter would neither unequivocally support Somoza or the revolutionaries. When Somoza was ousted, the Sandinistas ignored Carter. He likewise lectured the Shah of Iran, Mohammed Reza Pahlavi, on human rights, weakening him as his regime battled radical Islamic fundamentalists. Finally the shah was forced into exile and Ayatollah Ruhollah Khomeini's radicals took over, turning Iran into the first theocracy to replace any kind of monarchical or constitutional government in the twentieth century.

In a disturbing trend that would have powerful implications for President Reagan, it is worth noting that in both cases the Central Intelligence Agency and Carter's State Department were consistently wrong in their assessments, both of the status of the conflicts and of the motivations of the "revolutionaries." Well into 1979, the CIA assured Carter the Sandinistas couldn't win, and even if they did, the CIA viewed them as traditional Latin American thug strongmen, not ideologues. In Iran, as the French and Israeli intelligence services bombarded the CIA with warnings about the shah's demise, Carter's officials labeled them "alarmist" and never even passed them on to the president.[13] The CIA did not even have copies of Ayatollah Khomeini's works, and, in regards to the fundamentalism of the Islamic revolutionaries, a State Department official asked incredulously, "Whoever took religion seriously?"[14]

In the 1970s, both the CIA and State Department repeatedly
failed to assess threats in Nicaragua and Iran. In the case of the
rise of fundamentalist Islam, one State Department official asked,
"Whoever took religion seriously?"

Reagan did. Just six months after Jimmy and Rosalynn Carter visited Tehran, in 1978, the Gipper and Nancy, with Peter Hannaford, took a quiet trip to Iran. They began in Japan and Hong Kong, then slipped off to different locations in Iran, meeting with the US ambassador there, local dignitaries, and Iranian diplomats (but not the shah, at least not officially).[15] Upon his return, Reagan declared the shah a "staunch friend & ally" and expressed concern about the "erosion of American support" under Carter.[16]

Americans knew the nation was in trouble: 84 percent saw the United States on the wrong track and 67 percent said the United States was in "deep and serious trouble." Yet polls also showed Carter blowing out Reagan in the presidential race, 60 to 36 percent. Where was the truth? Certainly the economic indicators did not favor the president. Mortgage rates had shot up to 20 percent and median home prices had increased threefold, from $23,000 in 1970 to $62,000 in 1980.[17] Businesses, as well as individuals, had plunged into the red, including Chrysler that in 1979 posted a *$1 billion loss*, soon nearly matched by Ford (-$600 million) and General Motors (-$763 million). But foreign policy failures were more intrinsically tied to the floundering Carter administration.

Carter did not know (nor did the CIA know) that the shah was suffering from cancer at the time of his first visit and didn't learn of it for a year. By then the shah's grip on Iran had deteriorated quickly. He fled Iran on January 16, 1979, and the Ayatollah arrived two weeks later. A virtual pariah, the ailing shah and his retinue traipsed to Egypt, then Morocco, always pleading to come to the United States and its advanced medical care.

Carter's advisors pointed out that allowing him in could provoke the Iranian revolutionaries and that the mobs might take hostages. When the president asked if any of his advisors had an answer "as to what we do if the diplomats in our embassy are taken hostage,"[18] no one did. Apparently, no one suggested pulling them out or closing the embassy *before* admitting the shah, who was admitted into the US and arrived in New York on October 22. And contrary to the predictions of the CIA, on November 4, 1979, Iranian mobs swarmed into the US embassy in Tehran, taking sixty-seven Americans hostage. It was the beginning of a nightmare for Carter, as well as for the nation.

The American president had no immediate response. He knew a military foray would almost certainly kill all the hostages and be costly in military lives. Utterly helpless, Carter himself became a hostage to nightly newscasts that ran an ongoing ticker, "America Held Hostage, Day __." Although a rally-around-the-flag sentiment boosted his poll numbers initially, his support quickly eroded. In December, the Soviets, having already installed a Soviet-friendly Marxist regime in Afghanistan under Hafizullah Amin, discarded all pretense and invaded the country, deposing Amin and replacing him with a puppet, Babrak Karmal. The USSR described the events as an internal coup, but everyone knew Carter now was looking at two major foreign policy disasters in less than sixty days.

Reagan knew Carter was struggling abroad, especially when it came to the USSR. The public continued to oppose Soviet expansionism, with one poll showing three-quarters of Americans supported military intervention against the Soviets in the Middle East after the invasion.[19] But it was not the Soviet Union that gave the Gipper his opening, but Panama.

In yet another debacle—rooted in guilt over American actions—Carter looked for a way to hand over the Panama Canal to Panama (after declaring in the campaign "I would never give up full control of the Panama Canal"). Carter saw the canal as a "prime opportunity to apply moral values to foreign policy."[20] Response to the proposal was angry and overwhelming. Some senators reported letters coming in at a *5,000-to-1* margin opposing![21] Reagan's line consistently had been "we built it, we paid for it, it's ours, and we're going to keep it." Carter tried to persuade the Gipper to tone down his criticism by sending two emissaries to meet with him, but Reagan only held his fire for a single speech. The Republicans finally mobilized against Carter, sending out a fund-raising letter that netted $700,000 for the RNC...with Reagan's signature. Ads appeared in major papers saying,

"There is *no* Panama Canal. There is an *American* canal in Panama." Typically for Republicans, the money was never spent in a full-blown campaign, as the Senate minority leader, Howard Baker Jr. (R-TN), had decided to support ratification.

In his opposition to the Panama Canal, Reagan shifted among several positions, including allowing international control, and once joked that he would consider giving up the canal "if we could throw in the State Department."[22] Ultimately he settled on his original position that the canal was American. Several leading conservatives, including William F. Buckley, supported the treaty, and he and Dutch debated it on Buckley's *Firing Line* PBS show, where Reagan acquitted himself well. Fellow actor (and probably the Hollywood icon most associated with conservative positions) John Wayne argued in letters with Reagan over the canal, with Wayne supporting the treaty. After the treaty was signed on September 5, 1977, the ratification battle began, and a war of words between Duke and Dutch heated up. In November, Wayne wrote Reagan a "scathing" letter accusing him of playing politics.[23] "I'll show you point by goddamn point erroneous remarks [Reagan made]," Wayne thundered in another letter. But even he knew it was too late for Reagan to back down if he wanted to.[24] To Reagan, it was more than just a bad deal: it was a treaty subscribed to in defiance of the wishes of the voters. When informed on April 18, 1978, that the Senate had approved, Reagan was in Japan (on the trip that would end in Tehran). He told reporters that the vote was "a very extreme case of ignoring the sentiment of the people."[25]

CBS producer Norman Lear entertained the idea of a national debate between Reagan and a proponent of the treaty. It did not materialize, but CBS nevertheless gave Reagan an "extraordinary amount of time" to respond to Carter's Panama Canal address—something that today would be unheard of. In the end, the massive populist explosion against the treaties (one for turning over the Canal to Panama, one for the US leasing the Canal Zone) mattered. Senator Howard Baker of Tennessee received 22,000 letters, which were, by his own count, 98 percent opposed. He nevertheless voted for them. Both treaties passed the Senate by the narrowest margin possible—one vote above the two-thirds needed.[26] This was perhaps the first simmer of a thirty-year populist boil against the "Establishment" that would begin with Reagan and continue with Donald Trump, and it all came down to one simple fact: those in Washington, DC, just didn't care what the majority of Americans thought.

This "ruling class/country class" chasm (as Angelo Codevilla later called it) was similarly obvious in the divide between ordinary Americans and government in the case of the Soviet Union.[27] Carter's guilt-driven foreign policy continually ignored the elephant in the room—the USSR and its communist proxies—when it came to human rights. Democrat Senator Daniel Patrick Moynihan lamented the "administration speaks more about the abuses of human rights in Chile, the Philippines, Argentina, and Guatemala [than] in the Soviet Union."[28] In a seminal article in *Commentary* in 1979, "Dictatorships and Double Standards," Democrat Jeane Kirkpatrick of Georgetown University argued that Carter's administration had ceased to put American national interests first. "The failure of the Carter administration's foreign policy," she noted, "is now clear to everyone except its architects."[29]

Why wasn't it clear? Because Carter and his appointees to some extent shared the views of the socialists and communists abroad. Carter was not a communist, but his secretary of state Cyrus Vance told *Time* magazine that the president and Soviet premier Leonid Brezhnev had "similar dreams and aspirations about the most fundamental issues."[30] Carter's "similarity" could be seen in his appointees, such as UN ambassador Andrew Young. Just a few years earlier Young said, "It may take the destruction of Western civilization to allow the rest of the world to really emerge as a free and brotherly society," and if the Black Panthers needed to be the "revolutionary vanguard that God has ordained to destroy the whole thing," that was acceptable.[31] Carter's State Department saw pro-Soviet guerrillas in Africa as "liberation forces"; Iran's Ayatollah Khomeini would soon be considered a "saint." Britain, Young said, "almost invented racism"—a comment that Carter forced Young to apologize for to the British UN ambassador. It wasn't clear to Carter's administration, then, that his foreign policy was failing because he was invested in a foreign policy in which America did not emerge victorious and triumphant.

In short, Carter exhibited almost all the worst traits of a leader: apologetic and weak abroad; preachy and disdainful of Americans at home. And Reagan stood ready to fix America's 1976 mistake and contrast himself with the Georgian. He pounded Carter's weakness in his broadcasts, and the Georgian continued to give him ammunition, bloating the government by the day. The Federal Register gained an additional thirteen thousand pages in Carter's four years, and corporate giants like General Motors publicly complained they were spending vast amounts just complying with regulations. Ironically, a strange convergence of Ralph Nader's consumerism and Milton Friedman's libertarianism had produced an alliance that had started to deregulate airlines and trucking. But the changes—which Carter had little to do with—came too late to help him.

Reagan also was attuned to the broader changes in the electorate, especially the crushing burden of taxes. He saw it up close in California with the failed Proposition 1 and its 1978 much-simplified successor, Proposition 13, which limited the annual real estate tax on property to 1 percent of its assessed value. Prop 13 also capped property tax increases at 2 percent per year. The measure passed with 65 percent approval, and of course Carter was on the wrong side. He predicted "unemployment will go up in California," while the Congressional Budget Office likewise erroneously stated that Prop 13 would cause inflation to rise in the state. Reagan correctly characterized the tax revolt as a "prairie fire": following Prop 13's success, twenty other states introduced tax limitation measures. Congressman David Obey (D-WI) observed that news of Prop 13 caused "panic" in Congress. Polls showed more than three-fourths of Americans thought taxes were too high, and the weasel words "tax reform" used by so many legislators were discarded for "tax relief."

Indexing taxes had become a necessity with soaring inflation. Inflation rose, partly due to government spending and money printing and partly due to a series of price hikes by the Organization of the Petroleum Exporting Countries (which were not all Middle Eastern, and included Venezuela and African states). OPEC members, with Iran out, hiked their prices by 50 percent, an increase that economists said could cost up to one million US jobs. The American economy had already sputtered. Once massive energy costs were heaped on top, producers saw sales fall. Instead of wage and price controls as Nixon had tried, Carter used a system of rationing gas through federal allocations. Both had the same effect: long lines of drivers at gas stations, hoarding, and even fistfights. In July, a riot started in Levittown, Pennsylvania, over gas. A popular bumper sticker was CARTER—KISS MY GAS. Reagan took note and decided that deregulation of energy would be one of the first things he could do when he entered the Oval Office.

Carter gave another energy speech (he had delivered one in 1977), but his July 1979 televised speech was a classic in all the wrong ways. Before giving the "Malaise" speech (as it is called, though he never used the word), he had met with a potpourri of intellectuals, academics, and journalists at Camp David, confiding in one group that it was "inevitable" that there would be a lower standard of living in the US, that the "only trend is downward."[32] When he confronted the American public on TV, his grim countenance was a precursor to his shocking pessimism. Citing a "fundamental threat to American democracy," the public faced a "crisis of confidence.... that strikes at the very heart and soul and spirit of our national will." Carter's solution was for people to take no unnecessary trips and to use public transportation. Having just told Americans their greed and selfishness were the problem (their identity was not in "what one does, but by what one owns"), that they showed "a growing disrespect for government and for churches and for schools," the president concluded with no touch of irony by saying, "Whenever you have a chance, say something good about our country." While the response to the "Crisis of Confidence" speech was universally negative, Reagan, as usual, put things in perfect perspective: "People who talk about an age of limits are really talking about their own limitations, not America's."[33]

Politically, however, it seemed to make little difference: the Republicans' inability to capitalize on the Democrats' weakness was stunning. Liberal Henry Fairlie correctly observed that the "ineptness of this party has almost no parallel in history" and that the Democrats were still "without any real opposition."[34] In the 1978 midterms, Republicans gained a scant twelve House and three Senate seats. William Rusher, editor of *National*

Review, said the Republicans had "no more chance of controlling this country than the women's club of Newport, R.I."[35]

The movement needed a leader. It was waiting on Reagan.

Reagan, in fact, had been active the entire time but had not yet emerged as the "go-to" guy. He had shown in the 1976 primary fight that he could bring in donations, pulling in $5 million (more than either Carter or Ford). In February 1977, Reagan delivered a speech to the Conservative Political Action Conference (CPAC) in which he called for a "New Republican Party" that did not just meld together "the two branches of American conservatism into a temporary uneasy alliance, but the creation of a new, lasting majority."[36] He correctly defined conservatism as "common sense and common decency of ordinary men and women, working out their lives in their own way." When RNC chairman Bill Brock (no Reagan fan) asked the Gipper to sign the direct-mail fund-raising appeal to oppose the Panama Canal treaty, he did not allow Reagan to use any of the millions of dollars that flooded in. Dutch was furious, and Paul Laxalt, his top advisor, agreed that the Gipper would never raise another dime for the RNC until he was nominated.

Dutch also carefully skirted other races, even of some of his closest supporters. Jeff Bell in New Jersey upset the Establishment Republican Clifford Case in a primary there, pinning his positions on tax cuts and the Panama Canal. Even though Bell had worked for Reagan, and even though insiders such as John Sears advocated endorsing him, the Gipper had his sights set on the presidency and could not be thrown off stride by backing a losing candidate. And above all, Reagan had an astounding 95 percent name recognition among Americans. He wouldn't have to "introduce" himself to anyone.

Brock wasn't alone in trying to dissuade Reagan from running again. California pollster Melvin Field warned it would be best if neither Ford or Reagan was in the limelight.[37] And polls continued to show Carter would beat either Ford or Reagan, or that Ford would defeat the Gipper decisively among Republicans.[38] As usual, the pollsters were missing massive shifts in the electorate right under their noses. Where, right after Watergate, only 20 percent of Americans called themselves Republicans, by 1978 the GOP had made a stunning comeback to 40 percent in a Harris poll. Taxes, energy, and foreign policy were all reflecting a much different electorate than the one that put Carter in office. And again, while the elections concealed the groundswell—the GOP only gained three Senate seats and fifteen House seats—the trend was their friend. And Reagan had guessed right in not supporting Bell, who lost to former basketball player Bill Bradley.

And what of the mother's milk of politics, money? Reagan had loads of it, even without the RNC overflow. Right after losing the 1976 race, the Gipper formed a political action committee called Citizens for the Republic (CFTR) with over $1 million in leftover campaign funds. For anyone who paid attention, that in itself was a clear signal Reagan was running. As one supporter said, "He could have taken that money and bought a palomino ranch," but by plowing it back into the CTFR—headed by his loyal subordinate Nofziger—he kept his candidacy alive, firing off newsletters on a wide variety of issues.[39]

Carter continued to stumble, dropping a full 20 points in polls. By February 1978 he had plunged to 34 percent favorability. Economic news was dominated by soaring inflation (11 percent annual increase, with wholesale prices growing at a shocking 14 percent in the first months of 1979) and a plummeting stock market (a 200-point drop since Carter took office). When Harris polled on the economy, over half the population thought the US was in a recession.

Now the political landscape reverberated with Reagan's tune. Indeed, Dutch caught the attention of the media, which, lacking a position on which to attack him (as his were the most popular positions!), renewed its references to the Gipper's age. Carter's aides piled on, insisting he couldn't win the nomination because he was too old. And like the earlier attacks on his age, the new round had little impact. First, Reagan looked at least a decade younger than he was. (Later, when Reagan was president, I asked his commerce secretary, William Verity—about his same age—how Dutch had so much energy. And Verity learned the secret was bee pollen—Reagan took a daily dose of bee pollen.)[40] His physical health was superb, and he still had the winning, youthful smile. Contrary to some claims, Reagan did not dye his dark brown hair, which in photos came out black. Once he started to campaign, he constantly made jokes about his age. (After winning the nomination, he would jest at the Al Smith Memorial Dinner that he looked younger because he kept riding older and older horses.) In short, Reagan defused the age issue by putting it front and center.

Second, the public just didn't buy the media attacks: in November 1978 Reagan dashed ahead of Ford as the better candidate for the first time in a *New York Times* poll, and it was Reagan, not Ford, whom PBS chose to present a refutation to a multipart PBS series on John Kenneth Galbraith's book, *The Age of Uncertainty*. Even so, polls continued to show Carter easily dispatching the Californian.[41]

In dealing with the Soviets, Carter continued to publicly show weakness, ordering troop cuts, cancelling the B-1 bomber and the neutron bomb, and refusing to build the anti-missile systems allowed by the Anti-Ballistic Missile (ABM) Treaty. Speaker Tip O'Neill cited Carter as "the only president who doesn't have to rely on the Pentagon to make his military decisions."[42] While he meant it as a compliment, Americans saw it as anything but. (In one of his "stronger" moves, Carter beefed up spending for Radio Free Europe, which would play a significant role in Reagan's victory in the Cold War by blasting rock and roll music behind the Iron Curtain.)[43]

In fact, a bad situation in Afghanistan was rapidly getting worse. Adolph Dubs, the US ambassador to Afghanistan, was kidnapped and murdered in February 1979. Now, added to Carter's own vocabulary of weakness and decline, the press corps began to add "submissive" and "indecisive."

When Margaret Thatcher emerged as the leader of the Conservative Party in England, she met with Carter and explained her view of foreign policy, which he took as a lecture and instructed his staff never to schedule another meeting with a foreign opposition leader. The move was foolish, as Thatcher soon was the majority leader. When she won, becoming the first female prime minister there, Reagan—not Carter—was the first foreign politician to call with congratulations, but since he was not in office, he couldn't be put through for three days. Thatcher, who had come into office as a thoroughgoing conservative—she even sent a letter of thanks to economist Friedrich Hayek—immediately began to right Britain's ship against powerful odds. Her success would provide a policy lamp for Reagan to follow from across the ocean.

Hoping to score a diplomatic coup with the Camp David Accords between Israel and Egypt for a foreign policy victory, Carter failed again. Even his own biographer, however, admitted they were "at best a fragile framework for peace rather than a full peace agreement."[44] It took a Middle East trip by Carter to cement the accord, finalized by a March 1979 ceremony on the White House lawn. To Americans, this was meaningless if it wasn't reflected in falling energy prices, and as Carter sped off to Japan and Korea and vacationed in Hawaii, 90 percent of the gas stations in the New York City area were closed, as were 80 percent of those in Pennsylvania. His aide, Hamilton Jordan, wrote him: "People in gasoline lines [are] asking 'What in the hell is Carter doing in Japan and Korea when all the problems are here at home?'"[45] A popular bumper sticker of the day read "GOD BLESS AMERICA—AND PLEASE HURRY."

These pressures combined with poor—but largely misunderstood—advice from pollster Pat Caddell for Carter to address a nation "deep in crisis" that is "psychological more than material…marked by a dwindling faith in the future."[46] Caddell meant for Carter to lift and inspire Americans, but instead he harangued them about their shortcomings and dwelled on future limitations. It was the starkest contrast anyone could possibly paint between himself and Reagan. Carter even fretted in his diary, "I had already made four speeches to the nation on energy and they had increasingly been ignored."[47] This, of course, was Carter's problem: presidential speeches are seldom about an issue and almost always about inspiration to action. He responded to the dour reaction to the "Malaise" speech by inviting 150 people to Camp David where he reportedly "spent 90 percent of my time listening."[48]

Still, at that point the Gipper—while the Republican front-runner—was not alone in the Republican stable of candidates. Phil Crane, a congressman from Illinois, was smart and photogenic. Many hoped he could be a "younger Reagan" (still obsessing over Reagan's age). Indeed Crane had initially backed the Gipper, then reneged. One of the stronger potential opponents was the conservative Texas senator John Connally Jr., who could make important inroads in the South where Reagan's strength lay. Then there was Howard Baker, the Tennessee senator viewed as solid and moderate for his role in the Watergate hearings. George Bush, another Texan (though not nearly as conservative as Connally) and liberal Connecticut senator Lowell Weicker also threw their hats in the ring. Reagan remained the front-runner, a position that did not play to his strengths. He followed the strategy of his manager John Sears, acting like he was above the combat. Sears' strategy was foolish because it removed Reagan from what he did best: namely, interact with crowds. He didn't attend a New Hampshire fund-raiser, further raising questions about whether he was a serious candidate. Sears allowing him only a handful of "cameo appearances" (as pollster Richard Wirthlin called them).[49] The *Manchester Union-Leader* put it more succinctly, saying he'd been "Searscumcised."[50]

Worse, inside Dutch's campaign staff a power struggle was evolving. Since the formation of a committee to "explore" another presidential run, power had been shared among several of Reagan's California aides: Jim Lake, Mike Deaver, Lyn Nofziger, Richard Wirthlin, and Paul Laxalt— his national chairman—along with a relative newcomer, Charles Black Jr. The campaign manager was John P. Sears III, described as a "brooding Machiavelli," "Reagan's Svengali," and a moderate of "uncertain or dubious ideological convictions."[51] He was also a winner. Jeffrey Bell, a Reagan conservative who won the primary in New Jersey, called Sears "the most brilliant political strategist I've ever known."[52] Deaver's strength was public relations—"the producer of Reagan's public image."[53] As in almost all organizations, there was a power struggle, with Deaver and Nofziger on one side, pitted against Lake, Black, and Sears.

The showdown on November 26, 1979, at Reagan's home saw Nancy present along with Deaver, Lake, Black, and Sears. The Gipper expected a reconciliation at this gathering but in fact Lake, Black, and Sears arrived with a demand: "us or him," meaning Deaver. Reagan was stunned. He said to Lake, "Three weeks ago you told me both John and Mike were indispensable to my campaign, and now you're telling me that I have to choose between them."[54] Lake agreed, and said Sears was necessary. Deaver, ever the loyalist, did not force Reagan to make the choice: "I'll resign."[55]

Reagan was infuriated with his team after Deaver left, even descending to some mild profanity, but the incident moved Reagan to assume much more personal control over his campaign. It nevertheless drove a wedge between him and Sears, never to be repaired. Sears would eventually go, Deaver would return, and the Gipper came to rely on his own instincts about campaigning after that point, giving birth to the oft-invoked maxim, "Let Reagan be Reagan."

Returning to the speaking circuit, Reagan energetically contrasted himself with Carter more than his Republican challengers. Even when discussing the recent setbacks and disappointments for the nation, the Gipper never blamed the people themselves. It wasn't enough to win Iowa. Bush had virtually lived in the state (spending enough time, as one pundit quipped, to be a registered voter there). When the votes were tallied from the Iowa caucuses, although the Gipper exceeded his own turnout expectations, he still lost to George H. W. Bush by a meager 2,100 votes. Reagan may have been shocked by the outcome, but it prompted him to campaign more aggressively—and personally. He spent twenty-one consecutive days on the trail, mostly in New Hampshire interrupted by a few flights to South Carolina. His frenzy of activity seemed to be working, and he surged almost 20 points ahead of Bush after a Manchester debate. But the stuff of legend came with the subsequent Nashua debate. The *Nashua Telegraph* sponsored what was intended to be a two-man contest between Bush and the Gipper. To avoid violating campaign finance laws, the sponsors suggested having Bush and Reagan split the cost. Bush's campaign manager unwisely declined. Since Reagan's campaign was footing the cost, Sears thought the other candidates should be included as well. Others, except Connally (who was in South Carolina), agreed to come.

When Reagan, in one of his most-remembered lines, fumed "I paid for this microphone, Mr. Green," he got the name of the sponsor wrong. It was Jon Breen of the Nashua Telegraph. *But it didn't matter: the essence of the moment was Reagan's.*

All the candidates except Bush met in the Nashua High School gym, where the debate would take place, and Jim Baker—Bush's campaign manager—resisted. The deal, he said, was for a two-man debate. Reagan upped the ante, saying he wouldn't participate if the others weren't allowed to participate. In a stark example of Reagan thinking for himself, he rejected the advice of his team that said if he walked out it would look like he was afraid to debate. He "stalked" into the hall followed by, as Cannon called them, the "Nashua Four" to stand at the back of the stage with Bush off to the side looking gobsmacked. Shouts of "get them chairs" rang out. When Reagan finally spoke and tried to explain why the others should be included, the moderator and editor of the *Nashua Telegraph*, Jon Breen, tried to shut him up. "Turn Mr. Reagan's microphone off," he instructed the sound operator (who was a Reagan loyalist). Nothing happened. Then came Reagan's memorable line: "I paid for this microphone, Mr. Green." He got Breen's name wrong, but he got the mood of the crowd dead-on, and his righteous anger rippled through the crowd. David Broder of the *Washington Post* remarked, "Reagan is winning this primary right now."[56]

The event exposed one of the few times that Reagan allowed his deeper emotions to show publicly. Just as he was seen to weep only on a few occasions, likewise, Reagan kept his temper largely hidden. Cannon likened him (wrongly) to a mediocre football player who became aroused and dominated. In fact, Reagan didn't *need* public displays of emotions the way Bill Clinton did. He could convey his ideas without tears or angry outbursts. And reporters continued to miss the connections Reagan made with ordinary people who were not impressed with debate techniques but with that human factor that touched them. Reagan won New Hampshire by almost 30 points, humiliating the patrician Bush. And, breaking his own personal habit, the Gipper fired Sears, Black, and Lake, replacing Sears with William J. Casey.

Reagan's strategy changed dramatically. Sears wanted to sit on a lead and keep Reagan to the minimum number of events. Dutch, on the other hand, loved campaigning and drew energy from crowds. He complained to Nancy, "I go out and have these good days [on the campaign trail] and them I get these knots in my stomach when I come back here [to campaign headquarters]."[57] There were other issues, though, constraining the campaign: money. Under Sears' "pile it up early and coast" strategy, cash had been eaten up early and already the campaign was up against the federal spending limit of $17.6 million. Some two-thirds had been spent by the time the campaign finished in New Hampshire!

Still stewing about Deaver's departure, Dutch wanted to give his old California pal Ed Meese the job of chief of staff, for which he wasn't really fit, while keeping Sears as a campaign advisor. After further ruminating, and after Wirthlin's polls showed Reagan was well ahead in New Hampshire, he brought William Casey to oversee the finances. Casey, of course, was not a campaign manager, but after New Hampshire, everything seemed to turn around. Most of the other candidates dropped out, and Reagan had essentially won the nomination by the March 18 primary. With the nomination all but locked up, the Gipper enlisted Ford's support after a private meeting in Palm Springs. That left only Bush as the last outlier. There, Reagan had difficulties. He no longer respected Bush after Nashua, but pollster Wirthlin continued to push Ford or Bush for the veep slot, convinced Reagan needed some moderation there. As the convention opened on July 14, the Reagan team still played with both options. Ford's speech added further fuel to the fire, impressing the Reagan team. Dutch allowed his advisors to discuss the vice presidency with Ford's team at great length, even drafting remarks on the selection of Ford.[58] But the ex-president held out for powers not permitted the vice president, including more say in national security, and presented Reagan with a pair of cabinet choices that would have to accompany him, Henry Kissinger and Alan Greenspan.

The fact that Reagan's team went as far as it did with Ford was a testimony to the power within the party they thought the former president still held. It also spoke to the fact that in the frenzied hours leading up to the final announcement, few were thinking past January 20. After some of the initial details came back to the Gipper with the role Ford wanted to play, he called Ford and told him he needed an answer right away—which he knew Ford wouldn't give without all his conditions met. Ford said no. It was merely a ploy to get Ford to remove himself, and the ex-president played along. Reagan immediately turned to Bush, who was thrilled. So as to not shock the delegates who had been prepped to expect the "Dream Team" of Reagan/Ford, the Gipper had his aides leak the news so that it filtered out.

Expectedly, the media, including the so-called "conservative" press, pounced. The *Wall Street Journal* said the episode "struck a disquieting note about Mr. Reagan's staffing and decision-making ability," while others similarly piled on.[59] Meanwhile, Bush would prove an asset once the delegates got past his "voodoo economics" comment, which Ed Meese handled through a quip that Bush underwent an exorcism.

There was a second "exorcism" of sorts—this one within the family. Maureen Reagan had actively backed the Equal Rights Amendment. Dutch thought such rights were already covered under the Fourteenth Amendment. As the convention drew near, Mike Deaver and Lyn Nofziger feared Maureen might become a media focal point, a tool used to embarrass her dad. They met with her, pointedly asking, "What can we do to get you to stop supporting the ERA—at least during the campaign?" She replied that if her father would promise that in his first opportunity to appoint a US Supreme Court justice he would name a woman, Maureen would cease and desist until after the convention. Told this, Dutch replied, "Deal." Yet at the July convention, according to Michael Reagan, campaign officials "freaked out" when they saw Maureen wearing a button that said "ERA," handing out other buttons to anyone who passed. As they approached her, they saw in smaller letters below "ERA" the words "Elect Reagan Anyway." And sure enough, on August 19, 1981, Ronald Reagan nominated Sandra Day O'Connor of Arizona to be the first female to sit on the Supreme Court.[60]

In his acceptance speech, Reagan promised to balance the budget, reduce taxes, and build up the US military, and he invoked the words of Franklin Roosevelt as he spoke to the nation, holding up "a mirror of the past that reflected the days when the White House was the source of effective national leadership."[61] Then Dutch stumbled out of the gate with some ill-advised scheduling, some heckling in the South Bronx, where he finally controlled the situation by shouting, "I can't do a damn thing for you if I don't get elected."[62] At a VFW speech, he (as he often did) called the Vietnam War a noble cause. He undercut Bush when the latter was headed to mend fences with the Chinese communists by warning against abandoning Taiwan, causing the communists to fear he had returned to the "two China" policy.

Yet Reagan also knew that for the most part Americans don't pay attention to the election until after Labor Day, and he started the new leg of his campaign at Liberty Park, New Jersey, in the heart of the Democrats' stronghold. There, he sided with Polish labor leader Lech Wałęsa and expressed his support for the striking Polish workers against the communist government. Even when he seemed to be hitting on most cylinders, however, Reagan needed a top campaign director. Stuart Spencer was brought back, turning the spark plugs into fuel injectors.

Described as "combative, short, rumpled, profane, and blunt," Spencer spent most of his energy stoking Reagan's confidence. He was honest too. Reagan knew if "Stu" told him something, he wasn't being manipulative. By mid-September, Spencer's magic had worked. Reagan was either slightly ahead, tied, or slightly behind in the major polls. But then—as now—polls inaccurately sampled the *public* vs. the *voting public*, and even then, failed to really home in on the electoral votes. Wirthlin did. He knew Reagan could in fact achieve an electoral blowout, including leads in California, Texas, and Florida, three of the ten most populous states. Carter led in none.

Wirthlin and Spencer in particular knew Jimmy Carter would underestimate Reagan—just as almost every opponent did. As Dinesh D'Souza wrote,

> Carter and his advisors knew they had a difficult record to defend, but they did not believe they needed a defense. They reasoned that if the best and the brightest could not solve the problems of stagflation and the energy crisis, they must be insoluble. Instead they decided to make Reagan the issue. They were confident Americans would never elect...a washed-up actor whose political views were clearly outside the mainstream.[63]

Carter's team was indeed overconfident He wrote in his 1982 memoirs, *Keeping Faith*: "all my political team believed that [Reagan] was the weakest candidate the Republicans could have chosen.... and it seemed inconceivable that he would be acceptable as President."[64] Whether Carter directed what happened next is in dispute, but he certainly encouraged and permitted it. A congressman from Maryland, Parren Mitchell, said that Reagan sought the presidency "with the endorsement of the Ku Klux Klan."[65] No one who ever heard Reagan talk, or who knew him, had ever thought he had the slightest racist bone in his body. But one of Carter's own cabinet members had already warned that Reagan promised the "specter of white sheets." It was pure nonsense, and it reeked of Carter's desperation.

Reagan's advisors were in error in thinking Carter would let surrogates hurl these charges. As Election Day neared, a desperate Carter personally got in the mud. To paraphrase Marxist historian Charles Beard, Carter's rhetoric "foamed perilously near the crest" of nonsense. In Chicago on October 6 he warned voters that they faced a choice as to whether "Americans might be separated, black from white, Jew from Christian, North from South, rural from urban."[66] That was too much for even liberal news networks to take, and NBC called Carter's comments "mean and unpresidential," while ABC's Sam Donaldson opined that the president's reelection "is slipping away."

Such talk also pulled back the curtain on the Georgian's mean streak, which even his Democratic allies admitted to. Both Spencer and Wirthlin knew they could goad him to show this side of his personality more and more, and Wirthlin thought Carter had come "close to handing us the election that night."[67] Even the *Washington Post* referred to the "dirtiness factor."[68] At an airport, Reagan calmly responded, "I have two sons. I have a grandson. I have known four wars in my lifetime, and I think like all of you that world peace has got to be the principal theme of this nation."[69] When asked for a reaction to Carter's mudslinging, Reagan generously said he thought the president was a "badly misinformed and prejudiced man," but quietly told his aide that the attacks were an indication Carter knew he was losing.[70]

Reagan's campaign knew Jimmy Carter had a mean streak and carefully exploited it. When the Washington Post *referred to a "dirtiness factor" in Carter's personality, he was in trouble.*

Nevertheless, after a series of media hit pieces on Reagan, by mid-October Wirthlin showed Carter climbing back into the race. What Wirthlin didn't know—and what has continued to baffle pollsters at all-too-common intervals—is that polling fails to capture the views of individuals who are intimidated by the media or who are afraid to tell a stranger their choice in an election, especially if a candidate is disliked by the media. By late October, some 20 percent of Americans were undecided, giving tremendous hope to Carter's team. In reality, many—if not most—had in fact decided but weren't going to tell a pollster!

Throughout the campaign, a third-party candidate, John Anderson (who politically had been all over the map), ran to Reagan's left as a "moderate." As long as Reagan was the front-runner, no one saw any reason for him to debate Carter one-on-one. But when Wirthlin saw the polling change, he grew nervous. The Gipper had held out for Anderson to be included, which was consistent with the position he fought for with the inclusion of the other primary candidates in New Hampshire. Once Anderson's own poll numbers slipped, however, there could be no justification for keeping him in. On October 18, the Reagan team agreed to a two-man debate in Cleveland. This worried Caddell, who told Carter that the odds were against him even if he won "on points," but having insisted on the match for so long, Carter couldn't now refuse.

With the date set for a week before the election, it marked the latest debate ever in presidential campaign history—and if Reagan had his way, he would have moved it back even further, to the Monday before Election Day. Mysteriously, a briefing book containing extremely similar debate materials to the points Carter used had turned up in the hands of David Stockman, a Michigan congressman who stood in for Carter in the practice sessions. Stockman used the lines Carter himself would use, sometimes word for word. No one would have known, except Stockman offhandedly referred to the pilfered briefing book in front of an Optimist Club luncheon in Michigan the day of the debate.[71]

Carter was certain his mastery of policy specifics would expose the inept former governor: "I was confident I could hold my own" against the Great Communicator, Carter wrote.[72] He was shocked to find that his story of a conversation with his daughter, Amy, over nuclear weapons completely backfired. Carter also stumbled right into Reagan's trap when he accused Reagan of campaigning against Medicare. In one of the all-time classic political moments, the Gipper cocked his head with a smile and said, "There you go again." With four words, Reagan had made Carter look like a chronic fibber on national television, and the audience laughed along with him. The president was the child; the challenger was the adult. Carter, unsettled, chided Reagan for quoting Democratic presidents, and Reagan again good-naturedly responded, "I was a Democrat. I said many foolish things back in those days."[73] Then Dutch closed with a knockout, reviving Carter's own words from 1976. Looking at the camera, he said to the American public, "Ask yourself, are you better off than you were four years ago?" He really didn't have to say much more.[74]

Although Carter admitted "both sides felt good after the debate," almost all polls showed Reagan won by a margin of two-to-one. The Georgian wrote in his diary on October 28 that Reagan "apparently made a better impression on the TV audience than I did."[75] Further, negotiations with the Iranians—which at one point seemed promising—slowed to a crawl again, and Carter blamed his last-minute dip on "a wave of disillusionment [that] swept over the country."[76] Reagan beamed. He was in the home stretch of a fifteen-year quest and wouldn't be denied.

As the returns started coming in at 5:15 p.m. California time, both the Reagans were at their Pacific Palisades home. Dutch was just getting out of the shower as the networks started to show a landslide victory coming from the South and East, followed by a projection that Ronald Wilson Reagan would be the fortieth president of the United States. It was so obvious that Dutch had won an overwhelming victory that at 9:30 EST, Carter took the shocking step of calling him to concede before the polls were even closed in many states. Reagan was drying off, preparing for the evening at election headquarters. Nancy answered the phone, then handed it to the Gipper, who heard a White House operator say, "Governor Reagan? Please stand by for the president."[77] Later, at dinner with Neil, Mike Deaver, and others, Reagan beamed. "I bet there's a hot time in Dixon tonight," he said.[78]

Astonishingly, Jimmy Carter conceded the presidential election at 9:30 p.m. EST, before polls closed in many states, thereby affecting state and local elections all around the country.

Dutch had presented his values and policies to the American people, who had resoundingly endorsed them. The scope of Reagan's victory was breathtaking: he won the popular vote 51 percent to 41 percent, garnered more than eight million more votes, and carried a whopping forty-four states with 489 electoral votes to Carter's six states and 49 electoral votes. Across the board, the Republicans benefitted from the Gipper, picking up twelve Senate seats and gaining thirty-three in the House, although many of these races were razor thin. As the *Washington Post* anti-Reagan columnist David Broder wrote, "The election was a shocker."[79] Democrat Senator Paul Tsongas from Massachusetts glumly observed, "Basically, the New Deal died yesterday."[80]

To the Reagan team's great relief, there had been no "October Surprise" with the hostages being released. The campaign carefully avoided mention of the Iran situation in the last weeks. A subsequent utterly groundless hit piece from a member of Carter's National Security Council, Gary Sick, failed to provide any evidence of the Reagan campaign meddling in the hostage affair, but nevertheless the charge was feted with typical liberal hullabaloo in the media.[81]

While the final transition could have been thorny, particularly given the two candidates' dislike of each other, Reagan did not wish to be critical of Carter in public. He removed harsh tones regarding Carter in the inaugural address, and a lifetime of winning—and losing—roles in Hollywood had taught him not to alienate people unnecessarily. Surprisingly, the liberal press took Carter down several notches on its own, with *Time* magazine, which had chosen Reagan as "Man of the Year" in 1980, characterizing Carter as "bitterly resented" by the public and had reduced the American people to a "small people."[82] The administration had kept Reagan fully briefed on the Iranian hostage situation, mostly out of concern that if Carter struck a deal, Reagan might not abide by it. Reagan, for his part, did not return the favor, choosing to keep his strategy secret from the president in case he needed negotiating room later. Both strategies were sound, both ended up in the same place, and both men thought it preferable that the hostages be returned on Carter's watch.

The Gipper insisted that if indeed the hostage release occurred, Carter should get full credit—even if the news broke during the inaugural address, Reagan had instructed Michael Deaver to "tell me. Slip me a note. Interrupt me. Because if it happens, I want you to bring Carter up to the platform. I think it is outrageous that they are treating this president this way."[83]

On November 20, Reagan and Carter met alone in the Oval Office for the traditional briefing of the new president by the outgoing commander in chief. Reagan took no notes but received a copy of the 3" × 5" index cards Carter used for the briefing.[84] Carter, predictably, engaged in a wide-ranging lecture about situations all around the world, making a case to retain the Strategic Arms Limitations Talks (which limited the number of strategic missile launchers each nation could have), known as SALT II, and ending with a review of the hostage situation. And just as predictably, the Georgian was miffed that Reagan was not awed by Carter's mastery of the globe's trouble spots. He told one of his aides that the president-elect had "utterly no interest" in his pearls of wisdom. Just as typically, Reagan was generous to the president and described him as "helpful." Biographers— even those friendly to Reagan—ascribed it to his lack of attention to detail. Quite the contrary, even with notes, much of what Carter said would be irrelevant by the time Reagan took office, and his transition teams had already prepared extremely detailed issue papers on everything the Georgian discussed. Later, Reagan aides would recall they were impressed with the Gipper's description of the meeting and the detail he absorbed, and that once again, he had been underestimated.

At the time, Reagan was disproportionately focused on the economy, which had sunk even lower than during the campaign. Interest rates shot up to 21.5 percent—up an astonishing 13 percent in the previous year alone. Already his advisors were telling the Gipper that he would inherit the worst economy since FDR in 1933 (which has since become a standard campaign line for almost every candidate). New York congressman

Jack Kemp in November had sent the Reagan team a dark memo called "Avoiding an Economic Dunkirk," warning that things could go very badly in the first year of the new administration. Similar dire warnings were produced by Stockman and by pollster Richard Wirthlin, leading James Baker to quip that the administration had three goals, and all three of them are the economy.

In Reagan's worldview, defeating communism and stopping the Soviet Union was always at the top, but he understood that accomplishing those goals required economic growth be elevated to a key priority for three reasons. First, he had seen Nixon leave office mainly because the economy had tanked and deprived him of his electoral and congressional support. Had Nixon presided over a robust, growing economy, it's entirely unlikely he would have been forced out. Charges may have been leveled and, like Clinton twenty years later, a "trial" conducted in the Senate. As the Gipper himself would witness during Iran-Contra, a strong domestic economy covers a multitude of sins and purchases enormous public grace. Second, there was a powerful and oft-overlooked symbolic aspect of a capitalist nation embarrassing a communist state. Although Reagan would be out of office by the time the videos were shown, images of empty shelves in Soviet grocery stores did much to bring down the USSR. Of course, this symbolism only worked if Reagan could point to a clear counterexample in the United States. Finally, and most practically, the growing economy allowed the nation to ramp up military production. Pentagon budgets were not competing for domestic dollars. Although critics would point to the deficits (later a survey of twenty college textbooks found every one devoted extensive space to the deficits but virtually none to job growth under Reagan!), there were simply no observable ill effects from the 1980s deficits in the form of rapidly rising inflation or choked capital markets.

The economy, the economy, the economy. Everything Reagan wanted to achieve traced back to the economy. In retrospect, presidential historians argue, "By choosing the economy [Reagan] added simplicity to both policy-making and the policy process."[85]

If Carter was irked by his initial briefing of Reagan, Ron and Nancy had a similar reaction when they visited the White House a few days before the inauguration to inspect their future quarters. As Reagan recalled in *An American Life*, "We'd expected the Carters to give us a tour of the family quarters, but they had made a quick exit and turned us over to White House staff," an action the Reagans took as an "affront."[86] Later, the Gipper softened his judgment, offering that "I think we could sense a little of how President Carter must have felt that day.... It must have been very hard on him."[87] Carter, for his part, never concerned himself with how the Reagans felt, and Rosalynn's infamous quotation that Reagan "makes us feel comfortable with our prejudices" remains one of the nastiest and least-deserved comments ever uttered by a former First Lady.[88] It was further evidence of both Carters' "mean streak." Yet Reagan remained magnanimous, and at lunch after the inauguration, he announced that Carter's efforts to free the hostages after 444 days were successful and that the plane carrying the hostages had just cleared Iranian airspace. In *An American Life*, Reagan wrote that he "wished [Carter] had had the chance to make that announcement," a sentiment Carter never would have reciprocated.[89] Indeed, Reagan extended Carter a number of courtesies that were not required: when Anwar Sadat was assassinated, Reagan sent Ford, Nixon...and Carter to the funeral.

Carter's apologists insist that Reagan extended to the former president "the bare minimum" of respect.[90] Rosalynn groused, "There was no way I could understand our defeat. It didn't seem fair."[91] *Time* magazine would claim that Carter "used the presidency as a stepping stone to what he really wanted to do in life," which apparently was to be Moralist in Chief, but aside from quotes to the media—which especially in post-Reagan years would run to him for comments about Republican presidents—he largely disappeared.[92] There was one final shot, though, placed in stark relief years later in the Trump administration: in October 1981 the *Washington Post* reported that the Reagans wanted the Carters out of the White House before the inauguration because "Blair House, where Nancy was lodging... was *bugged*."[93] Further, the *Post* suggested that Carter listened to the tape himself. Carter supposedly was outraged because it damaged his pious image, telling the *New York Times* that "it really hurts me *in this country and throughout the world* to say I would...eavesdrop on the conversations of my successor" (emphasis mine).[94] Yet as Americans would later learn, it was not at all uncommon for some presidents to spy on their political opponents.

A half-million people poured into Washington to witness the inauguration, as one biographer noted, clogging the streets and overwhelming the subway system so much that attendants had to "throw open the turnstiles and let riders in free lest the system break down entirely."[95] Breaking tradition, Reagan took the oath of office on the west side of the Capitol, once again emphasizing his vision toward the future, and therefore he had a larger audience than most presidents—indeed, than most speakers to that point in history. Although the day was cloudy, the sky parted for sunshine as the Gipper took the oath, providing a natural example of a later Reagan theme, "Morning in America."

His inaugural speech addressed the economy, bringing the deficit under control, reminding his audience that government *is* the problem, and pointing to a new federalism with reinvigorated power in the states. He spoke of the heroes we see "every day going in and out of factory gates. Others, a handful in number, produce enough food to feed all of us and then the world beyond." We have every right, he insisted, "to dream heroic dreams." Closing with a reference to a soldier, a World War I member of the Rainbow Division, whom he mistakenly said was buried at Arlington National Cemetery, Reagan recounted Martin Treptow's words found in his diary: "I will work, I will save, I will sacrifice…and do my utmost, as if the issue of the whole struggle depended on me alone."[96] Reagan told his rapt listeners that the future would require "our best effort and our willingness to believe in ourselves, and to believe in our capacity to perform great deeds, to believe that together with God's help we can and will resolve the problems which now confront us. And after all," he closed, "why shouldn't we believe that? We are Americans."

Americans once again heard that they were the solution to the world's ills, not the cause, that they were…exceptional. If anyone doubted that there was a new sheriff in town, all doubt was removed.

Later, as Ron and Nancy dressed to start their round of nine inaugural balls, the family waited downstairs. Dutch came down in his white tuxedo with tails as the family looked on. He checked his appearance in the mirror, adjusted his tie, then as Michael Reagan recalled, "turned to us, jumped in the air, and clicked his heels—an astonishing achievement for a man almost seventy years old. 'I'm the president of the United States!' he announced with boyish glee."

And so he was.

9

Reaganomics

Reagan's presidency really began in the spring of 1980, when he and his campaign anticipated that to achieve what they wanted, they needed to have a full program in place. Most of all, this involved detailed budgets ready for Congress to debate. This gave birth to "Reaganomics," the economic blueprint crafted during the presidential campaign and enacted over the first two years of Reagan's presidency. This critical period is frequently ignored by biographers. Steven Hayward, who had the luxury of two volumes of 700 pages each, was able to include it. H. W. Brands, Reagan's most recent biographer, who gives six full pages to the baseless allegation that Reagan flew George H. W. Bush to meet with the Iranians to delay the release of the hostages, does not dedicate a single paragraph to the transition. Likewise, Edmund Morris's *Dutch* ignores the transition.

Yet since March of 1980, the Gipper had working groups in place, and throughout the summer they produced policy papers on all major issues—all thoroughly reviewed for budget impact. These were buttressed by the Heritage Foundation's army of scholars and researchers. In 1979, the Heritage Foundation trustees had drawn up a plan of action (eventually published as *Mandate for Leadership*) for the next president and approached both Reagan and Carter camps with the plan. Only Reagan responded. In July 1980, Meese met at a dinner party with the Heritage planners and indicated his boss's receptiveness to the project.[1] Ed Fuelner, Heritage's president, recalled it was important that the new administration have information other than what the outgoing people it would replace could provide.[2] But even the Heritage Foundation's own history, *The Power of Ideas*, admits that Reagan already had his tax plan developed separately. Teams had developed position papers on the B-1 Bomber, El Salvador, MX missile basing, the Law of the Sea Treaty, and virtually every key issue by November 1980.

Two days after the November election, draft *Mandate* copies were delivered to Meese, Martin Anderson, and Richard Allen. Reagan's people had already worked up most of them in their own major proposals. Some of this was overlap: Bill Bennett at Education, James Watt at the Interior Department, James Miller, and Paul Craig Roberts had been authors of parts of *Mandate*. In January, when he received the final study, the Gipper handed out copies to every member of his cabinet, and more than 60 percent of the *Mandate's* proposals would be implemented within the first year of the Reagan term. It could be said that Reagan provided the very blueprint that Heritage handed back to him months later!

Reagan's administration actually began in early 1980 with his meticulously researched and crafted transition policy planning. When he came into office, he hit the ground running.

Reagan's team also had been studying Carter's failures, especially during his own transition. In April 1980, for example, Peter McPherson wrote Meese about avoiding the "Ford & Carter problems" of disloyalty in subcabinet level personnel. All previous appointees had to go immediately, McPherson concluded, and even proposed a calendar like an NFL draft board with 150 names ready to go on Inauguration Day, with all criteria in place by January 1. He recommended having all 300 of the top positions cleared by the FBI by March and all 2,000 of the president's appointees by July.[3] In November 1980, the new administration was already circulating "A Regulatory Restraint Budget for the 1980s," which called for a process in which all budgets were evaluated for the impact of regulations they proposed.[4]

It was obvious to everyone that the most pressing issues were the budget and the economy. To that end, getting the budget director vetted and confirmed was a priority. Reagan's head of Executive Branch Management and Congressional Relations, William Timmons, who answered directly to Meese, told Meese on December 1, 1980 that it was "urgent" and "imperative" that Reagan name his budget director immediately.[5] The Gipper's teams had been planning budgets and taxes for months but knew they had to act with alacrity. As early as April 1980, one budget memo stated, "If a R[eagan] Administration is to have an impact on the budget for fiscal year 1982, it must formulate its taxing and spending priorities and communicate them to Congress before March 15." After that point, "it becomes almost impossible for the President, or even Congress itself, to realign Federal budget priorities."[6]

Reagan's approach marked a major change from Lyndon B. Johnson, Nixon, Ford, and Carter, all of whom had looked to raising taxes as a means of funding government growth. Of course, as was predicted, this led to runaway inflation. As Reagan's new budget director, David Stockman, would say, "The establishment had to be taught that you couldn't stop inflation with wage and price controls; you had to stop printing money," and that economic growth could not be achieved by expanding the welfare state.[7] Everything about the president's economic policies focused on inspiring people to save and invest, not borrow and spend. Jack Kemp, an early supply-sider, had introduced Reagan to economists Jude Wanniski and Arthur Laffer, and in California while he was governor they spent days reviewing basic supply-side concepts. As Joseph Wright Jr., Stockman's deputy in the Bureau of the Budget, noted, "There was a philosophy behind it— not just tax reduction."[8] Reagan had internalized these elements for some twenty years. Initially, in a sort of wild romantic fling, Stockman was a true believer, although some others (including Don Regan) were skeptical of the benefits of supply side.[9]

Reagan's team knew a pending increase in the debt ceiling loomed in March 1981, when unnamed senators warned it would "embarrass President Reagan by forcing him to increase the debt ceiling within a month after he is inaugurated."[10] Reagan, however, benefitted from a friendly and compliant group of Republican senators. Although many of the senators had their own tax bills they wanted to introduce, Reagan met with Bob Dole in mid-December 1980 and got Dole's agreement that Republican senators would hold off on their own plans until Reagan had introduced his.

Dutch's team thought Carter made another "fatal mistake" by not getting on good terms with the power brokers of the city. Reagan "not only wante[ed] to know them, but [wanted] to get this place working again."[11] The transition team prepared extensive dossiers on every key player. Democrat Senator John Stennis was described in a briefing manual prepared by Powell Moore, the Assistant Director for Congressional Relations of the Senate, as "a patriot" who "believes in 'one executive' and supports the President [and as] a symbol of Southern conservatism [who will] stick with you through thick and thin."[12] Republican Bob Dole—himself a future presidential nominee—"is very sensitive about his new role as Chair[man] of the Sen. Finance Comm. [and feels] there has not been enough consultation with him."[13]

As Dutch prepared to enter the arena, Carter remained very much in it and retained budget authority until January 20, 1981. He promised in a "farewell interview" to "strive to avoid embarrassing President Reagan," but he remained bitter and shocked. When Carter attended his final church service in DC, he had to tell friends there that "this isn't a funeral. We're not dead."[14] The liberal media remained in mourning as well, the depth of their defeat slowly dawning on them. Aware that Reagan's transition was moving briskly and efficiently, reporters couldn't attack the transition as incompetent and instead shifted to criticizing the size of the transition team. *Newsweek* referred to "A Bloated Transition" and claimed that Reagan needed 600 people compared to Carter's 350 four years earlier.[15] Predictably, the press claimed some of Reagan's appointees had "no apparent experience" and mentioned Phyllis Schlafly—who had enormous experience in a wide variety of jobs.[16] The point is that even in 1980, the so-called "objective" press was a thing of the past and had no ability to report honestly or fairly.

In the final organization of the transition, there were five groups with directors, along with special advisory committees for specific topics. The teams provided regular and timely reports—seventy-three in all—and briefed all nominees on departmental activities. Of the 650 personnel, most were one-dollar-a-year volunteers.[17] A "stylistic and political triumph for Reagan," one presidential scholar called the transition "the most carefully planned and effective in American political history," one that Harvard Business School made into a case study.[18]

These teams proposed an immediate federal hiring freeze upon assumption of office on January 20.[19] Meese had already received a recommendation to move as many federal employees out of DC as possible because of costs.[20] Carter's time bombs were only beginning to be acknowledged. The October budget resolution passed by Congress had set a spending limit of $633 billion and under current policies, the government was already set to spend $665 billion—which would be accounted to the Gipper, even though it belonged to Carter. The "new Administration," Timmons noted to Stockman, "will have been left with an even more serious situation for FY1982."[21] Stockman's staff was looking into even more cuts before the lights were turned on in his office and was assured "there is public support for such moves."[22] Many of Reagan's transition staff came in with a crusading spirit seeking to eliminate waste, indicating the deep commitment the Gipper had to reduce government. But Tony Dolan, who would later be a key speechwriter, cautioned against a "severe case of Washingtonitis." In the case of fraud, for example, he cautioned that the bureaucracy no longer even saw it as a problem.[23] (Fraud alone was estimated by a joint committee to constitute $5 billion to as much as $50 billion.)

Progress needed to occur fast, especially in the economic arena where Carter's legacy loomed over Reagan's teams like a cloud. In February, Murray Weidenbaum, already advising Reagan and soon to head the Council of Economic Advisers, laid out the basic understanding of the economy as the new administration viewed it. He warned that the economy was in the "worst state since WW II" and that it was "sapping the fundamental...strength of the nation." American workers, he added, were still productive—20 percent more than Germany and 50 percent more than Japan—but Reagan needed to enact "profound—even drastic—changes in Federal economic policies." The time for symbolism, he concluded, was over.[24]

David Stockman, Reagan's budget director, agreed with Weidenbaum's sentiments, especially the need for drastic action. He had famously sent around a memo, co-written by Congressman Jack Kemp, referring to an "Economic Dunkirk," and the language was symbolic: Stockman was thinking defensively.[25] He proposed a 30 percent tax reduction in installments, with the first installment due in 1981, the second in 1982, and the third on January 1, 1983, all based on the Kemp-Roth plan of reducing marginal tax rates across the board and with all income taxes indexed for inflation after the final cut.[26] The difficulty came in FY82, with Carter's $44 billion deficit looming, and the administration weighed a "go-slow" strategy over more than a year as opposed to a "first strike" strategy in which the administration would propose "a major, permanent fiscal stabilization plan—encompassing law revisions, program terminations, and consolidations…and other constraints on 'uncontrollables'" within the administration's first hundred days. The "go slow" approach meant that Reagan would be stuck signing off on a $1 trillion national debt sometime in 1981.

While tax cuts were the key to revitalizing economic growth, they were only one-fourth of Reagan's equation for full economic expansion, along with controlling inflation, deregulating industry, and cutting the size of government.

Tax cuts were key to reducing the deficits and debt through growth. No cuts, no growth. No growth, no debt reduction. During his confirmation hearings, Stockman said, "If we fail to cut taxes we have no hope during the next years of bringing the budget into balance." The current tax system had "debilitated" investment and savings.[27] In short, from well before he assumed office, Reagan not only believed in tax cuts as *the* key to prosperity and growth, but *had teams preparing a budget that would incorporate them as a key ingredient.* They were not "gimmicks," and everyone in the administration at the time—including Stockman, who would later disavow them—believed them utterly critical to growing the economy. Moreover, the necessity for action across the board, not partial "Band-Aids," was apparent. Never were they ever the sole ingredient. Again and again, Reagan and his team would place the tax cuts in the spectrum of four policies that were necessary: cutting the size of government, holding down the growth of the money supply, and deregulating the market.

Immediately after the election, Reagan quickly organized his staff and cabinet to accomplish this program. He bypassed his transition team leader, Ed Meese, in favor of James Baker for the chief of staff position.[28]

Meese had a reputation for being disorganized, and though his reputation for lacking organization was well deserved, at times he could rise to the challenge, guiding and directing a 650-person transition that was expertly divided into 73 teams that produced detailed and intricate issue papers so that Reagan came in as the best-prepared president in history. Baker was acutely sensitive to the political aspects of the chief of staff job, and Reagan knew he needed an insider to work with Congress. He was the ultimate "government man," not a revolutionary, viewing himself as a pragmatist who could cut deals. Baker made Deaver his deputy, which appeased conservatives. Moreover, Deaver seemed uniquely attuned to Nancy, and one of his unofficial tasks was keeping her placated. Later, he mused, "I always imagined that when I died there would be a phone in my coffin, and at the other end of it would be Nancy Reagan."[29]

Ultimately, Meese had to resign himself to a demotion with the title Counselor to the President for Policy with a cabinet-level rank. Baker promised to stay out of foreign policy, but he wanted a voice in domestic issues and claimed all authority over hiring and firing White House staff, and, most of all, he controlled the president's schedule. Baker also brought in an ally in Richard Darman, who headed the Legislative Strategy Group that served as the liaison to Congress. Darman, a Harvard grad, brought more of the "Establishment" into decision-making and was nearly universally distrusted. One critic circulated a joke about Darman: "Why do people take an instant dislike to Darman?…It saves time."[30] Darman's presence contributed to rumors of a "conservative/Establishment" split in the cabinet. In reality, there was a good intellectual and "ruling class/country class" balance. Meese and Baker, for example, both agreed to have the right to attend any meeting that the president attended, so long as Reagan consented. With Deaver in the mix, the "Troika" (as they were called) ensured that Reagan received strong, diverse views on a wide range of issues. Deaver tended to side with Nancy, so in a sense she was represented as well. For Reagan the delegator, this was an optimal situation. He could listen to a debate among the three and make a decision separately.

For secretary of state, Reagan selected Alexander Haig, a former NATO head and Nixon's prickly chief of staff during Watergate. Having a former military man at the head of State sent precisely the message that Reagan intended, but soon the perpetually scowling Haig had alienated virtually everyone. The choice for Defense, Caspar Weinberger, was something of a surprise. In California, "Cap" had been Reagan's budget director. He had acquired such a reputation for budget slashing that he was known as "Cap the Knife," an irony given the defense buildup of the Gipper's two terms. At Treasury, Reagan chose Donald Regan of Merrill Lynch. If not a "born-again" supply-sider, Regan was a dedicated tax cutter who brought with him a key cadre of supply-siders in Norman Ture, Bruce Bartlett, and Paul Craig Roberts. These men formed the core of a revolutionary group that was difficult to outflank by the traditional Keynesians or traditionalist conservative budget hawks. Malcolm Baldrige Jr.—who would die in office in a horse riding accident—headed Commerce. These were accomplished men, several from the private sector, and headstrong. They had frequent disagreements, but this was anything *but* a sign of "chaos." As Reagan explained, "The whole Cabinet argues in front of me. That was the system I wanted."[31]

The president's unwillingness to surround himself with "yes men" has frequently led biographers, especially Cannon, to portray Reagan as manipulated or easily swayed by the last—or loudest—voice in his ear. According to this view, Reagan, lacking the ability to study issues or prepare, simply drifted to the position of one of his advisors. Of course it was just the opposite: Reagan was usually (though not always) thoroughly prepared on almost every topic and above all knew his own mind. Many, though not all, would later admit they were wrong. Haynes Johnson of the *Washington Post*, one of Reagan's worst critics, said, "I thought Ronald Reagan was the most ignorant major candidate I'd ever seen running for president. I misjudged him. I was wrong."[32] Another liberal, John Patrick Diggins, listed Reagan among the three great liberators in American history alongside Abraham Lincoln and Franklin D. Roosevelt.[33] Moreover, as biographer Steven Hayward found, "Reagan exuded a magnetic field that tended to turn moderate Republicans by degrees into Reaganite conservatives," and offered as examples Caspar Weinberger and Richard Schweiker.[34]

In *An American Life*, Reagan said he didn't know what to expect on his first morning but that "the most immediate priority was dealing with double-digit inflation, high unemployment, and a prime interest rate of 21.5 percent."[35] Yet his first meeting on Monday, January 26, involved terrorism, with briefings by the FBI, the Secret Service, the CIA, and the Defense and State Departments.[36] To some degree this meeting demonstrated the reality that the economic recovery had to occur concurrent with a defense buildup and renewed presence on the world stage. That reality was particularly important, because Reagan's third objective behind improving the economy and rebuilding the military was reducing the size and scope of government. Over the course of the next eight years, Reagan would find that the political capital necessary to achieve the first two would leave nothing for the third. Reagan's revolution, while incomplete, had nothing to do with the Gipper being "insufficiently ideological" or lacking the "stomach for a serious assault on the New Deal" as David Stockman would later complain.[37] Reagan in no way lacked desire, but even without radical bureau-chopping, Reagan knew that the quickest way to shrink government's role in society was to grow the economy faster than government itself could increase.

Reagan found that to achieve two of his three major objectives—rebuilding the American economy and defeating the USSR—he would have to abandon his third goal of drastically reducing the size of the US government.

David Gergen insisted that Reagan's team was also intent on not repeating another of Carter's early mistakes, namely becoming unfocused through a "blizzard of proposals" being sent to the Hill.[38] Baker navigated this by making alliances with people in other departments or in Congress to address a specific task. Conservatives may have cringed at such talk, but the fact was nothing happened—in Washington or Hollywood—without such personal deal making. Baker's Texas roots stood him in good stead with a stable of Texas Democratic congressmen, who wanted assurances that if they supported the president, they would not be hung out to dry. They were reassured by Baker that if they supported Reagan's tax and economic policies, he would not campaign against them in 1982, and consequently they became the core of the "Blue Dog" democrats whose support proved crucial. Reagan, following Baker's lead, held sixty-nine meetings with 467 members of Congress in the first hundred days alone. Some of them said they saw more of the Gipper in four months than they saw of Carter in four years.[39]

Just a week after the inauguration, Reagan held a ceremony on the South Lawn to welcome home the fifty-two hostages from Iran and to express condolences to the eight families who had lost loved ones during Carter's failed rescue attempt. Recalling he "carried around a lump in my throat as big as a mountain," Reagan noted that a writer who had gone to Tehran shortly before the others were freed had also been arrested but not returned. Through Algerian and Swiss intermediaries, Reagan informed Iranian leadership that releasing the frozen Iranian funds—part of Carter's deal to obtain the hostages—would be implemented much more quickly if she was freed. While the administration never mentioned it publicly, several days later she also was released.[40] This would not be Reagan's last encounter with the mullahs in Iran.

Armed with the detailed reports that the teams had produced during the transition, Reagan came to view the pending economic crisis as an opportunity to renew the American spirit, not just fatten its wallet. Pollster Wirthlin reminded Reagan that his surveys showed Americans "demand a great deal from a president [but] they are willing to entrust him with considerable authority to lead."[41] If the president explained things simply, with a straightforward approach, he would be successful. Most important, the Gipper needed to "restore a sense of stability and confidence" to the economy.[42] John Maynard Keynes would call these the "animal spirits"; George Gilder, whose *Wealth and Poverty* would eventually become the Bible of the "supply side" movement, similarly thought confidence in the economy was far more important than any particular policy. Wirthlin's memo stated that Reagan had to offer a sense of hope, "that there is a light at the end of the tunnel."[43]

The Gipper was armed with more than just reports. He had already signed on to the Kemp-Roth tax reduction plan and had internalized the message that Gilder's *Wealth and Poverty*, which would not come out until May 1981, would champion. Indeed, Dutch would give a copy of the book to his entire staff and cabinet. But the ideas were already percolating inside

Reagan. Advisor Herbert Stein thought Reagan's economic views "were probably more precisely defined than those of any other recent [presidential] candidate."[44] Gilder, the grandson of Louis Comfort Tiffany, was raised in elite circumstances in Tyringham, Massachusetts, attending Exeter and Harvard. Unlike many of his status, he served in the US Marine Corps as a medic.[45] Originally a Ripon Society liberal Republican, Gilder slowly absorbed the ideas of Jude Wanniski (who in 1978 wrote *The Way the World Works*, another supply-side bible) and Robert Bartley, both nonacademic economics writers at the *Wall Street Journal* who offered sharp and accurate critiques of Keynesian economics.[46]

Gilder, Wanniski, Bartley, and others, in turn, all employed the "Laffer Curve," a theoretical construct that made the case that at a tax rate of zero and a rate of 100 percent, the government would receive no revenue. Therefore, Laffer argued, at some point (he didn't specify where), the government would enter a point of diminishing returns by raising taxes more, and, conversely, could get more revenue by lowering taxes.[47] Gilder ingested the elements of tax cuts that released entrepreneurs to invest. Supply-siders focused on savings and investment as opposed to consumption, tracing its heritage back to French philosopher Jean-Baptiste Say and his famous "Say's Law," which said supply creates its own demand because the cost of buying a product is already invested in its production. Keynes had argued just the opposite, namely that "sumps of wealth" and insufficient consumption had caused the Great Depression and that government spending would generate more consumption. *Wealth and Poverty*, like Laffer's work, emphasized "marginal" tax changes, that is, finding the tipping point at which a person will invest another dollar as opposed to hang onto it.

It's clear that when Reagan first read *Wealth and Poverty*, he was aware of its policy implications already. He knew of the success of President Warren G. Harding and his treasury secretary Andrew Mellon in the 1920s from his economic courses at Eureka. They slashed wartime taxes and produced a stunning economic explosion. After Harding died, American unemployment—as a direct result of the tax cuts—hit a record low 1.6 percent. Until recently falsely trashed by academics as the "cause" of the Depression, the era known as the "Roaring '20s" was one of the biggest expansions of the

American economy in history, and no small part of it was due to tax cuts. Any notion that Reagan was ill-prepared or poorly read was hogwash: he likely had a better economic education than either FDR or JFK, and certainly understood economics better than Nixon, Ike, Truman, or Carter. Reagan knew his history, and he knew his economics.

In *An American Life*, Reagan himself rejected the notion that he had only come to supply-side economics recently. He reminded people that his major in college was economics and that he had personally grasped the damage of high tax rates when he was working in Hollywood and saw 94 percent of his income going to the Internal Revenue Service. He claimed at one point he refused to do an additional picture, which would have put him in a higher tax bracket. When he invoked historical examples of tax cuts, he referred to John Kennedy and a Muslim philosopher from the fourteenth century, Ibn Khaldun, not to Harding, Mellon, or Laffer.[48]

Whichever were the more significant influences, tax cuts became the centerpiece of Reaganomics, the font from which all blessings flowed. The notion ran counter to established, entrenched Washington, to which every tax cut had to be "paid for." This was the static economic thinking Gilder warned about, in which there is a set pool of money to be divided into "defense," "welfare," "education," and so on. To remove some of that money through a tax cut meant that it had to be "made up" somewhere else. But Reagan knew that such static thinking was wrong—that tax cuts themselves generated more revenue due to changed perceptions. These ideas formed the basis of his inaugural address, that "progress may be slow, measured in inches and feet, not miles, but we will progress. It is time to reawaken this industrial giant, to get government back within its means, and to lighten our punitive tax burden."[49] Later, the phrase "America's New Beginning" would be introduced to Reagan's speech to the joint session of Congress.

New it was. Joseph Wright recalled the Office of Management and Budget's first encounter with the new president: "He came in and said, in effect, 'the Great Society is over.'"[50] Stockman organized a meeting in which, Wright noted, "we were all handed 100 new regulations Carter did which were 'Midnight Regulations.' Lynn Nofziger instructed the group to go through these." Wright asked, "Do you want comments?" Nofziger told them to go to the last page, which featured Reagan's signature and a single line: "Eliminate all of these." The "shortest meeting you could have with the president," Wright observed, "was to come in and propose a new regulation."[51] Indeed, Reagan's first official act was to sign an executive order eliminating price controls on oil and gasoline that were causing shortages.

In addition to the other influences on his economic ideas, Columbia professor Martin Anderson had informed Reagan's thinking since 1976. Anderson, who had earlier served as a special assistant to Nixon, served the Reagan administration as Assistant to the President for Policy Development, reporting directly to Meese. Anderson worked with Murray Weidenbaum for the first statement to the House Ways and Means Committee in February 1981 in which the "opportunity" message was again delivered. The president had "developed a combination of tax measures…designed to provide simultaneously the opportunity and incentive for people to increase their saving and work effort."[52] The administration emphasized that previous policies were "stop and go" and that new approaches would not view the economy as a "static national 'income pie.'" Taxes were an important part, but the key was a combination of all elements. It cannot be overstated: again and again, as in the "Preliminary Report to the Economic Policy Group" by John Rutledge and Lawrence Kudlow, everyone in the administration agreed that the budget cuts, tax cuts, and monetary control needed to be enacted simultaneously.[53] Reagan used the presidential address to focus the nation on the economic challenge, repeating the phrase that "we're in the worst economic mess since the Great Depression."[54] The budget was out of control, and the bureaucracy exploding. Everyone had a share in creating the problem, he noted, in the sense that the American people had steadily expected more out of government.[55]

Contrary to later assertions, especially by critics, no one in Reagan's administration—and certainly not the Gipper himself—ever said tax cuts would "pay for themselves." They all believed, however, that tax cuts were key to changing the national mood on investment and production.

On Wednesday, February 18, Reagan delivered his presidential address to the joint session of Congress to a "reception…more than I'd anticipated—most of it of course from one side of the aisle."[56] His budget went in immediately, and less than a week later he received good news from Stockman: both houses would embark on a major reconciliation bill. Stockman saw this as "a critical breakthrough" because it meant an up or down vote on a broad budget package, and because it avoided the "hopeless legislative swamp" that would result in each proposal referred to a separate committee.[57] Yet just a week later, Democratic congressman Dan Rostenkowski, chairman of the powerful Ways and Means Committee, sent a revised draft of the tax cuts back to the White House. Although Reagan found Rostenkowski's revisions unacceptable—the cuts were "too marginal…and too small" and were directed at specific groups—the president was giddy because "Rostenkowski is moving in our direction."[58] According to Elizabeth Dole's notes of a March meeting, Reagan said they had "made enormous progress in the scope of 2 ½ months" and changed the debate entirely from whether there would be any budget or tax cuts to "how much, how deep."[59]

Every step of the way, however, Reagan knew obstacles loomed. Even with his landslide victory, he entered office with only a 51 percent approval rating. He faced an overwhelmingly negative national press and television media. And, perhaps most important in terms of passing legislation, was that he had to overcome the Speaker of the House, another Irishman, Thomas Philip "Tip" O'Neill, a Massachusetts old-school pol who constituted the highest-ranking member of the Democrat opposition. New York Republican congressman John LeBoutillier called O'Neill "big, fat, and out of control—just like the federal government."[60] Reagan and O'Neill joked and got along privately, and when Reagan lay on a hospital bed after being shot, O'Neill "knelt next to [the] bedside, held the president's hand, and recited the Twenty-third Psalm with Reagan."[61] Nevertheless, when it came to politics, the bulbous-nosed Speaker was unrelenting in his resistance to Reagan's agenda, for O'Neill had a House majority of 243 to 192. In Reagan's corner, however, were around forty conservative Democrats under pressure to "do something" other than obstruct. Reagan's ambitious project of meeting with more than sixty senators and congressmen in the first three weeks helped cement relations with many of those "Boll Weevils" or "Blue Dogs" (as the conservative Democrats were called).[62]

The support of the Blue Dog Democrats infused Reagan with hope he could get his tax cuts through the House. Contrary to the claims of some historians, Reagan and his administration never said tax cuts would raise more revenue (especially in the short run) than was lost and never said they'd "pay for themselves."[63] Reagan and his team never wore rose-colored glasses, and no one stated that the tax cuts would by themselves address the deficit. Nor did any downplay any of the challenges they faced. In providing his testimony to the House Ways and Means Committee, Murray Weidenbaum noted that "over the near term—at least through mid-year—we expect that real growth will continue to be very sluggish and that inflation will continue near double-digit rates, seeing inflation as only falling below 5 percent by 1986."[64] Changing inflation, Weidenbaum argued, required changing expectations and the "psychology of the actors."[65] As the Economic Policy Group noted, "Success of these policies can be enhanced by immediate and clear announcement in order to reduce the public's inflation expectations by demonstrating that these policies represent a *clean break with the past*" (emphasis mine).[66] Further, gains in stock values generated by the president's program would represent the equivalent of a tax reduction.

No one disagreed on the combination of elements, which included significant spending cuts, monetary restraint, regulatory relief, and tax cuts. The disagreement came over the order and emphasis, with Reagan and Stockman favoring tax cuts first, while Federal Reserve chairman Paul Volcker and former Fed chairman Arthur Burns, who still influenced policy from his position at the American Enterprise Institute, sought spending cuts first. But Reagan was emphatic on doing both simultaneously, and as soon as possible—"and this means this year."[67] Public opinion polls showed between 65 and 70 percent supported the tax cuts, but only 55 to 60 percent supported the spending cuts. Craig Fuller, Reagan's assistant for cabinet affairs, told him that the House did not want to be viewed as "obstructionist" and could be counted on to pass the entire tax cut in one year. However, the planning groups expected it would be spread over three years.[68]

During this time, Reagan focused on winning over O'Neill, whom he described as "full of Irish warmth, a great storyteller," but who arrived at the

Oval Office "to set me straight on how things operated in Washington."[69] Quickly Reagan learned that O'Neill (and most of the Democrats) viewed him as the enemy who had come to dismantle the New Deal. He also got a quick lesson in how deceitful the Democrats were when it came to doing business. Reagan knew Congress had to raise the debt ceiling, which was not negotiable. But when he signed the debt ceiling increase, he was surprised to see the Democrats using it against him politically. This experience only reminded him of his Sacramento days and the importance of making an "end run" around Congress by going straight to the people. He would later say, "If we can't make them see the light, we can make them feel the heat."

In this, Reagan in 1981 had a monumental edge that Donald Trump would not have in a similar situation thirty-five years later: while the media was overwhelmingly liberal and oppositional, it still played the game by the basic rules of journalism (or, at least, tried to appear to play by such rules). A modicum of fairness still existed in the three major television networks, meaning that with a presidential address from the Oval Office, Reagan could indeed connect with average Americans watching on their televisions. It had worked in Sacramento, and Reagan thought it would work nationally. One of his first such addresses, in February, reiterated the message that there was no quick fix and that correction needed to begin immediately. The *Washington Star* noted that in outlining his plans for economic recovery, "President Reagan moved so easily among the fact and figures that they seemed his own discoveries [and] speaking with the quick fluency of the old sports announcer, he projected the kind conviction that, for the moment at least, can turn skeptics into believers."[70]

But such sentiments in the press were rare. *Newsweek* intoned, "Reagan's rosy vision [there was that word again!] depends on untested economic theories and entails a risky guide to the future," without noting that the "tested" theories had flopped disastrously or that Harding, Coolidge, and JFK had "tested" supply side before quite well.[71] *The Nation* claimed Reagan's budget would hurt the poor, saying "fairness is in the eye of the beholder," while the same day, *Time* acknowledged that easing the "tax squeeze" on savers was necessary but added "the question is how."[72] The media's strategy was to attempt to embolden the "moderates" in the Republican Party to resist, and then to peel off individual congressmen and senators with specific budget issues. Following a meeting with Senators Orrin Hatch, Dan Quayle, Paula Hawkins, Thomas Eagleton, and a dozen others, Reagan found some compromise possible.[73]

Reagan and his surrogates, using a packaged speech, touted returning the American economy to its greatness and creation of "the incentives that take advantage of the genius of our economic system."[74] Elizabeth Dole, charged with generating outside support for the economic package, marshaled all the conservative groups (who mailed some three million letters in support of the program), organized veterans groups' support, and staged countless seminars and briefings.[75] Reagan's team understood that they had to engage in an all-out public relations offense for their program—because the Left would certainly stage an all-out attack.

The freeze on federal hiring also played well with Middle America, who felt like much of the government's tax money was wasted. Reagan had asked every department to cut its budget at least 10 percent. Contrary to some biographers who claimed the Reagan program was, with cutting taxes first, doing the "easy" part that the public would approve of, in fact cutting taxes—not spending—was felt instantly and would boost confidence immediately. It was all about changing attitudes.

Cutting government growth was another matter. Dutch had put in place many business leaders committed, in principle, to reducing the size of government—only once in office, they suddenly couldn't find anything worth cutting! So that was when Stockman began circulating memos to reduce the funding of offices (or even defund them entirely). Any efforts to deal with the budget also had to confront the "entitlement" spending that was automatic: Medicaid; certain welfare spending; interest on the debt; and Social Security. The latter item had damaged Barry Goldwater in 1964, but neither he nor Reagan realized their best weapon against Social Security was FDR himself. The founder of Social Security had argued, in a 1935 speech, that government payments were only to be a supplement and sought legislation for "compulsory *and voluntary* annuities," such that "the Federal Government assume[d] one-half of the cost of the old-age pension plan, which *ought ultimately to be supplanted by self-supporting annuity plans*" (emphasis mine).[76] Even to this day, most Republicans—and likely all Democrats—are unaware that FDR was on record about replacing Social Security with private annuities.

Reagan never lost his verve for moving toward privatization, but his cadre of political advisors, especially Baker and Spencer, fretted about the political fallout. Baker was "determined to keep the president as far away from [Social Security] as possible."[77] Congress nevertheless drafted an initiative that would have constrained the growth of Social Security and reduced the deficit, which was badly needed. Pete Domenici (R-NM) and Senator Ernest "Fritz" Hollings (D-SC) arrived at agreement to freeze the Social Security cost-of-living adjustments (COLAs). But the effort was torpedoed by Baker and Stockman, who still viewed Social Security as untouchable ("the third rail" in politics).[78]

In fact, Stockman severely damaged the administration by concocting a scheme to get the budget shortfall back from Social Security funds after Congress passed the budget. While technically sound, the scheme gave the impression that Reagan was poised to cut Social Security itself. It had been the stated intent of Congress in 1968 when Johnson directed Social Security be placed into a "unified budget" to have shortfalls revert back to the general budget. Stockman knew that Congress had used the Social Security surpluses as perpetual cover to give the appearance of lower deficits than actually existed. Thus he wanted to take advantage of the same leeway Congress gave itself.

Reagan bristled. He wanted no shenanigans when it came to Social Security, feeling he had given his word during the campaign not to cut the program. In a March 17 meeting with Baker, Domenici, and others, the president listened patiently to the arguments on COLAs—which were accurate as far as they went, namely that reducing *future* outlays and reducing *increases* was not the same as a "cut." But perception is reality, and Reagan put it succinctly: "Compared to what [recipients] would expect to get there will be a cut from their expectation."[79] The fight Reagan expected—a political battle over Social Security—would be difficult. The challenge that came for him was far more desperate.

Heading out for a routine speech before a labor group on March 30, 1981, portended nothing unusual or ominous for the president. After he finished his speech at 2:25 p.m., he left with James Brady, the press secretary, Mike Deaver, and his Secret Service detail. The presidential limousine was first in line, just twenty-five feet from the hotel's VIP entrance and the follow-up Secret Service car, code-named "Halfback," was second. In the second car were a military aide carrying the "football" briefcase containing nuclear codes, the White House physician, and a senior staffer. James Brady was the first out the door to deal with the reporters, followed by Deaver, then Reagan with his two Secret Service guards. As Reagan reached the limo door, a reporter called out a question and the Gipper turned, smiled, and raised his left arm to wave away the question. Suddenly, at 2:27, there were two quick pops in succession, but few suspected gunfire. Deaver recalled smelling sulfur and "my reflexes took over. I ducked, the only one who did."[80] John Hinckley, an insane obsessive who wanted to date actress Jodie Foster, decided he would commit "suicide by police" by attempting to shoot the president and unloaded six shots in less than two seconds.[81] Press Secretary Brady was hit first, then DC police officer Thomas Delahanty. Deaver, who glanced at the president, recalled "a look of utter helplessness" before Jerry Parr, the Secret Service agent, covered Reagan with his body and then pushed him facedown into the limousine. By then Hinckley's third bullet missed entirely, and his fourth hit Secret Service agent Tim McCarthy, who also was shielding Reagan. After the fifth bullet missed, the final bullet ricocheted off the rear window edge of the limousine and hit the president under the arm just as Parr pushed him inside. It nearly hit him in the heart.

As civilians and Secret Service subdued Hinckley, the Secret Service radio recorded "Rawhide [Reagan] is OK," and the limo sped away.[82] Indeed, Parr thought Reagan was uninjured and initially directed the driver to head toward the White House. Meanwhile, Reagan noticed pain (the bullet had hit a rib) and thought perhaps Parr had broken a rib when he pushed him in the limousine. Parr, then thinking the rib had punctured a lung, diverted the car to George Washington University Hospital.[83]

Secret Service agent Jerry Parr saved Reagan's life with his quick decision to go to the hospital rather than the White House, even though he saw no visible wounds.

At the hospital, a call came in on the "White House Phone," and before long one doctor literally had three telephones under his chin. The staff quickly hustled another patient out of the prep room. No stretcher was available and Reagan insisted on walking in anyway, smiling and unassisted. But once inside, he collapsed. Later, in his *Diary*, Reagan recalled walking in and thinking, "Getting shot hurts."[84] His physician, Dr. Daniel Ruge, feared a heart attack and wanted the hospital's trauma team—not himself—to operate on him. Many did not even realize their patient was the president until Deaver, when asked for the address, blurted out "1600 Pennsylvania Avenue."[85] Even in the ER, some did not know that they had the president of the United States on the table.

Parr remained with Reagan and patted his head, making eye contact—he was the only one in the room the president knew. Between the Secret Service agents and the full emergency staff in the room, there was scarcely a place to stand, and the doctors had to clear the room of all but a couple of agents, who rushed back to don scrubs and masks. When Nancy arrived, he quipped, "Honey, I forgot to duck," then after being intubated scribbled, "All in all, I'd rather be in Philadelphia." But throughout, Reagan insisted he had trouble breathing. Deaver took Nancy to a small chapel in the hospital, then she joined the wives of Jim Brady and Tim McCarthy in an office on the second floor.

Though still conscious, Reagan neared shock. He later recalled that while the limousine was en route, he felt pain near his chest. Repeatedly he told the ER staff that he couldn't breathe—later writing "my fear was growing because no matter how hard I tried to breathe it seemed I was getting less and less air. I focused on that tiled ceiling and prayed."[86] Astoundingly, he then noted, "I realized I couldn't ask for Gods [sic] help while at the same time I felt hatred for the mixed up young man who shot me. Isn't that the meaning of lost sheep?"[87] Lying on the table—as far as he knew, close to death—the president prayed for John Hinckley's soul.

Although the team stabilized his blood pressure, the chief thoracic surgeon, Benjamin Aaron, decided that he needed surgery to stop the bleeding (the president had lost half his blood volume since he'd arrived). Once in the operating room, Reagan removed his oxygen mask and said "I hope you're all Republicans" to the doctors. Joseph Giordano, who was the most senior doctor and who had just arrived, was the head of the operating team (and a liberal Democrat). He replied, "Today, Mister President, we're all Republicans."[88]

As the doctors began working on Reagan, the staff addressed the question on everyone's mind: What would happen if Reagan died on the table? Baker and Meese had arrived at the hospital and conferred with Deaver. Baker placed a call to Reagan's personal physician, who assessed the president's condition as "stable." With that, Baker, Deaver, and Meese decided "right there" according to Deaver not to invoke the Twenty-Fifth Amendment and thereby transfer power to Bush, who had been in Fort Worth, Texas, addressing a cattleman's convention and was now en route back.

At the White House Situation Room, Caspar Weinberger, Alexander Haig, Richard Allen, and others met. Weinberger, fearing the Soviets might be linked to the shooting, questioned whether to raise the alert level at military bases. Haig reined him in, noting that sudden change in alert status might lead to a Soviet invasion of Poland. But then Haig, failing to understand the order of succession in the government, said that the "helm" of power was his chair (i.e., himself) in the Situation Room and that everything went through him. Meanwhile, in front of reporters, struggling spokesman Larry Speakes could not answer who was in charge of the government. When Haig heard that, he exploded, left the Situation Room, and grabbed Richard Allen to make a public statement. By all accounts, Haig looked bad—shaken, nervous—and he once again misstated the order of succession, claiming it was the president, vice president, and secretary of state—when in fact the Speaker of the House and the president pro tempore of the Senate were ahead of the secretary of state. Haig, answering a question as to "who's running the government right now," said "as of now I am in control, here at the White House."[89] Later Reagan, in his diary, would label him "paranoid" when it came to working with other cabinet officers.

Meanwhile, at the hospital, thoracic surgeon Dr. Ben Aaron finally found the bullet.[90] After a six-hour surgery, Reagan was out of the operating room and Vice President George H. W. Bush had arrived back at the White House, low-key and anticipating a return to "normalcy." Aaron met with Nancy and Deaver outside the operating room. "It took me forty minutes to get through that chest. I have never in my life seen a chest like that on a man his age," which he meant as a compliment.[91] Still in recovery, Reagan continued to have difficulty breathing, requiring Aaron to insert another tube through the first breathing tube to clear out debris. Reagan, coming to, tried to remove the breathing tube, but nurse Cathy Edmondson admonished him, saying, "You are going to have to let me breathe for you." The Gipper submitted.[92]

Dr. Dennis O'Leary, an administrator, was rounded up by Lyn Nofziger to write the official statement. "The president is in the recovery room…is in stable condition and he is awake," O'Leary began.[93] Actually, Reagan in the recovery room was on stage, "like an old trouper who had found the world's most appreciative audience." He dashed off notes to the nurses: "I'd like to do this scene again—starting at the hotel," and "Send me to L.A. where I can see the air I'm breathing."[94] Finally, at 6:15 the next morning, he left the recovery room, where they had kept him all night instead of sending him to a more traditional ICU bed. After the tube was removed from his throat, he was told things were going smoothly in his absence, and he asked, "What makes you think I want to hear *that*?" Nevertheless, he was given a bill for his signature—one reducing dairy price supports—constituting a very small victory for reducing government and his first legislative triumph. Reagan signed, somewhat wobbly, on his breakfast tray but proceeded to hold a one-man performance filled with stories and jokes. When the breathing tube was removed and everyone awaited his first words, Reagan asked, "What was that guy's beef?" referring to Hinckley.[95] Eventually, Marisa Mize, knowing he needed rest, said, "Now, Mr. President…you need to get some sleep. In the most polite way I know how, I'm putting this cover over your eyes and I want you to shut up and go to sleep."[96] And he did.

After thirteen days in the hospital, Reagan returned to the White House, where over two hundred members of the staff, the administration, and their families greeted him on the South Lawn. One critic noted that Reagan's survival "was taken not only as a personal triumph for Reagan but as a national one as well."[97] Although Nancy wanted him to keep his active hours limited, insisting he nap before he had evening events or speeches, Reagan pushed himself. On April 24 he went back to the Oval Office. At his first public appearance after the assassination attempt, to receive an honorary degree from Notre Dame, the audience gave him a sustained standing ovation. Deaver correctly noted that his entire demeanor in dealing with the attempt on his life provided him "carte blanche in his first term—his so-called Teflon coating."[98] His popularity soared from 53 percent to a whopping 73 percent within days. His courage under fire literally endeared him to Americans, and his charm in the hospital reassured the public they had not only elected the better man, but perhaps God's man. Certainly the Gipper thought so, recording in his *Diaries*, "Whatever happens now I owe my life to God and will try to serve him in every way I can."[99]

He would later return to God's purpose for his life. But in the short term, he had other thoughts: he began to carry a gun in his briefcase, even when he went on Air Force One. Novelist Brad Meltzer, doing research for a fictional work, interviewed a Secret Service employee in 2015. "I trust these [Secret Service] people…but if someone comes at me again, I want to be prepared," Reagan told the unnamed source.[100] It was the second time in his life Reagan "packed heat," the first being when he was threatened during the strike as head of SAG.

Returning to a normal routine was a different matter. Some sources claim he didn't recover his strength fully until December. While he slowly worked his way back to normalcy, both Nancy and Reagan's doctor carefully monitored his activity. Fortunately, between his well of public support and the absence of any international crises at the time, Dutch could pace himself and apply his energy to the main issue in front of him: the economy.

The Gipper's "greatest strength was the focus he brought to his task. His message never changed…. smaller government and lower taxes," as one biographer put it.[101] As liberal tax historian W. Elliot Brownlee observed, the president and his political operatives "concentrated their public messages on a deep, across-the-board, tax cut. As a political issue, the approach was decidedly successful."[102] Reagan's vision was never shaken, even when, in March—before the assassination attempt—staffers warned "the Administration's fiscal program is in danger of pulling apart at the seams. Remedial action is urgently needed."[103] Another memo complained that the administration "has *not* developed any fall back options; the ball is in Congress's court."[104] That was precisely where Reagan wanted it. There he could jawbone and buttonhole sympathetic congressmen, bringing them along a few at a time. And after the assassination attempt, his political capital soared, as did his approval ratings from the public, allowing him to cash in with fence-sitting Blue Dogs.

Reagan did not want any fallback positions in his economic policy. It was all or nothing. Success or failure.

Where the Gipper turned more to God in the aftermath of the assassination, Nancy took to consulting her horoscope. As she wrote, "I was devastated after the shooting.... Astrology was simply one of the ways I coped with fear." She reached out for help and comfort "in any direction" she could, praying, in her words "all the time" and talking with Billy Graham. While speaking with her old friend Merv Griffin, the talk show host mentioned an astrologer named Joan Quigley, whom Nancy had heard from before and who told her Dutch would win in 1980. Griffin told Nancy that Quigley had warned him about March 30, saying that it would be a "dangerous day" for him. Nancy later wrote in her memoirs that she relied on the astrologer as a "crutch," but only one of several. But immediately after the assassination attempt, she then developed a system of checking on travel days with Quigley and, if there were concerns, asking Deaver or, later, Don Regan, if plans could be adjusted. According to Nancy, Deaver not only acquiesced but himself said it was a "good idea" and while it could be nonsense, what was the harm? This was especially the case when it came to travel.[105]

She hid all this from the Gipper, until finally, years later, she told him. According to her, he responded, "If it makes you feel better, go ahead.... But be careful. It might look a little odd if it ever came out."[106] And, of course, it did. Although several news stories over the years had mentioned it, Nancy's astrology stayed below the radar until Don Regan—her archenemy—left the chief of staff job in February 1987 and wrote about it in his book. Some biographers, including Cannon, have blamed Nancy's interference in the schedule for some of Reagan's foreign policy missteps and for a poor performance in his first debate with Walter Mondale in 1984. Initially, while Nancy's "readings" remained a secret from Reagan and the world, her dabbling in astrology made little difference.

When it came to the economic plan, Reagan didn't need help from the stars. One thing the media and the Democrats could not stifle was confidence, which began to return almost immediately after Reagan took office. For example, by May 1981, the chief economist who produced the *Business Outlook* newsletter reported that consumer spending had grown 5 percent in the first quarter, including a whopping 22 percent increase in spending on durable goods. Spending on nondurable goods had fallen some, but gross private domestic investment shot up by almost 22 percent, "the highest rate of growth since…1977."[107] In other words, Reagan's long-term program of investment was working, even if in the short term, consumers were still struggling. This was borne out by comments from industrialists, such as Bill Verity of Armco Steel, who would later become Reagan's commerce secretary. Armco announced plans for a $1.96 billion expansion based on the anticipation of Reagan's policies.

However, the wild card was inflation. A major reduction in prices would benefit Reagan's program in a dramatic way. In May, economist Jerry Jordan sent Murray Weidenbaum a memo noting that the forecasts even from the private sector showed declining inflation and the likelihood that the velocity of money "in the near future will be below historical trends."[108] Even though he cautioned that lowering "the assumption of inflation even further would appear to be very 'Pollyannaish' to observers," in fact that's exactly what happened. Jordan also pointed out that the growth in real output was "much greater" than a superficial analysis would suggest.[109] Indeed, a June compilation of real GNP growth estimates by six private firms or universities found that they unanimously had the economy estimated to grow by 6.5 percent by April. Far from pushing overly favorable outlooks, the administration was more conservative than major independent estimates.[110] Marty Asher, who compiled the estimates from Georgia

State University, UCLA, Wharton, Chase Econometrics, Merrill Lynch, and Data Resources, noted that while the administration accepted the 6.5 percent growth rate, the real rate "was recently revised to 8.4%."[111]

As Reagan battled for his life, the budget process inevitably rolled on. Before the assassination attempt, Stockman had concocted a cost-saving device involving Social Security. He proposed to save $110 billion with a "fine print" clause that would increase the penalty for early retirees from 20 percent to a staggering 55 percent. Perhaps if this had been stair-stepped in, so that those around sixty years old and expecting to retire early could have prepared, it would not have been nearly as problematic. But Stockman (perhaps deliberately) did not explain it well to Reagan—who by then was still recovering from the gunshot wound of the assassination attempt—and definitely had purposefully hidden the language with as much "bureacratese" as he possibly could. When he presented the proposal to Reagan on May 11, in a grueling one-hour presentation, Reagan's eyes were "glazed by technical detail."[112] Further, Stockman called for phasing out early retirement since it was not a part of the original Social Security concept, and Reagan agreed—again, still not fully aware of the severe cut to early retirees.

Reagan wasn't the only one in the dark that day. Baker, Darman, and Meese were all blindsided and had in fact not taken the presentation as seriously as they should have because Reagan usually consulted them before reaching a final decision. Not this time. The Troika scrambled to undo the damage, immediately calling it "Schweiker's plan," but it was too late, and the *Washington Post* predictably ran a patently misleading scare headline, "Reagan Proposes 10% Cut in Social Security Costs."[113] The cut was only to a single element of the program, but David Broder, the *Post*'s resident Reagan-basher, didn't care: the words "Social Security" and "cut" in the same headline were all that mattered.

Though his hours were still limited and he was still weak, Reagan worked hard to give the appearance of recovering fully and rapidly. Two weeks after the assassination attempt, he was meeting with Democrats who were "with us on the budget.... [W]e seem to be putting a coalition together."[114] On June 4, he again recorded "[a] very good day. Met with Dem. Conservatives. Believe a majority of the 33 will support our tax program."[115] What Reagan discovered was that Carter had completely ignored not just the conservatives but almost everyone in Congress. Many noted a visit with Reagan was their first time ever in the Oval Office. Dutch made their visits memorable, slowly enlisting their support for his budget.

By then Reagan had listened to all the arguments about deficits and dismissed them, telling Alan Greenspan and Charles Walker, "I don't care." (Walker recalled that they "nearly fell out of their chairs.")[116] Of course, this was typical Reagan: keep the focus on the big picture, and details would take care of themselves. In the case of the deficits, Reagan understood that *no* Americans were moved by deficits they couldn't see, but tax cuts they could spend would generate growth, and growth was a major key to beating the deficits. It also returned the debate to spending, which after all was in the hands of Congress. "We can lecture our children about extravagance," he said, "*or* we can cure their extravagance simply by reducing their allowance."[117] Reagan exuded confidence, but he never avoided reality. His team was preparing numbers that were anything but "rosy" and were in fact underestimating both economic performance and the rate at which inflation was falling—as Weidenbaum put it, the "bright spot" in his analysis.[118] Internally they projected price increases to be at 4.1 percent in 1986, for example, but publicly the budget placed the level at 4.2 percent. Publicly Reagan's team published a money velocity rate of 5.5 percent for 1986, but internal estimates were for only 3.6 percent.[119] These memos provide a consistent and powerful rebuttal to any claims that Reagan's team "knew tax cuts wouldn't work" or were painting too optimistic of a picture of the economy. In reality, they were uniformly *understating real growth in public!*

Critics of the day and historians later complained that Reagan presented a "rosy" picture of his policies, while in fact his team almost always understated real growth and underestimated the beneficial effects of "Reaganomics."

Indeed, in his summary to Reagan in July 1981, Weidenbaum said the economy was "on a plateau," that real growth was "probably zero," and that aside from inflation falling, the economic news over the next two to three months would be "cheerless."[120] Over the long run, however, everything appeared to be on track, with business and consumer sentiment high and

capital spending up (in part thanks to oil investment due to Reagan's deregulation). Overall, Reagan was told the performance in the future would be
"quite strong."[121]

Foreign leaders knew there had already been a change and that Keynes's
"animal spirits" were loose. When Helmut Schmidt, chancellor of the Federal Republic of Germany (i.e., "West" Germany), visited in May, he saw in
America "a notion of 'upswing and optimism' whereas in Europe pessimism
reigns."[122]

Reagan's advisors continued to try to force him into budget balancing
through Congressional compromises that involved cuts in Social Security.
In mid-July, Reagan met with James Baker, who showed him yet another
proposed cut involving the elimination of a minimum Social Security benefit. Reagan saw through it as a "a pol[itical] trick by the majority Democrats
aimed solely at creating a 1982 election year issue for the Dem's [sic]."
Dutch refused to budge: "It will be taken as a test of my determination &
looked upon as a sign that I'll back down on the tough decisions."[123]

His intuition was correct: the public was behind him. On July 28,
Reagan noted his schedule was "unbelievable," meeting the entire day with
members of Congress, both in groups and individually. They told him their
phones were "ringing off the wall" and that while the votes were close,
"there is no doubt the people are with us."[124] The Gipper could forge ahead
on this confidence because of the long-term projections Weidenbaum and
Stockman were providing him—it wasn't blind faith. On August 4, Reagan
received from Congress the tax cut bill, which had passed overwhelmingly,
and now needed only his signature. The final version was a 5-10-10 cut
stretched over three years. It was a near total victory.

But as the bigger fight over cutting spending in the FY82–83 budget
dragged into September, Reagan grew concerned. The congressional coalition was breaking up over budget cuts, and "I think they have '82 election
jitters," he noted.[125] After his initial determination to stand on the Social
Security cuts, Reagan gave in. On September 23, he withdrew the reductions from consideration and admitted "we won't get all we ask for but
we'll do fairly well."[126] For hard-liners such as Stockman, it marked the first
capitulation to "big government" and the end of the revolution.

He had misread Reagan. The Gipper was not as revolutionary as Stockman thought but was far more complex. Having repeatedly brought Dutch variations of cuts to Social Security, Stockman was chagrined to conclude that Reagan was not interested in eliminating the program. And even as Reagan railed against the size and scope of government, he never criticized FDR personally or advocated a libertarian nonexistent government. While he saw many traps and weaknesses in the New Deal, he never campaigned on its full removal. He said:

> It is not my intention to do away with government. It is rather to make it work—work with us; to stand by our side, not ride on our back. Government can and must provide opportunity, not smother it; foster productivity, not stifle it.[127]

Moreover he saw that with the ominous cloud of the USSR looming, he could not reduce defense spending. Having started with four major priorities—restoring the American economy, rebuilding US defense forces, deregulation, and cutting government—one would have to go.

10

We Win, They Lose

An interesting set of negotiations took place on two occasions in 1981, and while the details remain buried, the principals do not. President Ronald Reagan met with Prince Bandar bin Sultan Al Saud of Saudi Arabia, ostensibly regarding the sale of AWACS (Airborne Warning and Control System aircraft) to the Kingdom.[1] To accomplish this sale, Reagan had to placate Menachem Begin, the prime minister of Israel. Reagan was unusually tight-lipped in his diary about the details of those negotiations, but in addition to the elusive "Middle East Peace" that every president has pursued since 1947, there was another issue weighing on his mind: oil.

A key to his strategy to defeating the USSR was the growth of American economic might and the undermining of the Soviet economy. The former depended, in part, on falling interest rates, and key to falling interest rates was a declining price of oil.

Oil prices had already tilted down, but beginning in mid-1981, they took a sharp turn even lower. Prices (adjusted for inflation) absolutely plunged, down to eighty-nine cents a gallon by 1986, despite OPEC imports falling by some two million barrels a day. Whether Reagan had demanded a quid pro quo for the AWACS and Prince Bandar got the message, whether it was the deregulation that Carter had initiated and which Dutch continued, or whether it was all coincidental, the impact was extremely beneficial for the Gipper's strategy—and deadly for the Soviets' ability to generate hard currency.

Three years before he became president, Ronald Reagan planned to defeat the Soviet Union, and to do so without a nuclear war.

Reagan knew this was their Achilles' heel. He studied it. According to NSC staff member John Poindexter, the president "loved seeing the raw intelligence on the Soviet economy," and Donald Regan agreed: "He just loved reading that stuff. He would take a big stack and read them one by one over the weekend."[2] When the CIA briefed president-elect Reagan in December 1980, the Agency, having missed on the Nicaraguan revolution and the rise of the Islamic radicals in Iran, for once got it right. The topic was the Soviet economy, and the report was music to the Gipper's ears. Economic prospects for the USSR, it began, "are gloomier…than at any time since Stalin's death." Its GNP over the previous two years was the lowest since World War II, its chances for a turnaround "bleak," and the economic problems would "get progressively worse as the decade passes."[3]

To anyone with an ounce of common sense, these assessments would have been obvious, but for years some economists, including Paul Samuelson in his famous textbook, *Economics*, had predicted the exact *opposite*. The Soviet economy, he explained, would catch up to that of the United States and even pass it—and he continued to predict this until 1989! He was not alone. MIT's Lester Thurow asserted the Soviet Union was "a country whose economic achievements bear comparison with those of the United States."[4] Economics textbooks routinely overestimated Soviet economic performance.[5] Liberal historian Arthur Schlesinger Jr. echoed the knowingly false reports of intellectuals who visited Russia in the 1920s when he wrote of his trip there: "I found more goods in the shops, more food in the markets, more cars on the street—more of almost everything."[6] As late as 1982, he said people who thought the USSR was on the verge of economic collapse were "only kidding themselves," while Samuelson said "it is a vulgar mistake to think that most people in Eastern Europe are miserable."[7] A prominent group of Soviet specialists predicted the USSR's economic growth would be 3.15 percent throughout the 1980s. Thurow, who proved perpetually wrong, referred to the "remarkable performance of the Soviet Union," and Columbia University's Seweryn Bialer insisted the USSR "is not now nor will it be during the next decade in the throes of a true economic crisis."[8] Oops.

Not only were all of these estimates by the learned elites wrong, they were grossly wrong. But for some time, they were echoed in the halls of the Central Intelligence Agency. As Herb Meyer, special assistant to CIA director William Casey recalled, the Agency "was monitoring Soviet strengths [but] it was not looking at Soviet weaknesses."[9] Indeed, Reagan may have been permanently stuck with simply goofy CIA estimates if not for his future vice president, George H. W. Bush, who took over as director of the Agency in January 1976. For years, the Agency had vastly underestimated the USSR's military strength in its National Intelligence Estimates (NIEs), and even when it increased its estimate of the numbers of Soviet missiles that would be deployed, the USSR exceeded the CIA's predictions.[10] Angelo Codevilla, a staffer on the Senate Intelligence Committee in the 1970s, later wrote, "Surely no failure of American intelligence compares in seriousness to this NIE's [misunderstanding] of the size, scope and purpose of Soviet Strategic forces between 1965 and 1979."[11] Part of this disconnect had to do with the CIA's estimates of the level of Soviet spending on defense, putting it at 6 percent (when later Leonid Brezhnev himself would publicly state the number was 15 percent). When Bush became the new CIA director in January 1976, he strongly suspected the numbers couldn't be correct and formed a "Team B" to review the estimates independently. Team B reported that the Soviets clearly were developing offensive missiles that were more accurate than thought and were preparing for a "Third World War as if it were unavoidable." Moreover, the Soviets expected to achieve military superiority in ten years that would allow them to aggressively pursue their expansionist goals.[12] Richard Pipes, a member of Team B, claimed Bush "fully identified" with the Team B point of view and expressed his impressions to Reagan as vice president.[13]

Bush may have supplied some evidence, but even before Reagan took office he intuitively knew "the Soviet Union…is up to its maximum ability in developing arms.… If we turned our full industrial might into an arms race, they cannot keep pace with us. Why haven't we played that card?"[14]

In 1981, after briefings from the CIA confirmed his views, he saw "great opportunities" to unravel the USSR's economy, and, a year later, in 1982, after receiving another briefing, he noted in his diary, "They are in very bad shape and if we can cut off their credit they'll have to yell 'Uncle' or starve."[15] As he recalled in *An American Life*, "The Soviet economy was being held together with baling wire; it was a basket case, partly because of massive spending on armaments."[16]

Certainly the Soviets knew their society was falling apart at the seams. Alcoholism was so rampant that annual spending on liquor was greater than what households spent on food, abortions were at record levels, life expectancy had dropped by six years between 1950 and 1970 (though the CIA missed it again, claiming the Soviets' public health record was "outstanding"), and even the KGB ran computer simulations showing the USSR was losing the Cold War. Only massive oil exports kept the economy afloat. One observer called the Soviet Union the "upper Volga with missiles."

Reagan's CIA director William Casey was the first in that office to hold views similar to the Gipper's. In May 1981 Casey echoed Reagan's "baling wire" assessment. Addressing the Business Council he said, "The Soviet economy is gasping under its inherent inefficiencies."[17] Casey delivered a report to Reagan that summer reiterating that "Soviet military leaders regard military strength as the foundation of the USSR's status as a global superpower and the most critical factor underlying [their] policy." Further, Casey's report noted, Soviet dictators saw the military investments of the past as "paying off" in advances "across the military spectrum" and viewed military power as "the actual instrument of policy" or a "critical complement to their diplomacy."[18] In Reagan's mind, if the Soviets saw the military as their strength, defunding it would be their fatal weakness. So Reagan was given the perfect stone with which to slay the giant without nuclear confrontation—a stone no other American president had even looked for, let alone tried to sling.

Initially, the strategy demanded an immediate buildup that, over time, would collapse the Soviet economy, the essence of which is found in the National Security Decision Directive (NSDD) 12, issued on October 1, 1981. It included:

- Making communications more secure;
- Modernizing the bomber fleet with two new bombers;
- Increasing the accuracy and payload of the Submarine Launched Ballistic Missiles (SLBMs) and the Submarine Launched Cruise Missiles (SLCMs), which meant development, then procurement of the D-5 longer-range missile;
- Deploying a larger land-based Intercontinental Ballistic Missile (ICBM) known as the MX. (This included replacement of existing ICBMs with one hundred MX missiles as soon as feasible, along with ballistic missile defense and either "airmobile basing" or "deep underground" bases.)[19]

The MX decision came within the 1982 budget fight, and Reagan saw it as essential. In NSDD 35 of May 1982, the directive flatly stated that development of the missile would be completed and one hundred operational missiles would be produced.[20] Getting the missile through Congress was a struggle, as Speaker Tip O'Neill "mounted an all out campaign" to kill the weapon, as Reagan confided in his diary.[21]

All these constituted the hardware of the Reagan strategy. All were deeply "game-planned" in the transition papers. But it was the "software" that constituted the most important component: Reagan's revolutionary approach to the Cold War. He repeatedly stated to reporters, who fretted the US was starting an arms race, that we already had an arms race, only one side was not racing. Asked once for his strategy, Reagan all too typically put it succinctly: "We win, they lose."

This marked a stark departure from the *détente* that had dominated the Nixon/Ford years, and from the more confrontational mutual assured destruction (MAD) standoff of the Eisenhower/Kennedy/Johnson era. More important, Reagan intended to do just that—win—*before his presidency even began.* In an interview with National Security Advisor Richard V. Allen, historian Paul Kengor asked if Reagan had a specific intent to defeat the USSR before he assumed office, and Allen said "yes."[22] Kengor was taken aback and said, "That's a big, big deal. Are you telling me that… in January 1977, Ronald Reagan told you that his goal was to take on and defeat the Soviet empire?" And again, Allen responded, "That's absolutely right. That's what I'm telling you."

In understanding Reagan, it is essential to realize two fundamental truths: he hated nuclear weapons and wanted to abolish them far earlier than even most of his supporters suggest, and he hated Soviet communism almost as much and knew that to accomplish the former, he'd likely have to also abolish the latter. Caspar Weinberger noted that Reagan saw the "two systems [as] not compatible," and Deaver said that, to the Gipper, "there was no ultimate gain in getting along [with the USSR]. We had to eliminate the threat."[23]

The MAD strategy of previous administrations had developed in large part because none could envision a way to defeat the Soviet Union, and therefore a "balance of terror" was all that remained. It meant, deep down, none truly *believed* the American economy could force the Soviets into retreat and surrender. These assumptions permeated every level of Washington and most of the peripheral think tanks and intellectuals. Thus, *every* agency, from the State Department to the CIA (pre-Casey), interpreted any action as "stabilizing" or "destabilizing." It amounted to two football teams on a field in which neither really wants to score, because that might cause the other to take more risks to score.

Reagan found this approach not only unacceptable but dishonest. First and foremost it presumed that both sides were equally committed to "parity," when to the Gipper it was blatantly obvious that the Soviets had been increasing their strategic advantage and growing it in ways that were inherently *destabilizing*. The construction of the SS-18 and SS-19 heavy missiles, for example, produced weapons specifically designed only to burrow into existing missile silos in a first strike. There was no other reasonable explanation for a design with singular massive warheads. Similarly, the deployment of the SS-20 mobile missiles, which could not even reach US soil, had the sole intent of de-linking America's European allies from the NATO alliance. Neither of these, in any conceivable scenario, contributed to the existence of parity or stability. Both pointed to Soviet aggressiveness and military expansion.

While putting the other pieces in place, Reagan had indicated his willingness to talk by sending veteran arms negotiator Paul Nitze to Geneva in 1982 to seek a compromise position on the SS-20s. Nitze proposed a plan to his counterpart, Yuli Kvitsinskiy, to meet informally and to find some interim agreement that would allow the US and its allies to forego placing the Pershing II missiles in Europe. Nitze did not understand this was far from what Reagan had in mind, and when he and Shultz reported back to Dutch on their progress in September 1982 Reagan finally got to say "*nyet*" to an arms deal. Nitze asked how he could go back with an even tougher deal, and Reagan said, "Well, Paul, you just tell them you're working for one tough son of a bitch."[24] He refused to pretend the SS-20s were anything but Soviet aggressiveness.

Reagan always wanted to tell the Soviets "nyet" to a bad arms deal, but the first opportunity he had to turn down such a deal came when his own negotiators exceeded their instructions.

The second reason Reagan thought the whole structure dishonest was that it continued to formalize and legitimize a fundamentally tyrannical and—in Reagan's view—evil communist regime. To not resist this, in Reagan's mind, was itself immoral.

It is important to understand that in 1981 Reagan was virtually alone in believing that the Soviets could be defeated. Robert Gates, deputy director of the CIA, said, "Reagan, nearly alone, truly believed in 1981 that the Soviet system was vulnerable, not in some vague, long-range historical sense but right then."[25] All of the strategy and policy options were thoroughly developed during the transition, and Reagan began implementing his vision immediately. He would fight the communists, to invoke Winston Churchill's phrases, "on the seas and oceans...on the beaches...in the fields...in the hills."[26] "Reagan's War," as Peter Schweizer put it, would be fought in the arena of religion, in the desert sands containing oil, in the heavens, and on the borders of Europe.

Of course, to the media, Reagan had no clue of what he was doing. A quick survey of headlines and comments will suffice:

- *Washington Post*: "100 Days and Still Groping for a Foreign Policy"
- *New York Times*: the administration has "set a record for confusion and contradiction in foreign policy"
- William Safire: Reagan was "embarrassingly unprepared on foreign policy"
- *National Review*: Reagan's policy in "disarray"[27]

In October 1981, Reagan signed the NSDD 13, in which he said, "We must be prepared to wage war successfully" for deterrence and must be able to deny the Soviet Union a military victory at *any* level of conflict.[28] But Reagan's real policy objective was established in NSDD 32, in April 1982, which stated that American policy was to "contain *and reverse* the expansion of Soviet control and military presence throughout the world.[29] It is worth noting that elements of Reagan's "rollback" plan were strongly opposed by Secretary of State Al Haig, Vice President George Bush, Chief of Staff James Baker, and Secretary of Commerce Malcolm Baldrige.[30] Achieving this rollback required ensuring access to space and the oceans, weakening the Soviet alliance system, and strengthening the US military. This would later be known as the "Reagan Doctrine"—or part of it—and its intention was not just to live with communism but to roll it back.

This was all Reagan. As Richard Pipes said, "I can attest that the direction of this policy was set by the president and not by his staff, and that it was vigorously implemented over the objections of several more dovish secretaries."[31] He set policy, Pipes noted, for "how we should think about our approach to the Soviet Union."[32] Bill Clark agreed: "The President played an extraordinarily active role" in drafting it, and "when it was done...the study and the decision were the President's."[33]

It is critical to step back at this point and remember that Reagan's loathing of nuclear weapons *and* communism, simultaneously, had not been a recent development. Contrary to many biographers' claims, it did *not* stem from Reagan's visit to NORAD in 1979, where he was told that when an incoming ICBM was tracked, "That's all we can do. We can't stop it."[34] According to the oft-repeated story, Reagan asked why, for all our military spending, we were helpless against an enemy missile attack. This supposedly propelled Reagan into his infatuation with SDI.

In fact, Reagan had called the Soviet Union "the most evil enemy that has ever faced mankind" in 1964, some twenty years before the "Evil Empire" speech.[35] Then, in 1967, as Governor, Reagan visited the Lawrence Radiation Laboratory in Livermore, California, at the invitation of Edward Teller.[36] At that time, Reagan received a briefing on the latest anti-missile capabilities, including the Sprint and Spartan, which relied on detonating their own nuclear warheads above the atmosphere to incinerate incoming ICBMs. Teller was certain Reagan had not heard of missile defense before, but Dutch asked "a dozen salient questions" and had "real interest in the subject."[37] Following the Teller meeting, as early as 1968, Reagan began arguing for the "development of effective defensive systems" against ballistic missiles.[38] His religious views supported his deep concerns about nuclear war. He accepted the biblical story of Armageddon and saw ICBMs as the instrument by which the end came.[39] Ed Meese recalled, "Almost as long as I have known him [Reagan] was very interested in some sort of defense against missiles."[40] Both Deaver and Weinberger observed Reagan had a commitment for a missile defense for a long time predating the NORAD visit.[41]

Nevertheless, he understood that as of 1981, he had limited options and the strategic arsenal had to be maintained. He also understood that in the short run, the most rapid way of responding to the Soviet threat was economic. The American economy had to be rebuilt, fast, and at the same time he had to kick the props out of the ailing communist structure.

First, Reagan intended to dry up Soviet funding. Fortunately, the United States had some control over the prices that the USSR could charge for its two most important exports: gold and natural gas. From Nixon's presidency to Carter's, the value of a sixty-pound gold ingot rose in retail value from $250,000 to $2.5 million, a tenfold increase that padded the account books of the USSR.[42] This was free money, made possible purely by the inflationist impulses of the West. Starting in 1981, though, gold prices dropped by almost 20 percent and then by 1984 fell again until prices stood at barely half of their record highs in 1980.[43] Soviet purchasing power abroad had been cut in half, merely by halting the rise of inflation, especially in the United States.

When it came to natural gas, Reagan meant to terminate, or at least slow down, the Europeans' participation in the Soviet natural gas pipeline.[44] This proved a thornier issue, as the United States did not have as much control in this arena. Struggling with high unemployment, the Western Europeans had reached a deal with the USSR to construct a 3,500-mile pipeline to deliver natural gas to seven countries of Western Europe. While initial construction income was lucrative, over the long term the pipeline meant that Europe's dependence on Soviet gas could rise by 20 percent.[45] Even worse from a strategic perspective, the USSR would generate $10 billion to $12 billion a year from the sale. At minimum the pipeline could provide another $6 billion a year to Soviet arms production.

Throughout early 1981, the Reagan administration battled the pipeline plan until, in September, the Europeans finally went ahead. French companies in particular had a number of contracts signed when François Mitterrand came into office. But even Britain's Margaret Thatcher supported the arrangement due to British firms' participation in the construction. "The question," she told the House of Commons, "is whether one very powerful nation can prevent existing contracts from being fulfilled; I think it is wrong to do that."[46] Reagan sympathized with the need for jobs on the part of the Europeans but knew, as Caspar Weinberger put it, "that what the Soviet Union needed…was hard currency [and] the construction of the pipeline would give them that."[47] On December 29, 1981, President Reagan prohibited direct involvement of US firms in the pipeline project. Coming at a time when the United States was struggling economically, this was a significant blow to companies such as Caterpillar Tractor, which lost a $90 million order, and General Electric, who saw its $175 million contract go up in smoke.

The European firms—many with US partners—had begun shipping, including Dresser Industries in France and John Brown, a turbine maker, in England. Nonaffiliated companies in Germany and Italy also began supplying the Soviets. Based on Reagan's order, the US had to issue "denial orders" to American companies involved, prohibiting them from further dealings with Europeans who had pipeline business. Soon, the denial orders created a firestorm, and Weinberger, Shultz, and Commerce Secretary Baldrige sprang into action to address the problem. To prevent John Brown from folding due to repercussions from the denial orders, Reagan approved a "clarification" that kept the British firm out of bankruptcy while the US negotiated a new arrangement. That came in February 1982, when Reagan issued NSDD 24 aimed at restricting or raising the costs of credits to Soviet-bloc countries. He also dispatched a team of negotiators to try to limit several European allies' sale of gas-related equipment to the USSR. Reagan expanded the sanctions further in NSDD 41. Needless to say, the Europeans, who had visions of Soviet petrodollars dancing in their heads, were none too keen on suddenly cutting ties to their newfound customers to the east. Mitterrand and the French were keenly aggrieved.

Shultz finally negotiated a revision under which the Europeans agreed to enforce stronger controls over strategically important goods, while restricting credits that subsidized the Soviets—which would also apply to US grain sales—in return for Reagan lifting his pipeline sanctions. In November, Reagan lifted the sanctions. In this negotiating process, the secretary of state learned that Ronald Reagan

> could be perfectly comfortable in taking a highly controversial and even unpopular position to bargain for other desired objectives.… a man ready to make trade-offs, a man who enjoyed and had a feel for the rhythm and timing of the bargaining process. This hard-line president combined a negotiator's instinct and common sense with tough views and staying power.[48]

At a cabinet meeting on June 18, 1982, almost all of Reagan's cabinet finally pressured him into concessions with the allies on the pipeline. Contrary to the view that Reagan was a puppet controlled by his advisors, Reagan finally stopped the discussion: "Well, they can have their damned pipeline," then looked around the table to the relieved members of the Establishment. But he then slammed his fist down on the table and added, "But not with American equipment and not with American technology."[49] Then he stood up and left.

The administration knew that the USSR was *already* facing declining energy production when Dutch took office. Reagan's very first executive order in January 1981 involved deregulating oil and gas, which in short order created a collapse in prices and a supply glut. This had an immediate effect on the USSR: in a June 1981 memo to the Council of Economic Advisers, Marshall Casse noted that the US embassy's Moscow expert on energy provided an outlook "for the next 20 years" which showed that the Soviets were facing "an energy shortage in the 1980s and probably the 1990s and know it." Moreover, the analyst "does not see clear evidence that new sources are being discovered and prepared fast enough to compensate for the decline in existing fields." He expected this would put "further strains" on the "faltering Soviet economy."[50] In other words, the Soviets were caught in a vise between Reagan's efforts to delay and derail the Trans-Siberian Pipeline (which they desperately needed to sell gas) and their own inability to produce enough oil.

The Gipper authorized "Farewell," a super-secret plan to "permit" the Soviets to steal certain technologies—which appeared genuine but were laced with catastrophic timers to cause them to fail down the road.

Others inside the National Security Council—Reagan's security advisory group that included the secretary of state, attorney general, defense secretary, CIA director, and others—were given full latitude by the president. They explored other ways to undermine the Soviet economy, including the super-secret "Farewell Dossier." It was the brainchild of staffer Gus Weiss, who had become aware of a Soviet spy program to steal American technology information. Through a defector named Vladimir Vetrov ("Farewell"), the CIA learned that the KGB had created a highly effective unit called Line-X to "plumb the R&D programs of Western nations." The Russians were essentially "running their research on that of the West, particularly the United States."[51] Casey and the NSC devised a plan to "intervene" and "supply some of these technologies and even add enticing new technologies to the shelf, but with a fatal catch: the technologies would appear genuine but later prove defective and destructive."[52] In 1982, Casey took Weiss's plan to Reagan, who was "enthusiastic" and immediately approved.[53] As Weiss noted in an article in the CIA journal *Studies in Intelligence*, "Reagan was the first president for whom this line of thought would have been even remotely acceptable."[54]

One of the key areas of focus in the sabotage was computers, a topic Reagan spoke little about yet which he intuitively knew was the key to winning the tech war. In NSDD 75, issued on January 17, 1983, Reagan struck at promoting change in the "internal system to reduce the power of the ruling elite." It stated that the United States would compete in "all international arenas…promote the process of change within the USSR, prevent technology transfer, and to avoid indirectly subsidizing the Soviet economy.[55]

None of this was lost on the Soviets. One former KGB official, Radomir Bogdanov, glumly admitted Reagan was "trying to destroy our economy," and in summer 1982, Soviet ambassador Anatoly Dobrynin quietly told William Clark, "You have declared war on us. Economic war." Clark, some twenty years later, admitted, "Yes, we had."[56] Even Reagan couldn't have hoped the "Farewell" program could have worked so magnificently. Just as he was giving in on the pipeline, at the other end—in Russia—products manufactured through Line X had started to arrive. Computer chips, turbines, plans for chemical plants, even aircraft designs were arriving. All were defective. Flawed software, programmed to fail at a designated time, brought about a massive explosion in the Trans-Siberian pipeline. This was described by former secretary of the Air Force Tom Reed as "the most monumental non-nuclear explosion," a blast estimated at three kilotons whose fires could be seen from space.[57] It cost the USSR hundreds of millions of dollars in lost revenue.

In its psychological impact, "Farewell" was paralyzing. The USSR now knew the technology it had been stealing was bogus…but which? As Reed explained, "Every cell of the Soviet technical leviathan might be infected. They had no way of knowing which equipment was sound."[58]

By November 1982, Reagan was tightening the screws across the board. He noted in NSDD 66 that the allies had all signed on to "key elements" of East-West trade, including an agreement not to sign new contracts for purchases of Soviet gas and a restriction on the sale or transfer of oil and gas equipment to the Soviets—all to be done before the Williamsburg Summit in May of 1983.[59] One of the CIA's senior economic warfare strategists, Henry Rowen, noted that the intent of this directive was to "cause such stress on the [Soviet] system that it will implode."[60] While the Europeans did not hold to their end of the agreements especially tightly, the strategy was still immensely successful, shrinking US high-tech exports to the USSR from 33 percent of all American exports to the Soviets in 1975 to a mere 5 percent in 1983. Meanwhile, American customs agents nabbed 1,400 illegal shipments ($200 million worth) headed to the heart of Russia.[61] In short, the Soviets couldn't buy Western technology and now they couldn't steal it, meaning they'd have to rely on their own invention—which had not proven too inspiring without Line-X to provide blueprints.

Having played the oil and pipeline cards, having built up American defenses, and having authorized the use of the "Farewell" catastrophic failure technologies, Reagan now employed the "God card." Reagan's faith had remained a constant, perhaps dipping only a little in his early Hollywood years. After surviving the attempt on his life, he trusted in God more than ever, telling people he believed he had been spared for a greater purpose. In his mind, that purpose was defeating Soviet communism.

In fighting the Soviet Union, Reagan was blessed with three key partners: Margaret Thatcher of Great Britain, Pope John Paul II, and Lech Wałęsa of the Solidarity movement in Poland.

In Karol Józef Wojtyła, Reagan found one of his staunchest allies. Elected by the College of Cardinals in 1978, Wojtyła became the first non-Italian to be elected pontiff since 1522 and the youngest in over a century. He chose the name John Paul II. A native Pole and the first pope from the Slavic East, John Paul knew well the oppression of communism, particularly under the heavy hand of the Soviets.[62] More than that, he was immensely popular in the West, with millions attending his sermons—his Mass in Manila brought between five and seven million people, and over half the population of Ireland turned out to hear him. John Paul's message did not fall on atheistic ears, especially in Poland, where over 90 percent of Poles at the time were still buried with Catholic rites, and where Sunday Mass was attended by over half of the population, even in the cities.[63] *Time* magazine admitted that attending Mass "became not only a religious act but a quiet sign of rebellion against the state."[64] Conservative and anti-communist, he shared with Reagan the fact that he had survived an attempt on his own life just two months after Hinckley tried to kill the president. The two men were a match made in heaven so to speak.

Increasingly directing his language to the "captured peoples" behind the Iron Curtain, the Gipper in particular began to address the Poles. Speaking before the AFL-CIO in April 1982, he warned of the communist government's attempts to control the new labor union in Poland: "You can take away their books, harass their priests, and smash their unions," he told the labor group, "[But] you can never destroy the love of God and freedom that burns in their hearts."[65] When Reagan visited Rome in June 1982, he and the pope met in the Vatican Library. A photo records the event with an almost mystical air, the pope bent over as in prayer, Reagan receiving the blessing. Each shared his near-death experience, and each noted to the other that they had been given "a spiritual mission," as Bill Clark called it, "a special role in the divine plan of life."[66] The pope shared Reagan's larger vision: it was more than about strengthening the new Solidarity movement in Poland—it was about liberating all of Eastern Europe.[67]

The pope and the president found the perfect leader in the person of Lech Wałęsa, a Polish labor activist who had been organizing boycotts of official rallies since the 1960s. Sporting a broad moustache, the charismatic Wałęsa organized illegal protests at the Gdańsk Shipyard that resulted in violent strikes that led to the deaths of more than thirty people. Fired from his job at the shipyard and constantly under communist surveillance, he continued his activism in the underground before leading a new strike committee that eventually became known as Solidarity. A rattled Polish communist government agreed to the Gdańsk Accord, giving Solidarity the right to exist and promising to reduce censorship. Almost instantly one million Poles left the communist party, suicides fell 30 percent, and drinking dropped substantially. An encouraged Gipper stoked the fires, saying in June 1981, "I think we are seeing the first, beginning cracks, the beginning of the end." Little did Dutch know that the Politburo was already contemplating letting Poland depart from the Warsaw Pact.[68] The Communist Party in Poland still thought it could stem the tide, however, and in 1981, General Wojciech Jaruzelski declared martial law and arrested Wałęsa and others.[69]

The pope had expressed his views, through Agostino Cardinal Casaroli, that change could not come in one country only, that "it would come at [the] same rate in all Eastern European countries."[70] Reagan may have nodded, but he had a bigger plan. Dutch intended to break the wall wherever he could and chose a more aggressive approach focused solidly on Poland.

He and John Paul II could do little for Wałęsa throughout this period except offer public moral support—but this again, in Reagan's case, was something no other president had done. Dutch was fomenting internal rebellion in a Soviet-dominated state, whereas Ike had backed off supporting the Hungarian Revolution and Nixon declined to support the Velvet Revolution. When martial law was imposed, Reagan saw Soviet fingerprints all over it and positively simmered. A December 21 NSC meeting saw Reagan at his best in a debate over Poland. Al Haig insisted the Soviets were "afraid to intervene because they know they can't hack it." He thought the USSR, instead, would ship food and otherwise try to bail out the Polish economy, but he did not think "that all is lost, that the Soviets are in charge, [or] that Solidarity is dead."[71] Haig warned, "If you slap on a full court press, then they can say to themselves they have nothing left to lose." Reagan disagreed. "That doesn't bother me at all. If we don't take action now, three or four years from now we'll have another situation.... I'm tired of looking backward." Vice President Bush urged Reagan to set the moral tone, saying "we are at an emotional turning point." Haig again raised the possibility of war over Poland, but Weinberger chimed in. While "the Soviets may take military actions against Poland…this is not world war."[72] Reagan concluded a combination carrot and stick approach would be best, for him to write Brezhnev a letter, reminding him of the stakes in Poland but offering continued trade. "Can he envision what it would be like if trade with the West were open?"

He sent the message to Brezhnev on the "hotline" on December 23, upbraiding him for intervening in what was clearly an "internal matter" and raising the Helsinki Accords, the 1975 Soviet-American agreement where each country pledged to observe human rights but also to respect the other nation's sovereignty. Brezhnev angrily responded that Americans could not "force their values" on the Polish people. These messages, of course, were hidden from the public eye, and it seemed to most observers that Reagan was doing very little. On the twenty-second, before the Brezhnev letter went out, Reagan had met with the Polish ambassador and his wife. They had defected when martial law was imposed and were impressed with the president's response. The ambassador urged Reagan to continue Radio Free Europe, then asked a special favor of the president—that he "light a candle and put it in the White House window tonight for the people of Poland." As Mike Deaver recalled, Reagan sprang up, went to the second floor, lit a candle, and put it in the dining room window.[73] When the ambassador and his wife departed, in what Deaver called "the most human picture" of Dutch's entire presidency, Reagan escorted them out into the rain, holding an umbrella over the ambassador's wife. She turned and wept on his shoulder.

President Reagan's symbolic and moral backing of Solidarity proved significant.

Wałęsa later praised him: "We stood on the two sides of the artificially erected wall. Solidarity broke down this wall from the Eastern side and on the Western side…. Your decisiveness and resolve were for us a hope." Reagan's backing "emboldened" and "encouraged" Wałęsa, and the Polish leader called Dutch an "inspiration."[74] Poland, according to biographer Brands, was Reagan's "first real test on foreign policy" that allowed him to "do what he always did best: state the case for freedom against those who would suppress it."[75]

In a remarkable, symbolic moment, Reagan walked the now-defected Polish ambassador and his wife through the rain to their waiting car. At the car door, Dutch held the umbrella over them as the ambassador's wife turned and wept on his shoulder.

Through Pope John Paul II, Lech Wałęsa, and Solidarity, Reagan perceived that Poland could be the crack in the East-bloc facade that he needed but that would take some prying for a while. He had one more ally to woo whose support would be crucial. But in the case of Margaret Thatcher, the courtship would require little effort at all.

Thatcher was the pre-Reagan Reagan. Coming to power in 1979, Thatcher was England's first female prime minister. Brezhnev called her the "Iron Lady" and she loved it. She was one of the first English politicians—and by far the most prominent—to have a grasp of Friedrich Hayek's free market theories, and she implemented them. Bringing the trade unions to heel, privatizing British industry, cutting taxes, and slashing regulation, Thatcher paved the policy path for Reagan to follow—although he needed no proof that his ideas would work. The British paid off 20 percent of their national debt, saw the number of stockholders rise fourfold, and chopped the top tax rate by half, resulting in rapid economic growth and the highest productivity in Europe for several years.[76]

When Thatcher saw the election results in November 1980, she was elated, describing the event as of "fundamental importance because it demonstrated that the United States, the greatest force for liberty that the world has known, was about to reassert a self-confident leadership in world affairs."[77] She regarded it as her "duty" to "reinforce and further President Reagan's bold strategy to win the Cold War."[78] Having met Reagan previously on two occasions, she knew he was a steadfast leader, but more—he was a soul mate. To the prime minister, Dutch not only advocated liberty and self-confidence, he embodied them. Reagan extended to Thatcher an invitation to be the first foreign head to visit America under his presidency, and when they met she found they agreed on almost every issue. Where they disagreed, she noted "there is no point in engaging in conflict with a friend when you are not going to win and the cost of losing may be the end of the friendship."[79]

Their friendship would be put to the test on two occasions, first when England sent a military expedition to reclaim the Falkland Islands from Argentina and again when the United States invaded the Caribbean Island of Grenada to oust Cubans who had begun building military installations there. Thatcher's grip on power, with her controversial and difficult free-market reorienting of the economy in its third year, was tenuous and her government was in danger of sinking. In stepped the Argentine government to throw her a lifeline.

Perhaps thinking Thatcher was preoccupied, in April 1982 the military junta running Argentina invaded the British territories of the Falkland Islands and South Georgia. Thatcher—and Britain—responded decisively and sent a naval task force to boot the Argentines out. Initially Reagan hoped to mediate between Britain and Argentina, a position the Iron Lady would not accept. She made it clear from the beginning that the United States would not be welcome as a mediator but "as a friend and ally."[80] Dutch knew in the end he would have to side with England and cited the NATO treaty in doing so. Reporters tried to paint the administration as uninformed of British actions. When he finally spoke to Parliament, Reagan stated his support for Great Britain unequivocally: British young men, he noted, "fight for a cause, for the belief that armed aggression cannot be allowed to succeed." The Gipper had deftly tied England's defense of a faraway island back to the Cold War.[81]

Arguably, the June victory came at a key moment for Thatcher, who found herself in a death struggle with Britain's unions. Victory not only bought her time, but public goodwill, and enhanced her international reputation. Now the Gipper had three powerful allies: one in politics; one in religion; and a union leader in a communist country.

It was fitting, then, that right after meeting with the pope, Reagan flew to England for a June 8, 1982, speech at Westminster. While many of Reagan's speeches rose to a level of greatness, the Westminster speech deftly and directly painted the Soviet Union as a massive failure and obstacle to human progress. He laid out a long-term program that would "leave Marxism-Leninism on the ash heap of history."[82] He observed that Karl Marx was right, that "we are witnessing a great revolutionary crisis.... But the crisis is happening not in the free, non-Marxist West, but...in the Soviet Union [which] runs against the tide of history." Item by item, Reagan ticked off the failures of the USSR: "A country which employs one-fifth its population in agriculture is unable to feed its own people," and "Overcentralized, with little or no incentives, year after year the Soviet system pours its best resource into the making of instruments of destruction." Whereas Jimmy Carter had used language of decline and failure to describe the United States, Reagan's Westminster speech described the Soviets in imagery of collapse with words such as "decay," "shrinkage," "crisis," "suffering," and "brutality." Then the Gipper also noted "there is a threat posed to human freedom by the enormous power of the modern state," indicating Reagan saw a potential threat looming that was even possibly greater than the USSR. He ended with a call for a "crusade for freedom that will engage the faith and fortitude of the next generation."

Liberals such as Lou Cannon, who was covering Reagan, couldn't believe their ears. Cannon described the speech as "wishful thinking, bordering on delusional."[83] Britons, on the other hand, were "reassured" by the speech and, as desired, the Soviets were rattled.[84] Some of the other European allies still needed persuading, but, of course, that's what Reagan was best at. In his first meetings with Helmut Schmidt, the German chancellor lectured him that "the West needs to be realistic regarding the possibilities for change in Eastern Europe."[85] He questioned the "organizational skills" of Poles and justified the communist regime's imposition of martial law. Canada's prime minister Pierre Trudeau announced his "impartiality" about what was going on in Eastern Europe and refused to support sanctions, while Norway fretted that Reagan might "exacerbate tensions"—the fallback excuse for doing nothing.[86]

Dutch was unmoved by his European colleagues' worries. It was America's responsibility, he told the North Atlantic Council, to nurture freedom abroad and not hoard it for itself.[87] In September 1982 he signed NSDD 54, which sought to encourage Eastern European nations to liberalize and reinforce their "pro-Western orientation." American policy would be "recalibrate[d]" to nations showing more independence from the USSR, which would involve debt rescheduling, International Monetary Fund membership, greater access to Western credit, and "Cultural and Educational Exchange and Informational Programs."[88]

According to NSC staffer Norman Bailey, in January 1983, Reagan officially put all the pieces together in a single document (NSDD 75) that outlined a fivefold strategy involving "economic, political, military, ideological, and moral" pillars.[89] In fact, however, there was a sixth element to Reagan's plan, one long overlooked by historians: a cultural pillar. His intuition told him we were already winning the culture war and that further effort could be decisive. He boosted spending for Voice of America/Radio Free Europe (VOA/RFE). According to Joseph Morris, a counsel for the agency overseeing VOA, there was a heated debate over whether the United States should be broadcasting rock and roll. Some thought the music itself lacked "class" and virtue and was "not representative of what the United States should be broadcasting." But others, according to Morris, said, "Hey fellas, wait a minute. This is precisely what we should be broadcasting." Rock and roll wasn't just a shiny object to attract the attention of the youth; it was, he noted, the *essence* of freedom. It was what America was all about, it was an entertainment genre that had been born and grown up without a dime of government support—it was truly "free market music."[90]

And so it was received on the other side of the Iron Curtain. Listeners huddled around shortwave radios in secret, picking up the broadcasts; they shared reel-to-reel tapes of rock, copying and recopying them; they purchased LPs for astonishing prices. One Romanian fan paid $150 in American dollars—a month's pay—for Simon & Garfunkel's *Parsley, Sage, Rosemary and Thyme* album. Soviet warlords knew how dangerous rock music was: spy Vasili Mitrokhin's smuggled notes revealed the anti-Soviet influence of music and warned that VOA/RFE broadcasts were producing "unhealthy signs of interest in...pop stars" and "almost surreal" levels of subversion in some Russian cities.[91] The Kremlin set up a government bureau, a Ministry of Rock, to co-opt and control it. Naturally, that failed.[92]

The music *was* the message seeping daily into the Soviet life. Kids there developed their own rock bands, copying the Americans. One rocker recalled hearing Bruce Springsteen's "Born in the USA" and remembered wanting to be...born in the USA. When Iron Maiden began its tour at Warsaw's Torwar Sports Hall, the crowd unfurled a massive "SOLIDARITY" banner, marking the complete fusion of rock and resistance to communism. Interestingly, though Poland was the symbolic center of the popular resistance to communism—and the country where Reagan placed most of his moral support—Hungary would be the place that first tasted freedom and was the "vanguard of rock liberalization."[93] Leslie Mándoki, a Hungarian rock drummer who escaped, later became a major German music producer who befriended Mikhail Gorbachev. When Gorbachev visited Mandoki's home after the Berlin Wall fell, he told Mandoki, "Rock music was fundamental to bringing down the Wall."[94]

Both Ron and Nancy were Beach Boys fans, a fact that would later surface during a dust-up involving Interior Secretary James Watt, but officially his musings on music were minimal. Other than his increased funding of VOA/RFE, Reagan never spoke much about the influence that America's music and pop culture were having. In retrospect, it was substantial and likely played a profound role in undermining the Soviets' ability to sustain long foreign wars, such as in Afghanistan.

Popularized in the book and film *Charlie Wilson's War*, the Afghan resistance received aid almost immediately under Reagan, who proclaimed "Afghanistan Day" on March 10, 1982.[95] "Every country and every people have a stake in the Afghan resistance," he announced, then signed it "in the year of our Lord nineteen hundred and eighty two."[96] A hard-drinking, womanizing Texas Democrat, Charles Wilson, through his powerful position on the House Appropriations Subcommittee on Defense (which funded the CIA), had begun increasing funding for the *mujahideen* sometime after 1980. Wilson was tenacious. His key contribution came in 1983 when he secured a $40 million dispensation to the freedom fighters that included anti-aircraft weapons. According to George Crile, who wrote *Charlie Wilson's War*, CIA officer Gust Avrakotos directly met with Wilson (which was contrary to CIA policy) and persuaded him to increase the budget even more. This took some doing in terms of changing policy, for the same people who told Reagan that trying to roll back communism in Eastern Europe was "destabilizing" similarly did not want the Afghans to actually defeat the Soviets—only bleed them out. That changed in March 1985 when Reagan signed NSDD 166, which changed the US objective in Afghanistan: it stated that the "ultimate goal of our policy is the removal of Soviet forces in Afghanistan," by improving "the military effectiveness of the Afghan resistance."[97]

Reagan had argued for arming the Afghan rebels with anti-aircraft missiles almost from the moment they were invaded, so supporting them was second nature.[98] While some aid arrived to the *mujahideen* quickly, the Stingers did not get into Afghan hands until June of 1986. Despite both Wilson's and Reagan's wrangling, the bureaucracy had dug its heels in, particularly at the CIA, where *even after presidential authorization*, Stingers were deliberately left out of a shipment.[99] Dutch emphatically told Bud McFarlane—by then national security advisor—"Do whatever you have to help the [Afghans] not only to survive but to *win*" (emphasis in original).[100] Bill Casey privately told one of his top lieutenants, "go out and kill me 10,000 Soviets until they give up."[101]

After that, money began flowing like milk and Bill Casey upped the ante whenever possible, including directing the killing of specific Soviet officers and even providing information on the residences of senior Soviet officers in Afghanistan to the *mujahideen*. Most of all, the money spigot was on, ultimately amounting to more than $2 billion—making it the largest covert action program in the history of the Agency. As one of the CIA agents on the ground recalled, "Whenever we needed another $20 million urgently...Charlie would find us $40 million." Arrival of substantial American cash combined with a remarkable secret alliance of Great Britain, Saudi Arabia, Israel, Egypt, China, and Pakistan enabled a stream of Soviet-made weapons (at first, so they couldn't be traced back to the US, until 1986 when Stingers began to arrive and the connection was hard to deny) to turn into a torrent of arms reaching the Afghan resistance. It marked the death knell of the Soviet invasion.[102]

Thus on every front, from supporting Solidarity to draining Soviet hard cash reserves to gaining the spiritual high ground to tapping into the desire of communist-bloc kids for freedom through rock music, Ronald Reagan mounted a frontal assault on the Soviet Empire. Like Grant, he advanced everywhere, simultaneously. "Those who can't skin, can hold a leg," instructed Grant to his generals. By 1983, the Gipper had the USSR set up to be skinned.

11

The Slog

Most modern presidencies have a period of euphoria, sometimes referred to as a "honeymoon," with Congress. Whether there is an actual period of congeniality and cooperation depends on the actual conditions under which the man assumed office. George W. Bush, entering by the slimmest of margins since Reconstruction, was viewed as illegitimate by the Democrats from the moment he entered the White House. "Selected, not elected" insisted Democrats after the US Supreme Court ordered vote recounts in Florida to stop, ensuring Bush won.[1] Reagan's successor, George H. W. Bush, and W's successor, Barack Obama, entered office with a great degree of support from both parties, with the losers viewing Bush's landslide warily and the Republicans seeking to avoid being labeled racist by opposing Obama.

At some point, though, most administrations settle down into the slog of battling over individual policies. In Reagan's case, the slog also involved riding out a deepening recession while Paul Volcker worked his inflation-squelching magic and the Gipper waited for the tax cuts to produce growth. Then the assassin's bullet hit, and though it removed Reagan from the fight for several weeks, it also bought him public sympathy and good will he may not have otherwise enjoyed. In short, it may have helped him through the slog.

Having shown he had the strength and grit to overcome John Hinckley's ricochet, Reagan had no sooner returned to active duty than he faced another crisis that would define his presidency. Oddly enough, it involved him going to war with one of the few unions who supported his candidacy: the Professional Air Traffic Controllers Organization, or PATCO. Founded in 1968, the 13,000-member union had labored under an increasingly creaky, outmoded system. And, naturally, PATCO sought the traditional union objectives of shorter hours and higher pay. Perhaps because the controllers had backed Reagan, perhaps because it was relatively early in his presidency, and perhaps because union officials thought that paralysis of the nation's air system would require a quick capitulation on the part of the administration, they called a strike on August 3, 1981. They thought they would be excluded from the prohibitions against government workers striking. They guessed wrong.

Like one of his heroes, Calvin Coolidge, who said "there is no right to strike against the public safety by anybody, anywhere, anytime," Reagan immediately declared the walkout a "peril to national safety" and ordered the controllers to return to their jobs. Only about 10 percent complied. On August 5, Reagan fired the rest. Two days later, Denis Prager of the Office of Science and Technology Policy provided a requested analysis of the strike to economic advisors Martin Anderson and Barbara Honegger in which he saw the strike as an "opportunity." Controllers had legitimate concerns about the nature of their job and its effects on health and longevity, as, historically, air traffic controllers were acutely affected by stress. However, PATCO had "shot itself in the foot" by focusing on money, for which "they have received little sympathy," and the president had the support of the public. Prager recommended that to address the health issues, Reagan create a task force on work conditions.[2] Reagan held fast. "I'm sorry, and I'm sorry for them," he said about firing the controllers. "I certainly take no joy out of this."[3] Reagan repeatedly reminded everyone that he led the first strike ever called by the Screen Actors Guild and that he was "maybe the first one ever to hold this office who is a lifetime member of the AFL-CIO"—but the private sector was not government.

Strikers were quickly replaced without any accidents or air incidents. There was some temporary pain: about half of the US flights were grounded, at a cost to the airlines of up to $10 million a day. PATCO badly misjudged the airlines themselves, seeing them as an ally and expecting the airlines to lobby Reagan. Within a week after replacements were hired, however, the major airlines had 75 percent of their planes back in the skies. United Airlines advertised, "United Airlines is still flying," and Delta Airlines trumpeted, "Delta is ready when you are."[4]

Transportation Secretary Drew Lewis recalled that the strike had "real national security implications," because without the controllers, American AWACS (Airborne Warning and Control System aircraft) couldn't go up.[5] Canadian flight controllers in Gander shut down in sympathy with their American counterparts. Lewis told the Canadian government that if Gander wasn't open in two hours, "the United States would never land there again.... 'They folded.'"[6] Reagan wrote in *An American Life* that the "members of PATCO were poorly served by their leaders [who] apparently thought I was bluffing."[7] While it took about two years to train a new crop of controllers, the administration discovered that the system had about six thousand more than it really needed to operate. Reagan had downsized government and the system "emerged safer and more efficient than ever."[8]

At the moment, it merely seemed like Reagan had handled a strike. But the decisiveness with which he confronted the first true national emergency he faced was noted internationally. Lewis observed "the Soviets and others in the world understood the implications of the strike" and referred to it as an "international event."[9] Ed Meese agreed, writing that "this action had a sobering effect on the Soviet leaders, who had become accustomed to seeing American Presidents back down before a serious challenge." Reagan's actions "convinced them that [he] was someone who had to be taken seriously."[10]

Many administration officials were convinced that Reagan's decisiveness in the PATCO strike had far-ranging effects abroad, especially on the Soviets, who knew he "was someone who had to be taken seriously."

Victory in the PATCO strike marked a noticeable peak in what for most presidents is a plateau of grinding daily work: endless speeches and public appearances, and a merry-go-round of meetings with foreign officials, trade groups, legislators, and friends with favors owed. As the Reagans settled into the presidential groove, a typical day began around 7:30 with a call from the White House operator. Ron and Nancy ate breakfast and read papers in bed—recall this was an age before the internet and iPads—or would turn on the morning news shows. Reagan always prepped for the day with his energy-boosting dose of bee pollen. Around 8:30 the president would head downstairs with a personal assistant and Secret Service guard, often met by his doctor, Daniel Ruge, who would do a quick health check.

Nancy recalled meetings staring at 9:00 a.m.; other members of the White House recalled Reagan getting security briefings long before that. A schedule of further meetings would fill the mornings after he met with the security team, along with more reading. Reagan had a light lunch on most days, and at any given time, the routine was interrupted by photo ops and urgent meetings with members of Congress. When possible, Dutch tried to leave the Oval Office by 5:00 p.m., and, especially after the assassination attempt, would work out before dinner. As often as not, evenings were consumed with formal/state dinners.

As in California, Reagan did not believe in staying at the office past 5:00 p.m., leading to charges he was lazy. *Newsweek* claimed "it is quite by design that he has chosen, in Cal[vin] Coolidge, a role model who slept eleven hours a day [and] took two-month vacations."[11] The schedule had nothing to do with energy and everything to do with attitude: Dutch simply believed that government should not consume every minute of a person's day, including the president's.

When they could, Ron and Nancy escaped to Camp David in Maryland, where they could ride. If there were no state dinners or other appointments, on Sunday nights Ron and Nancy—often with friends—would watch old movies. Camp David, of course, was always the fallback retreat: Rancho del Cielo was the ultimate getaway when it could be managed. Purchased in November 1974 for $527,000 just as Reagan was about to leave the governor's office, Rancho del Cielo ("Ranch in the Sky") was located north of Santa Barbara in the Santa Ynez Mountains. The 688-acre property was accessible only up a narrow, winding seven-mile road; the 1870s-vintage adobe house itself was somewhat underwhelming. It featured stables and corrals, and when the Reagans bought it, the property needed a lot of work. William ("Barney") Barrett, Reagan's driver as governor, helped the Gipper redesign the house itself, but more often than not Reagan personally cleared brush, painted fences, and otherwise rebuilt the ranch from the ground up. Outside the house, under the covered porch, was a table where Reagan signed arms-control agreements. Inside was his gun rack, from which he would select rifles to teach Mike to shoot when his son visited. Then there were the horses: with Ron and Nancy, riding was a requirement for a Secret Service agent.[12] Dutch truly loved physical labor and hard work—another factor that endeared him to the American public when photos of him in jeans with a chain saw began to circulate.

Four weeks after the assassination attempt, Reagan had returned to Congress to give an address. He was welcomed with a moving ovation from both sides of the aisle. Opening with comments about his brush with death and how the cards and letters poured in, he told of a child from New York who urged him to "get well quick" or "you might have to make a speech in your pajamas."[13] The Gipper, of course, used the occasion to lobby for more cuts and for a bipartisan passage of his ongoing economic program—still being resisted by the Democrats. In particular, they did not like his defense buildup. One item of interest may have escaped his congressional audience. Citing a successful mission by the latest space shuttle, he observed, "We tested our ingenuity once again, moving beyond the accomplishments of the past."[14] In July, after hosting Boll Weevil Democrats at a barbeque and making promises to a number of congressmen—including his future Afghanistan ally, Texas congressman Charlie Wilson (who said later he had been bought and would stay bought)—the House voted 238–195 for Reagan's budget, including the tax cuts. Forty-eight Democrats voted with the Gipper, as Tip O'Neill moaned, "I'm getting the shit whaled out of me."

Fortunes would turn, at least temporarily, for the "whaled" O'Neill. The focal point would be the budget deficit, especially the military's share in the shortfall. By the first half of 1982 the economy remained stalled: bankruptcies and foreclosures were high, there were warnings of bank runs, and even Alan Greenspan raised the specter of a 1929-style crash. America was still about two quarters away from turning things around: not until August would the Dow stabilize, and even then, unemployment hung on. Pollsters and pundits warned the Republicans were headed for big—possibly huge—losses in the House. Reagan's own approval numbers, so high after the assassination attempt, were eroding. He fought back against the media's "Reagan recession" mantra.

Without question the economy was languishing, and the media smelled blood in the water. CBS produced a documentary called *People Like Us*, narrated by Bill Moyers, providing heart-tugging stories of how Reagan's programs were creating suffering and hardship. The *New York Review of Books* chimed in, reporting "the stench of failure hangs over Ronald Reagan's White House."[15] Squeezing out inflation was every bit as painful as Reagan's team anticipated. Housing starts remained low, while business bankruptcies soared. Tip O'Neill crowed, "It's a shame that it takes the human tragedy of unemployment to show the Reagan economic nonsense for what it is."[16] Of course, O'Neill was giddy that the GNP was now falling at a rate of over 5 percent, and *Fortune* announced that investors were "terrified" by the tax cut.[17] Former treasury secretary W. Michael Blumenthal was "dismayed" by the big deficits, which, of course, hadn't bothered him when he was secretary.[18]

Stockman, whose purported loyalty to a "revolution" was always suspect, leaked damaging information to force a tax increase. Stockman saw himself as a perpetual revolutionary, yet his allegiances changed from his ultra-liberal early days to his supply-side conversion to, now, his recanting of supply-side doctrine. He seemed more interested in change for change's sake than in accomplishing a specific goal. By late 1981, when Reagan soberly concluded that the tax cuts would not offset the deficits, his response was to try to cut government further, not raise taxes. The Gipper reverted to his tried-and-true method of rousing the public: a national televised address, where he publicly gave up trying to overhaul Social Security after in May/June privately refusing to go along with Stockman's COLA increases. Instead, he called for a bipartisan commission under Alan Greenspan to make recommendations. Referring to a "number of threats" to the economy, Reagan told the public he would ask for another $57 billion in cuts, including abolishing the Departments of Energy and Education. Again, he urged the American people to lobby their representatives in Congress to "support them in making the hard decisions."[19] The Gipper's popularity sank.

Throughout late 1981 and early 1982, a civil war boiled inside Reagan's council of advisors. When Stockman first arrived in 1981, he thought Reagan was behind him in fomenting a massive revolution that would undo the New Deal, but after rebukes from the Gipper in the COLA increases, then when Dutch chose deficits over tax increases or more radical government funding, the budget director felt betrayed. At the same time, Weinberger at Defense thought Reagan was in his corner to expand the military. Various insiders lined up behind each. And at one time or another, each was right.

Both Weinberger and Stockman could be particularly manipulative, assaulting Reagan with multicolored charts, slanted statistics, and even, in Stockman's case, a phony "SAT test" that asked Dutch to choose from one of three spending levels on a range of fifty budget items. The "test" had as choices no cuts at all, moderate reductions, and draconian cuts. As any marketing psychologist will tell you, it's rigged: consumers almost always choose the middle option, as did Reagan. Stockman proudly noted his boss had flunked and increased the deficit by $800 million.[20]

These battles were unfortunately referred to by Richard Darman as "the struggle for the president's mind."[21] For biographers such as Lou Cannon, who believed Reagan was malleable all the time, this fit the mold. All of Reagan's important decisions were solely based on who had the cleverest presentation or who caught him at the right time. Reagan, Cannon insisted, was "poor at doing his homework," an utterly absurd comment given how much constant reading the president did, and one that does not line up with what insiders such as Shultz said about Dutch's preparation.[22] The fact was that no one, not even the supposedly brilliant Carter, could begin to keep up with the titanic stacks of information the agencies of the US government could churn out on a daily basis. Those who saw Dutch in action, up close, knew he was both studious and instinctive. George Shultz constantly was impressed with Reagan's "extensive preparatory effort" and his vision that always was well beyond that of his cabinet.[23] German chancellor Helmut Schmidt found in 1981 that Reagan understood arms control perfectly, and better than any of his predecessors.[24]

Reagan's system, honed by William Clark's "mini-memos," boiled down the voluminous Washingtonese into understandable essentials upon which the Gipper (or anyone else who read them) could formulate a decision.[25] Reagan's cabinet came to be in awe of him and his abilities to cut to the key issues, especially when it came to bringing the Soviets to heel in negotiations.

Yet within the cabinet, different forces tugged at the Gipper, usually in some way coming down to one person: Stockman. Shultz later complained that the thin-nosed, bespectacled Stockman was a "master of illusion" with "an encyclopedic knowledge of the budget" and "intellectual nimbleness" inclined to "displays of intellectual exhibitionism" who wanted to be viewed as Reagan's brain (a role later ascribed to Karl Rove in George W. Bush's administration).[26] Phil Gramm of Texas, a Democratic congressman who later switched parties to become a Republican senator, called Stockman the "smartest member of Congress." Stockman had actually turned down another cabinet position so he could head OMB, which was peculiar to say the least. Steven Hayward would call Stockman a "disastrous" appointment, the equivalent of "the Robert McNamara of the Reagan administration."[27] At the time, however, Stockman was portrayed as the boy genius of the Reaganites and targeted by *Newsweek* with a cover headline trumpeting, "Cut, Slash, Chop." Nevertheless, even as the administration basked in the glow of its first budget victories, Stockman warned his numbers showed they could not get to a balanced budget by 1986, when the deficit would reach $110 billion. Reagan's team could never get to a balanced budget with the existing level of congressional spending.

Aside from rejecting his fruitless attempt to reform Social Security, the Gipper stood behind Stockman on domestic issues, but he separated from him on defense. Stockman stewed over the fact that he could not force the president to chop the defense budget and increasingly saw Weinberger as his main competitor for the heart and soul of Ronald Reagan. (In time, Shultz would come to the same conclusion, albeit in a different arena.)

From 1980 to 1989, in real dollars, the military budget rose 50 percent, but those numbers were always murky. Depending on who was using them, they might include NASA budgets or other nonmilitary items. Whoever was torturing the numbers had great latitude in making them confess to whatever story was needed at the time. Yet Stockman persisted trying to reduce the size of government, presenting cuts of $100 million in other departments, which Reagan knew wouldn't fly. Dutch joked that Stockman had support, adding, "We won't leave you out there alone, Dave. We'll all come to the hanging."[28]

The notion of an "unprepared" Reagan who didn't do the background work was strongly disputed by his cabinet secretaries, who were always impressed at his understanding of the issues.

Meanwhile, Congress, finding itself at loggerheads, gave up on passing a budget and instead passed a continuing resolution in November 1981 that would fund the government at then-current levels until a budget compromise could be reached. That calm lasted only a month, when, in December 1981, David Stockman's interviews with *Washington Post* editor William Greider were published in an *Atlantic Monthly* article called "The Education of David Stockman."[29] Stockman had been blabbing to Greider for months at the Hay-Adams Hotel, starting immediately after Reagan rebuked his sharp cuts to Social Security. Stockman told Greider that the administration's policies would create large deficits and that he had used his prestidigitation at the Office of Management and Budget to conceal that fact. Of course, as shown in the administration's own internal documents, deficits were *always* projected and were *always* included in public budget presentations.

Later, in a memoir, Stockman claimed never to have been the "revolutionary" focused on rolling back the New Deal and instead portrayed himself as a traditional budget hawk. Much of this reflected his relationship with Greider; some was the result of bitterness at his plans being subordinated to larger realities. Whichever it was, by then his hatred for Reagan surfaced: "I considered him a cranky obscurantist whose political base was barnacled with every kook and fringe group that inhabited the vast deep of American politics."[30] Reagan embraced a "primitive, right-wing conservatism" and condescendingly referred to his speeches as "The Scrolls."[31] Not surprisingly, even many liberals couldn't stand Stockman. Senator Pat Moynihan, referring back to Stockman's college leftist-radical days, observed that "one day he arrives at Harvard preaching the infallibility of Ho Chi Minh [then] he turns up in Washington proclaiming the immutability of the Laffer Curve."[32] Many who came in contact with Stockman early on saw a man who was unstable, reckless, and untrustworthy, although Martin Anderson praised him as a "superb leader for OMB."[33]

In his new capacity as turncoat, Stockman insisted he never believed "just cutting taxes alone would cause output and employment to expand." Of course, as *all* the administration's internal documents presented earlier reveal, *neither Reagan nor his team ever made that argument* and in fact repeatedly make the exact opposite claim: that the program depended on four major elements, of which tax cuts were only one. Any scholar who has looked at the Reagan program has had the same takeaway. William Niskanen's subsequent book, *Reaganomics*, listed four major program objectives: tax relief, budget cutting, regulatory reform, and monetary tightening.[34] Michael Boskin's *Reagan and the Economy* identified six objectives, but they boil down to essentially the same four pillars.[35] But Stockman bought into the bogus "trickle down" criticism, telling Greider the tax plan was a "Trojan horse to bring down the top rate."[36] Liberal attackers in the media positively slobbered over Stockman's betrayal, including commentary on *CBS Evening News* and a story in the *New York Times*.

Nancy blew up when she read the piece. She demanded Dutch fire the traitor, and Meese agreed with her. Stockman's recollection of his face-to-face with Reagan after the story surfaced claimed Reagan was deeply hurt and asked how he could do that to him. As Stockman wrote, he offered his resignation, but Reagan said, "No, Dave, that's not what I want," and turned away. The president still needed him. But just as Stockman thought he had emerged unscathed, Reagan turned back and added: "Oh, the fellas think this is getting out of hand. They want you to write up a statement explaining all this and go before the press tomorrow afternoon."[37]

In the first place, no one—in the short term—knew the numbers as well as Stockman. Thus the appearance of keeping Stockman, as Steven Hayward points out, was "a shrewd political move" that suggested that perhaps there was nothing to Stockman's confessions. But Dutch himself later admitted he made a mistake by retaining the OMB director. It kept a subordinate on who no longer believed in the program and had the potential to do exceptional damage. Stockman remained at his post until 1985—by which time the recovery that he predicted couldn't occur was taking place.

From late 1981 through 1982, a full-blown debate raged about whether Reagan had oversold the *deficits*, not the tax cuts, and whether deficits were in fact as harmful as Dutch had claimed during the campaign. One of the Council of Economic Advisers, William Niskanen, delivered a paper in December 1981 arguing that inflation was not necessarily driven by deficits. At the time, Reagan had to disavow that, but Niskanen would be proven right.[38] Certainly at that point, a 5 percent tax cut wasn't going to turn any inflationary tide. What was working was Paul Volcker's tight money program, which had started to squeeze inflation. But Reagan's deregulation of gas and oil had also played a part. Once prices could attain their market level, they stabilized, then more production kicked in, and prices fell.

It is worth noting at this point that different factions, both within and outside the administration, favored different policy approaches and could agree for wildly different reasons. By and large, Reagan and his supply-side core wanted economic growth stemming from new investment and a sounder dollar. If deficits in the short term were the price for that growth, so be it. For them, tax increases were the last resort, for they would destroy confidence and investment. For many Washington traditionalists of both parties, a balanced budget was the golden chalice and was to be gained through tax hikes if necessary. They believed that Wall Street reacted to deficits, and that deficits would dry up investment. Some conservatives lobbied for tax increases for a totally different reason: Americans, they thought, would respond to tax hikes by demanding smaller government (which of course Reagan also wanted). Then there were no small number of venal Democrats, including O'Neill, who *knew* tax increases would throttle the Reagan program and were perfectly willing to tolerate high unemployment to win elections and get the Gipper out.

Assaulted from all sides by Wall Street budget hawks and less well-intentioned Democrats to give in to a tax hike, Reagan began to acknowledge that deficits were forcing the inevitable tax increase. He wrote on December 8, "We who were going to balance the budget face the biggest budget deficits ever," though, he noted, they would be "smaller in relation to G.N.P."[39] Two days later he recorded, after he rejected tax increases in a discussion with the Council of Economic Advisers, "Tax increases don't eliminate deficits and they increase govt. spending."[40] On the eighteenth, he confided in his diary, Senate leaders "are beginning to panic on taxes. They want us to raise or impose new ones. I'm resisting. D–n it our program will work & it's based on reduced taxes."[41] (Reagan never wrote out swear words in his *Diaries*.) Four days later, in yet another budget meeting, he recorded, "We've finally come together on the cuts—probably won't get all we ask for from Congress....The recession has worsened."[42] And so on.

By early January 1982 Republican House leaders were back "h–l bent on new taxes and cutting the defense budget."[43] Ten days later he "told our guys I couldn't go for tax increases [and that] I'd rather be criticized for a deficit than for backing away from our Ec[onomic] program."[44] After more negotiations, Reagan glumly concluded, the "Dems are playing games," and "it looks like the three weeks of budget talks got nowhere."[45] At one point, majority leader Jim Wright offered big spending cuts if Reagan would dump the third year of the tax cuts. Reagan snapped, "You can get me to crap a pineapple...but you can't get me to crap a cactus."[46]

Hayward claims Reagan was constantly negotiating, with his diary entries doctored to show he was "maneuvering for an advantage." By late 1982, when the Senate Republicans finally abandoned him, though, he had to acquiesce to a new tax increase outside of income taxes designed by Bob Dole, who was in the process becoming a hero to the media. Having cut taxes just a year and a half earlier, Reagan was now consigned to having to raise them. The tax increase, Reagan wrote, "is the price we have to pay to get the budget cuts."[47] He promptly vetoed a Democrat spending bill, and his veto was overridden with fifty-one timid Republicans voting with the

Democrats. It was his first veto override. If the Gipper ever believed Democrats when they promised spending cuts for tax increases, he now had his first lesson in their treachery.

Monetary growth constituted another arena, however, where the economic battles played out. When Dutch met with the chairman of the Fed only three days after he took office, Reagan stunned Volcker with a question that many Americans routinely had asked: "Why do we need a Federal Reserve?" He phrased it as though constituents had asked, but it was a shot across the bow that demonstrated that even the Fed wasn't immune to reforms—or possibly an audit. With his question the Gipper subtly made clear to Volcker he expected him to play ball.[48] Perhaps the Fed chairman—who was known to White House staffers as "Tall Paul" because of his 6' 7" frame—didn't need much prompting, as, after a new spurt of inflation in early 1981, Volcker tightened the money supply severely, knocking monetary growth to almost zero. Reagan understood what Volcker was up to and told editors that a consistent monetary policy was necessary—that the United States could not afford the "roller coaster effect" of previous years.[49] What neither Volcker nor anyone in Reagan's administration could predict, though, was that as Volcker clamped down on the money supply, the velocity of money would fall as well, causing overall inflation to decline faster than anyone thought possible—including Tall Paul.

Supply-siders beamed. In theory, this was precisely what was supposed to occur, as the value of holding financial assets—of investing in America—rose. Money shifted out of commodities such as gold and art and into companies. Yet nothing happened immediately and within months, the country drifted even deeper into recession as the money supply dried up. The tax cuts stimulated growth, but reining in inflation lowered the supply of money. Although the two elements ultimately worked together (leaving Americans, after 1983, with more dollars and more real value), in the interim, the recession took its toll on many Americans. Congress was trying to impeach...Volcker! But monetarists such as economist Milton Friedman backed Reagan and the Fed chief, and although most of Reagan's staff thought Volcker "is killing us" (as James Baker said) or was going to cost

Reagan reelection, intuitively the Gipper knew he was on the right track and intended to hold fast.

Only a few months earlier, O'Neill thought Reagan was beating him badly. Now he sensed a rebirth. He could bash Reagan for both deficits and stagnation, for both "draconian" cuts and for overspending, initiating a strategy that the *Baltimore Sun* called "aggressive victimology."[50] This technique involved rolling out a designated victim for whatever story the Democrats were pitching. If it was Reagan's "war" on Social Security, an elderly woman would be brought out in a wheelchair. For the CBS story "Hunger in America Is Back," the channel aired interviews with poor people alongside images of bread lines (even as some 22 million were receiving food stamps). Haynes Johnson at the *Washington Post* called supply-side ideas "old selfishness dressed up in new garb for the 1980s."[51]

The dirty little secret concealed by the media's relentless attacks was that social spending *grew* under Reagan. This was largely due to a trick legislators used called "baseline budgeting," where every year legislators presume the agency in question should start its next fiscal year from its existing baseline budget and work upward from there. It was (and remains) an outrageous process by which agencies never have to justify their *current* levels of expenditures and builds in more government growth automatically into the system.

Despite claims of "heartlessness" by the administration, social spending actually increased under Reagan.

Defense spending also increased, though proportionately nothing like what critics said. Relying on Caspar Weinberger, Reagan had asked for a significant military buildup in his 1981 budget: forty-eight antisubmarine aircraft (up thirty-four from Carter's budget), increasing tank production from thirty per month to ninety per month by 1985 and the number of attack helicopters from fifty-eight to more than 1,400 by 1984.[52] Most significantly, the administration was committed to building a 600-ship navy with fifteen carrier groups (up from twelve under Carter).[53] "Cap the Knife," as he had been known in Sacramento as Reagan's budget chief, suddenly appeared to be spending like a drunken sailor. Naturally, the media rushed to attack, with CBS News running a five-part hit piece documentary called *The Defense of the United States*. Typically, reports insisted defense spending would destroy the economy. Yet even with Cap's increases, the US was spending a smaller portion of its GNP on the military than it had done in the early 1960s. At that point Reagan had given in to cuts, though he justified it as "convinc[ing] the money mkt [sic] that we mean it" (i.e., balancing the budget) and "that means some cuts in defense."[54]

Lost in the slog was the fact that the administration had chopped federal regulations by about a third and brought far fewer antitrust suits, ending an era of excess litigiousness and resolving two large pending cases, AT&T and IBM. Against the advice of George Gilder, the government broke up AT&T into regional "Baby Bells" and lowered long-distance rates while allowing local rates to rise some. The case allowed new telephone service companies to grow, eventually providing more serious competition to AT&T. In 1982, the administration ended the IBM predatory pricing lawsuit, which caused the price of mainframes to fall as a host of new computing firms were providing genuine alternatives to IBM's products even with the "predatory pricing." But the Justice Department had less success in rolling back affirmative action, making only minor headway in a handful of cases. The more controversial AT&T and IBM cases were overshadowed by a tiff over Bob Jones University's policies of prohibiting interracial dating. After the US Supreme Court's ruling against Bob Jones, which the Reagan Justice Department had originally supported, then backed away from, Reagan quipped that the "right hand doesn't know what the far right hand is doing" sometimes.

Meanwhile—as it was poised to do without the tax hikes—the economy slowly started to recover. Reagan was right all along: if given time, the tax cuts and monetary restraint would produce prosperity. No tax hikes were needed. But the recovery did not arrive in time to save the Republicans in the 1982 elections. They lost twenty-six seats. Reagan expected this; he had known that at least a year of hardship would be needed to purge inflation and to allow America's economic engine to restart. Scholars found the elections in line with past performances for midterm congressional elections, and one professor said in perspective that it might be viewed as a "kind of political victory for Reagan."[55]

Unemployment finally began to fall while inflation fell faster, down to 5 percent by the end of 1981. Interest rates persisted somewhat longer, possibly because Volcker had kept rates unreasonably high to choke out inflation more quickly. This, of course, brought new calls for Reagan to dump Volcker, which he refused to do. As usual, liberal writers such as Lou Cannon and William Greider sought psychological motives to explain Reagan's unwillingness to relieve the Fed chairman. In their goofy interpretation, keeping the Fed chairman allowed Reagan to present Volcker as an "austere figure" who contrasted with the "generous king" in the person of himself.[56] A better question would be: Why would Dutch even want to meddle with Volcker's obviously successful program? The stock market was beginning to creep upward, factories were reopening, and gas prices were falling. Indeed, the press found itself with a problem: the "Reagan recession" had given way to the "Reagan recovery." Or as the Gipper himself joked, "The best sign that our economic program is working is that they don't call it Reaganomics anymore."[57]

Indeed, almost everything Reagan promised—except a balanced budget—came true. And that took liberals totally by surprise. Liberals hustled to provide statistics that would dampen the positive glow by noting the slower rate of growth in private wealth (though, interestingly, liberals would whine about a "decade of greed"), a declining value of the dollar, and unfavorable shifts in trade.[58] "The Declining Middle," moaned *Atlantic Monthly*. "The Disappearance of the Middle Class," complained the *New York Times*. They were right: based on real dollars, the middle class would shrink by five points from 1980 to 1990—except that the people moving *up* into the next highest wealth bracket accounted for all that change![59]

Almost always included in the criticism were the country's higher deficits and rising national debt. Yet George Gilder had already developed an interesting case in *Wealth and Poverty* about inflation and debt levels based on a market basket of goods going back to the 1400s. Inflation, it seems, periodically has giant bursts every 150 or so years, largely associated with major changes in human social organization. These included the commercial revolution in the 1400s, then the industrial revolution in the late 1700s. Another of these revolutionary growth spurts, which began in the 1970s and early 1980s, seems associated with the creation and rise of the computing industry. While rapidly escalating prices are a danger, these twenty- to thirty-year explosions seem more closely tied to inventive and innovative breakthroughs.[60] Citing research from Henry Phelps-Brown and Sheila Hopkins, Gilder observed that traditional prices failed to account for the changing "market basket of goods" and that fundamental shifts in what was measured by the goods were not always easily captured. And Reagan, without commenting on it extensively, found himself right in the middle of one of those explosions in the computer revolution.

Fantastic shifts in communications, through the introduction of cellular telephones, were already occurring thanks to computer chips. Steve Jobs and Steve Wozniak had created the first personal computer (PC), the Apple, in 1976, and founded the company of the same name in 1977. IBM released its first PC in 1981; just a year later, the home computer was named the "Machine of the Year" (instead of "Person") by *Time* magazine. By 1983, some ten million computers were in use in the United States; by 1986, that number was thirty million; and when Reagan left office, it was more than forty-five million. Computers were fundamentally reorganizing American life by the end of the Reagan years, and the potential, while obvious in some cases, was usually vastly underestimated.[61] However, whereas it was perhaps reasonable to think in the 1980s that the titanic shifts brought about by computers could "swap out" jobs in the industrial sector (and while undeniably growth occurred and productivity soared), no such direct exchange of labor occurred. Seen in the context of Reagan's willingness to engage in free trade, some decisions made in the 1980s (that will be addressed within subsequent chapters dealing with the Canada-United States Free Trade Agreement and Dutch's unwillingness to employ tariffs) simply did not pan out over time, despite the expectations of almost all involved.

Then, as now, ordinary Americans did not seem to fret as much about deficits as they did about weekly paychecks, and, from that perspective, "Reaganomics" was a home run. And, as often happens, ordinary people know what is occurring in their own lives without any help from the media.

During this period, news coverage of "Reaganomics" was overwhelmingly negative. Even *Time* magazine admitted that CBS, in particular, had been overly "antagonistic" (Reagan called it "a deliberate campaign" in his diary—which it was). It didn't matter. By late 1982, retail sales started rising and auto companies began recalling workers. Overall, the economy showed an 8.7 percent annual growth as early as the second quarter, and business investment—the key to supply side—rose almost as fast. Some forecasts had 1983 down for a 5 percent decline; instead, over the next twelve months private sector investment would shoot up over 23 percent. Dutch's approval numbers, once in the mid-30s, rose back over 50 percent.

In under two years, Ronald Reagan had survived the assassin's bullet, a major strike, the betrayal of a trusted confidant, and a solid year of haggling with the Democrats and the press. He was still standing, and was getting ready to take on an opponent more dangerous than Tip O'Neill.

12

Defeated, You Will Be!

Just as Reagan hitched up his pants for the main combat with the Soviet Union, he had a housekeeping duty to attend to.

In June 1982, drama king Al Haig had threatened to resign—again. This time, Reagan accepted.

Haig first pulled his resignation stunt on March 24, 1981. "Frankly," Dutch wrote in his diary, "I think he's seeing things that aren't there."[1] On other occasions, Haig made similar threats; then, in November, he called Reagan concerned about a Jack Anderson column saying he was about to be fired. Again, Dutch talked him off the ledge.

Haig knew Maggie Thatcher supported his opposition to the pipeline embargo and played that up. She complained about lifting the grain embargo—which helped American farmers—while pressing for an extension of the embargo on European firms building components for the pipeline. There was "a certain lack of symmetry," she told Haig. "Anything the West did must be designed to harm the Soviet Union more than ourselves."[2] Other Europeans were simmering about the pipeline pressures, yet Reagan thought he could persuade them on a trip to the G7 conference in June 1982. Dutch saw Haig up close on that trip as the secretary fumed about his quarters on Air Force One, resented the fact that Deaver always kept him from meeting with Reagan one-on-one, and quarreled constantly with Bill Clark.

Haig also had a talent for overstepping his rank, first by making the "I'm in control" comment during the assassination attempt, then by mistakenly standing in a receiving line at 10 Downing Street only to be personally admonished by Lady Thatcher. On June 14, after he and Clark engaged in new warfare over the Middle East upon returning from the G7 trip, Reagan called him into the Oval Office. The president upbraided Haig for sending instructions to Special Envoy Philip Habib outside of channels. Again, Haig offered to resign, but Reagan thought the two had an agreement to make it official after the election in November. Four days later, Clark and Weinberger presented Reagan with an NSC paper urging a strong stance on the pipeline. Some biographers argued the Gipper endorsed the position merely to "send Al Haig packing," but that seems unlikely. Reagan could have had his resignation anytime. He was in much the same position as Lincoln in 1862 when he held the resignations of all his cabinet members after they plotted a near coup against him.

At any rate, Haig was gone for the accumulation of sins, particularly the Habib communication. On Friday, June 25, 1982, Reagan wrote, "Today was the day—I told Al H. I had decided to accept his resignation then told the press." Indeed, the media was notified before either the Soviets or our allies were told via diplomatic channels. Although Reagan concluded his June 25 entry with "This has been a heavy load," one gets the sense that he was immensely relieved to have dumped Haig for George Shultz.[3]

In Shultz, Reagan had a true Establishment bureaucrat and, in twenty-first-century parlance, a "Swamp Creature." Schultz had served as secretary of the treasury under Nixon. Indeed, when the call came from the president, Shultz expected to be offered the Treasury slot. A globalist, and more of a liberal than Haig, Shultz ironically proved to be far more effective than his predecessor. For one thing, he didn't crave the spotlight, nor did he constantly want more power—though he did want the turf that was rightfully his, and he battled Judge Clark to get it. Shultz also could present less hard-line positions without offending Reagan, who knew exactly where he stood. He had also been a labor mediator and had swum in the same union waters Dutch had. Yet for all his perceived liberalism, Shultz did not entertain any notions of moral equivalency between the US and the Soviets.

Dutch had already allowed National Security Advisor Clark access to him after Clark replaced Richard Allen at the end of 1981, which made the entire decision-making process run much more smoothly. Clark could channel Reagan, knowing what he wanted without the president saying a word, and he widened the trio of close advisors who met regularly. Clark also insisted that every step be documented in the National Security Decision Directives (NSDDs). The result, as Martin Anderson put it, was "pure Reagan."[4]

By early 1983, the foreign policy team was closely watching Poland, the pipeline negotiations, Afghanistan, and, closer to home, developments in El Salvador and Nicaragua. There, Cuban and Soviet influence had produced insurgencies against thuggish governments that threatened to move communism onto the Central American mainland. In El Salvador, for example, the reigning military junta turned a blind eye to allied death squads that had killed a Catholic bishop, some nuns, and a relief worker. Unfortunately, the other side was comprised of leftist guerillas of equally murderous nature. Although the United States put in a handful of military advisors (fifty-five) and a small amount of aid ($2.5 million), any further assistance would have been portrayed as "another Vietnam"—precisely the phrasing Walter Cronkite used in a March 1981 interview.

An even worse situation was developing in Nicaragua, where the Marxist president Daniel Ortega—who worshiped Fidel Castro and Che Guevara—flatly proclaimed himself an anti-imperialist who looked admiringly at the USSR as the epitome of world progress.[5] But the administration did not "push" the Ortegas toward Marxism: they were full-blown radicals by the time the US even got involved.

As early as March 1981 Reagan had given approval to the CIA to stop Soviet arms shipments to El Salvador. Shortly thereafter the CIA came to him with a plan to assist resistance groups in Nicaragua. The request unsettled him because of the complex nature of the situation. Dutch wanted to support the anti-communist rebels but lacked the political support to do so overtly. He sought to offer covert aid—a measure soon nullified by the Boland Amendment. With images of Vietnam still fresh, Reagan wished to avoid direct involvement; the US could not expect to significantly affect the political situation in either El Salvador or Nicaragua by moral suasion or "nonmilitary" assistance. The group opposing the Ortega regime in Nicaragua, the "Contras," was too small in number to affect an overthrow, even with US aid, which became more problematic in December 1982 when the Democrats, trying to preemptively block Reagan from covert action in Nicaragua, passed the Boland Amendment (named for Massachusetts Democrat Edward Boland). Based on an amendment to the FY83 military budget that prohibited American support that had the "purpose of overthrowing the Government of Nicaragua," the amendment seemed to end any direct US involvement there. Astonishingly, though, the administration jumped behind the amendment, which passed the House unanimously—as Hayward noted, "the first sign of policy muddle."[6] Dutch's team thought it saw loopholes.

In evaluating Reagan's intervention in Latin America, it must be understood that in such civil wars—ideology aside—there are rarely any "good guys." Both sides in El Salvador and Nicaragua engaged in shocking brutality, and both sides had their versions of death squads. For that reason, *failing* to pick a side out of moral concerns—a Carteresque approach—was not an option. Reagan hoped to keep the lid on the Central American pot long enough to kick the props out from under the legs of Ortegas' patrons in the USSR. Without Soviet money, he reasoned, the Central American Marxists would either dry up or at the very least be forced to moderate.

Meanwhile, George Shultz had his hands full with another issue: the ever-boiling cauldron of the Middle East. Another conflict erupted there in June 1982 when upheaval in the Lebanese government allowed the Palestinian Liberation Army—the military wing of the PLO—to get a foothold in southern Lebanon as a staging ground for attacks against Israel. At the order of Prime Minister Menachem Begin, the Israel Defense Forces (IDF) entered Lebanon on June 6, swept the border of enemy forces, and then— to the shock of the administration—pressed on to Beirut. Ostensibly the IDF were after gunmen from the Abu Nidal terror organization who had tried to assassinate Israel's ambassador to England, but in practice this was a full-scale invasion.

Although Dutch liked almost everyone and even got along personally with his political rival Tip O'Neill, he did not care for the diminutive Begin and had little leverage with him. Making matters worse, the situation in Lebanon featured close to a half-dozen competing factions, including the Druze Christians, the Maronite Lebanese, the Lebanese Muslims, the PLO (a separate entity), the Israelis, and whatever remained of the "official" Lebanese military, not to mention a dozen individual militias sworn to particular leaders. Israel besieged Beirut, expelled the PLO, and ended Syrian control over the Lebanese government, supporting the newly installed Christian and pro-Israeli Lebanese government led by Bachir Gemayel. All might have been fine, except that Gemayel was assassinated in September 1982. In retaliation, the Lebanese Christian militias initiated attacks on Palestinian and Muslim groups. The IDF was not above allowing some of their allies in the area to have a free hand in zones they purportedly controlled, leading to the massacres of Palestinians and Shiites at Sabra and Shatila. Outraged international voices insisted the Israelis had permitted the slaughter, and the Begin government was forced to withdraw, leaving Lebanon to disintegrate into multi-factional civil war.

As a condition of the Israeli withdrawal from Lebanon, the United Nations was requested to provide a multinational "peacekeeping" force, which the United States agreed to. It included eight hundred American Marines put on the ground in August 1982. Hidden by the chaos was a very important fact. Before the IDF pulled out and handed control over to the Marines and the rest of the Multinational Force, it had smashed the Syrian military forces in Lebanon, shooting down almost one hundred aircraft. The implications in the larger Cold War were obvious: the Soviet military equipment was not up to snuff. Part of this deficiency would become shockingly apparent when Reagan later announced "Star Wars," namely the absence of computers in Soviet society and the lack of general availability of computing technology for what the military calls "C3" or command, control, and communications. Soviet General Nikolai Ogarkov noted with some distress that American kids "play with computers. Here, we don't even have computers in every office of the Defense Ministry. And for reasons you well know, we cannot make computers widely available in our society."[7] Shortcomings in the software of computing reflected other systemic weaknesses, most notably including a shocking lack of trust and autonomy. The United States had but one-seventh the general officers of the Soviet Union, with two times as many troops-per-officer in a platoon due to the absence of a trustworthy noncommissioned officer class.[8]

Anecdotal evidence from the IDF's encounters with Soviet equipment revealed a growing awareness in the Pentagon, the CIA, and the State Department that Reagan was onto something. Perhaps, indeed, the Soviet house of cards was ready to fall. In retrospect it is easy to see the outlines. First and foremost, Reagan understood more than any of his advisors—including, likely, Bill Casey—that, as Soviet military specialist William Odom wrote, "Marxism is itself a theory of war" and the *Communist Manifesto* "has this theory of war deeply imbedded in its text."[9] As Sigmund Neumann put it, "Marx and Engels can rightly be called the fathers of modern total war."[10] Going into the 1980s, what so many had ignored or missed entirely was that the foundations of Soviet military doctrine were offensive going back to the early formulations of proper Marxist warfare in the 1920s. In the postwar period, Soviet doctrine was based on the assumption that the USSR and its allies would confront the entire capitalist world. From 1949 to the 1970s especially, Soviet planners assumed "a future war would be nuclear, with massed use of nuclear weapons" and that "victory could be achieved in a world nuclear war."[11] Further, Colonel Ihor Smeshko told historian William Odom that he couldn't recall ever participating in a single military exercise that did *not* include the employment of nuclear weapons.[12] By the 1980s, some modifications had taken place so that Soviet doctrine now involved only "theater" or tactical nuclear weapons. In theory, these "theater" weapons were lower-yield, more contained nuclear weapons as opposed to "strategic" nuclear missiles that could level and irradiate massive areas at a time. Realistically, the destructive power was so tremendous that no army could safely move troops through an area recently struck by such destruction. It was a distinction that only existed in the war manuals. Nevertheless, it is worth noting that the Soviets seemed to disregard such distinctions and *always* planned for offensive war and *always* planned to use nukes.

Mikhail Gorbachev would later receive considerable credit for changing Soviet doctrine to a more "defensive" approach—which he did in 1987. But Odom found the doctrinal revision was almost entirely due to the collapsing economy, a view echoed by numerous Soviet officers. As recently as 1977, Leonid Brezhnev was still asserting that the USSR's goal was to "gain control of the two great treasure houses on which the West depends: the energy treasure house of the Persian Gulf and the mineral treasure house of central and southern Africa."[13]

Reagan and Moscow tested each other in the negotiations of the "Siberian Seven," and the Soviets found the American president could be trusted.

Reagan knew Brezhnev wasn't long for this world because of his age and rumors of his ill health. Dutch had been given insight on the man from Helmut Schmidt when the German chancellor visited in early 1981. "Brezhnev," confided Schmidt, was a typical Russian who, "'after reading Dostoyevsky and Pushkin' is 'cruel, abrupt, a great host, and emotional.'"[14] Schmidt continued: "I've seen him weeping...particularly when they played the German national anthem."[15] Reagan's opinion was less generous, sarcastically calling Brezhnev a "barrel of laughs." But the barrel died in November 1982, and Dutch skipped the ensuing funeral. One "evil emperor" was merely replaced by another, the seventy-one-year-old Yuri Andropov, who had come straight to the Politburo from the KGB. Shultz described him as "a cadaver." As they would do (with better justification) with Mikhail Gorbachev, the Western media tried to characterize the hard-bitten former spy Andropov as urbane and sophisticated, writing of his Western suits and his love of jazz. But, as spies would, he had led such a secretive life the CIA did not even know if his wife was still alive.

In 1978, several Russian Pentecostals in Moscow had managed to get inside the US embassy and claimed asylum. The "Siberian Seven" were Orthodox Old Believers who would not compromise with the godless government of the USSR. In December 1981, still living in the embassy basement, two of them, Avgustina and Lidia Vashchenko, had gone on a hunger strike and had to be sent to a hospital. Through Shultz, Reagan learned that the Soviets would consider releasing all the Pentecostals if the president did not make a public spectacle out of it. One or two at a time, they were allowed to leave, and, by July, all of the "Siberian Seven," as Shultz called them, were out of the USSR. Reagan, true to his promise, had not said a word.[16] Instead, he approved a new grain deal for the USSR. Shultz viewed the episode as a key test of Reagan's character by the Soviets: they found they could deal with him.

The US economy had regained its footing, and Reagan's early efforts to eliminate the Soviet Union had begun to pay off. He had shut down or delayed the Trans-Siberian Pipeline, greatly reducing Soviet cash reserves. His "Farewell" program had subverted Soviet espionage with leaks of deeply flawed technology. With Congressman Charlie Wilson's help in the House and the CIA team under Mike Pillsbury, Afghan rebels were starting to bleed the Soviet military in a foreign war. This set the stage for the Gipper to land three knockout blows, though the destructive impact they would have was not obvious at the moment.

Serious arms negotiations with the Soviets had begun in 1982 over the SS-20 Euromissiles, which the Soviets had started deploying under Carter. As part of Carter's initiative, the United States would counter the SS-20s by 1983 by sending 572 Pershing II and cruise missiles to bases across Europe. Once again, the design of a weapon reveals the strategy behind it. Soviet SS-20s were short-range (1,500 km) mobile missiles, intended not to be used against the United States but rather to intimidate European allies into fracturing NATO. Their mobility was a significant strategic problem in that if the Soviets knew our satellite paths, they could move the missiles immediately after the satellites passed over. The SS-20s' mobility thus made them invisible to and safe from preemptive strikes. While Carter's plan lacked perfect equivalence to the Soviets, the variety of missiles deployed was enough to restore deterrence.

Dutch knew there were more serious problems with Carter's response. First, persuading the European allies to actually deploy the American weapons was a different matter from getting them to sign a mere letter of intent. By fall of 1981, the anti-deployment forces in Europe had mobilized, protesting Reagan's "warlike" policies. Some of those in his administration, including NSC aide Richard Pipes, had made decidedly sober comments about the Soviets' doctrine of nuclear war, and at least one, T. K. Jones, an assistant secretary of defense, had theorized that the majority of Americans could survive a nuclear exchange if they could dig holes and "if there are enough shovels to go around."[17] Of course, these lines were published in a *Los Angeles Times* story, and the writer, Robert Scheer, quickly published a scare-ific book (*With Enough Shovels*) suggesting the administration actually wanted a nuclear war.[18] The irony of Scheer's book was that Pipes and Jones had merely expressed the logical extension of the MAD policy that every post-World War II president had lived by, while it was the man in the White House who was actually seeking to break from it.

Reagan dismissed the European peace movement as a "propaganda campaign" largely instigated and financed by the USSR. Critics scoffed, but by the time it became the "freeze" movement, he was at least partly right.[19] Subversion was not new to the Kremlin, which in 1976 had "extolled the value of encouraging the peace movement [to] weaken Western resolve," and Soviet rubles had funded the neutron bomb opposition in 1977.[20] The East German Communist Party was funneling $2 million a month to protest groups by 1981, while conveniently no West German "peace" groups took to the streets to protest the communists during the Polish crackdown.[21]

Caspar Weinberger and Richard Perle had developed a brilliant counterstrategy to deployment concerns, known as the "zero option" in which, in return for the Soviets withdrawing the SS-20s, the United States and its allies would forego deployment of the Pershing II and cruise missiles. In November 1981, Reagan had discussed the zero option for the first time, portraying the Soviets as arms-racing while the US stood at the starting gate. The zero option, he stated, "would be an historic step." For Reagan, though, eliminating the Euromissiles was a sideshow; the main event was achieving a reduction of the ICBMs and other strategic forces, for which he announced a new initiative that ditched SALT (Strategic Arms Limitation Talks) and moved to genuine reductions in nuclear forces. This was called START (Strategic Arms *Reduction* Talks). Even this, in Reagan's mind, was only to be an intermediate step to the complete elimination of nuclear weapons.

Liberals were horrified. Ask the Soviets to actually cut back weapons? Incendiary! Provocative! Leftist Strobe Talbott claimed it was a typical warmonger move to ensure no arms deal took place. Others, including the *Washington Post*, dismissed it as a "negotiating position" to be given away later. As usual, Reagan's critics did not take him seriously. In fact, Weinberger had already presented the zero option to NATO ministers in October. Moreover, Reagan was tipped off that Brezhnev, then scheduled to travel to West Germany, would present a new "freeze" option there. (He did.) Any "freeze" permanently "froze" all levels to the Soviets' advantage— precisely why they preferred it. Leftist groups such as the US Conference of Catholic Bishops, the United Presbyterian Church, and the Lutheran Church fell in behind the freeze, but even more conservative organizations such as the Southern Baptist Convention had signed onto a nuclear disarmament resolution.

Reagan had no intention of ceding the high ground to the religious left. On March 8, 1983, he enacted the second phase of his anti-Soviet offensive, appearing before the National Association of Evangelicals.

The Gipper's use of the phrase "Evil Empire" struck a nerve because most Americans had seen—or heard about— the movie Star Wars *and because Reagan, at least in attitude, resembled Luke Skywalker.*

At the core of Reagan's speech was language that shocked most of Reagan's advisors, for it employed a very well-known American movie theme to describe the USSR: "the Evil Empire." Virtually anyone who had seen the 1977 record-breaking George Lucas film *Star Wars* and its sequel (*The Empire Strikes Back*, 1980—with the final part of the trilogy, *Return of the Jedi*, appearing two months after Reagan's speech) knew that in fact the Soviet Union *did* resemble the evil Galactic Empire in the movie. *Star Wars* featured an evil emperor who could have been Leonid Brezhnev's brother, bent on dominating the world, resisted only by a "Rebellion," which called to mind the Revolutionary heroes of 1776. "Evil Empire" immediately captured in pop-culture phrasing the Cold War in ways that a more eloquent or reserved diplomatic terms might not, and for that reason it was exceptionally effective. And because it was effective, both the Washington

Establishment and the Left disintegrated into hysterics—including even some of the Gipper's staff, who preferred the nice, old "diplomatese" that never called a spade a spade. Shultz, for example, was "alarmed," and David Gergen thought the phrase "outrageous." The *New Republic* said it suggested Reagan was after a "holy war," and, predictably, the *New York Times* labeled it "simplistic theology."[22] Well, at least the *Times* figured out it was indeed theology and that there was a good and an evil at work!

Reagan took full responsibility for the line, inserting it after his speechwriters removed it. Later he quipped, "I made the 'Evil Empire' speech... with malice aforethought." To repeat: the speech was so despised because it connected so well. Whether Reagan ever saw *Star Wars* is not known—Michael said he hadn't spoken to him about it—but he absolutely knew that it was a cultural event shared by millions of Americans and that the story was one of good and evil, the bold colors in which Dutch always painted even as his more timid advisors called for pastels. If the USSR was the Empire, then America was the Rebellion; if Brezhnev was the Evil Emperor, it could only mean Reagan was Luke! These were *precisely* the kinds of appeals Reagan could make to the public over the heads of the media and even his own boxed-in advisors.

Across the pond, though, in the deepest reaches of the Soviet Union, Reagan's words had a different impact. Moscow police chief Arkady Murashev told the *Washington Post*, "It's true."[23] Writer Michael Novak, at a dinner many years later, heard a former Soviet general say, "That's what did it.... It *was* an evil empire. It was."[24] President Reagan's rhetoric had "badly shaken the self-esteem...of the Soviet political elites," reported another.[25] A member of the foreign ministry said, "Well, we are an evil empire."[26]

With the "zero option," Reagan had redefined the European strategy with a jab. By reframing the entire missile debate in spiritual/pop culture tones with the "Evil Empire," the Gipper landed an uppercut. He next was poised for the haymaker. Reagan planned to arm the public with a shield. Several of the NSDDs had already mentioned "strategic defenses" and shortly after the president signed NSDD 12 in October 1981, Weinberger had alluded to getting "something more effective than we have now." He then referred to some "brand new things that look quite promising."[27] All that remained was for Dutch, using Yoda's voice, to say, "Defeated, you will be."

In a comprehensive, and often revolutionary, strategy to defeat the USSR, Reagan launched offensives on all fronts: the Euromissiles, Afghanistan, economic warfare, and ballistic missile defense, or "Star Wars"— as well as the psychological "Evil Empire" references.

What is undeniable is that Reagan had been discussing defensive ballistic missile measures, including "directed energy weapons," with a number of people for some time. New Mexico senator Harrison Schmitt found him "most receptive" to new technologies in a private talk in late 1981.[28] Ed Meese, Richard Allen, and George Keyworth, Reagan's science advisor, used a 1981 planning session to begin a more formal study of missile defense. They communicated with former director of national intelligence Daniel Graham and physicist Edward Teller—whose own propensity ran toward space-based nuclear weapons that could destroy missiles. (Reagan utterly rejected such a path: indeed, when he and Teller met in September 1982, Teller committed the unforgivable sin of specifically requesting funds for an X-ray laser.) As early as NSDD 12 in October 1981, the United States had stated a commitment to effective ballistic missile defense. A broader study, begun in February 1982, resulted in NSDD 32, which formalized the strategy that April. Considered "essential to understanding the rest of the Reagan presidency," the new National Security Decision Directive makes clear Reagan's entire team had been thoughtfully and methodically considering missile defense for almost a year before he gave the "Star Wars" speech.

SDI, Reagan later wrote, "wasn't conceived by scientists," and indeed Teller admitted he thought he had had little influence on the president's thought.[29] In *An American Life*, Reagan observed that a "certain amount of mythology" surrounded Star Wars. One prominent factor influencing Reagan's steady gravitation toward defensive systems was the growing awareness that virtually no land-based missiles could be made invulnerable to enemy attack. The Gipper had inherited the MX missile, with its goofy and impossible "racetrack" basing, from Jimmy Carter. Quickly Weinberger concluded it was not practical and Reagan just as quickly discarded the basing mode—but not the missile itself. Weinberger toyed with an equally impractical "dense pack" basing in which the ICBMs would be clustered together to cause enemy missiles to commit fratricide, leaving the MX missiles somewhat intact. This involved faulty estimates, and the press labeled it "dunce pack" basing. Ultimately, Reagan realized that since *no* missile silo was "safe" from a first strike, the Soviets could build missiles cheaper than the United States could build secure basing. Unless…unless missile defense was involved. He gave up on novel ways to base the MX and in May 1982 had ordered production of one hundred "Peacekeepers" (as the MX missiles were called) with a December decision made to replace the existing Minuteman missiles in their silos.[30]

Reagan had been heading toward a structure that relied more heavily on defense and less on mutual assured destruction for some time. He hit the accelerator in March 1983. First, Reagan discussed it with the Joint Chiefs of Staff in late 1982, asking, "What if we began to move away from total reliance on offense to deter a nuclear attack" and move toward a "greater reliance on defense?"[31] (Martin Anderson would later note that Reagan signaled his choice of direction with a question.) Weinberger immediately tasked groups to explore missile defense, and the Joint Chiefs followed up for a February 1983 meeting. In his autobiography, *An American Life*, Reagan remembered this as "a couple of days," but the original instruction and the JCS response was more like a couple of months. It stood to reason that in light of the USSR's substantial advantage in ICBMs, the easiest way to minimize that advantage was to "attrit" (in the words of future Gulf War general Norman Schwarzkopf Jr.) large numbers of missiles after launch. Bud McFarlane on the NSC staff saw it as a "better way to compete" and to "have them spend a lot of money to keep up with us."[32]

Despite the myth that Reagan concocted Star Wars/SDI at the last moment himself, in fact his national security teams and the Joint Chiefs of Staff had been studying this option for months.

By February, Reagan had the Joint Chiefs in his corner, thanks to groundwork from Admiral James Watkins. The Chiefs endorsed a missile defense that would "move the battle from our shores and skies." General John Vessey Jr., in a discussion with Dutch, asked, "Wouldn't it be better to protect the American people than avenge them?"[33] Reagan liked the line so much he would later use it himself. This gave rise to another myth: that Reagan and his team saw missile defense as imminent. Quite the contrary, they all expected it to be incremental and of longer-term value. At the same time, however, he—and the Chiefs—all understood what the long-term program was *not*, namely, a technological quick fix that could deploy defensive weapons immediately. As Reagan said to his advisors immediately before the Strategic Defense Initiative speech, "If there is one thing I do not mean, by this [initiative is] a string of terminal defenses around this country."[34] Once again, though Dutch's vision may have been far, it was sharp: no matter how long it took, the goal was to destroy enemy weapons over *enemy* soil, so that even the collateral damage would be theirs alone. Contrary then to notions that Reagan's whole staff verged on rebellion over Star Wars, those who mattered most—the military, Clark, and McFarlane—were fully on board with the idea. Other elements of government, particularly the State Department, would pose a thornier problem, and State was deliberately kept out of the loop except for Shultz. Even then, the secretary was included gradually. While cautious, he understood its significance. Later, as the Strategic Defense Initiative was unveiled, Shultz would mostly seek to prevent language that might oversell the program, not to derail it.

Congress was another matter. Reagan understood members would "go public and grandstand" in their criticism. As he prepared to announce the program on March 23, the Gipper told McFarlane to keep "this tightly under wraps"[35] (the section dealing with the Strategic Defense Initiative was highly secret and referred to only as "the Insert"). Intuitively Reagan knew that such a fundamental change in defensive posture would have to be done in the style of FDR's "100 days"—that the mechanisms needed to be in place and the ship turned before anyone could mount serious objections. McFarlane and a handful of others drafted the speech and did not circulate it for the normal departmental vetting. But Reagan personally labored intensely on the speech, changing the "bureaucratic talk to people talk."[36] Meese, Deaver, and Baker all were involved and kept it mostly quiet, although Weinberger learned of it through Meese, who was "particularly enthusiastic."[37]

Reagan's instincts were right. Not only was Congress skeptical, but so were some of his closest allies—initially. Margaret Thatcher didn't like SDI, but, typically, over time, the logic of Reagan's positions won her over. She would later call it "the single most important [decision] of his presidency" but at the time worried that "it will make you look like you are going to launch a first strike."[38] Shultz, who similarly came to appreciate the genius of the proposal, at first thought it "destabilizing"—a favorite term for those who still did not see victory in the Cold War as possible. Shultz told Reagan, "I can see the moral ground you want to stake out, but I don't want you to put something forward so powerfully, only to find technical flaws or major doctrinal weaknesses."[39] Other critics, such as Richard Burt, were deliberate in wrongly describing the proposal as aiming at a "nuclear-free world," and even arms negotiator Richard Perle (again, predictably given his position) opposed SDI, although mainly on the grounds that it was "too abrupt" a change. Even Vessey and Watkins, who approved of the general proposal, were shocked at how quickly Reagan moved. They resigned themselves to tinkering with the language and dampening expectations. Weinberger, who favored the concept, likewise balked at the timing. Once again, Dutch leapfrogged the traditionalists with a piercing vision of the future and imposed tomorrow on today.

On March 23, 1983, Reagan delivered his "vision of the future" in which he urged Americans to turn to that "great industrial base" that made us strong. He admitted that what he proposed—"that we could intercept and destroy strategic ballistic missiles before they reached our own soil or that of our allies"—was a "formidable, technical task, *one that may not be accomplished before the end of the century*" (emphasis mine), but current technology had made such progress within the realm of feasibility. In a section of the speech often ignored, the Gipper noted that we already had technologies "to attain very significant improvements in the effectiveness of our conventional, nonnuclear forces," reiterating Reagan's dream of eliminating all nuclear weapons, with or without SDI. He concluded by calling upon American scientists to turn their great talents now "to the cause of mankind and world peace, to give us the means of rendering these nuclear weapons impotent and obsolete."[40]

The three key elements of the speech were that Reagan wanted to move away from nuclear weapons by any means possible; that SDI was a research program and admitted it could take twenty-five more years to see operability; and that he never talked of a "non-nuclear" world, only of America's ability to render ICBMs powerless. Shultz, writing of Reagan's "visionary ideas," noted that the president had the ability to "break through the entrenched thinking" and articulate the nation's most deeply rooted values and aspirations."[41] Two days later, Reagan signed NSDD 85, "Eliminating the Threat from Ballistic Missiles."[42]

What followed was one of the biggest cases of leftist critics shooting themselves in the foot possibly in all history. On March 25, the *New York Times* used a headline referring to SDI as "Star Wars."[43] For once, Reagan's intuition failed him. He hated the term, saying the media had "saddled him" with it, and he had *not* referred to space or space-based weapons in his speech.[44] However, the Gipper failed to understand that the pop culture was on his side. First, liberals merely assumed this would be the platform for defeating missile launches, meaning they had thought about it, meaning they knew it would work. Second, use of "Star Wars" in a derogatory form stemmed entirely from the experience of adult liberals who grew up in the 1950s and who had seen the term "Buck Rogers" used to describe anything that was fantastical and fantasy. Buck Rogers was a comic book and movie character who managed to fly around in space untethered with jet packs or rocket packs—often there was no difference—firing a "ray gun" at aliens. What was pure science fiction in the 1950s, however, had become scientific fact by the 1980s. The movie *Star Wars* had been a huge hit and an even bigger cultural influence. Most Americans had seen the space shuttles going into orbit on a regular basis and knew of lasers even if they hadn't personally seen one. In other words, Star Wars was far from a fantasy in people's experience. Reagan himself had once acknowledged the rapid technical change in another setting. In a discussion with young activists, a student lectured Reagan: "You grew up in a different world. Today we have television, jet planes, space travel, nuclear energy, computers," to which Reagan quipped, "You're right....We didn't have those things when we were young. We *invented* them."[45]

Reagan's apprehension about the term "Star Wars" came from his fear that it would conjure up images of destruction and space war, while he insisted the program as he envisioned it "only destroys other weapons, [it] doesn't kill people."[46] It was unrealistic for him, or anyone, to think any weapon designed to "kill weapons" wouldn't eventually be turned on people. Here the American public was actually ahead of Reagan due to pop culture. So, contrary to the assessments by historians such as Paul Kengor—that the name hurt the program—it was a net benefit. It allowed average people to grasp an idea they had seen countless times in movies and to simplify an extremely complex technical question in terms of good and evil, which had been the Gipper's goal all along. He should have thanked people like Helen Thomas, who insisted on using the term.[47] Most of all, the fact that the Soviets—who hadn't been on the right side of culture since Lenin went into his tomb—hated the Evil Empire description was another cue that the phrase was on target.

Uncharacteristically, Reagan failed to perceive that the term "Star Wars" worked to his benefit, as it made difficult technical issues of missile defense easily accessible to ordinary Americans while aligning him with the hero Luke Skywalker.

Moreover, for years the Soviets had been experimenting with lasers and directed energy weapons. *Aviation Week & Space Technology* had run countless stories about Soviet tests, and while they remained just tests, a typical American could reason that, well, they were the Soviets after all and they *should* be a few years behind us.[48] In 1987, Dutch referred to these efforts as the "Red Shield" program—one included "everything from killer satellites to the modernized ABM defenses that ring Moscow. More than 10,000 Soviet scientists and engineers are working on military lasers alone, with thousands more developing other advanced technologies, such as particle beam and kinetic energy weapons."[49] He had sat on the information for years. As word of Soviet research leaked out, over time it became increasingly difficult to argue that Star Wars couldn't work: after all, why would the Soviets be pouring so much time and effort into a dead end? Reagan had them. He had the moral high ground of ending MAD; he had the cultural iconography of being Luke fighting against the Evil Empire; and he had the grudging scientific admission that the Soviets themselves thought the idea feasible.

What he didn't know at the time was that SDI sent shock waves through the Kremlin, more than he could imagine. At the time, the Soviet ambassador Anatoly Dobrynin said Reagan was opening a new phase of the arms race. Soviet leadership, he noted, called it a "real threat" and his leadership "was convinced that the great technical potential of the U.S. had scored again."[50] The new premier Yuri Andropov said SDI was irresponsible and "insane." Over time, the true impact of SDI would produce even more candid comments from the Evil Empire. Alexander Bessmertnykh, foreign minister under Mikhail Gorbachev, said Star Wars "frightened us very much" and had a "long-lasting impact."[51]

Beneath Star Wars itself lay Reagan's original economic hypothesis: that the Soviets' economy was ready to fold. Diplomat Andrei Gromyko glumly agreed, saying "behind all this lies the clear calculation that the USSR will exhaust its material resources…and therefore will be forced to surrender."[52] Underlying *those* assumptions by the Soviet leaders was another myth that many in the West had bought into but which the Russians realized was never the case, namely that the Red Army had more or less defeated Hitler without the West. While the Soviets hurled hundreds of divisions against the Germans, as Dave Dougherty and I wrote in *A Patriot's History of the Modern World*, for the United States "the statistics of production…were nothing short of staggering. Ford alone outproduced all of Italy in total wartime goods," and American factories in four years turned out over three hundred thousand aircraft and thirty-one fleet and light aircraft carriers.[53] Soviet leaders knew this far better than Western liberals: in the key months of November–December 1942, almost all of the heavy tanks defending

Moscow were American or British, and the best Soviet fighter plane was the Bell P-39 Airacobra.[54]

Thus, even the most brainwashed Soviet leader knew that if the USA turned on the jets, figuratively speaking, the USSR would be left in the dust. Colin Powell would observe, "The opponents of SDI did not want us to aggressively pursue the research because, Lord forbid, we might be able to do it."[55] Andropov acknowledged SDI meant the Soviet Union "will just stop being a superpower." While Star Wars might not be operationally feasible in the near term, he noted, "in 10 to 15 years the situation might change" and "whether the system is practicable or not, it is a real factor."[56] Or, in other words, SDI was indeed practicable.

It is also irrelevant whether the Kremlin actually believed that Star Wars was an offensive system (as they always claimed) or a defensive system as the Gipper insisted. Either way, they had to address it, and that meant spending more money. Their creaking economy sputtered even more.

As Reagan came to his decision on SDI in 1983, he was turning another screw on the Soviets: the final deployment of the cruise and Pershing II missiles that had been planned for some time. Nevertheless, the deployment did not happen without effort: it was a commitment Reagan had built meticulously from the beginning of his presidency. When Reagan had first met with European leaders about the Theater Nuclear Forces [TNF] or Euromissiles in 1981, he had even then been reassured of their commitment. Ambassador Emilio Colombo of Italy, according to NSC meeting minutes, said the deployment "presented no problems." Then, he boasted, Italy's position "helped bring Germany along." Without Italian help, Colombo told Reagan, the Germans "might have found it very difficult to proceed" with the Pershing II deployments.[57] When German chancellor Helmut Schmidt met with Dutch three months later, *Germany* took credit for calming down the Europeans, saying "reassurances are required for [other countries] not so much for England and [Germany] but for others." The minutes recorded that Schmidt jokingly said, "Belgium [is] so dysfunctional [Schmidt] suggested NATO deploy Flemish missiles in one part and French in another!" Schmidt admitted to Reagan "there is a wrong perception of you" and he recommended a presidential visit to Europe to "let people understand you are not…a cowboy…. Am I too blunt?"[58]

Of course, Reagan thought not. He relished honesty, and he couldn't care less who got credit for aligning the allies. By 1981, he had gotten a firm commitment from three of the most critical allies for the deployment—Thatcher, Schmidt, and Colombo. By 1983, further German and British elections solidified the decision, and although Helmut Schmidt was forced out of office on the issue of the missiles, his successor followed through anyway.

Then came the reaction: in October 1983 some three million protestors took to the streets of Europe, including 400,000 in Bonn and 250,000 in Stuttgart. The Euromissile deployments had united "virtually every leftist group in existence," including "an enthusiastic…assortment of feminists [and] environmentalists" who, aligning behind the "freeze" mantra, "mounted a prolonged siege of…Greenham Common."[59] While many of the protesters were no doubt sincere, they were also to some extent Soviet dupes. One KGB agent boasted that "it was us, the KGB residency, who brought a quarter of a million people out onto the streets." Subsequent researchers have argued that while the Soviets *tried* to gain more of a foothold, the peace organizations were competent enough to organize their own protests without any outside help.[60] Regardless of who organized the protests, the Euromissiles were deployed. The Soviets had failed to stop them.

Then, almost out of nowhere, two disconnected events realigned the thinking on both sides of the Iron Curtain. First, on August 31, 1983, a South Korean airliner, Flight 007, left Anchorage, Alaska, for Seoul, South Korea. It wandered into Soviet airspace at the same time as a US spy plane was conducting reconnaissance. The pilot of KAL 007 had not switched off autopilot, and the plane was tracking back to an Anchorage beacon that was down for maintenance. As a result, KAL 007 drifted 175 miles off course into Soviet airspace and was not picked up until the plane had actually turned back toward international airspace. The radars that should have picked up the Boeing jet further out were inoperable, but the local Soviet officials had "lied to Moscow trying to save their ass," one defector told the television show *60 Minutes*.[61] Interviews later showed that the head of the Soviet Air Defence Forces ordered that the craft be shot down, thinking it was an American spy plane. The commander at the Soviet air base, Anatoly Kornukov, was more cautious. When interceptors were finally launched, they caught up with KAL 007 and fired warning bursts, hoping for a response. The bursts were apparently not seen by the pilot, who had already changed course, leading the Russians to think he was engaged in evasive maneuvers. Now Kornukov became adamant the plane be shot down. By the time the interceptors fired, KAL 007 was in international airspace and one of the Soviet pilots admitted he saw the running lights of a civilian aircraft. The Soviets began to lie more from that point on. A US spy flight, Cobra Ball, had been hundreds of miles away from KAL 700 and in fact was already back on the ground when the missile was fired, so claims that the Soviets thought the airliner was a "spy plane" were specious.

Reagan responded with outrage, calling the act an "atrocity," a "massacre," and a "crime against humanity." The administration took the unusual step of releasing intercepts of Soviet communications between the pilot and ground control and also played some of the tape in a televised address. Despite the rhetoric, the Gipper's responses were measured. Many called for expulsion of Soviet diplomats, but Reagan responded with verbal attacks, now mentioning the shoot-down in almost every public speech. George Will, ever hawkish, sneered, "Thank God it is not December or some dunce would suggest dimming the national Christmas tree."[62] On September 7, Shultz publicly humiliated Gromyko at a scheduled meeting. The point was made, but the Gipper came away with another conclusion: the events "made me more aware than ever of the urgent need for a defense against nuclear missiles."[63] After all, he ruminated, even if the shoot-down was an error, "if somebody could make that kind of mistake" with a single missile, "what about a similar miscalculation by the commander of a missile launch crew?" And "once a nuclear missile is launched, no one could recall it."[64] So once again the "simple minded" Dutch had gone from a narrow, deadly incident to the biggest of all pictures, incisively pulling everything back to his vision of a strategic defense.

In October, Reagan sent another message, this time in response to communist provocation in the Caribbean. The little island of Grenada was taken over by Marxist radicals, as on October 19, Cuban-backed rebels inside Grenada murdered prime minister Maurice Bishop, imposed martial law, and trapped one thousand Americans (seven hundred of them students at St. George's School of Medicine) on the island. Reagan had in fact warned about developments on the island in his March 23 SDI speech, alluding to Cubans who were in the process of "building a ten-thousand-foot runway," when Grenada didn't have an air force. Reagan's hands were tied, however, until he received a formal request on October 21 from six of Grenada's neighbors specifically asking for the US to invade the island and kick the Cubans out. Reagan blazed into action: "Do it," he said.[65] By not giving Congress a chance to dither, Reagan was able to act with urgency.

As the ships were set in motion, Reagan spoke to the American public, justifying Operation Urgent Fury on three grounds. First, "and of overriding importance, to protect innocent lives, including up to a thousand Americans.... Second, to forestall further chaos. And third, to assist in the restoration of conditions of law and order [over] a brutal group of leftist thugs [who] violently seized power."[66] Justifying action as members of an organization of states, taken under the auspices of an existing treaty, Reagan had staked out all the high ground. Later, when a critical press demanded his reaction to a predictable censure from the United Nations, Dutch grinned and said, "It didn't upset my breakfast at all."[67]

A task force composed of Marines, Rangers, and SEALs, already on its way to Lebanon, was diverted to Grenada in Operation Urgent Fury. Troops went in on October 25, sweeping the Cuban forces out and liberating the students. "We blew them away," observed the task force commander.[68] Indeed, although the Cubans constituted no more than a weak sparring partner, the symbolic significance was that to a small degree the demon of Vietnam had been vanquished. America had exercised military force in a just cause and won easily. Learning a lesson from Vietnam, the press was barred from the operation for several days, a ban that doubtless contributed to the operation's success. Before the media could whip up an anti-war furor as it had in Vietnam, the conflict was over. This time, a student—one much the same as those who had marched against the Vietnam War at Reagan's Berkeley—disembarked the airplane bringing him home, fell to his knees on the tarmac, and kissed American soil on camera.

Grenada displayed many things to the Soviets, first and foremost that the United States military had not gone into decline since Vietnam. There were some issues with the compatibility of the radios between the services during the invasion, and in a well-known incident, one commander had to find a land telephone line and place a call through an operator using his credit card to get air support. But overall the disparate units of the American military performed well. And it was undeniably a quick, complete *victory*. Second, it swept away any notions that Reagan would not act decisively when confronted by Soviet aggression. Third, despite media howls and liberal fulminations, the "splendid little war"—to steal a descriptor of the Spanish-American War—demonstrated that the free world indeed looked to the Gipper when in distress.

Nevertheless Dutch had to endure another angry call from Margaret Thatcher. She still steamed over the tardy American support for Britain in the Falklands a year earlier and now was surprisingly "angry" as Dutch put it. Thatcher described it differently, recalling she wasn't "in the sunniest of moods."[69] Thatcher justifiably fumed that she had not been given a heads-up of the invasion (Reagan cited "leaks" and the need for secrecy as preventing him from calling her). She mistakenly saw the Grenada strike as intimately linked to the truck bombing of the Marine barracks in Lebanon (as discussed in the next chapter)—internal administration papers show almost no connection of the two in the eyes of Reagan's advisors. Thatcher was miffed that the US had decisively stepped in to right a wrong in what was once a British sphere of influence, when England clearly could not. Following a tense phone call with the prime minister, the president came out of the Oval Office and, in a classic understatement, told Howard Baker, "Mrs. Thatcher has strong reservations about this."[70] Nevertheless the frictions of the pipeline and Grenada only strengthened the bonds between the Gipper and the Iron Lady, convincing both they could be completely honest about their own interests without sacrificing the partnership against the Evil Empire.

Earning the trust of the Soviet dictators, however, was a different matter. Throughout Reagan's first three years in office, he had delivered personal letters to Kremlin leaders, first to Brezhnev in 1981, then, in July

Reagan's father, Jack, his mother Nelle, and his brother John Neil (nicknamed "Moon").

As a lifeguard on the Rock River, young Ronald Reagan saved seventy-seven people who were in danger of drowning.

During World War II, Reagan was an officer in the film unit known as "Fort Roach" in Culver City.

The love of Reagan's life was Nancy Davis. The two were exceptionally close, even to the exclusion of their children.

Reagan campaigned on rebuilding the American economy, and found his ideas were well supported among working Americans.

Enormously popular with rank-and-file Republicans, the Gipper was a born campaigner.

Reagan's charm, self-deprecation, and movie-star looks made him difficult to hate, even for his most fervent political enemies.

Having defeated George W. Bush in the 1980 primary, Reagan named Bush as his running mate. Over the years, it proved to be one of Reagan's best decisions. Bush was an utterly loyal vice president who frequently would be the only one in meetings of cabinet officials who would take Reagan's side in an argument.

Reagan was not above lobbying members of Congress or Senators personally, and probably experienced one of his greatest failures when he did not quickly move to shore up the nomination of Robert Bork to the US Supreme Court.

Reagan found his greatest ally in the Cold War in British Prime Minister Margaret Thatcher.

Reagan and Nancy, departing for Camp David. While a getaway from Washington, Camp David was never as relaxing as the Ranch (Rancho del Cielo). 1982.

In Pope John Paul II, Reagan found the perfect spiritual ally, one who had immense influence even behind the Iron Curtain. 1987.

Once considered a "cowboy," Reagan quickly dissipated any concerns on the part of foreign leaders about his competence or sincerity in achieving peace. May 8, 1985.

On the campaign trail, Reagan was as comfortable with children as with political bosses. 1984.

Reagan's family in a rare White House family photo; in fact, there were not a great number of family photos due to friction with Reagan's children.

Reagan and Gorbachev met many times, with no meeting more important than their meeting in Geneva, when they retired to a more intimate location where they learned they could trust each other.

Reagan, an avid rider, was asked to do a publicity shot for a campaign. When he appeared in his English riding clothes, his managers were horrified. They told him they wanted a cowboy, and Reagan dutifully changed into western riding gear—but he frequently rode in English jodhpurs and with an English saddle.

Reagan before the Berlin Wall in 1987 when he uttered his timeless line,
"Mr. Gorbachev, tear down this wall!"

On his trip to Moscow in 1988, Reagan sought to deliver a remarkable message on Christianity and faith to the "godless Soviets," even discussing Christianity with Soviet Premier Mikhail Gorbachev.

"Morning in America": In 1984, Reagan's reelection slogan was "Morning in America," and it resonated with a revived America, whose self-image was restored from the dismal Carter years.

No one ever questioned whether Ronald Reagan bled red, white, and blue.

1983, to the ailing Andropov. Dutch proposed a new overture to improve relations, including an "interim agreement" to reduce the number of Euromissiles. Andropov responded but rejected Reagan's proposal, insisting French and British nuclear forces be included in all discussions. The Gipper's response to each of these rejections was the same: "Well, at least they're talking." The Soviets knew he was willing to discuss matters, to negotiate. After Reagan met privately with Soviet ambassador Anatoly Dobrynin in August, the president wrote a friend, saying that the dialogue with the Soviets was much further along than the public knew.[71] Reagan could hear the music; he just needed the right dance partner.

13

Misjudgment

Few new administrations have faced as many foreign policy challenges in as short a time as Reagan's did: the Euromissile deployment, the KAL 700 crisis, the Grenada invasion, the Lebanon war. Reagan surmounted most of these challenges brilliantly, such as in Grenada, where he and his team had avoided military conflict with the USSR while reestablishing American moral and military authority. But not every challenge was met with triumph. It was in Lebanon that the Reagan presidency suffered the darkest day of its eight years. Understanding the disaster that subsequently unfolded in Lebanon requires some background on numerous diplomatic and military actions in the region.

Let's return to 1981. The Syrian government had installed Soviet surface-to-air missiles in Lebanon, and Iraq neared completion of a nuclear reactor. Reagan still hoped to find a peaceful solution in the region—as so many others had. He appointed a special emissary to the region, Philip Habib, who carried a reputation as a "diplomatic troubleshooter." Habib's original tasking from Reagan in March of 1981 was to negotiate an agreement between Syria, Lebanon, and Israel. Saudi Arabia finally joined the mediation on the Syrian/PLO side and neared a cease-fire when, on June 7, the Israeli Air Force launched Operation Babylon. American-made Israeli jets bombed Saddam Hussein's Osirak nuclear plant, then under construction near Baghdad, and destroyed the facility. Prime Minister Menachem Begin only informed Reagan after the attack. He argued that the facility was nearing completion and therefore, as JFK had in Cuba in 1963, he had to stop construction before one of the Middle East's worst dictators got a nuclear weapon. Reagan fumed. "I can understand his fear," Dutch wrote in *An American Life*, noting in his diary that he "should have told us.... We could have done something to remove the threat."[1]

Dutch rebuked Israel for the attack (or, at the very least, for not alerting the United States to it). Begin's response was sharp: "Mind your own business." American-Israeli relations were badly strained by the attack.[2] Besides the fact that an ally undertook a potentially major destabilizing strike, at issue was the fact that the Israelis employed American-made planes. Some in Reagan's cabinet expressed outrage that Israel had indeed violated the agreement involving the sale of the airplanes not to use them for offensive purposes. But the Gipper also noted that he "had no doubt that the Iraqis were trying to develop a nuclear weapon" and decided that if Congress determined Israel had violated the terms of the sale, he would grant a presidential waiver.[3]

The American-Israeli relationship got worse after the sale of the AWACS to Saudi Arabia that same year, whereupon Begin railed at the president: "Are we a vassal state of yours? Are we a banana republic?"[4] Reagan hoped Begin would "regard [the sale of the AWACS] as a gesture showing that we desired to be evenhanded."[5] Eventually, Reagan saw the AWACS sale as absolutely critical for peace in the Middle East and later said he spent more time on that issue than any other.

Tensions in Lebanon continued to fester, with the "claims and counterclaims in the region...astounding and insurmountable."[6] The PLO continued to shell Israel relentlessly; Syria continued to claim it had an ancestral right to Lebanon; Christian minorities were small and unsafe in most Muslim states; a few hundred miles east, Iran and Iraq engaged in war of "stunning carnage"; and no Muslim nation wanted to house the PLO "refugees"—not Syria, not Egypt, not Saudi Arabia. They posed only a drain on local services and constituted a destabilizing alien force inside any nation, especially given their persistent demand to exterminate the state of Israel! As was his wont, Reagan tried to cut through the obfuscation and find an action item, which had served him so well in dealing with the Soviets, rebuilding the economy, liberating Grenada, and deploying the Euromissiles. Lebanon was different. A report would later describe it as "a country beset with virtually every unresolved dispute afflicting the peoples of the Middle East.[7] Whereas Winston Churchill famously said of Russia that it was a riddle, wrapped in a mystery, inside an enigma, the same was true of Lebanon, except that it was all contained inside a box also holding a bomb.

Israel's invasion of Lebanon in June prompted Reagan to dispatch Habib—who returned after the Osirak bombing—on a second mission to rescue Lebanon. Habib called for both Israel and the PLO to withdraw and a multinational force of Americans, French, and Italians to separate the combatants. It was a plan fraught with peril, which Reagan recognized: "I'm afraid we are faced with a real crisis," he wrote in his diary.[8]

That proved an understatement. Weinberger immediately opposed the move, arguing a buffer force was fine if both sides had agreed to have it separate them, but otherwise, it became a target. The Marines, he insisted, were too lightly armed and had an undefined mission, and the Marine brass opposed the mission—but saluted and obeyed orders. When the Multinational Force (MNF) arrived on August 20, Ronald Reagan made the biggest mistake of his presidency.

The ghosts of Korea, Ghana, and the Congo, with their "collective action" through the United Nations in particular, haunted the mission. Such "peacekeeping missions" were seldom approved in the first place unless, ironically, peace had already been decided and there was little risk of violence.[9] Later, studies would show that the insertion of "peacekeeping" forces actually increased the likelihood of continuing war.[10] In Reagan's time, however, leaders on all sides firmly (and falsely) believed that "peacekeepers" could somehow separate combatants who genuinely wanted to eradicate each other. Dutch had inherited from Eisenhower the tradition of inviting the United Nations to participate, if often secondhand, in American national security decisions.

In the midst of these discussions came palace intrigue worthy of the Tudors. Reagan's team, on their own, attempted a reshuffling of the top positions due to almost debilitating infighting and frustration that neither the "traditionalists" nor the "conservatives" could seem to attain victory. It began with NSC advisor Bill Clark, who, like Al Haig, had become some-thing of a pain to the president and a perpetual enemy of James Baker and George Shultz. Meanwhile, for different reasons, Caspar Weinberger and Shultz were constantly at odds. The men were of different temperaments: Weinberger was a lawyer, Shultz a mediator (with anyone but Cap, it seemed). They fought during the Nixon administration and often stumbled onto each other's turf. Shultz claimed to want military knowledge so he could share it with the president, without caring that it was the job of the secretary of defense. And by the time the fateful decision came to leave the Marines in Lebanon, Bud McFarlane temporarily sided with Shultz to keep them in place. But McFarlane's support wouldn't last long. By late 1983, many of these actors—all justifying their actions as aiding the Gipper—had begun to leak to their favorite reporters. It got so bad that Clark, who, as Nancy observed, always seemed after a position in the administration other than the one he had, wanted out. He hoped to leave without giving the impression of bailing on the president. Meanwhile, the leaking contin-ued, leaving both Reagan and his military commanders furious.

On September 13, 1983, a leaked story about a change in the rules of engagement for the Marines appeared in the *Washington Post*. Accord-ing to the story, Marines were authorized now to call in Beirut air strikes. The military branches, especially the Marines, actually welcomed the leak because it put enemy gunners on notice that they could no longer shell Marine positions at will. But Clark believed that Bud McFarlane, who sup-posedly leaked the story, was at risk of assassination by Lebanese groups as a result. This was not entirely untrue, as almost every American official who traveled to Lebanon was at risk of assassination. Still, it distorted the situa-tion and raised the drama quotient. Clark certainly didn't think McFarlane was at risk in the United States, but he did see an opportunity to stop the leaks once and for all. With Meese in agreement, Clark stormed into the Oval Office and demanded Reagan launch a leak investigation through the attorney general, even to the point of lie detector tests. Deaver learned of the plan and informed Baker, viewed by Meese as the source of a number of leaks. They tried to minimize the damage and squelch the polygraphs. Reagan's staff bordered on internal war: Shultz and Bush were horrified about the prospect of polygraphs, believing they would completely erode all trust within the administration. Nevertheless, in a move that unsettled many, the FBI questioned various staffers.

Into this mix stepped James Watt, the controversial interior secretary. In the summer of 1983, Watt ended the tradition of having the Beach Boys and the Grass Roots perform each Fourth of July concert at the National Mall on an alternating basis. Watt claimed the bands attracted the "wrong element" and instead invited Reagan's friend Wayne Newton. Not only were Reagan and Nancy Beach Boys fans, but there was a firestorm that threatened to portray Reagan as culturally clueless. Watt had to apologize. In fact, Watt had never mentioned the Beach Boys by name, and it was the Grass Roots, not the Beach Boys, who had been the scheduled band to perform in 1983. Watt's memo was apparently referring to the 1982 concert where he received complaints about the Grass Roots.[11]

Now Watt, in September, put his foot in his mouth again. Attempting to tout the "diversity" in his department, he said, "We have every kind of mix you can have. I have a black, I have a woman, two Jews, and a cripple." Political correctness had not then become what it is today, but even for 1983 such comments were the kiss of death. Senator Paul Laxalt, a westerner and one of Reagan's staunchest allies on the Hill, was told by Nancy that Watt had to go and began searching for suitable alternatives. It dawned on Meese, Weinberger, Casey, and Clark himself that this was their golden ticket: move Clark to Interior and put someone else in as National Security Council advisor. That "someone," to some of the internal plotters, was Baker, whom Clark suspected of being the leaker. Baker's deputy chief of staff Mike Deaver would move from his deputy position to chief of staff. Quietly the musical chairs were discussed with Shultz, Nancy, and others, though after the initial suggestion of moving Clark to the Department of the Interior, he was kept out of the loop, as was Meese. Shultz approved of the reshuffle as a means to return foreign policy to more "traditional" approaches. Nancy saw the removal of Baker as streamlining her input. Most operated out of limited information as to the "palace coup," and everyone who was in on the musical chairs thought it would benefit Reagan. Deaver and Baker thought that the day after Reagan announced

Clark's new position, on October 13, 1983, he would then announce the remainder of the staffing changes.

Initially Dutch seemed supportive and was to announce the changes at a National Security Planning Group Meeting, which, in such a public forum, would make reneging on the plan much more difficult for Reagan.

Then, when Deaver and Baker suggested announcing the changes a day after announcing Clark's new position on October 13, 1983, the Gipper began to have misgivings. Clark was agreeable to going to Interior but hated the prospect of Baker—whom he thought was the leaker—in his NSC spot. The more Reagan ruminated about the proposed restructure, the less he liked it and he finally called in Baker and Deaver. As he typically would, Reagan laid responsibility on nonexistent others for his own decision. "The fellas," he told them, "have a real problem with this [reorganization and] I want to think about it over the weekend." When Baker offered to withdraw the announcement Deaver had drawn up, Reagan got personal: "No. I said I would think about it over the weekend and I will."[12] Deaver took the rejection of his placement as chief of staff personally, and Reagan noted in his dairy that "Mike was pretty upset" after the meeting. It was the second time Reagan had seemingly "chosen" someone else over Deaver— the previous time in the dust-up with John Sears in the campaign—and Deaver mistakenly thought he had a closer relationship with the Gipper than he did. (It must always be kept in mind Peggy Noonan's observation that Reagan didn't have friends in Washington, only employees, and that he carefully kept the wall up with everyone, including Deaver.) Jeane Kirkpatrick was the early favorite to replace Clark at NSC, but she and Shultz were more at odds than even he and Weinberger. Instead, everyone agreed on Deputy National Security Advisor Bud McFarlane, a compromise candidate who, while hawkish, lacked Clark's personal knowledge of Reagan and the president's instincts.

Dutch later wrote in his memoirs that he made a critical mistake and should have appointed Baker to the NSC post, calling it a "turning point" in his administration. "I had no idea at the time how significant it would be."[13] Clark agreed to go to Interior, but Baker made up his mind to leave the White House when possible.

In the midst of these machinations, on September 28, 1,746 Marines arrived on Lebanese shores, along with approximately the same number of French and Italian troops. As they promised, the Israelis withdrew, whereupon Druze and Muslim militias battled openly, what remained of the Lebanese Army disintegrated, and Shiite Muslims from Iran made their way into Lebanon. Weinberger arranged for the Marines to stay at the Beirut Airport.

Five months earlier, Shiite operatives had detonated a car bomb at the US embassy in Beirut, killing sixteen Americans, including the CIA's top Middle East researcher. The bombing should have registered on Reagan's usually acute antennae as evidence that no conventional deal would be possible in this war zone. An accident of history likely prevented the Gipper from acting on his instincts: Habib, who had proven quite successful, notified the president he wanted to retire and in his place, Reagan temporarily sent Shultz. A reliable and often relentless secretary of state, Shultz was a throwback to the Eisenhower style of diplomacy in that he was a staunch anti-communist but one who recognized the limits of military power. At times, this led him to fail to understand Reagan's powerful instincts for how much military power—or, at least, the show of it—could be effective in dealing with the USSR. Shultz had come to Reagan with a warning from Richard Nixon—"watch out for him...after a while he'll be disloyal."[14] Nixon was wrong in this case, but the truth was neither Habib nor Shultz could pull a peaceful bacon out of that fire.

Shultz's plan for Lebanon was to get Reagan to "work on the Syrians" through King Hussein of Jordan.[15] Dutch thought highly of the king, writing in his diary "His Majesty is a solid citizen" and was "our hope to lead the Arab side and the P.L.O." (Reagan always used periods when referring to the Palestinian Liberation Organization.)[16] Where he trusted the king, Reagan was more cautious with Egyptian president Hosni Mubarak, worrying that he was "playing a game" in Lebanon and seeking to cut up the country with Syria.[17] McFarlane replaced Habib as the special envoy in July and immediately went to work trying to withdraw the American forces.

Administration strategy flowed through a "Lebanese Working Group" that still saw Lebanon through the lens of Syrian aggression. In September the group had warned about a "suicidal attempt to go after a U.S. vessel" in the Mediterranean.[18] Warning that the Syrian strategy through such an attack would be to "draw [in] the U.S." and "hurt the IMF," the working group laid the groundwork for the ultimate disaster by warning that the event would "lay the trap" and "force [the] US to escalate." For that reason, it argued, the "US cannot reverse [its policy and] cannot withdraw."[19] The Working Group continued to see things through traditional, "state-boundary" eyes, referring to working with Arab "moderates" and all too often falling back on the Soviet bogeyman to explain often ethnic and sectarian conflicts that had little to do with the Cold War.[20] The Joint Chiefs still expressed concern about the peacekeeping forces, and they increasingly recommended redeploying the Marines offshore on ships. At the same time, the Joint Chiefs proposed sending the battleship *New Jersey* to the Lebanese coast to provide firepower. Shultz, who, like Haig, was never timid about offering a resignation, opposed the move as unduly provocative.

Even as the Working Group met, American casualties began to pile up—a mine here, a firefight there, and constant mortar fire from the time they arrived. Reagan fretted, "We may be facing a choice of getting out or enlarging our mission."[21] Throughout September he made personal phone calls to the family of every American serviceman killed in Lebanon, recording them as "difficult, terrible calls."[22] Earlier that month, the Israelis had withdrawn from their positions on the heights overlooking Beirut—positions quickly occupied by a variety of rival Islamic militias. And at that critical moment of September 1983, the KAL 700 crisis absorbed much of the administration's attention—though not Weinberger's: he saw the Marines as "sitting right in the middle of a bull's-eye."[23]

During the day between the decision to invade Grenada and the Beirut Marine barracks bombing, Reagan himself was a peripheral participant in a surreal hostage situation at a Georgia golf club.

Not only were three crises brewing more or less simultaneously—Lebanon, KAL 700, and Grenada—but now a personal crisis of sorts hit

Reagan. Dutch was on a golfing outing in Georgia on October 21, 1983, when the Grenada assistance calls came through. Reagan agreed that the invasion should occur four days later. The following morning, a gunman named Charles Harris drove his truck through the golf club gate, took over the pro shop at the course, and held seven hostages, including White House aide David Fischer. Harris demanded to speak with the president face-to-face, so Reagan hustled back to his armored limousine and placed a call to the gunman. "This is the president of the United States. This is Ronald Reagan. I understand you want to talk to me."[24] Harris responded with silence. Reagan tried three more times before the Secret Service took him back to his cottage. Two hours after the incident started, police captured Harris and freed the hostages—after he had let one go to buy a six-pack of beer![25]

At a little after two o'clock in the morning Georgia time, Reagan's phone rang. It was Bud McFarlane, relaying the news from Washington that an Islamic terrorist had driven a truck laden with explosives past the guard posts at the Beirut airport and blown up the Marine barracks there, killing 241 US Marines. It was the bloodiest day in Marine Corps history since Iwo Jima. A simultaneous attack killed fifty-eight French paratroopers at their location two miles away. The blast at the Marine barracks also killed Robert Ames, the CIA's chief analyst in the Middle East, and eight other CIA officials. Shultz, who was also along on the golf outing, huddled with McFarlane and the president, who immediately returned to Washington. He called it the "worst day of my presidency" but did not terminate the Grenada invasion. Although the decision to invade Grenada occurred Friday, congressional leaders were not informed until Monday evening. Tip O'Neill mistakenly thought the invasion was a knee-jerk reaction to the barracks bombing.

Amidst all this, and despite the cabinet reshuffle, Reagan found himself supervising subordinates who were constantly battling. If George Shultz thought removing Judge Clark would end his troubles, he was mistaken. Instead, he and Caspar Weinberger increasingly were at odds. Cannon, in particular, lays the majority of the blame for the Lebanese debacle on their power struggles, which "wore down Reagan."[26] Cannon's view, however, largely relied on his own interpretation of Reagan as lacking control over his subordinates, as "remarkably uninformed, almost innocent, about the way his staff did its business."[27] (It was precisely such low-level tinkering that preoccupied Carter to the point of incapacity.)

Disagreement exists over the level of Reagan's engagement in meetings, largely stemming from his tendency to let the proponents of various positions hash it out without interfering, then coming to a decision at the end. Cannon found him disengaged, even sleepy. Brands termed Reagan an "apt pupil" who would sit silently for long periods of time until Meese would summarize the discussion with a string of directed questions, followed by a final summary from Dutch.[28] As we have seen, though, Reagan was actively engaged in the meetings that mattered to him, especially on the Soviet Union. He was less engaged during budget discussions, where fuzzy numbers talk made all but Stockman and Don Regan drowsy. Yet even then, Dutch would elevate the discussion back to his principles and vision, challenging the attendees to "find me a way to get there."

This obsession with the infighting and "sausage making" led even sympathetic biographers into a larger trap. While Reagan would never solve the organizational issues—indeed, they would nearly bring down his administration through Iran-Contra—after Lebanon he did begin to understand a deeper threat that no previous president had even noticed: radical Islam. For this he has received virtually no credit.

To an extent, everyone (including Reagan) at the time was singing from the wrong sheet of music. They all still interpreted radical Islamic terrorism in terms of traditional Cold War or small-state conflicts, ignoring the religious aspects of the new terrorism. This could be seen in the original "Peace Plan" Reagan had rolled out a year earlier, focused on using Jordan as the point of leverage. Given that Jimmy Carter's Camp David Accords still seemed to be working, and given that the world seemingly had entered into an era of "multinational" actions followed by agreements that all celebrated, the momentum seemed to be on the side of such optimistic overtures. Weinberger, who had always opposed inserting the Marines, now complained that the first withdrawal of the Marines and the MNF in September had allowed the massacres at Sabra and Shatila. Habib disagreed, noting that Italian troops were stationed immediately outside the camps and could have prevented the slaughter.[29]

The second insertion of troops, however, had been opposed by the Joint Chiefs (who had also opposed the first) and Weinberger, who likened the American position to a referee in a prizefight within punching range of both fighters. Shultz favored the MNF and, as Clark recalled, seemingly the rest of the cabinet—apart from Cap—did as well. Weinberger years later said that it was "terrible to be proven right under such horrible circumstances."[30] Moreover, he later took responsibility for muffling the voices of the Joint Chiefs, saying no one ever firmly told Reagan the US would face disaster if the Marines weren't removed.

Although the CIA could confirm the barracks attack originated from the Hezbollah-controlled Beqaa Valley, the Agency remained unsure of exactly who carried out the bombing. A planned French-American assault on a staging camp was aborted at the last minute—by Weinberger. The radicals at the camp had been alerted and expected the attack. "None of us is afraid....We want to see our God," one blustered on CNN. "We welcome the bombs of Reagan."[31] Few in the White House fully grasped the apocalyptic overtones in these boasts, even as cables from the US embassy revealed that the *Iranians* expected to be attacked in response to the bombing and Iranian radio wanted such an attack "because we seek *martyrdom*" (emphasis mine).[32] Such comments underscored the Islamic context of the conflict, and even government-run radio in Beirut referred to the dead American and French troops as "martyrs"—the first time a multinational force casualty had ever been so categorized.[33] A January 1984 CIA briefing called the "Terrorist Threat to US Personnel" warned that "Shiia extremists are increasingly willing to sacrifice their lives in attacks on the MNF. They are confident they are serving the will of Allah."[34]

Still, Reagan was not yet perceiving the struggle as one involving a shame-honor culture or a religious battle but rather clung to the Cold War framework. On October 27, 1983, in a televised address, Reagan again wove KAL 700, the Grenada invasion, and Lebanon into a Cold War tapestry: "The events in Lebanon and Grenada, though oceans apart, are closely related. Not only has Moscow assisted and encouraged the violence in both countries, but it provides direct support through a network of surrogates and terrorists."[35] Earlier, after the embassy bombing, he had argued if the United States "cut and run...we'll be sending one signal to terrorists everywhere. They can gain by waging war against innocent people."[36] Aside from Weinberger, this view was largely shared inside the administration. According to another cable, "the stakes in Lebanon, if we are driven out...[are that] the radicals, the rejectionists...will have won," although this was still defined within the context of the US-Soviet conflict. "The message will be sent that relying on the Soviet Union pays off."[37] It is also noteworthy that in many of his justifications for SDI, Reagan cited the risk of action by a "Middle East madman," likely with Muammar Gaddafi or Saddam Hussein in mind.

In the initial aftermath of the bombing, Reagan benefitted from strong public sympathy, including from groups such as Al-Mojaddedi of the Islamic Unity of Afghanistan Mujahideen and the Federation of Islamic Association of the US and Canada. Similarly, the National Federation of Syrian-Lebanese American Clubs supported the effort in Lebanon, and the National Association of Arab Americans, which had originally opposed American involvement, fell in behind Reagan after the Sabra and Shatila massacres.[38] Over time, however, opposition grew from both the Left and from conservatives such as the publisher of *Conservative Digest*, Richard Viguerie.

Slowly Reagan began to develop a new framework in which to view the Middle East. After the bombing he wrote, "I still believed that it was essential to continue working with moderate Arabs to find a solution to the Middle East's problems," indicating he knew there were some not-so-moderate Arabs out there.[39] But he added, "I was beginning to have doubts whether the Arab world, with its ancient tribal rivalries, centuries of internecine strife, and almost pathological hatred of Israel" could ever support genuine peace efforts, notwithstanding individuals such as King Hussein.[40] Although he would not fully employ the term "radical Islamic terrorism," he came close. In December 1983, the administration developed the term "state-sponsored terrorism" to describe Iranian-supported terrorist activities. In taking even these modest steps, Reagan was rowing against the tide.

A March 1984 NSC meeting on terrorism, which supported the language used in the April NSDD 138 ("Combating Terrorism"), did not mention Islam, Islamic, or Islamic radicals.[41] The NSDD did, however, approve pre-emptive attacks on individuals involved in or planning terrorist attacks.[42] A year later, in NSDD 180 ("Civil Aviation Anti-Terrorism Program") the administration expanded the use of US air marshals.[43]

Reagan seemed alone by inching toward the subject. He said in a March National Security Planning Group meeting on the Iran-Iraq war, "We can't afford another Beirut. Most likely, we will get another terrorist attack," indicating that he well understood the nature of the first one.[44]

Reagan tasked Vice President Bush to head up a task force on terrorism in February 1985, which for the first time used the phrase "Islamic radicals" in a reference to Iran.[45] The paper, "Middle East Terrorism: The Threat and Possible US Responses" provided by the Directorate of Intelligence stated flatly that "Iranian-sponsored terrorism is the greatest threat to U.S. personnel and facilities in the Middle East."[46] That October, the Director of Intelligence submitted an analysis that expanded upon the Islamic radicalism comment. Secret and untitled, the analysis observed that "Middle Eastern terrorists do not see themselves" in traditional political ways, and instead "the community of Muslims always had [a] resort to terrorism as a vehicle of religio-political change."[47] It further argued that Muslim terrorists saw "their particular group as possessing the only totally true version of the path of virtuous behavior," and the Islamic terrorist "sees himself as the defender of right against evil and also thinks of himself as a...kind of soldier in a just war, not as a criminal."[48] It was an astoundingly accurate assessment of what would later be called "radical Islamic terrorism," and it brought a remarkably vitriolic backlash. Former ambassador Edward Peck wrote in the margin that the analysis was "a piece of...fecal material," while another unidentified commentator on the circular called it "less-than-helpful sociobabble."

The views expressed in the analysis by the intelligence directorate were not fashionable. As late as 1987, in a National Security Planning Group meeting, after listing all the terror threats that year, no one bothered to mention that they were all related by one factor: Islam.[49] Dutch even then still believed he could work with individual Muslim regimes and could support the *mujahideen* in Afghanistan to evict the Soviets. In 1986, he sent Clark to Baghdad to meet with Saddam Hussein to persuade him to stop supporting terrorist training cells outside of Iraq. And "Charlie Wilson's War" supporting the Afghan rebels continued to blur the lines of allies and potential enemies.

If the decision to put the Marines in harm's way constituted a fatal misjudgment, Reagan compounded the error by withdrawing them. As McFarlane would later argue, it sent a message to the terrorists that the United States had neither the will nor the means to respond to such attacks.[50] Indeed, after the first attack a Middle Eastern paper, *An-Nahar*, predicted that America's failure to respond to the embassy bombing would only lead to more attacks.[51] Few could have foreseen Osama bin Laden in 1996 cite Lebanon as an example of Americans' inability to "fight long wars." This, he claimed, "was proven in 1983 when the Marines fled after two explosions."[52] When bin Laden sat for an interview in 1998 with reporter John Miller of *Esquire*, he called America a "paper tiger" and recalled Beirut, where after "a few blows [America] would run in defeat."[53]

Weinberger had begun arguing (again) for withdrawal almost immediately after the bombing, only now he had the support of the press. He received further ammunition from the subsequent report that blamed the commanders on the scene for housing too many men in a single building and for inadequate security and barricades. It was indirectly a criticism of Reagan and the entire policy, though the report admitted that originally it was expected that the Marines would operate in a "relatively benign environment." That was true only so long as the Israelis remained in place—a sort of buffer to the buffer. Reagan thought the officers had suffered enough and spared them from further military justice. Pressure still built, however, to remove the Marines, which Dutch resisted, observing correctly that once the Americans left, Lebanon would simply fall to pieces. While Reagan was on a speaking trip, the National Security Planning Group met. All were in agreement, save Undersecretary of State Lawrence Eagleburger and Shultz. The United States could still provide air and fire support, but land troops needed to be withdrawn as soon as possible. Dutch reluctantly agreed.

When Reagan announced it to the press, it was in the form of "decisive new steps" that involved training of the Lebanese Army—itself a tall order, given that there was no Lebanese government at the time.

From start to finish, the Lebanese intervention proved a misjudgment of the highest order. Dutch was still surrounded by advisors who, without exception, swam in the waters of the US-Soviet interpretations of Middle Eastern conflict. Over time, the truck bomb attack led the United States and other governments to install more secure vehicle barriers around high-density targets overseas, but not every facility could be protected, as the 1996 Khobar Towers bombing in Saudi Arabia would reveal. The Gipper had fundamentally challenged and reoriented much of the thinking toward Cold War strategy and the economy. And Reagan, more than any prior president, had moved in the direction of seeing radical Islam for what it was. But completely reshaping the understanding of Islamic radicalism in the Middle East would prove a bridge too far.

14

Red, White, and Blue Dawn

"A merica is back," Ronald Reagan beamed in his second inaugural address, "standing tall." A more upbeat, inspirational message couldn't be imagined. The change could be felt. It could almost be tasted. The United States of America was a different nation than the America of 1979, which was, to paraphrase Arlo Guthrie, depressed, suppressed, repressed, oppressed sitting on the Group W Bench. Dutch had already restored the morale of the nation—especially the military—and despite Beirut, much of the shadow of Vietnam had been erased with the light of Grenada and Reagan's recovering economy. As Americans' own perceptions improved, like a seesaw, Soviet views of their own relative strength buckled.

Some things Americans barely or never saw played a key role in changing Soviet perceptions as well. In early 1982, just as the administration submitted its economic recovery plan, the first of twenty-four planned Trident submarines, the USS *Ohio*, slipped quietly into the water to undergo sea trials. The results were spectacular: America's own anti-submarine warfare (ASW) forces couldn't find the sub! Since American ASW technology was held to be at least five years ahead of Soviet capabilities, this singular sea trial forced a stunning reevaluation of the entire nuclear force by the US Navy and the entire national security apparatus across a wide spectrum of activities.[1] The Trident was a ballistic missile submarine capable of firing up to twenty-four C-4 missiles, each with up to eight multiple-reentry warheads. Each missile had a range of 4,600 miles. A single Trident was capable of laying waste to most of the USSR's cities. And the sub could prowl the oceans undetected by the most advanced naval technology in the world. Suddenly it was no longer necessary to accelerate production of a longer-range sub-launched ballistic missile (SLBM), because patrol lanes could be moved almost a thousand miles closer to the USSR, improving accuracy. Suddenly the MX basing question took on a vastly reduced urgency. And just as suddenly, Dutch had, with the decision to follow-through on the Euromissile deployment, nearly offset the entire Soviet strategic missile advantage *before* introducing Star Wars.

When a second Trident sub, the *Michigan*, became operational in September 1982, just these two alone carried enough ballistic missiles to eradicate virtually every major Soviet city. More important, however, they were virtually invisible to Soviet sonars and ASW technologies, drastically changing the balance of power. Worse for the Soviet leaders, a CIA analyst later observed that "the Soviets had learned a disturbing lesson about what Washington *could* do in a wartime situation.... [but] Moscow did not know what the U.S. *would* do."[2]

Few observers then, or historians since, debate that Reagan had changed perceptions at home and abroad well before his reelection campaign. Even the Soviets admitted that the Gipper "restored America's belief that it is capable of achieving a lot.... [and Reagan] is giving America what it has been yearning for. Optimism. Self-belief. Heroes."[3] The Soviet writer might have added, "Luke Skywalker." What the Soviet writer alluded to, without stating it, was that even before the internet, the world had dramatically shrunk. Rock music's ability to penetrate the Iron Curtain proved this: "Music shrank the world," observed rock producer George "Shadow" Morton.[4] East-bloc dictators found it more difficult every year to keep Western ideas, products, and culture out. For communists to compete in the new world of public opinion, the images of aged, thuggish men in uniform swapping sloppy kisses did not play well. New images were needed—especially to compete with the seemingly perpetually effervescent Reagan.

To that end, the KGB made an attempt to meddle in the 1984 presidential election and to renew their efforts to impose a "nuclear freeze." Dr. Helen Caldicott of the left-wing group Physicians for Social Responsibility was a particularly willing dupe and one whom Reagan's daughter, Patti, brought to the White House to meet her father after the MX speech. Caldicott promised to reveal nothing publicly about her talk with the president, a promise she immediately broke.[5] Of more significance was the near-treason of Senator Ted Kennedy, who, through a third party, passed along a message in May 1984 to Soviet premier Yuri Andropov. Kennedy requested that Moscow invite him for a personal visit in July to "arm Soviet officials with explanations of problems of nuclear disarmament so they may be better prepared" in appearances in the United States.[6] While Kennedy was actively trying to stop Reagan's reelection, Hollywood weighed in with a $7 million television movie *The Day After*. Aired in November, the show depicted a nuclear war as seen from Lawrence, Kansas, featuring lots of people being vaporized and plenty of radiation sickness. Eventually, ABC's crew admitted it was a pro-disarmament movie with a rather large budget. Dutch found it "profoundly depressing," and David Gergen, prone to hysteria in the first place, called it "potentially the most powerful thing ever shown on American television" (apparently forgetting the 1977 *Roots* miniseries on slavery).[7] Yet polls showed it had no impact on people's views, at least of Reagan or American defense policy.[8] Reagan personally was popular, and his policies were working.

In 1984 the administration leaked news of a successful—but phony—SDI test intended to make the USSR spend money.

It didn't hurt that the administration engaged in a bit of SDI "disinformation" in the summer of 1984. A test of Star Wars had been planned in which there would be four attempts to shoot down a missile launched from California with another missile. While the first three attempts failed, the fourth test was a success, or so it seemed. Only in 1993 did "unnamed" Reagan officials confirm that they had rigged the test with a homing beacon on the missile. Peter Schweizer confided to historian Paul Kengor that indeed the test had been planned with the intent of diverting Soviet resources against SDI. Just two years earlier, the earliest anyone predicted having any kind of operational hardware was the 1990s. While judging the immediate Soviet reaction is impossible, it certainly reinforced Reagan's original intent of showing the USSR that the productive and inventive capability of the United States was on display.[9] As we will later see, internal memos show that while SDI technology would not be ready for a while, it was nevertheless proceeding at an "astonishing" pace.[10]

Reagan's aggressiveness in Grenada, evicting the Cubans as if flicking a fly, rattled the communists. Dutch's policies had a way of projecting back onto the Soviets exactly what they themselves planned. From 1978 to 1980, with their large SS-18 and SS-19 missiles, the Red missile forces had increasingly been designed for "first-strike" (code words for "surprise attack") capabilities. That window had shut when Reagan deployed the B-1s, the Tridents, and other systems. Likewise, the Soviets had engaged in sweeping military exercises in June 1982 designed to intimidate the Europeans by simulating an invasion of Europe with nuclear weapons. Yet in November 1983, when the US and its allies did the same thing (in an exercise called Able Archer), the jittery Soviets concluded this might be a pretext for a Western "first strike." A heated argument within the Politburo ensued between Andropov and Andrei Gromyko, which resulted in the Soviet dictator instructing the KGB to look for signs of an American surprise attack. Many, including French president François Mitterrand and Soviet spokesman Georgi Arbatov, feared the world was closer to nuclear war than in the Cuban Missile Crisis due to Soviet paranoia.

Far from being a warmonger, Reagan's aversion to nuclear weapons, and to even thinking about nuclear war, caused him to dodge his briefing on the "Single Integrated Operating Plan," which constituted the procedures for launching counterattacks in the event of such a strike, for a year and a half! He was "nearly the first modern president not to receive the SIOP briefing" within his months upon taking office, and, when the briefing finally came, he recorded it in his diary as "sobering."[11] Here, again, was the Reagan paradox: while his enemies in the West portrayed him as "Hitler" and as some "Dr. Strangelove" president—virtually a cowboy riding an ICBM—he was personally obsessed with abolishing nuclear weapons and quite literally worried that Armageddon was not just real but imminent. As Steven Hayward notes in his magisterial *Age of Reagan*, Hal Lindsey's book

The Late Great Planet Earth was a number one bestseller in the 1980s, and more than a few evangelical preachers had prophesied the "End Times" were upon us. Reagan confided in his diary in June 1981, "I swear I believe Armageddon is near," and in 1983 wrote to former speechwriter Peter Hannaford that he had been "wondering about some older prophecies...having to do with Armageddon." He added, "Don't quote me."[12] As late as 1987 Reagan again mentioned Armageddon, expressing concern about the slow process of arms control during a top-secret NSC meeting:

> There has to be an answer to all these questions because some day people are going to ask why we didn't do something now about getting rid of nuclear weapons. You know, I've been reading my Bible and the description of Armageddon talks about destruction, I believe, of many cities and we absolutely need to avoid that. We have to do something now.[13]

Dutch wasn't alone in his administration in his view that Armageddon might be real and had to be avoided. Caspar Weinberger, speaking to a Harvard audience in 1982, confided "I have read the Book of Revelation and, yes, I believe the world is going to end—by an act of God, I hope—how every day I think that time is running out."[14]

Again and again, Reagan reminded his cabinet and arms-control negotiators that maintaining a balance of terror was not acceptable. In a 1987 NSC meeting he reiterated his view that the "whole [arms control] thing was borne of the idea that the world needs to get rid of nuclear weapons.... we *can't win a nuclear war and we can't fight one....* We need to keep in mind that's what we're all about" (emphasis mine).[15] Reagan expressed surprise when the CIA told him the KGB was paranoid about a US attack, telling McFarlane, "I don't see how they could believe that—but it's something to think about."[16] He even joked about "what the h–l have they got that anyone would want?"[17]

Shortly after the first Pershing and cruise missiles were deployed in late 1983, the Soviets stormed out of the START and Geneva talks. Dutch shrugged it off: "They'll be back." Having smacked the Soviets on the snout, though, in his January televised speech he extended a hand with a carrot, insisting on engagement and good-faith negotiations. He ended with an imaginary conversation between two couples, one Russian and one American, in which they found they shared common interests, dreams, and challenges. Yet this was in many ways a throwback to several Dutch daydreams about getting the Soviet dictators on Air Force One, showing them America, allowing them to touch down anywhere and see the prosperity. Reagan always maintained the Beatles' message that "We Can Work It Out" at the same time he realized the reality of the "Evil Empire." Part of the newfound carrot approach, however, lay in the renewed strength of the American economy, which gave the United States a flexibility it had not previously had.

More than four million new jobs had been added since the "Reagan Recession" bottomed out and the economic indicators began their long rise. By the end of 1984, the GDP would hit a pace for the fastest growth in thirty-four years. Driving this economic rebirth, in part, was the continued digital revolution. Computers started to replace human calculations, record keeping, and inventory tracking. Apple released its Macintosh.

Dutch similarly seemed revitalized. After he had fully recovered from the assassin's bullet—and possibly because of that rehabilitation—the Gipper had hit the weight room regularly, often sandwiching in a workout before or after dinner. *Parade* magazine featured him on the cover, pumping iron at age seventy-three, and his chest (already unbelievably tough for surgeons to cut through three years earlier) had expanded by two more inches. When on the ranch, he continued to chop wood, cut brush, and ride horses, further obscuring his age (though by now he wore a hearing aid, ostensibly from the nearby gunshot in his acting years).

Reagan's very appearance was a stark reminder of the contrast between the two sides in the Cold War, for less than a month after his televised speech, Dutch's counterpart, Yuri Andropov, abruptly passed away. Again, Reagan sent Bush to the funeral, saying, "I don't want to honor that prick."[18] The "prick's" successor, Konstantin Chernenko, died just a month later, causing Dutch to ask Nancy, "How am I supposed to get anyplace with the Russians if they keep dying on me?"[19] Fortunately, Shultz had been able to develop a diplomatic gait with Andrei Gromyko, the Soviet minister of foreign affairs, and, following Reagan's televised address, the secretary of state noted that despite having an "ugly dialogue" with the Soviet official it was his "best meeting with Gromyko by miles."[20] Just before Chernenko died, the Soviet leader sent a letter to Reagan that left Dutch with a "gut feeling" he should meet with the Soviet premier in July. The Soviets rejected the overture.

After the events in Grenada and Lebanon, Reagan visited Japan, delivering the first speech by an American president to the Japanese Diet. He received an enthusiastic welcome, interrupted twenty-five times by applause, and used the speech to reiterate his belief that "a nuclear war can never be won and must never be fought." His relationship with Japanese prime minister Yasuhiro Nakasone strengthened further from their meeting at the Williamsburg summit.

From Japan, Reagan flew to Korea, receiving another moving welcome before attending a state dinner where he again condemned the despicable shoot-down of KAL 700. Taken to the Demilitarized Zone (DMZ), he observed through field glasses the North Korean phony Propaganda Village with its cluster of building facades. "It looks like a Hollywood back lot, only not as important," he joked.[21] In a speech to troops of the 2nd Infantry Division, charged with the lonely job of guarding the DMZ, he mistakenly called the commanding general who introduced him "colonel," to the roar of laughter by the soldiers. He then again humorously told them how much they were appreciated back home and that Americans knew "about having to stay awake on guard duty when you'd rather be at a movie." Lou Cannon, covering the trip, groused that "nothing in the trip had been left to chance. Everything had been planned, produced, orchestrated, recorded and flown out."[22] To the pundits, when every aspect was worked out in detail, Reagan was "orchestrated," and when anything was not, there was "internal friction" in the White House.

Reagan was not finished with Asia, visiting China from April 26 to May 1, 1984, and receiving information and advice by phone from Richard Nixon, the first US president to go to China. Nixon emphasized, as only he could, using "Red" China as a counterweight to the Soviet Union. Resting up for a couple of days at the ranch before departing, Reagan first touched down in Hawaii. Although the Chinese leaders had agreed to carry his speech on April 27 in Beijing, instead they feared the message of freedom and edited out key passages, including a phrase in which Reagan said America succeeded due to two great forces, "faith and freedom." But he repeated the "faith" message again in Shanghai the following day. At the time, the trip was considered a success. The president thought China was "on the road to capitalism" and that in any businesses Americans created in China, "capitalism will be there in these plants."[23] Reagan had no idea his words would reach millions of young Chinese. But the year after Reagan stepped down, student-led protests associated with the '89 Democracy movement rose up at Tiananmen Square, during which protestors demanded "Government of the People, by the People, and for the People." Fang Lizhi, one of the leading voices of democracy, told biographer Dinesh D'Souza that the Chinese were "inspired by the idea of the American revolution that Reagan championed."[24]

From June 1–10, Reagan made a trip to Europe that included a visit to his ancestral homeland, Ballyporeen, Ireland. Speaking on June 3, he referred to the "Irish-American tradition" and worried that he would "drown everyone in a bath of nostalgia."[25] Then he went to Normandy to celebrate the fortieth anniversary of D-Day, where a procedural issue threatened to mar the arrival. Reagan's team had wanted the speech to begin at 7:00 p.m. EST in the United States, where it could compete with the Democratic convention in prime time. But Mitterrand wanted to welcome the president to Omaha Beach at 4:00 p.m. EST (10:00 a.m. local). Normally having the host country welcome the president first would be desirable, but Reagan's staff discussed matters with the French ambassador, reminding him that earlier that year Reagan had extended Mitterrand a lavish welcome at the White House, and the famous Pointe du Hoc speech went off as the American delegation planned. By all accounts, this speech, partly crafted by Peggy Noonan, was one of the greatest of Reagan's career. Dutch, his back to the English Channel and framed in flowers, stood on the point of the rock where in 1944 US Army Rangers had climbed up a sheer 130-foot cliff under heavy fire to destroy a gun emplacement—that was not there. (The Germans had withdrawn the guns earlier.)

"When one Ranger fell," Reagan somberly reminded the audience of American veterans who were present, "another would take his place.... One by one the Rangers pulled themselves over the top [and] began to seize back the continent of Europe.... These are the boys of Pointe du Hoc.... These are the champions who helped free a continent. These are the heroes who helped end a war."[26]

There was not a dry eye, even among the cynical press and stoic Secret Service agents. The Gipper had, in a speech for the ages, talked of timeless heroism that had driven the three hundred Spartans to save Greece from the Persian hordes, of the grim dedication of the Alamo defenders who saved Texan independence, and of the determined, rugged Marines who held Khe Sanh against daunting odds at the peak of the Vietnam War. It was somewhat symbolic that Reagan spoke here, at Pointe du Hoc, where the matchless courage bore no real impact on the outcome of the conflict. The actual result of the fight, he knew, was not what was important after all.

Later, Reagan laid a bouquet of flowers on the grave of Theodore Roosevelt's son, Brigadier General Theodore Roosevelt Jr. As the oldest man on the beaches that day and the only general in the first wave, Roosevelt was awarded the Medal of Honor for his battlefield decision to "start the war from right here" after landing in the wrong spot. (Already in poor health and wading ashore with a cane, Roosevelt died a month after landing on Utah Beach.)[27]

Dutch delivered another speech at Omaha Beach that afternoon in the official ceremonies—and it was another triumph. He ended with, "We will always remember. We will always be proud. We will always be prepared, so we may always be free." Though Reagan spent the war in Los Angeles, he spoke as if he had returned to the scene of battle. To Reagan, as the previously discussed flap about the death camp footage pointed out, war *footage*—which was 100 percent real—differed from movies, a distinction his critical biographers fail to grasp. Men who died in war footage film really died.

The great stage of the foreign tours provided the setting for Reagan's reelection campaign. Cannon and other biographers typically ascribed Reagan's landslide reelection in 1984 to his personality, the fact that Americans liked him, and his ability to play a winning role. But there was something else: in the 1980s, the television media still largely reported actual news, not commentary. Thus, extended versions of Reagan's speeches abroad and at home were usually televised. Since the general public still received the overwhelming amount of its news via the three television network newscasts and the local newspapers, Reagan could often get his points across simply through speaking events. Whether it was "acting" or a more subtle understanding of American popular media of the day, Dutch used the medium that would yield the best results.

Modern Americans would not recognize this type of coverage, for in the twenty-first century, no politician (and certainly no conservative) is given large blocks of uninterrupted time to state his case. Quite the contrary, nowadays a typical "newscast" would begin with a hyperbolic headline, follow that with less than fifteen *seconds* of a president speaking, then give way to a panel of four to five "experts," all of whom are bitterly opposed to any conservative principle. Those today who long for a more traditional televised speech to explain policy objectives are barking up the wrong decade's tree.

So was it "acting" at all? Was Lincoln "acting" when he adapted to the stump-speech debate style of the day, invoking God and the Bible at every opportunity? Or was it "acting" when FDR took to the radio—again, uninterrupted by commentators—to relay his goals for America? Such charges miss the essential genius of Reagan in identifying and perfecting the communication medium of the day, along with all of its "stage setting" and visual signaling. They also completely ignore the reality that when a politician is in front of a camera he still has to say *something*. And the "something" Reagan had to say connected with real people across party lines. Cannon himself quoted a voter (a retired brewery worker in Texas) who said, "He really isn't like a Republican....He's more like an American."[28] Yet this is precisely the genius of a great politician—that he makes potential political opponents believe they agree with him on the issues, regardless of party.

To merely ascribe Reagan's fantastic success to "communication skills" would be a profound misjudgment. He comprehended and then leveraged a more fundamental trend, a genuine realignment in American politics that had occurred after 1976 when the Republicans had crashed to their lowest point in recent history. Reagan's stunning election in 1980 had been explained away as "Carter was just bad." Indeed he was. But the funny thing about winning is that it tends to inspire others to win with you, a phenomenon easily observed on any sports team. When a "winner" arrives—a Roger Staubach in football or a Michael Jordan in basketball—he lifts average teams to new heights. The mood Reagan inspired among many (though not all) Republicans was that perhaps they were not consigned to being the minority party forever.

A classic example of the new dichotomy was the minority leader Robert Michel of Illinois, the epitome of the "go-along-to-get-along" Republican and a golf-playing buddy of Tip O'Neill. Michel was more than comfortable with a Republican minority so long as the party got a few bones thrown its way and was invited to all the cocktail soirees. He despised partisanship, which the Democrats always defined as disagreeing with them. Newt Gingrich of Georgia, however, was a new breed, a Reagan congressman who loved ideological debate and had no small lust for power. He waded into a highly volatile floor debate over the "Dear Comandante" letter that the congressional Democrats had sent to Nicaraguan communist dictator Daniel Ortega in April 1984. Gingrich attacked the letter as "cross[ing] the bounds from legitimate opposition to American policy to a deliberate communication of that opposition to a foreign government."[29] Gingrich's floor debate with O'Neill—where the Irishman called the Georgian "un-American" backfired—was captured on the C-SPAN network. Like everything in American life ever since the McCarthy hearings, video lent a powerful emotional impact to stories that mere words could never convey. Trent Lott, a young Republican congressman who himself would become quite "Michel-esque" after dwelling in the Swamp for many years, insisted that the Republicans were completely united in their anger against the despotic Democrats. Even the *Washington Post* commented on the apparent shift from meekness to partisan strength among the minority party.

In fact, a realignment of sorts had been gaining momentum for a while. Despite Republicans losing seats in 1982, a White House memo noted that in the Senate the GOP won 41 percent of the elections, compared with a

"6th-year average" of 34 percent; that the Republicans gained eight gover-nors when the party in power had never gained governorships in a modern off-year election; and that the House loss of five seats represented the small-est six-year loss since 1866.[30] Moreover, the Senate losses were extremely narrow, and the GOP lost every one. But, the memo noted, the "realign-ment is real." Republicans expanded control of the statehouses from sixteen to twenty-four, won a "Sun Belt Sweep" of governor's races, and most important, had brought party identification to parity—something unheard of in 1976. Reagan himself ended the campaign at a 67 percent approval rating, raising Republican strength in every category from its 1980 levels.[31]

So the realignment was real and had been in place, and it gained speed with Reagan. Of course, the media dislikes having clear sides drawn because liberals almost always appear more "reasonable" when they are not confronted with an aggressive challenger who makes them defend their views, which was exactly what Reagan (and, now, Newt) did. However, to argue, as Steven Hayward has, that Reagan started a "conservative counter-revolution" probably goes too far in that many of these "Reaganites" were little more than deathbed converts. *Many* Establishment Republicans pre-tended to embrace Reaganism as long as the polls were on their side. But how many Goldwater Republicans were left in the Senate after Goldwater himself retired in 1986? Several were traditional conservatives, including John Warner of Virginia, Howard Baker of Tennessee, and Bob Dole, men who still Bible-thumped on deficits but ran away from the so-called "social issues." Of the new visionary Reaganites, only a handful—such as Gingrich in the House—could be found. Probably the most conservative senator in 1984 was also the oldest: Strom Thurmond of South Carolina, who arguably was the oldest senator on the planet! The most Reagan-like were Alan Simpson of Wyoming, Paul Laxalt, and the new incoming Democrat Phil Gramm of Texas, who would eventually become a Republican. Then, as today, most senators kept their distance from any "revolution" talk and gratefully accepted Dutch's support when it came to their campaigns.

When considering the Gipper's reelection campaign, it is interesting to note that the polls at the time again failed to capture the sentiment of real Americans. In February, polls indicated that only 38 percent of those surveyed approved of Reagan's foreign policy. As late as October, Reagan still languished below 50 percent in some polls that showed him behind in potential matchups with Democrats. (Other polls had him well ahead, however, crushing Democrats by 20 points. "It looks so good it's frightening," one campaign aide said.)[32] Beneath the flawed top-layer statistics, however, there was a mass of data showing Reagan would smash any challenger: he was viewed as a "leader," especially after his smackdown of PATCO and his glowingly successful foreign trips. Then there was the popularity issue. People just liked Reagan, a detail ABC picked up in exit polls that showed two-thirds of the voters—even those who voted against him—liked the president personally.[33]

It is easy to ignore the issues and focus on Reagan's personality. America's economy was "sizzling" with 7.4 percent growth and only 3.2 percent inflation by July 1984, and while the long-term damage of pure "free trade" would be hidden for almost two decades, temporarily Reaganomics had brought some revival to the Rust Belt. New manufacturing jobs constituted about 25 percent of all new jobs created during the recovery, while industrial state unemployment fell (by 8 percent in Michigan, and in selected cities such as Youngstown, Ohio, and Rockford, Illinois, by six to eight points there as well). Private capital investment was up, and the Japanese threat from its state-directed industry conglomerates had already started to slow.[34]

This was no small point. Japanese automakers had vied with their American counterparts and almost put Chrysler out of business (Carter saved it with a bailout in 1979). Toyota was challenging General Motors for the position of largest automaker in the world, and, in shipbuilding, robotics, electronics, and steel, Japanese firms took the lead or attained parity with their American counterparts. Indeed, American "Big Steel" had lost market share since the 1960s—mostly to Japan—falling behind foreign rivals in technology while suffering from higher labor costs. Between 1974 and 1986, steelmaking jobs fell by 337,000, and in Dutch's first term, the industry saw total capacity fall by 30 percent.[35] The carnage was shocking, as one-fourth of all US steelmakers went bankrupt and 75 percent of all steelworkers lost their jobs. Some of this involved industry shifts as automakers moved to lighter plastics and composites, and as Reagan took office, already companies such as Nucor were opening "minimills" that would soon surpass traditional steelmaking in productivity.[36] That took time, however, and in the 1980s criticisms of Reagan's policies by Ira Magaziner, Robert Reich, and Lester Thurow raised questions of whether a "new economy" could ever replace the industrial jobs.[37]

Over time, some of the critics' concerns would prove sound, but at the time, they were seemingly proven wrong by the computer and high-tech revolution that had gripped the world and which was centered in America. Once again, it took George Gilder to explain that manufacturing was playing an increasingly smaller role in the world economy (though in hindsight it is clear that Gilder understated the significance of manufacturing, especially for national security purposes).[38] He argued that Japan had succeeded in the first place by creating *more* competitors, not fewer, and in Reagan's lifetime the Japanese economy would turn "relentlessly bleak," falling to 1.5 percent a year growth.[39] Further, under Reagan's watch—but without any government "assistance" or interference—a new computer industry had sprung up that would dominate the world. While voices such as Magaziner and Reich called for an "industrial policy" that would control and direct fields that included high-tech, new industry dynamos like Intel were rattling out "a string of chips that increased processing power by *1,000 percent in less than seven years.*"[40] An industry that hadn't even existed just fifteen years earlier, the personal computer industry, soared to world dominance in Reagan's terms. Similar revolutions were occurring in optics, fiber cables, cellular phones, and communications. A whole new region sprang up to replace what was increasingly called the "Rust Belt": Silicon Valley.

As Reagan's trade and taxation policies took hold, the computer revolution was easy enough to see, but the side effects of the deindustrialization and "reindustrialization" were not. Obscured by both the job growth in the tech industries and the sudden weakness in Japan's industrial policy, Reagan's economy fed the surging information society without simultaneously restructuring the traditional industries. By whipping inflation and cutting taxes, Reagan had saved millions from bankruptcy and perhaps even bread lines. Liberals grew so desperate for a counter to the Reagan-induced growing prosperity that under Representative Richard Gephardt and Senator Bill Bradley they even proposed a massive flattened tax code revision, putting the top rate at 30 percent. The appeal was lost on the eventual Democratic candidate Walter Mondale.

Although eight Democrats would seek the nomination, and Mondale would win it, the airiest bubble enveloped the candidate of the good-looking playboy Gary Hart (né Hartpence), the senator from Colorado. He had the looks and physical appeal to challenge Dutch—which only the most thickheaded would any longer say did not matter. He was young. And he supposedly was a "new Democrat," which was a term that had not really come of age yet (but would with Bill Clinton eight years later). Hart briefly captured the hearts of many Democrats with his ill-defined policies, but soon his bizarre biography caught up to him (he changed his age and his name and failed to mention he had separated from his wife—twice). Hart's womanizing was not the issue it would become three years later, when he was caught on a yacht called the *Monkey Business* with actress Donna Rice, but the other peculiarities quickly drove his front-running campaign down. That was not to say Mondale's campaign exactly rose: he won the nomination much by default, the way Bob Dole would the Republican nomination in 1996.

As a former vice president to Jimmy Carter, the silver-haired, chiseled-faced Mondale was hopelessly saddled with the Georgian's policies, and his party had moved steadily further left since Reagan became president. Worse, Jesse Jackson and his "Rainbow Coalition" had done exceptionally well in states with large black populations, pushing Mondale further to the Left. To answer the threat from Jackson, Mondale named a woman, Geraldine Ferraro, a representative from New York, as his vice presidential pick (for the first time in history). As if his über-liberal platform wasn't enough to alienate undecided voters, in his acceptance speech Mondale promised to raise taxes. As Mondale basked in the cheers of the convention, he quietly said to Congressman Dan Rostenkowski, "Look at 'em; we're going to tax their ass off."[41]

When Dutch could escape the "play it safe" shackles his campaign team put on him, he observed of Mondale, he "sees an America in which every day is tax day, April 15...we see a day in which every day is Independence Day."[42] As his classic political ad, "Morning in America," was rolled out, its metaphorical images of renewal couldn't be more clear. "Today," the ad said, "more men and women will go to work than ever before in our country's history.... [and the nation has] inflation at less than half of what it was just four years ago....Why would we ever want to return to where we were less than four short years ago?" Why indeed. Later, a second powerful ad called "The Bear in the Woods" featured a grizzly bear prowling across a landscape with the narrator soberly saying, "There is a bear in the woods. For some people, the bear is easy to see. Others don't see it at all. Some people say the bear is tame. Other say it's vicious and dangerous. Since no one can really be sure...isn't it smart to be as strong as the bear?" Taken together, the "Morning/Bear" ads perfectly played Reagan as the candidate with hope and vision, yet with reassuring common sense.

Reagan has been criticized by friend and foe alike for running a defensive campaign, what one biographer called the "political equivalent of the four-corner stall in basketball." Steven Hayward lamented this as "one of the greatest lost opportunities in American politics to break the opposition party and bring about a lasting and fundamental realignment." Ironically both the Reagan supporter (Hayward) and skeptic (Cannon) accuse the Gipper of being lazy, but from different perspectives. To Hayward, Reagan didn't want to push his "revolution" far enough, and to Cannon, the Gipper "coasted through the campaign, relying on the glow of the economic recovery and his identification with...a 'mythic America'"—which Cannon apparently saw as a bad thing.[43]

Both Reagan and his advisors knew, however, that his policies had only just taken effect, that the economy—while growing—was still fragile, and that his foreign policy overtures hadn't begun to truly bear fruit. Why did Reagan not mention SDI in the campaign, as some insisted he should have? A better question would be: why would he tout a research project in its infancy that could either collapse entirely or suffer a string of technological pitfalls before it matured? Why did Reagan not campaign on cutting government growth and lowering taxes further? Perhaps because his own staff had received a cold bath of reality when trying to make even incremental changes to Social Security. Dutch had expended almost every ounce of his political capital in his first term securing the tax cuts he had. Most of all, Reagan knew that if the Republican Party itself wasn't yet fully behind his revolution, they could not articulate it to the American public. In show business, the "elevator pitch" needs to be one line, and that line in 1984 was "It's Morning in America."

Dutch ran a logical, highly successful campaign, marred only by ongoing questions of his age, which were made worse by a debate performance in Louisville with Mondale. The Democrat arrived at the debate prepared to hammer all of the administration's projections and predictions when it came to the budget (still not realizing that deep down Americans *don't care* about the budget or deficits, only about prices and wages). He said Reagan's team "missed the mark by nearly $600 billion." But Reagan deftly replied that Mondale didn't have a plan for balancing the budget: he had a plan for raising taxes, which was accurate. Unfortunately, when asked directly if he had a plan to raise taxes (which all administrations have in reserve), Reagan trotted out his "there you go again" line to laughter and applause. But Mondale was ready: "You remember the last time you said that?" Reagan replied he did. Mondale said he had used that in a debate about cutting Medicare and "you went out and tried to cut $20 billion out of Medicare." Mondale got his own laughs. By all accounts, Reagan was flustered, confused, and lost his train of thought in his closing remarks, admitting he "flattened out." Privately he told his wife, "I was terrible," and Nancy recalled it as "a disaster."[44] To critics, the meandering and confusion indicated Reagan was, in fact, mentally impaired and too old.[45]

Nancy was furious, lashing out at aides for over-preparing her husband with statistics. Dutch's staff, on the other hand, blamed the candidate for not studying enough. Reporters burned up the phones to find psychologists and aging experts who could explain Reagan's weak performance, and the *Wall Street Journal* asked, "Is Oldest U.S. President Showing his Age?"[46] The *New York Times* chimed in, saying, "Age may have been a factor."

Reagan blew the issue out of the water in the second debate, where he certainly expected a question about his age. When asked if he was up to the challenge—at his age—of going days with little sleep like John Kennedy did in the Cuban Missile Crisis, Dutch said it wouldn't be a problem at all and added, "I want you to know that I will not make age an issue of this campaign. I am not going to exploit, for political purposes, my opponent's youth and inexperience." It was every bit as much a "there you go again" line as he had with Carter. The audience laughed, and even Mondale laughed. How well Reagan did, or did not do, in the second debate was erased with the joke, which again reminded the public how much they liked the Gipper over a guy who wanted to talk deficits and taxes.

Armed with the "Morning in America" ad and a knockout in the second debate, Reagan embarrassed Mondale, winning forty-nine of fifty states—he lost Mondale's home state of Minnesota—and crushed him in the popular vote, 59 percent to 41 percent. Again, on paper the shift looked like a revolution, as just twenty years earlier, the "pre-Reagan Reagan," Barry Goldwater, had been similarly beaten by twenty points. Thus, a thirty-eight-point shift in two decades was significant. Political observer Michael Barone thought the election had already been won by the time Reagan delivered his D-Day speech, and advisor Ed Rollins placed the turning point even earlier, when the troops were withdrawn from Lebanon. Regardless, he had won every age group. The stock market soared. The Gipper dryly noted that the press "is now trying to prove it wasn't a landslide or should I say a mandate?"[47] Unfortunately, the numbers in Congress said that the Republicans had no widespread endorsement. They gained only fourteen seats (versus the thirty-three they won in 1980). It was not enough to offset the 1982 losses in the House, and Reagan ran seventeen million votes ahead of the Republicans in the House. They actually lost two seats in the Senate. O'Neill raced to the microphones to insist "There is no mandate out there," and the New York Times promptly parroted "Poll Finds Reagan Failed to Obtain Policy Mandate."[48]

Contrary to the urging of hard-knuckled pols like Ed Rollins and Newt Gingrich, Reagan had avoided a polarizing realignment. He did not even use the language of further revolution in his speeches by the end of the campaign, speaking in FDR-ish appeals to hands-across-the-aisle. "Join us," Reagan intoned. "Come walk with us down that new path of hope and opportunity." He did not mount a major offensive to build up the

Republican Party, nor was it in his DNA to shatter his former party, the Democrats. Indeed, many voters cited Reagan's "leadership" and ability to work with Congress as one of the main factors determining their vote. His appeal to a national vision of hope was seemingly symbolized by the Los Angeles Olympic Games, which for the first time transported the Olympic torch from Greece to Los Angeles via thousands of runners handing the torch off over an eighty-two-day period. The Olympic torch—an international symbol—suddenly was transformed into Lady Liberty's torch in a new burst of patriotism and nationalism.

Against this, the Democrats rolled out the old hate-filled playbook. O'Neill said "the evil is in the White House at the present time [in the form of] a man who has no care and no concern for the working class of America."[49] And once again, the media played along, referencing the divisions and "breach" between the two sides as the worst ever, while calling Republicans "far-right" or "conservative" far more often than they used terms like "far-left" or "liberal" to describe Democrats. It never stuck to Dutch: he was too honest, too genuine. This was seen in his consistency of speech and thought for twenty years. As H. W. Brands correctly observed, "Reagan had never faltered. He refused to change his message [using] the same images and even some of the same phrases he had employed in his 1964 speech." Ultimately, Brands concluded, "What had been dismissed as delusion won new appreciation as vision."[50]

Moreover, Reagan's vision was already being reflected in the popular culture. Andrew Breitbart, cofounder of the Drudge Report and Breitbart News, would later utter the maxim that "politics is downstream of culture," meaning that the society has to adopt a position before politicians can effectively legislate. This, after all, was the essence of one of the four pillars of American exceptionalism, that with "common law," God put the law inside the hearts of the people, and their leaders merely enacted and enforced that which was already adopted. Reagan's America saw a new burst of films depicting "hard body" heroes that differed sharply from Clint Eastwood's classic *Dirty Harry* movies. In 1970s action movies, the heroes might solve the crime, but the corrupt and incompetent individuals who enabled the criminals in the first place remained in power. The heroes of

Reagan's presidency, however, were "thrust forward into heroism [not] in defiance of their society but…of their governments and institutionalized bureaucracies." In such films as *First Blood* ("Rambo," 1982) and *Rambo: First Blood Part II* (1985), *Missing in Action* (1984), and *Robocop* (1987), the heroes were "pitted against the bureaucracies that have lost touch with the people."[51] This was a key theme of Reaganism: the need to decrease the size of government and to redirect the government to serve the people. *Die Hard* (1988) and *Lethal Weapon* (1987), far from calling for the elimination of the police, saw outsiders as seeking to return law enforcement to its original greatness. (Indeed, Bruce Willis, in *Die Hard*, begs the police—the "cavalry," as he calls them—to hustle to Nakatomi Plaza and deal with the bad guys.) One author likened Reagan himself to Robocop.[52] In *Red Dawn* (1984) and *Top Gun* (1986), bold patriotism was on full display, again with good-looking, young, healthy actors and actresses.

Similarly, the Reagan '80s celebrated the human physique with the rise of the exercise industry and aerobics (as seen in the film *Perfect* [1985]) and featured the rise of a former Mr. Universe (Arnold Schwarzenegger) into the biggest box-office draw of the decade. Such images were reaffirmed in Reagan himself: as one *Time* magazine reporter described it:

> Ronald Reagan lifted the double-edged ax above his head and slammed it into the tree branch lying on the ground…and kept swinging for two full minutes. His face glistened with sweat…. In his faded denim shirt, leather gloves, scuffed boots and cowboy hat, he looked fit and even young.[53]

Intellectuals fumed that Reagan, with his own workout regimen, had become a "collective symbol" of individual action and self-sufficiency. It was, in the eyes of some analysts, a rejection of the weakened and feminine Carter years—a president who had made them feel "puny."[54] But in overcoming the assassin's bullet, Dutch showed that events that could have defeated a lesser man—"or, more to the point, a lesser body"—were unable to overcome him.[55] Now he had dismissed a second Democrat challenger with ease.

Despite two serious thumpings in the last two presidential elections and, going back to Nixon, two landslides out of four, the inclination might be to view the Democrats as collapsing, or to view them as in disarray. In the twentieth century, however, each political party had its own period of bad fortune and each time the proverb ascribed to Count Metternich applies: "The Democrats are never as strong as they appear, and never as weak as they appear." Reagan's success had made the Democrats, at least temporarily, try to hide their radicalism with stage managing, including lots of American flags. If the Republicans had not yet bought into a conservative counterrevolution, neither had the Democrats yet accepted that their brand of liberalism would not sell in most of America. But those were lessons for another election.

In the election's aftermath, Reagan did not march back into the Washington temple and overturn the K Street vendors' tables or drive out the bureaucrats with his riding crop. Instead he engaged in the far more immediate task of bringing the USSR to heel once and for all. His landslide gave him increased credibility and leverage, both with the Soviets and with some recalcitrant Democrats back home. In late October, Edmund Morris observed the christening of the USS *Theodore Roosevelt*, a state-of-the-art, powerful warship with its flyover of F-14s that screamed, "*Tremble, you sons of Soviet bitches!*"[56] Morris's reaction was typical of that of many Americans to a highly visible incarnation of American power—except the carrier, for all its weaponry, paled in comparison to the power of the nuclear-armed *Ohio* that had launched into the water two years earlier. It was an object lesson about the tips of icebergs.

Fittingly, on an icy cold day in January, Dutch took his second oath of office, then attended eleven balls. Then, as if to dunk the basketball, two weeks later Reagan delivered an "oratorical triumph" in his State of the Union that had "senior Democrats shaking their heads in admiration."[57] His landslide had the Soviet Union shaking in a much different way.

15

Foxes, Henhouses

Entering his second term, Dutch knew he was slowly winning the Cold War. A CIA briefing told him the Soviets were already seeing their gains eroded.[1] They had lost the battle to stop deployment of the MX missile, failed in their "freeze" offensive against the Euromissiles, and could not prevent the new B-1 bombers and *Ohio*-class subs from being produced and deployed. Most of all, they now faced the astronomically expensive SDI program. Although several in Reagan's National Security Council continued to view SDI merely as a tradeoff—a giveaway in arms-control negotiations—in Dutch's mind, the system would be built regardless, fully in keeping with his "trust, but verify" approach to arms-control talks. In all their discussions, the NSC members kept coming back to one inescapable conclusion: Star Wars was a breakthrough no matter how it was used.

A final tipping point occurred through more natural processes. Konstantin Chernenko, the Soviet dictator, died on March 11, 1985. Reagan was informed that Mikhail Gorbachev was the new "head man." Western media celebrated him as "young," but that was silly: "Gorby" (as talk show host Rush Limbaugh called him) was in his mid-fifties and merely seemed young compared to the dinosaurs that had held the reins of power before him. He was somewhat different than his predecessors, though *not* the radical alternative to communism that many Westerners portrayed him as being. The CIA's Robert Gates recalled thinking that Gorbachev was "a leader who was prepared to make tough decisions" but, of course, so was

Stalin.[2] As before, Reagan skipped Chernenko's funeral and sent Bush (who adopted the slogan, "You die, I'll fly").

At the time, Reagan was awaiting minor surgery to remove a polyp from his intestine. After the initial examination, though, doctors found a golf-ball-sized mass in his colon and feared it was "precancerous," so they suggested removing it right then. Nancy insisted on being the one to tell him, with the good news being that he wouldn't have to drink the GoLytely regimen that cleared out the bowels again. Of course, the Gipper replied with a joke: "Does this mean I won't be getting dinner tonight, either?" Indeed he didn't. But after the growth was removed, it was found to be malignant, and Nancy was crushed. The doctors told her, however, "prospects are for a full recovery and a normal life," and they had excised the tumor before it got to any surrounding tissue. During this time Nancy had communicated in guarded language with Don Regan, the new chief of staff, who later assumed that the scheduling of the surgery had to do with astrology. In *My Turn*, Nancy emphatically denied that and reviewed the schedule of events at the hospital. But this was just the first indication that life with the new chief of staff would be more difficult than with James Baker.[3]

With Dutch in the hospital, it fell to George Bush (who was in Geneva at the arms-control meetings) and George Shultz to attend the Chernenko funeral and subsequent reception. Reagan had given Shultz specific instructions to get quite frank and personal with Gorbachev, to feel him out. Both Bush and Shultz were immediately impressed with the new Soviet leader and wondered if, finally, change might be possible. Gorbachev insisted to the American delegation that the USSR did not have "expansionist ambitions" (even as his troops were in Afghanistan and while his country was supporting Nicaragua's socialist government). He also alluded to the previous past cooperation in World War II as a "bright page in the history of Soviet-U.S. relations."[4]

While Gorbachev's sophistication and openness to seeing the errors of communism have been overblown by sympathetic Western writers, he was certainly the first Soviet leader to appreciate the very tenuous economic position in which the USSR was enmeshed. Whether he was or wasn't able to admit the theoretical failures of Marxism-Leninism, he was smart enough to know that very soon his cardboard structure would fall down around his ears if he didn't so something, and fast. Even before he became premier, Gorbachev won Margaret Thatcher's endorsement. "I like Mr. Gorbachev," she told Shultz. "We can do business together."

In fact, however, the Soviet Union had blinked back in November of 1984, when, on Thanksgiving, it was announced that Andrei Gromyko and Shultz would meet in Geneva the following January to enter into new, wide-ranging arms-control talks. Shultz noted "a sense of excitement [that] an effort of immense significance" was upon the two nations.[5] That December, after a letter from Chernenko was delivered to Reagan urging the elimination of all nuclear weapons in space, Dutch saw an opening. The NSC held meetings to outline the specifics of the discussions and Reagan again was adamant that all nuclear weapons should be eliminated and that the US—and he hoped the Soviets—would move toward strategic defense over time. Shultz dragged his feet, arguing strategic defense "was not everything." He still did not see the Gipper's big picture.

Instead, Shultz thought the US was already "pulling away in the competition" merely through traditional weapons and thought the deployment of the Euromissiles constituted the turning point. However, he admitted that piling on SDI and the president's landslide victory meant "the Soviets were going to be left at the station as the train pulled out."[6] Over time, repeatedly, in NSC planning group meetings, Reagan would reiterate the goal of moving to purely defensive weapons, only to have one of the staffers (in this case, Kenneth Adelman) argue to retain nuclear weapons for use in Europe.[7] Reagan and Shultz, however, found a chink in the Soviet negotiating armor they could exploit. The Soviets had simply failed to keep their word. "Noncompliance" would be the crowbar with which they would pry open Russia's negotiating vault.

A January 1984 NSC meeting had warned of an "expanding pattern of Soviet non-compliance," followed by a February 1985 NSDD called "Soviet Noncompliance With Arms Control Agreements (C)."[8] In May 1985, Reagan issued one of the most important NSDDs of his tenure, NSDD 172, called "Presenting the Strategic Defense Initiative."[9] Soviet noncompliance was a "very serious concern," and the document cited phased-array radars and increases in mobile missiles. Over the long run, the Soviets' persistence in clinging to offensive weapons threatened even traditional deterrence. SDI offered a way out, "respond[ing] directly to the ongoing and extensive Soviet anti-ballistic missile effort [which] provides a necessary and powerful deterrent to any near-term Soviet decision to expand rapidly." There it was. Reagan had successfully invoked *Soviet* defensive buildup to justify the inevitability of Star Wars!

Reagan insisted that negotiations would be aggressive and flexible in seeking to reduce nuclear weapons but that "we will protect the potential offered by the SDI research program to alter the adverse, long-term prospects we now face." For the purposes of arms-control negotiations, SDI was "wholly compatible with the Anti-Ballistic Missile (ABM) Treaty." No one was under any illusions: the USSR "will certainly attempt to protect [its] massive, long-term investment." However, the Soviets fully understood that "the SDI program—and most especially, that portion of the program which holds out *the promise of destroying missiles in the boost, post-boost, and mid-course portions of their flight*—offers the prospect of redressing Soviet offensive advantages," advantages which had been acquired over many years and with the vast expenditure of resources (emphasis mine).[10]

America's negotiating strategy in presenting the SDI program nationally was "not to seek superiority" but to assure stable deterrence. Once again, lest anyone claim the Reagan administration was overly optimistic about the timetable or challenges involved in Star Wars, the NSDD noted that "research will last for some years" and will be "carried out on a broad front of technologies" with "initial development decisions [that] could be made in the early nineties." And again, contrary to critics who insisted SDI was pursuing a single approach (i.e., lasers), the administration noted, "We do not have any preconceived notions about the defensive options research may generate," and it would "not proceed to development and deployment unless the research indicates that defenses meet strict criteria." Those criteria included defenses that were survivable and cost-effective, but the administration emphasized that it was too early to "speculate on the kinds of defensive systems [to be used]—whether ground-based or space-based."

The singular goal was to destroy attacking enemy missiles before they could reach their targets. Once the research had borne fruit, the US would consult with allies about deployment and to negotiate with the Soviets, but that would "in no way be interpreted as according the Soviets a veto over possible future defensive deployments." But, the document concluded, "for the foreseeable future, offensive nuclear forces and the prospect of nuclear retaliation will remain the key element of deterrence."[11]

In one sweeping statement, Reagan's team had addressed a reasonable strategy for the present with a visionary and clever approach for a transition to a new defensive posture. As with all great conflicts, the immediate impact was not clear outside the National Security Council's chambers. Over the next year, as the battle raged in Afghanistan, it would be joined by contests from the negotiating tables in Geneva to the jungles of Central America.

El Salvador and Nicaragua were closely tied together.[12] Early in his administration Reagan had dispatched fifty-five military advisors and $25 million in aid to the El Salvadoran government. Leftists pounced on "another Vietnam" (seemingly their only criticism of anti-communist efforts abroad). Nearby Nicaragua had suffered from an insurgency by the Sandinista rebels who, despite the assurances of Western liberals, were dyed-in-the-wool Marxists. Dutch originally hoped to squash the rebels through economic growth stemming from the Cancun summit of October 1981, but the State Department drug its heels, leading to Reagan upping the ante with the Caribbean Basin Initiative.

Prosperity can indeed work as a buffer against communism, but it takes time and there were no quick fixes in Nicaragua. Reagan's team didn't take Nicaragua that seriously at first, and the Ortega brothers who ran the country sensed weakness in Washington. Reagan signed a "presidential finding"—a document finding an emergency need to conduct an operation or engage in buying or selling materials—in 1981 authorizing the CIA to conduct covert operations to interdict arms shipments to El Salvador and at the same time plan to arm the resistance movement against the Ortegas in Nicaragua. In December 1981, the NSC proposed military aid to Nicaraguan exiles, but almost all agreed that the "Contras," as they were called, were too small to be effective. Although the United States was restricted from overthrowing a sovereign foreign government, that had not stopped any administration from "making suggestions." Democrats in the House, whose own presidents JFK and LBJ had more than flaunted these rules, were determined to keep Reagan from doing the same. Congressman Edward Boland (D-MA), who chaired the House Intelligence Committee, attached an amendment to the 1981 Pentagon budget known as the Boland Amendment that banned any American support "for the purpose of overthrowing the Government of Nicaragua."

The administration accepted the Boland Amendment because there were other, more restrictive measures being discussed in Congress and it was the best of several bad options. Moreover, Reagan's team thought they could still fund the Contras within the language of the amendment, rather than immediately challenging it in court as an unconstitutional limitation on executive powers. After new elections in El Salvador in 1985 retained José Duarte in El Salvador, Congress voted continued El Salvador assistance but turned down aid to Nicaragua, just as the Contras were making headway against the Ortegas. Fortunately, the US invasion of Grenada had caused the Soviets to rethink additional aid to the Sandinistas. Unfortunately, the State Department still thought the Contra cause hopeless and argued for negotiations. When word leaked out to Congress of various CIA-backed assistance for the Contras, virtually all support evaporated. All funds tied to direct or indirect paramilitary operations in Central America were yanked. Following passage of the Senate's version of the FY85 budget, even tighter (likely unconstitutional) restrictions were placed on aid to the Contras. Dutch was stuck: he couldn't veto the budget because he needed the economy to keep humming and needed the military spending against the USSR.

Reagan's subordinates began scheming for ways to circumvent Congress's restrictions on aid to the Contras almost immediately, including finding ways to entice Saudi Arabia to serve as a money funnel.

Outwardly, Reagan opted for negotiations with the Ortegas. It had been at that point in April that the House Democrats had penned their "Dear Comandante" letter to Daniel Ortega—an outrageous act but, in the end, irrelevant in terms of Nicaraguan policy. A June 25 NSC meeting, though, showed how frustrated many in the administration were about finding some way to help the Contras. Some, including Caspar Weinberger and Jeane Kirkpatrick, wondered if the president couldn't persuade anti-communist neighbors to send aid, essentially becoming a funnel. James Baker and Shultz thought that notion was not only illegal but likely would result in impeachment charges. In short, the Contra issue was viewed as an extremely dangerous pitfall from the beginning.

There was exactly such a dangerous scheme already unfolding, thanks to discussions between Reagan and his NSC advisor Bud McFarlane about how to fund the Contras. McFarlane had tasked his staffer, Marine Colonel Oliver North, to devise a plan. North's byzantine arrangement had Saudi Arabia sending money to bank accounts held by the Contras in Miami. It was the opening note in a disastrous subterfuge that would envelope the Gipper in the most damaging event of his presidency. Already, other unrelated notes could be heard from seemingly unrelated regions: only two weeks after the Marines had left Lebanon in 1984, CNN's Beirut bureau chief, Jeremy Levin, was kidnapped, as was, a week later, the CIA station chief, William Buckley. Another dozen Americans would be kidnapped in the next year, with the CIA unable to even figure out who was doing the kidnapping, let alone secure their release. The Marine withdrawal had turned out to be no withdrawal at all, only an exchange of military targets for civilians. While these abductions would provide a drip-drip-drip of pressure on Reagan to act, as of early 1985 they remained largely unseen and, unfortunately for those taken, largely unimportant in the larger geopolitical struggle taking shape.

All attention focused on the new head of the Soviet Union, Mikhail Gorbachev, who was, in his first meeting with George H. W. Bush at Chernenko's funeral, highly disturbed by Star Wars. He told Bush the Soviets had no intention of fighting the United States, calling those who held such views "madmen," insisting that "history [would] judge" which system was better.[13] Like Reagan, Gorbachev had grown up in humble means—though that was common in the USSR—but unlike Dutch he went to his nation's elite university and then immediately into politics. Far from the "different" kind of communist leader that many have portrayed him as being, Gorbachev—much like Dutch did with FDR—romanticized his predecessors' vision. He spoke glowingly of Lenin and his "lofty moral strength..... Lenin lives on in the minds and hearts of millions of people."[14] His wife, Raisa, was an even more devout Marxist-Leninist than he was, and she, like Nancy Reagan, supported her husband in his political ambitions.[15]

Great misunderstanding surrounds Gorbachev and his role in ending the Cold War. Had he not come along, the outcome for the USSR would not have changed: it was on a meteor-like trajectory to impact the ground and disintegrate. All Gorbachev changed was how big the crater would be. Indeed, some political scientists—trying to minimize the Gipper's role—have claimed that his "rhetoric and policies...delayed the reconfiguration of the Soviet outlook" in the Gorbachev era.[16] If that was the case, then Reagan *greatly accelerated* Soviet decline and in fact was more likely to have forced Gorbachev into increasingly weak positions!

Yet historians insist on giving the Soviet dictator superhuman powers of transformation. According to a popular textbook, *Nation of Nations*, "Gorbachev's reform policies led not only to the collapse of the Soviet empire but also the breakup of the Soviet Union itself," while another, *America: A Narrative History*, claimed Gorbachev "backed off Soviet imperial ambitions" (which, presumably, is why it took him three years to evacuate Afghanistan).[17] *Unto a Good Land* echoes other liberal textbooks' assessments: "Perhaps more important [than Reagan], under a new, younger leadership, the Kremlin allowed long-dormant forces of change to emerge and drive the U.S.S.R. toward democracy and a market economy."[18] (It bears repeating that Gorbachev was only "young" by comparison to his immediate predecessors, and his "reform" policies were brought about entirely by the pressure Reagan had exerted.) Even left-wing historian John L. Gaddis admitted that SDI "contributed to the rise of Gorbachev."[19]

Did Reagan "create" Gorbachev? Historians and many former Soviet leaders themselves suggest Gorbachev was selected specifically to counter Ronald Reagan.

Others, including Dutch's labor secretary Bill Brock and historian Stephen Ambrose, suggested Reagan deserved credit for the rise of Gorbachev.[20] Some Reagan biographers go even further, suggesting Reagan's policies were deliberately directed to advancing the Soviet leader. Paul Kengor, who had access to the personal files of Judge Clark, noted in January 1984 that "another few months of 'standing tall' should restore the arms balance and *very likely influence the rise of a less dangerous Soviet leader*" (emphasis mine).[21] It is true that Gorbachev had advanced through the ranks long before Dutch entered the Oval Office. And it is equally true that Central Committee movers and shakers like Yegor Ligachev had already reoriented the Party into *"perestroika"* (restructuring) before Gorbachev assumed power by reorganizing the regional party secretaries. But Ilya Zaslavsky, who would later be elected to the democratic Russian parliament, called Reagan the "father of perestroika."[22] A Central Committee member, Yevgeny Novikov, recalls Soviet leaders speaking about perestroika "as early as 1982...*particularly in light of the American buildup*" (emphasis mine).[23] Nevertheless, others, relying on much older evidence, have continued to maintain that Reagan's election emboldened the hard-liners and slowed adoption of "new thinking."[24]

Virtually all the Soviet leadership knew that the Soviet state was crumbling, that its young men were less eager to fight for Mother Russia, and that its economy was in tatters. Those social and economic strains had already affected the Soviet military, where even hard-line communists saw that their system, with its iron grip on information, could not cope with a new computer age where ideas were almost instantly shared. The night before he was elevated to general secretary, Gorbachev told Raisa, "We cannot go on living like this."[25] Top officers shared this view, concluding that "significant cuts in military spending" were needed.[26] Yegor Ligachev said "after April 1985 we faced the task of curtailing military spending [because] the economy could not breathe normally with a military budget that comprised 18 percent of the national income."[27] Moreover, top Soviet arms-control negotiators realized that conceptually Star Wars had been a game changer. Sergei Tarasenko drafted a memo to the foreign ministry saying SDI gave the US the "upper hand" because it "offered the prospect of a *morally preferable alternative to nuclear deterrence*" (emphasis mine).[28]

At Chernenko's funeral, George H. W. Bush had raised the prospect of a Reagan-Gorbachev summit. "Ronald Reagan," he said, "believes that this is a very special moment in the history of mankind. You are starting your term [and he] is starting his second term…. President Reagan is ready to work with you." The Soviet premier agreed to consider the possibility when Bush invited him to come to the United States. Shultz positively gushed about Gorbachev as a "different kind of leader," a view Bush shared, but with a little more caution, noting that Gorbachev would "package the Soviet line for Western consumption much more effective[ly] than any (I repeat any) of his predecessors."[29] You could almost read between the lines the words of Reagan's future admonition: "Trust but verify." Gorbachev's willingness to deal seemed to be confirmed when his letter arrived on Reagan's desk on March 24. It was the same day an American major was shot in Potsdam, Germany by a Soviet sentry. Despite first aid from the Soviets to the stricken soldier, Major Arthur Nicholson died. Hoping the incident could be separated from the larger disarmament mood that was flowering, the United States did not respond to the shooting. Gorbachev's letter seemed to further Reagan's idea of a face-to-face meeting. Ultimately, Gorbachev asked for a summit in Geneva in November. Reagan enthusiastically agreed, and the two would meet at a chateau near Lake Geneva.

If the meetings with the Soviets would eventually prove to be Dutch's greatest triumphs, in the near term he was about to encounter a series of potholes largely caused by a major reorganization of his cabinet. Cabinet departures are common after a first term, partly because secretaries get worn down by the bitter infighting and 24/7 work schedule, and partly because they suddenly have great market appeal in books and speeches that presents a once in a lifetime opportunity to make a great deal of money.

After the election, in late November 1984, Treasury Secretary Don Regan had laid a new tax reduction plan on Reagan's desk, with the gains coming from restructuring of the existing system and the perpetual Shangri-La of "closing loopholes." Regan had come from the world of Wall Street. His plan offered the president a way to reduce the existing fourteen tax brackets to just three, with a top marginal rate of 35 percent. To "make up" the revenue—in Washingtonese, allow Congress to keep spending as much money—Regan's plan drastically closed loopholes and taxed certain luxury items, including boats. Many business deductions that the public thought were abusive were eliminated.

The Establishment responded with its most potent weapon: the leak. Using leaks in all the major papers to reveal the painful parts of the plan, the media and the Democrats hoped to scuttle it before it got out of port. Reagan, who had not run on another major tax reform, didn't have the heart for a new fight, nor did his foot soldiers. Regan was dismayed, thinking the president was bereft of good advice. Put another way, Don Regan thought Ronald Reagan had flat been lucky in his first term. But after a particularly egregious leak in the *Washington Post* that included cabinet comments on the plan, Regan exploded and dictated his resignation letter. When Dutch received it, he called Regan back and said, "I can't accept your resignation [and] I'm tearing it up right now and burning it in the fireplace."[30] The Gipper went on to tell Regan, "You're the only friend I have around here." Indeed, in January 1984, Ed Meese had moved to the Justice Department to replace William French Smith, who had resigned.

At the same time Don Regan was finding the Treasury job too boring, James Baker was being ground down by the demands of being chief of staff. It was, next to the presidency, probably the hardest job in Washington. Regan and Baker met about the leaks—which Regan had scolded Baker over—where Regan brought up the idea of switching jobs. The two men agreed to think about it. When Baker was able to convince his immediate team to join him at Treasury, he and Regan agreed to swap positions, then brought Mike Deaver in to get Nancy on board. They drafted a memo to Deaver beginning with "It's time for a change." Baker, they noted, would be quite good at manipulating the legislators for the tax plan. Regan, meanwhile, would institute discipline on the budget from his chief of staff position. By the time the pair formally met with Deaver, he had already sounded out Nancy and had her full approval. Next, they collectively met with Reagan in the Oval Office to present the plan.

Biographers seem surprised that Dutch agreed to the switch with few questions and no opposition. Yet it is entirely unrealistic to think that Nancy had not warmed the president up to the concept long before they formally presented it. In her memoir, *My Turn*, Nancy appeared to be trying to cover her role in the original reorganization. She later wrote, "If, by some miracle I could take back one decision in Ronnie's presidency, it would be his agreement in January 1985 that Jim Baker and Donald Regan should swap jobs…. It seemed like a good idea at the time."[31] By then, Nancy had almost become a de facto fourth member of the "troika." After the job shift, she increasingly chafed at Regan's attempts to expand both his role and his image, and once, after getting wind of Regan suggesting he should take Marine One to the hospital to visit Dutch as he recovered from the polyp removal, she blew up. Calling Regan personally, she asked if it was true, and he confessed he had thought about it, whereupon he wisely backed off and came by car.[32] Ed Rollins would joke to Regan that his job was to "take Mrs. Reagan's shit," but a serious problem was indeed worming its way into the administration between Nancy's interference and Regan's overreach.

Meanwhile, George Shultz and Caspar Weinberger were constantly at each other's throats, to the point that in late 1984 Shultz tried to bring about another cabinet shuffle. Meeting with Reagan in late 1984, Shultz told Dutch "the two of us are unable to work congenially…. You should take one or the other."[33] Critics point to Reagan's refusal to choose between the two as evidence of weakness. It was quite the opposite: the Gipper needed a hawk in the Pentagon and a dove at State. This was the very character of the institutions. Reagan didn't need the two to "work together" so much as to each present their points of view and allow Reagan to choose. George Washington was in precisely the same position with Thomas Jefferson and Alexander Hamilton. Actually, Washington's position was worse: Jefferson and Hamilton hated each other personally, while at least Shultz and Weinberger were congenial. Critics have assumed this lack of consensus allowed authority to devolve to McFarlane and that McFarlane saw his job as resolving differences of policy before they came before the president.

However, when it came to Central American policy, McFarlane found himself with a growing role, reshaping the NSC staff itself and relocating critical NSC functions to a separate new office. And, as always (and as Reagan warned) the new office began to take on a life of its own, eventually employing 186 people, many of whom really had no tasks. One of McFarlane's key advisors was his deputy, Lieutenant Colonel Oliver North, who favored bold—and often rash—plans when it came to foreign affairs. (When a freighter packed with North Korean weapons was bound for Nicaragua, he suggested boarding it and seizing all the arms, which amounted to piracy.) North, a Vietnam veteran and fierce anti-communist, focused within the NSC on terrorism and special operations, eventually taking leadership roles on El Salvador and Nicaragua. Reagan liked North because he offered direct advice without the "on the other hand" kinds of advice Dutch got from everyone else.

The president made clear that McFarlane was to report to Regan, but McFarlane soon attempted to exercise authority and power beyond the limited duties of his position. This irritated Shultz as well as Regan. When McFarlane informed the Gipper of Chernenko's death—without first going through Regan—he got a severe dressing down. A four-way game of tug-of-war ensued, with Reagan in the middle, pulled at by Cap, Shultz, Regan, and now McFarlane. Contrary to the claims of the NSC advisor, the decision to reinvigorate the arms talks with the Soviets was a mutual decision pushed by all four.

Don Regan, in the meantime, was already committing his first error as chief of staff in preparing Reagan's D-Day trip. The new German chancellor, Helmut Kohl, had earlier complained about being excluded from the World War II commemorations and wanted to show support for the postwar order. Kohl asked Reagan if he would participate in a ceremony at a wartime cemetery in Germany, then privately asked if he would visit Dachau. Dutch handed the request over to Regan, who turned the matter over to State. Mike Deaver personally led a team to Germany to look at sites. Kohl's staff had selected Bitburg, a wartime cemetery in the chancellor's home state. Although Deaver's staff asked if any SS were buried at Bitburg and were told no, neither Deaver nor his staff pursued the matter with gusto. Next, Reagan himself thought it better to focus on the future and not visit Dachau—which he insisted was a private, not a state, invitation. That ignited a storm of responses. It got worse when, in talking with broadcasters, Reagan referred to "young men [who were] victims of Nazism... even though they were fighting in German uniform, drafted into service to carry out the hateful wishes of the Nazis."[34] Prior to the event, Reagan portrayed them as "victims, as surely as the victims in the concentration camps." This was an extreme comparison, though Dutch was simply trying to say something nice about the Germans. Once it was discovered that Waffen-SS were buried at Bitburg, the controversy spiked. Before leaving for Germany, Reagan invited Elie Wiesel, one of the best-known Holocaust survivors, to the White House to calm the waters. Wiesel accepted the invitation, then at the White House politely called Dutch out, saying "symbols are important" and strongly insisted that he find "another site." Bitburg, he said, "is not your place. Your place is with the victims of the SS."[35]

Reagan, however, was receiving strong pressure from Kohl, who in an interview noted that to cancel the visit would offend Germans. A poll showed over 70 percent of Germans favored the visit to the cemetery. The chancellor made a last-minute call to the White House to ensure that the event would go as planned. By then, Dutch felt he could not turn back. But Reagan's team did add a visit to the Bergen-Belsen concentration camp to the itinerary.

On May 5, 1985, before beginning with a meeting of G7 leaders in Bonn, Reagan and Kohl met privately, with the chancellor telling Dutch the president had "won the heart of Germany by standing firm on this." It seemed that the German people agreed, based on their turnout for the motorcades. When Reagan finally arrived at Bergen-Belsen, however, he was met by hecklers. Reagan dismissed them with "It's a free country," then laid a wreath that read "The People of the United States of America" at the stone monument.[36] Reagan was joined by ninety-year-old General Matthew Ridgway, who had commanded the 82nd Airborne during World War II. After placing the wreath, the Gipper shook hands with the general, stood silently for a trumpet salute, and left. He made comments at the nearby Bitburg Air Base, but not at the cemetery itself.

Despite scathing criticism from Jewish groups and the press, the Gipper held fast. He received strong support from Bush and, of course, Kohl. Reagan said, "We're here because humanity refuses to accept that freedom of the spirit of man can ever be extinguished," then concluded with "we can, and must pledge: never again."[37]

The mess was widely viewed as Regan's fault and seen as a mistake Baker wouldn't have made. Regan, in turn, blamed Deaver, and some inside the White House blamed Kohl for setting up the president. But the Gipper's subsequent faux pas in his remarks were his own. He asserted a moral equivalency between draftees and those killed, occasionally by those very draftees. To Reagan, it was a matter of diplomacy. An ally had invited him to a ceremony: "We won and we killed those soldiers. What's wrong with saying 'let's never be enemies again'? Would Helmut be wrong if he visited Arlington Cemetery on one of his U.S. visits?"[38] Kohl, according to Reagan, "may very well have solved our problem re the Holocaust" by making an official invitation to visit a concentration camp. He also told Dutch that the remarks about the dead soldiers were well received in Germany and that to cancel the cemetery visit would have been a disaster.[39]

When it was all over, Nancy blamed everyone but Dutch for the blowup: she blamed Regan for scheduling it; she blamed Kohl for "not getting us out of it." Her Ronnie? She was "proud of [him] for following his conscience."[40]

Regan took from the episode that Reagan had a unique leadership style, which kept the president distanced from the mechanics of making the sausage. "This was the first tough presidential decision which I had been an eyewitness as Chief of Staff," he wrote, adding that he thought Reagan came through with "flying colors" by "choosing the future over the past. He saw the bigger issue as his credibility, as a leader who—even privately—kept his word to his ally."[41] Direction and end results were all that were important. Other presidents, especially Carter, had become notorious for getting their fingers in every possible pie. But Regan and others were often astounded at how few direct orders Reagan issued. Quite the contrary, he was able to persuade and direct people largely through questions ("don't you think?") or even the tone of his voice. Frequently, his decision would be passed off as "the fellas think. . . ." People would leave meetings with him saying "he wants this," or "he wants that," often without Dutch ever giving a clear oral directive. Yet his leadership style was every bit as effective as if he did give explicit instructions. When he needed to, Reagan set out all his goals in his speeches and the NSDDs and expected everyone to conform to his management style. In cabinet meetings and National Security Council meetings, the Gipper typically let his lieutenants speak until he wanted to redirect the discussion, occasionally with a story (which some had heard before and cringed at). But Reagan had read his Bible and knew that "faith cometh by hearing"—not *having heard*—but hearing and hearing again. Dutch constantly reminded everyone where he stood and where they needed to end up.

Bitburg may have damaged the Gipper temporarily. But as Dinesh D'Souza noted, Reagan's own comments provide more of an insight to what he was thinking, that it "should be a time of healing," that he "didn't feel that we could ask new generations of Germans to live with this guilt forever without any hope of redemption."[42] As D'Souza put it, "Reagan's argument was both an ethical and a practical case for reconciliation. His contention was that the West was in a better position to resist the contemporary evil of totalitarianism by permitting postwar fraternity of free nations on an equal basis." Ultimately, the public respected the president all the more as someone who would not be deterred even when confronted by intense opposition.[43] Although he didn't know it at the time, in this instance as well as the Freeze and the Euromissile Crisis, the Gipper was battling a new psychological state among German youth, whom historian Tony Judt called "Hitler's children." Judt argued the new, younger Germans rejected their parents' generation as soulless and identified with America and the West "in no small measure [deriving from] a wish to avoid…'Germanness.'" As a result, he concluded, in their children's eyes the older Germans "stood for nothing."[44] At the time, however, Reagan stood with the postwar generation who still wanted to be Western. Indeed, as Hungarian activist and rock musician Leslie Mándoki told me, "We all wanted to be *American*." Dutch got that.

A more serious storm was converging on the administration from two fronts—Central America and the Middle East. By 1985, the prospects for the Contras to overthrow the Sandinista government of the Ortegas had gone from slim to almost none. American failure to deliver support had not helped, and in March Reagan wrote in his diary that the "Nicaraguan problem continues to fester." Only about half of the Contras even remained in Nicaragua itself, with the rest driven to Honduras by a sixty-thousand-man Sandinista army supported by Soviet helicopters. It was a jungle version of Afghanistan, without US aid. Reagan lobbied King Fahd of Saudi Arabia to help the Contras, and the king obliged by sending more than $30 million to the beleaguered fighters—though McFarlane did not divulge all details of the aid to Shultz or Weinberger.

A Nicaraguan election, also held in November 1984, left the Sandinistas in power but under a cloud of vote fraud. The leading opponent, Arturo Cruz, withdrew from the race amidst allegations of Sandinista disruption of polling places and press censorship. He even visited Washington, embarrassing Democrats who had up to that point seen him as useful foil for Sandinista victories in Nicaragua. Although Dutch still referred to the Contras as the equivalent of the founding fathers, he could not sell the American public this time. Realizing his limits, Reagan declined Pat Buchanan's strong urging to make a national speech on Nicaragua. However, the Democrats did give in on one point: humanitarian aid would be permitted. Before the vote could be taken, however, a full-fledged communist offensive was mounted, with peace groups and liberal organizations mobilizing to stop any aid. A flustered Caspar Weinberger muttered, "I simply cannot understand why a Communist regime so close to our borders has so much support in Congress."[45] Dutch went further, describing O'Neill as "irrational" on Nicaragua. Even the Republicans in Congress proved intransigent and Reagan got "tired of foreign policy by a committee of 535."[46]

The Saudi monarch visited Washington in February 1985, after Saudi Arabia had received Stingers and other air defense weapons it wanted. Without prompting, King Fahd volunteered to send another $24 million to the Contras. McFarlane and Weinberger were aware of the Saudi offer, but they again kept Shultz out of the loop. Critics complain that no one briefed Congress, but then no one had briefed Congress on the massive aid Charlie Wilson was funneling to the Afghans, either.[47]

The vortex bringing together the Middle East and Central America gained speed in June 1985 when TWA Flight 847 from Cairo to San Diego was hijacked after a stop in Athens and taken to Beirut (where some passengers were allowed to leave in return for fuel) and then on to Algiers. There, twenty more passengers were released in exchange for more fuel, then the plane lifted off for Beirut again. Having beaten almost all of the passengers, at Beirut the hijackers shot a US Navy diver, Robert Stethem, and threw his body on the tarmac. More terrorists joined the hijackers there, then the aircraft flew *again* to Algiers (where sixty-five more passengers and five female crew members were released). The kidnappers received worldwide television coverage for demanding the release of over seven hundred prisoners the Israelis had captured in Lebanon and a few held in Kuwait. Then they landed in Beirut yet again.

When Reagan learned of the hostage crisis, he canceled a planned trip to the ranch and issued a restatement of America's policy of refusing to deal with terrorists. Israel enunciated the same policy. The terrorists removed the hostages and dispersed them throughout Lebanon with groups associated with the Hezbollah factions linked to the Iranians, making any rescue attempt (such as the Israelis had achieved at Entebbe in 1976) nearly impossible. Briefed by the NSC, Reagan found there were few options, although a phrase emerged from the discussions—"war on terrorism"—that Shultz favored, one which would later lead down entirely different roads in a subsequent presidency.

Essentially helpless, Reagan allowed the diplomats to pursue negotiations with Syria's Hafez al-Assad, who exerted enough pressure to obtain the release of the hostages on June 30. Israel released its prisoners thereafter—rightly claiming it had already made the decision to let them go just prior to the kidnapping.

After all the turmoil of TWA 847, there still remained seven other Americans prisoners kidnapped in 1982. Unlike Muslim kidnappings of the 1800s by the Barbary Pirates, which had been mostly for the purposes of gaining payments from families or states, the new wave of kidnappers had something much different in mind. For them, hostages were both bargaining chips for policy changes and object lessons for infidels. Reagan fully understood the first motive but was still slow to appreciate the second. One of those still held was a Catholic priest named Lawrence Jenco. Just before the TWA 847 hostages were released, Reagan had met with Jenco's family in Illinois, where the petulant Jencos harangued the president for not doing enough. Of course, they were fully aware that hostages spread throughout a foreign land were difficult to find and impossible to rescue, but they used the photo op to bash Reagan regardless. Dutch was somewhat shaken, and the president's advisors were furious, one calling the family "real motherfuckers."[48] Far more important to US interests than Father Jenco, unfortunately, was William Buckley, the CIA station chief grabbed on March 14, 1985, for he stood to reveal methods and names to America's enemies.

On July 1, word of the return of the TWA hostages reached the White House, and after an angry exchange with TWA officials, the plane was rerouted to Andrews Air Force Base and the families quickly informed and sent there instead of the original arrival point of New York City. When the hostages arrived, Reagan delivered remarks vowing retribution on those who had killed Robert Stethem. "There will be no forgetting," he solemnly warned. A few days later, he upped the ante, saying, "The American people are not going to tolerate…intimidation, terror, and outright acts of war against this nation [especially coming from] the strangest collection of misfits, Looney Tunes, and squalid criminals since the advent of the Third Reich."[49] While he had aptly characterized the enemies of America perpetrating these deeds, he had still not included another descriptor that tied all these "misfits" together: Islamic radicals.

Jenco was finally released in late July. His captors drove him to a village and alerted the Americans, who found him "taped like a mummy." According to the debriefing team, he had been "treated like an escaped lunatic with tape and cotton still sticking to his head and clothes."[50] These reports weighed heavily on Dutch.

It was against this background that a critical meeting took place. Reagan was in the hospital recovering from his polyp surgery when he recorded in his diary that there were "some strange soundings coming from the Iranians."[51] (He added, "miracle of miracles I had my 1st food by mouth. Only a couple of spoonfuls of broth, Jello, some water & ½ cup of tea.") Bud McFarlane, with Donald Regan present, visited him the next day detailing the latest developments in the Middle East, most notably the ongoing war between Iran and its neighbor Iraq.

The two nations were divided by sectarianism within Islam (Shiite Iran versus Sunni Iraq). The Soviets had thrown in behind Saddam Hussein in Iraq, the smaller of the two nations in population, but, because of Soviet help, the more militarily advanced. Despite five years of massive casualties—especially on the part of Iran—the war had yielded neither side an advantage. Reagan's policy, as set forth in NSDD 114 of November 1983, had been to not take sides but to "undertake whatever measures may be necessary to keep the Strait of Hormuz open."[52] Iran needed weapons and technology, which opened the door for a very dangerous opportunity. (Contrary to the claims in *Landslide*, there is no NSDD of May 1985 related to Iran or in any way suggesting other nations "fill a military gap for Iran.")[53]

In the hospital meeting between McFarlane and Reagan, the NSA director briefed the president about the potential for negotiations that might release the remaining hostages. Reagan (according to Regan) said, "Yes, go ahead. Open it up."[54] On July 18, Reagan recorded, "I'm sending Bud to meet with [the Iranians] in a neutral country."[55] The rest of the cabinet had weighed in strongly against any deals that called for exchanging arms in any way for hostages. Shultz called it "contrary to our interests" and "particularly perverse." Weinberger, who seldom agreed with Shultz, concurred, denouncing the scheme as "almost too absurd to comment on… It's like asking Qaddafi to Washington for a cozy chat."[56] Despite the fact that as late as mid-1985, Reagan himself continued to hammer Iran as an international version of Murder, Incorporated, increasingly the hostages weighed on him, to the point that he said at one meeting, "I don't care if I have to go to Leavenworth: I want the hostages out."[57]

It is also important to keep in mind that the Israelis had, with the able support of Democratic congressman Charlie Wilson, already helped coordinate weapons sales through the Egyptians to the *mujahideen* for the administration. Thus the lines delineating what was in fact an "arms for hostages" exchange were becoming increasingly blurred with every subsequent negotiation. At that point administration officials were reintroduced by the Israelis to an Iranian expatriate named Manucher Ghorbanifar, a man the CIA had "burned" as a bad contact years earlier. Ghorbinafar intimated that further arms transfers to the Iranians, particularly TOW anti-tank missiles, would result in the release of more hostages—a proposal raised at an August 6 NSC meeting. Bush and Reagan were willing to explore the deal, while Shultz and Weinberger staunchly opposed, arguing the deal would likely be illegal. While the president made no clear decision at the meeting, he recorded in his diary "rumors" that some of the hostages would be released but added *"We have no confirmation whatsoever"* (emphasis mine).[58]

Reagan's willingness to move forward on such sketchy evidence and questionable legality was justified, in part, by a hope on his part that relations with Iran might be restored. There were also suggestions that "moderates" inside Iran might be supported and encouraged. Regardless, the "arms for hostages" concept was now fully embedded as US policy. The administration, Shultz warned, had inadvertently created a "hostage-taking industry." Worse, any pretense that the missiles were intended for Israel— who just happened to transfer them to Iran—was immediately dispelled when two weeks later just under one hundred weapons were sent straight to Iran. No hostages were freed, however, and word returned that Iran wanted four hundred *more* missiles.

An exchange of a shipment through Israel in September saw a single hostage released: Reverend Benjamin Weir, who "displayed all the hallmarks of Stockholm syndrome" and praised the captors while criticizing the administration.[59] The Iranians dangled more hostages in front of the Americans, but with ever-increasing demands, including the release of jailed terrorists. And while America kept hoping for the return of Buckley, he was already dead (a fact the CIA did not yet know). At the same time, supposed "moderates" inside Iran, including the new speaker of Iran's Parliament, Akbar Hashemi Rafsanjani, had been thought to have helped pressure the Lebanese terrorists to release their hostages. How "moderate" Rafsanjani or any of them were was dubious, and their role in the release of

Weir could not be confirmed by the CIA. When no further hostages were freed, a depressed McFarlane resigned, leaving Oliver North to take over the arms transfer operations under John Poindexter. North continued to frame the initiative in terms of concern for the hostages, even drafting a formula of missiles shipped for captives released.[60]

It bears repeating, though, that *everyone* on every side of the hostage/arms/Iran/Middle East debate was operating on flawed assumptions about the nature of the so-called "moderates" throughout the region and the radical "Islamic Republic" that called itself Iran. It is true that there were secular dictators and generals who were Muslim in name but who first and foremost ensured their own survival, that of their families, and of their regimes (leading Tahseen Bashir, an Egyptian diplomat, in 2002 to call most of the Middle Eastern nations "tribes with flags").

Those leaders were not "moderates," and at best they obscured the true nature of the radical threat that indeed was based in fundamentalist Islamic teaching. Reagan had already started to express doubts about the nature of Islam after Lebanon, but he never came full circle to connecting radical tenets of the Koran with actual state actions. Those insights came only later to McFarlane, who later explained that he wanted to believe in "Iranian moderates" because it was logical in Western terms: "There ought to be moderates in Iran," he noted. But while it was logical, "It is not, I think, the reality."[61] Indeed, Shultz and others feared that rather than strengthening the moderates, new arms would improve the position of the radicals.

Steven Hayward, an admirer of Reagan's, makes three noteworthy points about these discussions involving the hostages and Iran. First, the central issue on Reagan's mind at the time was the upcoming summit with Gorbachev. Second, the Iran arms deal debunks the notion that Reagan was a puppet in the hands of his secretaries, for *all* of them opposed the arrangement and it went ahead precisely because the Gipper wanted it to. And third, Dutch wanted it to go forward because he let his heart rule his head, and his sympathy for the plight of the hostages outweighed the long-established and prudent policies that forbade such exchanges.[62] Shultz recalled the plight of the hostages weighed on Reagan constantly. "He worried about them personally," Shultz said. "It just drove him crazy." He was the most powerful man in the world, with massive intelligence and military resources at his beck and call, and yet helpless. Reagan subsequently signed a formal "finding" and authorized the plan to free the five remaining hostages, but he ominously noted in his diary, "It is a complex undertaking with only a few of us in on it. I won't even write in the diary what we're up to."[63]

Matters were further complicated by the resignation of McFarlane in December 1985 and his replacement by John Poindexter. Both men were present for a crucial NSC meeting that month wherein the president was briefed on a resumption of the Iran talks. This entry provided the best evidence to that point that Reagan was fully informed of the entire scheme. In January of 1985, Reagan signed NSDD 159, the "Covert Action Policy Approval and Coordination Procedure" under which "all covert actions undertaken [by the CIA] must be authorized by a Presidential Finding."[64] But before his departure at the NSA, McFarlane had attended to that detail by moving control of the Iran planning from the CIA to the NSC. Now there was no oversight over the operation except what McFarlane (then Poindexter) chose to show to Reagan.

In October another terrorist act—the hijacking of the cruise ship *Achille Lauro* by member of the Palestinian Liberation Front—threatened to add dozens of new hostages to the mix. Possibly realizing they were about to go head-to-head with the US Navy, they hightailed the *Lauro* to Port Said and handed themselves over to the Egyptians in return for safe conduct to a friendly state—but not before they pushed wheelchair-bound Leon Klinghoffer into the Mediterranean. An outraged Reagan sent F-14s to intercept the Egyptian transport plane with the hijackers and forced them down at a NATO base in Sicily, an action that sent patriotic chills through large numbers of Americans. Finally, a blow had been struck against terrorists! He called Mrs. Klinghoffer and she and other passengers had to travel to Rome to identify the hijackers.

When the next element of the hostage initiative unfolded in January 1986, Reagan described it as "a highly secret convoluted process" in which Israel would free twenty Hezbollah captives who "aren't really guilty of any bloodletting" and sell twenty TOW missiles (which the US would replace) to Iran in return for five hostages and a pledge from Iran of no more kidnappings.[65] This deal required yet another presidential "finding" to stay within the law, which Poindexter produced on January 6. At the NSC meeting the following day, neither Poindexter nor Reagan mentioned the "finding."[66]

With Iran losing the war against Iraq, Poindexter believed that all the interim steps needed to be bypassed and the United States needed to sell arms directly to Iran. North and Poindexter cleverly restructured the initiative to exclude Israel altogether and sell arms directly to Iran. Weinberger continued his objections, and Poindexter on January 16 held a meeting in which Weinberger wanted the Defense Department lawyers to look at the proposal. No one in the DOD apparently ever reviewed it, though the CIA director William Casey the following day claimed they had. The pro-sale group referred to Weinberger as "Doctor No" and Shultz as "Doctor I Don't Want to Know."[67]

The following day set the program in stone. On January 17, 1986, Poindexter, at an NSC meeting, handed a new "finding" to Reagan identical to the one given the president ten days earlier, but with a cover memo from North and Poindexter indicating the arms would be sold directly by the United States. Reagan signed it without looking at the cover memo and noted in his diary, "I gave the go ahead."[68] He then started drinking his GoLytely for his next polyp checkup.

The same NSC meeting included a draft opinion from Attorney General William French Smith allowing Reagan to sell arms directly if "the CIA, using an authorized agent...purchased arms from the Defense Department...and then transferred them directly after receiving appropriate payment from Iran." Again, there was the obligatory reference to working with "moderate elements within and outside the Government of Iran."[69] Reagan was still convinced the exchanges involved only TOW anti-tank missiles.[70] But this was his third finding in a six-week period that approved arms sales despite his publicly stated position otherwise.

While there is no doubt Reagan approved the arms sales or that the White House concealed the sales from Congress, there remains considerable doubt as to why. The most likely—and commonly accepted—answer is that Reagan desperately wanted the hostages released. A second view, espoused in Lou Cannon's biography, is that Reagan had to be protected from himself by loyal surrogates—all of whom had left by 1984. Without question, the shakeups within the NSC and the departure of some of the most devout Reaganites played a role. More than just policy advisors had left: Michael Deaver, notorious for looking out for Reagan's political image, had departed in May of 1985. Contrary to claims that Reagan would have employed a political calculation to stop the arms-for-hostages exchanges, Reagan's own words—including the threat to let them put him in Leavenworth—indicate otherwise. Clearly Dutch *knew* both the legal and political impact of what he was doing, and in his mind, the hostages mattered more.

Likewise, some biographers harp on the "infighting" among Reagan's cabinet and senior staff. *This was nothing new.* Abraham Lincoln's cabinet constantly fought with each other and with him. George Washington's closest advisors were constantly at each other's throats, each trying to undermine the other. In more recent times, cabinet officials and staffers frequently resign because the battles become too fierce.

Ultimately most biographers ignore the obvious: Iran-Contra occurred because of Ronald Reagan's fundamental faith in the American people. It informed his dealings with the Soviets, whom he could call the "Evil Empire" in the abstract while insisting that in personal meetings he and any given Soviet leader could work things out. He thought it inconceivable any of them truly desired war—that was just the Marxism-Leninism talking. A similar dynamic had led him to be manipulated by Poindexter and North. Poindexter by that time had become fully convinced that the only way the hostages could be released was through arms shipments, but he also had bought into the notion (possibly exaggerated by North and even Casey) that there were "moderate" voices in Iran with whom more important deals could be struck. North, on the other hand, was searching for ways to fund the Contras and saw an opportunity with the money left over from the arms transfers. Reagan may have understood incompetence, but he never dreamed his own staff would deliberately subvert him, his presidency, or his ideals for their own agendas.[71]

As Ronald Reagan stood on the brink of his monumental success in dealing with the Soviets, he had opened the henhouse door, not only letting in the foxes, but keeping their presence a secret from his most trusted watchdogs. The only possible outcome was disaster, but it would not be the only one about to strike his administration.

16

Disasters

Optimism permeated the administration, continuing through mid-1985, despite some of the internal squabbling. Reelection showed the public had great confidence in Reagan. The economic expansion continued. Job growth continued (and would persist throughout the year). Oil prices began to drop, not only benefitting consumers but ratcheting up pressure on the USSR's cash flow. Inflation continued to fall.

Gloomsters warned about a merger wave (thirty mergers/acquisitions of $1 billion in 1985 alone versus twelve in the previous decade, although some of that was a factor of inflated prices), and the new villains to them were "corporate raiders" like T. Boone Pickens. In fact, new forms of equity instruments had arisen, most notably the "junk bond," that enabled the cellular telephone industry to establish itself and helped finance the tech boom. Overall, the stock market benefitted from the new takeover activity. But its rise allowed the Democrats and the Left to begin invoking the "decade of greed" indictments against the Reagan boom. It was truly all they had.

These complaints fed Washington's desire to increase taxes, always embraced by the Democrats and now often supported by some Republicans under the guise of "balancing the budget." This rationale for tax increases had never worked in American history: government always found more ways to spend any additional money, and deals that supposedly would result in spending reduction never saw the cuts materialize.

Nevertheless, the pressure on Dutch to address the deficit was increasing. Worse, it was *Republicans* who stopped a line-item veto proposal in 1985. When another budget Reagan delivered to Congress was declared "dead on arrival," the Gipper bristled, shooting back word that any tax increase he received would meet the same fate.

A great deal of optimism in early 1985 came from the opportunities to finally make progress on arms control with a new Soviet leader. Few suspected that the next eighteen months would witness a variety of technological and political disasters—not just in the United States, but in the Soviet Union as well.

The Strategic Arms Limitations Talks (SALT II) were about to become obsolete, as the United States' new Trident subs would put it over the limits. And, of course, as both sides knew, the USSR was already cheating whenever possible. SALT was to expire at the end of the year, so an opportunity existed to engage in new talks, with negotiations aligned with Reagan's goal of actually reducing the number of nuclear weapons.

Before George Shultz met with Andrei Gromyko in January, the National Security Planning Group met in December to review objectives. Minutes reflected that the goal was to "begin the process of [using] strategic defense to make the world safer."[1] McFarlane, who opened the meeting, reminded all that "SDI is not only important for our future, but it provides a hedge against a Soviet breakout of the ABM Treaty." The goal in Geneva, he noted, was to continue to shift from greater reliance on offense to defense. Shultz, who noted that he was "the person who was going to do the talking in Geneva," needed to know what to say. At that point President Reagan observed that "we and the Soviet Union may be coming together more than many people realize....We must show them defenses are not threatening." Moreover, the goal had to be a "zero option" of nuclear weapons, and Shultz heartily concurred. Reagan again insisted that Shultz "link research on SDI to making nuclear weapons obsolete." As the meeting ended, McFarlane noted that the Russians were counting on the president not being able to "sell" the SDI program to the public. Dutch adjourned by noting that everyone could start by cancelling their subscriptions to the *Washington Post.*[2]

Shortly thereafter, the president issued a highly unusual NSDD with quite specific instructions for the negotiations. Normally NSDDs were reserved for broad strategy directions, not for details of specific meetings, but Reagan felt it important enough that he *not* allow Shultz too much wiggle room. The prevailing issue was Star Wars: "The overriding importance of SDI," the NSDD stated, "is that it offers the possibility of radically altering…dangerous trends" and moving to a "more stable basis of deterrence." If the promise of SDI was achieved, it continued, "the Soviet advantage accumulated over the past twenty years at great cost will be largely neutralized." Therefore, Shultz was expressly directed "to avoid a 'space only' forum" and in no uncertain terms instructed to protect SDI.[3]

When Shultz met with his counterpart, Andrei Gromyko, later that month, he indeed held firm on SDI, forcing the Soviets to agree to new rounds of meetings that (supposedly) put everything on the table, including the Euromissiles, space-based weapons, and all strategic weapons. What the Russians still did not understand, however, was that SDI was never a bargaining chip because the US viewed it not as a "space-based weapon" but as a defensive system. "I feel," Reagan wrote, "the Soviets came to the table because they finally decided it was in their best interest to do so."[4]

For years—and well before he became president—Reagan harbored a sense that while the "godless communists" were evil as a system or as a government, individual godless communists could be reasoned with. He spoke frequently of getting one of the Soviet leaders in an airplane, setting it down in any town the man chose, and showing him how ordinary Americans lived and prospered. As matters would turn out, he was exactly right. His one-on-one encounters with Gorbachev were profound. As the SALT II expiration loomed, Reagan decided to dismantle two of the Poseidon submarines to remain within the broad outlines of the treaty, although formally the United States was no longer going to abide by it. While this seemed to be backing down, the fact was the Poseidons were well past their shelf life, and there were concerns over the obsolescence of their reactor cores. The obsolescence of the Poseidons had been one of the driving factors in the approval and design of the Tridents; keeping the older subs on line would have required massive refits, when it was more prudent and cost-effective to simply build *Ohio*-class subs later.

Then, as if by a stroke of fate, Chernenko died and turned the reins of power over to Gorbachev. Dutch, of course, wasn't fooled by all the happy talk surrounding the new Soviet dictator, and, as we have seen, with good reason. As he wrote in his diary in June, "I'm too cynical to believe [he's different]."[5] Asked by publishers if he thought "Gorby" would be different, he reiterated, "I don't think there's any evidence that he is less dominated by their system and their philosophy than…the others. But it isn't true that I don't trust anyone under seventy."[6] Rather, the Gipper emphasized, the *situation* had changed (largely because of his policies) and the Soviets now had an incentive "I believe…to try and, with us, negotiate a reduction of armaments."[7] Reagan sent Gorbachev a letter on March 11 assuring him of Dutch's commitment to engage in serious discussions, and the Soviet leader replied two weeks later with a promise not to "let things come to the outbreak of nuclear war."[8] After further talks between Gromyko and Shultz, the two superpowers agreed on a date of November 19–20 for their leaders to meet in Geneva. Reagan had his long anticipated face-to-face.

*Reagan had to balance two contradictory views he held:
On the one hand, he knew the USSR was an "Evil Empire."
On the other hand, he felt its individual leaders might be
reasonable men with whom he could negotiate.*

Subsequent exchanges of letters revealed just how obsessed the Soviets were with SDI. Reagan calmly reminded Gorbachev at every turn that the USSR had its own ABM system and that all focus should be on reducing and eliminating offensive weapons. A June exchange exposed a somewhat hostile Gorbachev insisting on de-linking human rights violations from the talks, while designating SDI as space-based weapons.[9] He further tipped his hand by replying to his own reply a mere twelve days later (June 22) in which he said "the 'star wars' [sic] program—I must tell you this, Mr. President—already at this stage is seriously undermining stability."[10] Those familiar with Soviet newspeak quickly understood that "undermining stability" was code talk for "we are getting weaker." Gorbachev wrote again on September 12, trying another tack, this time a reduction of all ballistic missiles by half but a complete ban on "space attack weapons."[11] Sensing the Soviets' eagerness, even desperation, Reagan led the NSC through a September 20 meeting in which he again pointed out the weakness of the USSR's economy, recalling the words of Richard Nixon that "we want peace. They *need* peace." But Weinberger still thought that reality was a ways off. Dutch again focused on the salient point: SDI, he said, "may very well be our most important leverage. I am prepared, once any of our SDI programs proved out, to then announce to the world" that the US would "integrate defensive weapons into our respective arsenals [which] could even lead to a complete elimination of nuclear weapons." Again, he reiterated that the United States was "ready to internationalize these systems."[12]

Gorbachev wasn't interested in sharing SDI any more than his predecessors were interested in sharing the atomic bomb with an international body. Of course, the USSR had its own defensive missiles (which were nuclear). The hypocrisy and irrationality grated on Reagan, who wrote, "They are raising h--l about our research & they've been at it for 20 yrs. & we're just starting."[13] What was Gorbachev's motivation to stick to a position he was almost sure to lose with? First, for all his "openness" and "Western-ness," Gorbachev was, after all, a communist. He believed (as most advocates of big government do) that the problem wasn't the system, only the men at the controls. *He* could apply a smarter approach. Hence, he had said in a December 1984 speech that the USSR needed "serious scientific recommendations on the application in contemporary conditions of such economic levers as price, cost, profit, credit, and certain others."[14] Yet there is no indication he actually understood the terms "price," "cost," or "profit," nor was there any hope that "science" could provide the answers in a communist context. He told his first Politburo meeting he was "deeply devoted to the idea of collective work" and what "we need is...more socialism."[15] Ultimately, as Milton Friedman pointed out, it was difficult if not impossible to maintain an authoritarian political system with a free market: markets demand freedom of information, which works precisely in opposition to government control. Furthermore, Soviet history was the history of fraud, of deceit. Steel mills and other production facilities kept two sets of books—one for the *apparatchiks* who inspected them, and a genuine set so the managers knew the true performance of the plant. Yet the impossibility of true reform from the top was apparent even to Soviet economists, who visited the West for tips in the early 1990s before the system fell.[16] While the younger members of the Communist Party were searching for help somewhere, they still saw Gorbachev as in line with basic communist teachings.

Still, the West (especially its liberals) was mesmerized by Gorbachev and his supposedly revolutionary programs of *glasnost* ("openness" or "transparency") and *perestroika* (economic restructuring). In fact, the first elements of *perestroika* were more onerous than what was already in place, as individuals were prohibited from receiving any income outside their official job, completely removing profits from home gardens. Predictably, supply fell as incentives for production vanished. Margaret Thatcher summed up Gorbachev: "He doesn't understand that the system is the problem."[17] After Shultz explained the communist system's fatal flaws—especially when it came to information being necessary for efficient pricing—Gorbachev's response said it all: "You should take over the planning office here in Moscow."[18] The premier was still looking for "the right man."

And, just like Marx, Gorbachev was thoroughly hypocritical: when he came to the US for a visit, he brandished an American Express Gold Card—prohibited in the USSR. Of course, after the Cold War ended, he enthusiastically accepted a large advance from Doubleday to publish his memoirs.

A mythology surrounds Mikhail Gorbachev, namely that he was a liberal and a reformer. In fact, he remained a firm believer in communist principles and to the end remained convinced that the Soviet system only needed "the right man" in control.

The chief benefit of the profound failure of communism, even under a "new reformer" such as Gorbachev, is that it forced him to confront the USSR's contradictions in foreign policy, where, as he told the Eastern

European communist leaders, they could not expect Soviet military force to bail them out any longer. This marked the end, at least philosophically, of Leninism and its necessary expansionism. (Indeed, a smart man, as Gorbachev was, must have appreciated the irony of Lenin's thesis that capitalism had to expand to survive, when it was obvious that only through expansion could the failures of communism be camouflaged.)[19] Afghanistan was the first to go, in late 1985, when he gave Afghan president Babrak Karmal a year to develop his own defense forces. Gorbachev had never supported the Afghan invasion, but as he would soon learn, withdrawing from a country was much more difficult—even for a dictator—than invading it.

Reagan kept hammering, now more than before, about the Soviet's possession of defense systems that they claimed not to have. He continued to present himself as open to serious arms reductions. At the same time the hostage situation had receded from the headlines. Dutch's approval shot up to 65 percent, providing wind at his back for the trip to Geneva. The Gipper had never before been so prepared for a meeting. Robert Gates and Bill Casey briefed Reagan, who, according to one observer, had "spotty command of historical facts" but was aware of gaps in his understanding and enthusiastically requested the information: "I want the best minds in the country, Republican or Democrat, academics or diplomats, to give me in-depth knowledge," as he told McFarlane.[20] Given briefing papers every Friday, Reagan read them fully all weekend. McFarlane noted "he would devour them, annotate them…quiz his experts…obsess about getting more information." These reports put lie to the notion that Reagan was uninformed or had poor study habits. Some sources have reported that statistics were lost on Reagan, but he was keenly focused on how *people* were affected by Soviet policies, including levels of alcoholism, social breakdown, and basic living conditions. That kind of information told him more about his bargaining position than how many bombers each side had.

Modern presidents—especially after Richard Nixon—have realized the critical nature of what information they do, and do not, leave behind. Before the Geneva trip, Reagan took what Martin and Annelise Anderson called "an unusual step" of writing a long memo to himself.[21] Certainly he didn't need this, nor would he take it with him. There was only one purpose in writing the memo: to leave an after-the-fact "press conference" for history and for that memo to show that he had his own ideas about the agenda—not that of the State Department, which continued to try to influence him. Dutch reviewed Gorbachev's character, the goals of each side (noting that the Soviets want to "reduce the burden of defense spending that is stagnating the Soviet economy"), the role of SDI (it "forces them to revamp, and change their plan at great cost"), and negotiating tips ("You're unlikely to ever get *all* you want").[22] He closed with, "And so we take leave of historic Geneva, and I get the h__l out of there and head for the ranch. Happy Thanksgiving Comrades!"

Geneva marked perhaps the most important moment in Ronald Reagan's life up to that point—not that surviving getting shot was a small feat!—but the summit would put to the test once and for all every one of Dutch's most cherished notions about America and himself. He was acutely aware that he was carrying the hopes of millions of his fellow citizens. The talks would prove, once and for all, which of his two contradictory views of the Soviets were correct—the "Evil Empire" characterization or the "reasonable man" interpretation...or if, perhaps, both were. "Summits" had been part and parcel of presidential diplomacy since Franklin D. Roosevelt met with Winston Churchill and Josef Stalin in Tehran in November 1943 at the Soviet embassy. A meeting between John Kennedy and Nikita Khrushchev in June 1961 left the young American leader chastened and reeling, but it prepared him for further confrontations with the Soviets. Ronald Reagan had no intention of looking like John Kennedy. The notion of a summit played on the American romantic notion of reasonable men talking things out.

Gates observed that Reagan went to Geneva "holding better cards than any president meeting his Soviet counterpart since Eisenhower."[23] Indeed, Casey and Gates thought that Shultz and Weinberger were aiming too low, that greater opportunities lay in Geneva. And the Gipper was likely fortunate to have had Chernenko and Andropov die on him, because they were hardly reasonable men. Then again, after years of union negotiations, Dutch knew how to play the long game. It was, in the end, Gorbachev whose preconceptions were changed, and he said in 1987 that leaders "also represent human qualities, the interest and aspirations of common people, and…can be guided by purely normal human feelings and aspirations."[24] One cannot imagine such a comment coming from Stalin, who would watch a movie with tears in his eyes one moment and order the execution of hundreds of people the next.

As Reagan noted, "When you have peace, you have disarmament." He went into the meetings with the Russian leader in hopes that a personal exchange might open more ideas for discussion. Both conservatives and the liberal media fully expected Reagan to get snookered, and the administration complained in an NSDD attachment that "our negotiating position continues to be undermined by unauthorized, and often inaccurate or distorted 'information' from the news media."[25] Expectations for Reagan were low: one congressman quipped that the summit "was orchestrated to make Reagan think that his highest second-term achievement will be the Nobel Peace Prize."[26] Knowing Gorbachev would come out swinging against SDI, Reagan planned to go on offense with human rights and force the Soviet leader on defense. But he needed to do so in a way that allowed Gorbachev to look strong before the Politburo—the same tactic JFK used in the Cuban Missile Crisis when he publicly acknowledged Khrushchev's more conciliatory letter while acting as if he hadn't seen the more hard-line message. Dutch suggested the US give "consideration up front to what they want" before moving to our terms.[27] Again, Gorbachev was the one on the clock and needed a quick victory to solidify his tenuous hold on power. The US military buildup alone gave Reagan the edge, which was compounded by the economic deterioration of the USSR and, finally, pushed to the maximum by Star Wars. Gorbachev's own aide warned him not to provoke Reagan, lest he incite the "hawks" back in the US and "yielded the advantage to Reagan before the first handshake."[28] Arms-control director Kenneth Adelman watched in awe as "Reagan took [Gobrachev] to the cleaners."[29]

A student of the stage, Reagan controlled the imagery from the outset. He stood outside the Maison de Saussure where the meetings were held, in bracing cold, without an overcoat or hat. Gorbachev arrived in his massive limousine and crawled out in a thick jacket and pillbox hat, looking all of ten years Dutch's senior. The ruddy-faced Reagan walked down the stairs to greet him, making it appear all along as if Gorbachev had come to the Gipper's house for dinner. Then, in a private session, the two men exchanged frank views for an hour. (The length of the session, slated for fifteen minutes, excited the press.) Those were merely opening positions, and neither yielded, but in the plenary session Gorbachev got defensive about the Soviet economy, telegraphing his weak position. When Reagan's turn came, he firmly poured out a list of Soviet treaty violations and reminded the premier of the USSR's missile defense program. Increasingly, Gorbachev got more irritated at Reagan's pounding at the Soviet Union's expansionist ideology, finally denying their invasion of Afghanistan was an offensive move.

Repeatedly Gorbachev returned to SDI as an attempt to militarize space. And just as forcefully, Reagan returned to the untrustworthy nature of agreements with the USSR. Again, Reagan insisted Star Wars was a research program about a purely defensive weapon and that it represented the future of real arms limitations. By then, the Soviet leader was annoyed, flustered, and on his heels. He asked how they should proceed, and Reagan jumped at Gorbachev's early proposal of a 50 percent reduction in nuclear weapons, allowing the negotiators to decipher the technical details of what kind of bomber counted for what. When Gorbachev again raised SDI, Reagan again said it was defensive and that the United States would be willing to share it. Then came history's moment.[30]

Dutch suggested he and Gorbachev take a walk outside, away from the arms-control wonks and the diplomats. They ended up inside a boathouse, sitting next to a fireplace, when Dutch pulled out a working paper based on Gorbachev's own ideas, centered on the 50 percent reduction. Gorbachev yet again returned to SDI. Reagan rejected it, saying defensive weapons weren't part of the arms race and, besides, if they were successful at eliminating nuclear weapons, who would need defensive ones? He once again emphasized the defensive nature of the SDI research and said that after World War I, when the Europeans had all banned poison gas, they nevertheless kept their gas masks.

Still, Gorbachev didn't know that he could trust the Americans not to turn Star Wars into the Death Star, though he used different terminology.

But Dutch fell back on the shared technology suggestion, for which Gorbachev had no answer. Gorbachev continued to hammer at SDI, and Reagan continued to hold firm—which was an unusual tactic for the generally conciliatory Americans. They walked back from the boathouse, whereupon Dutch urged Gorbachev to come to America and meet with him in Washington, and Gorbachev reciprocated by inviting the American president to Moscow.

On the second day, Reagan broached the subject of human rights violations, and predictably Gorbachev cited discrimination against women in the United States. Reagan deflected by citing the limits of the legal process, causing Gorbachev to claim Dutch was using the political process as an excuse. The session gained little, although Shultz thought, based on the two men's grim expressions, that again Reagan had come out ahead.

Fireworks came in the third general session, when Gorbachev yet again returned to SDI and Reagan smacked the arguments back so fast the two men interrupted each other. But Reagan had Gorbachev on his playing field and said since SDI would take years, why not focus on what was in front of them—cutting nuclear arsenals. In fact, the Gipper said to a shocked Gorbachev, why stop at 50 percent? Why not eliminate all nuclear weapons? After mentioning Star Wars yet again, Gorbachev retreated, adding, "I don't agree with you, but I can see you really mean it" about Reagan's position on defensive weapons. Dutch, a third time, came back to Gorbachev's own proposal: Why not cut now and conduct missile defense research and visit that when it was further down the road? At that key moment, Gorbachev suggested a break to study Reagan's proposal (in reality, his own), less an SDI agreement.

Shultz and Reagan both knew he had gained the advantage, but Dutch knew it was important not to embarrass the Soviets. When Reagan walked into a meeting with his staff, he had taken one arm out of his sleeve and hid it behind his back. Staff noticed the empty sleeve and asked, "Where is your arm?" Reagan looked at the empty sleeve and feigned surprise: "It was here before I met Gorbachev." At dinner, Gorbachev got "really belligerent," but Reagan held his ground and suggested they list all their areas of agreement. He requested that the two leaders put out a joint statement, but Gorbachev refused, saying such a statement of agreement was not justified (despite the fact that they indeed had agreed on each of Reagan's points). After more turmoil among staffs, the two men indeed finally stood together to issue a statement summarizing an agreement to a 50 percent cut in nuclear weapons and an interim agreement on the intermediate Euromissiles. Dutch was the victor in almost every respect.

He followed up immediately. From Rancho del Cielo, where he went after Geneva, he wrote another personal letter to the premier—"I finally met a Soviet leader I could talk to," he wrote—arguing for practicality, insisting SDI would never be used in a first-strike scenario, and bringing up Afghanistan again.[31] The US would offer to help the Soviets withdraw, he noted, in a way that would maintain Soviet interests. Another summit was set for the following year. Little did he know that the first encounter convinced Gorbachev that Reagan was a "dinosaur." The change of scene to the fireside alleviated the tension, but by the end of the private chat, Gorbachev felt like Dutch had given him a "take it or leave it" list of demands. Still the Soviet leader began to see a "human factor" at work and thought they could still agree.[32]

Shrewdly, Gorbachev asked the United States to join him in a moratorium on nuclear testing—immediately after the USSR did its own tests—and put the ball in Reagan's court. The Pentagon opposed a moratorium, arguing that it needed tests to gauge the reliability of new systems. Although Reagan rejected a moratorium, he knew that Gorbachev had finally scored a public relations coup, calling it a "h__l of a propaganda move."[33] Ambassador Dobrynin arrived with an offer for another summit, which Reagan thought would occur later that summer.

Even before those exchanges occurred, the disasters started. America's space program had become largely a series of space shuttle missions to engage in orbital experiments. While the majesty and mystery of landing on the moon had passed, there was still excitement with each new shuttle liftoff and landing. And the launch of the space shuttle *Challenger* on January 28, 1986, was special: a schoolteacher, Christa McAuliffe, would be the first civilian in space. Minutes after launch, however, abnormal white streaks began to appear from the engines; then, within seconds, the

Challenger blew up, parts of the rocket motors careening wildly away from the explosion cloud. All members of the crew died instantly.

Then-national security advisor John Poindexter reached George H. W. Bush first with the news—Reagan was practicing his State of the Union speech in the Oval Office—and together they told the president as they flicked on the television to see the footage. Instead of the State of the Union message to the nation, Reagan delivered a moving tribute to the crew. He made reference to the *Apollo I* disaster in 1967 when the United States suffered its first loss of space travelers on their launch pad. In closing, Reagan quoted the lines from a famous poem by John Gillespie Magee Jr. about aviation, "High Flight," ending with "We will never forget them, nor the last time we saw them, this morning as they prepared for their journey, and waved goodbye, and 'slipped the surly bonds of earth' to 'touch the face of God.'"[34] Although the Gipper told speechwriter Peggy Noonan he had failed, in fact his address went down as one of the finest speeches in American history.[35]

Obscured in the tragedy was a profound strategic issue, in that the United States had begun an important internal secret debate about the future of the shuttle system *before* the *Challenger* disaster. During Carter's term, the United States Air Force had started studies on post-shuttle vehicles, formalizing it in 1982 with a directive from General Lawrence Skantze of the Aeronautical Systems Division, ordering advanced planning. NASA and the Defense Advanced Projects Research Agency (DARPA) had each embarked on their own studies, with all three combining in a 1985 commitment to build an experimental spacecraft that relied heavily on scramjets.[36] After watching the laborious shuttles crawl out to their launch pads, then sit endlessly, all agencies involved wanted "routine" access to space. Virtually nothing could be done in space until that was achieved, and the shuttles had been failures. But air-breathers like the X-30 Aero-Space Plane, being researched, or new heavy-lift rockets were increasingly seen as necessary due to the entirely un-routine nature of shuttle flights. In October 1987, an internal memo refuting an earlier *Washington Post* editorial cited "seemingly endless increases in Shuttle and Space Station cost estimates."[37]

Only days after the *Challenger* explosion, Reagan delivered his State of the Union address to Congress, where he spoke of moving forward "with research on a new Orient Express that could, by the end of the next decade, take off from Dulles Airport, accelerate up to twenty-five times the speed of sound, attaining low Earth orbit or flying to Tokyo within two hours." This was a reference to the Aero-Space Plane research project and a clause inserted by Dana Rohrabacher. In reality, hypersonic capability was not even remotely close to testing, let alone practical use. The fact that the program received significant funding reflected the concerns everyone had about "routine" access to space, so much so that former astronaut Harrison Schmitt was asked to prepare a briefing for Reagan on future directions for space policy. Although he did not actually present the briefing until January 1988, Schmitt's recommendations included cancelling the International Space Station program, temporarily relying on the shuttles, and refocusing America's space program on a more visionary goal: settling Mars.[38] It was a shockingly audacious plan, and one that would have reenergized the American space program, which instead drifted into nothingness until it was virtually canceled by Barack Obama in 2010, only to be revived by President Donald Trump in 2017...with a focus on Mars.[39]

In his *Challenger* speech, Reagan had taken a jab at the Soviets by noting, "We don't keep secrets and cover things up." It was an ironic phrase in that a much larger calamity would occur at a small city on the Ukraine/Belarus border on April 26, 1986, when one of the reactors at the Chernobyl Nuclear Power Plant exploded after a safety test. Plumes of radioactive fission materials gushed into the atmosphere, drifting over the western USSR and Europe and exposing thousands of people. The Soviets evacuated the city—but not for two days. Whatever Gorbachev's intentions personally were, the first official announcement in the USSR didn't come until April 28. Reagan received a briefing two days later, noting "as usual the Russians won't put out any facts but it is evident that a radioactive cloud is spreading beyond the Soviet border."[40] He offered assistance to Gorbachev, but others pounced on the problems inherent in a communist system. On the one hand, Gorbachev looked weak, and on the other hand, he looked incompetent, unable to manage his own bureaucracy. He claimed the "tragedy of Chernobyl was exploited."[41]

Shortly before Chernobyl's reactors blew up, another hot spot had erupted in Libya, in the form of its unstable leader, Colonel Muammar Gaddafi. Though professing to be a Muslim, Gaddafi was, like Saddam Hussein of Iraq, part of a generation of "secular" Middle East military thugs. He wore his army uniform, loved pomp and demonstrations, and, of course, was ruthless. For years, the National Security Council had been worried by Libya. As early as December 1981, Reagan had enacted a new policy toward Libya based on information that Gaddafi was plotting terror attacks on American targets. As a result, Al Haig had requested American companies to leave that nation (thirty-five firms did) and the US ended all travel to Libya.[42] Gaddafi had emerged as a major client of Soviet arms and a general mischief-maker: some reports suggested he was trying to acquire nuclear power. From 1978 to 1981 he had invaded neighboring Chad.

The 1981 policy remained in effect until 1985, when Gaddafi imposed himself in the Rome and Vienna airport attacks, pledging support to the various communist factions involved, and labeling the terrorists heroes. Then he declared the Gulf of Sidra to be Libyan territory (well past the accepted twelve-mile international boundary) and dubbed the zone the "Line of Death." Dutch would have none of it, calling the Libyan dictator "a madman…harassing our planes out over international waters, and it's time to show the other nations there—Egypt, Morocco, et al.—that there is a different management here."[43] The US Navy promptly sailed the USS *Nimitz* and its task force into the zone in March 1986. As US ships and aircraft crossed the "Line," Libyan planes flew up and engaged in a nonfatal dogfight, then small patrol boats attacked the battle group. Three Libyan ships were disabled or sunk, two Libyan planes shot down, and American forces disabled or destroyed numerous Libyan radar installations. Gaddafi's defeated forces withdrew.[44] When the sleeping Reagan wasn't awakened and informed for six hours, the press began its normal huffing and puffing. Dutch waved it off: "If our planes were shot down, yes, they'd wake me up right away. If the other fellow's were shot down, why wake me up?"[45]

The "madman" wasn't finished, however, putting out a "hit" on Reagan. The president laughed it off. After all, he had been threatened by professionals—mobsters associated with American unions! On April 2, TWA Flight 840 from Los Angeles to Cairo was bombed, killing four Americans, including an infant. A group claiming responsibility cited "American imperialism" in the Gulf of Sidra, but direct links to Libya were not apparent. Then Gaddafi sent agents to bomb the La Belle nightclub on April 5 in West Berlin. The club was a popular hangout for American military personnel. One American was killed (plus two others) and over two hundred wounded.

Dutch had had enough. On April 15, Reagan ordered fighter-bombers from England and strike aircraft from carriers in the Gulf of Sidra to strike various targets in Libya. Several allies, including France and Spain, refused overflight or basing, which made the operation more time-consuming and difficult, but the raid continued nonetheless. Six main target areas were struck, including the barracks at Bab al-Azizia, where Gaddafi and his family had a residence. Whether any of Gaddafi's immediate family died—the matter remains in dispute—the dictator got the message. Gaddafi dropped his bluster for years, and any operations that terrorists associated with him were laundered through far more layers of deniability. Less than a year after the Libyan raid, Ed Meese noted that increased cooperation around the world against terrorism "stems from the success of our attack on Libya."[46]

Reagan asserted that the evidence of the bombing was indisputable, that the strike was a part of a larger war on terrorism (although still Reagan had yet to accept the Islamic element), and that America would retaliate if attacked by terrorists. The National Security Planning Group meeting of August 14 later that year reiterated the Gipper's resolve, stating "it is absolutely necessary that there be no delay in hitting Qadhafi [sic] again when the evidence links Libya to a terrorist act."[47] An NSC follow-up memo of April 26 contained an extensive list of Libyan-related terrorism, which showed Gaddafi's fingerprints on some two-dozen incidents over the previous seven years.[48] If anything, Reagan had acted with restraint and forestalled a more serious involvement there for another two decades.

Reagan had found success in Libya, but two other disasters were unfolding, though neither of them would be apparent for some time. First, the continuing policy quagmire known as Nicaragua festered throughout early 1986. Poindexter referred to it as a dilemma that required rewinding the clock to the day the Sandinistas took power. A January NSC meeting cited improvement in the democratic resistance in Nicaragua: it "remains potentially strong, and with additional support is capable of bringing significantly increased pressure to bear on the Sandinista regime." However, the status of the internal opposition within Nicaragua was "precarious," and American policy had to ensure that it stayed in the country and that its plight be publicized.[49] Reagan reviewed major options at a May National Security Planning Group meeting.[50] Congress, as he knew, was insisting on negotiations in exchange for money, but in fact the administration did not want an agreement with the Sandinistas, fearing that—like all communists—they would break the deal after obtaining what they wanted. Weinberger cautioned, "We just have to make sure that the negotiations don't get out of our control"—a tall order given that virtually all negotiations with communist states in the past had been less than "controlled." Pressure on the "Contadora" group (Columbia, Mexico, Panama, and Venezuela), which launched an initiative in 1983 to resolve the conflicts in Central America, might have prevented a bad deal, but Weinberger feared that if the Contadoras reached a separate agreement without the US, "We'll never get anything out of Congress."[51]

During the meeting the prospect of getting funds from other countries was again raised. Weinberger urged the group to "try everything.... We should try every country we can find...If the contras [sic] are out of business in July, we will have to fight there ourselves some day." Oliver North, who had accompanied Poindexter to the meeting, noted that the 1986 intelligence authorization allowed overtures from the State Department to other nations about providing Contra aid. Casey, seeing the direction this was heading, noted that "until now we have not involved the president," and there was no discussion about the previous Saudi support given the Contras. Yet at that time, North already was siphoning funds from the sale of TOW missiles. He drafted a key memo to

Poindexter explaining what he was doing and urging "the President approve the structure depicted above."[52]

At first, Poindexter would claim he did not receive this—North's shredder worked overtime after the scheme was discovered—and said he told North not to put anything in writing about the plan. North claimed he was given no such instructions. Poindexter claimed to have had had an uneasy feeling, possibly from knowing North's temperament, and deliberately walled it off. He told Don Regan, "I didn't want to know. I was so damned mad at Tip O'Neill…[for] dragging the Contras around, I didn't want to know."[53] Later, however, Poindexter admitted he knew about the scheme and "didn't see anything illegal about it." In fact, he found the idea clever, "like a gift from Iran," and deliberately did not inform Reagan for purposes of "plausible deniability." He was willing to take the risk, rather than the president.[54] McFarlane, North, and Poindexter had planted an IED for Reagan, set to explode at any moment.

A second time bomb came as an inheritance of Carter's policies in Haiti and Cuba. Reagan's dealings with these immigration issues, which soon encompassed illegal aliens from Mexico, expose a myth that conservatives have propagated, namely that a reluctant Reagan was pushed into signing off on the Simpson-Mazzoli bill. Archival documents tell a much different story—one in which the Reagan administration from the beginning had accepted a policy of allowing Mexican illegal immigrants to stay. However, this approach was largely buried under the more immediate concerns of Haiti and Cuba, which requires us to review developments in Haiti and Cuba since 1981 when Reagan took office.

Under Jean-Claude "Baby Doc" Duvalier's dictatorship in Haiti, oppression had driven thousands of "boat people" to board small vessels and to seek asylum status in the United States. By 1979, more than 15,000 had arrived and, after a review, were found to be not political refugees but economic immigrants. Therefore, they were ineligible for asylum status. Then in 1980, another 40,000 to 80,000 Haitians tried to join the 125,000 Cubans who escaped Cuba in the Mariel boatlift. A flustered Carter created the "Cuban/Haitian Entrant (Status Pending)" to define the new immigrants and prevent their deportation according to law. New Haitians trying to enter would be turned away.

Reagan enforced this policy, returning seized boats to Port-au-Prince, Haiti. Virtually all of the next wave of 25,000 immigrants were intercepted and returned. Meanwhile, it was discovered that many of the Mariel boatlift immigrants had not been political escapees but 25,000 criminals from Fidel Castro's jails—an episode brought to cinematic life in the famous Al Pacino film *Scarface*.[55] This produced a serious political problem for Reagan, in that a central holding area for 950 of the worst of the Cuban thugs—described as "mentally ill, alcoholics, homosexuals and social misfits [who] would be opposed by any state to which they were moved"—was currently Fort Chaffee, Arkansas, where Governor Frank D. White had been a staunch administration ally.[56] White (who beat an up-and-coming future president Bill Clinton) desperately wanted the criminals removed, but all five of the alternative sites had similar concerns about housing the Cubans.

The significance of the Haitian/Cuban issues cannot be overstated, as they became the basis for the Simpson-Mazzoli Act that would become one of Reagan's worst legacies. Simpson-Mazzoli can be directly traced to a memo from Kenneth Cribb to Edwin Meese, Martin Anderson, and Craig Fuller in July 1981 called "Immigration Policy."[57] The memo admitted there were 3.5 million illegal aliens present, creating "problems for themselves as well as for the country" because the aliens were exploited by sweatshops, strained American services, and required more detention facilities. The memo suggested implementing a new temporary worker program with Mexico on a two-year trial basis. Most importantly, the memo argued *for full legal status* for all illegals in America at that time under the classification "renewable term temporary resident."[58]

Nevertheless, in most of the immigration discussions, the primary focus was on Haiti and Cuba, not Mexican immigrants. For example, in the July report of the President's Task Force on Immigration and Refugee Policy, the first task was to address Cuba/Haiti: "All agencies agree that we should seek legislation," the memo noted, "to authorize Cubans and Haitians who arrived before October 1980 to apply for permanent resident status after residing here two years." But it also argued that the administration should pursue negotiations to restrain further Haitian illegal immigration. While recommending detaining undocumented aliens upon arrival, the memo left open the question as to where to put them. Fort Chaffee was again suggested as a possible site, but the memo concluded there were "no good answers to the…problem." A recommendation to negotiate with Cuba for the return of the prisoners to Castro's island could not have been made with much seriousness.[59]

Perhaps the unwillingness to raise the "amnesty" question in 1981 arose from the fact that, overwhelmingly, the American public opposed it. Reagan's pollster Richard Wirthlin conducted polling in May 1981 for the administration and found that 92 percent said greater efforts should be made to halt the influx of illegals—and a very significant majority opposed further Mexican immigration no matter how he changed the wording.[60] Similarly, a May national study showed 61 percent of Americans favored reducing the numbers of *all* immigrants, and 20 percent wanted to stop immigration entirely. Even more astounding, a *Los Angeles Times* poll in April 1981 found that 75 percent of the jobless would take menial work at a minimum wage, putting to rest the notion there "were jobs Americans won't do."[61] No wonder the administration wanted Congress to take the lead.

> *Reagan's administration had virtually conceded*
> *an early form of amnesty in 1981, long before negotiating*
> *the matter with Congress.*

Beyond the Cuban/Haitian aspects of immigration, the next most serious question was the temporary alien workers, where "all agree[d] there should be some form of a new temporary worker program," with a call for a large number (fifty thousand a year) getting worker status under a pilot program. (It should be noted that in bureaucracies, no pilot program ever fails; by the nature of creating it in the first place, the assumption is that it would succeed if only it could find Gorbachev's "right man.") Shockingly, the memo also advanced the position that illegals who had been here "for a considerable period of time" should be allowed to apply for a permanent status. The "larger issue," however, involved whether Reagan should propose legislation to establish employer sanctions. What is most revealing about these documents is that (1) the administration had agreed to grant permanent residence status to millions of illegal aliens *before* negotiations even began with Congress, and (2) that point number one was not considered to even be the "larger issue"![62]

Perhaps even more astonishing from the viewpoint of 2018, the liberal press overwhelmingly criticized Reagan for failing to install a program of employer verification. The task force that had looked into immigration had mixed reactions to issues of worker identification. One approach was to make Social Security cards the basic form of identification, but that had considerable opposition from conservatives, who feared government intrusion. Ultimately, no system emerged, which meant, the *New York Times* pontificated, that it would be impossible to decide which aliens that entered could stay in the United States. No system could be "cohesive or even coherent" if it failed to deal with worker identification.[63] "Card tricks," the *Washington Post* called the administration's proposed policy: "Without relying on some fair, accurate and simple means of distinguishing legal migrants from illegals, proper enforcement...becomes hopeless."[64] And the *Chicago Tribune* warned the welfare system was just "a haven for illegal aliens."[65] In short, the major media was attacking Reagan for not cracking down harder on illegal immigration—a position 180 degrees opposite of where they stand today!

In June 1981, an illegal immigration and refugee paper was submitted to the president. It argued for "providing for large scale legalization [which] makes a major move in the direction of eliminating the subclass of illegals (3-5 million) currently in this country." It recommended sanctioning employers who "knowingly" hired illegals and advocated new Social Security cards for a "tracking system." Despite recommending legalization for illegals, the paper noted that Americans wanted greater enforcement of immigration laws and cited no public outcry to legalize those already here.[66] It was one of Reagan's biggest blind spots in his entire tenure. On July 30, 1981, Reagan issued a statement on immigration policy ahead of his submission to Congress of his legislative package. The president noted that "both the United States and Mexico have historically benefitted from Mexicans obtaining employment" in America and claimed "illegal immigrants in considerable numbers have become productive members of our society and are a basic part" of our workforce. However, he warned, "we must not encourage illegal immigration."[67] Unfortunately, that was exactly what he had done.

The administration had just engaged in extensive talks with Mexico about the issue. A confidential memo in May noted that the government of Mexico (GOM) hoped to "keep the widest possible opportunity for the greatest number of Mexicans to be able to work in [the US]" Indeed, the American embassy in Mexico observed that the José López Portillo administration had sought to delay serious discussions and to even avoid negotiations about immigration until Reagan took office, fearing that the US would take unilateral action. Mexico, the embassy noted, had internal problems trying to police migration to America and thought "imaginative approaches" would be needed to make any kind of guest worker program function.[68] By the time the new Mexican president Miguel de la Madrid arrived for a visit in August 1986, the administration had a new set of criteria by which to judge Mexico. Bill Casey's statistics showed the previous five years of estimates had resulted in a "grim outlook for economic and political stability" there, and Madrid hoped to emphasize the positive changes.[69] Still, Casey's analysts found, the Mexicans had overstated their oil reserves, and on a broader scale they "are not ready to make the structural changes needed to put their economy on a sound footing.... [P]oor economic conditions in Mexico will contribute heavily to a growing surge of illegal aliens across our southern border."[70]

Republican Senator Alan Simpson and Democrat Congressman Romano Mazzoli finally got the legislation moving in 1985 with a bill that curbed illegal immigration with stronger border controls and employer sanctions while extending amnesty to those already here. The bill made it illegal to hire illegals knowingly, putting the onus on employers to guarantee employees' immigration status without providing any means to do so (attempts at providing employers with means to verify status were rebuked by Congress on anti-regulatory grounds). It turned "a personnel manager into a special agent of the INS," said one labor lawyer.[71] The amnesty process allowed illegal aliens already here to become citizens if they paid a fine, paid back taxes, proved they had not committed any crimes, and showed they possessed a minimal knowledge of English.

Reagan signed Simpson-Mazzoli into law on November 6, 1986. Later, critics would insist this was merely the foot in the door that opened to allow millions of new Democrat voters into the country (and, looking at the subsequent path of California, they may have had a point). Moreover, with no imposing barrier on America's southern border, there was simply no way to ensure a curb on subsequent immigration. The entire fight would be reengaged in 2007 under George W. Bush, and again in the presidential election of 2016 when Donald Trump would vow to build a wall. But the unfortunate significance of the 1986 legislation is that it was *Reagan's proposal* and had been his basic outline, with the goal of amnesty, for five years when it was finally enacted.[72] Later, Dutch would claim the Democrats duped him and failed to live up to their enforcement agreements—yet Reagan's own policy papers had minimal enforcement mechanisms.

The cultural and political repercussions of the disaster that was Simpson-Mazzoli would not become apparent until Reagan had long left the political stage. Few even noticed the bill at the time because another near-catastrophe had bubbled up to boiling level. Once again, this disaster began with the issue of the hostages. This time, however, structural changes occurring inside the Reagan administration came close to bringing the presidency down.

But 1986 seemed good to Reagan. Aside from the *Challenger* tragedy, he and the nation were on a roll. Geneva was a tremendous success. His approval numbers were up. The economy was booming. There seemed to be hope for new talks with Gorbachev. On the Fourth of July 1986 he unveiled the renovated Statue of Liberty on its hundred-year anniversary, and even *Time* magazine was complimentary, noting he had moved from "success to success" and "inhabits his moment in America with a triumphant…ease…hitting home runs."[73]

17

You Could Have Said Yes

Wrestling with multiple disasters at home and abroad, Reagan nevertheless expected 1986 to bear much fruit. In February Dutch celebrated his seventy-fifth birthday and, with the exception of a few recurring intestinal polyps, seemed to be the picture of health. So did the American economy. Not only were businesses humming (as of January with thirty-seven months of growth) and increasing numbers of Americans returning to work (unemployment down to 6.9 percent from over 10 percent when Reagan took office), oil prices were finally starting to drop, falling to almost half of what a barrel of oil had cost just five years later. This, of course, severely stung the USSR, which needed the revenue, and prompted Gorbachev to blame Reagan for forcing the price of oil down: "We know who began this process of cutting prices," he said, "and whose interest it is in."[1]

While oil prices began to fall not long after the Geneva summit, the windfall the United States received from falling energy prices was not such a simple matter and certainly was no quid pro quo. After the second Arab oil shock that followed the Iranian revolution, prices had shot up again from $13 a barrel to $34 a barrel.[2] At that point, many OPEC members grew concerned that prices might go so high as to permanently damage demand. This dramatic increase in prices led to an investment boom and temporary price inflation in oil services. New investment poured into the North Sea, Alaska, and Mexico, and American oil supplies had started to increase throughout Reagan's first term. As Paul Volcker tightened the money spigots, prices rose and energy demand fell, declining by as much as half globally from 1978 to 1985. Producers, especially in the Middle East, began to face dwindling market share and, by 1983, North Sea oil wells were producing more fuel daily than Algeria, Libya, and Nigeria combined. In a panic, OPEC met in London in 1983 and agreed to a historic price cut of 15 percent. Thus, in a roundabout way, Reagan's goal of reducing the Soviets' cash reserves was being realized: their oil revenues fell—painfully so.

Don Regan's arrival as chief of staff enabled him to lobby more forcefully for his personal agenda goals, most notably tax reform. He wanted to reduce rates but also "close loopholes," a favored Washington term that means "remove from the tax code beneficiaries you don't like." Reagan agreed, seeing it as a continuation of the first-term tax cuts: "We must radically change a system that still treats people's earnings, similar incomes, much differently regarding the tax they pay."[3] When the FY86 budget came up in the spring of 1985, the deficit hawks were at it again, seeking another round of spending cuts to reduce the deficit by over $50 billion. But there was a poison pill: a one-year freeze in the cost-of-living adjustments (COLAs) for Social Security recipients. Again, this skirted Reagan's pledge not to cut Social Security, but he agreed to the package submitted by Kansas senator Bob Dole. Tip O'Neill saw his opportunity to leverage the cuts for higher taxes. Reagan exploded and told O'Neill, "Do you think I am going to let Mondale say, 'Look, I told you I was right?' Never!"[4] He then announced he would oppose the COLA freeze, aware that Democrats were just lurking in the weeds to pounce on any retreat on his pledges not to touch Social Security. Senators such as Dole and Warren Rudman felt hung out to dry by Reagan's position shifts, which was typical of lawmakers used to presidents caving in on their commitments.

As with all things in Washington, the initial forays were just that. Soon new negotiations were undertaken around a deficit control bill named for Senators Phil Gramm of Texas and Warren Rudman of New Hampshire (Gramm-Rudman). This bill purported to force automatic cuts to balance the budget—yet it only affected "discretionary" spending (i.e., it did *not* include entitlements, welfare, Social Security, or Medicare, namely the very programs that were blowing up the deficits). Its passage in December 1985 allowed Congress to dodge the most difficult and divisive decisions.[5] The Supreme Court found the law unconstitutional in June 1986 by virtue of the fact it had the comptroller general exercise a function belonging to the executive. Congress hustled to fix the flaw and Reagan signed it. None of this solved the problem of an overspending, out-of-control Congress or the absence of a line-item veto.

Midterms approached, placing still more pressure on Congress to act. It did so with a far-reaching tax reform bill that greatly simplified the code and lowered the top rate from 50 percent to 35 percent, with lower brackets at 25 percent and 15 percent. Although the Treasury plan suggested eliminating state and local tax deductions, which would have severely affected high-tax states such as New York, that proposal was dropped. Another point of contention was the high corporate tax rate, which many wanted to *increase*. Reagan refused. Provided some new provisions under what was called "Treasury II" in May 1985, which preserved the lower individual rates and lowered the corporate rate from 46 percent to 33 percent, Dutch took to the airwaves to again sell a tax plan. He noted that the new plan was as different from America's current system as a Model T was from a space shuttle, then added, "I should know—I've seen both."[6] He then embarked on a tour to sell the new program, noting that America's current system had become so complex even Albert Einstein couldn't fathom it. He added, "You know, it's said that his hair didn't look that way until after he experienced his first tax form."[7] Dutch had the prefect line for every audience. At a high school he spoke to those who might already have part-time jobs. He said if the tax system were a song it would be "Gimme Shelter," and if it were a movie, it would be *Take the Money and Run*.

The tradeoffs in the proposed plan involved slightly higher taxes on investment income but larger reductions in various tax rates on investment itself. Knowing they couldn't oppose the popular Reagan, the Democrats tried to reframe the debate as them *siding* with Reagan against "big business." This response had the effect of sparking urgent and frenzied lobbying efforts to preserve the tax breaks contained in the infamous "loopholes."[8] As administration economist William Niskanen noted, support for the plan was broad but not deep, and by the time the House committees finished with it, the plan had added a fourth 38 percent rate for the highest incomes. Worse, the bill had a combined effect of increasing the tax rates on new investments by about 16 percent, leading business to oppose the bill.

Defeated in the House committee the first time, Reagan's team went into overdrive. Baker, who had helped sponsor the second iteration of the bill, stewed that Don Regan was insufficiently involved and wrote to Dutch insisting that he make passage his top priority. The president met with House Republicans and gave them a twofold promise: the bill *would* be fixed in the Senate, but he would veto it if he received it in its present form. His lobbying finally moved the bill to the Senate in December 1985, ironically on a voice vote alone! (Tip O'Neill had expected Republicans to insist on a roll call, but none did.)

There, it faced a different, but familiar, opposition. Senate Finance Committee Chairman Robert Packwood (R-OR) stated, "I rather like the tax code as it is."[9] Nevertheless, Packwood agreed to embark on a radical strategy of starting with a clean bill, which "changed the dynamic of the issue."[10] At one point, the senator even announced to the press that there would be no committee business over the weekend; then, after the reporters departed, he held a secret meeting on Saturday that hammered out the details so well that it passed the committee 20–0. After a number of tweaks that lowered the corporate rate to 33 percent and reduced the number of business deductions (including the infamous "three martini lunch"), the Senate passed its version 97–3. The conference committee worked through the summer to finalize the details of the final bill, in which individual rate cuts were a little lower, business rates a little higher, and the corporate rate was capped at 34 percent. All in all, it was close to the original Treasury proposal, and Reagan praised Congress's work for "eliminating unnecessary loopholes."[11] The Tax Reform Act of 1986 passed the House on September 25, 1986, sailed through the Senate the following day, and was signed by Reagan on October 22. It was based on the "fairness, growth, and simplicity" that he had advocated before the nation in May.[12] George Gilder called the tax bill the "greatest victory of the Reagan Revolution"—all this coming from a president who supposedly was adrift when he started his second term.[13]

Reagan's second great economic achievement, after the 1981 tax cut, was a revision of the tax code that once and for all killed the oppressive taxation in America that had been brought about by the New Deal and Great Society.

After all the smoke cleared, individual rates stood at 28 percent, down from a nearly unbelievable 70 percent when Dutch took office. Corporate rates fell from 46 to 34 percent—still high compared to other nations, but a significant improvement. Some individual oxen were gored. But Reagan knew the score. "I feel like we just played the World Series of tax reform and the American people won."[14] On the political battlefield, the Republicans won the working class over: Democratic candidate Gary Hart said tax reform "got away from us and it's theirs now," referring to the Republicans.[15]

Victory over the Soviets was not quite as obvious yet, at least not to the West. Inside the USSR, though, the system was coming apart at the seams. In January, Gorbachev proposed eliminating all nuclear weapons by the year 2000—a cover to get out of the Euromissile quicksand. By October 1986, he flatly told the Politburo that deploying the SS-20s in the first place was a mistake. It failed to split the Western alliance and boxed the Soviet Union into a corner where it would look weak if it unilaterally withdrew the missiles. His solution was to try to get some concession out of Reagan for something he already wanted to do. Of course, Gorbachev always knew that the Soviet Union's massive land army and conventional forces had been one of the main rationales for a policy of the American nuclear "linkage" with Europe in the first place, and he offered no overtures toward reducing that imbalance.

Reagan and Gorbachev had continued their pen-pal relationship since Geneva. Each time Gorbachev would bring up the issue of SDI, Dutch would insist it wasn't up for discussion except as a defensive system employed by both nations. In a response to Gorbachev after the "abolition" missive, Reagan suggested the Soviets begin by getting out of Afghanistan and urged his counterpart to help him "find a solution" to eliminate strategic weapons.

By that time, fissures in the Reagan team were deep. Many of the more dovish members wanted to remain in the SALT II treaty, which the Gipper disdained as more of the same. Although in 1985 Reagan said the United States would abide by the agreement, by April 1986 he noted in his diary that he met with a number of congressmen who wanted to ditch SALT II and noted, "Frankly I'm ready. The Soviets are guilty of about 30-odd violations & show no signs of making any redress."[16] Weinberger, wrestling with the swap-out of new Trident subs for the aging Polaris and Poseidons, argued for leaving the treaty. Reagan sided with him and announced on May 23 that the US would not abide terms of SALT II, citing multiple violations of the agreement by the Soviets. Of course, to the perpetually myopic news media—which only saw disarmament as possible by unilaterally getting weaker—the action was a "blunder" and "deplorable" and portended the likelihood that there would never be a reduction in nuclear arms.[17] But Dutch knew where he was going and the press didn't.

Larry Speakes, Reagan's press secretary (who had succeeded Jim Brady in March 1981) found that the so-called "conservative" media was every bit as biased as the liberals. His former boss and communications director, David Gergen (in the Clinton years christened "David Rodham Gergen" by Rush Limbaugh for his fawning over the First Couple), had resigned in December 1983 and pestered Speakes so much he referred to Gergen (whom he nicknamed "Tall") as a "distraction." George Will was worse, turning on Reagan "whenever it suited him." After the Daniloff episode (which we'll get to below), Will wrote that the Reagan administration was "nothing but air."[18]

All along, the Gipper reiterated that he was not interested in "arms control" or even parity, but *reduction and elimination* of nuclear arms. This was never possible under SALT II, and it certainly wouldn't occur if anything blocked SDI. Reagan was bringing the US Congress, the Soviets, and the world along kicking and screaming.

He may not have known, but strongly suspected that American policies were having their desired effect behind the Iron Curtain. In the spring of 1986, at the Twenty-Seventh Communist Party of the Soviet Union Congress, Gorbachev lamented that Afghanistan was becoming a "running sore."[19] (This was months before the first Stingers were delivered.) Shultz, who was almost always initially wrong but ultimately came down on the winning side, thought 1986 would be the year of "maximum leverage" because support for SDI would decrease as costs rose.[20] In fact, over time, SDI became more popular as people saw the technology was feasible, especially with early laser tests in the airborne laboratory—but that would come later. Reagan had several factors working on his behalf, most importantly that the Soviet economy was continuing to crumble. Gorbachev, seeking to demonstrate his commitment to *glasnost* and to appease Reagan's incessant human rights prods, released dissident Anatoly Shcharansky on February 11. (Reagan noted in his diary that he was beloved in the Soviet gulags: the prisoners "like me.")

Gorbachev, despite facing many old-line Stalinist hard-liners, nevertheless attempted to open himself to the West by reading many banned Western books, including Churchill's memoirs. Rock and roll was already popular *within* Russia, and the regime struggled with controlling bootleg music and above all American clothing, especially blue jeans. Shultz thought the Soviets were "on the ropes" by mid-1986. Chernobyl still festered, its impact fully hitting the Soviet military elite, who "were forced to rethink their predictions of a favorable outcome to a major nuclear strike."[21] Gorbachev later called it a "historic turning point," causing him to admit "the system as we knew it could no longer continue."[22] Once again, the USSR's weakness in the information age was exposed—not only with the Soviets' inability to *get* information, but to control information from slipping in and out. It was not a good look for a totalitarian dictatorship.

Still, to the outside, the USSR looked like a colossus. It continued to produce heavy missiles, continued to test specialized radars in violation of arms-control agreements, and continued to produce new lines of strategic bombers and subs. Its own financial situation notwithstanding, Gorbachev's Soviet Union kept propping up the governments of Nicaragua and Vietnam with over $3 billion in loans in 1986.

Both Reagan and Gorbachev knew the real score. After Gorbachev's post-Geneva letter, Reagan delivered his own missive in July 1986 offering a small concession, a promise not to withdraw from the ABM Treaty for seven and a half years. Rather than receiving it as a step forward, Gorbachev (who wanted a twenty-year exception) blasted it as unacceptable, provoking "grave and disturbing thoughts." Nevertheless, he was shaken, and then further jarred, by the Daniloff case.

In August 1986 the FBI had arrested a Soviet spy, Gennadi Zakharov. The Soviets responded by arresting an American journalist in Moscow named Nicholas Daniloff, charging him with espionage. Dutch fumed, calling it a "frame up" in a letter to Gorbachev. "There are no grounds for Mr. Daniloff's detention," Reagan warned, cautioning that "it can only have the most serious and far-reaching consequences for the relationship between our two countries" if he were not freed.[23] The Soviet leader refused to back down, insisting Daniloff had conducted "impermissible activities," a response that irritated Reagan even more, calling it "arrogant," adding, "I'm mad as h–l."[24] As more information emerged, however, and as Shultz conferred with the State Department's legal advisor, the secretary concluded Daniloff was sloppy, if not guilty. But after Reagan was briefed on the new information, he held fast until Abraham Sofaer, the State Department lawyer, explained to Reagan that the truth didn't matter, only the evidence in the case—and that looked bad for Daniloff. Explaining that Daniloff had been drawn in by the CIA and could be looking at a lifetime in a Soviet prison, Dutch had the same emotional reaction as he did with the hostages, even to the point that he referred to the American reporter as a hostage.[25] Later, Reagan vented to Eduard Shevardnadze, the foreign minister of the USSR. "I enjoy being angry," Dutch wrote.[26]

Gorbachev realized he had pushed matters too far and beat a hasty retreat, using a September letter to urge another personal, private meeting between the two—not to supplant the planned Geneva sequel. At home, however, Gorbachev played both sides, telling his Politburo that he had to give the Americans something, which he would then use to pressure them in the world press if Reagan did not meet them halfway.

With Gorbachev's overture, Reagan allowed Shultz to cut a deal for Daniloff. The Soviet leader tossed in permission for human rights activist Yuri Orlov and his wife, Sidney, to leave. Dutch agreed to the one-on-one at a neutral site, Reykjavik, Iceland, in October. Gorbachev, however, vacillated between confidence and fear. "The Americans need this meeting.... Elections are just around the corner," he reassured his comrades."[27] Yet immediately before the trip to Iceland, he advised his ministers, "If we do not compromise on some questions, even very important ones, we will lose the main point [and] be pulled into an arms race beyond our power, and we will lose this race."[28] In this, the Soviet leader made the same mistake as almost all totalitarians, mistaking democracy for mobocracy and assuming that every leader is *only* driven by getting reelected. Reagan, especially now in his second term, was all but immune to these pressures.

Though Reagan was fully in the driver's seat, his policies wreaking havoc on the Soviet economy and his firm stance on SDI all but assuring him an advantage in the negotiations, the Gipper was coming under heavy fire from American conservatives. *National Review* had devolved into perpetual hand-wringing over the possibility Reagan might seek an arms-control treaty at all costs, and Dutch had even advised Shultz to quit reading *Human Events* because it was so critical of their work. Lyn Nofziger told Reagan that conservatives feared the president would "be conned into giving away the store" in negotiations.[29] George Will, as usual, sniped at the president at every opportunity.

Conservatives had been suspicious of Reagan since the transition, fearing the influence of several "RINO" (Republican in Name Only) holdovers from the Nixon administration or from the Romney/Bush camps. Their fears never materialized, but from time to time they reemerged, never more so than with the Reykjavik "non-summit." Repeatedly Reagan announced he would not use SDI as a negotiating tool. "SDI is no bargaining chip," he reiterated.[30] In reality, most of the "RINOs" were far behind Reagan in vision, failing to see he had the ultimate tool to win, not perpetuate, the Cold War.

Dutch approached the Iceland meeting as well prepared as ever, briefed on more than thirty specific issues by his team and arriving at Reykjavik two days early to prepare. Recalling his days of bitter negotiations as the head of SAG, Reagan preferred a freewheeling discussion, a format where he thought he would have the advantage.[31] Shultz, for example, had urged Reagan to be "positive, self-confident, and commanding...The American people are all for it."[32] While still viewing the Iceland meeting as a scene-setter for the "real" summit to come later, Shultz's high praise of Reagan would have no doubt surprised his critics. He noted "the policies you set in motion six years ago have put us in the strong position we are in today."[33] Some had concerns that Gorbachev's objectives were poorly understood—meaning Dutch would have trouble penetrating them. This was a sound concern. Gorbachev was indoctrinated into believing that "in the U.S. governing circles they do not want to allow a relaxation of tensions, a slowing down of the arms race."[34]

The meeting in Reykjavik, Iceland was intended as a "pre-summit," but both Reagan and Gorbachev plunged into wheeling and dealing and were anxious to end the arms race.

Several biographers have provided blow-by-blow coverage of Reykjavik, and a complete rehash of every detail of the meeting is not necessary here. The basics, however, reveal two dogged foes, each seeking a solution to the larger threat while holding fast to their ideologies. When the "pre-summit" commenced on Saturday, October 11, the Soviet goals became clear quickly.

Gorbachev said all questions were on the table, including human rights, and that he was "most eager" to present new arms-control proposals. He cited having too many variations under discussion at once and thought the two leaders could talk specifics. Reagan jumped at the opportunity, suggesting they seek a goal of reducing their arsenals to 5,500 nuclear warheads each. Then, having suggested a discussion of particulars, Gorbachev immediately dodged, instead noting that it brought up the issue of verification. For the first time, Reagan hit Gorbachev with the Russian proverb *Doveryai no proveryai* ("Trust, but verify"). The Soviet leader said he knew the proverb, then leaped back into generalities. Dutch had called his bluff, and Gorbachev had blinked.

Gorbachev was seeking a widespread large agreement on principles that he could use in a worldwide propaganda campaign. Reagan didn't bite: almost immediately the meeting turned from a simple one-on-one pre-summit to a top-level negotiation. Dutch brought up the arcane—but important—issue of "throw weight" (destructive force). Numbers meant little if overall destructiveness was not reduced. Gorbachev seemed willing to deal and offered flexibility in limits on ICBMs if the United States would limit sub-launched missiles, and he relented on the issue of on-site inspections. He also agreed to Reagan's "zero option" with regards to full removal of the Euromissiles and offered to remove British and French arsenals from the discussion. These were all significant concessions. All hinged, however, on the third major issue of SDI: Gorbachev originally wanted the US to commit to the ABM Treaty for twenty years (Reagan had proposed seven and a half years). Now he lowered the bar to ten years, limiting all SDI research to "laboratories." As it turned out, this was likely the most important word in the entire summit.[35]

Gorbachev had been urged to hold the line on SDI testing: "If there is no testing," a Soviet preparation memo noted, "there will be no SDI."[36] He continued to harbor the notion that SDI was a first-strike advantage. Reagan was incredulous. How could the United States have first-strike capabilities if—by their own agreement at the meeting—they greatly reduced or eliminated all nuclear weapons? But Gorbachev refused to respond, merely urging Reagan to consider the new proposals.

After retreating to meeting rooms at the US embassy, the American delegation was ecstatic, with Paul Nitze calling it the "best Soviet proposal we have received in twenty-five years." Without any concessions, the Soviets had moved on every issue save one: SDI. Reagan liked what he heard, but he knew the stumbling block would be SDI and didn't share his team's glee. At a second meeting that afternoon, Reagan, Shultz, Gorbachev, and Shevardnadze began with a review of the positive elements that had been raised in the morning session, and Reagan went right to the key: Gorbachev's hostility to SDI.[37] Dutch reiterated his offer to share SDI with the Soviet Union—a position Gorbachev found ridiculous. One nation did not share its drilling equipment, machine tools, or any other advantage with its rivals. The rhetoric grew heated, and Shultz recalled tempers flaring. However, he did make further concessions on intermediate-range missiles. Then Reagan produced a new list of dissidents he wanted freed or allowed to leave the

USSR, to which Gorbachev replied, "We will examine these lists carefully, as we always do." Reagan, mending fences, said, "I know that." Working groups were tasked to handle the details of the proposed 50 percent reduction in strategic weapons. Mostly Nitze and Chief of the General Staff Sergei Akhromeyev led the discussions, hammering out capabilities and numbers of bombers, ICBMs, cruise missiles, and other weapons. They produced an agreement that still had elements of obscurity in the definitions of strategic vs. offensive weapons. Nevertheless, the final agreement called for a reduction of nuclear warheads the superpower arsenals to six thousand each.

The defining moment came the following day, on October 12. Reagan began by stating that he could not retreat from his policy on SDI. He insisted the ABM Treaty was flawed and a relic of mutual assured destruction. "I do not understand the charm of the ABM Treaty," he told Gorbachev. The Soviet leader then played an unusual card, offering that a "unique situation" has been created for compromise, one that did not exist earlier. "I simply did not have that capability then. I am not certain that I will still have it in a year or [two or three] years," he stated.[38] Whether it was a threat or an opportunity, Reagan reminded him that he was in the "same position."

Reagan returned to the premise that the Soviet Union rested on, attempting to get Gorbachev once and for all to renounce Marx and Lenin. He restated the basic foundations of communist expansionism and *worldwide* conquest as being necessary for success, although he gave Gorbachev an out: "Maybe you have not managed to express your views on this yet, or maybe you do not believe it. But so far you have not said it," meaning Gorbachev had not yet aligned himself with Marx and Lenin publicly. Instead—likely because he *did* still cling to the antiquated, failing doctrine—Gorbachev simply snorted, "So you are talking about Marx and Lenin again." Nevertheless, he mildly endorsed national self-determination (a form of rejecting international revolution) and instead changed the subject to Reagan's rhetoric, homing in on the Westminster speech and the "Evil Empire" comment. "What does it mean politically?" he asked. "Make war against us?" Reagan shot back, "No." Gorbachev replied, "But that is exactly what you said before Reykjavik." Nevertheless, he returned to SDI and again Reagan held firm: no compromise on Star Wars.

The two continued well past the originally scheduled limits of the meeting and Gorbachev anxiously asked, "What are you going to do?" Shultz offered to outline their agreements on arms reductions, which Gorbachev rejected. Then he suggested a break for the ministers to "propose something." Again, negotiators went to work with an outline of a ten-year commitment to the ABM Treaty (instead of Reagan's proposed five) and an elimination of all strategic nuclear weapons, which would undermine Gorbachev's opposition to Star Wars. When Dutch and the Soviet premier met again at 3:30, Reagan bored in: "If you feel so strongly about the ABM Treaty, why don't you dismantle the radar you are building at Krasnoyarsk in violation of the treaty?" Once again, Reagan exposed the hypocrisies of the Soviet position, and Gorbachev had to ignore the question. He became frustrated, unable to move the president off SDI. The Gipper was aware of his bargaining strength and tried to lighten the mood with some banter about the two of them getting together a decade later and destroying the last missiles. After smiling, Gorbachev wondered if he would live that long, citing "dangers…still ahead": "I still have to meet with President Reagan, who I can see really hates to give in."[39]

After reviewing yet another proposal late in the afternoon, Gorbachev's ears perked up when he noticed Reagan had eliminated the word "laboratories" in his discussion of SDI testing. Did Reagan "omit the mention of laboratories deliberately?" he asked. "Yes," responded Dutch. "It was deliberate. What's the matter?" Gorbachev knew he wouldn't win the point. Reagan suggested a breathtaking proposal, one that neither his critics nor his supporters would have believed could come from him (showing how few really knew the Gipper): "By the end of two five-year periods all nuclear *devices* would be eliminated, including bombs, battlefield systems, cruise missiles, submarine weapons, intermediate-range systems, and so on."

Gorbachev's fateful response was, "We could say that, list all those weapons," and Shultz pounced: "Let's do it." Gorbachev said, "Well, all right. Here we have a chance for an agreement." But then during a break at the last moment the premier returned to the issue of SDI testing in "laboratories," which Shultz likened to "giving away the sleeves on your vest." When Reagan raised the historical point of nations keeping gas masks even after banning poison gas, an exasperated premier said, "Yes, I've heard all about gas masks and maniacs, probably ten times already....It still does not convince me."[40] Gorbachev had suddenly backtracked. In the next face-to-face he said, "What you propose is something we cannot go along with. I've said all I can." Reagan was stunned. Just moments earlier, Gorbachev had committed to the elimination of all nuclear weapons in ten years, and now he was reneging over SDI testing outside of laboratories? Dutch blew up and said, "Are you really going to turn down a historic opportunity for agreement for the sake of one word in the text?" Gorbachev tried to butter up Reagan, saying, "If we sign a package containing major concessions by the Soviet Union...you will become, without exaggeration, a great president." But if not, "let's part...and forget about Reykjavik. But there won't be another opportunity like this. At any rate, I know I won't have one."

Neither flattery nor threats moved Reagan when it was obvious Gorbachev would throw away the deal over SDI testing in laboratories only. At that point, Reagan jotted down a note to Shultz: *Am I wrong?* Shultz bent over and whispered, "No, you are right." The president stood up and said to Shultz, "Let's go, George."

The parties walked out to a breathtaking cold and a breathless news media, each offering apologies. Reagan wondered if "we'll ever have another chance like this and whether we will meet soon."[41] An embarrassed Gorbachev, aware he had been the stumbling block, meekly replied, "I don't know what more I could have done," and Reagan coldly stated, "You could have said 'yes.'"

Press Secretary Larry Speakes thought Dutch looked "grim and downcast" and suddenly was concerned for his health, and Don Regan said, "I was in the presence of a truly disappointed man."[42] As reporters crushed in, Reagan curtly said, "There is going to be no statement." He walked Gorbachev to his limo. The Soviet premier said, "I'm sorry it didn't work out," and a bitter Reagan replied, "It could have worked out if you had wanted it to." Gorbachev tried to soften things again. "I hope to see you in the United States," he offered, but Dutch demurred. "I don't know that there is going to be a meeting in the United States." Then he climbed in his own limo.[43]

As Dutch left, he was noticeably downcast. Speakes blamed the "mistakes" of Reykjavik on insufficient time to prepare, but then noted that Reykjavik was only viewed as a failure because "we raised the media's expectations too high" and because Reagan was fatigued. Don Regan, in the car with the president, tried to cheer him up but warned Reagan was looking "grim and angry" and that it wouldn't play well with the staff.[44] Handed a speech for when he would give a public statement, Reagan was distracted, still upset according to Regan. He "shuffled the speech cards, changing the order…then shuffled them again."[45] He couldn't get over how nearly the two leaders had come to a major agreement. Looking at Regan, Dutch put his thumb and forefinger just inches apart and said, "We had been 'that' close."[46]

Arriving at the airport, Dutch mesmerized Regan with his ability to learn the speech in mere minutes, literally memorizing the last lines as the band played "Hail to the Chief." Within seconds he transformed himself into the confident, cheery president everyone expected to see when he strode up to the podium. He joked about calling Nancy and telling her he'd be late, hoping she'd understand. "In about six and a half hours, I'll find out." Describing the talks as "frank," "hard," and "tough," Reagan nevertheless insisted they were "extremely useful" and that he and the Soviet premier "made more progress than we anticipated." Nevertheless, he noted, they had one area of disagreement, SDI, which he would not and could not concede.[47]

Gorbachev delivered his news conference to a typically fawning press. The *New York Times* described him as "leaning forward in his seat and slashing the air with his right hand," speaking "without notes for an hour."[48] The liberal arms-control experts and Reagan critics in the press had a field day, some blaming Shultz. ("Arms Talk Disaster," blared the London *Telegraph*.) Hawkish allies, such as Margaret Thatcher, were horrified. She wanted to "get the Americans back onto the firm ground of a credible policy of nuclear deterrence."[49] Republican House whip Dick Cheney frantically called negotiator Ken Adelman: "What the hell have you guys done?"[50] Nixon fumed that Reykjavik was another Yalta. Democrats, of course, piled on with Senator Al Gore calling the meeting a "fiasco" and Senator Gary

Hart claiming Reagan was more interested in building Star Wars than in arms control.

But the director of the US Information Agency, Charles Wick, thought Reagan had just won the Cold War, and in a separate press conference Gorbachev was already spinning: "In spite of all the drama Reykjavik is…a breakthrough."[51] As the CIA's Robert Gates would later assess the summit, "Gorbachev took a very high-stakes, high-risk gamble to set up [Reagan], ambush him, and kill SDI," and he failed.[52] Aaron Wildavsky, a political scientist, had a more accurate assessment of the criticism: the deal was made without input from the intellectuals. Even Shultz, hardly a true believer in SDI, thought Star Wars ensured a commitment to any arms agreements going forward.[53]

The Soviets had already started to drop SDI as the bottom-line bargaining chip **before** *the Reykjavik summit.*

Historians from both sides of the political spectrum—Tony Judt from the Left and Paul Johnson from the Right—are skeptical about the role of SDI, or, at least subordinate it to internal conditions within the Soviet Union.[54] Yet neither historian sufficiently weighs the crushing pressure Reagan had *already* brought on the Soviet empire by the time Gorbachev could enact his "reforms," nor the box in which he had placed the Soviet leader. In fact, for a relatively tiny military research investment—the cost of perhaps two Trident subs by then—Reagan had driven the Soviet leader to offer to cut his entire strategic force by half, merely for a promise that the United States wouldn't continue with *research!*[55] Moreover, to conclude Reagan came out the winner, one only has to look at Gorbachev's near-frantic push for continued negotiations. After Reykjavik, Gorbachev was all bluster, contending that he forced Reagan into revealing his bottom line. It was a facade. Gorbachev was weaker having left Iceland than before, only now he had shown his willingness to trade the USSR's major advantage in the Cold War: its missiles.

In fact, foreign policy advisor Anatoly Chernyaev had already begun recommending that Gorbachev move off SDI since mid-summer.[56] Others suggested that the hard position on SDI was added later, or that there was even a fallback position allowing SDI that the Soviet military failed to communicate to Gorbachev before Reykjavik.[57] Ultimately, though the obstacle of the word "laboratories" was removed by Richard Perle, who asked about laboratories in space. Almost immediately, a Soviet scientist (speaking with full authority from Moscow) conceded SDI testing could be conducted from space.[58] As Shultz observed, Gorbachev had already caved in on the truly important issues of weapons reductions. All else after that was fluff. In February 1987, the Soviets quietly eliminated any limits on SDI testing in return for an intermediate forces treaty with the Euromissiles. And despite the initial public relations coup that Gorbachev seemed to enjoy, *Newsweek*'s polling saw Reagan rising, emerging from Iceland "a winner." No doubt to the consternation of *Newsweek* editors, the public saw Reagan more committed to arms control than Gorbachev.

Reagan's victory at the negotiating table did not immediately translate into gains at the ballot box in the 1986 midterms, but it may have staved off losses. The Republicans lost eight seats and control of the Senate, but only a mere five House seats (compared to the average loss of over forty for a sixth year in office). A number of the races, especially in the Senate, were razor thin, but power had shifted nonetheless. Even without what was to follow, future progress of the Reagan agenda with an obstructionist Senate—whose arcane rules and filibusters made it a much more serious impediment to enacting a program than Tip O'Neill's House ever was—did not look promising. In the hands of political opponents, however, the Senate could be much more than obstructionist given the right ammunition. And a story in a Beirut newspaper running on Election Day 1986 handed the Democrats all the ammunition they could possibly need.

18

Watergate, Part Deux

From a vantage point of forty years, it is easy to see that Reagan emerged from Reykjavik the victor and that, in many ways, the downhill slide of the USSR was irreversible after that. Gorbachev offered everything, received nothing, and returned to a decaying economy suddenly jolted further by falling international oil prices. SDI research continued, the Pershing and cruise missiles were still in place, and Afghanistan was a quagmire.

At the time, however, much of this was murky. To the Western press, it looked like Reagan either had failed or had almost given up America's strategic defenses. Even Reagan's press secretary Larry Speakes thought Reykjavik was a bust. Dutch returned home to an unfriendly Senate and a second term that had recently not been good to American presidents. For the Gipper, it was about to get worse. A lot worse.

It began when an Election Day story in an Arabic-language paper in Lebanon was picked up by the US press. It claimed that Robert McFarlane, before his departure, had been shipping arms to the Iranian government, even to the point of flying to Tehran in person (which he had, though the story got the date of his trip wrong). These arms deliveries had been tied to the release of American hostage David Jacobsen (taken in May 1985), despite the existence of an arms embargo against Iran. The day after the story appeared, Akbar Hashemi Rafsanjani delivered a speech to his parliament repeating the claims (but with the erroneous date). When Jacobsen was finally released on June 2, 1986, Reagan brought him and his family in for a photo op and was directly asked about the arms-for-hostages story by the press. He responded that he couldn't answer without endangering the remaining hostages.[1] Jacobsen, standing next to the president through a series of hostile questions, remarked to Reagan when they went inside, "My God, Mr. President, these people are savages."[2] After Jacobsen left, Don Regan said to the president, "We're between the devil and the deep [and if] these hostages don't materialize soon, you're going to have to speak up."[3]

So began the public unfolding of what would be called the "Iran-Contra" scandal. There were three essential elements to this affair, and while none were pleasing to Reagan supporters, none directly pointed to criminality on the Gipper's part. First, over a period of two to three years, Reagan had convinced himself that his administration was not trading arms to Iran for hostages but rather providing arms to intermediaries carrying out negotiations. *They* were the ones trading the arms. It is irrational, illogical, and circuitous, but that was what Reagan believed. This justification nevertheless still violated Reagan's own publicly stated policy, but it did not violate a law so far as Reagan knew and was informed. However, second, Reagan was deliberately deceived and willfully denied evidence from his subordinates John Poindexter and Lieutenant Colonel Oliver North, not only about a diversion of funds (which was, without a doubt, illegal) but also as to the details of weapons sales to Iran. Finally, Reagan was led to believe by subordinates (some of whom engaged in wishful thinking and others who genuinely thought they saw an opportunity to improve relations) that so-called "moderates" inside Iran could be elevated within that government and possibly even gain power there.

All of it originated with the plight of the hostages. Some people in DC knew that Bill Casey, McFarlane, and then Poindexter and North had sought foreign funding of the Contras and that at the same time Reagan was deeply troubled by the ongoing hostage situation. No one, as of 1986, had put the two together. The Boland Amendment had barred direct American aid to the Contras but permitted soliciting support from foreign countries—support Saudi Arabia had been providing for years.

Reagan had battled Congress over support for the Contras, but the issue simply did not resonate with the American public. Reagan's own pollster found that almost two-thirds of Americans opposed direct aid and bluntly told Dutch, "Our people do not support what we're trying to do in Nicaragua."[4] When the outside pipeline slowed, McFarlane and then North tried to find innovative ways to keep the funnel open. As noted earlier, throughout 1986, more missiles flowed to Iran. By early 1986, North had been working with Ghorbanifar and his Iranian friends, though with few results. During that time, he conceived of a way to divert money from the arms transactions to Contra aid. He delivered a memo to Poindexter that included a paragraph "explicitly detailing the diversion plan."[5] It must be kept in mind the murky origins of the arms transfers in the first place, as at one time or another the administration gave three different policy goals: obtaining release of the hostages, opening a political dialogue with Iran, and encouraging moderates within that country. And it must also be kept in mind that through Charlie Wilson, the US was employing *multiple* third-party nations to transmit arms to the *mujahideen* in Afghanistan, and that those transfers were increasing.

By late 1985, however, all but the arms-for-hostages element had vanished. Since McFarlane did not leave a written record, Reagan's credibility rested on who knew what, and when. These shipments were technically legal under the Arms Export Control Act of 1985, so long as the administration notified Congress of any sale that exceeded $14 million, even if such shipments were made by another nation that had acquired arms from the United States (i.e., Israel). And while the president could send arms to whomever he wished as part of the intelligence covert action clauses of the National Security Act, prior to such shipment he was required to make a "finding" that such a transfer was in the national interest, then notify Congress in a timely manner. In no case did such reports go to Congress. Aside from Regan and McFarlane—and then later Poindexter and North—no one knew about the shipments. However, it soon became apparent that no one knew who knew the details about anything.

Originally the plan was for an intermediary—Israel—to deliver all weapons, then the United States would resupply what Israel had sold. But when Robert McFarlane resigned on December 4, 1985, and was replaced by Admiral John Poindexter, matters changed dramatically. Lieutenant

Colonel Oliver North, then a military aide to the NSC, recommended eliminating the middleman and selling the arms directly to Iran, then sending some of the proceeds to the Contras. Under Poindexter, North found himself with exceptional autonomy. In November of 1985, McFarlane informed the president that a shipment of Hawk anti-aircraft missiles had been sent to Iran and that all hostages would be released. But Poindexter had told White House lawyers that in fact the Hawk shipment had not occurred. Casey was telling yet a different story: that no one in the US government knew of an *Israeli* Hawk sale. What finally became apparent was that Oliver North had been encouraging concealment at all levels.

Soon members of the administration were confused and on the defensive: Speakes asked Peter J. Wallison—then Regan's counsel at Treasury—if a president could violate his own executive order, namely the one about exporting arms to a terrorist state. Wallison, because of Reagan's trust in him, found himself suddenly at the heart of the controversy. Regan was sure the issue had been run by the attorney general, but Wallison asked that it be reviewed by the AG again. Wallison met with Pointdexter, who lied to him about the sales, leading Wallison to conclude "I may have had the dubious distinction of being the first person outside [North, McFarlane, and Poindexter] to be lied to about the president's role in the Iran arms sales matter."[6]

By then, Don Regan was begging Nancy to get involved and persuade her husband to tell the whole truth and withhold nothing. "He's going down in flames if he doesn't speak up," he warned. She refused and, according to Regan, cited her "friend," the astrologer, as saying "it's just *wrong* for him to talk right now."[7] Here was a case of Nancy Reagan's inherent distrust of Regan working against the interests of her husband.

With the story now public at least in some form, Reagan met with his national security team on November 10 and reiterated the press's claim that "we are violating our own law about arms sales to Iran."[8] He then met with leaders of Congress, who were skeptical, but given Reagan's history of only telling the truth to them, they accepted it. Regan thought by that time the president had convinced *himself* he was telling the truth. In the past Reagan had commented on the dishonesty in the media in his diary, but then let it go. Now, however, he increasingly dwelt on it. "This whole irresponsible press bilge about hostages and Iran has gotten totally out of hand," he wrote. "The media looks like it's trying to create another Watergate"—which it was.[9] That, however, did not make the charges any less true or damaging.

The most serious problem was that Reagan was relying on Regan as his chief of staff to keep him apprised, and Regan's information was limited. As his counsel, Wallison noted, "He had very little knowledge about how the initiative was actually carried out."[10] Worse, when North and Poindexter eventually left the White House and refused to testify about the closely held initiative, neither the president nor his staff could get accurate information. Regan on his own could not force Poindexter to come clean, and Poindexter repeatedly cited the safety of the "moderate" Iranians as reason to avoid full disclosure. North fed this notion, even claiming the "moderates" were an underground opposition close to toppling the mullahs—a ridiculous claim. North had been so successful with his misrepresentations in fact that in the November 10 national security meeting, Reagan spoke of the "moderates" who would be endangered by disclosure. Wallison warned Regan that the president needed to waive executive privilege immediately and that a cover-up would possibly be fatal.[11]

Indeed, now the Nicaraguan "leg" of the scandal was giving way. The Sandinistas shot down a cargo plane carrying weapons for the Contras that was chartered by North on October 5. One of the crew and the sole survivor, Eugene Hasenfus, was displayed for the cameras by the Sandinistas. He revealed that the mission had originated with the CIA in El Salvador. Yet Reagan was telling reporters "there was no government connection with that at all." Administration officials had testified to Congress that there was no US involvement with the Contras until the Boland Amendment restrictions were lifted on October 17. The ball was rapidly spinning out of control by the time Reagan made a public speech a month later, on November 13. As his key advisors, including Poindexter, Regan, speechwriter Pat Buchanan, and press secretary Larry Speakes met, everyone but Poindexter urged transparency. Poindexter continued to stall, urging a briefing only of Congress or otherwise quarantining information. At the last moment, however, Oliver North was added to the speechwriting team—an odd choice for discussions at that level. Another speechwriter, Tony Dolan, had warned Wallison that North was "going to cause you enormous problems someday."[12] The team hotly debated whether the line that "all laws have been complied with" was true. Many knew it wasn't, but Poindexter's deputy Alton Keel insisted that the attorney general had cleared it, and just three days earlier Reagan himself had said the same thing. Moreover, Reagan had not made a "finding" yet and thus was technically in possible violation of two laws.

Reagan's public address on the matter began informally, almost breezy: "I know you've been reading, seeing, and hearing a lot of stories the past several days attributed to Danish sailors, unnamed observers at Italian ports and Spanish harbors" and, especially "unnamed government officials.... Well, now you're going to hear the facts from a White House source, and you know my name." He then dove in, explaining how a "secret diplomatic initiative" which was "extremely sensitive" had been underway for eighteen months. The Gipper listed several reasons, including renewing a relationship with Iran, ending the Iran-Iraq War (which had *never* been a central consideration in any of the discussions), eliminating state-sponsored terrorism, and obtaining the release of all hostages. He did not include empowering the Iranian "moderates."

He then came to the charge that the US shipped weapons to Iran as ransom payment for Americans held hostage in Lebanon and that his administration had "secretly violated American policy against trafficking with terrorists." Reagan then stated "those charges are utterly false.... The United States has not swapped boatloads or planeloads of American weapons for the return of American hostages. And we will not."[13] Dutch then promptly contradicted himself, admitting that he authorized the transfer of "small amounts of defensive weapons and spare parts for defensive weapons to Iran" but described this transfer as a "gesture." He claimed they could fit inside a "small cargo plane," which was untrue, but added (most likely accurately) that the numbers of weapons could not affect the military balance between Iran and Iraq.

Dutch cited progress toward releasing the hostages—some of whom had come home—then cited the strategic importance of keeping Iran out of the Soviet Union's orbit. Again, while this was true, and certainly the CIA had discussed it, Iran's position vis-à-vis the USSR was not a major discussion item when the shipments were approved. He explained that he had sent Bud McFarlane to Iran with "explicit instructions" to open a dialogue, that the discussions had continued thereafter, and the release of David Jacobsen was an indication they were bearing fruit. (He neglected to mention that other hostages had since been seized and that by all counts the net number of hostages had *increased* by one since the talks began.) Reagan cited his attack on Gaddafi as evidence that he had not gone soft on terrorism and then insisted the administration broke no laws. "The actions I authorized were, and continue to be, in full compliance with federal law." This, of course, *would* have been true if he had alerted Congress and been aware of the changes in the finding and then apprised Congress of that change as well.

All in all, Reagan's speech explained some elements to the American people but generated such a smokescreen of irrelevant policy mishmash that it guaranteed a hostile reception. Shultz was aghast: the president still did not appreciate what was going on under his nose and was outraged that Poindexter had buffaloed the president with incomplete or slanted reports. Reagan told the American public what he knew to be true and had properly advised Congress based on what he had been told. But it was far from the truth. As far as Dutch was concerned, the negotiations were all going through a third party, thus no real "arms for hostages" has transpired. Second, he was convinced that the arms that were sold were serving the twofold purpose of enhancing the stature of the Iranian "moderates." Third, he was often not clear if the US was directly providing the arms or if they were still flowing through Israel. While he was authorized to deliver "findings" to Congress that would make almost any of the direct deals legal, they all were nevertheless in stark violation of the administration policy of "not negotiating with terrorists." Reagan's statement that all laws were followed not only committed the administration officials to supporting his claim—which was technically false—but "represented the first major step…down the path to a cover-up," as Wallison noted. Certainly the press didn't miss this either. Both the *New York Times* and *Washington Post* had four stories each about the speech and the implications it carried. Even the *Wall Street Journal* noted that Reagan did not address the legal issues.

Reaction abroad was much the same. An internal summary from the US Information Agency to Poindexer on November 24 on foreign responses to the speech said the president "did not put to rest the distinct concerns of Europeans, Arabs or Israelis." It continued: "Europeans fear the consequences for East-West relations…if the President is unable to bounce back"—ironically the same Europeans that had portrayed Reagan as a "cowboy!" The Europeans "are concerned that the President's ability to govern over the next two years may be seriously damaged by American public and congressional reaction."[14] European views that Reagan had to prove he had not "irrevocably lost…momentum" were not salved by the press conference. As for the Arabs, admission that Israel was involved only confirmed their suspicions. Overall, the foreign press described the president, unlike his "usual optimistic natural self," as "fumbling," "rambling," and "confusing."[15]

Insiders knew the Iran-Contra scandal was serious when pollster Richard Wirthlin met with attorney Peter Wallison and asked for the definition of "high crimes and misdemeanors."

Insiders knew there was trouble. Richard Wirthlin met with Wallison and said that the Iran deal was of Watergate proportions and even asked him what "high crimes and misdemeanors" were. A frustrated Regan found himself unable to overcome Poindexter's claims to the president that the hostages would be endangered by further release of information. By November 16, the press had assumed its blood-in-the-water position and the *Times* ran eight Iran stories. Reagan's staff looked to backfill his assertions by concluding that he was on safe ground so long as a "finding" existed in January 1986 and so long as weapons shipments to Iran occurred after August when the amendment to the Arms Export and Control Act went into effect—but even then, the value had to be under $14 million or the administration would have had to report it. Unfortunately for Reagan, an assembly of all the general counsels revealed a September 1985 shipment, which was prior to any "finding." (No one had yet turned up the August 1985 shipment by Israel.) Demands by the counsels for answers, including a simple timeline, were refused by Poindexter. Now the NSC advisor had become a dangerous gatekeeper to the president of the United States, sealing him off from his own White House lawyers!

The whole affair started to indeed resemble Watergate's origins, in which John Dean (the most likely perpetrator and mastermind) became Nixon's main source of information.[16] Under what Ed Rollins called a "siege" mentality, the White House reluctantly agreed to hold a news conference (Regan claimed Nancy Reagan cleared the date with her astrologer first).[17] A news conference on November 19 revealed a president who did not know the facts of his own policy team. Regan described the president at this news conference as "over-briefed but underinformed, uncertain of the facts [and] concerned with keeping secrets that were already bubbling up onto the front pages all over the world."[18] Reagan admitted his advisors disagreed with each other and again raised the safety of the hostages and the go-betweens. Reagan again took responsibility, stating, "I weighed their views...I decided to proceed. And the responsibility for the decision and the operation is mine and mine alone."[19] That statement would have been fine if Reagan had known the particulars of what he was admitting responsibility for. He understood that "some profoundly disagree with what was done." Again, however, he cited the goals of bringing "Iran back into the community of responsible nations, ending its participation in political terror, bringing an end to that terrible war, and bringing our hostages home" justified taking risks. Now, however, he had directed that no further sales be made to Iran and that Congress be provided with all relevant information. In an answer to a question, Dutch reiterated, "There was no deception intended by us." Rather, he again cited the "great risk" to the hostages if word leaked out.

As the questions came in like bricks, Reagan was accused of violating his own policy and of lying to America's allies about the embargo. Asked by Sam Donaldson if the president could "repair" his image, Dutch shot back, "I'm the only one around who wants to repair it." For a half hour, Reagan continued to dance through a minefield of the 1985 sales, the violation of the embargo, and whether the TOWs altered the balance of the war. By that point, Reagan asserted that the arms were not traded for the hostages but for good will, or a "token of good faith"—a remarkably thin line. But he did repeat a point the press deliberately seemed to miss, namely that the US government was not dealing with the Iranian government but with individuals who had (or, at least, were thought to have) a chance to change policy internally. Had he not been so buffeted, he might have cited Ted Kennedy's message to the USSR before the 1984 election as a similar approach to elicit foreign intervention in an American election. When offered an escape route, to admit that the policy was a mistake, Reagan dug in his heels, saying, "I don't think a mistake was made. It was a high-risk gamble.... We still have made some ground. We got our hostages back—three of them. And so, I think what we did was right, and we're going to continue on this path."

Which "path" Reagan referred to wasn't clear—the path of interacting with the questionable "moderates" or the practice of selling weapons to a terrorist state. A frustrated Shultz, who rightly felt he had been forced into the position of point man for a lie, insisted on a face-to-face with Dutch after the news conference and point-by-point listed the errors in the speech. Shultz recalled the president was "shaken" but listened intently. Even before Shultz arrived, the press office put out a correction that there was indeed a third country, Israel, involved, but he still clung to the "token amounts" of "defensive arms" that were shipped—still a lie. Indeed, one of the reporters at the news conference corrected Reagan when he said that the TOW was a shoulder-fired missile (he was thinking of the Redeye—an honest enough mistake, but nevertheless, one more damning fact that made it appear as though Reagan was either clueless or covering up).[20]

As biographer H. W. Brands points out, Reagan's natural optimism, which was most often his greatest ally, came with a serious side effect. When truly bad news came (as it had in Sacramento with his chief of staff), Reagan was prone to dismiss it and focus on the positive. This trademark characteristic had defined Dutch and set him apart from the gloomster Republicans of the past. The trait made the Gipper "almost unsinkable emotionally."[21] But it also led him to listen more closely to those who praised his performances, which in turn shaped the behavior of his subordinates who did not wish to deliver bad news...or bad reviews! Neither Shultz nor Weinberger nor Regan fit in that category, but since all three had been kept out of the Iran arms sales loop, none could step in. Finally the internal information dam broke.

Regan received a top secret envelope containing a copy of a chronology (that he had badgered Poindexter about for days). This chronology, however, was false, and that fact provided "tangible evidence that a cover-up was underway."[22] More bad news was incoming. While preparing for testimony to the Intelligence Committees of the Senate and House the next day, William Casey casually stated that no one in the government knew about the sale of the Hawk missiles by the Israelis in 1985—this was a blatant lie, in that both North and Casey himself indeed had knowledge of it. Shultz maintained that the president *had* been told about the Hawk shipment in November 1985. Ed Meese, at West Point giving a speech, was frantically called back to work out the inconsistencies of the two stories in advance of a meeting on Monday, November 24, that would include Casey, Poindexter, Regan, Bush, Shultz, and Weinberger. In other words, Reagan would finally have the principles together with the right questions in front of them—except it was too late.

The following day's NSC meeting alerted Reagan to "a thing" having to do with "Israel and some Hawk missiles in the Iran mix that has to be straightened out." Attorney General Meese "assured" Dutch he was "in the clear legally on what we were doing."[23] In fact, Meese had only offered a nonbinding temporary opinion and was still conducting his "straightening out the inconsistencies" work when on Saturday, November 22, Assistant Attorney General William Bradford Reynolds was in North's office reviewing documents. Reynolds had come across an April 1986 memo reviewing the TOW missile sale in September 1985. North wrote "$12 million [of the proceeds] will be used to purchase critically needed supplies for the Nicaragua Democratic resistance." Meese was assigned to conduct a quick inquiry to be ready for the Monday morning (November 24) NSC meeting. The attorney general stormed over to meet North the next day, only to have North weave an even more elaborate lie about the Israelis financing the

Contras. The attorney general knew better and saw that it could immediately lead to articles of impeachment, telling Regan instantly about "things the president did not know" including a diversion of funds.[24] Meese and Regan quickly met with the president before the NSC meeting, telling him, "It's a terrible mess....I have a few things to button up.... But it's going to be bad news." According to Regan, Meese did *not* mention the diversion of funds then.[25]

After the November 24 meeting in the Situation Room, where Reagan and Shultz "got everything out on the table," Reagan then again met with Meese and Regan. Meese told the president of the illegal transfer—a smoking gun. On one of the arms shipments the Iranians paid Israel a higher purchase price than they were getting and the difference was put in a secret bank account. Out of a $30 million payment, the United States government received only $12 million, and exactly where it was, while unknown, had nevertheless been controlled by North.

As Meese related this, the color drained from the president's face. Regan recalled his skin went "pasty white." Reagan later wrote in his diary, "Our Col. North (NSC) gave the money [from the Iran arms sale] to the 'Contras.' This was a violation of the law against giving the Contras money without authorization from Congress. North didn't tell me about this."[26] He grimly concluded, "Worst of all John Poindexter found out about it & didn't tell me. This may call for resignations." Of course, Poindexter didn't "find out" about anything—he was involved in the planning and cover-up, as was North. McFarlane had written to North in November, "I hope to daylights that someone has been purging...[certain sensitive files] on the episode."[27]

Regan later wrote, "Nobody who saw the President's reaction that afternoon could believe for a moment that he knew about the diversion of funds before Meese told him about it."[28] Regan then received the expected phone call from Nancy. He recalled she was "furious" and that "there was no mistaking her message: Heads would roll." Regan "had the impression that mine might very well be among them."[29]

Later, James Baker would argue that Reagan made a serious strategic error by not giving an indignant press conference where he lambasted

Poindexter and North. By failing to show genuine anger at his two sub-ordinates, it led people "to believe that they must have been acting at the President's direction....This was exacerbated by him calling North a national hero," meaning that Dutch "lost the opportunity to get mad."[30]

Although Reagan blamed the media for what was ultimately his own fault, calling it "irresponsible press bilge," he knew the press was aiming at a second coming of Watergate. The media found its elixir, and new Wood-wards and Bernsteins now perched behind every microphone, hoping to be the instruments that led to an impeached or disgraced president. In the next three months, the *New York Times* and *Washington Post* alone would pub-lish over one thousand stories on Iran-Contra. Michael Kinsley gleefully reported "having a good time." It was, he confided, "the kind of episode we all live for," while *Time's* Hugh Sidey observed, "Young reporters all over town have visions of Pulitzer Prizes dancing in their heads."[31] So-called friendly papers, such as the *Wall Street Journal*, basted Reagan: "If some malicious Merlin were trying to concoct a scheme that...would undermine American principles, policies, people, interests and allies, it would be hard to conjure up anything more harmful" than what the president did.[32] In the end, Reagan had done it to himself. By addressing the nation the first time without a full review and understanding of how he was being played, Dutch set himself up for the expected reaction. His poll numbers dropped immediately, especially on the "trust" question, with his overall approval sinking over 20 points in a few weeks (the largest one-month decline in Gallup's polling history). In particular, the speech did not work. Only 14 percent believed his denials and by February 1987 he bottomed out at 40 percent. Regan found the president "baffled by his loss of credibility" because in his mind he was telling the truth. The administration had dealt with intermediaries, not with the Iranians themselves.[33]

Having told the American people once that he had no knowledge of the arms sales, Reagan now had to deal with the new diversion of money to the Contras. With the memo that Reynolds turned up—followed by North's flimsy explanations—Don Regan knew the administration was on a precipice. He had already come to the conclusion that Poindexter and North had to go, immediately, telling Wallison that the situation "looks like

Watergate." Wallison noted that for the first time, the chief of staff looked "genuinely worried" that he was dealing with a matchbox that "went well beyond managing a political or public-relations problem."[34] Reagan's team immediately planned for a new, serious review, but first things first: Regan met Poindexter in the hallway and demanded his resignation that morning. Poindexter offered no resistance and insisted he had not told Reagan. It was unanimously decided that a bipartisan commission would be the best approach (instead of having the attorney general look into it). Reagan asked what Poindexter's reaction had been and was told he knew about North's activities but didn't look too closely. The president was stunned, asking both Meese and Regan what the conspirators were thinking. Neither had an answer.[35]

North was also dismissed. Later, he would claim without any evidence that Reagan was aware of the diversion of funds and "enthusiastically" approved. In fact, his "diversion memo" as it was called, had boxes at the bottom for those who read it to indicate so with a check mark. The copy that Meese's team found had no check mark for Reagan's name. While it is possible he had checked *another* copy of the memo that North shredded, neither North nor anyone else could prove Reagan ever saw it. At any rate, now Reagan—who had been portrayed as out of touch for five years by his enemies—was now universally portrayed as knowing and controlling everything in his administration. But they had made their case too well.

In the first news conference after Reagan was briefed on the Poindexter deceptions, the president began with a statement and Meese then handled the Q&A. Saying he had requested the attorney general to conduct an internal review, Dutch admitted he "was not fully informed on the nature of one of the activities undertaken in connection with this initiative." He announced that Poindexter had resigned, that North had been terminated, that Justice would continue its ongoing probe, and that he would appoint a special review board to conduct a separate investigation. Reagan admitted that implementation of his Middle East policy "was seriously flawed." He then turned things over to Meese without taking questions.[36] Meese's own comments noted that the investigation was in its early stages, but that, in the course of moving arms to Israel and then to "representatives of Iran," money that was received in those transactions was made available to the Contras.[37]

A brief hush fell over the room. Asked why the president wasn't told, Meese replied he was told as soon as it was discovered but that he had known nothing until Meese's report. But then Meese walked into land mines of his own when asked who else knew, and he said only North. "What about CIA director Casey?" Meese repeated that no one else knew. When asked how high the cover-up went, Meese replied "it did not go any higher than [Poindexter]."

In the immediate aftermath, no one took it harder than Nancy, who lost ten pounds and who swung between depression and anger at "her Ronnie's" aides and, especially, Regan. She even arranged for "special meetings" with William Rogers and Robert Strauss—two long-time Washington Establishment types, but, at the moment, outsiders—to get advice from them. When they met with the Reagans, they proved of little assistance, except they reinforced the notion that Regan was a poor chief of staff. Nancy didn't find the president very responsive to their suggestions.[38] Rogers and Strauss weren't the only ones telling Dutch to dump his team. Both Deaver and Stu Spencer met to advise the Gipper and both told him to "fire my people," as he put it, including "top staff and even cabinet."[39] Reagan could not agree with their recommendations and told some Republican lawmakers the same thing, that if others "are named I'll take action, but I'm not going to change my team."[40]

Already the issue of testifying before the committees had come up. At an NSC meeting on December 16, 1986, the cabinet unanimously agreed Reagan should not testify.[41] As for other members of the administration, Bill Casey had a seizure the day before his scheduled appearance before the Senate committee and, after surgeons removed a malignant tumor, subsequently lost his ability to speak. It was awkward, to say the least, to fire a man who lay on his deathbed, but the CIA post was no small matter. Nancy increasingly began to involve herself, much to Regan's displeasure, constantly calling him about replacing Casey. An irritated Regan chided her, noting that it was Christmas and it would not look good for the president to fire someone under such circumstances. A full-blown argument ensued, leaving Nancy determined to get rid of Don Regan, Bill Casey, and even speechwriter Pat Buchanan.[42] Thus, at a critical moment when Reagan needed his team fully united and on the same page, his wife was hard at work trying to fire anyone within walking distance of the White House.

As the Nancy-Regan hostilities simmered, the president held firm that he was not firing his chief of staff. If, on the other hand, Regan wanted to leave, that was his business. Previously Dutch had energetically worked to keep Shultz on the job through several show resignations, as he had with Haig. But the Gipper knew that getting on the wrong side of his wife was not the best policy, especially when she had a point. Regan *had*, for whatever reasons, failed to get all necessary information to the president. He *had* failed to properly supervise and oversee Poindexter. And he had, at various times, attempted without success to expand his job description. Wallison, Regan's lieutenant, made a valiant effort to burnish his boss's image, saying the president was "fortunate to have had a chief of staff who so willingly took the heat."[43] Don Regan, however, suffered the fate of any subordinate in a firestorm—especially one who had made no allies in the administration and who had rightly or wrongly alienated the president's wife.

Originally the plan was for Regan to leave after the Tower Commission report came out. But new dustups with Nancy, including one where he hung up on her (the second time he had done that), led to another round of "Don bashing" in the Reagans' private quarters. The final nail in Regan's coffin came on a Monday, February 23, 1987, meeting when a new director of communications, Jack Koehler, was appointed without a sufficient vetting. When Koehler's participation in a Nazi group in Germany came up, the media feeding frenzy blamed Nancy. Regan piled on, saying it was her choice, and thus her responsibility to do the background check. Dutch would have none of that. "I was the one who wanted him," he sternly told his chief of staff.

Dutch then obliquely raised the issue of Regan's resignation: "I think it's time we do that thing that you said when we talked in November," referring to Regan's promise to resign after the commission report came out.[44] Regan replied, "I'll stick by that. I'll go whenever you say." The president noted the report was coming out Thursday and added, "I think it would be appropriate for you to bow out now." Regan exploded. "What do you mean, *now*? This is Monday before the report. You can't do this to me, Mr. President. If I go before that report is out, you throw me to the wolves." He insisted Reagan owed him better treatment than that, and Regan was right.[45] Dutch requested Regan's opinion: "What do you think would be right?" Regan suggested the following week, after the report came out, when he would take his chances.

Regan wasn't going to go quietly, though, and unloaded about Nancy, telling the president that she was "meddling" in the administration's affairs and said, "I thought I was chief of staff to the president, not to his wife." He then admitted that he was "very bitter about the whole experience. You're allowing the loyal to be punished."[46] The president backed off. "Well, we'll try to make that up by the way we handle this. We'll make sure that you go out in good fashion."[47]

All departments had been instructed to cooperate fully with the Tower Commission and with the congressional investigations. There was one problem: neither North nor Poindexter would cooperate, pleading the Fifth Amendment. When the Tower Commission reported its findings in the last week of February, while highly critical of Reagan's management and lack of oversight, it nevertheless confirmed that the president had not been fully informed. Proper policies were not followed by the NSC, again because Reagan had not properly supervised and controlled it. Shultz, Weinberger, and of course Poindexter and McFarlane, all came in for harsh rebukes. In the end, however, the president was cleared of any illegalities for both the arms transfers and the cash diversions. Dutch met with the Tower commissioners twice, the first time stating he had approved the Israeli TOW shipments in August 1985, which ran against what Regan had stated in testimony. Before the second interview, the president met with Bush, Regan, and Wallison and went over the timeline, and they convinced Reagan that he had not approved that shipment. The Gipper admitted to being surprised. They reviewed the discussion that day, and Dutch concluded that Regan was right.

In his testimony before the board, however, after Reagan informed them he had changed his mind—and that in subsequent discussions with others he found he had not authorized the missiles—he astonished everyone by asking Wallison, who had helped draft a memo of talking points, for "that piece of paper that you gave me this morning." The Tower commissioners were shocked and now were concerned that any of the president's memories on this issue were of little value. Reagan told them, "I don't remember—period."[48] His diary for the period August 11 through September 1 had only one cryptic reference to any action that could even be remotely interpreted as approving of a sale of missiles: He wrote of

> a "secret" phone call from Bud MacFarlane [sic]. It seems a man high up in the Iranian govt. believes he can deliver all or part of the 7 Am. kidnap victims to Lebanon sometime in early Sept. They will be delivered to a point on a beach north of Ripoli & we'll take them off to our 6th Fleet. *I had some decisions to make about a few points—but they were easy to make.* [emphasis mine][49]

When Reagan told the commissioners he did not have any "personal notes or records to help any recollection on this matter," he was likely telling the truth. Although there could be some elasticity in the phrase "decisions to make about a few points" and it could conceivably involve approval of TOW missiles, Reagan was fairly meticulous about using specifics for missiles in other references to transfer. The actual details of this reference remain buried.

Dutch received his share of hammering in the Tower report, but Regan was the main nail. It concluded that the chief of staff, "as much as anyone, should have insisted that an orderly process be observed.... He must bear primary responsibility for the chaos that descended upon the White House."[50] In the end, the president himself was excused of anything more than lax management. As promised, Regan prepared to resign the next Monday, but a leaked story stating Howard Baker would succeed him (Brands pins the leak on Nancy) threw him into a rage and he resigned in a one-page letter, not even responding to Reagan's request to stay a few days to help with the transition.

When he was sure Regan was out, Dutch noted, "My prayers have really been answered," and after Regan's impetuous note, Nancy claimed it was the first night in weeks that she slept well.[51] Regan, to the end, thought everything was about him, orchestrated to "humiliate me."[52] Both Nancy and Regan had so personalized their vitriol that for either of them, seeing reality was impossible. Dutch, caught in between, had to remove his chief of staff, who, for all his imperiousness, got a bum deal. Nevertheless, chiefs of staff come and go and President Reagan would not suffer for replacing Don Regan. It was ironic that Regan's fate had in part resulted from his aggressiveness in accumulating power. Regan, in fact, wasn't nearly as damaged by Iran-Contra as was Bud McFarlane, who attempted suicide in February 1987 by overdosing on Valium.

One more speech to the American public was necessary, and on March 4, 1987, Reagan addressed the country with a full mea culpa.[53] This one was different from all previous speeches as president, because for the first time Dutch did not automatically have the public on his side. He had to win them over. He admitted being silent on Iran for too long and that it had cost him the confidence of the American people. *The Tower Commission Report* gave him the opportunity to break his silence. Immediately, Reagan had reestablished credibility by not contesting the commission. He noted that the Tower Commission's "findings are honest, convincing, and highly critical; and I accept them." Reagan noted his anger at "activities undertaken without my knowledge," but he was "still accountable for those activities.... I'm still the one who must answer to the American people for this behavior...[and] as the Navy would say, this happened on my watch."[54] He denied knowledge of the funds North shipped to the Contras. But when it came to his view that there were no arms-for-hostage deals, he told the public, "My heart and my best intentions tell me that was true, but the facts and the evidence tell me it was not." There would be, he said, "no more freelancing by individuals when it came to our national security." He concluded by noting that, when you make a mistake, "You take your knocks, you learn your lessons, and then you move on." By admitting he made mistakes, Reagan belatedly did what he needed to do to rebuild his bond with the public.

Reagan's friend, Canadian prime minister Brian Mulroney, once said Dutch was "in communion with the American people."[55] No event showed this better than the Gipper's address, which instantly repaired the breach with the public. Although overnight polls suggested he hadn't succeeded, very quickly he rebounded. Americans still liked him: by now they knew his halls and gates, stairs and doorways. They always *wanted* to like him. Within months he was back over 50 percent. Moreover, as Steven Hayward pointed out, this was the only time in history a president came back twice "from two…steep swoons in public esteem" (the first being the 1983 economic recovery).[56] But if the public was back on Reagan's side, the Democrats in Congress still saw an opportunity for impeachment.

The irony was that by the time Reagan delivered his mea culpa address, Congress had changed the law and now approved the policy Reagan had followed in violation of the previous law. Further, changes in the law now would criminalize a prior policy. For example, Reagan had used multiple "cut outs" to send Stinger missiles to Afghanistan, which was funded and a policy which Congress approved of, but Congress was now seeking charges against Reagan for doing the same thing with Nicaragua. Yet while Reagan had chafed at the Boland Amendments (there were ultimately three), he had not vetoed them or brought on a court fight because it would have shut down the government. This was another area where Dutch had stood on the precipice of utterly crushing, once and for all, the perennial power Democrat congresses have lorded over Republican presidents (or vice versa). In the 1990s, Bill Clinton would bring the Newt Gingrich-led Congress to heel through a clever public relations campaign with the aid of willing allies in the media over a government shutdown. Reagan, however, had been in a far stronger position to have won the fight in 1983 through 1985, having a big lead over Congress in public approval and possessing a clear advantage in communicating his position. Still, it was an arcane and complicated issue, the public had not in any way favored Central American involvement, and Reagan rightly worried about the defense budget being unnecessarily limited. Thus he unwisely agreed to the Boland Amendments and their claim on his executive powers.

Democrats salivated over the fund transfers to the Contras, when the arms-for-hostages was a more serious issue. Then again, they knew they could not pin any illegality for the latter on Reagan. Senator Daniel Inouye of Hawaii headed the investigation and homed in on the Contra aspect of the scandal. Democrats promptly withheld further Contra aid that had passed the year before. Now North, McFarlane, and Poindexter were lined up to become the new Watergate baddies. Unfortunately for their strategy, the Democrats agreed to a joint investigation with the House and Senate, which played into Republican hands in the House. But their key error came in offering Oliver North immunity for his testimony—without knowing in advance what he would say because they also foolishly waived a deposition prior to his testimony. If they thought North would sell out Reagan, they were gravely mistaken.

On July 17, 1987, Lieutenant Colonel Oliver North appeared before the committee decked out in his uniform and resplendent with medals. The mere contrast between the snappy officer and the somewhat disheveled counsels questioning him was immediately obvious. North attacked the opposing counsels early, challenging their understanding of covert operations and the dangerous position the United States had in the world. He was Colonel Jessup of *A Few Good Men* right up to the point Jessup blew his stack under questioning from Tom Cruise—but North never blew. Indeed, he threw veiled jabs at the president because he *didn't* know: "The president ought to be aware of what a handful of people did to keep the Nicaraguan resistance alive at a time when nobody in Congress seemed to care." But he saved his best bombs for Congress: "Plain and simple, Congress is to blame [for the problems in Nicaragua] because of the fickle, vacillating, unpredictable, on-again off-again policy toward the Nicaraguan Democratic Resistance."[57] As great a communicator as Reagan was, North captured the essence of the Contras' cause in a mere six days.

It worked for North. The public liked him, and his presentation of the Nicaraguan conflict was a winner. Reagan wrote in his diary that "the witch hunt against him has made him a national hero."[58] One *Newsweek* poll said nearly half of the public thought the committee members were harassing him, and after North's testimony, public opinion on Nicaragua itself shifted to Reagan's position. Terrified Democrats knew they had stepped in it and began to look for an escape route. His testimony ended, only to be followed by that of Poindexter, who took full responsibility: "The buck stops with me." Reagan was ecstatic, writing that it was the "bombshell" he'd been waiting seven months for.[59] With great disappointment the *Washington Post* noted "there will be no impeachment," and the foreign press noted that the inquisitors had been unable to score a single point.[60] A flat statement issued by the committees noted they could "make no determination as to whether any particular individual involved in the Iran-Contra Affair acted with criminal intent or was guilty of any crime."[61] Neither North nor Poindexter would ever be charged with any serious crimes related to the actual Iran-Contra Affair, although there were convictions for both men for lying to Congress, and North was eventually found guilty by a criminal court of accepting illegal gifts. Those charges emerged from the subsequent investigation by Special Prosecutor Lawrence Walsh.

Dutch followed up with an August 1987 speech in which he contradicted Poindexter, saying "the buck does not stop with Admiral Poindexter...it stops with me." He noted that he "let my preoccupation with the hostages intrude into areas where it didn't belong," that he was "stubborn in pursuit of a policy that went astray," but reiterated he "did not know about the diversion of funds," a point that had now been accepted by Congress. There would be internal changes, he concluded. Then he took Richard Nixon's advice and never spoke of Iran-Contra again. Congress quietly voted more Contra aid in February 1988, and the whole Central American issue ended in a stalemate. Eventually the forces of democracy would toss out the Sandinistas when they foolishly listened to American media predictions that they could win a popular vote. It was a harbinger of Mikhail Gorbachev's foray into actual democracy years later.

19

Craters to Peaks

Dutch may have thought he had dodged enough bullets in his lifetime with the end of Iran-Contra, but he hadn't reached the depths of the crater yet. Two more bombs would fall before he started the final ascent that would grace his last presidential days.

First, since 1985 he had battled an unwinnable public relations issue over the newest public health concern, AIDS. Known at the time as the "gay plague," AIDS (acquired immune deficiency syndrome) was little understood and had only been officially labeled and described in the early 1980s. Clinically, it was overwhelmingly associated with homosexual behavior and drug abuse, especially use of hypodermic needles, and was tied to human immunodeficiency virus (HIV). Not all HIV-positive people showed symptoms, and some, such as basketball star Earvin "Magic" Johnson, lived an apparently normal life for years with HIV. At the time, however, little was understood about the transmission and course of the disease. Reagan first took serious notice of it when his acquaintance, former movie star Rock Hudson, died in October 1985. The Gipper wrote that he had learned from television that prior to his death Hudson was in a Paris hospital "for treatment of AIDS."[1]

When Reagan entered office, the Centers for Disease Control identified 3,700 AIDS cases, almost all in San Francisco and New York, but it indeed was a plague that was expanding at terrifying rates. Within seven years there would be over 82,000 confirmed cases (with almost half that number of AIDS-related deaths) and this was the tip of the iceberg, since homosexual men especially were hesitant to even report the disease. After Hudson's death, Reagan received a briefing from his White House physician and grew concerned that in fact a serious epidemic was taking shape. Whether Reagan increased or decreased funding for AIDS research is a matter for those who want to debate budgeting terminology, but suffice it to say there was no giant spike to find the "cure for AIDS" that Reagan claimed was one of his "highest public-health priorities."[2] The fact was, AIDS was still poorly understood—many physicians still thought it could be transmitted through tears or saliva—and was still overwhelmingly identified with the homosexual community. Speechwriter Pat Buchanan had written in 1983, before joining Reagan's team, that "they have declared war on nature and now nature is exacting an awful retribution."[3] In February 1986, Reagan instructed Dr. C. Everett Koop, his surgeon general, to prepare a report of the AIDS epidemic. Lou Cannon described Koop as facing "the AIDS epidemic with the uncompromising honesty that was characteristic of his career."[4]

Koop's report came out in October 1986. It correctly noted that only changes in personal behavior could control the spread of AIDS and corrected the notion that AIDS could be contracted through casual contact. Koop's report was well received by Jerry Falwell, who invited Koop to speak at Liberty University, but Koop's support of condoms and other protections were disdained by many in the administration. Some feared that support of condom use promoted promiscuous sex. By April 1987, Reagan called AIDS "public health enemy number one" and delivered a speech to the American Foundation for AIDS Research. He said AIDS "affects us all" and that those who carried the AIDS virus should not have to wear a "scarlet A." He admitted that "we're still learning about how AIDS is transmitted" but that it could not be acquired from "swimming pools or drinking fountains [or] shaking hands or sitting on a bus."[5]

The Gipper's remarks were groundbreaking. Since the disease had only clearly been identified since his election, he obviously was the first president to address it. Critics in the homosexual lobby and biographers viewed Reagan's approach to AIDS as a missed opportunity. He "hesitated in speaking out," "should have done more," and "did not care enough about the AIDS problem to muster the best scientific information available."[6] Koop, of course, was in possession of *some* scientific information, but he was hardly the final authority on AIDS in 1986 or 1987.

Reagan's call for mandatory testing in federal prisons was greeted with harsh responses, with the concern that insurance companies would cancel policies if someone was diagnosed—indeed a likelihood, but hardly different from other serious diseases at the time. Conservatives in his administration were badgering him not to normalize homosexuality, while AIDS activists wanted him to do just the opposite. While Dutch was sympathetic to the plight of any sick person, and while he had extensive contact with homosexuals in the film industry, he still believed in the Bible and its strictures against the practices. Mark Madsen of the California Medical Association noted after the speech that while he wanted Reagan to say "a great deal more," he nevertheless appreciated "him coming out and talking about it. Considering this was his first major talk on AIDS, I'd give him a B+ for effort."[7]

As Reagan struggled with the little-understood epidemic, he was oblivious to a more immediate threat to his administration and legacy in the form of a new US Supreme Court vacancy. He had honored his promise to Maureen Reagan for her support in the 1980 nomination by naming a woman, Arizona's Sandra Day O'Connor, to the Supreme Court at his first opportunity. In mid-1981, Associate Justice Potter Stewart announced his retirement. Reagan, who had at one point said he would name a woman as "one of his first" appointments to the court, received a list of recommendations from the Justice Department with no women on it. He promptly returned it with the instructions that he wanted to name a woman. Period. In O'Connor, the Department of Justice found a reasonably conservative female from the Arizona Supreme Court but one whose views were, nevertheless, relatively unknown. Responding to concerns that O'Connor wasn't sufficiently hard-line enough in her abortion positions, Reagan wrote to one evangelical that he was reassured by her that she found abortion "abhorrent" and that it was a proper subject for legislation.[8] When conservative Chief Justice Warren Burger resigned in 1986, Reagan moved

William Rehnquist into the chief justice position and replaced Rehnquist as an associate justice with Antonin Scalia, a brilliant circuit court judge who would become viewed as the leading intellectual light of the conservative position on the court. But Scalia merely replaced another conservative and the balance of the court wasn't affected.

Lewis Powell's retirement, however, was a different story. Nominated to the court by Richard Nixon and viewed as a swing vote, he was thought to have provided the key vote in the *Regents of the University of California v. Bakke* (1978) case that upheld affirmative action. It outraged conservatives, who contended he had gone out of his way to save a policy of flimsy legal basis. With his retirement came an opportunity to shift the court to the right in a significant way. Expecting no opposition, Reagan nominated Robert Bork, a judge who had been on his short list for years. Bork's brilliant legal mind should have made the Judiciary Committee no match for him. As they say in football, "that's why you play the game." Bork—and Reagan—were in for a shock.

As the Gipper said when he announced Bork's nomination, "We're fortunate to be able to draw upon such an impressive legal mind."[9] Initially, even most Democrats thought he would be confirmed. But the entire process of confirming Supreme Court nominees was about to take a disgraceful turn, beginning with Ted Kennedy's speech on that same day called "Robert Bork's America." Kennedy claimed women would be "forced into back alley abortions," that segregated lunch counters would return, and that Bork was "reactionary."[10] Kennedy's assault was designed to be a claxon to liberal groups, warning them they were about to lose a swing court to a permanently conservative court. His efforts were aided by Democrat stalling, turning a normal forty-day delay from nomination to hearings into a seventy-day span, giving the Left time to mobilize.

Mobilize they did. As Steven Hayward put it, the "public campaign of the activist Left was stunning in its breadth, depth, and dishonesty."[11] It's entirely likely the Left learned its lesson with the long, dragged-out campaign for the Equal Rights Amendment in the early 1970s, where the Right slowly galvanized its voters behind the efforts of Phyllis Schlafly.[12] This time the response would be brutal, immediate, and completely effective. Reagan and his team were taken entirely by surprise, and to their discredit their overconfidence in Bork's abilities and obvious qualification had played a part in Reagan's failure to lay the proper groundwork.

Newspaper ads appeared instantly, with even the biased *Washington Post* admitting that the anti-Bork campaign "did not resemble an argument so much as a lynching."[13] Yet, even after the initial onslaught, conservatives and the administration sat on their hands, expecting decency and consideration from liberals. It would not be forthcoming. Hayward again captured it appropriately: "The sheer demagoguery and dishonesty of the assault were breathtaking."[14] Democratic senator after senator, having once piously announced that ideology had no place in the confirmation process, now attacked Bork simply for his views, not his competence. And the reason was obvious: as a press spokesman for Jimmy Carter noted, "We are depending in large part on the least democratic institution…in government to defend what…we no longer are able to win…in the electorate."[15] No one in Reagan's administration—save perhaps Pat Buchanan—really grasped this sea change until it was too late. In July Dutch wrote, "We'll get Bork confirmed…but it will be a battle."[16] Yet Reagan did not start calling senators with support until September 30 and never lobbied the southern Democrats who might prove the swing votes.

Bork did himself no favors with his appearance, his clinical bearing, and his puzzling answers to low-hanging curveball questions. He appeared to be an intellectual seeking a spot on the highest court for mental stimulation, and even his supporters admitted he failed to connect. In retrospect, some Reagan scholars such as Hayward argue that far from supporting "original intent," Bork's textual literal approach to the Constitution concerned many and that his approach to "judicial restraint" was not in keeping with the true conservative notion of original intent.[17] By the time Reagan was informed that the opposition had fifty-one votes, he said Bork "has a decision to make…I have made mine. I will support him all the way."[18]

Nevertheless, even with their reservations, few conservatives would have thought that the judge being "borked" (unfairly punished for his ideology) was desirable, and, following his rejection by four votes in the Senate, one of the brightest men ever nominated for the highest court position in the land was summarily dismissed. Reagan blew up and considered not even appointing someone else, then thought about a recess appointment of Bork. But he mostly had himself to blame. Neither he nor his conservative advisors had truly appreciated the new era of vicious politics the desperate Democrats had foisted on America. A cornered animal is extremely dangerous, and even after Iran-Contra, Reagan's popularity had made conservatism so widely popular that New Deal notions were not only being reconsidered but rejected across a broad swath of the American landscape.

Indeed, the Bork nomination exposed Reagan's greatest weakness, the same shortcoming that afflicted him in the Iran-Contra episode, yet from a different perspective. Reagan simply believed that most people were inherently good. His unwillingness to delve into the character and nature of his hero, Franklin D. Roosevelt, was perhaps central to his weakness. Roosevelt's lamentable history of deception, his use of the levers of power to crush his political enemies, and his class warfare haunted Dutch's own political legacy, and Reagan, for all his complaints about "big gubmint," never once criticized FDR. The Gipper possessed political skills second to none, empowered by acute intuition, but he had a blind spot not only for where modern liberalism had arrived in the 1980s, but for where it had started under his hero. Repeatedly, this caused him to underestimate the ruthlessness of his enemies as much as they underestimated his abilities. How could the Left so viciously and callously destroy the reputation of not only an innocent man but of an exemplary legal jurist? To Reagan, such behavior was nearly incomprehensible, and only grudgingly accepted after repeated lashings and key defeats at the hands of the Left. Reagan all too frequently believed the liberals would in the end "play fair" and let their humanity surface. One of the great ironies of Reagan's presidency was that he had more success appealing to that human quality with the Soviets than he did with his Democrat opponents.

After Bork, Reagan nominated the supposedly uncontroversial Douglas Ginsburg, hoping to go "the extra mile to ensure a speedy confirmation." Unfortunately, the nominee was discovered to have smoked marijuana in his youth—much like almost every young person of that age.[19] For any other Republican, Ginsburg's pot smoking would have amounted to nothing, but because of Nancy Reagan's "Just Say No" anti-drug campaign, he became unacceptable and Reagan withdrew his name. In his third choice, Anthony Kennedy, Reagan received the support for the nomination he wanted, a 97–0 approval. That, in itself, should have concerned him. Kennedy would later prove every bit as "swingy" as Powell.

The Bork fiasco consumed much of Washington's attention during the summer, and just as it came to an end, the stock market staged a spectacular crash. Markets are driven by fear and greed and can be spooked or fed quickly by the right mix. By the fall of 1987, some outlets, including the *Harvard Business Review*, claimed the stock market was overvalued. There was little doubt it was becoming more volatile. Even the president of the New York Stock Exchange expressed concern, with several stock-predictors chiming in to warn of a crash. James Baker made the rounds of the talk shows to suggest the administration saw a strong dollar as the problem and that foreign countries were taking advantage of the US with their trade surpluses.

A sell-off began in early October, with the market dropping 6 percent the first week, then 12 percent more the second, then on Friday October 16, a true panic hit. Monday was worse, with many stocks finding no buyers at all and unable to open for trading. The tape ran over two hours late and the Dow fell a shocking 508 points. In just three days, the Dow had lost almost 770 points, a 30 percent drop (by comparison, the Great Crash of 1929 saw the market fall only 13 percent).

Federal Reserve Chairman Alan Greenspan was well aware of the 1929 crash—both its reality and the myth that it "caused" the Great Depression. He also knew that most economists thought that a tight money policy was a major contributing factor. When Reagan was questioned by reporters, he replied with an accurate line that "there is nothing wrong with the economy," but one which sounded eerily like those used by Herbert Hoover in 1929. Dutch reminded everyone that employment was up to record highs, that productivity and manufacturing were up, and that "the economic indicators are solid." Congressional Democrats, of course, saw only an opportunity to increase taxes—their favorite pastime—and leaked their message to liberal reporters who harangued Reagan with it. He was peppered with questions about "compromising" on raising taxes. (Once again, it bears noting that Democrats are never hammered with question after question about "compromising" on *cutting* taxes.) Nevertheless, whether it was the perception that Reagan might be open to raising taxes to address the budget deficit—again, which seldom if ever actually worked—the reporters and the markets seemed placated and the following week the nation's financial markets stabilized. Greenspan had leaned on the bankers to continue lending, and indeed the fundamentals of American business were solid.

Financial historian Richard Sylla concluded that roughly half of the trading the day of the crash involved a "small number of institutions with portfolio insurance."[20] Big institutions dumped, and arbitragers, looking at the Chicago futures market, were buying futures in Chicago and selling for cash in New York City. But the Fed's own study in 2006 downplayed the role of portfolio insurance and instead found no consensus on the causes, noting that "uncertainty and herd behavior also contributed to the crash."[21] After-the-fact surveys at the time also suggested that technical analysis, not portfolio insurance, played a more important role. One study found no single news story affected investor behavior.[22] John Maynard Keynes's maxim mentioned in an earlier chapter likely captured the situation best: the "animal spirits" of capitalism still directed financial events.

As usual, the market recovered and "people forgot about it in the months after," with the Dow back to 1987 levels by 1989.[23] Over the hundred-year history of the stock market, the 1987 crash was a blip—a big blip, but still only a blip in steadily increasing values. At the time, however, the Democrats once again pounced, thinking they had finally found the smoking gun to defeat Reaganomics. "The voodoo chickens...have come home to roost," crowed Senator Al Gore, while leftist economist John Kenneth Galbraith saw the crash as the "end product of Arthur Laffer's supply-side economics and Milton Friedman's experiment with monetarism."[24] The real "end product" that was coming "home to roost" was continued growth under Reagan's policies. America's GDP grew by 3.4 percent in 1987 and shot up 6.1 percent in the fourth quarter after the crash. Consumer confidence rebounded quickly, and, as the *Financial Times* observed, "the prophets of doom had been confounded."[25]

It was critical for Democrats to find a means to say the Age of Reagan was over, first emphasizing Iran-Contra, then the Bork rejection, then the crash. Some conservatives joined in, frustrated that Dutch had seemingly given up on reducing the size of government. This, supposedly, had been the motivating factor in David Stockman's betrayal.

A frustrated Stockman had found resistance to downsizing everywhere when he first sought to reduce the size of government. A typical example was at the Energy Department, which candidate Reagan had promised to eliminate, and at Transportation, where Secretary Drew Lewis accused Stockman of "seeking power for himself" via deregulation and demanded to know, "What kind of bureaucracy are you building up over at OMB?"[26] Stockman railed against Reagan for not working harder to chop government spending, claiming the Gipper was not up to the task. Stockman had warned that "forty years…of promises, entitlements and safety nets issued by the federal government to every component and stratum of American society would have to be scrapped or drastically modified," and Reagan simply wouldn't rule with the iron hand necessary to accomplish the revolution.[27]

The reality, as Reagan learned, was quite different and more complicated. Consider this 1988 exchange with the Office of Management and Budget and the Commerce Department over forty-three congressional add-on programs, totaling $73 million, that could be cut. In response to a request from Budget Director James Miller on what wasteful and/or unnecessary spending could be identified, Commerce replied that 51 percent "has already been obligated. Of the remaining $36.1 million, Commerce intends to comply with $23.9 million as earmarked and partially comply with another $1.1 million." But of the remaining money, Commerce either claimed the money was in other programs or departments or that it was still planning to use the reminder in some way. In short, Commerce genuinely planned *no* cuts.[28] Even though one of Reagan's very first orders, on January 27, 1981, was a memo to all departments ordering that they reduce spending on consulting contracts, office redecoration, and any other nonessential items, soon they slipped back into their bloated ways.[29] Stockman had a point: trimming at the margins was a far cry from eliminating entire departments, such as Energy and Education.

Disillusion set in with many conservatives over the inability to reduce government. They failed to understand the reality that no individual, and no administration, had unlimited resources of time, talent, and energy. Rebuilding the economy, eliminating regulations, and most of all defeating communism—all the while beset by normal upheavals such as the market crash or political obstructionism such as the Iran-Contra hearings—consumed virtually everything the administration, and Reagan himself, had. It was simply unrealistic to think that everything could get done equally fast, or equally effectively. The president had failed to put forward a market-oriented solution to catastrophic health care, had deftly avoided any Social Security reform, and had given up fighting for the line-item veto. He once remarked that subsequent generations might have to do some of the heavy lifting and that he couldn't do it all.

Congress felt its oats, though, sensing that perhaps Dutch was weakened, and overrode two Reagan spending vetoes. But the Democrats in Congress failed to override a more important Reagan reform: the Federal Communications Commission's repeal of the so-called "Fairness Doctrine." A dinosaur regulation dating to the time when access to news was limited to a handful of broadcasters, the Fairness Doctrine supposedly required equal time for both sides of any political argument. Based on the presumption that the airwaves were public property and should be regulated in the public interest, the doctrine in fact eliminated serious and controversial points of view for fear of a regulatory crackdown that could put a local broadcaster out of business, resulting in a "chilling effect" on free speech (as the FCC noted). In part thanks to freedom from the Fairness Doctrine, a new voice appeared on the national airwaves in 1988 that revolutionized talk radio and immediately galvanized conservatives: Rush Limbaugh. His show, far more than the limited-circulation *Washington Times*, became the first truly national opposition media to the "Big Three" of ABC, CBS, and NBC—and they did not like it. Rush made no secret of his admiration for the Gipper, calling him "Ronaldus Magnus" and providing real-time counterarguments to left-leaning news stories. As he would frequently put it, he eliminated the Left's monopoly on the news media.

In addition to dealing with conservative disillusionment and liberal recalcitrance, Reagan had hurdles to overcome in his personal world. The first involved his adopted son, Michael Reagan. Because Michael was adopted by Dutch and Jane Wyman, he did not spend nearly as much time around his father as Patti or Ron would, though perhaps no less than Maureen. His parents divorced when he was three, and when Michael was old enough, he went to a youth camp after school each day. He came to view the man who ran the camp as a father figure, but for nearly a year, the counselor began sexually abusing Michael on automobile rides, as well as photographing him naked.[30] Michael never told his parents, but as the Gipper ran for president, Michael worried that the photos would emerge. The molestation began to show itself in "an enormous load of rage, guilt, and fear," Michael wrote.[31] "I knew I had to get away from my mother," he told a Christian Broadcast Network interviewer. "I had to get away from God. I thought he abandoned me."[32] He feared his wife would leave him if she found out. Then, in 1987, he was offered an impressive advance for a tell-all book. During interviews with his ghostwriter, he decided he had to tell his wife and, most of all, his father about the molestation.

On April 12, 1987, Michael, his wife Colleen, and his kids visited Rancho del Cielo. Ostensibly they were there for his daughter's fourth birthday party, but Michael's real reason for the visit was a talk with his father, the president. He walked with Ron and Nancy to the edge of a lake when Nancy said, "We know you're writing a book. What's in the book we should know about?" Michael revealed the abuse he had suffered years earlier. When he finished his story, as he recalled, "Dad was angry. 'Where is this guy? I'll kick his butt!'"[33] "Why didn't you tell me before?" Reagan asked his son. Michael explained that he was afraid his father wouldn't like him anymore. "Oh, Michael," Dutch replied, "You should have known better." Later, Michael's sister, Maureen, saw her brother at a state dinner and added that if she could find the camp leader who committed the abuse "there'd be a whole lot of physical trouble."

Michael's revelation began a long road of reconciliation between father and son. Seven months later, though, Dutch would be hit with news about his wife that was every bit as troubling. During a mammogram, a lump was found in Nancy's breast. An immediate biopsy was performed, as the president and Nancy's brother Dick stood by. The cancer was minimal, but Nancy lost a breast. The First Lady did not have to undergo any further chemotherapy or radiation treatments, but when he received the news of the mastectomy, Reagan recalled "how desperately Nancy had hoped this would not be the case."[34] Not long after, Nancy's mother died in Phoenix.

During this personally troubling and difficult time, Reagan was about to achieve a cataclysmic victory. On October 27, just as the Reagans—with Nancy still in a weakened state—were preparing to leave for Phoenix, the president held a conference call with George Shultz in which he was told that the Soviet ambassador, Eduard Shevardnadze, "speaking for Gorbachev," would be arriving for meetings on [the Intermediate Nuclear Forces, or "Euromissiles"]." As Reagan wrote in his diary, "The Soviets blinked."[35]

In fact, they had blinked at Reykjavik, but few knew it. As early as September, Shultz noted in a National Security Planning Group meeting that Reagan "has had success in imposing the full U.S. agenda on the Soviets."[36] Compared to the 1984 meetings with Gromyko, where "little [was] going on," Shultz observed that "Now...there is a lot going on in each of the four areas [of negotiation], human rights, bilateral, regional issues, and arms control."[37] Reagan, who had a habit of constantly reminding everyone of the big picture, spoke up. "You've got to remember that the whole [arms control] thing was born of the idea that the world needs to get rid of nuclear weapons.... we can't win a nuclear war and we can't fight one....We need to keep in mind that's what we're about."[38] The Gipper, of course, had a story. "I have a friend," he said, "who tells me that in the Soviet Union their right-wingers are starting to call Gorbachev 'Mr. Yes' because he agrees with everything that I propose."[39]

While Reagan's success at Reykjavik had changed much, his ongoing "advance on every front" approach involving energy had contributed to the slow squeeze on the USSR. Energy policy, to Reagan, was another weapon to be wielded against the Soviet economy. Reagan's first executive order on January 28, 1981, was to deregulate gas and oil, removing all allocation controls on the production of domestic oil and refined petroleum that

Nixon had put in place in 1973.[40] Then, in NSDD 87, Reagan laid out a vision for domestic and international energy policy.[41] Energy historian Daniel Yergin observed that the net effect of Reagan's deregulation was to allow Americans to command world prices for the sale of US crude, and, subsequently, the high prices brought into production new supplies in the Gulf of Mexico, the North Slope of Alaska, and internationally.[42] While prices originally rose, the high prices brought in more producers, and very quickly a glut appeared—a glut that would cripple the USSR. Producers either had to cut production to prop up prices or cut prices drastically in an attempt to gain market share. But the Soviets could not do the former; they depended too heavily on oil dollars. The Saudis, on the other hand, could easily do the latter, and in 1985 they dramatically increased production, sending prices tumbling.

Reagan's team also dealt with other oil-related issues. In meeting after meeting about Libya, the administration had postponed for as long as possible a decision on an embargo and ban on American business there. As late as December 1983 Reagan told McFarlane he had "come down on the side of permitting sales" of equipment to Libya. "To do otherwise is an empty gesture."[43] With Libya out of the mix, more emphasis was placed on an agreement with Saudi Arabia, which led to their agreement to substantially increase its production, and quickly.[44] Infuriated Soviet ministers shot off a letter to King Fahd, warning against pushing prices lower and offered secret meetings in Geneva to push up prices. Of course, the Soviets' troubles were not all the doing of Reagan's policies: the ongoing Iran-Iraq war continued to see tankers and refineries struck and supplies slowed. Saudi Arabia responded by requesting Reagan step up the American presence in the Gulf to protect shipping. By early 1986, Saudi production of oil was ten million barrels a day, pushing prices down further. While Saudi Arabia felt no negative effects from the lower prices—having made it up by increased production—the Soviets could not match their increased production. Prices fell to as low as eight dollars a barrel.

This price collapse would have been significant for Dutch's goals in and of itself, but when combined with the stall tactics he had used related to the natural gas pipeline, it had a near-fatal effect. And it was no coincidence that George Shultz, who rode herd on all these negotiations, had a background in energy from his days with the Bechtel Corporation. Indeed, he was the ideal person to straddle the administration's twin free market and national security concerns. Reagan pushed hard to help his allies as well, hoping to give them commercial channels to natural gas that would deny the Soviets further sales of their product. However, his efforts there failed—probably the only aspect of Reagan's entire energy policy that was not a success.

Dutch wasn't satisfied. In September 1986, the president announced "we will undertake a high-level review of America's energy-related national security concerns."[45] The review, headed by John Herrington, assessed energy into the 1990s. Reagan placed one stipulation on the recommendations: that they be revenue neutral so that they "would not reopen basic issues already considered in tax reform."[46] In addition to the opening up of the ANWR (Arctic National Wildlife Refuge), the proposals included increasing the net income limitation on depletion allowances and reducing the minimum bid requirement on federal leases."[47] Other initiatives the president proposed, but which were not adopted, included repealing the windfall profits tax and seeking comprehensive natural gas control. Another proposal to Reagan from his National Security Council included an expansion of nuclear power.[48] Yet one recommendation that Reagan did not take was that of filling the Strategic Petroleum Reserve while prices were low.

That proved a minor point compared to his audacious CUSFTA (Canada-United States Free Trade Agreement), an early arrangement that would later be the basis for Bill Clinton's North American Free Trade Agreement (NAFTA). Originally discussed at the March 1985 meeting between the president and Prime Minister Brian Mulroney in Quebec City, the plan originally had envisioned including Mexico. Ultimately Mexico refused to participate, so CUSFTA finally resulted in negotiations solely between the United States and Canada designed to tie the two countries together in an integrated web of oil and natural gas production, as well as distribution infrastructure, that would serve as an insurance policy against future disruptions in oil supply from the Middle East.[49] Negotiators dealt with not only gas and oil, but with electricity, coal and coke, and uranium. The recommendation to Reagan was that the "U.S. should attempt to negotiate language in the final FTA with Canada which will allow for the greatest degree of free trade in energy between the two countries."[50] CUSFTA was not concluded until 1988, and it set the stage for future NAFTA negotiations, but by that time all of Reagan's other policies had severely crippled the Soviet Union.

Pressing on the arms-control front, Reagan increasingly found that his earlier meeting in Iceland with Gorbachev had turned out to be more favorable than even he originally thought. As Ambassador Max Kampelman noted in an NSPG meeting in October 1987, preparing for the Shultz-Shevardnadze meetings in Moscow, the Soviets were already down to a limit of 60 percent of the total weapons on each leg of the TRIAD. "Mr. President," he said to Reagan, "you got this in Reykjavik.... This is certainly one of the accomplishments of that meeting."[51] The issue came up as to whether Reagan was deliberately trying to "restructure" the Soviet Union's forces. He slyly answered, "Yes," but added if they wanted "land-based stuff, so what?" It was an answer that stemmed directly from his understanding that with SDI, the "land-based stuff" would become increasingly useless, and that indeed it was preferable that they restructure toward "land-based stuff."[52] Typically, some of his advisors failed to see the longer-range picture, particularly Weinberger's future successor as secretary of defense, Frank Carlucci, who called the land-based missiles the most destabilizing. Quite the contrary: in Reagan's mind, shooting down missiles from fixed launch locations was far easier than dealing with submarine-launched missiles, which might be fired from windows that SDI wasn't specifically covering.

For Dutch, the goal was to remain on offense at all times, across all fronts. He visited Germany in June 1987 and he saw the opportunity to "restructure" the Soviet Union in a fundamental way. While his advisors again cautioned a nonconfrontational approach, Reagan—as he always did—saw a stage. It was, perhaps, the most powerful and profound stage from which to blast the Soviets for their oppressive, closed system: the Berlin Wall. Standing with the Brandenburg Gate as a backdrop, the president delivered the lines for the ages:

General Secretary Gorbachev, if you seek peace, if you seek prosperity for the Soviet Union and Eastern Europe, if you seek liberalization, come here to this gate! Mr. Gorbachev, open this gate! Mr. Gorbachev, tear down this wall![53]

Reagan repeated those exact words many times in the ensuing weeks.[54]

Reagan's Berlin address marked an interesting bookend: in John F. Kennedy's administration, the Berlin Wall went up and he traveled to Berlin to give his famous "Ich bin ein Berliner" speech in June 1963, where he said, "Freedom has many difficulties and democracy is not perfect, but we have never had to put a wall up to keep our people in, to prevent them from leaving us."[55] Now, the Gipper was demanding that the supposedly enlightened and "modern" Gorbachev put his money where his mouth was. It constituted a propaganda victory that Gorbachev couldn't match, exposing him as yet one more dictator in a steady line of dictators.

Gorbachev already knew he had a PR problem and had hoped for more openness, but he couldn't move fast enough in the sclerotic Soviet system. He was, as he wrote in his memoirs, exasperated that Reagan wouldn't give him the flexibility and time to do things at his own speed.[56] Quite the contrary, Dutch forced the pace, as cable traffic from Moscow showed, in which the Soviets suggested the East Germans might begin to allow travel to the West. Equally important, the State Department was emboldened, "treating Reagan's call as a policy."[57]

Gorbachev's empire was coming apart at the seams, and the Gipper knew it. Poland continued to exert pressure on the communists, the Soviet economy had not shown any benefits from *perestroika*, and Afghanistan was a disaster. Although Gorbachev had privately decided to extricate the USSR from the Afghan morass in 1985, nevertheless, here he was, two years later, still explaining to Soviet mothers why their sons were not coming home. William Odom, who wrote the finest summary of the decline of the Soviet military, claims that Gorbachev lagged behind his arms-control negotiators in their ideas for eliminating nuclear weapons. Internally, his advisors noted that he had come back from Reykjavik buoyed by the prospect of peace and that he never again referred to Reagan as a "fool and a clown."[58] Odom dated Gorbachev's first fundamental change in perception to February 1986 when, for the first time, he spoke of an understanding that "society's interests are higher than class interests."[59] He had already been informed that victory in Afghanistan was not possible because no "revolutionary base" existed there. Symbolically, however, Afghanistan was momentous, for it was the first time the USSR had been forcibly evicted from a country that it had invaded and the only time it had been driven out or stopped without the apparent influx of US forces or materials. It also marked the public exposure of the fallacy of Lenin's view of capitalism—that capitalism had to expand or die. Now it was clear, without expansion communism would die.

The final insult came on May 28, 1987, when Mathias Rust, a West German teenager, flew a small Cessna airplane undetected from Helsinki to Moscow, circled the Kremlin several times, then plopped the plane down at Red Square. Rust's prank shocked the Soviet military to the bone. If a Cessna piloted by a kid could—*without trying*—evade the vaunted Soviet air defense system, what would happen if American B-1s or new "stealth" bombers attacked with deadly intentions? Gorbachev used the incident to fire hard-liner Cold Warrior generals, to demand once and for all the Soviet Union withdraw from Afghanistan, and to take a much more suspicious approach to the iconic Soviet military. Details soon emerged that the Air Defence Forces had not been integrated, that they lacked spare parts, and that they had no real capacity to track low-flying, ground-hugging aircraft, such as the B-1s or cruise missiles, at all. After the Rust flight, ordinary Soviet citizens no longer believed in the superiority of their own military.

Had Reagan been unaware, or unappreciative, of these weaknesses in Gorbachev's position, matters might have turned out differently. But he knew he had the Soviet leader and his party structure reeling. At the September 1987 National Security Planning Group meeting where Reagan had reminded the cabinet that the goal was to eliminate all nuclear weapons, the focus was on the Euromissiles. Weinberger called the mobile ICBMs "the most fundamental issue" and that we should "have no mobiles. There is no way we can verify them."[60] Shultz dismissed mobile missiles and wanted to focus on START, but Weinberger insisted there was no reason to give in to Soviet demands on anything. Reagan ended the heated September

NSPG meeting with an interesting revelation: "You know, I've been reading my Bible and the description of Armageddon talks about destruction, I believe, of many cities, and…. we have to do something now."[61] Once again, Dutch had boiled down the argument to its most basic element: the negotiators had to get past numbers of platforms and warheads and reach fundamental agreements about the commitment to, and in the direction of, arms reduction.

Internally Gorbachev was in some trouble, and the Reagan administration even worried that his six-week disappearance meant he had been removed in a coup. But to Reagan's relief, Gorbachev resurfaced and announced that he would consider negotiating on the Euromissiles in a separate treaty. As usual, he wanted to leverage this to take SDI off the table, but privately he knew that the SS-20s had been a mistake. "I would even go so far as to characterize [the deployment of the SS-20s] as an unforgivable adventure," he wrote, in that the Euromissiles, with their limited range, threatened only Europe, while their counterparts—the Pershing II and cruise missiles—could reach the USSR itself, and in less than ten minutes.[62] Those weapons threatened the Soviet Union "more gravely" than any other American system.

When Reagan sent Shultz to Moscow to prepare for START talks, the secretary found Gorbachev was ready to deal on the Intermediate-Range Nuclear Forces (INF) separately. A surprised Shultz enthusiastically helped draft the outlines of a deal. Gorbachev pushed for a deal by year's end. (The NATO ministers had all signed on to such a deal in June.)

Chancellor Kohl actually spurred the agreement by announcing in August that the Federal Republic of Germany would dismantle its seventy-two Pershings and not replace them if the superpowers could come to an agreement. By September, the two sides had a rough outline of what would become the Intermediate-Range Nuclear Forces Treaty.

Reagan gleefully accepted an INF deal but still pressed for full reductions in strategic weapons and reminded his negotiators he wanted a START deal. Weinberger, who later wrote "I had proposed the [INF] treaty in the first place," expressed concerns about the Euromissile negotiations insofar as Gorbachev connected them to SDI.[63] By then, he had resigned as a result of prosecution related to Iran-Contra (even though he had opposed the sale) and Frank Carlucci, his deputy, had taken over as the secretary of defense. Reagan told his security team that he could sense they were about to finish the task of getting a full arms-reduction agreement before he left office. All was ready for the Soviet leader's visit to the United States in early December.

While some tough negotiating remained—"a good rousing meeting," was how Dutch recorded it in his diary—no one could doubt that the "atmosphere was electric with a sense of historic importance," as Shultz recorded.[64] On December 8, Reagan and Gorbachev signed the INF Treaty in Washington, in which all mobile systems in Europe would be eliminated in the next three years. The INF Treaty constituted a landmark: never before in human history had the combatants agreed to the elimination *and destruction* of an entire class of weapons, let alone nuclear weapons. Inspection teams were created and subsequent memoranda provided for observers from each side to watch the weapons physically being dismantled and cut up.[65] At the signing ceremony, Reagan went out of his way to insert Russian stories and concluded with his phrase of "trust, but verify," to which Gorbachev replied, "You repeat that at every meeting."[66] "I like it," Reagan said, turning the microphone over to Gorbachev, who said he and Reagan had "covered a seven-year-long road," with only the final step to be taken—signing the document.

After the ceremony, Gorbachev engaged in a public relations offensive by getting out of his limo and meeting Washingtonians on their lunch hour. Naturally, he was mobbed, and the media swooned. There was a luncheon and an event with the who's who of American (mostly leftist) elites that included Carl Sagan, Robert De Niro, John Denver, Paul Newman, Yoko Ono, Gus Hall, Cyrus Vance, George Kennan, Brent Scowcroft, Norman Mailer, John Kenneth Galbraith, and, of course, Henry Kissinger.[67] Novelist Joyce Carol Oates, at the luncheon, couldn't contain herself: "The things he said were almost too good to be true." Mary McGrory called Gorbachev "a leader to make Americans weep."[68] Conservative hard-liners who never appreciated Reagan's foresight, such as George Will and Pat Buchanan, whined that Reagan had given away the store and that the signing of the

INF Treaty was the day America lost the Cold War. Once again, the Gipper was underestimated; once again, he won an astounding victory.

Raisa Gorbachev was less clever and chided Nancy about homelessness in America. Nancy was offended by far more than Raisa's snide comment. Three weeks earlier, she had invited the Russian First Lady on a tour of the White House, and Raisa had ignored it. When she finally took the tour, Raisa continued her rude remarks, calling the White House a "museum." As Nancy recalled in her memoir, "once or twice, she even lectured me on the failings of the American political system."[69] Nancy Reagan understood politics and certainly had a sophisticated grasp of issues, but she believed her role was not to serve as the spokeswoman for those: that was "her Ronnie's" job. Thus, she did not debate Raisa, and when she met Mikhail Gorbachev for the first time, at first she wasn't impressed: "I felt a certain coldness from him." But over dinner, "he warmed up considerably [and] the more I saw him, the more I liked him." She found he had a good source of humor. Dutch typically jibed Gorbachev in an "I know who you really are" context. In Geneva, Reagan had told a story of an old Russian woman who came to the Kremlin to see Gorbachev and told him, "We must have a more open society..... In America, anyone can go to the White House and [say to] President Reagan...'I don't like the way you're running the country.'" Reagan continued, "'My dear lady,' replies Gorbachev, 'You can do the very same thing right here in the Soviet Union. Anytime you like you can come into my office and tell me that you don't like the way President Reagan is running his country!'"[70] Gorbachev laughed—and not just out of politeness.

Raisa's annoying attitude never seemed to bleed over to her husband, who continued to impress Americans as an ordinary guy, whether in closed groups with government audiences or on the street. Most liked him, and typically the media continued to have its "gorbasms" (as Rush Limbaugh called them). When the Soviet leader finally departed, he informed Reagan he would end financial support to Nicaragua. The summit left Reagan feeling the two men had personally connected and that negotiations were indeed on the right track. If "Gorby" had been the star of the summit, though, the entire affair had been produced and directed by Ronald Reagan.

20

Missionary to Moscow

"**D**o you believe in it?" came the question.

"What?" asked the president.

"Do you believe in it?" was the reply, again.[1]

Ronald Reagan knew his wife's consultations with an astrologer had become public after Don Regan published his scathing 1988 tell-all book ridiculing his *bete noire*, Nancy, for following her horoscope and meeting with Joan Quigley, an astrologer. The issue had come up back in his first run for the presidency, and the Reagan team thought they had it quashed. Now Regan, out of spite, had opened up the can of worms again.

In *My Turn* (1989), Nancy did not mention her earlier flirtations with astrology, suggesting that while Joan Quigley contacted her during the 1980 campaign, they had only spoken by phone.[2] Nancy had seen Quigley on a panel of astrologers on the Merv Griffin show but did not remember meeting her (Griffin said he introduced the two). Lou Cannon claims in *Governor Reagan* that both Ron and Nancy consulted their horoscopes daily during his years in Sacramento, and Reagan himself, in *Where's the Rest of Me?* mentioned a "good friend" Carroll Righter, who wrote a syndicated column on astrology and confirmed that "every morning Nancy and I turn to see what he has to say."[3]

Cannon lent more weight to the issue of astrology than most other biographers (Steven Hayward barely mentions it in Reagan's prepresidential years, *The Age of Reagan*, a seven-hundred-page book).[4] According to

Cannon, however, Reagan always had a superstitious streak in him, carrying lucky pennies and knocking on wood. Of course, since the assassination attempt on him, Reagan always carried a pistol with him as well, so there was that! Paul Kengor, the best chronicler of Reagan's spiritual life, discovered a letter from Joan Sieffert, the president of the Pittsburgh chapter of Reagan's fan club in 1974, when Sieffert had a dream of Reagan being shot while entering a car. Her letter to Nancy about the dream prompted a call from Nancy.[5] Whether this pushed her further into astrology Kengor is reluctant to say, but he noted that Nancy Reagan never abandoned Christianity and saw no conflict between it and astrology.

In Cannon's narrative, Nancy had deeply involved herself in scheduling through Mike Deaver. According to Nancy, right after the assassination attempt Merv Griffin had called her to say that Quigley could have prevented the attempt on Reagan's life, that "the president should have stayed home," as Merv related Quigley's words.[6] A distraught Nancy told Merv, "*I could have stopped it!*" and called Quigley. From there on, she began to have regular discussions with the astrologer—though Nancy did not use the term "readings." "Joan was a good listener," Nancy wrote, and saw her as a "kind of therapist."[7] Nevertheless, she insisted on multiple occasions that astrology never interfered with politics and was only used to adjust schedules on some occasions, that it was not true that, as Don Regan claimed, "virtually every major move and decision the Reagans made during my time as White House Chief of Staff was cleared in advance with a woman in San Francisco who drew up horoscopes."[8] Kengor notes that Reagan himself scheduled key events, often against the advice of his staff, such as at Reykjavik.

However, no one doubts that *some* events were first cleared with Quigley. Deaver was exasperated, unable to tell others why events were moved, delayed, or canceled. Privately he called Quigley "Madam Zorba." He told Cannon that people would "come in with perfectly reasonable ideas" but he couldn't accommodate them because of Quigley's recommendations to Nancy, and that "I couldn't talk about why we were doing what we were doing."[9] Quigley's influence was perhaps most felt in the Bitburg trip, in which Nancy moved the ceremony from the morning to the afternoon and delayed the departure from Bonn by twenty minutes because it was "dangerous" to be in the air earlier. When Deaver confronted her about inconveniencing six hundred people, Nancy shot back, "I'm talking about my husband's life."[10] Deaver, on yet another part of the Bitburg trip, told Nancy he was changing the timing of an event when in fact he did not.

When word of Nancy's astrology consultations publicly surfaced with publication of Don Regan's book *For the Record* in early 1988, it sparked a major controversy. Nancy claimed she was badly hurt by the revelations and took his claims in the book as a personal attack.[11] Reagan was, of course, protective of Nancy ("I'll be damned if I'll just stand by and let them railroad my wife").[12] When pressed on whether he believed in astrology, Reagan said no changes were "ever made on the basis of whether I did nor did not conduct this [consultation]." It was "smoke and mirrors, and we made no decisions on it," then he added, "I don't mean to offend anyone who does believe in it or who engages in it seriously." Specifically asked, "Do you believe in it?" Reagan responded, "I don't guide my life by it, but I won't answer the question the other way because I don't know enough about it to say if there something to it or not." He denied that the attempt on his life could have been prevented by astrology.

Reagan suffered a strong backlash from evangelical Christians when the news of Nancy's astrology dabbling came out, including letters from Pat Boone and a petition with twenty-five thousand signatures urging him to disassociate himself immediately.

The issue hardly died down. Reagan's Christian supporters were concerned. Pat Boone, his friend, wanted him to "remove any association" with astrology.[13] George Otis, the head of High Adventure Ministries, who had met with Reagan, Pat Boone, and others in his Sacramento home in 1970, reminded the Gipper that "God's Powerful Word came [saying] you were to become President of the United States." Now Otis sent in petitions with over twenty-five thousand signatures urging the Reagans to reject astrology and "renounce the practice of Astrology in the White House."[14] The *Atlanta Constitution* proclaimed, "Reagans' Stargazing Concerns the Christian Right" and claimed that the Southern Baptist Convention might withdraw its invitation to Reagan to address the group.[15] Cal Thomas called the Reagans' flirtation with horoscopes "the last straw for a lot of religious people.... [Reagan] used to say, 'The answer to all life's problems can be found in the Bible.' I guess he put God on hold and consulted Jeane Dixon."[16]

Few, however, deserted Reagan over this; most believed Nancy that her dabbling in astrology was an outgrowth of her concerns after the assassination attempt, that it was just one minor part of her life, and that her husband was not significantly involved and never based decisions on the stars. Instead, they paid attention to Reagan's actions—his unending support for pro-life issues, his Christlike concern for the human suffering of the hostages, his gentleness and persistent kindness even to his nasty enemies, and his repeated professions of his faith in God.

For instance, after he was shot, Reagan did not mention astrology but instead said to his pastor, Donn Moomaw, "I'm ready to meet God because I have a Savior."[17] Further, Reagan had told Terence Cardinal Cooke, not long after the assassination attempt, "I have decided that whatever time I have left is for Him.... Whatever happens now I owe my life to God and will try to serve him every way I can."[18] These were hardly the words of a stargazer.

While he may not have stared at the stars, Dutch had his vision firmly fixed on the future. His quest, as always, remained ending the arms race— or, at least, taking significant steps to do so—before he left office. He had one more shot at Gorbachev. While still pushing for START, Reagan still thought he could make major inroads into the Soviet arsenal and even into the USSR itself. He sent Shultz to Moscow in February, and the secretary of state met with dissident Andrei Sakharov, now a free man (as free as any Soviet citizen could be). Shultz then got down to brass tacks, meeting with Shevardnadze, who regaled him with human rights abuses in the US. By then, Shultz and others in the American delegation nearly laughed at such nonsense and often wondered if the Soviets themselves even believed it any longer.[19] Moreover, Soviet officials knew they had lost the propaganda war and that their claims of an "advanced" or "enlightened" society fooled no one. Reagan's humor, rolled out at every speech—even when Gorbachev was present—had its acid tip. At the Washington summit, Reagan told a story of an American scholar taking a cab to the airport in the USSR. The Soviet driver asked, "When you finish your schooling, what do you want to do?" The young man answered, "I haven't decided yet." Then the American asked the cab driver, "When you finish your schooling, what do you want to be?" The cab driver answered, "They haven't told me yet." That, Reagan said, was the difference between the two systems.[20]

Gorbachev blanched, and Shultz predictably was "disturbed and disappointed." After all, "this was not the moment for it"—in Shultz's world. But in Reagan's world, the advantage was to be pressed, even at the cost of diplomatic formalities. This stuck with the Russians, and had since Reagan's early "Evil Empire" comments, which still weighed on them in 1988. When Suzanne Massie, a Reagan advisor, met with Dutch in March 1988, she said the Soviets all but begged her—coming from the highest levels—for Reagan to state publicly that he had disavowed the "perception of Soviet international behavior" that had prompted the "Evil Empire" speech.[21]

Typically, Reagan did just the opposite, piling it on in an April speech before Shultz met with Gorbachev in Moscow. While he was positive that American relations had improved with the USSR, he nevertheless was under no "illusions on our part" about the Soviet system. There was a "moral and spiritual point" to be made, and, most of all, it was still a fact that "the differences that separated us and the Soviets were deeper and wider than just missile counts."[22] In short, Dutch delivered a pre-summit message to Gorbachev: just because you and I get along personally does not mean that your ideology doesn't belong on the ash heap of history. According to Shultz, back in October during the INF discussions, he noticed a change in Gorbachev, even from the more mellowed leader who left Reykjavik. "The boxer has been hit," Shultz wrote.[23] When Reagan's "differences" comment hit Gorbachev back in Moscow, he "flew into a tantrum," according to Shultz.[24]

Reagan's unceasing "punches" to Gorbachev about human rights, freedom, and the differences in the two societies irritated "Gorby" profoundly... because he knew they were true.

Senators had started debating the INF Treaty as Reagan prepared to go to Moscow, and a last-minute inclusion of "futuristic weapons" threatened to derail the ratification. Shultz suspected that conservatives were behind it, particularly Senators Dan Quayle and Jesse Helms. When Shultz informed Reagan that the main opposition was on the Right, he "could only shake his head in dismay."[25] But on May 27, the Senate finally assented to the treaty 93–5. START would prove much more difficult, and now time was working against Reagan, as he said in a February 1988 interview.

Still, both Reagan and Shultz agreed that they would not sign a deal just for the sake of a deal. In March 1988, at a National Security Planning Group meeting, Shultz worried about working against a deadline of a summit, but, addressing the president, added, "I have no fear that we will go bananas and grab a bad deal off the table under your leadership."[26] Dutch agreed, but replied they needed to "go for the gold." His experience as a labor union negotiator said to "put down what the ideal agreement would be," then set bottom lines. However, "there are things that we simply can't retreat on. One of them is verification." He thought the Soviets "feel they need START," that they have "an innate eye to protect the homeland at all cost, and it may be they recognized after Chernobyl that facing the nuclear forces they face, they can't do this [i.e., ever consider a nuclear exchange]. So I think we must press." Virtually all of the cabinet members in the meeting fully agreed with Reagan, a harmony he had not enjoyed for some time.

Not only did Reagan not moderate his tone, he ratcheted up the pressure. In his February 1988 "Address to the Citizens of Western Europe," the Gipper said he had told the Soviet leadership he was serious about freeing Europeans. He had made his Berlin proposals nine months before, and "the people of Berlin and all of Europe deserve an answer," he stated. Reviving his by-now historic phrase, "tear down this wall," Reagan essentially spoke directly to Gorbachev: "Make a start. Set that date, bring it down." Only this would satisfy real, genuine *glasnost*, he implied.[27] Dutch's comments threw Gorbachev into a rage, but when he calmed down, the general secretary reassured Shultz, "The Soviet Union does not pretend to have the final truth. We do not impose our way of life on other people."

435

Therefore, on May 29, 1988, when Air Force One sat down at Vnukovo International Airport in Moscow, Dutch was friendly and conciliatory. He stood next to Gorbachev for a press event, where he was asked by Sam Donaldson if he still thought the Soviet Union was an evil empire. "No," replied Reagan. "I was talking about another time in another era." They went to the Grand Kremlin Palace building and climbed the Grand State Staircase, where they were greeted with a giant painting of Lenin. "I sort of expected him to be there," Reagan said, smiling. Gorbachev and Reagan then made remarks in St. George's Hall. It was a Sunday, and Dutch ended his comments with, "Thank you and God bless you." A translator's notes recorded that "the heretofore impregnable edifice of Communist atheism was being assaulted before their very eyes."[28]

As the two men headed off for their one-on-one meeting, Reagan again raised the issue of religious freedom in the Soviet closed society. "What if you ruled religious freedom was part of people's rights?" he asked the general secretary. It was a stunning question. No one would have dared to seriously ask Nikita Khrushchev or Joseph Stalin such a question. But Dutch went further, telling Gorbachev that such a declaration would make him a hero, "and much of the feeling against your country will disappear like water in the hot sun." He even promised to keep his own role quiet if Gorbachev were to undertake such reforms (just as he had done with the release of the "Siberian Seven").

At first Gorbachev bobbed and weaved. Baptized as a child, Gorbachev now did not believe in God and typically tried to turn the question back to violations of civil rights in America. Reagan would have none of it and then drove the point home personally. His own son, Ron, was an agnostic. If the Gipper could serve Ron a gourmet dinner and ask him at the end, do you believe there was a cook, Reagan asked Gorbachev what the answer would be. The Soviet dictator, head of the empire of "godless communism," said the answer had to be yes.[29] Reagan repeated the story without Ron's name in remarks the following day at Spaso House.

His remarks there were inspiring and soaring, and once again injected with a spiritual tone:

I want to give you one thought from my heart.... I have to believe that the part of history of this troubled century will indeed be redeemed in the eyes of God and man, and that freedom will come to all. For what injustice can withstand your strength, and what can conquer your prayers?

He then again ended with "God bless you."[30]

One almost might have thought Reagan was on a mission to convert Mikhail Gorbachev personally, a sort of Billy Graham crusade into the heart of communism. When the two men met again, Reagan gave the premier a videotape of a movie, *Friendly Persuasion*, a 1956 Gary Cooper film about Quakers caught in the American Civil War and the necessity of listening to God. Then, after dinner, Reagan concluded yet a third time with "God bless you." The Name of the Lord had likely been mentioned in the halls of the Kremlin more times in Reagan's visit than in the previous forty years.

Dutch, the evangelist, was not finished. After another set of negotiations on May 31, Reagan and Gorbachev walked in Red Square. Gorbachev attempted to lead the Gipper to Lenin's Tomb, but Reagan politely steered him away. The images of the two men before St. Basil's Cathedral could not have been staged better by Jack Warner himself. The highlight of the day, however, came when the president spoke to students at Moscow State University, the Soviet equivalent of Harvard. Though not carried live by Soviet television, excerpts were edited and broadcast later.

Reagan's trip to Moscow often seemed like a Billy Graham crusade designed to lift the godless communists out of their hopeless mire.

If the Berlin Wall speech is Reagan's best remembered—if only for a few lines—the Moscow State speech was viewed by even the Soviets as a "tour de force" and his "finest oratorical hour."[31] Always aware of the scene, Reagan stepped before a huge marble bust of a scowling Lenin—which he recalled as being fifty feet high—turned to briefly consider it, then loudly sighed. Playing off Franklin Roosevelt's "Four Freedoms," Dutch dove right back into faith. Americans are "one of the most religious peoples on Earth," he said, explaining that every American town is dotted with "dozens of churches" and "families of every conceivable nationality worshiping together." The students must have been stunned to hear a sermon coming from the president of the United States. But Reagan tied everything together by noting that liberty was "not earned but a gift from God" and that the United States sought to share that gift with the world."[32] One aide recalled the response as "almost electric, the way he touched the students there."[33] As Dutch received a standing ovation from the young communists, Reagan joked that he turned back to Lenin and saw the statue weeping.

Yet Dutch's sermon was not over. That night at a dinner, again at Spaso House, he launched into the Boris Pasternak poem "The Garden of Gethsemane," where Peter heard, "put your sword in its place, O man." Reagan concluded with the admonition that "we will work together that we might forever keep our swords at our sides."[34]

In retrospect, there is little question that Ronald Reagan saw his mission to Moscow as not one of saving Russia's economic life through capitalism, but of saving its very soul. One could have called the Gipper the Apostle to the atheistic communists and it would have been appropriate. Astonishingly enough, it seemed to have an effect. As Paul Kengor points out, Gorbachev increasingly began to invoke God's name in Reagan's presence ("God help us," or "Let us pray God that..."). These were amazing phrases coming from a nation that had *banned* God, and which, under Marxism, saw the Divine as the source of pain, suffering, and inequality to be banished from all sensible societies. Reagan, after his Moscow trip, returned energized, "infectious," and told Deaver: "He believes." A stunned Deaver knew Dutch meant Gorbachev. "Are you saying the general secretary of the Soviet Union believes in God?" Reagan answered that he didn't know for certain but that "I honestly think he believes in a higher power."[35] Whether he did or did not believe, it is interesting that church leaders began to appear on Soviet television not long afterward. They had never been allowed to appear before Reagan's historic visit.[36]

Official meetings between Gorbachev and Reagan now took a back seat to the intangible movement toward freedom that occurred in Moscow, although the Gipper did take one last opportunity to reverse Marx's maxim, saying to Gorbachev, "The principle of the economy had to be that as you produce, so you earn."[37] Reagan told Margaret Thatcher that it was possible "we are entering a new era in history, a time of lasting change in the Soviet Union." After Reagan's departure, Gorbachev faced new internal opposition, much of which had started with an article written in a Soviet newspaper in the spring of 1988. The article, which challenged Gorbachev's *glasnost* and *perestroika*, called "I Cannot Forsake My Principles," prompted a heated debate in the Politburo, where Gorbachev noted that in fact the article was a prime example of his new "openness" of divergent thought. He started to criticize Stalin and other Soviet leaders, and he allowed dissident writings, including those of Solzhenitsyn, to appear. Whether it was Reagan's influence or not, Gorbachev announced in June 1988 that there would be elections for the body governing the USSR and that the Supreme Soviet would be replaced with an elected Congress of People's Deputies involving elections by secret ballot.

Elections? Secret ballots? In the Soviet Union? There could be no question that whether through military pressure or moral suasion, Ronald Reagan was having a profound influence on the Land of Lenin. Brian Crozier, writing in *National Review*, called the announcement "a gigantic funeral service: the burial of a doctrine."[38] Another, however, might have seen it as a baptism.

Even after Iran-Contra, conflict in the Middle East seemed to remind Americans that peace in that region remained distant. Israel continued to skirmish with neighbors, and the Iran-Iraq war labored on. In May 1987 an Iraqi airplane had fired two missiles at an American ship, the USS *Stark*—an attack the Iraqis claimed was an accident. The *Stark*'s radars and defensive systems failed to track the missiles. Only one of the missiles detonated, but the ensuing explosion was enough to kill thirty-seven crew and wound another twenty-one. The *Stark*'s captain was recommended for a court-martial for failing to take proper defensive measures and shoot down the aircraft. A year later, another American warship off the shore of Iran in international waters, the USS *Vincennes*, picked up an incoming aircraft. Repeated calls to identify "friend or foe" failed, and when the plane reached a dangerous limit, the *Vincennes* followed the procedures the *Stark* had not: the aircraft, an Iranian passenger plane that had veered off course, was destroyed and over three hundred passengers killed. *Proceedings*, the US Naval Institute's magazine, featured columns debating whether the captain acted properly, but he was ultimately cleared, and Reagan thought the captain had followed the only reasonable course.

America's political cycle is unrelenting, and no matter who is in the Oval Office, others want in. George H.W. Bush's patient waiting was over, and it was his turn. He had been a faithful vice president and, in many ways, one of Dutch's closest advisors on some occasions. Now the Gipper had to reward him, though during the primaries Reagan had to keep an arm's-length distance so as to not appear to play favorites. Still, Bush was the expected GOP nominee and had allied himself as closely as possible to Reagan during the campaign. He wrapped it up early, taking a slate of primaries on Super Tuesday in March, ensuring him the nomination at the Republican Convention in August in 1988.

When the Gipper strode on stage for one last national political hurrah, the crowd exploded. Returning to his imagery that had served him his entire political life, Reagan told the delegates, "It was our dream that together we could rescue America and make a new beginning, to create anew that shining city on a hill." Americans, he said, had elected him to make "our nation strong enough to preserve world peace and freedom and to recapture our national destiny." While the challenge had been great, "Americans were used to rising to challenges. And so they had risen during the last eight years."

The auditorium erupted and the cheers prevented him from continuing for some minutes. Reagan finally added, "And George was there." But the Reagan crowd changed from chants of "Reagan! Reagan!" to one embarrassing for both Dutch and the nominee: "Four more years! Four more years!" Reagan again turned the attention to his vice president, describing Bush's task force that eliminated regulations, then reminded the delegates that the battle was still ongoing. Speaking to Bush, he said, "Go out there and win one for the Gipper." Another eruption.

Reagan concluded with a personal touch. He would be leaving for California, where he would mend fences, ride his horses, and clear brush. But, he added, "If the fires ever dim, I'll leave my phone number and address behind just in case you need a foot soldier." Finally, as he prepared for his exit, he said, "I'll be there, as long as words don't leave me and as long as this sweet country strives to be special during its shining moment on earth."[39]

Poor George Bush. There was nothing he could possibly say the following night that would outshine the Gipper. Needless to say, the delegates went wild, with nonstop applause and screaming. Had there been no constitutional amendment, Reagan easily would have walked into a third term.

Bush certainly knew he had to tie his fortunes to Reaganism, and especially to Reaganomics. He declared, in one of the most famous "come back to bite you" sound bites of all time, "Read my lips: no new taxes." Bush had come a long way from "voodoo economics" and now pretended to be an ardent fan, even as the "real" Bush told the convention he wanted a "kinder, gentler nation," a subtle dig at Reagan's budget tightening. An outraged Rush Limbaugh would remind his listeners that conservatism *was* the kinder ideology!

If George H. W. Bush could conceal his liberal nature behind Reagan and his achievements, the reverse was not true for his Democrat opponent Michael Dukakis, former governor of Massachusetts. The diminutive Greek governor—once dubbed "Zorba the Clerk"—ducked the label "liberal," and even leftist *Washington Post* writer David Broder admitted that the Democrats needed to say less about issues to win. Dukakis's vice-presidential choice, Congresswoman Geraldine Ferraro, said that for a Democrat to succeed, "you can be a liberal, but you can't say you're a liberal."[40] Sidney Blumenthal, a virulent left-wing writer, glumly observed that Dukakis was "a man for all vacuums." But Dukakis had far more than liberalism working against him: his record in Massachusetts was atrocious, including his policy of providing prison furloughs for violent criminals. The Willie Horton incident helped further mobilize people against Dukakis when a convicted murderer named Willie Horton raped a woman and stabbed her fiancée while he was out on a furlough during a life sentence without parole. Horton told *USA Today*, "I am for Dukakis."[41]

Much has been made of Bush's landslide victory of 426 electoral votes to 111 for Dukakis as a third term for Reagan. Yet neither 1984 nor 1988 were mandates to do any more than what Reagan had already been doing. Clearly the support for Republican positions in Congress had not seen a sudden shift. And it must be remembered that, as of November 1988, for all intents and purposes the Soviet giant was as formidable as ever and the Cold War was still very much on.

For those who had eyes to see, however, there were powerful signs appearing all over the communist bloc. During the summer of 1988, Poland's puppet dictator, General Wojciech Jaruzelski, responded to massive strikes by Solidarity by allowing opposition candidates to fill one-third of the legislature's lower house and allowing the one hundred senate seats to be open to elections. In a scenario frequently repeated in communist states, the democratic opposition mobilized far faster than expected and in far greater numbers than Western media claimed was possible. Solidarity-associated candidates took all but one of the senate seats and filled all thirty-five lower house seats, and by August the first non-communist prime minister since World War II took office. When Reagan visited Warsaw in 1990, after the Berlin Wall had fallen and Poland was free, he stopped in Gdańsk—the center of Solidarity's resistance—where he received a hero's welcome as shipyard workers and well-wishers sang "Sto Lat" ("May He Live 100 Years").[42] Poles had started a movement to rename public spaces after Reagan, and he was named an honorary citizen of Gdańsk and Krakow. On November 21, 2011, Poles erected the Ronald Reagan monument in Warsaw. The statue of Dutch was unveiled by Lech Wałęsa. Everywhere the air was filled with memories and appreciation for the man about to leave Washington. Margaret Thatcher visited DC, partly to officially congratulate Bush, but unofficially to say goodbye to her long-standing ally and friend. Other than Nancy, only Thatcher ever called Reagan "her Ronnie."

On January 11, 1989, Reagan delivered his farewell address to the nation. As always, it was friendly and folksy. "We've been together eight years," he opened, "and soon it'll be time for me to go.... It's been the honor of my life to be your president." He now got to return to "California, the ranch, and freedom." He then told a story about a ship, a refugee, and a sailor, in which Vietnamese boat people encountered the USS *Midway*. A sailor spotted the boat and a small launch was sent to rescue them. As the boatload of refugees neared the huge carrier, one of the Vietnamese spotted the sailor on deck and shouted, "Hello, freedom man." It struck Reagan that in the 1980s the United States had rediscovered its freedom. Dutch reminisced about the "Reagan revolution," saying, "Well, I'll accept that, but for me it always seemed more like the great rediscovery."

He then recalled a moment during his trip to Moscow:

> Nancy and I decided to break off from the entourage one afternoon to visit the shops on Arbat Street—that's a little street just off Moscow's main shopping area. Even though our visit was a surprise, every Russian there immediately recognized us and called out our names and reached for our hands. We were just about swept away by the warmth. You could almost feel the possibilities in all that joy. But within seconds, a KGB detail pushed their way toward us and began pushing and shoving the people in the crowd. It was an interesting moment. It reminded me that while the man on the street in the Soviet Union yearns for peace, the government is communist. And those who run it are communists, and that means we and they view such issues as freedom and human rights very differently.[43]

Regrets? Yes, he cited the deficit, but then observed, "I've had my share of victories in the Congress, but what few people noticed is that I never won anything you didn't win for me." Of all his accomplishments, Dutch said he was proudest of a "resurgence of national pride that I call the new patriotism." This patriotism, he warned, had to be "informed," and he obliquely suggested that education in America was failing to explain how the United States was exceptional. Specifically urging a new commitment to teaching history "based not on what's in fashion but what's important," Reagan noted that "all great change in America begins at the dinner table." He urged parents to teach "what it means to be an American," and if the parents didn't do it, the children should "let 'em know and nail 'em on it. That would be a very American thing to do."

Ending his magisterial speech with yet another reference to the shining city on a hill, he wasn't sure even after all these years he had properly conveyed the message. In his mind,

> it was a tall, proud city built on rocks stronger than oceans, windswept, God-blessed, and teeming with people of all kinds living in harmony and peace; a city with free ports that hummed with commerce and creativity. And if there had to be city walls, the walls had doors and the doors were open to anyone with the will and the heart to get here. That's how I saw

it, and see it still. And how stands the city on this winter night? More prosperous, more secure, and happier than it was eight years ago. But more than that: after two hundred years, two centuries, she still stands strong and true on the granite ridge, and her glow has held steady no matter what storm. And she's still a beacon, still a magnet for all who must have freedom, for all the pilgrims from all the lost places who are hurtling through the darkness, toward home.

Concluding, Reagan commended all Americans: "We've done our part.... My friends: We did it. We weren't just marking time. We made a difference. We made the city stronger, we made the city freer, and we left her in good hands. All in all, not bad at all."

Winding up with a few interviews with "a jillion P.C.s [personal communications], & letters to sign," Dutch prepared for a dinner where his official portrait would be unveiled. When he saw it, Reagan wasn't thrilled and said the artist "feels that way & is going to make some changes."[44] The following day, he had his final haircut while at the White House, then met with seven hundred members of the staff as the Marine band played "Auld Lang Syne." "Lots of tears," he noted. On January 19, he ended his diary entry with the simple line, "Tomorrow I stop being President."

Then, on January 20, 1989, after a few more photos, he made one last survey of the Oval Office. General Colin Powell, now military advisor, entered: "Mr. President, this is my last briefing for you. I can tell you that the world is quiet today." Reagan replied, "That was nice of you, General. That was a nice thing to say."[45] Dutch conducted another goodbye meeting with yet more staff from ushers to gardeners, then took the limo to the Capitol for Bush's swearing in.

He walked with Nancy to Marine One—now technically named "Nighthawk Two" since he was an ex-president—snapped off a final salute, and turned to give a final wave to the country he had restored. At Andrews Air Force Base on "Special Air Mission" (as Air Force One was renamed), he plopped down and said to the group that accompanied him, "Well, let's set our watches [for California time]."

Ronald Reagan ended his presidential diary with "Then home & the start of our new life."

21

Ebony Veil

Ronald Reagan left office more popular than when he was elected, something Carter, Ford, Nixon, Johnson, and Truman had all failed to achieve. When he touched down in California, an awaiting band played "Happy Trails," the famous Roy Rogers and Dale Evans song. Soon they arrived at 668 St. Cloud in Bel Air, a house purchased by friends for when Reagan retired, which the Reagans bought from them for about $3 million. It was next door to the iconic mansion used in the television series *The Beverly Hillbillies*, and while the Reagans were hardly "hillbillies," their residence was considered the cheapest in the neighborhood.

Reagan's longtime assistant, Fred Ryan, had found him a new presidential office in Century City, which he decorated with appropriate pictures and a small glass dome containing John Hinckley's bullet with the inscription, "This is it!"[1] Ryan, who had been named chief of staff for the post-presidential years, had located the office in 1988 while searching anonymously. Marvin Davis, the owner of Fox Plaza, told him the space was filled, but when Davis learned Ryan was working for Reagan, the room immediately became open—even as the movie *Die Hard* was wrapping up there. A Secret Service agent found "all the props up.... spent gun shells on the ground, fake broken windows."[2]

In his farewell meetings before he left Washington, Reagan used to tell audiences that he planned to "lean back, kick up my feet, and take a long nap. Now, come to think of it, things won't be all that different after all!"[3] In fact, although Dutch was scheduled to take two weeks off, he bounded into the office after only a few days and was back to work. Ryan had no choice but to schedule meetings and calls. Reagan handed him a list of names, which the chief of staff didn't recognize. Dutch said, "Well, they've been calling." Incorrectly installed phone lines had sent callers right past the receptionist to Reagan and he would answer, "This is Ronald Reagan." Usually the caller would ask for an appointment and the ex-president would dutifully jot down the information. Ryan noted, "The average John and Jane Q. Citizens [found] themselves on the line with the former president."[4]

One of the visitors to Reagan's Century City office in 1992 was president-elect Bill Clinton, who was forty-five minutes late. Dutch good-naturedly tried to give Clinton some advice on wasteful spending, but Clinton would have none of it.

When not in the office or on the ranch, Reagan was under some pressure to raise money. In the twenty-first century, the term "the Swamp" came to refer to Washington, whose denizens (far more than even in Reagan's time) mysteriously got rich while in DC. But Reagan returned to California needing a steady income. His Bel Air house wasn't cheap, nor was the Century City office. He found that, as before his presidential run, speaking opportunities abounded and paid well. His regular fee was $50,000 per speech, not at all exorbitant, and he occasionally made up to $2 million per talk. Then there was his book, *An American Life*, based on his diaries, for which he commanded an advance of $5 million. Nancy had her own bookings as well, at $30,000 per speech.[5]

But Reagan also found his retirement interrupted by continued legal demands relating to the Iran-Contra culprits. He was besieged with petitions and informal requests to pardon Oliver North. Just before Reagan left office, even Shultz argued that Reagan should issue a pardon so that North's trial did not drag out national secrets.[6] In fact, Dutch was convinced the judge was not going to permit that and decided against the pardon. He was subpoenaed to testify in North's trial, yet feared that an appearance would violate executive privilege—even if it involved an *ex*-president. In the end, he decided against appearing in that it would "set a precedent that a president doesn't have a right to impose on other presidents."[7] When North was convicted, Reagan stayed quiet. Poindexter's legal team was next, seeking the former president to testify for their client. In February 1990, responding to an order from Judge Harold Greene, Reagan testified via videotape in a closed courtroom, where he responded to over 150 pre-delivered questions. For the most part, Reagan said he either didn't know or had no memory of events at that time. Poindexter was convicted, but the more ominous picture that emerged was one of a confused witness with memory problems.

Meanwhile the special counsel, Lawrence Walsh, was still seeking Reagan's conviction. A bitter partisan, Walsh had gained indictments against North, Poindexter, and McFarlane, all with his eye on Dutch. After viewing the Poindexter trial tape, Walsh had to know that any attempt to question Reagan would make him appear a bully.

Dutch's health had started to decline. The seventy-nine-year-old was in New Mexico at the ranch of friend Bill Wilson over the Fourth of July 1989 when he was pitched from a horse.[8] His head struck a rock, and he was immediately flown to Tucson. Doctors found no broken bones, and after a short time he was released. Back in Los Angeles, however, he had further tests, which revealed a blood clot on the brain. Again, he was released, but the ex-president remained under watch. On their annual trip to the Mayo Clinic in Minnesota, where both Ron and Nancy had physicals, a new clot was discovered and doctors recommended a procedure to drill holes in his head to drain excess fluid. While in good humor as always—he removed his baseball cap for reporters to see the shaved part of his head and quipped, "I guess my barber can have the week off"—it was a serious issue. In a moment that spoke to the future, Boris Yeltsin, who would be the first non-communist to win a free election to lead Russia, visited him while he was in the hospital. The visit portended an earthshaking changing of the guard to come in the former Evil Empire.

Reagan was released, but this time Nancy thought he had been permanently affected by the riding accident: "I've always had the feeling that the severe blow [from the fall] hastened the onset of Ronnie's Alzheimer's."[9] Risk factors for Alzheimer's include head injuries, so she may have been correct.

While at times the "old" Ronald Reagan was there for everyone to see, he struggled more often than not. He did a book tour for *An American Life* in 1990, making the talk show rounds, and generally hosts tried to assist him, even when he fumbled. Those attuned to the "real" Reagan saw a change. His book, however, was a hit, reaching the top of the bestseller lists and bringing in needed income.

Reagan was cognizant enough of the fall of the Berlin Wall to appreciate that it was the result of his efforts—though he would never personally take much credit for it. He and Gorbachev had maintained their correspondence, and when the Russian leader was in America, he made it a point to invite Reagan to a meeting in San Francisco. Dutch and Nancy both went and subsequently invited Gorbachev to the ranch. After another rewarding exchange, they visited Gorbachev in Moscow. There, the Soviet premier told Reagan—a former US president and the man who called his country the "Evil Empire"—"We, the people in Soviet society, hold you in tremendous respect and esteem."[10] Gorbachev's use of the term "the people in Soviet society" could have been a slip, but it was an interesting reference that indicated change: the government no longer was "Soviet society." Reagan appreciated the compliment and issued Gorbachev a veiled caution: "Freedom can bring out passions between groups of people that may boil over. When they do, cool and calm decisions are called for by leaders, so as to lower temperatures all around." Dutch's vision once again was sound as a dollar: before long, the entrenched forces of the Soviet military would react to the increasing democratization of the USSR with a coup that failed. Reagan urged Gorbachev to *ally* with the United States, an unthinkable position just ten years earlier. "Together," he noted, "our great size can be used in the service of all humankind."[11]

Before visiting Moscow, Reagan had a mandatory stop to make in England. There, his old friend Margaret Thatcher knighted him. From England he had gone to France, where Jacques Chirac inducted him into the Academy of Moral and Political Sciences. Subsequent stops included Rome, where Dutch again met with his ally, John Paul II, and then to Poland to celebrate with Lech Wałęsa.

Other than the ruins of the Berlin Wall, no monument better captured the spirit of Reagan than the stately Reagan Presidential Library, which began construction in 1988 and was dedicated on November 4, 1991. After looking at over twenty locations, the Reagan Library team had originally settled on a site at Stanford University. Dutch vetoed that in favor of a site at Simi Valley, where the land was donated by developers Donald Swartz and Gerald Blakeley. Perched on a tall hill, it commands a view of the Pacific and the entire valley. Built at a cost of $57 million, the Mission-style building was the largest of all presidential libraries at an original 153,000 square feet but was expanded to include the 90,000-square-foot hangar for Air Force One, Marine One, and the presidential limousine in a giant pavilion. In addition to a gift shop (which banned Edmund Morris's *Dutch* for its blatant inaccuracies and approach), a walking tour of memorabilia from Reagan's life, and a cafeteria, the library (as do all presidential libraries) housed the documents and papers of the administration, operated under the National Archives and Records Administration. It also contained the offices of the Ronald Reagan Presidential Institute and Foundation, which served as guardians of the Gipper's legacy. In the back of the library, facing the Pacific, was a space for two tombs, one for Ron and one for Nancy. For anyone to be buried at the library, however, required the library director Ralph Bledsoe to expend no small amount of time and energy preparing the paperwork. Also near the rear of the main entrance stood a giant section of the Berlin Wall, a permanent monument to Reagan's vision. The entire design of the facility, from its scenic view to its open courtyard, made it a masterpiece among presidential libraries. At the dedication, four former presidents—Richard Nixon, Gerald Ford, Jimmy Carter, and Reagan—plus then-incumbent George H. W. Bush smiled and posed for photos. It was the first time in history that five presidents had been in the same location. In the months that followed, Reagan would surprise visitors by showing up and strolling through the library.

The eighty-year-old Reagan seemed his old self: he continued to ride horses, work hard physically on the ranch, make speeches, and regularly go to his office. While his successor George Bush had campaigned hard as a conservative and had completed Reagan's goal of enacting a START

Treaty, which Bush and Gorbachev signed in July 1991, there were signs that the "Reagan Revolution" was losing steam. Bush never had the same unwavering support that the Gipper enjoyed and was just one mistake away from losing many Reagan Republicans. He made two. First, in 1990 he signed a bill he had supported and favored, the Americans with Disabilities Act, a civil rights law that prohibited discrimination based on disabilities. Not only did this again expand federal power over the private sector, but it opened up endless lawsuits—including one by a handicapped stripper who claimed discrimination because she could not use a "shower" prop on a stripper stage—against ordinary businesses incapable of paying for major renovations. Then Bush, under pressure from the Democrats about the deficit, found himself reneging on his "Read My Lips" pledge of no new taxes. Agreeing to a Democrat deal (which the Democrats failed to keep), Bush exchanged immediate tax increases for promises of spending cuts that never materialized. Combined with the onset of a mild recession, Bush ensured the end of the Reagan revolution and guaranteed himself a one-term presidency.

When it came time for Reagan to endorse Bush again, however, the Gipper—ever the Republican warrior—stepped up to the plate making yet another patriotic appeal. "After all America had accomplished" in his own two terms and in Bush's first, "its best days are ahead."[12] Though he could still deliver a speech, and though the crowd still loved him with chants of "Rea-gan, Rea-gan," Dutch was a different man. He and Nancy remained active, riding, working, playing golf. But in July 1992, just prior to the convention, he had been required to testify before Lawrence Walsh's seemingly never-ending Iran-Contra investigation.

The testimony was disturbing, revealing that Reagan's memory was fading fast, even for the most basic questions, such as who his secretary of state in 1985 was or whether McFarlane was still on his staff then. "I can't remember," "I take your word for it," and "I think so but I can't swear anymore," Reagan answered, not just once or twice, but in question after question. Even obvious queries that Walsh tried to lead Reagan through proved futile for the prosecutor. After one series, Reagan said, "It's like I wasn't president at all."[13] When Walsh finally ended his six-year witch hunt—five years after the president he was investigating was out of office, and two presidents later—his report found Reagan guilty of no wrongdoing but cited him for lax oversight. Walsh harrumphed through a report that ultimately had no evidence to incriminate Reagan. Dutch's attorney, Theodore Olson (who would be solicitor general under George W. Bush and whose wife, Barbara, was on Flight 77 when it flew into the Pentagon on 9/11) called the Walsh report a "fantasy."[14]

Reagan continued to comment on current events, particularly on defense policy under the new Clinton administration after Bush lost in 1992. When Clinton ended funding for Star Wars in 1993 under the guise of "re-conceptualizing" it due to the demise of the Soviet Union (another of Reagan's great victories), Dutch told graduates of the Citadel, "If we can protect America with a defense shield…we should by all means do so." A perceptive Reagan noted if "Washington thinks we are no longer at risk, they need to open their eyes."[15]

Slowly, however, friends and acquaintances started to notice that Reagan was slipping. At his eighty-second birthday party in 1993, he delivered the same toast twice verbatim to a baffled room. Nancy tried to cover up his memory issues, and after his 1993 Mayo Clinic exam a month after the Walsh testimony, the doctors did not provide any details about Reagan except to say that the physicians found him to be in excellent health. But soon he couldn't remember the name of his ally Phil Gramm, he could barely get through a speech at his eighty-third birthday party in Washington, DC, and in the spring of 1994, his personal doctors grew concerned. Up to that point, he had passed memory tests, but they now were "seeing memory loss that was more than age-appropriate."[16] Nancy decided to request additional tests that August at the yearly exam. The diagnosis confirmed her worst fears: Alzheimer's disease, a devastating, nonreversible deterioration of the brain. However, claims that he was "losing it" during the presidency because he forgot a name or date—or, as he did in Brazil when he toasted Colombia—would have been sloughed off under any other president.[17]

Nancy Reagan was informed of the diagnosis back in Bel Air on a Saturday morning, just before the 1994 election, by Dr. Oliver Beahrs,

Dutch's doctor from the Mayo Clinic. She phoned Fred Ryan and asked him to come to be there when Reagan was told the following day. The two of them accompanied the doctor when he delivered the crushing diagnosis to the ex-president. Reagan "took it in stride" and understood what he was facing. According to Craig Shirley, who chronicled the Gipper's final years, Reagan "almost immediately" went to a small round table and "pulled out a piece of paper and a pen." Ryan asked what he was doing and Dutch replied, "Well, I guess we've got to tell some people about this."[18]

He wrote the final letter himself—choosing not to dictate it—in his own hand. It remains one of the more touching documents in American history and bears complete reprinting here:

Nov. 5, 1994

My Fellow Americans,

I have recently been told I am one of the millions of Americans who will be afflicted with Alzheimer's disease.

Upon learning this news, Nancy and I had to decide whether as private citizens we would keep this a private matter or whether we should make this news known in a public way.

In the past Nancy suffered from breast cancer and I had my cancer surgeries. We found through our open disclosures we were able to raise public awareness. We were happy that as a result many more people underwent testing. They were treated in early stages and able to return to normal, healthy lives.

So now, we feel it is important to share with you. In opening our hearts, we hope this might promote greater awareness of this condition. Perhaps it will encourage a clearer understanding of the individuals and families who are afflicted by it.

At the moment I feel just fine. I intend to live the remainder of the years God gives me on this earth doing the things I have always done. I will continue to share life's journey with my beloved Nancy and my family. I plan to enjoy the great outdoors and stay in touch with my friends and supporters.

Unfortunately, as Alzheimer's Disease progresses, the family often bears a heavy burden. I only wish there was some way I could spare Nancy from this painful experience. When the time comes I am confident that with your help she will face it with faith and courage.

In closing let me thank you, the American people, for giving me the great honor of allowing me to serve as your President. When the Lord calls me home, whenever that may be, I will leave with the greatest love for this country of ours and eternal optimism for its future.

I now begin the journey that will lead me into the sunset of my life. I know that for America there will always be a bright dawn ahead.

Thank you, my friends. May God always bless you.

Sincerely,
Ronald Reagan

As Shirley points out, Reagan must have appreciated the historic nature of his letter because he rarely dated personal letters in handwritten communications. He handed it to Ryan and said, "I guess we should get this typed up." Nancy called the children to relate the diagnosis, and during halftime of the Notre Dame-USC football game, it was announced on national television. Later, Reagan informed the board members of the Reagan Library and personally called friends.

Over the next few years, he continued to go to his Century City office and to visit the library and, of course, go to Rancho del Cielo with Nancy. Increasingly the kids came to visit Reagan at the ranch, but, as Nancy noticed, she would begin to talk to her husband about memories only to catch herself because she would start to say, "Honey, remember when?"[19] At Richard Nixon's funeral in 1994, a tall, healthy-looking Reagan made an appearance, but friends and acquaintances could tell he was slipping.

Dennis LeBlanc, who had been on Reagan's security detail as governor, was hired by the Deaver/Hannaford firm upon Reagan's retirement. He was a friend and came to the ranch frequently. He had been with the Gipper virtually all day several times, helping him do chores. At the end of a physical day, Dutch would say, "We did good today," then discuss their chores for the following day.[20] Steve Colo was the head of Reagan's Secret Service detail and was informed by the doctors after the Alzheimer's diagnosis, "You and your team need to understand that there's going to be some changes." Indeed, Reagan still liked to drive the pair of old jeeps (one with a license plate that read "GIPPER") and ride his favorite horse, El Alamein. Ironically, given his reputation as a cowboy, Reagan often rode English, not western style. At one point early in his run for governor, Reagan posed for a picture in his jodhpurs and high boots with an English saddle, horrifying Lyn Nofziger, who knew that Americans wanted a real cowboy. So Reagan changed, reappearing in Levi's, boots, and a Stetson. Nofziger was happy.

John Barletta, Reagan's closest Secret Service agent, rode frequently with Reagan and even wrote a book about it—*Riding with Reagan: From the White House to the Ranch*. Barletta recalled that a normal ride was over two hours. While Dutch was president, he used to jump his horses, a move that not only concerned Barletta for the president's safety but which required the Secret Service to jump with him! When Reagan reconsidered "for the good of the American people," Barletta said, "Sir, every time you take that jump, I have to take it with you. So on behalf of the Secret Service, I thank you."[21]

After Reagan's Alzheimer's diagnosis, Barletta knew it was only a matter of time until the rides came to an end. At first, Barletta saw the Alzheimer's effects in small ways, such as when he was called in by Reagan. Pointing to the cinch, Dutch said, "John, I know I'm supposed to do something with this, but I can't think of it. Would you help me?" Barletta saw that the Gipper was having trouble remembering how to buckle it, and had it wrong. Often, Reagan would take something in his hand but forget what to do with it. Barletta would help with that too.

The final ride came when El Alamein began acting up. Barletta had to scamper off his own horse and walk next to the president, as otherwise El Alamein was going to pitch him. After the ride, Barletta met with Nancy. "Mrs. Reagan, I don't want to do this," he said. "John," she replied, "we've talked about it." Barletta glumly walked to the house and found Dutch sitting by the fire. "Mr. President," he began, "we had a lot of trouble out there this morning, didn't we?" Reagan responded, "Yeah, I did." (Even in his condition, Reagan would not allow the agent to accept any of the blame.) Barletta continued, "It's just at the point where this riding isn't working out. Sir, I don't think you should ride anymore."

The agent knew this had to tear Reagan up: he loved riding. Instead, Dutch got up, put his hands on Barletta's shoulders, and said, "It's okay, John. I know." Barletta was taken with how, despite the terrible news for him, Reagan "was trying to make *me* feel okay."[22] Agent Steve Colo, in charge of the Reagan detail, had already taken Dutch's pistol—which he had carried since he got shot—out of the Gipper's briefcase. On August 14–15, the Reagans made their last visit to the ranch as a couple. Karl Mull, a hand, noted, "No riding—no work. President has obviously slowed down."[23] Barletta said that on the last visit Reagan slept almost the whole way up and did not recognize the ranch: "I thought we sold this place," he said to Nancy.[24]

Dutch's medical care and inability to provide any more income took its toll on Nancy every bit as much as the emotional drain of his illness. In 1996 Nancy put out feelers to sell the ranch. She soon reached an agreement with Young America's Foundation (YAF) to transfer it for approximately $6 million. YAF, which was a powerful supporter of the president, created a Reagan Ranch Center in Santa Barbara that showcased the story of the ranch and its place in Reagan's life and maintained the ranch itself some twenty miles away. YAF's actions were important for preserving this part of Reagan's life, as the Clinton administration had failed to protect the Reagan ranch as a historic site.

One by one, friends disappeared from Reagan's memory, including Deaver. The president's old friend visited Dutch in 1997 and noted that, while the ex-president was dressed in a blue suit and looked good, "It didn't take long to realize that [he] had no idea who I was." The president, Deaver noted with sadness, was reading a picture book about Robert E. Lee's horse.[25] Michael Reagan, who had grown much closer to his father after the diagnosis, recalled it got to the point where Reagan couldn't talk, and said in 1999 that he hadn't said his name in two years. In 1997, Ron Reagan had admitted his father hadn't recognized him for years. Yet he remained "very lovable" according to Maureen, and Mike could always expect his dad to open his arms for a big hug.[26]

Nancy made an appearance at the 1996 Republican Convention, speaking to an audience who loved Reagan and who, like her, wished they could all have the "old" Ronnie back instead of the candidate they had to put forward that year. Although he would still golf and go to lunch until 1999, he finally went into seclusion in 2001 and the Century City office was closed. In January 2001, while at home, Dutch fell and broke his hip. He was rushed to the hospital for surgery and thereafter was rarely seen in public again. When out in a park, while he didn't speak much with adults, Reagan always talked with children—an ironic final phase for someone who spent such little time with his own children. One of the last people to see him in public, a mother, recalled he was "very gray and very thin."[27] Maureen Reagan died of cancer in August 2001, and Nancy attended her funeral alone. Joanne Drake, who still handled PR requests, found herself with little to say: "He's ninety-three years old. He's had Alzheimer's disease for ten years," she would tell reporters.

Likewise, Nancy made the trip alone to Norfolk in 2001 for the christening of the USS *Ronald Reagan*, then again in 2003 for the ship's commissioning. She also received the Congressional Gold Medal in 2002 on their behalf. Apart from these trips, she found herself at Dutch's side almost without break. Her trips for lunch with her friends had to be at restaurants close to home in case she needed to quickly return. Before long, Dutch was permanently bedridden. In May 2004, word went out to the close set of Reagan confidants that the time was growing near. For three weeks, Reagan's eyes were closed.

A funny thing about presidents, especially since the JFK assassination: people plan for their deaths from the moment they assume office. So it was with Ronald Reagan. Jim Hooley, a long-time advance man, had been assembling the protocol for the Gipper's death since 1981. Yet ironically, Ronald Reagan lived to an older age than any other US president and outlived all of those who were originally chosen to be his pallbearers. Due to the pallbearers dying, Hooley had to continuously revise the funeral plans.

At the Reagan home, Patti, Mike, and Mike's kids had gathered around Reagan's bed, ready for the worst. But the Gipper hung on, and eventually they left to rest. Ron arrived that night. Patti recalled the final moments in her book *The Long Goodbye*:

> My brother [Ron is] sitting beside the hospital bed.... His hand is resting on our Father's back—a back grown thin, the bones sharp and narrow as twigs [and his] breathing even more ragged.... Several moments we think this is it. We tighten the circle around him.... He inhales sharply;

he makes a snoring sound and we laugh through our tears [but just] before one o'clock we know that this really is it. His breathing is telling us.... His face is angled toward my mother's. He opens his eyes—both eyes—wide. They are focused and blue. They haven't been blue like that for more than a year.... My father looks straight at my mother, holds onto the sight of her face for a moment or two, then gently closes his eyes and stops breathing.... [My] mother whispers "That's the greatest gift you could have given me."[28]

Ronald Reagan slipped his mortal coil at 1:09 p.m. Pacific time on June 5, 2004, as the ebony veil descended. Michael, called back, had not arrived in time for his father's passing.

A military honor guard arrived to protect the remains of the president, while a media gaggle appeared outside the Reagan home as word went out. President George W. Bush's eyes welled up—he had been around Reagan as a young man with his father—and he ordered the nation's flags to half-staff. Reagan's casket was transferred to the funeral home around five that evening. From there, an intricate farewell was scheduled for the American people.

From the funeral home, Reagan's body would take a back-and-forth journey from California to DC. First, it would be taken to the Reagan Library where citizens could pay respects, then he would be flown to Washington to lie in state at the US Capitol. There would be a service at the National Cathedral, then he would be transported back to California for a ceremony at the library where he would be buried facing west. A Secret Service agent stayed with the body at all times.

At the private rites at the Reagan Library, citizens lined the forty-mile route, displaying homemade signs in a spontaneous outpouring of love. Thousands of cars from all over the Southwest were already lining up on the Ronald Reagan Freeway. The motorcade passed under a massive American flag that firefighters displayed between two fire engines and then arrived at the Library. A military procession with the coffin preceded Nancy to the library; then, after a short service, the building was opened for private citizens to enter. They came at a rate of two thousand people per hour, with only the sound of weeping penetrating the quiet. Shuttle busses ran people up from parking lots at a nearby community college, and many mourners waited as long as three hours to get on the bus. The library visitations were to end at 6:00 p.m. but thousands remained outside and the hours were extended until 10:00. Even after the "population of a good-sized city" had passed by, thousands of others were turned away. [29] Planners had estimated about 60,000 mourners would show up to Simi Valley, but over 118,000 passed by Dutch's casket at the library.

A stunned media did not know what to make of the spectacle. For years reporters had dismissed Reagan's connection with the American people as "good communication skills." Underestimating the love and support for President Reagan would not be limited to the planners at the Reagan Library. As Dutch was flown to the Capitol to lie in state, planners there estimated the crowds would only be in the thousands.

The president would lie in state in the Capitol Rotunda, one of only twenty-eight people to do so. Most, but not all, were presidents (including Lincoln, Garfield, McKinley, Harding, Taft, Hoover, Kennedy, Johnson, then later, Ford). Non-presidents to lie in state included Senator Henry Clay, Generals Douglas MacArthur and John Pershing, and the unknown soldiers of both world wars and the Korean War, as well as J. Edgar Hoover and other prominent individuals, such as Pierre L'Enfant, Admiral George Dewey, Billy Graham, and Vice President Hubert Humphrey. Lying in state did not de facto constitute a "state funeral," and both Nixon and FDR had state funerals without lying in state. Naturally, coming just three years after 9/11, the funeral would become a massive security event.

Reagan's plane arrived on June 9. From the airport, the president's coffin was taken to Constitution Avenue, where it was placed on a caisson for the official procession. Amidst twenty-one-gun salutes, the transport arrived at the Capitol for a 7:00 p.m. funeral service. Members of the current and Reagan administrations and the diplomatic corps attended; there was a secret "Do Not Admit" list that included Oliver North. Margaret Thatcher, a surprising attendee given her health, upon leaving curtsied and "gently touched the flag."[30] After the service, the doors of the Capitol opened to the public, with five guards from the service branches rotating every thirty minutes. Plans called for the Rotunda to be open Wednesday night, Thursday, and Thursday night, closing on Friday morning. Officials thought that amount of time would be sufficient for all to pay their respects.

Were they ever mistaken!

Outside, a line of ordinary people began to grow, and, even as it became clear that all would not get inside before Friday, people still waited and the line still grew. By 9:00 a.m. after the Wednesday night service, Capitol Police estimated that already thirty thousand had passed the coffin. Even in death, however, the petty partisanship still remained: the AFL-CIO refused to close on Friday, the national day of mourning—for the only president to ever head a labor union! The vast crowds who showed up to pay their respects, however, showed how out of touch the union was: when it came time for the funeral procession to take the body to National Cathedral for the final service, Park Police estimated 104,684 had passed the coffin. Another 1,324 were admitted into the West Front Lawn.[31]

The procession moved to the Cathedral Church of Saint Peter and Saint Paul, better known as the Washington National Cathedral. People were admitted by tickets to a service that Reagan had wanted to be led by the Reverend Billy Graham. But the famed evangelist's health was too fragile, and Senator John Danforth, an Episcopalian minister, handled the service. Inside the cathedral was the "largest gathering of past and present officialdom the world had seen" for several decades. In addition to Gorbachev, Lech Wałęsa, former presidents Carter, Ford, and Bush, and current president George W. Bush, 25 other heads of state were present, along with 180 ambassadors or foreign ministers.[32] Almost every living cabinet member of Reagan's administration was in attendance. Nancy and the family entered and moved to the front, and then the casket was brought in. Speakers included former president Bush, the current president Bush, former Canadian prime minister Brian Mulroney, and Margaret Thatcher, who said

> With the lever of American patriotism, he lifted up the world. And so today, the world—in Prague, in Budapest, in Warsaw and Sofia, in Bucharest, in Kiev, and in Moscow itself, the world mourns the passing of the great liberator and echoes his prayer: God Bless America.... We here still move in twilight, but we have one beacon to guide us that Ronald Reagan never had. We have his example.[33]

Former president George H. W. Bush observed that it would not take one hundred years to thank God for Reagan. But his son, President George Bush, provided even more emotional comments:

> Ronald Reagan belongs to the ages now, but we preferred it when he belonged to us. When he saw evil camped across the horizon he called that evil by its name. There were no doubters in the prisons and gulags, where dissidents spread the news, tapping to each other in code what the American president had dared to say. There were no doubters in the shipyards and churches and secret labor meetings, where brave men and women began to hear the creaking and rumbling of a collapsing empire.... In his last years he saw through a glass darkly. Now he sees his Savior face-to-face.[34]

After the service, the coffin was taken to Andrews Air Force Base for his final trip to California. As the plane flew over Tampico, Illinois, it dipped its wings in honor of Dutch's hometown. Landing at Point Mugu's naval air station, a Marine band struck up "Hail to the Chief." Ronald Reagan made his final trip to his library. Once again, an unmatched spontaneous demonstration of affection occurred as hundreds of thousands of people lined the thirty miles from Point Mugu to the Reagan Library. Jim Lake, the son of Reagan's press aide Jim Lake, watched in stunned silence at "farm workers in the fields...stopped working and stood...with their hats held over their hearts," and at fire engines with giant American flags flying, and people saluting, most of them crying.[35] Arriving at a sea of flowers, Nancy and the family took their places as the sun literally set in the west. Three Reagan children spoke, though just earlier Patti had told *Newsweek*, "I resented the country at times for its demands on him, its ownership of him."[36] As the final speaker concluded, the sun set.

Despite having had nonstop coverage all week, Reagan's funeral was one of the ten most watched events in the history of broadcasting. The coverage of the death of the first president to die in the twenty-first century was seen by twenty-one million viewers.[37]

That night, at a private event at the Bel Air Hotel, the family met with many of the dignitaries who had attended the funeral. The following morning, Michael Reagan saw Margaret Thatcher at breakfast. As the two spoke,

Lady Thatcher mused about what would have happened if Ronald Reagan had taken the presidency in 1976. What additional victories would they have won? Michael responded that in fact the Cold War would have lasted longer because his father needed allies to bring down the Iron Curtain, yet in 1976, none of them were in place—not even the Iron Lady. Pope John Paul II did not arrive until 1978, and Thatcher herself didn't get elected prime minister until 1979, when Wałęsa came on the scene. And Gorbachev, perhaps the final piece, didn't attain power until 1985. "It took all of you," Michael told Thatcher, "working together, to end the Cold War. I think God's providence put you and Dad and every other player in position at just the right moment in history."[38]

Michael was right to a point. Possibly without some of Dutch's allies, he might not have achieved what many thought impossible. For the most part, however, it was Reagan's vision and energy that carried them, that steadily weakened the USSR so that Wałęsa *could* be successful, or so that the message of John Paul II *could* be received. It was Radio Free Europe that slowly eroded the militaristic Soviet culture and had East-bloc kids longing to be Americans...not kill them. It was Reagan's secret war in Afghanistan that handed the Soviets their first postwar military defeat. Reagan designed the energy policies that stripped away the USSR's hard cash. Reagan followed through on the Euromissiles, forcing Gorbachev to the bargaining table. And most of all, Reagan—almost alone in his faith—pushed SDI into existence as a research project, knowing that above all other initiatives, it posed a threat to the Soviet Union that would force its collapse.

On the domestic front, Reagan, often with only a handful of advisors, believed in the supply-side tax cuts that could revive America. His energy revolution greatly eased the oil crunch that had plagued America for a decade. Deregulating as much as he could, Reagan freed America's powerful economic engine.

Even where he made mistakes, as with the Contras or the hostages, they were done for humane reasons—liberating people both specifically and in the abstract. While the Marine barracks bombing was a horrible mistake, it caused Reagan, alone among almost all other political leaders, to begin to see Islam as the root cause of terrorism in the Middle East. The

United States would suffer greatly because his successors did not examine and expand upon those views.

Above all, Reagan was the first president since John F. Kennedy to appeal to Americans' sense of exceptionalism and greatness as a people. JFK looked to the moon; Dutch looked to a peaceful earth. Neither apologized for America's greatness or, most of all, for America's goodness. Both called on citizens to recommit themselves to the American dream and to the vision of a greater—not lesser—future. After the Vietnam War, Watergate, the energy crisis, and Jimmy Carter's crisis of confidence, Americans threw off the mantle of weakness and doubt, fear and helplessness, and won one for the Gipper.

Acknowledgments

Because the key contributions of this book come from Reagan's papers, it goes without saying that I owe the greatest debt of gratitude to the archivists and staff of the Ronald Reagan Presidential Library and National Archives and Records Administration in Simi Valley. None assisted me more by digging out lost citations or pointing me to the most relevant files than Jennifer Mandel. Thanks also to Michael Pinkney for help in identifying photos.

Valerie Yaros, archivist and historian at the Screen Actors Guild/American Federation of Television and Radio Artists, saved me from countless errors and pointed me to key documents in Reagan's Hollywood years. Likewise, the University of Dayton provided research support for many trips to the Reagan Library.

Special research help on the topic of energy was provided by Frederick Cedoz, once a student and now an oil executive in his own right. Thanks also to David Culbert, who directed me to fascinating research on Leni Riefenstahl's reception in Hollywood. As mentioned in the introduction, this book did not rely heavily on interviews: that is well-plowed ground. But I did benefit from discussions with Michael Reagan, Joseph Wright, the late William Verity, Craig Shirley, Joe Morris, John Morris, and Robert Barthelemy of the X-30 program. Also thanks to Ron Robinson and Young America's Foundation for allowing me time at the Reagan Ranch. Once again, thanks to all the rock and rollers who gave me their time in filming

Rockin' the Wall. Brett Smith provided the iconic artwork of "Morning in America."

Any book is a collaborative effort among writer, agent, editor, and publisher. Thanks to my agent Roger Williams for his continued faith in me; to Jon Ford, my excellent editor; and to Post Hill Press and Anthony Ziccardi for seeing this to fruition.

Appendix: Brothers Separated by Three Decades?

To many Reaganites, comparisons with Donald Trump, the forty-fifth president of the United States, are sacrilegious. For many true believers, the brash and occasionally profane Trump is as far from the good-natured, funny, self-deprecating Gipper as possible. But the comparisons bear examining and are far more extensive than one might think.

Age

At the time of their elections, each man was the oldest president to ever assume office (Reagan at sixty-nine, Trump at seventy). Reagan, more than Trump, was tagged with lacking energy, or was said to need a nap in the afternoon. (Few sixty-nine-year-olds don't!) His close associates however marveled at his energy and stamina, and his love of physical work on the ranch was a source of amazement. Trump, on the other hand, is one of those rare people who survives on just a few hours sleep a night. I interviewed Steve Bannon, Trump's strategist, in 2016 and asked an aide, "Does he sleep?" and the aide replied, "Not much." I said, "How about Trump?" and the aide said, "Less than Bannon."

Path to the Presidency

Lou Cannon wrote, "No other president ever reached the White House by the road that Ronald Reagan traveled, and the path he traveled is no longer there."[1] Trump proved Cannon wrong. Both men took a nonpolitical route to the White House, with Reagan the "more political" of the two, having served as governor of California. Still, each for the better part of his life was something other than a politician (and, in Trump's case, was *never* a politician).

Showbiz

Both Reagan and Trump had a strong show business background, Reagan obviously in movies, then *General Electric Theater* and *Death Valley Days*, and Trump in *The Apprentice*. These were the only two American presidents to hold a SAG/AFTRA card for something other than a cameo or bit part. Although each man internalized the lessons of show business differently, both clearly knew the importance of stagecraft—Reagan with his televised speeches, Trump with his rallies.

Revolutionary Means of Communicating to the Public

Reagan ascended at the high point of television, when homes still got their programming from one of three sources: ABC, NBC, or CBS. This proved crucial, as the networks—because of this structure—*had* to carry presidential addresses as part of their "public service" commitment. Thus, Reagan could go over the heads of the news media of the day through forty-five-minute national speeches that were seen by very large segments of the American public. Rarely did these fail him—his first Iran-Contra speech and his earlier plea for help for the Contras were about the only two instances where Reagan failed to elicit enough pressure on Congress to force action.

Trump emerged in a totally different era, where the big three networks had lost massive market share to cable television and the internet and where many viewers were completely "unplugged" from networks, watching entertainment and news on handheld devices. In the primaries, Trump found he did not need to spend massive advertising dollars on ads that ran on traditional television because it was wasted money. (Indeed, subsequent studies would find that his opponent in the general election outspent him roughly ten-to-one, yet lost.) Instead, Trump turned to free media coverage generated by his blustery personality...but the media willingly played along and gave him millions of dollars worth of free coverage. Then there was the new phenomenon, Twitter, which at the time was a forum limited to 140 words. Trump, even more than Barack Obama, mastered Twitter, and his Tweets went out daily to over one hundred million Americans. At one time in the primary, Trump had more Twitter followers than every other Republican candidate in the race *put together*.[2]

Perhaps even more than free media and Twitter, Trump realized that, just as Dutch had gone over the heads of the established media, so he also could make an "end run." He held dozens of giant rallies, sometimes two a day. These were denigrated as "preaching to the choir," but the experts missed the key element of Trump's rallies, which was their penetration of local markets via *local* news that carried with it no additional commentary by "talking heads." In market after market, Trump got his message out despite 93 percent negative coverage by the mainstream media.

Reagan had not faced nearly as hostile a media in the 1980s—but he did not have friends in the press. Each man had to neuter news coverage, or reshape it, to have any chance at success.

Government by Advisors

Both Reagan and Trump were accused of being mere puppets for more powerful advisors. To reporters such as Lou Cannon, Reagan was directed by George Shultz, Ed Meese, Jim Baker, and Mike Deaver. To modern pundits, Trump can't possibly design policies—they *must* have been done by H. R. McMaster, or Rex Tillerson, or even his son-in-law, Jared Kushner. Both assessments rest on the misunderstanding of how many decision-makers operate. Reagan and Trump both wanted disparate voices in their administrations. They sought out, if not "no" men, at least advisors who would not just go along to impress the boss. Anyone watching *The Apprentice* would have seen this at work in Trump's assessment of those he chose to win the apprenticeship. In meetings, Reagan would frequently let every advisor at the table have his say, sometimes arguing with each other. He would end the meeting, often with a story that left everyone puzzled about whether he understood the issues. Then a decision brief would be provided that would precisely capture the positions and the direction the president intended to take. Likewise, Trump turned his generals loose, freed his secretary of state to bring him deals, and took positions that even his chief of staff did not like—but only after he had input from everyone.

Divorced

Both men were divorced before coming into office, the only two American presidents to have had failed marriages. Both had adult children when they assumed the presidency. Both were strongly supported by the religious and evangelical community. Both won surprisingly easy victories in their first national election. Both had to deal with a special prosecutor.

Underestimated

Both Reagan and Trump were continually underestimated during their political lives. Both men played on that factor and even thrived because of it.

Most of all, though, each man's love for America was undeniable. There is a photo of Reagan kissing an American flag, and a photo of Trump hugging Old Glory. Each man spoke with love, reverence, and awe of the United States and its heritage. Whereas Barack Obama would enter in jogging clothes, neither Reagan nor Trump would enter the Oval Office without a coat and tie. Only the most rabid partisans would fail to admit that both men wanted only the best for the United States of America.

Despite these many similarities, there were of course some significant differences, mostly of temperament. Dutch was generally self-deprecating and used humor as a weapon. That had been honed during hundreds and hundreds of speeches in his union and GE days. Trump, a construction magnate, had battled unions on the ground and grumpy stockholders in the boardroom. He was much more prone to sarcasm and responded to attacks rather than dismissed them with a joke. Reagan rarely got even, though his diaries show a few instances where, when he felt betrayed, he vowed never to help a fellow Republican again. Trump was quick to fire back, but also quick to forgive. Several of his earlier political critics, including Senators Ted Cruz, Ron Johnson, and Lindsey Graham, were within a year viewed as key allies.

Endnotes

INTRODUCTION

1. Dinesh D'Souza, *Ronald Reagan: How an Ordinary Man Became an Extraordinary Leader* (New York: Touchstone, 1997), 7.
2. Ibid., 8; and William Strauss and Neil Howe, *Generations: The History of America's Future, 1584 to 2069* (New York: William Morrow, 1991).
3. H. W. Brands, *Reagan: The Life* (New York: Doubleday, 2015).
4. D'Souza, *Ronald Reagan*, 9.
5. Ibid., 37.
6. Craig Shirley, *Last Act: The Final Years and Emerging Legacy of Ronald Reagan* (New York: Nelson Books, 2015), 80.
7. Peggy Noonan, *When Character Was King: A Story of Ronald Reagan* (New York: Penguin, 2001), 50.
8. Ronald Reagan, *Abortion and the Conscience of the Nation* (Nashville: Thomas Nelson, 1984).
9. Steven F. Hayward, *The Age of Reagan: The Fall of the Old Liberal Order, 1964–1980* (New York: Three River Press, 2001), 631–32.
10. Lou Cannon, *President Reagan: The Role of a Lifetime* (New York: Simon & Schuster, 1991).
11. "Instructions for the Shultz-Gromyko Meeting in Geneva," 1 November, 1985, National Security Decision Directive (NSDD) 153, Box 1, Folder 151-160, Reagan Library (RL).
12. Cannon, *Governor Reagan: His Rise to Power* (New York: Public Affairs, 2003), 470.
13. Jim Kuypers, *Partisan Journalism: A History of Media Bias in the United States* (Lanham: Rowman & Littlefield, 2013). A useful study would be to record the number of reports of Barack Obama's painful gaffes—saying there were "fifty-seven states" or calling a US Navy corpsman a "corpse-man" with those of George W. Bush or Donald Trump, who was castigated merely for calling a "category 5 hurricane" a "class 5 hurricane."
14. Brands, *Reagan: The Life*, 734; and Noonan, *When Character Was King*, 41.
15. Noonan, *When Character Was King*, 12–13.

CHAPTER 1

1. Reagan himself in *An American Life* (New York: Pocket Books, 1990), 22, remembered the building as a bank, but at the time the Reagans first lived there it was a bakery. By the time the Reagans moved back, First National Bank had taken the space. Thanks to Joan Johnson, manager of the Tampico website "The Wisp" for this clarification.

2. Anne Edwards, *Early Reagan: The Rise to Power* (London: Taylor Trade Publishing, 1987), 25.

3. Peter Hannaford, *Reagan's Roots: The People and Places That Shaped His Character* (Bennington: Images from the Past, 2012), 1.

4. For example, Peter Wallison, Reagan's former Treasury counsel, claimed Reagan had "no peculiarities of personality; there was nothing particularly colorful about him" and that his "*only* interest was policy" (*Ronald Reagan: The Power of Conviction and the Success of His Presidency* [Boulder: Westview Press, 2004]). To Wallison, Reagan "was a kind, old-fashioned, formal, and intelligent man" and "a shy man who did not like to talk about himself." Yet these do not constitute the *absence* of personality—quite the contrary. They appear so in our modern, celebrity-obsessed, reality-TV culture, but in fact they are the essence of personality—an essence shared by millions of people at one time when it was not fashionable to talk about oneself or to constantly emote, anticipating the ubiquitous camera will be focused on "me." With the exception of blustery individuals such as Samuel Colt, Theodore Roosevelt, or P. T. Barnum, Reagan was typical of generations of Americans who let their lives do the talking. What others saw as "personality" was more often than not a series of often serious (and occasionally fatal) character flaws that individuals such as Andrew Jackson, Franklin D. Roosevelt, John F. Kennedy, Lyndon B. Johnson, and more recently Bill Clinton and Barack Obama exhibited but overcame to one degree or another.

5. William Strauss and Neil Howe, *Generations: The History of America's Future, 1584–2069* (New York: William Morrow, 1991), 261–3.

6. Edwards, *Early Reagan*, 33–34.

7. Ibid., quoting the *Tampico Tornado*.

8. Reagan, in his autobiography, embellished by adding to Jack's comment, ". . . who knows, he might grow up to be president someday." But no one else recorded this. (Reagan, *An American Life*, 23).

9. Ibid. However, Reagan said ". . . as soon as I could, I asked people to call me 'Dutch.'" In fact, the family had taken to calling Ronald "Dutch" long before he was old enough to ask for the name.

10. Edwards, *Early Reagan*, 33.

11. Recently renamed "Reagan Park."

12. Edwards, *Early Reagan*, 35; and *Tampico Tornado*, February 4, 1984.

13. Hannaford, *Reagan's Roots*, 19.

14. Ronald Reagan with Richard G. Hubler, *Where's the Rest of Me?*, (New York: Dell, 1965), 11.

15. Edwards, *Early Reagan*, 57.

16. Reagan, *An American Life*, 24.

17. Ibid.

18. Scott Derks, *Working Americans, 1880–1999: Volume I: The Working Class* (Lakeville: Grey House Publishing, 2000), 115, 128.

19. Ibid., 128.

20. Derks, *The Value of a Dollar: Prices and Incomes in the United States, 1860–2009* (Amenia: Grey House Publishing, 100–2.

21. Edwards, *Early Reagan*, 57.

22. Reagan, *Where's the Rest of Me?*, 16; and Edwards, *Early Reagan*, 36.

23. Although Patti Davis, Reagan's daughter, later claimed "he couldn't really *rely* on his father," the things expected of men and fathers in that time differed substantially from post-World War II men. As long as fathers paid the bills and provided necessary discipline, that was often viewed as all that was needed to perform one's fatherly roles (Patti Davis interview, *Ronald Reagan: A Legacy Remembered*. Produced by the History Channel. United States, 2003. Documentary.). In short, measuring Dutch and Jack's relationship by twenty-first or even late twentieth-century standards would be inaccurate.

24. Edwards, *Early Reagan*, 42.

25. Reagan, *Where's the Rest of Me?*, 19–20, 42.

26. Ibid.

27. Ibid., 25.

28. Patti Jones, "The Brainy Benefits of Bedtime Stories," July 9, 2015, http://ladywiththealligat.wixsite.com/literacy-resources/single-post/2015/07/09/The-Brainy-Benefits-of-Bedtime-Stories. "There's a clear indication of a neurological difference between kids who have been regularly read to and kids who have not," notes G. Reid Lyon, a scholar cited in the article.

29. Reagan, *Where's the Rest of Me?*, 11.

30. Reagan, *An American Life*, 24.

31. Ibid., 25.

32. William became surly when drunk and, in 1912, became so ill with alcohol problems (including delirium) Jack feared he might hurt himself or someone else. After five years of petitioning for a legal declaration of insanity for William, the court approved the petition, and William was committed, dying in the institution in 1925.

33. Reagan, *Where's the Rest of Me?*, 14.

34. Ibid.

35. Edwards, *Early Reagan*, 36.

36. Edwards incorrectly has his entry as February 1916, but it was later that year.

37. Reagan, *An American Life*, 24.

38. Neal Gabler, *Walt Disney: The Triumph of the American Imagination* (New York: Vintage, 2006), 11.

39. Ibid., 18. As Gabler wrote, "It was not just the homely appearance of Marceline or the cultural rites of passage he experienced there that Walt Disney loved and remembered and would burnish for the rest of his life; it was also the spirit of the community. In Marceline people cared for one another and were tolerant of one another." Everything "was done in a community help," Walt said. "One farmer would help the other, they'd go and help repair fences" (Ibid., 13).

40. Edwards, *Early Reagan*, 39.

41. Ibid., 38.

42. Paul Kengor, *God and Ronald Reagan* (New York: ReganBooks, 2004), 8.

43. Ibid., 8. Also see information at the Reagan Boyhood Home, 816 South Hennepin Ave., Dixon, Illinois.

44. Edwards, *Early Reagan*, 62–63, citing *Motion Picture*, 1937.

45. United States Department of Health and Human Services, "Great Pandemic: The United States in 1918–1919," archived March 5, 2009, https://cybercemetery.unt. edu/archive/allcollections/20090305010427/http://vietnamese.pandemicflu.gov/pandemicflu/envi/24/_1918_pandemicflu_gov/index.htm.

46. Hannaford, *Reagan's Roots*, 29.

47. Edwards, *Early Reagan*, 39.

48. Reagan (*An American Life*, 24) recalled contracting pneumonia while in Chicago, but he also wrote that "while I was recuperating one of our neighbors brought me several of his son's lead soldiers," suggesting it is likely that he had the wrong location. He recalled that when he finally felt better, "The sun streamed through the window and I felt like a king with an army of 500" (Edwards, *Early Reagan*, 40).

49. Joan Johnson, "Tampico, Illinois" *Illinois Heritage*, January February 2011), cited in Hannaford, *Reagan's Roots*, 36–37

50. Edwards, *Early Reagan*, 42.

51. Kengor, *God and Ronald Reagan*, 7.

52. Reagan, *Where's the Rest of Me?*, 20.

53. Ibid., 21.

54. Ibid., 23.

55. Edwards, *Early Reagan*, 45. A useful snapshot of Nelle Reagan is in Gordon P. Gardiner, "Nelle Reagan: Mother of Ronald Reagan, President of the United States," *Bread of Life* 30 (May 1981): http://breadoflifemagazine.com/pages/198105.html.

56. Edwards, *Early Reagan*, 55.

57. Reagan, *Where's the Rest of Me?*, 24. In contrast, one searches in vain for similar "feel-good" memories of Bill Clinton in his autobiography, *My Life* (New York: Knopf, 2004), although George W. Bush's memoir (*Decision Points* [New York: Crown, 2010], 5–6) contains similar nostalgic memories of Bush's childhood in Midland playing baseball with his father.

58. Reagan, *Where's the Rest of Me?*, 25.

59. Edwards, *Early Reagan*, 53.

60. Ibid., 53.

61. Reagan, *Where's the Rest of Me?*, 13.

62. Kengor, *God and Ronald Reagan*, 17. Kengor established Reagan's age as eleven when he was born again, although Reagan himself once said he was twelve.

63. Ibid., 18

64. Reagan wrote this to Wright's daughter-in-law, Jean H. Wright, on March 13, 1984, copy in the Dixon Public Library. See Reagan's reference to the book in *An American Life*, 32.

65. As Lynne Doti and I note in *American Entrepreneur*, the myth of Horatio Alger that the Left cites—that there are no "rags to riches" stories in America, misses the point of the Horatio Alger books entirely in that the stories did *not* depict someone getting ahead by hard work, but rather in almost every occasion by a fortunate meeting with a man of means. In other words, the Horatio Alger stories were all about "who you

know." (Larry Schweikart and Lynne Pierson Doti, *American Entrepreneur* (New York: Amacom, 2009), 190–92.

66. Kengor, *God and Ronald Reagan*, 21; and Harold Bell Wright, *That Printer of Udell's* (New York: A. L. Burt Company Publishers, 1903), 118–19, 206.

67. Kengor, *God and Ronald Reagan*, 23; and Wright, *That Printer of Udell's*, 122–23.

68. Kengor, *God and Ronald Reagan*, 23.

69. Reagan, *Where's the Rest of Me?*, 12.

70. Ibid., 12.

71. Kengor, *God and Ronald Reagan*, 28.

72. Norman E. Wymbs, *Ronald Reagan's Crusade* (Lauderdale-by-the-Sea: Skyline Publications, 1997), 154–55, 164–65; and Kengor, *God and Ronald Reagan*, 30.

73. Kengor, *God and Ronald Reagan*, 31; and Wymbs, *Ronald Reagan's Crusade*, 158.

74. Kengor, *God and Ronald Reagan*, 34.

75. Edwards, *Early Reagan*, 63.

76. Reagan, *An American Life*, 39–40.

77. Ibid., 39.

78. Ibid., 40.

79. Reagan, *Where's the Rest of Me?*, 28.

80. Edwards, *Early Reagan*, 64.

81. Ibid., 65.

82. Ibid.

83. Reagan, *Where's the Rest of Me?*, 27.

84. Ibid., 27.

85. Ibid., 28. Marc Eliot, in *Reagan: The Hollywood Years* (New York: Harmony Books, 2008), claims, based on a plaque in Dixon, that all the victims were women. But in fact, as seen in the news story cited in Edmund Morris (*Dutch: A Memoir of Ronald Reagan* [New York: Modern Library, 1999], 62), at least one of those was a man. Eliot, wading into heavy waters of psychoanalysis, claims that Reagan was really seeking Margaret's approval and her elevation of him to hero status. He cites Nancy Reagan's skepticism about his feats, but in fact evidence has surfaced for two of these rescues, plus the little girl at his inauguration party, which is caught in photographs.

86. Morris, *Dutch*, 62.

87. "I Never Think of Him as Ronald," *Dixon Telegraph*, June 18, 2011.

88. Hannaford, *Reagan's Roots*, 62–63.

89. Edwards, *Early Reagan*, 65.

90. Reagan said this to Joseph A. Pecorato, president of the US Lifesaving Association, July 17, 1986. Kengor interview with Pecorato on October 6, 2004 (Kengor, *The Crusader: Ronald Reagan and the Fall of Communism* [New York: ReganBooks, 2006], 325. Pecorato mentioned this previously in a letter published in the *Lifeguard*, the official publication of the US Lifesaving Association, Autumn 1986).

91. Ron Reagan, in *Ronald Reagan: A Legacy Remembered*. Produced by the History Channel. United States, 2003. Documentary.

92. Kengor, interview with Bill Clark, July 17, 2003, in Kengor, *The Crusader*, 325.

93. Edwards, *Early Reagan*, 66; and *Dixonian* (1928): 92.

94. Edwards, *Early Reagan*, 69.

95. Ibid., 71–72.

96. Ibid., 74.
97. Reagan, *Where's the Rest of Me?*, 29.
98. Stephen Vaughn, "The Moral Inheritance of a President: Reagan and the Dixon Disciples of Christ," in eds. Michael W. Casey and Douglas A. Foster, *The Stone-Campbell Movement: An International Religious Tradition* (Knoxville: University of Tennessee Press, 2002), 248–68.
99. Reagan, *Where's the Rest of Me?*, 30.

CHAPTER 2

1. Anne Edwards, *Early Reagan: The Rise to Power* (London: Taylor Trade Publishing, 1987), 81–82.
2. *Pegasus,* 41, no. 1, September 24, 1928.
3. Ronald Reagan, *An American Life* (New York: Pocket Books, 1990), 46.
4. H. W. Brands, *Reagan: The Life* (New York: Doubleday, 2015), 20.
5. Reagan, *An American Life,* 45; and Ronald Reagan with Richard G. Hubler, *Where's the Rest of Me?* (New York: Dell, 1965), 31.
6. Edwards, *Early Reagan,* 87.
7. Reagan, *Where's the Rest of Me?*, 32.
8. Ibid., 32.
9. Edwards, *Early Reagan,* 87.
10. Ibid.
11. Edwards, *Early Reagan,* 88.
12. Larry Schweikart and Lynne Pierson Doti, *American Entrepreneur* (New York: Amacom, 2009), 296–300.
13. Ibid., 296.
14. James Bovard, *The Farm Fiasco* (San Francisco: Institute for Contemporary Studies, 1989), 13.
15. Edwards, *Early Reagan,* 91.
16. Reagan, *Where's the Rest of Me?*, 37.
17. Ibid.
18. Ibid.
19. Ibid., 39.
20. Reagan, *An American Life,* 49.
21. Larry Schweikart and Lynne Pierson Doti, *Banking in the American West from the Gold Rush to Deregulation* (Norman: University of Oklahoma Press, 1991), 105; and Lee J. Alston, Wayne A. Grove, and David C. Wheelock, "Why Do Banks Fail? Evidence from the 1920s," *Explorations in Economic History 31* (1994): 409–431.
22. Mark Guglielmo, "Illinois Bank Failures During the Great Depression," unpublished paper, 2002, http://s3.amazonaws.com/zanran_storage/www.uic.edu/ContentPages/25537147.pdf.
23. Alvin S. Felzenberg, "Calvin Coolidge and Race: His Record in Dealing with the Racial Tensions in the 1920s," *New England Journal of History* 55 (Fall 1988): 83–96.
24. Reagan, *An American Life,* 54.
25. Ibid.
26. Lou Cannon, *Governor Reagan: His Rise to Power* (New York: Public Affairs, 2003), 32.
27. Ibid.

28. Hannford, *Reagan's Roots,* 97.
29. Stephen Vaughn, "The Moral Inheritance of a President: Reagan and the Dixon Disciples of Christ," in eds. Michael W. Casey and Douglas A. Foster, *The Stone-Campbell Movement: An International Religious Tradition* (Knoxville: University of Tennessee Press, 2002), 248–68 (quotation on 254).
30. Reagan, *An American Life,* 57.
31. Edwards, *Early Reagan,* 112.
32. Reagan, *Where's the Rest of Me?,* 60.
33. Reagan, *An American Life,* 61. In his earlier book, *Where's the Rest of Me?* Reagan noted that simply growing older had sent them along "divergent paths" and that "our love and wholesome relationship did not survive growing up," 55.
34. Reagan, *Where's the Rest of Me?,* 56.
35. Edwards, *Early Reagan,* 172.
36. Ibid., 122, 172.
37. Reagan, *Where's the Rest of Me?,* 60.
38. Ibid.
39. Ibid., 62.
40. Edwards, *Early Reagan,* 125.
41. Scott Derks, *The Value of a Dollar: Prices and Incomes in the United States, 1860–2009* (Amenia: Grey House Publishing, 2009), 206.
42. Reagan, *Where's the Rest of Me?,* 66.
43. Ibid., 63.
44. Ibid.
45. Reagan, *An American Life,* 66.
46. Ibid., 67.
47. Ibid.
48. Burton Folsom Jr., *New Deal or Raw Deal?* (New York: Threshold, 2008), 79.
49. Reagan, *An American Life,* 69.
50. In *Early Reagan,* Edwards claims the batter was Augie Galan (137), the same batter Reagan identified in *Where's the Rest of Me?* (79). But Reagan says the batter was Billy Jurges in *An American Life* (73). The only scoreless game in the last innings with Dean pitching against the Cubs was on August 31, 1934, and Galan batted five times. Reagan also said it was a "scoreless tie," but there was no such game. Rather it was scoreless over the last three innings. Thanks to Jake Jacobs for this insight.
51. Reagan, *An American Life,* 74.
52. Reagan, *Where's the Rest of Me?,* 71.
53. Ibid., 80.
54. Edwards, *Early Reagan,* 155.
55. Eliot, in *Reagan: The Hollywood Years,* claims Reagan left "on purpose" because he "believed unavailability in Hollywood somehow made him more desirable" (49). There is no substance to this, other than his quip in the telegraph about a "childish trick." The fact was Reagan had to return. He had promised the station he would, had no other money or source of income in Los Angeles, and had already made it clear he would not leave Des Moines until he had another job.
56. Edwards, *Early Reagan,* 156.

CHAPTER 3

1. He would eventually film the similarly named *Murder Is In the Air* (1940).
2. Brian Taves, "The B Film: Hollywood's Other Half," in *Grand Design: Hollywood as a Modern Business Enterprise, 1930–1939*, ed. Tino Balio (Berkeley: University of California Press, 1995).
3. Anne Edwards, *Early Reagan: The Rise to Power* (Lanham: Taylor Trade Publishing, 1987), 169.
4. Marc Eliot, *Reagan: The Hollywood Years* (New York: Harmony, 2008), 53. Eliot applies questionable psychoanalysis to imply that Reagan was embarrassed by his film career, observing that while movies consumed up to a third of Reagan's life, he only dedicated one-fourth of his books to his film career and made self-deprecating jokes about his films. More likely, Reagan rightly thought in *An American Life* that his role in history was as a president, not as an actor, and that it was his presidential career most people who read his book were interested in. As for *Where's the Rest of Me?*, he clearly intended it as a political "introduction" to the public and again emphasized his time as president of the Screen Actors Guild in order to reassure everyone that he was not inexperienced.
5. Eliot suggests Reagan wanted to marry Travis, but this seems unlikely. He was just starting a film career and was seeing that he could date a number of leading ladies. Similarly, Eliot downplays Reagan's acting ability as lacking "heat" (a descriptor he uses several times), arguing that Jack Warner thought Reagan possessed the all-American looks and appeal that would keep the censors off his back.
6. Edwards, *Early Reagan*, 169.
7. Even today, most actors—especially some of the most politically vocal—do not have college educations. Some, such as the popular actress Jennifer Lawrence, even dropped out of high school.
8. Edwards, *Early Reagan*, 174.
9. Eliot, *Reagan: The Hollywood Years*, 73.
10. Eliot claims that Wyman's real birth date was 1917, which differed from that frequently reported (1914) and added years to her age so she could legally work full time as an actress. (*Reagan: the Hollywood Years*, 81), but Edwards notes that would have made her nine in first grade. Wyman herself said in 1980 that 1914 was her actual birthdate, while her birth certificate says January 5, 1917.
11. Edwards, *Early Reagan*, 188.
12. Ibid., 192.
13. Ibid., 193.
14. Eliot, *Reagan: The Hollywood Years*, 84.
15. Joe Morella and Edward Z. Epstein, *Jane Wyman: A Biography* (New York: Delacorte Press, 1985), 51.
16. Ronald Reagan with Richard G. Hubler, *Where's the Rest of Me?* (New York: Dell, 1965), 116.
17. Ibid., 118–9.
18. Eliot, *Reagan: The Hollywood Years*, 101.
19. Edwards, *Early Reagan*, 193.
20. Ibid., 207. Although Edwards gives no source for Wallis's comment, it comes from O'Brien's autobiography, *The Wind at My Back: The Life and Times of Pat O'Brien* (Garden City: Doubleday, 1964), 240–241.

21. Eliot, *Reagan: The Hollywood Years*, 116.
22. Ibid., 117.
23. Edwards, *Early Reagan*, 230.
24. Morella and Epstein, *Jane Wyman: A Biography*, 52.
25. Ibid., 53.
26. Eliot, *Reagan: The Hollywood Years*, 134.
27. Reagan, *Where's the Rest of Me?*, 153.
28. The aircraft carrier USS *Ronald Reagan* flies the flag of the 323rd Cavalry in her hangar bay today (courtesy of Michael Reagan).
29. Edwards, *Early Reagan*, 235; and Reagan, *Where's the Rest of Me?*, 117.
30. Ibid., 235; and Hobe Morrison, "9 Lives Are Not Enough," *Variety*, September 3, 1941, https://ia800509.us.archive.org/22/items/variety143-1941-09/variety143-1941-09.pdf.
31. Reagan, *Where's the Rest of Me?*, 9.
32. Ibid.,10.
33. Eliot, *Reagan: The Hollywood Years*, 143.
34. Edwards, *Early Reagan*, 250.
35. New research revealed that Wayne applied to serve in the Office of Strategic Services (the World War II equivalent of the CIA) and was accepted into a field photographic unit, but his estranged wife did not deliver the letter and never told him about it. (Wayne's application for entrance into the OSS, http://www.archives.gov/press/press-kits/american-originals-traveling.html#wayne.) Wild Bill Donovan, the head of OSS, gave Wayne a commendation, and Wayne begged John Ford in May of 1942 to get him in the war. "Have you any suggestions on how I should get in? Can you get me assigned to your outfit, and if you could, would you want me? How about the Marines?…. I hate to ask for favors, but for Christ sake you can suggest can't you?" (Dan Gagliasso, "John Wayne, World War II and the Draft," Breitbart News Network, February 28, 2010.)
36. "Henry Fonda Quotes," IMDB, http://m.imdb.com/name/nm0000020/quotes. See also James E. Wise and Anne Collier Rehill, *Stars in Blue: Movie Actors in America's Sea Services* (Annapolis: Naval Institute Press, 1997); Larry Schweikart and Michael Allen, *A Patriot's History of the United States*, 10th anniversary ed. (New York: Sentinel, 2014), 620–21; James E. Wise and Anne Collier Rehill, *Stars in the Corps: Movie Actors in the United States Marines* (Annapolis: Naval Institute Press, 1999); James E. Wise and Paul W. Wilderson III, *Stars in Khaki: Movie Actors in the Army and the Air Services* (Annapolis: Naval Institute Press, 2000); and Gary L. Bloomfield and Stacie L. Shain with Arlen C. Davidson, *Duty, Honor, Applause: America's Entertainers in World War II* (Guilford: Lyons Press, 2004).
37. Communists had been fiercely anti-involvement prior to June, but when the USSR was attacked, they changed positions almost immediately. Indeed, when one group of anti-war marchers received news that the Soviet Union had been invaded, they literally turned their "stay out of Europe" signs around and painted "Join the War NOW" on the reverse sides. See Paul Kengor, *Dupes: How America's Adversaries Have Manipulated Progressives for a Century* (Wilmington: 2010), 135-59.
38. Eliot, *Reagan: The Hollywood Years*, 150. See also Neal Gabler, *Walt Disney: The Triumph of the American Imagination* (New York: Vintage, 2006). In the *Gibbons v. Ogden*

case, the United States Supreme Court essentially ruled against both parties (who were contesting which state, New York or New Jersey, could authorize a ferry charter across the Hudson River). The court held that interstate waterways were the sole jurisdiction of the federal government and that neither company had a valid charter.

39. Martin Kent, Ray Loynd, and David Robb, *Hollywood Remembers Ronald Reagan* (unpublished), cited in Eliot, *Reagan: The Hollywood Years*, 345. "That's all he talks about," Wyman told Cummings, "how he's going to save the world" (Ibid.).

40. Eliot, *Reagan: The Hollywood Years*, 154.

CHAPTER 4

1. Anne Edwards, *Early Reagan: The Rise to Power* (London: Taylor Trade, 1987), 266.

2. Gary L. Bloomfield and Stacie L. Shain, with Arlen C. Davidson, *Duty, Honor, Applause: America's Entertainers in World War II* (Guilford: The Lyons Press, 2004), 317.

3. Marc Eliot, *Reagan: The Hollywood Years* (New York: Harmony, 2008), 169.

4. David Culbert, "German Films in America, 1933–1945: Public Diplomacy and an Uncoordinated Information Campaign," in *Cinema and Swastika: The International Expansion of Third Reich Cinema*, eds. David Welch and Roel Vande Winkle (London: Palgrave, 2011), 306–317, especially n. 36.

5. Thomas Doherty, *Projections of War: Hollywood, American Culture, and World War II* (New York: Columbia University Press, 1993), 20. See also Michael E. Birdwell, *Celluloid Soldiers: Warner Bros.'s Campaign Against Nazism* (New York: New York University Press, 1999).

6. Cooper C. Graham, "'*Olympia*' in America, 1938: Leni Riefenstahl, Hollywood, and the Kristallnacht," *Historical Journal of Film, Radio & Television* 13, (October 1993): 433–50. Disney's best biographer, Neal Gabler, doubts that Disney saw the film due to Hitler's unpopularity. He was reluctant to even view *Olympia* for fear of political repercussions. (Neal Gabler, *Walt Disney: The Triumph of American Imagination* [New York: Vintage, 2006], 449.) According to Gabler, Riefenstahl visited the studio on December 8, 1939, at the invitation of Jay Stowitts, and spent the day with Walt. They viewed a discussion session of *Fantasia*, then she offered to have a print of *Olympia* sent over for Walt's viewing. Then, according to Riefenstahl, he hesitated and said, "If I see your film then all of Hollywood will find out by tomorrow," and even feared a boycott. Later, he claimed he didn't know who she was when he issued the invitation for a visit. However, that certainly did not preclude him from *earlier* seeing a print of *Triumph of the Will*, and the film and its techniques were well known. At this point, in light of any positive evidence, it should be concluded that Disney never saw *Triumph of the Will* in the 1930s. In 1938, Riefenstahl made a trip to Hollywood with her next film, *Olympia*, in which all images of Hitler were edited out, but found an even more chilling reception.

7. Stephen Vaughn, *Ronald Reagan in Hollywood: Movies and Politics* (Cambridge: Cambridge University Press, 1994), 113. Before long, Walt Disney would exceed Arnold's wildest expectations with his visually stunning *Victory Through Air Power* 1943 animated feature. Even Disney, though, would be surprised to find that it was not waves of bombers but a single plane carrying a single bomb that effectively ended the war with Japan.

8. Bloomfield, Shain, and Davidson, *Duty, Honor, Applause*, 325.

9. Eliot, *Reagan: The Hollywood Years*, 162.

10. Ibid., 171.

11. Joe Morella and Edward Z. Epstein, *Jane Wyman: A Biography* (New York: Delacorte Press, 1985), 65.

12. Edwards, *Early Reagan*, 270.

13. Ibid., 293.

14. Mark Betancourt, "World War II: The Movie," *Air & Space*, March 2012, http://www.airspacemag.com/history-of-flight/world-war-ii-the-movie-21103597/?onsite_source=airspacemag.com&onsite_campaign=photogalleries&onsite_medium=internal&onsite_content=World+War+II%3A+The+Movie&page=4.

15. Lou Cannon, "Dramatic Account About Film of Nazi Death Camps Questioned," *Washington Post*, March 5, 1984.

16. Cannon, *President Reagan: The Role of a Lifetime* (New York: Simon & Schuster, 1991), 386–489. Cannon relies on secondhand relating of a conversation that required foreign-speaking sources to not only understand with perfect clarity but to relate through subordinates to him. Rather than Reagan doing the conflating, it seems much more likely that there were tiny misunderstandings and mistranslations of what Reagan said. Since Cannon was not there, one must side with Reagan.

17. Edwards, *Early Reagan*, 282.

18. Eliot, *Reagan: The Hollywood Years*, 181.

19. Morella and Epstein, *Jane Wyman: A Biography*, 99.

20. Ibid., 107.

21. Ibid., 71.

22. Ibid., 89.

23. Wyman interview in *Los Angeles Daily News*, June 18, 1946.

24. Edwards, *Early Reagan*, 294.

25. Ronald Reagan with Richard G. Hubler, *Where's the Rest of Me?* (New York: Dell, 1965), 190. Neither Edwards nor Eliot mentions this aborted strike.

26. Vaughn, *Ronald Reagan in Hollywood*, 125.

27. Ibid., 131.

28. Edwards, *Early Reagan*, 303. Moon was an informant doing small jobs for the FBI at the time, such as observing license numbers at meetings. One night, Dutch insisted Moon join him for coffee at midnight. Moon found him in a car when Reagan explained that a woman at another studio had been strategically "recommending" people to the HICCASP board every time an opening appeared. Reagan tracked down the minute books and found that she had cleverly packed the board with communists (Ibid., 304). Reagan also knew, likely through Neil, that the FBI had HICCASP under surveillance.

29. Vaughn, *Ronald Reagan in Hollywood*, 123.

30. Ibid., 124.

31. Ronald Reagan, *An American Life* (New York: Pocket Books, 1990), 113.

32. Eliot, *Reagan*, 182.

33. Reagan, *An American Life*, 115.

34. Eliot, *Reagan: The Hollywood Years*, 184.

35. Reagan, *Where's the Rest of Me?*, 191.

36. Ibid., 192.

37. Ibid., 192.

38. Vaughn, *Ronald Reagan in Hollywood*, 133.
39. Ibid., 132, says that Reagan "remained with the organization another three months after De Havilland's resignation" (around August 1). Various HICCASP standing committees showed that more than a month later, the executive council ratified him for membership on its labor committee—but that could be lag time related to processing paperwork or an unawareness that the resignation letter had come in. Since official records show his resignation date as August, this could be the acknowledgment of the resignation, not his submission, which he said he sent by telegram the night that the de Havilland resolution failed in the executive council. Roosevelt's resignation is dated the ninth.
40. Ibid., 139.
41. Edwards, *Early Reagan*, 312. Edwards has the wrong date for the meeting, which was called *on* October 1 *for* October 2. Thanks to Valerie Yaros, the historian/archivist for the Screen Actors Guild, for clarifying this. (E-mail from Yaros to the author, August 24, 2015.)
42. Eliot, *Reagan*, 188–89.
43. Reagan, *Where's the Rest of Me?*, 200.
44. Vaughn, *Ronald Reagan in Hollywood*, 140. Eliot claimed the studio gave Reagan the .32 and wrote that he could find no record, but in fact the police gave it to Reagan. Eliot, however, admits the weapon was real: Jimmy Stewart saw Reagan with it. But Eliot has Reagan already packing the .32 at the September speech at the Hollywood Legion Stadium.
45. In *Where's the Rest of Me?*, Reagan gives no date for this meeting but says it occurred "two days later" after describing the meeting at Ida Lupino's house that he and Holden attended, where he spoke and referred to his talk as a "dress rehearsal of the same report" he gave to the mass SAG body (197). In fact, as noted, Reagan made *two* speeches to the guild at Hollywood Legion Stadium, one on October 2, and one on December 19.
46. Seldom have such well-documented events been made so incomprehensible by writers, including Reagan himself. Eliot (*Reagan*, 191) claims Reagan had his .32 by the time he made this speech (which was correct). But the speech at Hollywood Legion Stadium was on December 19, not in September as Eliot maintains, or October as Reagan recalled, and by then Reagan had been carrying his .32 for two months. As for the size of the membership in the audience, Vaughn puts the number in attendance at 1,800, not 3,000, but Eliot's detailed final vote tally confirms the larger number.
47. Reagan, *Where's the Rest of Me?*, 201.
48. Eliot, *Reagan*, 191.
49. Gerald Morne, *Class Struggle in Hollywood, 1930–1950: Moguls, Mobsters, Stars, Reds and Trade Unionists* (Austin: University of Texas Press, 2001), 199.
50. Morella and Epstein, *Jane Wyman: A Biography*, 116.
51. Ibid., 121.
52. Eliot, *Reagan: The Hollywood Years*, 205.
53. Morella and Epstein, *Jane Wyman: A Biography*, 122.
54. Ibid., 123.
55. Ibid.
56. Edwards, *Early Reagan*, 354.

57. Morella and Epstein, *Jane Wyman: A Biography*, 124.

58. Ibid., 127.

59. Nancy Reagan with William Novak, *My Turn: The Memoirs of Nancy Reagan* (New York: Random House, 1982), 82. According to Nancy, Reagan came from a generation that believed "you married once, and that was it. For better or worse. And if you made a mistake and your marriage wasn't what you hoped it would be, you suffered in silence" (82). The difficulty with Nancy's assessment of this is that Reagan seemed to suffer only minimally.

60. Edwards, *Early Reagan*, 347.

61. Ibid.

62. Ibid., 348.

63. H. W. Brands, *Reagan: A Life* (New York: Doubleday, 2015), 94. Brands, who managed to short shrift many of the important episodes in Reagan's life, found space to dedicate four full pages to Howard Lawson's testimony before Congress.

64. Vaughn, *Ronald Reagan in Hollywood*, 156.

65. John Earl Haynes and Harvey Klehr, *Venona: Decoding Soviet Espionage in America* (New Haven: Yale University Press, 2000); Christopher Andrew and Vasili Metrokhin, *The Sword and the Shield: The Mitrokhin Archive and the Secret History of the KGB* (New York: Perseus, 1999), 128, 130–34, 148, 164, and for just a few of the spies; M. Stanton Evans, *Blacklisted by History: The Untold Story of Senator Joe McCarthy and His Fight Against America's Enemies* (New York: Crown, 2007).

66. Paul Kengor, *God and Ronald Reagan: A Spiritual Life* (New York: ReganBooks, 2004), 23.

67. Peter Hannaford, *Reagan's Roots: The People and Places That Shaped His Character* (Bennington: Images from the Past, 2012), 110.

68. Burton W. Folsom Jr. *New Deal or Raw Deal? How FDR's Economic Legacy Has Damaged America* (New York: Threshold Books, 2008), 56–57; Larry Schweikart and Lynne Pierson Doti, *American Entrepreneur* (New York: AMACOM, 2009), 307–10; and Stephen J. DeCanio, "Expectations and Business Confidence During the Great Depression," in *Money In Crisis: The Federal Reserve, the Economy, and Monetary Reform*, Barry N. Siegel, ed. (San Francisco: Pacific Institute, 1984).

69. Kengor, in *God and Ronald Reagan*, cites Kleihauer's impact on Reagan stemming from a discussion in the 1930s the two had after Reagan addressed the church's men's group and condemned fascism. "I think your speech would be even better if you also mentioned that if communism ever looked like a threat, you'd be just as opposed to it as you are fascism," 51. Reagan admitted he hadn't thought much about communism as a threat but within a short time, after denouncing fascism, added "there's another 'ism,' communism, and if I ever find evidence that communism represents a threat to all that we believe in and stand for, I'll speak out just as harshly against [it] as I have fascism" (52). Suddenly Reagan noted that the room was dead silent: he had failed to appreciate the inroads the far left had already made into the community, and he later, as president, thanked Reverend Kleihauer for the wake-up call.

70. "A Labor Sunday Message—1944," *The Christian Challenger*, 3, September 10, 1944; "Dr. Kleihauer Says," ibid., 2, June 20, 1946; and "Panhandlers and Preachers," all in Hollywood-Beverly Christian Church Library. The Hollywood Christian Church merged with the Beverly Christian Church in 1934 to form the Hollywood-Beverly Christian Church.

71. Hedda Hopper, "Mr. Reagan Airs His Views," *Chicago Tribune*, May 18, 1947. The words were almost an exact copy of Kleihauer's, spoken more than a decade earlier.

72. Edwards, *Early Reagan*, 358.

73. Eliot, *Reagan: The Hollywood Years*, 232–33.

74. Nancy did not mention the Schary dinner in her book. She recalled her first meeting with Reagan as stemming from her meeting with Mervyn LeRoy about her name appearing in "one of the Hollywood papers" (*My Turn*, 78). LeRoy suggested he contact Reagan about the mistake, then said, "Come to think of it…you two might really hit it off. I'll have Ron call you." (Ibid.,79.) Reagan then called her, and they agreed to meet at LaRue's, which, to Nancy, was the first time they met.

75. Nancy Reagan, *My Turn*, 78.

76. Ibid., 81; and Eliot, *Reagan: The Hollywood Years*, 236.

77. Nancy Reagan, *My Turn*, 81.

78. Marc Eliot provides another interpretation—that Nancy wanted to "redeem" Reagan from his previous bad marriage just as her mother had done with Loyal Davis. Eliot claims that "she wasn't about to let a few 'dalliances' stand in the way of what she had in store for him, meaning of course for them. Greatness" (*Reagan: The Hollywood Years*, 236). This view over-psychoanalyzes Nancy. She was thinking, as Sinatra sang, "Love and Marriage." When Reagan drove her to the ranch he bought, he said, "You know, you really should buy a house. It would be a terrific investment, and you're just throwing away your money by paying rent" (Nancy Reagan, *My Turn*, 83). A crushed Nancy recalled, "I had been thinking along the lines of *joint* ownership."

79. Edwards, *Early Reagan*, 405.

80. Ibid., 407.

81. Ibid., 395.

82. H. W. Brands erroneously has Reagan arriving at the dinner with Nancy months later, after her mistaken identity problem, on "a pair of canes," but by then, Reagan's leg was healed. (Brands, *Reagan: The Life*, 109).

83. Eliot, *Reagan: The Hollywood Years*, 238.

84. Edwards, *Early Reagan*, 431.

85. Nancy Reagan, *My Turn*, 136. It's interesting that neither Vaughn nor Brands even mention Patti's birth in their books.

86. Eliot, *Reagan: The Hollywood Years*, 287.

87. Ibid., 288.

88. Reagan, *An American Life*, 125; and Edwards, *Early Reagan*, 447.

89. Nancy Reagan, *My Turn*, 141.

90. Biographer Brands doesn't even have an index entry for "family life." Reagan's relationship with his children, but especially Patti, was the subject of much controversy when he later became president and she had drifted into left-wing views. Nancy rationalized her behavior as Patti being "used by people with their own political agenda," but clearly Patti had been a liberal much of her life. Nancy also described Patti's distance from her father as "unresolved feelings" (*My Turn*, 137–39). But Reagan's distance from his children was real—and substantial. Michael Reagan—whom admittedly the Gipper had not seen on a regular basis for some time—recalled an incident when as president, Reagan spoke to his high school graduation. Michael posed in a group with his father in cap and gown, and after the picture Reagan introduced himself to

everyone in the group…including Michael, saying, "Hi, my name's Ronald Reagan. What's yours?" Michael took off his cap and said, "Dad, it's *me*. Your son, Mike." (Edmund Morris, *Dutch: A Memoir of Ronald Reagan* [New York: Modern Library, 1999], 518.) Morris somewhat snidely noted that none of Reagan's kids got a college degree, though Michael became a successful talk show host and Ron Jr. danced with major ballet companies. Maureen had an unsuccessful run for the US Senate, then met an early death through cancer. Morris's condescension aside, Reagan came from the Depression/World War II-era school of parenting, where it was the father's job to supply money, a home, and security and the wife's job to handle parenting tasks. He was typical of his age and, like many fathers of that generation, distant emotionally. Compared to modern expectations of fatherhood, Reagan would have been a failure, but by the standards of the day, he was quite the norm.

91. Interviews with Michael Reagan, various dates 2017.

CHAPTER 5

1. Thomas W. Evans, *The Education of Ronald Reagan: The General Electric Years and the Untold Story of His Conversion to Conservatism* (New York: Columbia University Press, 2006), 11; and Ronald Reagan, *An American Life* (New York: Pocket Books, 1990), 132.

2. Reagan, *An American Life*, 126.

3. Anne Edwards, *Early Reagan: The Rise to Power* (Lanham: Taylor Trade Publishing, 1987), 452–53. Evans, without taking sides, notes that it is disputed whether anyone else was considered for the GE job and that while Reagan said the show was created with him in mind, Edwards claims others were considered. Both could be true.

4. Marc Eliot (*Reagan: The Hollywood Years* [New York: Harmony, 2008]) said that Wasserman did not present the package to Reagan until it was finalized, not wanting to build up hopes. Eliot further claims—without a source cited—that Reagan was "ninth on the list of nine possibilities" (276), and that the others included Kirk Douglas, Eddy Arnold, and Walter Pidgeon. Douglas, of course, was just coming into his prime and had yet to make *Gunfight at the O.K. Corral*, *Paths of Glory*, *In Harm's Way*, or one of his greatest hits, *Spartacus*. Pidgeon was past his prime, as was Arnold, but "ninth out of nine" could just as likely been an alphabetical list as a prioritized list. Nevertheless, it's common in Hollywood to design a story, film, or show with one actor or set of actors in mind but with the awareness that flexibility is required. Paramount wanted an established star like Jack Nicholson or Robert Redford to play the role of Michael Corleone in *The Godfather*, Johnny Depp was reportedly offered the role of Ferris Bueller before Matthew Broderick, and Julia Roberts was the choice for Leigh Anne Tuohy in *The Blind Side*, a part for which Sandra Bullock won the Oscar. It's entirely possible that the "package," as Reagan called it, was indeed meant for him but that others were waiting in the wings if he developed prima donna-itis.

5. Eliot, *Reagan: The Hollywood Years*, 277.

6. Edwards, *Early Reagan*, 453.

7. Harold Evans overstates Boulware's influence on Reagan (Evans, with Gail Buckland and David Lefer, *They Made America: From the Steam Engine to the Search Engine, Two Centuries of Innovators* [New York: Little, Brown, & Company, 2004]). While their ideas were quite similar, and while no doubt Boulware wished to manipulate and

direct Reagan, the Gipper doesn't even mention Boulware in either of his biographies. H. W. Brands (*Reagan: The Life* [New York: Doubleday, 2015], 123–124), Reagan's most recent comprehensive biographer, discusses Boulware's role as head of GE public relations, but does not suggest Boulware's ideas percolated into Reagan. Quite the contrary, Reagan on his own came to resemble Boulware in his appreciation for American business and the threat of communism in unions—which he knew about.

8. See Evans, Buckland, David Lefer, *They Made America*, 318–33. Edmund Morris (*Dutch: A Memoir of Ronald Reagan* [New York: Modern Library, 1999]) doesn't mention Boulware in his index, despite having talked with Reagan extensively—probably more than any other living author.

9. Evans, *Education of Ronald Reagan*, 59, citing an interview with Dunckel.

10. Edwards, *Early Reagan*, 457.

11. Evans, *Education of Ronald Reagan*, 64.

12. Ronald Reagan, remarks at the annual National Prayer Breakfast, February 4, 1982.

13. Dinesh D'Souza, *Ronald Reagan: How an Ordinary Man Became an Extraordinary Leader* (New York: Touchstone, 1997), 42.

14. As a biographer, I have witnessed this countless times, especially in a family where each member will have different recollections of dates and times or other specifics. Often a paper document—a plane ticket or travel calendar—sorts it out. Most people have experienced this in a profound way, convinced that an episode occurred one way when the details showed something else entirely.

15. Edwards, *Early Reagan*, 457.

16. Evans, *Education of Ronald Reagan*, 60. See the recollection of the event from his traveling aide Ed Langley, "Reagan Philosophy Changed," *Knoxville Journal*, July 14, 1980. Franklin Roosevelt had used the phrase before, but today it is almost uniquely connected to the Gipper.

17. Eliot, *Reagan: The Hollywood Years*, 286.

18. Evans, *Education of Ronald Reagan*, 62.

19. Langley, "Reagan Philosophy Changed"; and Reagan, *An American Life*, 128–29.

20. Ronald Reagan with Richard G. Hubler, *Where's the Rest of Me?* (New York: Dell, 1965).

21. Ibid., 297.

22. Ibid., 129.

23. Ibid., 297.

24. Ibid.

25. Evans, *Education of Ronald Reagan*, 66. In *An American Life*, Reagan placed the development of more politically oriented speeches a little later in the tour (129–30).

26. Larry Schweikart, *48 Liberal Lies About American History (That You Probably Learned in School)* (New York: Sentinel, 2009), 239–44.

27. Reagan, *Where's the Rest of Me?*, 303.

28. Evans, *Education of Ronald Reagan*, chapter 8, deals in depth with Beilenson's influence on Reagan's Cold War thinking. While Beilenson was important in honing Reagan's thoughts, it was clear already from the Gipper's confrontations with the radical communists in the unions that they were not capable of playing by normal rules and therefore contained an element of malevolence in their very core.

29. Fabius was a Roman general known for his "slow-down" tactics that delayed the march of Hannibal to Rome in the Punic Wars. "Fabian Socialism" was a slow creep, as opposed to the revolutionary brand of communism advocated by Lenin.

30. Paul Lettow, *Ronald Reagan and His Quest to Abolish Nuclear Weapons* (New York: Random House, 2005), 14.

31. "Speech to Engineers: Actor Reagan Hurls Blast at Liberals," *Corpus Christi Caller*, February 23, 1962, in Ronald Reagan Presidential Library (RL), "Miscellaneous Collection" (also called "Vertical File").

32. Reagan, "Losing Freedom by Installments," *Qualified Contractor*, November 1961, in RL, "Miscellaneous Collection."

33. Reagan, "Commencement at Eureka College," June 7, 1957; and Kengor, *God and Ronald Reagan: A Spiritual Life* (New York: ReganBooks, 2004), chapter 8.

34. Reagan, *Where's the Rest of Me?*, 305–6.

35. Ibid., 306.

36. Reagan, *An American Life*, 137.

37. Ibid., 137.

38. According to Eliot, Nancy cherished a nonexistent notion of "an extended, never-ending honeymoon" with "Ronnie" and struggled with the place of the children in it (Eliot, *Reagan: The Hollywood Years*, 301).

39. Ibid., 299.

40. Ibid., 298.

41. Valerie Yaros to the author, e-mail, April 14, 2007, in author's possession.

42. Ibid.

43. According to Edwards (*Early Reagan*, 320), Reagan claimed that the strike ended "in June" between "soup and salad" at one of the large Hollywood dinner parties when he sat next to the new studios' PR head for the strike, Anna Rosenberg, who then passed on the union's final proposal to MGM's Joe Vogel. Vogel then called Reagan for a private meeting (as other meetings were going on simultaneously) and four days after that, everyone arrived at the deal. But Reagan never used the June date—obviously the strike was over by April. See Reagan, *Where's the Rest of Me?*, 319–20.

44. Eliot, *Reagan: The Hollywood Years*, 307.

45. Ibid., 318.

46. Edwards, *Early Reagan*, 440.

47. Ibid., 441.

48. Think for example of an actor such as Lorne Greene, who would be hard-pressed to headline a major movie, but who was perfect as Ben Cartright on *Bonanza*, then again as Commander Adama in *Battlestar Galactica*. Or, later, think of David Duchovny, who had an iconic role as Fox Mulder on in the sci-fi show *The X-Files*, then later as the drunken, womanizing Hank Moody in *Californication*. When the film industry went into a recession in the twenty-first century, television once again provided a soft landing through the cable outlets, where even an Academy Award-winning star such as Matthew McConaughey made news by appearing in the series *True Detective*. H. W. Brands entirely mischaracterizes the MCA/SAG deal, portraying it as a battle over union jurisdiction between SAG, the American Federation of Television and Radio Artists, and Actors' Equity, with its umbrella called the Television Authority or TVA. According to Brands, Reagan was concerned that the TVA was "a stalking horse"

for the communists and resisted the "one big union." Reagan, Brands insists, "spent much of two years fighting the single-unionists" (Brands, *Reagan: The Life*, 116). In fact, whether it was one or many unions mattered little to Reagan when it came to extending the working careers of actors, and by 1952, the communist elements within Hollywood had taken on less of a threat in his mind than high levels of industry unemployment.

49. Interview with Chet Migden, June 3, 1998, SAG-AFTRA Archives, Los Angeles, CA.
50. Ibid. Edwards dedicates no small amount of space to the SAG meetings at the time of the strike and final vote, putting to rest the notion that there were "missing minutes" of a meeting in which Reagan supposedly met a near-insurrection led by Leon Ames. In fact, Migden claimed, the minutes were only misfiled and were discovered in October 1980, and Ames was not even present. There was no "insurrection"—there wasn't even a protest. Migden did note that there was a different meeting during the strike that was heated, but that the guild (and Reagan) stayed out of it (Edwards, *Early Reagan*, 470).
51. Randy Roberts and James S. Olson, *John Wayne, American* (New York: Free Press, 1995), 533.
52. Evans, *Education of Ronald Reagan*, 163.
53. Ibid., 164.
54. Ibid., 166.
55. Reagan, *An American Life*, 140–41.
56. Ibid., 142; and JohnJ2427, "Reagan—A Time for Choosing," Youtube video, 4:15, https://www.youtube.com/watch?v=lvg7lRsCVJ8.
57. *Los Angeles Times*, November 29, 1964.
58. Brands, *Reagan*, 750; and *Los Angeles Times*, November 11 and 15, 1964.
59. Reagan, *An American Life*, 145.

CHAPTER 6
1. Larry Schweikart and Michael Allen, *A Patriot's History of the United States: From Columbus's Great Discovery to America's Age of Entitlement*, 10th anniversary ed. (New York: Sentinel, 2014), 724–37; Lewis B. Mayhew, ed., *Higher Education in the Revolutionary Decades* (Berkeley, CA: McCutchan Publishing, 1967); Schweikart and Dave Dougherty, *A Patriot's History of the Modern World Vol. II: From the Cold War to the Age of Entitlement, 1945–2012* (New York: Sentinel, 2013), 220–21; Chester E. Finn Jr., *Scholars, Dollars, and Bureaucrats* (Washington, DC: Brookings Institution, 1978), 21; Roger Kimball, *Tenured Radicals: How Politics Has Corrupted Our Higher Education* (New York: Harper & Row, 1990); Ellen Schrecker, *No Ivory Tower: McCarthyism and the Universities* (New York: Oxford, 1986); David Steigerwald, *The Sixties and the End of Modern America* (New York: St. Martin's Press, 1995); and Peter Collier and David Horowitz, *Destructive Generation* (New York: Summit, 1989).
2. *Washington Post*, June 17, 1965.
3. *Los Angeles Times*, December 17, 1965.
4. Thomas W. Evans, *The Education of Ronald Reagan: The General Electric Years* (New York: Columbia University Press, 2006), 175.
5. Anne Edwards, *Early Reagan: The Rise to Power* (Lanham: Taylor Trade Publishing, 1987), 489. Edwards cites a phone call during 1964 during an interview with Sheilah

Graham but does not give a specific date. Neil, Ron's brother, said that he held out "a long time" after that suggestion (Ibid.).

6. Steven F. Hayward, *The Age of Reagan: The Fall of the Old Liberal Order, 1964–1980* (New York: Three Rivers Press, 2001), 97.

7. Evans, *Education of Ronald Reagan*, 173. The professors were impressed with Reagan's library of books on political philosophy and history as well as with his intellectual abilities.

8. Interview with Michael Reagan, September 5, 2017.

9. Ibid.

10. Evans, *Education of Ronald Reagan*, 178.

11. Matthew Dallek, *The Right Movement* (New York: Free Press, 2000), 210.

12. The same dynamic worked for Hillary Clinton in 2012, when her opponent was Senator Bernie Sanders. While the real policy differences between the two were minimal to nonexistent, Clinton could portray herself as a more "traditional candidate" in the primary.

13. H. W. Brands, *Reagan: The Life* (New York: Doubleday, 2015), 152.

14. James Piereson, *Camelot and the Cultural Revolution: How the Assassination of John F. Kennedy Shattered American Liberalism*, 2nd ed. (New York: Encounter Books, 2013).

15. Schweikart and Lynne Pierson Doti, *American Entrepreneur: The Fascinating Stories of the People Who Defined the Business of the United States* (New York: Amacom, 2009), 324–27.

16. Ibid., 325; and Henry R. Nau, *The Myth of America's Decline: Leading the World Economy into the 1990s* (Oxford: Oxford University Press, 1992).

17. David Halberstam, *The Reckoning* (New York: William Morrow & Co., 1986).

18. Hayward, *Age of Reagan: Fall of the Old Liberal Order*, 87.

19. Schweikart and Allen, *A Patriot's History of the United States: From Columbus's Great Discovery to the War on Terror* (New York: Sentinel, 2004), 686.

20. Hayward, *Age of Reagan: Fall of the Old Liberal Order*, 87.

21. Ibid., 105.

22. Brands, *Reagan: The Life*, 170–1.

23. Ibid, 155.

24. Lou Cannon, *Governor Reagan: His Rise to Power* (New York: Public Affairs, 2003), 282.

25. Ibid., 284. Again, the similarities between Reagan and Donald Trump are striking. As Cannon explained of Reagan, "He typically sought more, much more, than was attainable, then settled for the best deal he could get" (284). Trump would be described as staking out a radical position, all the while desiring something much more reasonable that he would eventually obtain.

26. Even Brands called Brown's budget an "egregious fiction" (*Reagan: The Life*, 157).

27. Hayward, *Age of Reagan: Fall of the Old Liberal Order*, 160.

28. Paul Kengor and Patricia Clark Doerner, *The Judge: William P. Clark, Ronald Reagan's Top Hand* (San Francisco: Ignatius Pres, 2007), 62.

29. Brands, *Reagan: The Life*, 157–58. Brands notes another obstacle for Reagan, namely his distaste for "chumming" with the local politicians of both parties after hours, claiming "the governor was expected to socialize." Unlike previous governors, though, Reagan didn't particularly *want* to be in Sacramento, went home every night to dinner

with Nancy and the kids, and was not a drinker. In this way, again, he would very much presage Donald Trump, who had little in common with the "swamp dwellers" in Washington. But many of the California legislators saw their time in Sacramento as an extended bachelor party away from their wives and were put off by Reagan's fidelity to Nancy. Even when the Reagans would have some of the legislators over to their home, they weren't comfortable. Reagan thus suffered from a piety gap that had afflicted men such as John Adams, who rubbed those who "wanted to sin, and sin greatly" the wrong way (Schweikart and Allen, *A Patriot's History of the United States*, 140). Such attitudes were alien to Reagan, who, as he headed out of the office at night, would poke his head in the door of his staff and say, "All right, everybody, it's time to go home to your spouses and families!" (Kengor and Doerner, *The Judge*, 73). Reagan failed to understand that many of them didn't *want* to go home and enjoyed their "adult" free time.

30. Kengor and Doerner, *The Judge*, 63.
31. Hayward, *Age of Reagan: Fall of the Old Liberal Order*, 165.
32. Carl Ingram, "Aide Defends Mini-Memos," *Sacramento Union*, June 16, 1967.
33. Lee Edwards, *Reagan: A Political Biography* (San Diego: Viewpoint Books, 1967), 205–206.
34. Lou Cannon, "Reagan's 'Inner Cabinet' at Work: County's Clark in Key Role," *Ventura County Star-Free Press*, February 26, 1967, D7.
35. "Reagan Gives a Surprising Performance: Not Great, Not Brilliant, but a Good Show," *New York Times*, December 10, 1967.
36. Kengor and Doerner, *The Judge*, 66.
37. Joe Cannon, *Ronnie and Jesse: A Political Odyssey* (Garden City: Doubleday, 1969), 182.
38. Dinesh D'Souza, *Ronald Reagan: How an Ordinary Man Became an Extraordinary Leader* (New York: Free Press, 1997), 67.
39. Fred Barnes, "American Conservatism: Ronald Reagan, Father of the Pro-Life Movement," *Wall Street Journal*, November 6, 2003; and Lou Cannon, *Governor Reagan* (New York: Public Affairs, 2003), 208–14.
40. William Clark, foreword ("Ronald Reagan: Lifeguard") in Ronald Reagan, *Abortion and the Conscience of the Nation* (Sacramento: New Regnery Publishing, 2000), 10.
41. Lou Cannon, *Governor Reagan*, 242.
42. Ibid., 248.
43. Gladwin Hill, "Lawyer Revamps Reagan's Regime," *New York Times*, September 10, 1967. Note the use of the term "regime" for a Republican, when no Democratic government would be described as a "regime."
44. Cannon, *Governor Reagan*, 251–54.
45. Kengor and Doerner, *The Judge*, 70.
46. Ibid., 75.
47. Ron Reagan on his parents in *American Experience*, episode "Reagan," aired 1998, on PBS.
48. Caspar Weinberger, *In the Arena: A Memoir of the 20th Century* (Washington, DC: Regnery, 2001), 149–52, 161; and Lou Cannon, "Reagan Loses Valuable Aide in Clark," *San Jose Mercury-News*, December 1, 1968.
49. Kengor and Doerner, *The Judge, 78.* Cannon appears to have embellished. Kengor and Doerner, Clark's biographers, do not even mention the final four months before Clark

departed, nor does Brands even have an index entry for Phil Battaglia or discuss Clark in reference to the final four months.

50. Hayward, *Age of Reagan: Fall of the Old Liberal Order*, 162.

51. Tony Judt, *Postwar: A History of Europe Since 1945* (New York: Penguin Press, 2005), 417; Schweikart and Dave Dougherty, *A Patriot's History of the Modern World Vol. II: From the Cold War to the Age of Entitlement, 1945–2012* (New York: Sentinel, 2013), 216; and Patricia G. Steinhoff, "Student Protest in the 1960s," *Social Science Japan*, March 15, 1999, 1–6.

52. Schweikart and Allen, *A Patriot's History of the United States*, 725–28.

53. Lou Cannon, *Governor Reagan*, 285.

54. Lyn Nofziger, *Nofziger* (Washington, DC: Regnery Gateway, 1992), 64.

55. Lou Cannon, *Governor Reagan*, 285. Cannon dismissed Reagan's view that there was a "conspiracy" among the campus radicals. Perhaps there were no meetings, but many, if not most, had read or ingested the essence of the Abbie Hoffman tactics in use on all campuses, which did not call for organized collusion to all pursue the same objective with the same methods.

56. Ibid., 288.

57. Ibid., 290.

58. Ibid., 291.

59. Ibid., 291.

60. Lou Cannon, *Governor Reagan*, 292.

61. *Los Angeles Times*, June 14, 1969; and Brands, *Reagan: The Life*, 173–74.

62. Leroy F. Aarons, "Student Revolution Breaks New Ground—Bank Burned," *Washington Post*, May 3, 1970; and Doug Shuit and William Drummond, "Violence, Arson, Hit UC Santa Barbara for 2nd Night," *Los Angeles Times*, February 26, 1970.

63. Tim O'Brien, "Supervisors Ask Governor to Send Guard into I.V.," *Santa Barbara News-Press*, June 11, 1970.

64. "What About Ronald Reagan?" *CBS Reports*, aired December 12, 1967 on CBS; and Tom Wicker, "Reagan's Role in '68," *New York Times*, July 8, 1966.

65. "The Making of a Candidate: A Look at the Reagan Room," *U.S. News & World Report*, July 24, 1967, 53.

66. *National Review*, December 26, 1967.

67. Michael Beran, *The Last Patrician: Bobby Kennedy and the End of American Aristocracy* (New York: St. Martin's Press, 1998), 150.

68. Ibid., 150.

69. Andrew Gilder, "Reviving Republican Liberalism," *The New Leader*, October 24, 1966. The canard of "permanent minority status" is rolled out every time a conservative is likely to win. Similar warnings were issued about Trump in 2016—when the party immediately began to *increase* voter registrations following his election.

70. *The Lou Gordon Program*, aired on WKBD, August 31, 1967.

71. Hayward, *Age of Reagan: Fall of the Old Liberal Order*, 173.

72. Jonathan Aitken, *Nixon: A Life* (Washington, DC: Regnery, 1993), 330; and Hayward, *Age of Reagan: Fall of the Old Liberal Order*, 174.

73. *U.S. News & World Report*, September 11, 1967.

74. Joe Cannon, *Ronnie and Jesse*, 264.

75. Hayward, *Age of Reagan: Fall of the Old Liberal Order*, 211.

76. Reagan, second inaugural address, January 4, 1971, governors.library.ca.gov.

77. Charles Murray, *Losing Ground: American Social Policy, 1950-1980* (New York: Basic Books, 2015).

78. Brands, *Reagan*, 180. Although it was a joke, Reagan demonstrated that even he—a hard-core conservative—failed to understand that the "general welfare" phrase *only* applied to business aspects of the US Constitution, i.e., the US government should promote business and thereby promote the general welfare. See Larry Schweikart, *What Would the Founders Say?* (New York: Sentinel, 2011).

79. Cannon, *Governor Reagan*, 349.

80. "Governor's Welfare Proposals Scored by Democrat Leaders," *Los Angeles Times*, March 4, 1971.

81. Cannon, *Governor Reagan*, 351.

82. Murray, *Losing Ground*.

83. The literature on the impact of welfare, particularly AFDC, on wealth-building and families is extensive. See Irwin Garfinkle and Robert Haveman with David Betson, "Earnings Capacity, Poverty, and Inequality," Institute of Research on Poverty, US Department of Health, Education, and Welfare, monography series (New York: Academic Press, 1977); Patrick F. Fagan and Robert Rector, "The Effects of Divorce on America," *Heritage Foundation Backgrounder* no. 1373 (June 5, 2000); Stuart Butler, *Out of the Poverty Trap* (New York: Free Press, 1987); Allan Reynolds, "The Ominous Decline in Work Incentives," *Jobs & Capital* (Fall 1994): 9–17; and "Welfare Transfers in Two-Parent Families: Labor Supply and Welfare Participation under AFDC-UP," National Bureau of Economic Research, Working Paper no. 4407, July 1993.

84. George Gilder, *Men and Marriage* (Gretna: Pelican, 1992). *Men and Marriage* was first published in 1986.

85. Cannon, *Governor Reagan*, 359.

86. Ibid., 360.

87. As usual, pundits and intellectuals cited "abundant good luck" as the reason for Reagan's triumphs. Frank Levy of the Urban Institute, in a 1977 paper called "What Ronald Reagan Can Teach About Welfare Reform," claimed the caseload was going to stabilize anyway (an unprovable assertion, but always convenient).

88. Cannon, *Governor Reagan*, 378.

89. Ronald Reagan, "Reflections on the Failure of Proposition #1," *National Review*, December 7, 1973.

90. Peter Schrag, *Paradise Lost: California's Experience, America's Future* (New York: Free Press, 1998), 132.

91. Lou Cannon, *Governor Reagan*, 381.

92. Ibid., 386.

93. Ibid., 388.

94. *Baltimore Sun*, November 18, 1975.

95. Len Colodny and Robert Gettlin, *Silent Coup* (New York: St. Martin's Press, 1991).

CHAPTER 7

1. H. W. Brands, *Reagan: The Life* (New York: Doubleday, 2015), 186.
2. Ronald Reagan, *Reagan, In His Own Hand*, eds. Kiron K. Skinner, Annelise Anderson, and Martin Anderson (New York: Free Press, 2001).
3. "Oil I," June 15, 1977, in ibid., 320.
4. "Communism, the Disease," May 1975, in *Reagan, In His Own Hand*, 11–12.
5. "Two Worlds," August 7, 1978, in *Reagan, In His Own Hand*, 14.
6. "The Russian Wheat Deal," October 1975, in *Reagan, In His Own Hand*, 30.
7. "Welfare," January 9, 1978, in *Reagan, In His Own Hand*, 394–95.
8. Brands, *Reagan*, 191.
9. "Rockefeller's Panel Nears Probe Wind-Up," *Port Arthur News*, June 2, 1975, https://newspaperarchive.com/port-arthur-news-jun-02-1975-p-1/.
10. Lou Cannon, *President Reagan: The Role of a Lifetime* (New York: Simon & Schuster, 1991), 396, claims Ford's naming of Rockefeller was the decisive moment that convinced Reagan to run in 1976.
11. Gerald Ford, *A Time to Heal: The Autobiography of Gerald R. Ford* (New York: Harper & Row, 1979), 294–95.
12. Ibid.
13. Ronald Reagan to Gerald Ford, telegram, 7 October, 1974, in Reagan, Ron W.H.C.F. Name File, Box 2608, Gerald Ford Presidential Library (FL).
14. Ibid.
15. Halberstam, *The Reckoning*.
16. Steven F. Hayward, *The Age of Reagan: The Fall of the Old Liberal Order, 1964–1980* (New York: Three Rivers Press, 2001), 413.
17. Henry Kissinger, *Diplomacy* (New York: Simon & Schuster, 1994), 766.
18. Daniel Patrick Moynihan, *A Dangerous Place* (Boston: Little, Brown, 1978), 56.
19. R. Emmett Tyrell, *Public Nuisances* (New York: Basic Books, 1979), 237. Reagan, in his November 8, 1977, radio address "SALT," referred to Brezhnev's statement. (Skinner, Anderson, and Anderson, *Reagan: In His Own Hand*, 75.)
20. Angelo Codevilla, *Informing Statecraft: Intelligence for a New Century* (New York: Free Press, 1993), 223.
21. Hayward, *Age of Reagan: Fall of the Old Liberal Order*, 423.
22. Ibid., 436.
23. Ibid., 440.
24. Lou Cannon, *Governor Reagan: The Rise to Power* (New York: Public Affairs, 2003), 386.
25. Jules Witcover, *Marathon: The Pursuit of the Presidency, 1972–1976* (New York: Viking, 1977), 70-72.
26. Ron Nessen to Bob Hartmann, 15 April 1975, in Reagan, Ron W.H.C.F. Name File, Box 2608, FL.
27. James M. Cannon, *Gerald R. Ford: An Honorable Life* (Ann Arbor: University of Michigan Press, 2013), 397.
28. Michael Reagan with Joe Hyams, *On the Outside Looking In* (New York: Zebra, 1988), 30, 33, 96, 122–24, 142–43, 147; and Maureen Reagan, *First Father, First Daughter* (Boston: Little, Brown, 1989).

29. *The New Republic*, January 3, 1976; Barry Farrell, "The Candidate from Disneyland," *Harper's Magazine*, February 1976, https://harpers.org/archive/1976/02/the-candidate-from-disneyland/; and "Taking Reagan Seriously," *Chicago Daily News*, November 21, 1975.

30. Hayward, *Age of Reagan: Fall of the Old Liberal Order*, 454.

31. Jim Shuman to Ron Nessen, memorandum, 21 November 1975, in Reagan, Ron W.H.C.F. Name File, Box 2608, FL.

32. Ibid.

33. Terry O'Donnell to Dick Cheney, memorandum, 23 January 1976, in Reagan, Ron W.H.C.F. Name File, Box 2608, FL.

34. "Campaign Plan, 08/29/1975 (President Ford Committee Campaign Plan)," in Robert P. Visser, Legal Counsel for the President Ford Committee: Papers 1972–1978, General Subject File, FL.

35. Ibid.

36. Ibid.

37. Ibid.

38. James M. Cannon, *Gerald R. Ford*, 391.

39. "Part II (cont'd) Delegate Strategy," General Subject File, Campaign Plan, 29 August, 1975, in Visser, FL.

40. Ibid.

41. Jeffrey Hart, "White House Report," *National Review*, March 19, 1976.

42. Lou Cannon, *Governor Reagan*, 410–11, relates a story where at a press conference Reagan told the story of Doris Miller, the black sailor at Pearl Harbor who manned a machine gun and shot down up to five Japanese planes. He didn't use Miller's name but used this as an example of how the armed services had been integrated. Except Miller was a messman at the time—and while he wasn't a sailor, the fact is that Miller indeed advanced integration in the armed forces.

43. Hayward, *Age of Reagan: Fall of the Old Liberal Order*, 463.

44. Ibid., 465.

45. Ibid., 466.

46. Lou Cannon, *Governor Reagan*, 424.

47. Ibid., 430.

48. Hayward, *Age of Reagan: Fall of the Old Liberal Order*, 476.

49. Ibid, 481.

50. Edward L. Schapsmeier and Frederick H. Schapsmeier, *Gerald R. Ford's Date with Destiny: A Political Biography* (New York: Peter Long, 1989), 201–211.

51. Lou Cannon, *Governor Reagan*, 431.

52. Hayward, *Age of Reagan: Fall of the Old Liberal Order*, 478.

53. Ibid., 480.

54. *Newsweek*, August 30, 1976.

55. *National Review*, September 1976. The irony of *National Review* criticizing Reagan for not being conservative enough is all the more noteworthy since in 2015–2016 the magazine, now as *National Review Online* or *NRO*, sharply attacked the Republican nominee Donald Trump on grounds he wasn't conservative enough when he held almost exactly the same positions as every Republican up to Dwight Eisenhower had

held, and most of the same positions as Reagan. But, like Reagan, he was an "outsider" who was not invited.

56. Lou Cannon, *Governor Reagan*, 434.

57. See Joel Pollak and Larry Schweikart, *How Trump Won: The Inside Story of a Revolution* (Washington, DC: Regnery, 2017), for examinations of polling errors during the 2016 election. Pollster Richard Baris, of People's Pundit Daily poll—the most accurate pollster of 2016 who had Hillary Clinton at +1.5% nationally yet losing the key states of Ohio, Florida, North Carolina, Michigan, and Pennsylvania has consistently argued that pollsters misidentify "likely" voters, particularly conservative voters. One error, for example, in Suffolk polling, involved asking for the "youngest voter in the home"—a dead certain way to rig a poll to be more Democrat friendly. Polling in Wisconsin was off by an *average* of six points! No pollster, including PPD, correctly called Wisconsin for Donald Trump, and only PPD and Trafalgar (which did not poll nationally) correctly called Michigan and Pennsylvania for Trump. All pollsters missed badly (an average of 4 points) Trump's margin of victory in Ohio (9.5).

58. Hayward, *Age of Reagan: Fall of the Old Liberal Order*, 483. Hayward claims Reagan benefitted by not winning, and that the Panama crisis would have been extremely difficult for him. The Gipper called Omar Torrijos, the Panamanian leader, a "tinhorn dictator" and insisted the canal was and would always be American property and the Canal Zone American territory. "We bought it, we paid for it, it's ours, and we're going to keep it," he said (Lou Cannon, *Governor Reagan*, 422).

CHAPTER 8

1. Larry Schweikart, *Seven Events That Made America America* (New York: Sentinel, 2010), 5–33.

2. Lincoln does not fit the notion of a popular candidate in that there were four political parties in the 1860 election and the popular vote was against him. It is more fitting to say he was on the cutting edge of a revolution that had not yet reached a majority of Americans.

3. "Politicians Find G.O.P. Fighting for Its Survival," *New York Times*, November 24, 1976, https://www.nytimes.com/1976/11/24/archives/new-jersey-pages-politicians-find-gop-fighting-for-its-survival.html.

4. Peter G. Bourne, *Jimmy Carter: A Comprehensive Biography from Plains to Postpresidency* (New York: Lisa Drew, 1997), 270.

5. Interview with Jimmy Carter, *Playboy*, November 1976.

6. Bourne, *Jimmy Carter*, 371.

7. Steven F. Hayward, *The Age of Reagan: The Fall of the Old Liberal Order, 1964–1980* (New York: Three Rivers Press, 2001), 514.

8. Ibid., 521.

9. Craig Shirley, *Reagan Rising: The Decisive Years, 1976–1980* (New York: Broadside Books, 2017), 62; and Jimmy Carter (speech excerpts), "Carter: 'Oil and Natural Gas…Are Running Out,'" *Washington Post*, April 19, 1977, https://www.washingtonpost.com/archive/politics/1977/04/19/carter-oil-and-natural-gas-are-running-out/de4c4a51-4418-4224-b388-3fcc5d63e631/?noredirect=on&utm_term=.c3fd512d1921.

10. Carter, "Oil and Natural Gas…Are Running Out."

11. Bourne, *Jimmy Carter*, 430.
12. H. W. Brands, *Reagan: The Life* (New York: Doubleday, 2015), 226.
13. Hayward, *Age of Reagan: Fall of the Old Liberal Order*, 554; Michael Ledeen and William Lewis, *Debacle: The American Failure in Iran* (New York: Alfred A. Knopf, 1981), 126; and Gary Sick, *All Fall Down: America's Tragic Encounter with Iran* (New York: Penguin, 1986), 43.
14. Hayward, *Age of Reagan: Fall of the Old Liberal Order*, 554.
15. "RR AND MRS. R'S SCHEDULE (13–30 April, 1978), Governor's Office Files, GO 178, Foreign Travel (Ronald Reagan) - Far East/Iran, 04/13/1978-04/30-1978, Reagan Library (RL).
16. Ronald Reagan, *Reagan in His Own Hand*, eds. Kiron K. Skinner, Annelise Anderson, and Martin Anderson (New York: Free Press, 2001), 113–14.
17. Hayward, *Age of Reagan: Fall of the Old Liberal Order*, 610.
18. Ibid., 601.
19. Jay Winik, *On the Brink* (New York: Simon & Schuster, 1996), 100; and Hayward, *Age of Reagan: Fall of the Old Liberal Order*, 606.
20. Bourne, *Jimmy Carter*, 382.
21. Adlai Stevenson III received 5,600 opposed and only 5 in favor (Hayward, *Age of Reagan: Fall of the Old Liberal Order*, 546).
22. Ronnie Duggar, *On Reagan: The Man and His Presidency* (New York: McGraw-Hill, 1983), 273.
23. Randy Roberts and James S. Olson, *John Wayne, American* (New York: Free Press, 1995), 611. Wayne had been brought into the debate almost by accident, placing a phone call to Panama's president Omar Torrijos, congratulating him on the treaty. Torrejos told the *New York Times*, but once the information was out, Duke had to bone up on the aspects of the agreement. He still concluded it was a reasonable deal, "moderniz[ing] an outmoded relationship with a friendly and hospitable country" (610).
24. John Wayne to Ronald Reagan, 11 November 1977, Executive File, Jimmy Carter Presidential Library (CL).
25. Hayward, *Age of Reagan: Fall of the Old Liberal Order*, 548.
26. Shirley, *Reagan Rising*, 105, 112.
27. Angelo M. Codevilla, "America's Ruling Class—and the Perils of Revolution," *American Spectator*, July 16, 2010.
28. Burton I. Kaufman, *The Presidency of James Earl Carter, Jr.* (Lawrence: University Press of Kansas, 1993), 370–71.
29. Jeane Kirkpatrick, "Dictatorships and Double Standards," *Commentary*, Fall 1979, https://www.commentarymagazine.com/articles/dictatorships-double-standards/.
30. *Time*, "Vance: Man on the Move," April 24, 1978, http://content.time.com/time/magazine/article/0,9171,916105,00.html.
31. *National Review*, February 18, 1977.
32. Hayward, *Age of Reagan: Fall of the Old Liberal Order*, 575.
33. Jimmy Carter, "Crisis of Confidence," in Larry Schweikart, Dave Dougherty, and Michael Allen, *The Patriot's History Reader: Essential Documents for Every American* (New York: Sentinel, 2011), 385–92; and Hayward, *Age of Reagan: Fall of the Old Liberal Order*, 579.

34. "Dank Victory," *The New Republic*, November 18, 1978.

35. Shirley, *Reagan Rising*, 45.

36. Reagan, "The New Republican Party," February 6, 1977, Reagan 2020, The Patriot Post, http://reagan2020.us/speeches/The_New_Republican_Party.asp.

37. Shirley, *Reagan Rising*, 67.

38. Ibid., 114.

39. Lou Cannon, *Governor Reagan: His Rise to Power* (New York: Public Affairs, 2003), 440.

40. Author interviews with William Verity, various dates, 1999–2000. See also Schweikart, *Marriage of Steel: The Life and Times of William and Peggy Verity* (Boston: Pearson Custom Publishing, 2000), 56.

41. For example, in January 1979, Gallup showed Carter with a 22-point lead over Reagan.

42. Bourne, *Jimmy Carter*, 396.

43. *Rockin' the Wall*. Produced by Schweikart and Mark Leif. United States, 2010. Documentary.

44. Bourne, *Jimmy Carter*, 436.

45. Ibid., 441.

46. Pat Caddell, "Of Crisis and Opportunity," April 23, 1979, Powell Paper, Box 40, (CL).

47. Bourne, *Jimmy Carter*, 442; and Jimmy Carter, *Keeping Faith: Memoirs of a President* (New York: Bantam, 1982), 115.

48. Bourne, *Jimmy Carter*, 444.

49. Hayward, *Age of Reagan: Fall of the Old Liberal Order*, 628.

50. Ibid., 635.

51. Ibid., 630.

52. *Weekly Standard*, February 5, 2001, 21.

53. Hayward, *Age of Reagan: Fall of the Old Liberal Order*, 633.

54. Cannon, *Governor Reagan*, 448.

55. Ibid., 449.

56. Ibid., 460–61.

57. Cannon, *Governor Reagan*, 464.

58. Hayward, *Age of Reagan: Fall of the Old Liberal Order*, 664.

59. Ibid., 671.

60. Michael Reagan, *Lessons My Father Taught Me: The Strength, Integrity, and Faith of Ronald Reagan* (West Palm Beach, FL: Humanix Books, 2016), 50–51; interviews with Michael Reagan, various dates, 2017.

61. Cannon, *Governor Reagan*, 476.

62. Ibid., 478.

63. Dinesh D'Souza, *Ronald Reagan: How an Ordinary Man Became an Extraordinary Leader* (New York: Touchstone, 1997), 82.

64. Carter, *Keeping Faith*, 542.

65. Cannon, *Governor Reagan*, 487.

66. Hayward, *Age of Reagan: Fall of the Old Liberal Order*, 699.

67. Ibid., 699.

68. Edward Walsh, "Carter Criticizes Reagan on Arms Control," *Washington Post*, October 7, 1980.

69. Cannon, *Governor Reagan*, 491.

70. Ibid., 492.

71. It was never determined how the Reagan team got the files, although some speculated that a Kennedy associate, Paul Corbin, who received a check from William Casey for $1,500 for "research," supplied the briefing book. However, Corbin had never been to the White House or the Carter campaign offices, so there was no smoking gun. However, in 1983, the materials were found in David Gergen's files, and Gergen had been on Reagan's debate preparation team.

72. Carter, *Keeping Faith*, 564.

73. Craig Shirley, *Rendezvous with Destiny: Ronald Reagan and the Campaign That Changed America* (Wilmington: ISI Books, 2009), 540.

74. Carter was delusional about the state of the economy, writing in *Keeping Faith*, "Reagan and the press are playing up the so-called economic emergency. As a matter of fact, with the exception of interest rates, everything is going surprisingly well," 589.

75. Ibid., 565.

76. Ibid., 567.

77. Shirley, *Rendezvous with Destiny*, 576.

78. Cannon, *Governor Reagan*, 511.

79. Steven F. Hayward, *The Age of Reagan: The Conservative Counterrevolution, 1981–1989* (New York: Three Rivers Press, 2009), 21.

80. Ibid., 22. David Broder called the election a "tidal wave" and said an anti-Washington, anti-Establishment storm was entirely missed by the elites. It would be precisely the same attitude that missed the anti-Washington/anti-Establishment wave that swept Donald Trump into office in 2016. See Joel Pollak and Schweikart, *How Trump Won: The Inside Story of a Revolution* (Washington, DC: Regnery, 2017).

81. Brands (*Reagan: The Life*) dedicates almost six pages to this non-event.

82. Cannon, *President Reagan: The Role of a Lifetime* (New York: Simon & Schuster, 1991), 103.

83. Michael K. Deaver with Mickey Herskowitz, *Behind the Scenes* (New York: William Morrow, 1987), 100.

84. Cannon, *President Reagan*, 105.

85. This created, as another scholar noted, a "unified political management" of all issues, even noneconomic issues. See Wallace Earl Walker and Michael R. Reopel, "Strategies for Governance: Transition and Domestic Policy Making in the Reagan Administration," *Presidential Studies Quarterly* (Fall 1986): 734–60; and H. Helco, "One Executive Branch or Many?" in *Both Ends of the Avenue*, ed. Anthony King (Washington, DC: American Enterprise Institute, 1983), 44.

86. Reagan, *An American Life* (New York: Pocket Books, 1990), 225.

87. Ibid., 225–26.

88. Quoted in Tara McKelvey, "Close Encounters," *New York Times*, January 22, 2006, https://www.nytimes.com/2006/01/22/books/review/close-encounters.html.

89. Reagan, *An American Life*, 227.

90. Bourne, *Jimmy Carter*, 476. Interestingly, biographers such as Bourne omit all of Carter's slights to Reagan, including Rosalynn's "comfortable with our prejudices" comment.

91. Jimmy Carter and Rosalynn Carter, *Everything to Gain* (New York: Random House, 1987), 9.

92. And, to add insult to injury, the blind trust in which Carter's assets had been placed was broke when he finally saw the ledgers.

93. Paul Taylor, "Carter Plans to Sue The Post Over Blair House Bugging Story," *Washington Post*, October 9, 1981.

94. Anthony Lewis, "Abroad At Home; 'One Little Tattler,'" *New York Times*, October 19, 1981.

95. Brands, *Reagan*, 256.

96. Treptow was buried in Wisconsin and the staff discovered the error too late to change the essence of Reagan's speech, which alluded to Arlington. Of course, the media pounced on this factual error while ignoring the more substantial symbolic truth.

CHAPTER 9

1. Lee Edwards, *The Power of Ideas: The Heritage Foundation at 25 Years* (Ottawa: Jameson Books, 1997), 41–68.

2. Ibid., 42.

3. Peter McPherson to Ed Meese, 31 April, 1980, Box 20, Folder Early Planning, Reagan, Ronald 1980 Transition Papers, 1979–1981, Reagan Library (RL).

4. Ed Schmults, Background, "A Regulatory Restraint Budget for the 1980s," 18 November, 1980, Alpha File 5(3), Box 16, [51.], Transition Papers 1979–81, RL.

5. Memorandum from William Timmons to Ed Meese, 1 December, 1980, "W.H." Misc., Box 34, Reagan, Ronald 1980 Transition Papers, 1979–81, RL.

6. Memorandum by Eric Hemal, "RE: The Reagan Administration and the Congressional Budget," 13 April, 1980, Reagan, Ronald 1980 Transition papers, 1979–81, RL.

7. H. W. Brands, *Reagan: The Life* (New York: Doubleday, 2015), 260.

8. Interview with Joseph Wright, June 15, 2015.

9. Regan, clearly disliked by Brands, seemed miffed that he had little personal time with the Gipper and claimed that he had not been informed as to what his goals were, or what the president expected out of him. But Regan was a Wall Street banker, and considered smart. Reagan should *not have had to* brief him often on the goals or objectives. All he had to do was read a speech. Regan early on would begin to undermine the supply-side basis of the Reagan administration (Brands, *Reagan*, 262–63).

10. Darrell M. Trent to Ed Harper, "Debt Ceiling Status," 11 December, 1980, Transition Action Papers, A.031-A.059 (A.044), Box 20, [51.], Transition Papers 1979–81, RL. The same debt ceiling increase would confront President Donald Trump in 2017 under similar circumstances.

11. Lou Cannon, *President Reagan: The Role of a Lifetime* (New York: Simon & Schuster, 1991), 103.

12. Memorandum for President-Elect From Powell Moore, Assistant Director of Congressional Relations - Senate, 5 December, 1980, in Folder President-Elect Reagan Briefing Manual from December 8–13, 1980, Box 21, Transition Papers 1979–81, RL.

13. Ibid.

14. "Farewell Interview," *San Antonio Express*, in "Trudy Feldman," Box 18, Reagan, Ronald 1980 Transition Papers, 1979–81, RL.

15. Tom Morganthau, "A Bloated Transition," *Newsweek*, December 29, 1980.

16. Even at six hundred people, some were inevitably left out of the transition process, including supply-sider Paul Craig Roberts, who complained about being left out, and

businessman Lewis Lehrman, who sent Meese an unsolicited detailed memorandum on "How to Organize President-Elect Reagan's Program During an Economic Crisis" (Paul Craig Roberts to Edwin Meese, 10 November, 1980, in Reagan, Ronald 1980, "Transition Papers, 1979–81"; and Lewis Lehrman to Edwin Meese, 11 November, 1980, Series II, Director of the Treasury (Ed Meese), Subseries A, Correspondence, incoming Alpha C, Box 13, RL.

17. William Timmons to Edwin Meese, 6 January, 1981, in Transition Papers, Series I, Director of Transition (Ed Meese), Series II, Subseries A, Correspondence Memorandums & Correspondence (2), RL.

18. Cannon, *President Reagan*, 86, 111; and Wallace Earl Walker and Michael R. Reopel, "Strategies for Governance: Transition and Domestic Policy Making in the Reagan Administration," *Presidential Studies Quarterly* (Fall 1986): 734–60 (quotation on 739). Typically, Walker and Reopel inject "The Reagan strategy was not always a well designed blueprint. Often events and decisions became strategy fortuitously," yet offer no examples.

19. "Transition Action Paper," 19 December, 1980, in 1980 Transition Papers, 1979–81, Series II: Director of Transition (Ed Meese), Series II, subseries C Amin & Planning, Box 20, Folder A.060-A.078, RL.

20. Transition Timmons Papers, 1980 Transition Papers, 1979–81, Series III: Deputy Director for Executive Branch Management (William Timmons), Series III, Subseries B, Reports, Box 35, RL.

21. Memorandum from Bill Timmons to David Stockman, 15 December, 1980, in 1980 Transition Papers, 1979–81, Series III, Deputy Director for Executive Branch Management (William Timmons), Series III: Subseries D; Issue Clusters; Sub-Subseries 3: National Security (D. Abshire) Box 79, Folder "Stockman Budget Taskforce NSG," RL.

22. Ibid., Timmons to Stockman.

23. Memorandum from Anthony R. Dolan to Ed Meese and Bob Barrick, 7 January, 1981, in Transition Papers, 1979–81, Box 5, RL.

24. Memorandum from Murray Weidenbaum to the President, 6 February, 1981, "Sudit of U.S. Economy as of 1/20/81," in Anderson, Martin Files, Series I: Subject File, Economic Recovery Package (2 of 7), Box 12, RL.

25. As biographer Steven Hayward noted, Jack Kemp preferred the term "Economic Inchon," but people were less familiar with the battle. However, Inchon was a daring offensive maneuver, while Dunkirk was a withdrawal, and as Winston Churchill noted, "Wars are not won by great evacuations." Hayward quips that when trouble came in the Reagan years, Stockman "sought the first lifeboat" (Steven F. Hayward, *The Age of Reagan: The Conservative Counterrevolution, 1980–1989* [New York: Three Rivers Falls, 2009], 58).

26. Memorandum from David Stockman to Economic Policy Coordinating Committee, 1980 Transition Papers, 1979–81, Series II, Director of Transition (Ed Meese), Series II, Subseries C, Admin, Box 20, Folder A.069, RL.

27. Transition Update, 8 January, 1981, in Reagan, Ronald 1980 Transition Papers, 1979–81, Series II: Director of Transition (Ed Meese), Subseries A: Correspondence memorandums & Correspondence (2), RL.

28. Brands, *Reagan*, 241–42.

29. Hayward, *Age of Reagan: Conservative Counterrevolution*, 40.

30. Ibid., 40.

31. Ibid., 9.

32. Paul Duke, *Beyond Reagan: The Politics of Upheaval* (New York: Warner Books, 1986), 122–23.

33. John Patrick Diggins, *Ronald Reagan: Fate, Freedom and the Making of History* (New York W. W. Norton, 2007), xx.

34. Hayward, *Age of Reagan: Conservative Counterrevolution*, 43.

35. Ronald Reagan, *An American Life* (New York: Pocket Books, 1990), 230.

36. Ronald Reagan, *The Reagan Diaries*, ed. Douglas Brinkley (New York: HarperCollins, 2007), 1.

37. David A. Stockman, *The Triumph of Politics: How the Reagan Revolution Failed* (New York: Harper & Row, 1986), 9.

38. Cannon, *President Reagan*, 111.

39. Ibid., 114. Democratic congressional members would say the same things of Donald Trump and Barack Obama in 2017.

40. Reagan, *An American Life*, 236–37.

41. Cannon, *President Reagan*, 108.

42. Ibid. This was precisely the success that both FDR and Donald Trump had with the economy, FDR insisting there was nothing to fear but "fear itself" and Trump promising to "make America great again!" In Trump's case particularly, investment and job creation started immediately, whereas at best FDR can be credited with stopping a worse collapse—although the academic jury is still out on that. Many point to Roosevelt's subsequent policies as perpetuating the Great Depression long after a normal recovery would have set in. See Larry Schweikart and Michael Allen, *A Patriot's History of the United States: From Columbus's Great Discovery to the Age of Entitlement* (New York: Sentinel, 2014), 580–90; and Burton W. Folsom Jr. *New Deal or Raw Deal? How FDR's Economic Legacy Has Damaged America* (New York: Simon & Schuster, 2008).

43. Cannon, *President Reagan*, 108.

44. William Fellner, *Essays in Contemporary Economic Problems, 1981–2* (Washington, DC: American Enterprise Institute, 1981), 58.

45. George Gilder, "George Gilder is on a Ken Fisher Kick," *Forbes*, December 14, 2006, https://www.forbes.com/2006/12/14/fisher-gilder-telecosm-pf-guru-in_gg_1214 soapbox_inl.html; and Gilder and Bruce Chapman, *The Party That Lost Its Head* (1966). Gilder later recanted what he wrote in 1966, saying that the "'right wing extremists,' as I confidently called them, were right on almost every major policy issue from welfare to Vietnam to Keynesian economics and defense—while I...was nearly always wrong" (Gilder, "Why I am Not a Neo-Conservative," *National Review* 23, 219–20.)

46. Jude Wanniski, *The Way the World Works: How Economies Fail—and Succeed* (New York: Basic Books, 1978). Wanniski's Smoot-Hawley thesis was provocative and compelling. It took time for scholars to determine that the specific impact of the tariff was not likely enough to cause the Crash. But there remained a case for the effect of the pending tariff on expectations.

47. Critics would later scoff at the "Laffer Curve," often claiming it was drawn on a napkin at dinner, without noting that the Dayton, Ohio Engineers' Club, featuring the work

of some of the most famous engineers and inventors in the country, displays numerous tablecloths where brilliant designs were sketched, or that the elements of the Beatles' classic "Yesterday" were similarly written on a napkin.

48. Reagan, *An American Life*, 231–32.
49. Ibid., 227.
50. Interview with Joseph Wright, June 15, 2015.
51. Ibid.
52. "Ten Questions and Answers on the President's Economic Program," Economic Recovery Package (1 of 7), Anderson, Martin Files, Box 12, Series 1: Subject File Economic Policy Group-Energy (3), Murray Weidenbaum Statement to House Ways & Means Committee, 24 February, 1981, RL.
53. John Rutledge and Lawrence Kudlow, "Preliminary Report to the Economic Policy Group," 22 January, 1981, in Anderson, Martin Files, Box 12, Series 1: subject File Economic Policy Group, RL.
54. Brands, *Reagan: The Life*, 263.
55. In fact, with a couple of exceptions, the federal government per capita had grown since the age of Jefferson, then accelerated once Martin Van Buren ingeniously linked winning elections to the "spoils system" in 1824. Abraham Lincoln had to deal with lines of federal job-seekers while fighting the Civil War. With the Pendleton Civil Service Act, which "reformed" the process, the spoils system hardly ended. Rather it was expanded from giving jobs to individuals to promising jobs to groups. Reagan was battling a century-old system embraced by both parties as a means of maintaining power and would soon find that significantly cutting government would be nearly impossible within the system (Schweikart, *Seven Events That Made America America* [New York: Sentinel, 2010], 5–23).
56. Reagan, *The Reagan Diaries*, 5.
57. Memorandum from David Stockman to Jim Baker and Ed Meese, "Status of Legislative Strategy," 23 February, 1981, in Fuller, Craig L. Files, Series III, Budget Planing and Review, OA 4691, Box 1, Folder [Economic Budget Policy 1981], RL.
58. Notes on "Tax Rate Cuts" discussion, no date [February 1981], Dole, Elizabeth Files, Series III, Economic Policy Program, Box 65, Folder (1 Economic Recovery Program 1 (3)), RL.
59. Notes on "Tax Rate Cuts" discussion, Dole, Elizabeth Files, RL.
60. Hayward, *Age of Reagan: Conservative Counterrevolution*, 35.
61. Ibid., 140.
62. Dick Kirschten, "Reagan: No More Business as Usual," *National Journal*, February 21, 1981, 300, 302–3.
63. Dinesh D'Souza (*Ronald Reagan: How an Ordinary Man Became an Extraordinary Leader* [New York: Touchstone, 1997]) said, "Critics of supply-side economics, including some conservative skeptics, have tried to discredit the doctrine by attributing to supply siders in the Reagan administration the view that a reduction in tax rates would produce an overall increase in government revenues, so the tax cut would 'pay for itself.' This *obviously didn't happen*" (emphasis mine) (116). First, D'Souza does not cite Reagan or any Reagan official for such a claim. Second, revenue rose by over 20 percent, meaning the tax cuts did produce an overall increase in government revenue. Likewise, Michael Boskin wrote in *Reagan and the Economy: The Successes, Failures,*

and Unfinished Agenda (San Francisco: ICS Press: 1989), xv: "It is important not to be distracted by the…1980 campaign statements.… [when] the Reagan campaign team was saying, *or implying*, that a large tax cut would raise revenue, that inflation could be sharply reduced without a recession, and that tens of billions of dollars of expenditures could be cut out of the budget without injury to anyone except a few bureaucrats. *None of these things turned out to be true*" (emphasis mine). Again, it most certainly was true that the large tax cut raised revenue. According to US federal budget figures, revenues increased 22 percent from 1982 to 1988. They increased every year after 1984 following the recession. So claims that the tax cuts did not "raise revenues" are simply wrong. See "Budget of the United States Government," https://www.govinfo.gov/app/collection/BUDGET/ .

64. "Ten Questions and Answers," RL.
65. Economic Briefing by Murray Weidenbaum, Donald Regan, and David Stockman, 18, February, 1981, Box 65, Economic Recovery Program I (1), RL.
66. Rutledge and Kudlow, "Preliminary Report."
67. Draft Speech to the Joint Session, 2nd Draft, 17 February, 1981, Anderson, Martin Files, Series I, Subject File Economic Recovery Package (2 of 7), Box 12, RL.
68. Fuller's Handwritten Notes for Meetings, n.d. but circa 23 February, 1981, Fuller, Craig L. Files, Series III, Budget Planning & Review, OA 4691, Box 1, Folder [Economic/Budget Policy 1981], RL.
69. Reagan, *An American Life*, 233.
70. "The Emerging Style," *Washington Star*, February 23, 1981.
71. "Sizing Up the Program," *Newsweek*, March 2, 1981.
72. "Reagan's Budget Battle," *The Nation*, May 11, 1981; and Christopher Byron, "Easing the Tax Squeeze on Savers," *Time*, May 11, 1981, http://content.time.com/time/magazine/article/0,9171,949140,00.html.
73. An untitled memorandum, n.d., in Craig Fuller's files noted: Hawkins is "adamant about not including the community mental health program (her favorite) in the block [grants]," but Chairman Hatch's strategy was to "reorganize and redefine the blocks" to hold together a majority. See Fuller, Craig L. Files, Series III, Budget Planning and Revision, OA 4691, Box 1, Folder [Economic/Budget Policy April 1981], (1), RL.
74. "Surrogate Economic Policy Speech: Speakers Bureau," 16 March, 1981, Anderson, Martin Files, Series 1, Economic Policy Group - Energy (3) Box 12, Document #4, Economic Policy Package (7 of 7), RL.
75. Memorandum, Elizabeth Dole to Morton C. Blackwell, 30 March, 1980, Doc. #7, in Dole, Elizabeth Files, Series III, Economic Recovery Program, Box 65, "Economic Recovery," (3 of 4), RL.
76. Franklin D. Roosevelt, "A Message to Congress on Social Security," January 17, 1935, https://www.ssa.gov/history/fdrstmts.html.
77. Cannon, *President Reagan*, 244.
78. Ibid., 245. It did not help that Stockman was contemptuous of the New Mexico senator, calling him John Maynard Domenici.
79. Ibid., 247. Note that Cannon has only an interview source on this, Stephen Bell. While not an anonymous source, nevertheless one must wonder if other participants recalled the meeting the same way.

80. Michael K. Deaver with Mickey Herkowitz, *Behind the Scenes* (New York: William Morrow, 1987), 16.

81. Hinckley in fact had stalked *both* Jimmy Carter and Ronald Reagan during the campaign. See *The Shooting of Ronald Reagan*, produced by National Geographic. N.d. Documentary, https://www.dailymotion.com/video/x2yh9l9.

82. Secret Service Radio Audio Clip at "Attempted Assassination of Ronald Reagan," https://en.wikipedia.org/wiki/Attempted_assassination_of_Ronald_Reagan#Assassination_attempt.

83. Parr's wife worked right across the street and came running, horrified her husband was injured or dead (*Shooting of Ronald Reagan*).

84. Ronald Reagan, *The Reagan Diaries*, single volume edition, ed. Douglas Brinkley (New York: HarperCollins, 2007), 12.

85. Del Quentin Wilber, *Rawhide Down: The Near Assassination of Ronald Reagan* (New York: William Morrow, 2011), 107–8.

86. Reagan, *The Reagan Diaries*, 12.

87. Ibid.

88. Wilber, *Rawhide Down*, 147.

89. "Shooting of Ronald Reagan."

90. *The Saving of the President, 1981*, produced by George Washington University Medical Center (1982: WJLA-TV7), https://www.youtube.com/watch?v=P2Wr3UPR5CU.

91. Deaver, *Behind the Scenes*, 23.

92. Wilber, *Rawhide Down*, 200.

93. Ibid., 203.

94. Deaver, *Behind the Scenes*, 23.

95. Wilber, *Rawhide Down*, 210.

96. Ibid., 211.

97. Susan Jeffords, *Hard Bodies: Hollywood Masculinity in the Reagan Era* (New Brunswick: Rutgers University Press, 1994), 30.

98. Deaver, *Behind the Scenes*, 27.

99. Reagan, *The Reagan Diaries*, 12.

100. "An 'Incredible Revelation': Reagan Carried a Gun After Attempted Assassination, Author Says," Fox News, June 15, 2015, http://www.foxnews.com/politics/2015/06/15/incredible-revelation-reagan-carried-gun-after-attempted-assassination-author.html.

101. Brands, *Reagan*, 270.

102. W. Elliot Brownlee, *Federal Taxation in America: A History*, 3rd edition (New York: Cambridge University Press, 2016), 184.

103. "Financial and Economic Update—A Report on the Current Situation," 17 March, 1982, [Economic/Budget Policy 3/82] (2 of 2) OA4691 in Fuller, Craig Files, RL.

104. "Legislative Strategy Agenda," RGD-3/24/82, March 24, 1982, in Fuller, Craig Files, RL.

105. Nancy Reagan with William Novak, *My Turn: The Memoirs of Nancy Reagan* (New York: Random House, 1989), 40–42.

106. Nancy Reagan, *My Turn*, 43.

107. *Business Outlook*, 20 May, 1981, in Anderson, Martin Files, series 1, Subject File Congressional Budget Office - C- Issues (5), Box 9, Folder "Council of Economic Advisers" (2 of 3), RL. The author of the newsletter, Dr. James Smith, noted, "Some observers do

not realize how the entire program fits together as a package. A particular problem for some has been understanding that the proposed tax cuts are not inflationary."

108. Jerry Jordan to Murray Weidenbaum, "Discussion Points Regarding the 1981–86 Forecast," 23 May, 1981, in Anderson, Martin: Files, Series 1, Subject File, Congressional Budget Office, Box 4, C, Issues (5) Folder "Council of Economic Advisers" (1 of 7), RL.

109. Jordan to Weidenbaum, "Discussion Points Regarding the 1981–86 Forecast."

110. Marty Asher to Murray Weidenbaum, "The Evolution of First Quarter GNP Forecasts," 8 June, 1981, in Anderson, Martin: Files, Series 1, Subject File, Congressional Budget Office, Box 9, (1 of 3), Folder "Council of Economic Advisers," RL.

111. Asher to Weidenbaum, "Evolution."

112. William A. Niskanen, *Reaganomics: An Insider's Account of the Policies and the People* (New York: Oxford University Press, 1988), 38.

113. "Reagan Proposes 10% Cut in Social Security Costs," *Washington Post*, May 13, 1981.

114. Reagan, *The Reagan Diaries*, 17.

115. Ibid., 23.

116. Charls [sic] Walker, "Summary of Discussion," *American Economic Policy in the 1980s*, Martin Feldstein, ed. (Chicago: University of Chicago Press, 1994), 224–25.

117. Ronald Reagan, economic speech—address to the nation, February 5, 1981, in Kiron K. Skinner, Annelise Anderson, and Martin Anderson, *Reagan: In His Own Hand: The Writings of Ronald Reagan That Reveal His Revolutionary Vision for America* (New York: Free Press, 2001), 490.

118. Murray Weidenbaum to the President, "The Economy—Early July 1981," 6 July, 1981, in Anderson, Martin: Files, Series 1, Subject File, Congressional Budget Office, Box 9, Folder "Council of Economic Advisers" (2 of 3), RL.

119. "Annual Averages," 6 July, 1981, in Anderson, Martin: Files, Series 1, Subject File, Congressional Budget Office, "Council of Economic Advisers," Box 9 (1 of 3), C, Folder "Issues" (5)," RL.

120. Weidenbaum to the President, "The Economy."

121. On December 15, Weidenbaum told the National Press Club that interest rates had come down because of "restraint" and that while he anticipated several more months of poor economic statistics, there were "powerful forces" reversing the current direction, most notably the tax cuts. Murray Weidenbaum, "The Challenges of Making Economic Policy," 15 December, 1981, in Anderson, Martin: Files, Series 1: Subject File, Congressional Budget Office, C, Issues (5), Box 9, Folder "Council of Economic Advisers," (3 of 3), RL.

122. Memcons–President Reagan, 21 May, 1981, Box 48, Exec Sec NSC, Sub Files [Chancellor Helmut Schmidt of FRG], RL.

123. Reagan, *The Reagan Diaries*, 31.

124. Reagan, *The Reagan Diaries*, 33.

125. Ibid., September 21, 1981, 39.

126. Ibid., 40.

127. Ronald Reagan, inaugural address, 1981.

CHAPTER 10

1. See, for example, Ronald Reagan, *The Reagan Diaries*, single volume ed., ed. Douglas Brinkley (New York: HarperCollins, 2007), 33 and 40.

2. Paul Kengor, *The Crusader: Ronald Reagan and the Fall of Communism* (New York: ReganBooks, 2006), 118.

3. "USSR: Economic Issues Facing Leadership: An Intelligence Assessment," January 2, 1981, CIA Historical Collection on Ronald Reagan https://www.cia.gov/library/readingroom/docs/CIA-RDP83B00140R000100020026-5.pdf. Note that the document is dated 1981, but this is the written version given shortly before.

4. Peter Schweizer, *Reagan's War: The Epic Story of His Forty-Year Struggle and Final Triumph Over Communism* (New York: Anchor Books, 2002), 143.

5. Jim Rose, "Paul Samuelson's Repeated Predictions of the Soviet Union Economy Catching Up with the USA," January 24, 2015, https://utopiayouarestandinginit.com/2015/01/24/paul-samuelsons-repeated-predictions-of-the-soviet-union-economy-catching-up-with-the-usa/; David M. Levy and Sandra J. Peart, "Soviet Growth & American Textbooks," December 3, 2009, https://ssrn.com/abstract=1517983 or http://dx.doi.org/10.2139/ssrn.1517983. As they reported in "economese," "What we find is over-confidence in the potential for Soviet growth and an asymmetric response to past forecast errors." See Paul Samuelson, *Economics: An Introductory Analysis* (New York: McGraw-Hill from 1961 to 1989), Robert Heilbroner, *The Economic Problem* (Englewood Cliffs: Prentice Hall, from 1968 to 1970), or George Leland Bach, *Economics: An Introduction to Analysis and Policy* (Englewood Cliffs: Prentice Hall, from 1954 to 1980).

6. Schweizer, *Reagan's War*, 143.

7. Peter Schweizer, *Victory: The Reagan Administration's Secret Strategy That Hastened the Collapse of the Soviet Union* (New York: Atlantic Monthly Press, 1994), xiv–xv. Actually, the people in Eastern Europe *were* miserable. In filming *Rockin' the Wall* during 2009 (Produced by Schweikart and Mark Leif. United States, 2010. Documentary), my crew interviewed a wide range of rock and roll musicians who played behind the Iron Curtain. Asked to describe what they saw, their almost unanimous single-word response was "grey." They found a general lack of spirit: "You would look in the eyes," said Joyce Kennedy of Mother's Finest and "see nothing there, no color in the cheeks. My big thing was the spirit. There was just nothing there, it was 'get up, go through the motions every day.'"

8. Schweizer, *Reagan's War*, 143.

9. Kengor, *Crusader*, 120.

10. Steven F. Hayward, *The Age of Reagan: The Fall of the Old Liberal Order, 1964–1980* (New York: Three Rivers Press, 2001), 422; and Angelo Codevilla, *Informing Statecraft: Intelligence for a New Century* (New York: Free Press, 1992).

11. Codevilla, *Informing Statecraft*, 233–4.

12. Richard Pipes, "Team B: The Reality Behind the Myth," *Commentary* (October 1986): 34.

13. Anne Hessing Cahn, *Killing Detente: The Right Attacks the CIA* (University Park: Pennsylvania State University Press, 1998), 161.

14. "Reagan: 'It Isn't Only Washington That Has a Compassionate Heart,'" *National Journal*, March 8, 1980, 392.

15. Reagan, *The Reagan Diaries*, 75.

16. Ronald Reagan, *An American Life* (New York: Pocket Books, 1990), 237.

17. William Casey, Speech to the Business Council, May 9, 1981, in Mark B. Liedl, ed., *Scouting the Future: The Public Speeches of William J. Casey* (Washington, DC: Regnery, 1989), 8, 16–24.

18. "Soviet Goals and Expectations in the Global Power Arena," National Intelligence Estimate, 11-4-78, 7 July, 1981, Reagan Library (RL).

19. National Security Decision Directives, Box 1, Folder NSDD 11-20, NSDD 12, 1 October, 1981, RL.

20. National Security Decision Directives, Box 1, Folder NSDD 31-40, NSDD 35, 17 May, 1982, RL.

21. Reagan, *The Reagan Diaries*, 240.

22. Kengor, *Crusader*, 54, and full interview segment reprinted on 334, n61.

23. Paul Lettow, *Ronald Reagan and His Quest to Abolish Nuclear Weapons* (New York: Random House, 2005), 26.

24. John F. Matlock, *Reagan and Gorbachev: How the Cold War Ended* (New York: Random House, 2004), 41–45; and Paul Nitze, *From Hiroshima to Glasnost: At the Center of Decision* (New York: Weidenfeld, 1989), 366–98.

25. Robert Gates, *From the Shadows* (New York: Simon & Schuster, 1997), 197.

26. Winston Churchill, Speech before the House of Commons, June 4, 1940, https://en.wikipedia.org/wiki/We_shall_fight_on_the_beaches.

27. Steven F. Hayward, *The Age of Reagan: The Conservative Counterrevolution, 1980–1989* (New York: Three Rivers Press, 2009), 99.

28. NSDD 13, 19 October, 1981, National Security Decision Directives, Box 1, Folder 11-20, RL. Subsequent NSDDs 23 (3 February, 1982) and 26 (25 February, 1982) determined that "deterrence" consisted as providing for survival of 80 percent or, later, a "substantial portion" of the US population in the event of a nuclear attack.

29. NSDD 32, 20 May, 1982, Box 1, Folder 31-40, RL.

30. Kengor, *The Crusader*, 129. Haig later fumed Reagan was dedicated to the "quixotic goal" of stopping the pipeline (Lou Cannon, *President Reagan: The Role of a Lifetime*, 2nd ed., [New York: Public Affairs Books, 2000], 167.

31. Richard Pipes, "Misinterpreting the Cold War," *Foreign Affairs*, January/February 1995, https://www.foreignaffairs.com/reviews/review-essay/1995-01-01/misinterpreting-cold-war-hardliners-were-right.

32. Pipes, "Misinterpreting the Cold War."

33. Kengor, *Crusader*, 130.

34. D'Souza, *Ronald Reagan*, 174. Many others repeated this, including Lou Cannon.

35. Ronald Reagan, speech reprinted in the *Shreveport Times*, March 1, 1964; "No Place to Escape To," *Monitor*, September 1964, 32; Ronald Reagan speech to Chicago Executives' Club, *Executives' Club News* (Chicago: Chicago Executives' Club, March 26, 1965), 8; Ronald Reagan, "Freedom Is Not Spelled with an 'S'," *Proceedings of the International Newspaper Advertising Executives and the California Newspaper Advertising Executives Association 1965 Join Meeting*, 12, all in "Miscellaneous Collections, Vertical File," RL.

36. Edward Teller with Judith L. Shoolery, *Memoirs: A Twentieth Century Journey in Science and Politics* (Cambridge: Perseus Publishing, 2001), 509.

37. Lettow, *Ronald Reagan and His Quest*, 19.

38. Ronald Reagan, Speech in Amarillo, Texas, 19 July, 1968, in "Miscellaneous Collections, Vertical File," RL.

39. Adriana Bosch, *Reagan: An American Story* (New York: TV Books, 2000), 219–20.

40. Lettow, *Ronald Reagan and His Quest*, 21.

41. Ibid., 22.

42. *Wall Street Journal,* July 10, 1980; and Paul Johnson, *Modern Times: A History of the World from the Twenties to the Nineties,* 2nd ed. (New York; HarperCollins, 1991), 525.

43. "Gold Prices for 200 Years," Only Gold, last updated December 10, 2018, http://onlygold.com/m/Prices/Prices200Years.asp.

44. NSDD 24, 9 February, 1982, Box 1, Folder 11-20, RL.

45. George P. Shultz, *Turmoil and Triumph: My Years as Secretary of State* (New York: Charles Scribner's Sons, 1993), 135.

46. Ibid., 136.

47. Paul Kengor, *The Crusader,* 122.

48. Shultz, *Turmoil and Triumph,* 145.

49. Kengor, *The Crusader,* 150, quoting Roger Robinson, who was present in the room.

50. Marshall Casse to the Council of Economic Advisers, 12 June, 1981, in Anderson, Martin Files: Series 1, Subject File "Congressional Budget Office," C, "Issues" (5), Box 9, Folder "Council of Economic Advisers," (2 of 3), RL.

51. Kengor, *The Crusader,* 124.

52. Ibid., 124.

53. David E. Hoffman, "Reagan Approved Plan to Sabotage Soviets," *Washington Post,* February 27, 2004.

54. Gus W. Weiss, "The Farewell Dossier: Duping the Soviets," https://www.cia.gov/library/center-for-the-study-of-intelligence/csi-publications/csi-studies/studies/96unclass/farewell.htm.

55. NSDD 75, 17 January, 1983, Folder 71-80, RL.

56. William Clark, "President Reagan and the Wall," Speech to the Council of National Policy, San Francisco, California, March 2000; Don Oberdorfer, *The Turn* (New York: Poseidon, 1991), 76; and Kengor, *The Crusader,* 141.

57. Thomas Reed, *At the Abyss: An Insider's History of the Cold War* (New York: Ballantine Books, 2004), 268–69.

58. Ibid., 269. Reed recalled another psyops, in which William Clark flew to Caracas and Brasilia to warn the presidents of Venezuela and Brazil about "impending" American actions against the Soviet base in neighboring Surinam. Horrified Latin Americans, rather than risk the big brother from *El Norte* coming in, quickly drove the Soviets out. But it came at the cost of Clark leaving the White House for the Interior Department (271–72).

59. NSDD 66, 29 November, 1982, https://www.reaganlibrary.gov/digital-library/nsdds.

60. Schweizer, *Victory,* 125–27.

61. US Department of Commerce, International Trade Administration, "Quantifications of Western Exports of High-Technology Products to Communist Countries Through 1983" (Washington, DC: Government Printing Office, 1985, 28–29).

62. One Italian reporter noted "the Soviets would rather have Aleksandr Solzhenitsyn as Secretary-General of the U.N. than a Pole as Pope" (Hayward, *Age of Reagan: Conservative Counterrevolution,* 116).

63. Johnson, *Modern Times*, (1991), 701–2.
64. *Time*, January 4, 1982.
65. Reagan speech to AFL-CIO, April 5, 1981.
66. Kengor, *The Crusader*, 134.
67. Carl Bernstein, "The Holy Alliance," *Time*, February 24, 1992.
68. Timothy Garton Ash, *The Polish Revolution: Solidarity*, 3rd ed. (New Haven: Yale University Press), 328.
69. Lech Wałęsa, *A Way of Hope* (New York: Henry Holt, 1987), and his *The Struggle and the Triumph: An Autobiography*, trans. Franklin Philip (New York: Arcade, 1992).
70. Memcons: President Reagan, 15 December, 1981, Box 49, Exec Sec NSC: Subject File [Augostino Cardinal Casaroli], RL.
71. Minutes of the National Security Council meeting, 21 December, 1981, RL; and Martin Anderson and Annelise Anderson, *Reagan's Secret War* (New York: Crown Archetype, 2009).
72. Minutes of the National Security Council meeting, 21 December, 1981, RL.
73. Michael K. Deaver with Mickey Herskowitz, *Behind the Scenes* (New York: William Morrow, 1987), 142.
74. Paul Kengor interview with Lech Wałęsa, April 5, 2005, in *The Crusader*, 290–1.
75. Brands, *Reagan*, 343.
76. Johnson, *Modern Times*, 744.
77. Margaret Thatcher, *The Downing Street Years* (New York: HarperCollins, 1993), 157.
78. Ibid.
79. Ibid., 158.
80. Alexander M. Haig Jr., *Caveat: Realism, Reagan and Foreign Policy* (New York: Scribner, 1984), 272.
81. Ronald Reagan, address to members of the British Parliament, June 8, 1982, http://www.heritage.org/europe/report/20-years-later-reagans-westminster-speech.
82. Ibid.
83. Lou Cannon, "Reagan Radiated Happiness and Hope," *George*, August 2000, 60.
84. Steven Rattner, "Britons Reassured by Reagan's Visit," *New York Times*, June 10, 1982, https://www.nytimes.com/1982/06/10/world/britons-reassured-by-reagan-s-visit.html; and Kengor, *Crusader*, 143.
85. Schweizer, *Reagan's War*, 168.
86. Ibid.
87. These principles were outlined in NSDD 54, "United States Policy Toward Eastern Europe," 2 September, 1982, National Security Decision Directives, Folder 51-60, RL.
88. Ibid.
89. Norman A. Bailey, *The Strategic Plan That Won the Cold War: National Security Decision Directive 75* (McLean: The Potomac Foundation, 1998), iii.
90. *Rockin' the Wall*. Produced by Schweikart and Mark Leif. United States, 2010. Documentary; and Larry Schweikart interviews with Joseph Morris, various dates, 2009. Reagan was not known as a music aficionado. He liked Sinatra and the classic singers of the 1950s. But while in the White House, there was a monthly program called "In Concert at the White House" that ran on PBS. These were live concerts with every genre of music, from pop to jazz, opera to country. I personally worked an "In Concert at the White House" near the Reagan Ranch in 1984, where I served as the van driver

for opera star and hostess Beverly Sills and that month's performing group, Merle Haggard and the Outlaws. The event was held in a friend's barn and in attendance were Bo Derek, Mike Connors (*Mannix*), Ron Ely (*Tarzan*), and, sitting immediately behind me, Fred MacMurray (*My Three Sons*).

91. Christopher Andrew and Vasili Mitrokhin, *The Sword and the Shield: The Mitrokhin Archive and the Secret History of the KGB* (New York: Basic Books, 1999), 548.

92. Larry Schweikart, *Seven Events That Made America America* (New York: Sentinel, 2010), chapter 5, "A Steel Guitar Rocks the Iron Curtain," 117–50. Ironically, by the early 1970s, rock and roll was criticized by radical leftists in America for *failing* to cause a revolution here. See Peter Doggett, *There's a Riot Going On: Revolutionaries, Rock Stars, and the Rise and Fall of the '60s* (New York: Canongate, 2007).

93. Schweikart, *Seven Events*, 137.

94. *Rockin' the Wall*. Produced by Schweikart and Mark Leif. United States, 2010. Documentary. Schweikart interviews with Leslie Mandoki, various dates, 2009; and Mark Stein and Schweikart, *You Keep Me Hangin' On: The Raging Story of Rock Music's Golden Age* (n.p.: Lightning Source, 2012).

95. George Crile, *Charlie Wilson's War: The Extraordinary Story of the Largest Covert Operation in History* (Atlantic Monthly Press, 2003); and Ann Scott Tyson, "Sorry, Charlie. This is Michael Vickers's War," *Washington Post*, December 27, 2007, http://www.washingtonpost.com/wp-dyn/content/article/2007/12/27/AR2007122702116.html.

96. Proclamation 4908, "Afghanistan Day," March 10, 1982, in *The Public Papers of President Ronald Reagan, 1982, in Two Books, January 1 to July 2, 1982*, vol. 1 (Washington, DC: Government Printing Office, 1983); and "Welcome Ceremony for President Mohammed Zia-ul-Haq," December 7, 1982, in ibid. Zia stated "history will remember you as Reagan the Peacemaker" and was grateful for "knowing you as a man of God."

97. NSDD 166, "U.S. Policy, Programs and Strategy in Afghanistan," 27 March, 1985, in National Security Decision Directives (NSDDs), Folder 161-170, RL.

98. Kengor, *The Crusader*, 258.

99. Ibid., 260.

100. Ibid.

101. Vernon Loeb, "Undercover to Hard Cover" *Washington Post*, December 12, 1998; and Milt Bearden and James Risen, *The Main Enemy: The Inside Story of the CIA's Final Showdown with the KGB* (New York: Ballantine Books, 2003).

102. Milt Bearden minimized the role of Wilson: "Ironically, neither [Gust] Avrakotos nor [Charlie] Wilson was directly involved in the decision and claims any credit" for the Stinger sales, despite the fact that it was precisely the Stinger that was the focus of the film *Charlie Wilson's War* (2007, directed by Mike Nichols) based on the same book. See Bearden and Risen, *The Main Enemy*, 211–12, 278.

CHAPTER 11

1. In fact, when the results were recounted by several different news services, Bush won in every variation except one.

2. Denis Prager to Martin Anderson and Barbara Honegger, "Air Traffic Controllers Strike," 7 August, 1981, in Anderson, Martin Files: Series 1, Subject "Air Traffic Controllers Strike," Box 1, Reagan Library (RL).

3. Warren Brown, "U.S. Begins Firing Striking Air Controllers, Five Jailed," *Washington Post*, August 6, 1981, https://www.washingtonpost.com/archive/politics/1981/08/06/us-begins-firing-striking-air-controllers/07c17a9e-1e8c-498c-978a-deb1324854ef/?noredirect=on&utm_term=.1a7a19bc9055.

4. Carole Shifrin, "Airlines Report Traffic is Picking Up," *Washington Post*, August 8, 1981, https://www.washingtonpost.com/archive/politics/1981/08/08/airlines-report-traffic-is-picking-up/99826dc0-e2ca-4a44-9239-feb6e0ecf0fe/?utm_term=.bd436b5cff7f.

5. Peggy Noonan, *When Character Was King: A Story of Ronald Reagan* (New York: Penguin, 2001), 223.

6. Ibid., 224.

7. Ronald Reagan, *An American Life* (New York: Pocket Books, 1990), 283.

8. Ibid.

9. Noonan, *When Character Was King*, 224.

10. Edwin Meese III, *With Reagan: The Inside Story* (Washington, DC: Regnery, 1992), 18.

11. *Newsweek*, January 26, 1981.

12. Information on daily routines and the ranch comes from Nancy Reagan with William Novak, *My Turn: The Memoirs of Nancy Reagan* (New York: Random House, 1989), 244–59; interviews with Michael Reagan, various dates, 2017; and Reagan Ranch Foundation, Santa Barbara, California.

13. H. W. Brands, *Reagan: The Life* (New York: Doubleday, 2015), 297.

14. Ronald Reagan, address to Congress, April 28, 1981.

15. *New York Review of Books*, October 7, 1982.

16. Steven Hayward, *The Age of Reagan: The Conservative Counterrevolution, 1980–1989* (New York: Three Rivers Press, 2009), 185.

17. A.F. Ehrbar, "What the Markets are Telling Reagan," *Fortune*, October 19, 1981.

18. *Wall Street Journal*, October 31, 1981.

19. Hayward, *Age of Reagan: Conservative Counterrevolution*, 187.

20. Lou Cannon, *President Reagan: The Role of a Lifetime* (New York: Simon & Schuster, 1991), 152–53.

21. *New York Times*, December 12, 1981.

22. Cannon, *President Reagan*, 155.

23. George P. Shultz, *Turmoil and Triumph: My Years as Secretary of State* (New York: Charles Scribner's Sons, 1993), 355.

24. Memcons, President Reagan, 21 May, 1981, Box 48, Exec Sec NSC - SubFiles [Chancellor Helmut Schmidt of FRG].

25. Cannon blamed the assassination attempt for limiting Reagan's hours during a "critical learning period" of his presidency (*President Reagan*, 156).

26. Shultz, *Turmoil and Triumph*, 256–57. Ironically, Shultz praised Reagan's mastery of foreign affairs but thought him not up to snuff on economic issues.

27. Hayward, *Age of Reagan: Conservative Counterrevolution*, 84. Stockman was in fact never a conservative and voted 80 percent of the time with John Anderson. He supported abortion, opposed prayer in public schools, and had been a member of the hated Ripon Society.

28. Dinesh D'Souza, *Ronald Reagan: How an Ordinary Man Became an Extraordinary Leader* (New York: Touchstone, 1997), 99.

29. William Greider, "The Education of David Stockman," *Atlantic Monthly*, December 1981, accessed December 10, 2018, https://www.theatlantic.com/magazine/archive/1981/12/the-education-of-david-stockman/305760/.

30. David Stockman, *The Triumph of Politics: Why the Reagan Revolution Failed* (New York: Harper & Row, 1986), 89.

31. Hayward, *Age of Reagan: Conservative Counterrevolution*, 85.

32. Daniel Patrick Moynihan, *Came the Revolution: Argument in the Reagan Era* (San Diego: Harcourt, Brace, Jovanovich, 1988), 6.

33. Martin Anderson, *Revolution: The Reagan Legacy* (New York: Harcourt Brace, 1988), 236, 263.

34. William Niskanen, *Reaganomics: An Insider's Account of the Policies and the People* (New York: Oxford University Press, 1988), 4.

35. Michael Boskin, *Reagan and the Economy: The Successes, Failures, and Unfinished Agenda* (San Francisco: ICS Press, 1989), 52–53.

36. Hayward, *Age of Reagan: Conservative Counterrevolution*, 189.

37. Stockman, *Triumph of Politics*, 1–4; and Brands, *Reagan*, 322–23.

38. Hayward, *Age of Reagan: Conservative Counterrevolution*, 191.

39. Reagan, *The Presidential Diaries*, ed. Douglas Brinkley (New York: HarperCollins, 2001), 53.

40. Ibid., 54.

41. Ibid., 57.

42. Ibid., 57.

43. Ibid., 61.

44. Ibid., 64.

45. Ibid., 82; and Hayward, *Age of Reagan: Conservative Counterrevolution*, 207.

46. Hayward, *Age of Reagan: Conservative Counterrevolution*, 208.

47. Reagan, *Presidential Diaries*, 96. He found it ironic that on August 19, Tip O'Neill made a speech to Republicans explaining why they should support their president (99).

48. Hayward, *Age of Reagan: Conservative Counterrevolution*, 193.

49. Public Papers of the President, Meeting with Editors, October 16, 1981.

50. Fred Barnes, "TV News: The Shock Horror Welfare Cut Show," *Policy Review* (Spring 1983): 57–73.

51. Haynes Johnson, *Sleepwalking Through History: America in the Reagan Years* (New York: Norton, 1991), 111.

52. Caspar Weinberger, *Annual Report to the Congress On the FY 1983 Budget, FY 1984 Authorization Request and FY 1983–1987 Defense Programs*, February 8, 1982.

53. Hayward, *Age of Reagan: Conservative Counterrevolution*.

54. Reagan, *The Reagan Diaries*, ed. Douglas Brinkley, single volume ed., (New York: HarperCollins, 2007), 37. This was remarkably akin to President Bill Clinton asking his "War Room" advisors, "You mean to tell me that the success of my program and my reelection hinges on...a bunch of f__king bond traders?" (Bob Woodward, *The Agenda: Inside the Clinton White House* [New York: Simon & Schuster, 2005], 73).

55. Robert C. Rowland and Rodger A. Payne, "The Context-Embeddedness of Political Discourse: A Re-Evaluation of Reagan's Rhetoric in the 1982 Midterm Election Campaign," *Presidential Studies Quarterly* (1984): 500–511.

56. Lou Cannon, *President Reagan: The Role of a Lifetime* (New York: Simon & Schuster, 1991), 274.

57. D'Souza, *Ronald Reagan*.

58. Cannon, *President Reagan*, 275–76.

59. US Bureau of the Census, *Statistical Abstract of the United States* (Washington, DC: Government Printing Office, 1995), 474, 481–3.

60. See George Gilder, *Wealth and Poverty* (New York: Bantam, 1981); and Henry Phelps-Brown and Sheila Hopkins, *A Perspective of Wages and Prices* (London: Taylor and Francis, 2013).

61. George Gilder, *Microcosm: The Quantum Revolution in Economics and Technology* (New York: Free Press, 1990).

CHAPTER 12

1. Ronald Reagan, *The Presidential Diaries*, ed. Douglas Brinkley (New York: HarperCollins, 2007), 11.

2. Margaret Thatcher, *The Downing Street Years* (New York: HarperCollins, 1983), 255.

3. Reagan, *The Presidential Diaries*, 90–91. Reagan thought Haig was "sound...on the complex international matters but...utterly paranoid with regard to the people he must work with" (Steven F. Hayward, *The Age of Reagan: The Conservative Counterrevolution, 1981–1989* [New York: Three Rivers Press, 2009], 251).

4. Paul Lettow, *Ronald Reagan and His Quest to Abolish Nuclear Weapons* (New York: Random House, 2005), 63.

5. See the comments of his brother, Humberto, and others in Paul Hollander, *Anti-Americanism: Irrational and Rational* (New York: Oxford University Press, 1992), chapter 5 and his *Political Pilgrims: Western Intellectuals in Search of the Good Society* (New York: Harper Colophon, 1981).

6. Hayward, *Age of Reagan: Conservative Counterrevolution*, 268.

7. Leslie H. Gelb, "Who Won the Cold War?" *New York Times*, August 20, 1992, https://www.nytimes.com/1992/08/20/opinion/foreign-affairs-who-won-the-cold-war.html.

8. William E. Odom, *The Collapse of the Soviet Military* (New Haven: Yale University Press, 1998), 40.

9. Ibid., 2.

10. Ibid., 1.

11. Ibid., 70, interviewing members of the Soviet General Staff in 1992.

12. Ibid.

13. Hayward, *Age of Reagan: Conservative Counterrevolution*, 271.

14. Memcons—President Reagan [5/21/81], Box 48, Exec Sec NSC: Sub. Files [Chancellor Helmut Schmidt of FRG], RL.

15. Memcons-President Reagan [5/21/81], Box 48, Exec Sec NSC: Sub. Files [Chancellor Helmut Schmidt of FRG], RL.

16. George P. Shultz, *Turmoil and Triumph: My Years as Secretary of State* (New York: Charles Scribner's Sons, 1993), 168–71.

17. Robert Scheer, "U.S. Could Survive in Administration's View," *Los Angeles Times*, January 16, 1982.

18. Robert Scheer, *With Enough Shovels: Reagan, Bush, and Nuclear War* (New York: Random House, 1982).

19. Robert Gates, *From the Shadows* (New York: Simon & Schuster, 1996), 261.

20. Peter Schweizer, *Reagan's War: The Epic Story of His Forty-Year Struggle and Final Triumph over Communism* (New York: Anchor, 2002), 181.

21. Jeffrey Herf, *War by Other Means: Soviet Power, West German Resistance, and the Battle of the Euromissiles* (New York: Free Press, 1991).

22. Hayward, *Age of Reagan: Conservative Counterrevolution*, 288.

23. "Dead Souls," *New York Review of Books*, December 19, 1991.

24. Michael Novak, "The Return of Good vs. Evil," *Wall Street Journal*, February 7, 2002.

25. Hayward, *Age of Reagan: Conservative Counterrevolution*, 289.

26. William C. Wohlforth, ed., *Witnesses to the End of the Cold War* (Baltimore: Johns Hopkins University Press, 1996), 20; and Paul Kengor, *God and Ronald Reagan*, 233–270.

27. Lettow, *Ronald Reagan and His Quest*, 56.

28. "Washington's New Push for Missile Defense," *Fortune*, October 19, 1981.

29. Ronald Reagan, *An American Life* (New York: Pocket Books 1990), 547

30. National Security Decision Directive (NSDD) 35, "The M-X Program," 17 May, 1982, Folder 31-40, in National Security Decision Directives, Box 1, RL.

31. Martin Anderson, *Revolution: The Reagan Legacy*, 2nd ed. (Stanford: Hoover Institution Press, 1990), 97.

32. Robert C. McFarlane, "Effective Strategic Policy," *Foreign Affairs*, Fall 1988, 33–48 (42).

33. Lettow, *Ronald Reagan and His Quest*, 98.

34. Frances Fitzgerald, *Way Out There in the Blue: Reagan, Star Wars and the End of the Cold War* (New York: Simon & Schuster, 2000), 206.

35. Robert C. McFarlane and Zofia Smardz, *Special Trust* (New York: Caddell & Davies, 1994), 320; Greg Herken, *Cardinal Choices: Presidential Science Advising from the Atomic Bomb to SDI*, rev. ed. (Stanford: Stanford University Press, 2000), 211; and Lettow, *Ronald Reagan and His Quest*, 102. Lettow cites this as "uncharacteristic" of Reagan in that he gave orders rather than nudging with a question.

36. Reagan, *The Reagan Diaries*, ed. Douglas Brinkley, single volume ed. (New York: HarperCollins, 2007), 139.

37. Lettow, *Ronald Reagan and His Quest*, 103.

38. Thatcher, *Downing Street Years*, 435; and H. W. Brands, *Reagan: The Life* (New York: Doubleday, 2015), 418.

39. Shultz, *Turmoil and Triumph* (New York: Charles Scribner's Sons, 1993), 249–56. Shultz, not a scientist, at first opposed SDI on scientific ground, arguing that the Joint Chiefs "were not equipped to make this kind of proposal. They are not scientists" (249).

40. Ronald Reagan, address to the nation on defense and national security, March 23, 1983, http://www.atomicarchive.com/Docs/Missile/Starwars.shtml.

41. Shultz, *Turmoil and Triumph*, 263. As Lettow notes, Reagan never took credit for any of his ideas or programs, save one: SDI. In a long pair of discussions on March 25 and 29, he laid out a very clear path as to exactly how missile defense could lead both sides to de-nuclearize—the closest he ever came to saying "Star Wars"—would do away with nuclear weapons (Lettow, *Ronald Reagan*, 118).

42. NSDD 85, 25 March, 1983, "Eliminating the Threat from Ballistic Missiles," Folder 81-90, National Security Decision Directives, Box 1, RL.

43. Francis X. Clines, "Democrats Assert Reagan Is Using 'Star Wars' Scare to Hide Blunders," *New York Times*, March 25, 1983, https://www.nytimes.com/1983/03/25/world/democrats-assert-reagan-is-using-star-wars-scare-to-hide-blunders.html.

44. Tony Dolan, Reagan's speechwriter, is one of the few to challenge this view, telling Dinesh D'Souza that "Reagan never minded when critics called his program 'Star Wars,' a term that made conservative backers of SDI bristle. Reagan knew that the term 'Star Wars' was used with the intention of making the very concept of missile defense seem fanciful. But Reagan was convinced that the American people wouldn't see it that way.... [and he] cheerily pointed out that 'Star Wars' reminded Americans of one of their favorite movies—one in which the forces of good conquer the forces of the dark side" (Dinesh D'Souza, *Ronald Reagan: How an Ordinary Man Became an Extraordinary Leader* [New York: Touchstone, 1997], 177). However, Dolan, speaking with D'Souza years later, is the only one to have such a memory. Kengor, on the other hand, described the term as a "huge PR problem" (Paul Kengor, *The Crusader: Ronald Reagan and the Fall of Communism* [New York: ReganBooks, 2006] 182).

45. D'Souza, *Ronald Reagan*, 71.

46. Kengor, *The Crusader*, 182.

47. See the presidential news conference of January 9, 1985, for example, where Thomas insisted on calling SDI "Star Wars."

48. See, for example, Clarence A. Robinson, "Soviets Push for Beam Weapon," *Aviation Week & Space Technology*, March 2, 1977; "G.A.O. Warns of Lag in Space Research," *New York Times*, February 16, 1981; Robinson, "Beam Weapons Effort to Grow," *Aviation Week*, April 2, 1979; "Soviet Union Developing Laser Antisatellite Weapon," *Aviation Week*, June 16, 1980, 60-61; William H. Gregory, "Exotic Weapons Challenge," *Aviation Week*, July 28, 1980, 6-7; and dozens of other citations in D. Douglas Dalgleish and Larry Schweikart, *Trident* (Carbondale: Southern Illinois University Press, 1984), 450–51.

49. Ronald Reagan, remarks to administration supporters at a White House briefing on arms control, Central America, and the Supreme Court, November 23, 1987; and Kengor, *The Crusader*, 179.

50. Anatoly Dobrynin, *In Confidence* (New York: Times Books, 1995), 528.

51. William C. Wohlforth, *Witnesses to the End of the Cold War*, 13–14.

52. Andrei Gromyko, *Memoirs* (Garden City: Doubleday, 1989), 307.

53. Schweikart and Dave Dougherty, *A Patriot's History of the Modern World Vol. I: From America's Exceptional Ascent to the Atomic Bomb, 1898–1945* (New York: Sentinel, 2012), 353.

54. Ibid., 353–56.

55. Deborah Hart Strober and Gerald S. Strober, eds., *Reagan: The Man and His Presidency: The Oral History of an Era* (Boston: Houghton Mifflin, 1998), 244.

56. Oleg Grinevky, "The Crisis That Didn't Erupt: The Soviet-American Relationship, 1980–1983," in Kiron K. Skinner, ed., *Turning Points in the Cold War* (Palo Alto: Hoover Institution Press, 2008), 71.

57. Minutes of meeting with Prime Minister Emilio Colombo, 12 February, 1981, NSC, NSPG Mtg Minutes and Presidential Memos, Folder "Memcons—President Reagan [2/12/81], Box 48, Executive Secretariat, NSC: Subject File [Italian PM Emilio Colombo], RL.

58. Minutes of meeting with Chancellor Helmut Schmidt, 21 May, 1981, NSC, NSPG Mtg Minutes and Presidential Memos, Folder "Memcons—President Reagan [2/12/81], Box 48, Executive Secretariat, NSC: Subject File [Chancellor Helmut Schmidt of FRG], RL.

59. Tony Judt, *Postwar: A History of Europe Since 1945* (New York: Penguin Books, 2005), 591.

60. Christopher Andrew and Oleg Gordievsky, *KGB: The Inside Story* (New York: HarperCollins, 1990), 585.

61. Red Air Force pilot Aleksandr Zuyev on *60 Minutes*, aired on CBS January 3, 1993. Available to watch at https://www.youtube.com/watch?v=_glEQuvurFQ.

62. Hayward, *Age of Reagan: Conservative Counterrevolution*, 311.

63. Reagan, *An American Life*, 585.

64. Ibid., 584.

65. Ed Magnuson, "D-Day in Grenada," *Time*, November 7, 1983, http://content.time.com/time/magazine/article/0,9171,949850,00.html.

66. Ronald Reagan, remarks to Eugenia Charles, October 25, 1983.

67. Ronald Reagan, comments to reporters, November 3, 1983.

68. Richard Harwood, "Tidy U.S. War Ends: 'We Blew Them Away,'" *Washington Post*, November 6, 1983, https://www.washingtonpost.com/archive/politics/1983/11/06/tidy-us-war-ends-we-blew-them-away/1dc47588-0f13-40c8-afbd-23528fb62759/?utm_term=.61c40248c332.

69. Thatcher, *Downing Street Years*, 332.

70. Brands, *Reagan*, 401.

71. Ronald Reagan to Paul Trousdale, 23 May, 1983, in Martin Anderson, Annelise Anderson, and Kiron D. Skinner, eds., *Reagan: A Life in Letters* (New York: Free Press, 2003), 409.

CHAPTER 13

1. Ronald Reagan, *An American Life* (New York: Pocket Books, 1990), 413.

2. Ibid., 419.

3. Ibid., 413.

4. David K. Shipler, "Begin Contends U.S. Policies Treat Israel Like a 'Vassal,'" *New York Times*, December 21, 1981, https://www.nytimes.com/1981/12/21/world/begin-contends-us-policies-treat-israel-like-vassal-haig-retains-high-hopes-for.html.

5. Larry Schweikart, *Seven Events That Made America America* (New York: Sentinel, 2010), 153; and Reagan, *An American Life*, 410.

6. Schweikart, *Seven Events*, 156.

7. *Report of the Department of Defense Commission on Beirut International Airport Terrorist Act*, October 23, 1983. It is worth noting that even in this report, the word "Islamic" doesn't appear.

8. Ronald Reagan, *The Reagan Diaries*, ed. Douglas Brinkley, single-volume edition (New York: HarperCollins, 2007), 87–88.

9. See Brett D. Schaefer, "United National Peacekeeping: The U.S. Must Press for Reform," *Heritage Foundation Backgrounder* 2182, September 18, 2008; and James Dobbins, et al., "The U.N.'s Role in Nation-Building: From the Congo to Iraq," RAND Corporation, 2005, http://www.rand.org/pubs/monographs/2005/RAND_MG304.pdf.

10. Roy Licklider, "How Civil Wars End: Questions and Methods," in Roy Licklider, ed., *Stopping the Killing: How Civil Wars End* (New York: New York University Press, 1993), 3–19.

11. The following year, Nancy personally invited the Beach Boys to perform. On July 4, 1985, the Beach Boys played to 750,000 on the National Mall, an action Mike Love called the greatest moment of his life.

12. Lou Cannon, *President Reagan: The Role of a Lifetime* (New York: Simon & Schuster, 1991), 431–33.

13. Reagan, *An American Life*, 448.

14. Edmund Morris, *Dutch: A Memoir of Ronald Reagan* (New York: Modern Library, 1999), 462–63.

15. Reagan, *An American Life*, 440.

16. Reagan, *The Reagan Diaries*, 218; and Reagan, *An American Life*, 440.

17. Reagan, *An American Life*, 441.

18. ."Lebanese Working Group," September 1983, Richard S. Beale Files, Box 90403, National Security Council (NSC), Reagan Library (RL).

19. "Lebanese Working Group," September 1983.

20. NPSG 0072, "October 14, 1983 (Middle East), Box 2, Executive Secretariat, NSC: National Security Planning Group, RL.

21. Reagan, *An American Life*, 445.

22. Ibid., 447.

23. Cannon, *President Reagan*, 421.

24. Francis X. Clines, "Reagan Unhurt as Armed Man Takes Hostages," *New York Times*, October 23, 1983, https://www.nytimes.com/1983/10/23/us/reagan-unhurt-as-armed-man-takes-hostages.html.

25. Reagan, *An American Life*, 452.

26. Cannon, *President Reagan*, 402.

27. Ibid., 423.

28. H. W. Brands, *Reagan: The Life* (New York: Doubleday, 2015), 328.

29. David C. Martin and John Walcott, *Best Laid Plans: The Inside Story of America's War Against Terrorism* (New York: Touchstone Books, 1988), 95.

30. PBS interview with Caspar Weinberger," 2001, http://www.pbs.org/wgbh/pages/frontline/shows/target/interviews/weingerger.html.

31. Robin Wright, *Sacred Rage: The Wrath of Militant Islam* (New York: Touchstone, 2004), 54.

32. Cable 2025, printed 14 December, 1983, Folder "Lebanon, Marine Explosion, October 23–November 3, 1983," (4), Box 41, Executive Secretariat, NSC: Country File, RL.

33. Cable from US embassy in Beirut, in "Lebanon, Marine Explosion, October 23–November 3, 1983," (4), Box 41, Executive Secretariat, NSC: Country File, RL.

34. "The Terrorist Threat to US Personnel in Beirut," 12 January, 1984, in Cable from U.S. Embassy in Beirut to Middle East and major embassies, Box 43, Executive Secretariat, NSC, Country Fil, RL.

35. Reagan, address to the nation, October 27, 1983. In *The Terror Network: The Secret War of International Terrorism* (New York: Henry Holt, 1981), Claire Sterling had made the case that the Soviet Union was behind most international terrorism, ignoring the rise of Islamic fundamentalism.

36. Cannon, *President Reagan*, 398.
37. "Lebanon Bombing, 23–24 October, 1983," Box 41, Executive Secretariat, NSC, Cable Files, RL.
38. See the letters of support in the ND016 Files, RL.
39. Reagan, *An American Life*, 463.
40. Ibid., 463.
41. National Security Planning Group (NSPG) 0086, 2 March, 1984, Executive Secretariat NSPG Meeting File [Combating Terrorism], RL.
42. NSDD 138, 3 April, 1984, "Combating Terrorism," in National Security Decision Directives (NSDDs), Box 1, Folder 131-40, RL.
43. NSDD 180, 19 July, 1985, "Civil Aviation Anti-Terrorism Program," NSDD, Box 1, Folder 181-90, RL.
44. NSPG 0087, 30 March, 1984, Executive Secretariat, NSC: NSPG Meeting File [Iran-Iraq War], RL.
45. "Middle East Terrorism: The Threat and Possible U.S. Responses," 15 February, 1985, Directorate of Intelligence, in North, Oliver Files: Racbox 9, "NSDD on Vice President's Task Force" (1 of 3), RL.
46. Ibid.
47. "DIA Analysis," 18 October, 1985, in North, Oliver Files: Box 32, Folder "Incoming 10/27/1985 - classified," RL.
48. Ibid.
49. NSPG, 24 February, 1987, 1 of 2, Executive Secretariat, NSC: NSPG File [Terrorism], RL.
50. Robert C. McFarlane, "From Beirut to 9/11," *New York Times*, October 22, 2008, https://www.nytimes.com/2008/10/23/opinion/23mcfarlane.html.
51. "Marine Explosion, October 23–November 3, 1983," Box 41, Executive Secretariat, NSC: Country File, RL.
52. Mark Silverberg, "Paper Tiger," September 18, 2006, http://www.marksilverberg.com/articles/paper-tiger/.
53. John Miller, "Greetings, America. My Name Is Osama Bin Laden," *Esquire*, February 1999, 96–103; and John Miller, Michael Stone, and Chris Mitchell, *The Cell: Inside the 9/11 Plot and Why the FBI and CIA Failed to Stop It* (New York: Hyperion Books, 2003).

CHAPTER 14
1. D. Douglas Dalgleish and Larry Schweikart, *Trident* (Carbondale: Southern Illinois University Press, 1984).
2. Steven F. Hayward, *The Age of Reagan: The Conservative Counterrevolution, 1981–1989* (New York: Three Rivers Press, 2009), 328.
3. Vladimir Simonov, "Political Portrait of Ronald Reagan," *Literernaturnaya Gazeta*, May 25, 1988, cited in Paul Kengor, *The Crusader: Ronald Reagan and the Fall of Communism* (New York: ReganBooks, 2006), 202.
4. *Rockin' the Wall*. Produced by Schweikart and Mark Leif. United States, 2010. Documentary.
5. Ronald Reagan, *An American Life* (New York: Pocket Books, 1990), 566.

6. V. Chebrikov to Yuri Andropov, May 14, 1984, in Paul Kengor, *Dupes: How America's Adversaries Have Manipulated Progressives for a Century* (Wilmington: ISI Books, 2010), Appendix A, 503–5.

7. Hayward, *Age of Reagan: Conservative Counterrevolution*, 335.

8. Stanley Feldman and Lee Sigelman, "The Political Impact of Prime-Time Television: 'The Day After,'" *Journal of Politics* (1985): 556–78.

9. Kengor, *The Crusader: Ronald Reagan and the Fall of Communism* (New York: Regan-Books, 2006), 210–11.

10. NSPG 0143, 3 February, 1987, 2 of 3, Executive Secretariat, NSC: NSPG Meeting File [SDI], Reagan Library (RL).

11. Beth A. Fischer, *The Reagan Reversal: Foreign Policy and the End of the Cold War* (Columbia: University of Missouri Press, 1997), 121.

12. Hayward, *Age of Reagan: Conservative Counterrevolution*, 331; and Ronald Reagan to Peter and Irene Hannaford, February 10, 1983, in Martin Anderson, Annelise Anderson, and Kiron Skinner, eds., *Reagan: A Life in Letters* (New York: Free Press, 2003), 278.

13. National Security Planning Group Meeting, 8 September, 1987, NSPG 0165, Executive Secretariat, NSC: Meeting File [Review of US Arms Control Positions], RL.

14. Weinberger quoted in Hayward, *Age of Reagan: Conservative Counterrevolution*, 680n101.

15. NSPG 0165.

16. Don Oberdorfer, *The Turn from the Cold War to a New Era: The United States and the Soviet Union, 1983–1990*, rev. ed. (Baltimore: Johns Hopkins University Press, 1998), 67.

17. In November 1983, Herbert Meyer, the vice chairman of the National Intelligence Council, wrote a memorandum to CIA director William Casey called "Why is the World so Dangerous?" which answered with the conclusion that American strength had now "fundamentally changed the course of history in a direction favorable to the interests and security of ourselves and our allies," and predicted that if present trends continued, "we're going to win the Cold War" within the next twenty years. But he also predicted the Soviets would become more dangerous as they found themselves becoming extinct. See Herbert E. Meyer, "Why is the World So Dangerous?" memorandum to William Casey, November 30, 1983, https://www.cia.gov/library/readingroom/document/cia-rdp88t00528r000100020008-2 .

18. Jack Matlock, *Reagan and Gorbachev: How the Cold War Ended* (New York: Random House, 2004), 87.

19. "Where's the Rest of Him?" *New York Times*, November 18, 1990.

20. George P. Shultz, *Turmoil and Triumph: My Years as Secretary of State* (New York: Charles Scribner's Sons, 1993), 468–70.

21. "Reagan's Asian Takes Are in the Can," *Washington Post*, November 15, 1983.

22. Lou Cannon, *President Reagan: The Role of a Lifetime* (New York: Simon & Schuster, 1991), 478. What Cannon would say about candidate Hillary Clinton in 2016, when vast empty halls were carefully edited and cut *by the news outlets themselves* to present a fake image of well-attended events, is not known.

23. Cannon, *President Reagan*, 482.

24. Dinesh D'Souza, *Ronald Reagan: How an Ordinary Man Became an Extraordinary Leader* (New York: Touchstone, 1997), 171.

25. "President Reagan: Remarks to the Citizens of Ballyporeen, Ireland, June 3, 1984," posted by MCamericanpresident March 30, 2011, video, 3:15, https://www.youtube.com/watch?v=4bQVxdhitok.

26. Ronald Reagan, Speech on the 40th anniversary of D-Day, June 6, 1984, http://www.historyplace.com/speeches/reagan-d-day.htm.

27. Stephen E. Ambrose, *D-Day, June 6, 1994: The Climactic Battle of World War II* (New York: Simon & Schuster, 1944), said Col. James Van Fleet gave a similar order, but Roosevelt made the decision.

28. Cannon, *President Reagan*, 495.

29. Hayward, *Age of Reagan: Conservative Counterrevolution*, 356–58.

30. "Elections Results Talking Points," Coy, Craig P.: Files, Racbox 1, Box 1, Folder "Burn Bag," (1 of 3), n.d., circa 6 November, 1986, RL.

31. Ibid.

32. Hayward, *Age of Reagan: Conservative Counterrevolution*, 375.

33. Cannon, *President Reagan*, 496.

34. Schweikart and Dave Dougherty, *A Patriot's History of the Modern World, Vol. II: From the Cold War to the Age of Entitlement, 1945–2012* (New York: Sentinel, 2013), 426–27; Warren Brookes, "The Silent Boom," *The American Spectator*, August, 1988.

35. John P. Hoerr, *And the Wolf Finally Came: The Decline of the American Steel Industry* (Pittsburgh: University of Pittsburgh Press, 1988), 600–607.

36. Richard Preston, *American Steel* (New York: Prentice-Hall, 1991).

37. Ira Magaziner and Robert B. Reich, *Minding America's Business: The Decline and Rise of the American Economy* (New York: Harcourt Brace Jovanovich, 1982); and Lester Thurow, *The Zero-Sum Society* (New York: Basic Books, 1968).

38. George Gilder, *Recapturing the Spirit of Enterprise* (San Francisco: CS Press, 1992) and his *Microcosm: The Quantum Revolution in Economics and Technology* (New York: Simon & Schuster, 1989); James Wallace and Jim Erickson, *Hard Drive: Bill Gates and the Making of the Microsoft Empire* (New York: Wiley, 1992); and Walter Isaacson, *Steve Jobs* (New York: Simon & Schuster, 2015).

39. Scott Callon, *Divided Sun: MITI and the Breakdown of Japanese High-Tech Industrial Policy, 1975–1993* (Stanford: Stanford University Press, 1995), 2, 201; Schweikart and Lynne Pierson Doti, *American Entrepreneur: The Fascinating Stories of the People Who Defined Business in the United States* (New York: Amacom, 2009), 430–31; and Michael Sheridan, "Japan Falls into Spiral of Despair," *London Sunday Times*, February 22, 2009, https://www.thetimes.co.uk/article/japan-falls-into-spiral-of-despair-0r736qcxs39.

40. Schweikart and Doti, *American Entrepreneur*, 398.

41. Jeffrey H. Birnbaum and Alan S. Murray, *Showdown at Gucci Gulch: Lawmakers, Lobbyists, and the Unlikely Triumph of Tax Reform* (New York: Random House, 1987), 35.

42. Hayward, *Age of Reagan: Conservative Counterrevolution*, 377.

43. Cannon, *President Reagan*, 494.

44. Ronald Reagan, *The Presidential Diaries*, ed. Douglas Brinkley, single-volume ed. (New York: HarperCollins, 2007), 271; and Nancy Reagan, *My Turn: The Memoirs of Nancy Reagan* (New York: Random House, 1989), 266. Reagan confided in his diary that after the debate "I didn't feel good about myself" but the next day after a rally said he left Louisville "not feeling too bad" (*The Presidential Diaries*, 271).

45. Brands, *Reagan*, 453–54.

46. "New Question in Race: Is the Oldest President Showing His Age?" *Wall Street Journal*, October 9, 1984.

47. Reagan, *The Presidential Diaries*, 277.

48. Hayward, *Age of Reagan: Conservative Counterrevolution*, 388.

49. Ibid., 383–84.

50. Brands, *Reagan*, 457–58.

51. Susan Jeffords, *Hard Bodies: Hollywood Masculinity in the Reagan Era* (New Brunswick: Rutgers University Press, 1994), 19.

52. Ibid., 20.

53. Robert Ajemian, "Where the Skies Are Not Cloudy . . ." *Time*, January 5, 1981 http://content.time.com/time/magazine/article/0,9171,922303,00.html.

54. John Mihalic, "Hair on the President's Chest," *Wall Street Journal*, May 11, 1984, 30; and Roger Rosenblatt, "Out of the Past, Fresh Choices for the Future," *Time*, January 5, 1981. http://content.time.com/time/magazine/article/0,9171,922299,00.html.

55. Jeffords, *Hard Bodies*, 29. Jeffords points out Reagan was the only president in American history who was hit by an assassin's bullet not only to survive, but to survive "in character."

56. Edmund Morris, *Dutch: A Memoir of Ronald Reagan* (New York: Modern Library, 1999), 507.

57. Ibid., 514.

CHAPTER 15

1. National Security Planning Group, NSPG 86-109, 5 December, 1984, Executive Secretariat, NSC: NSPG Meeting File, Box 3, Reagan Library (RL).

2. Robert M. Gates, *From the Shadows: The Ultimate Insider's Story of Five Presidents and How They Won the Cold War* (New York: Simon & Schuster, 2007), 328.

3. Nancy Reagan with William Novak, *My Turn: The Memoirs of Nancy Reagan* (New York: Random House, 1989), 230–35.

4. George P. Shultz, *Turmoil and Triumph: My Years as Secretary of State* (New York: Charles Scribner's Sons, 1993), 529.

5. Ibid., 500.

6. Ibid., 510.

7. NSPG 0143, 3 February, 1987, Executive Secretariat, NSC; National Security Planning Group Meeting File [Arms Control and SDI], RL.

8. NSDD 121, 14 January, 1984, National Security Decision Directives, Box 1, RL. Also see the NSDD for 6 February, 1985.

9. NSDD 172, "Presenting the Strategic Defense Initiative," 30 May, 1985, in NSDDs, 171–80, RL.

10. NSDD 172, RL.

11. Ibid.

12. Steven F. Hayward, *The Age of Reagan: Conservative Counterrevolution, 1984–1989* (New York: Three Rivers Press, 2009), 260.

13. H. W. Brands, *Reagan: The Life* (New York: Doubleday, 2015), 465.

14. Mikhail Gorbachev, *Perestroika* (New York: Harper & Row, 1987), 25.

15. Paul Kengor, *The Crusader: Ronald Reagan and the Fall of Communism* (New York: ReganBooks, 2006), 218.

16. James Graham Wilson, "Did Reagan Make Gorbachev Possible?" *Presidential Studies Quarterly* (September 2008): 456–75.

17. James West Davidson et al., *Nation of Nations: A Concise Narrative of the American Republic, Vol. II: Since 1865*, 3rd ed. (New York: McGraw-Hill, 2002), 952; and George Brown Tindall and David Emori Shi, *America: A Narrative History*, brief 6th ed. (New York: Norton, 2004), 1196.

18. David E. Harell, et al., *Unto a Good Land: A History of the American People* (Grand Rapids: William B. Eerdmans, 2005), 1142.

19. John L. Gaddis, *The United States and the End of the Cold War* (New York: Oxford University Press, 1992), 225.

20. Kenneth W. Thompson, ed. *Leadership in the Reagan Presidency, Pt. II: Eleven Intimate Perspectives* (London: UPA Press, 1993), 119; Stephen P. Ambrose, "How Great Was Ronald Reagan? A Symposium," *Policy Review*, Fall 1988, 30.

21. Kengor, *The Crusader*, 219.

22. Peter Schweizer, *Victory: The Reagan Administration's Secret Strategy That Hastened the Collapse of the Soviet Union* (New York: Atlantic Monthly Press, 1994), 198.

23. Ibid., 198.

24. James Graham Wilson, "Did Reagan Make Gorbachev Possible?" *Presidential Studies Quarterly* (September 2008): 456–75. Virtually all of Wilson's sources were from memoirs and documents published in the 1990s and long eclipsed by newer studies.

25. William E. Odom, *The Collapse of the Soviet Military* (New Haven: Yale University Press, 1998), 89; and Michael Ellman and Vladimir Kontorovich, *The Disintegration of the Soviet Economic System* (London: Routledge, 1992).

26. Odom, *Collapse of the Soviet Military*, 91.

27. Yegor Ligachev, *Inside Gorbachev's Kremlin* (New York: Pantheon, 1993), 329.

28. Odom, *Collapse of the Soviet Military*, 100.

29. George H. W. Bush and Brent Scowcroft, *A World Transformed* (New York: Knopf, 1998), 4.

30. Don Regan, *For the Record: From Wall Street to Washington* (New York: Harcourt Brace Jovanovich, 1988), 236–45.

31. Nancy Reagan, *My Turn*, 267.

32. Jane Mayer and Doyle McManus, *Landslide: The Unmaking of the President, 1984–1988* (Boston: Houghton Mifflin, 1988), 114.

33. Ibid., 55.

34. Ronald Reagan, remarks to broadcasters, April 18, 1985.

35. Elie Wiesel, comments at White House, April 19, 1985.

36. Brands, *Reagan*, 482–83.

37. Ronald Reagan remarks at Bergen-Belsen, May 5, 1985.

38. Ronald Reagan, *An American Life* (New York: Pocket Books,1990), 377.

39. Ibid., 378.

40. Nancy Reagan, *My Turn*, 63.

41. Regan, *For the Record*, 262–63; and Peter J. Wallison, *Ronald Reagan: The Power of Conviction and the Success of His Presidency* (Boulder: Westview, 2004), 71–2.

42. Ronald Reagan, remarks to regional editors, April 18, 1985, and interview by foreign radio and television reporters, April 29, 1985; and Dinesh D'Souza, *Ronald Reagan: How an Ordinary Man Became an Extraordinary Leader* (New York: Touchstone, 1997), 234.

43. D'Souza, *Ronald Reagan*, 235.

44. Tony Judt, *Postwar: A History of Europe Since 1945* (New York: Penguin, 2005), 417; and Larry Schweikart and Dave Dougherty, *A Patriot's History of the Modern World Vol. II: From the Cold War to the Age of Entitlement, 1945–2012* (New York: Sentinel, 2013), 215–16.

45. Hayward, *Age of Reagan: Conservative Counterrevolution*, 431.

46. Ronald Reagan, *The Reagan Diaries*, ed. Douglas Brinkley, single-volume ed. (New York: Harper Collins, 2007), 314; and Reagan report to Congress, 10 April, 1985, RL.

47. Mayer and McManus, *Landslide*, 80–81. According to critics such as Mayer and McManus, all of Reagan's trouble stemmed from a directionless campaign that ran on attitude, not issues. When McFarlane gave Reagan a thick binder with a number of issues to tackle in his second term—supposedly for him to select only a couple—Reagan typically wrote, "Let's do them all." But in fact, presidents can and often do take on many different initiatives at one time.

48. Ibid., 103.

49. Ibid., 106.

50. "Hostages: Father Jenco Release," 26 July, 1986 (a), North, Oliver Files, Box 11,

51. Reagan, *The Reagan Diaries*, 343.

52. NSDD 14, 26 November, 1983, National Security Decision Directives, Box 1, 11-20, RL.

53. Mayer and McManus, *Landslide*, 124.

54. John Tower, *The Tower Commission Report* (New York: Bantam, 1987), 26.

55. Reagan, *The Reagan Diaries*, 343.

56. Shultz, *Turmoil and* Triumph, 793–94; and *Report of the Congressional Committees Investigating the Iran-Contra Affair* (Washington, DC: Congressional Budget Office, 1988), 148; Caspar Weinberger, *Fighting for Peace* (New York: Time Warner, 1991), 363–64.

57. Ronald Reagan, remarks to the American Bar Association, July 8, 1985; and Michael Ledeen, *Perilous Statecraft* (New York: Scribners, 1988), 127.

58. Reagan, *The Reagan Diaries*, 348.

59. Hayward, *Age of Reagan: Conservative Counterrevolution*, 439.

60. *Report of the Congressional Committees Investigating the Iran-Contra Affair*, 171.

61. Mayer and McManus, *Landslide*, 125.

62. Hayward, *Age of Reagan: Conservative Counterrevolution*, 441–42.

63. Reagan, *The Reagan Diaries*, 374.

64. NSDD 159, 18 January, 1985, "Covert Action Policy Approval and Coordination Procedures," Box 1, Folder "NSDD 151-60," RL.

65. Reagan, *The Reagan Diaries*, 381.

66. Lou Cannon, *President Reagan: The Role of a Lifetime* (New York: Simon & Schuster, 1991), 636.

67. Ibid., 637.

68. Reagan, *The Reagan Diaries*, 384.

69. "USG" (United States Government): Finding Pursuant to Section 662 of the Foreign Assistance Act of 1961," January 17, 1986, National Security Archive, cited in Brands, *Reagan*, 553.

70. Reagan, *The Reagan Diaries*, 384.

71. This was another area in which Reagan differed greatly from Richard Nixon: Reagan fundamentally trusted people until they proved untrustworthy; Nixon distrusted them even after they showed loyalty.

CHAPTER 16

1. National Security Planning Group (NSPG) Meeting, 5 December, 1984, Executive Secretariat, NSPG, 86-109, Box 3, Reagan Library.
2. Ibid.
3. NSDD 138, 1 January, 1985, "Instructions for the Shultz-Gromyko Meeting in Geneva," National Security Decision Directives (NSDD), Box 1, Folder "NSDD 151-160," RL.
4. Ronald Reagan to Alan Brown, 22 January, 1985, in Martin Anderson, Annelise Anderson, and Kiron Skinner, eds., *Reagan: A Life in Letters* (New York: Free Press, 2003), 413.
5. Ronald Reagan, *The Reagan Diaries*, ed. Douglas Brinkley, single-volume ed. (New York: HarperCollins, 2007), 332.
6. Martin Anderson and Annelise Anderson, *Reagan's Secret Wars: The Untold Story of His Fight to Save the World from Nuclear Disaster* (New York: Crown, 2009), 207.
7. Ibid., 208.
8. Ibid., 209.
9. Mikhail Gorbachev to Ronald Reagan, 10 June, 1985, Executive Secretariat, NSC: Head of State File: Records, 1981–1989, USSR "General Secretary Gorbachev," Box 40, RL.
10. Mikhail Gorbachev to Ronald Reagan, 22 June, 1985, Executive Secretariat, NSC: Head of State File: Records, 1981–1989, USSR: "General Secretary Gorbachev," Box 40, RL.
11. Mikhail Gorbachev to Ronald Reagan, 12 September, 1985, Executive Secretariat, NSC: Head of State File: Records, 1981–1989, USSSR: "General Secretary Gorbachev (859009), Box 40, RL.
12. Minutes of National Security Council, 20 September, 1985, Executive Secretariat, NSC: NSC Meeting Files: Records, 1981–1989, Box 913 03, RL.
13. Reagan, *The Reagan Diaries*, 357–58.
14. Archie Brown, *Seven Years That Changed the World: Perestroika in Perspective* (Oxford: Oxford University Press, 2007), 60–61; and Steven F. Hayward, *The Age of Reagan: The Conservative Counterrevolution, 1981–1989* (New York: Three Rivers Press, 2009), 422.
15. Moshe Lewin, *The Gorbachev Phenomenon: A Historical Interpretation* (Berkeley: University of California Press, 1988), 120.
16. At one such meeting, the author was discussing a transition to a market economy with these top Soviet economists. "One approach," I said, "would be to have the government announce on Monday that it would establish a value—whatever it is—on a factory, then issue shares of ownership for that factory to every employee. They could do what they wanted with the shares." One economist with a puzzled look replied, "You don't understand. No one believes anything the government says."
17. Hayward, *Age of Reagan: Conservative Counterrevolution*, 424.

18. George Shultz, *Turmoil and Triumph: My Years as Secretary of State* (New York: Charles Scribner's Sons, 1993), 591.

19. Larry Schweikart and Dave Dougherty, *A Patriot's History of the Modern World Vol. II: From the Cold War to the Age of Entitlement: 1945–2012* (New York: Sentinel, 2013), 31.

20. H. W. Brands, *Reagan: The Life* (New York Doubleday, 2015), 503.

21. Anderson and Anderson, *Reagan's Secret Wars*, 223.

22. Ronald Reagan, *An American Life* (New York: Simon & Schuster, 1990), 637.

23. Robert Gates, *From the Shadows: The Ultimate Insider's Story of Five Presidents and How they Won the Cold War* (New York: Simon & Schuster, 1996), 342.

24. Hayward, *Age of Reagan: Conservative Counterrevolution*, 447.

25. NSDD 183, 8 August, 1985, "Meeting with Soviet Leader in Geneva (U)," National Security Decision Directives, Box 1, NSDDs 181–90, RL.

26. Hayward, *Age of Reagan: Conservative Counterrevolution*, 448.

27. Jack Matlock, *Reagan and Gorbachev: How the Cold War Ended* (New York: Random House, 2004), 150–54.

28. Hayward, *Age of Reagan: Conservative Counterrevolution*, 450.

29. Kenneth Adelman, Oral History, Miller Center, University of Virginia, https://miller-center.org/the-presidency/presidential-oral-histories/ronald-reagan.

30. Anderson and Anderson, *Reagan's Secret War*, chapter 15, contains extensive accounts of the discussions.

31. Reagan, *An American Life*, 640–41.

32. Mikhail Gorbachev, *Memoirs* (New York: Doubleday, 1996), 405–9.

33. Reagan, *The Reagan Diaries*, January 15, 1986, 383.

34. Ronald Reagan, "Explosion of the Space Shuttle *Challenger*," address to the nation, January 28, 1986, https://history.nasa.gov/reagan12886.html.

35. Peggy Noonan, *What I Saw at the Revolution* (New York: Random House, 1990), 254–55.

36. Schweikart, *The Hypersonic Revolution: Case Studies in the History of Hypersonic Technology Vol. III: The Quest for the Orbital Jet—The National Aero-Space Plane Program (1983–1995)* (Washington, DC: Air Force History and Museums Program, 1998), 13–33.

37. Memorandum from Robert K. Dawson to the Director, Office of Management and Budget, 7 October, 1987, in Crippen, Dan L. Files, Office of the Chief of Staff, Series 1: Subject File L (Legislative Strategy) - P (Polygraph), Box 2, Folder "NASA (National Aeronautics and Space Administration,)" RL.

38. Harrison H. Schmitt, "The Space Station Dilemma," Briefing for Howard Baker, Chief of Staff, 7 January, 1988, in Crippen Dan L. Files, Office of the Chief of Staff, Series 1: Subject File L (Legislative Strategy) - P (Polygraph), Box 8, Folder "NASA (National Aeronautics and Space Administration,)" RL.

39. Tariq Malik, "NASA Grieves Over Canceled Program," nbcnews.com, February 2, 2010, http://www.nbcnews.com/id/35209628/ns/technology_and_science-space/t/nasa-grieves-over-canceled-program/#.XB2phlxKjIU. What was missing from the discussion was SDI, where heavy lift was crucial and where the shuttles were incapable of providing the transport capability needed. (Indeed, the Strategic Defense Initiative Office had a partner role in the Aero-Space Plane.) Over time, the discussions of space

exploration often had to take lift requirements of SDI into consideration when examining policies.

40. Reagan, *The Reagan Diaries*, April 30, 1986, 408.

41. Gorbachev, *Memoirs*, 412.

42. NSC 00038, 21 January, 1982, Executive Secretary, NSC Meeting File [Libya], RL, citing a Reagan directive of 8 December, 1981.

43. Reagan, *The Reagan Diaries*, 22.

44. Joseph T. Stanik, *El Dorado Canyon: Reagan's Undeclared War with Qaddafi* (Annapolis: Naval Institute Press, 2003); and Robert E. Venkus, *Raid on Qaddafi* (New York: St. Martin's Press, 1992).

45. Reagan comments, August 20, 1981.

46. National Security Planning Group, 24 February, 1987, 1 of 2, Executive Secretariat, NSC: NSPG File [Terrorism], RL.

47. Memorandum of Conversation, "NSPG on Libya," 14 August, 1986, NSPG 0137, 2 of 2, Executive Secretariat, NSC: NSPG Meeting File [Libya], RL.

48. Memorandum to Thomas F. Gibson from Rodney B. McDaniel, "Chronology of Terrorist Attacks: U.S-Libyan Relations," 26 April, 1986, in Coy, Craig P. Files, RocBox 1, Box 1, Folder "Libya Strike Follow Up" (2 of 3), RL.

49. National Security Council Meeting on Nicaragua, 3 January, 1986, DRF/Contra-Military Activities (3 of 12), North, Oliver L. Files, Racbox 4, RL.

50. Minutes of National Security Planning Group meeting, 16 May, 1986.

51. Brands, *Reagan: The Life*, 558.

52. Daniel K. Inouye and Lee H. Hamilton, *Report of the Congressional Committees Investigating the Iran-Contra Affair, with Supplemental, Minority, and Additional Views* (Washington, DC: Government Printing Office, 1987), 199.

53. John Tower, *The Tower Commission Report* (New York: Bantam, 1987), 54–55.

54. Brands, *Reagan*, 559.

55. Craig L. Fuller to the President, "Report of the President's Task Force on Immigration and Refugee Policy/CM 62," in Anderson, Martin Files, Series 1: Subject File H Issues (2) - Immigration and Refugee Policy, Box 19, "Illegal Aliens" (1 of 2), RL.

56. Memorandum for the President from Craig L. Fuller, 1 July, 1981, in Anderson, Martin Files Series 1: Subject File H issue (2) - Immigration and Refugee Policy Box 19, "Illegal Aliens," (1 of 2), RL.

57. Memorandum from Kenneth Cribb to Edwin Meese, Martin Anderson, and Craig Fuller, "Immigration Policy," 27 July, 1981, in Anderson, Martin Files, Series 1: Subject File H Issues (2) - Immigration and Refugee Policy, Box 19, Folder "Illegal Aliens" (2 of 2), RL.

58. Ibid.

59. Memorandum to the President from Craig L. Fuller, July 1, 1981, in Anderson, Martin Files Series 1: Subject File H issue (2) - Immigration and Refugee Policy Box 19, "Illegal Aliens," (1 of 2), RL.

60. Memorandum from Richard Wirthlin to Edwin Meese, James Baker, and Michael Deaver, 28 May, 1981, RE: Immigrants, in Anderson, Martin Files Series 1: Subject File H issue (2) - Immigration and Refugee Policy Box 19, "Illegal Aliens," (1 of 2), RL.

61. *Los Angeles Times*, April 6, 1981.

62. Memorandum to the President from Craig L. Fuller, 1 July, 1981, in Anderson, Martin Files Series 1: Subject File H issue (2) - Immigration and Refugee Policy Box 19, "Illegal Aliens," (1 of 2), RL.

63. "Bad Advice on Immigration," *New York Times*, July 21, 1981, https://www.nytimes.com/1981/07/21/opinion/bad-advice-on-immigration.html.

64. "Card Tricks," *Washington Post*, July 21, 1981.

65. "Welfare System a Haven for Illegal Aliens," *Chicago Tribune*, April 12, 2017.

66. Frank Hodsoll to Martin Anderson and Michael Uhlmann, untitled draft revision of immigration and refugee paper, 9 July, 1981, in Anderson, Martin Files: Series 1.

67. Statement by the President, 30 July, 1981, in Anderson, Martin Files: Series 1, Subject File H Issues (2) - Immigration and Refugee Policy, Box 19, Folder "Illegal Aliens," (2 of 3), RL.

68. Confidential memorandum from the Ambassador in Mexico to the Secretary of State, 1 May, 1981 in Anderson, Martin Files: Series 1, Subject File H Issues (2) - Immigration and Refugee Policy, Box 19, Folder "Illegal Aliens," (2 of 4), RL.

69. NSC 0000135, 11 August, 1986, Executive Secretariat, NSC: NSC Meeting File [Visit of Mexican President De La Madrid], RL.

70. Ibid.

71. *Crain's Chicago Business*, October 27, 1986.

72. David Miller to the Attorney General, "Consultations Concerning the Immigration Task Force," in Anderson, Martin Files: Series 1, Subject File H Issues (2) - Immigration and Refugee Policy, Box 19, Folder "Immigrants - Illegal Aliens" 2 of 2, RL.

73. Lance Morrow, "Ronald Reagan: Yankee Doodle Magic," *Time*, July 7, 1986, http://content.time.com/time/magazine/article/0,9171,144460,00.html.

CHAPTER 17

1. Steven F. Hayward, *The Age of Reagan: The Conservative Counterrevolution* (New York: Three Rivers Press, 2009), 465.

2. Daniel Yergin, *The Prize: The Epic Quest for Oil, Money & Power* (New York: Simon & Schuster, 1991).

3. Ronald Reagan, address to the nation, May 28, 1985.

4. Hayward, *Age of Reagan: Conservative Counterrevolution*, 469.

5. Historian John Ehrman called it "one of the most disgraceful and irresponsible laws ever passed." See *The Eighties: America in the Age of Reagan* (New Haven: Yale University Press, 2005), 131.

6. Ronald Reagan, address to the nation, May 28, 1985.

7. Ronald Reagan comments at Williamsburg, May 30, 1985.

8. For a blow-by-blow account of the bill, see Jeffrey H. Birnbaum and Alan S. Murray, *Showdown at Gucci Gulf: Lawmakers, Lobbyists, and the Unlikely Triumph of Tax Reform* (New York: Vintage, 1988).

9. William A. Niskanen, *Reaganomics: An Insider's Account of the Policies and the People* (New York: Oxford, 1988), 96.

10. Hayward, *Age of Reagan: Conservative Counterrevolution*, 476.

11. Niskanen, *Reaganomics*, 100.

12. Ronald Reagan, address to the nation, May 28, 1985.

13. Hayward, *Age of Reagan: Conservative Counterrevolution*, 477.

14. Ronald Reagan remarks on signing tax reform, October 22, 1986.
15. Hayward, *Age of Reagan: Conservative Counterrevolution*, 477.
16. Ronald Reagan, *The Reagan Diaries*, ed. Douglas Brinkley, single-volume ed. (New York: HarperCollins, 2007), April 17, 1986, 406.
17. *Chicago Tribune*, June 23, 1986; and Albert Gore Jr., "Why Mr. Reagan Blundered on SALT," *New York Times*, June 1, 1986, https://www.nytimes.com/1986/06/01/opinion/why-mr-reagan-blundered-on-salt.html.
18. Larry Speakes with Robert Pack, *Speaking Out: Inside the Reagan White House* (New York: Charles Scribner's, 1988), 141–42, 244.
19. Paul Kengor, *The Crusader: Ronald Reagan and the Fall of Communism* (New York: ReganBooks, 2006), 260.
20. George Shultz, *Turmoil and Triumph: My Years as Secretary of State* (New York: Charles Scribner's Sons, 1993), 690.
21. Hayward, *Age of Reagan: Conservative Counterrevolution*, 488.
22. Mikhail Gorbachev, "Turning Point at Chernobyl," *Project Syndicate*, April 14, 2006, http://www.project-syndicate.org/commentary/gorbachev3/English.
23. Reagan, *The Reagan Diaries*, 435; and Ronald Reagan to Mikhail Gorbachev, 4 September, 1986, Reagan Library (RL).
24. Reagan, *The Reagan Diaries*, 435–36.
25. H. W. Brands, *Reagan: The Life* (New York Doubleday, 2015), 566.
26. Reagan, *The Reagan Diaries*.
27. Hayward, *Age of Reagan: Conservative Counterrevolution*, 492.
28. Notes on Politburo advisory group by Anatoly Chernyaev, September 22, October 4, and October 9, 1986, in National Security Archive, cited in Hayward, *Age of Reagan: Conservative Counterrevolution*, 695.
29. Hayward, *Age of Reagan: Conservative Counterrevolution*, 495; and Deborah Strober and Gerald Strober, *Reagan, the Man and His Presidency: The Oral History of an Era* (Boston: Houghton Mifflin, 1998), 347.
30. Ronald Reagan, address to the nation, July 12, 1986.
31. George P. Shultz, memorandum to the president, 2 October, 1986, https://nsarchive2.gwu.edu//dc.html?doc=3402665-Document-04-Shultz-memo-to-Reagan-Reykjavik.
32. Ibid.
33. Ibid.
34. Brands, *Reagan*, 570.
35. The American transcript of the summit is available online: Memorandum of Conversation, https://nsarchive2.gwu.edu//dc.html?doc=3131925-Document-29-The-White-House-Memorandum-of.
36. Hayward, *Age of Reagan: Conservative Counterrevolution*, 499.
37. Memorandum of Conversation, 11 October, 1986, https://nsarchive2.gwu.edu/NSAEBB/NSAEBB203/Document11.pdf.
38. Transcript of Gorbachev-Reagan Reykjavik Talks on October 12, 1986 (English translation), July 12, 1993, https://nsarchive2.gwu.edu/NSAEBB/NSAEBB203/Document12.pdf.
39. Ibid.
40. Ibid.
41. Hayward, *Age of Reagan: Conservative Counterrevolution*, 507.

42. Speakes and Pack, *Speaking Out*, 142; and Don Regan, *For the Record: From Wall Street to Washington* (New York: Harcourt Brace, 1988), 350–52.

43. Speakes and Pack, *Speaking Out*, 142–43.

44. Regan, *For the Record*, 350–53.

45. Ibid.

46. Ibid., 351.

47. Ronald Reagan, remarks at Keflavik, October 12, 1986.

48. Philip Taubman, "The Iceland Summit: 'A Difficult Dialogue'; Gorbachev Angrily Accuses Reagan of Scuttling an Accord at Reykjavik," *New York Times*, October 13, 1986, https://www.nytimes.com/1986/10/13/world/iceland-summit-difficult-dialogue-gorbachev-angrily-accuses-reagan-scuttling.html.

49. Margaret Thatcher, *The Downing Street Years* (New York: HarperCollins, 1993), 472.

50. Hayward, *Age of Reagan: Conservative Counterrevolution*, 509.

51. Ibid., 507.

52. Robert Gates, *From the Shadows: The Ultimate Insider's Story of Five Presidents and How they Won the Cold War* (New York: Simon & Schuster, 1996), 408.

53. Shultz, *Turmoil and Triumph*, 775.

54. Tony Judt, *Postwar: A History of Europe Since 1945* (New York: Penguin Books, 2005), 600–601; and Paul Johnson, *Modern Times: A History of the World from the Twenties to the Nineties*, rev. ed. (New York: HarperCollins, 1991), 748–49.

55. Strober and Strober, *Reagan, the Man and His Presidency*, 356.

56. Robert D. English, "The Road(s) Not Taken: Causality and Contingency in Analysis of the Cold War's End," in *Cold War Endgame*, ed. William C. Wohlforth, (University Park: Penn State University Press, 2003).

57. Raymond Garthoff, *The Great Transition* (Washington, DC: Brookings Institution Press, 1994), 289 n103; and William C. Wohlforth, ed., *Witnesses to the End of the Cold War* (Baltimore: Johns Hopkins University Press, 1996), 311 n2.

58. Hayward, *Age of Reagan: Conservative Counterrevolution*, 511–12.

CHAPTER 18

1. Ronald Reagan remarks to the press, November 7, 1986.

2. Don Regan, *For the Record* (New York: Harcourt, 1988), 27.

3. Ibid., 28.

4. Steven F. Hayward, *The Age of Reagan: The Conservative Counterrevolution* (New York: Three Rivers Press, 2009), 522.

5. Ibid., 525.

6. Peter J. Wallison, *Ronald Reagan: The Power of Conviction and the Success of His Presidency* (Boulder: Westview Press, 2004).

7. Regan, *For the Record*, 30.

8. Ronald Reagan, *The Reagan Diaries*, ed. Douglas Brinkley, single-volume ed. (New York: HarperCollins, 2007), November 10, 1986, 449.

9. Reagan, *The Reagan Diaries*, November 12, 1986, 450.

10. Wallison, *Ronald Reagan*, 181–82.

11. Ibid.

12. Ibid., 182.

13. Ronald Reagan, address to the nation, November 13, 1986.

14. Memorandum from Marvin L. Stone to John M. Poindexter, "President Reagan's Iran Policy Press Conference," 24 November, 1986, in Coy, Craig P. File, RacBox 1, Box 1 [Iran-Contra, Reactions to], RL.

15. See the summary of foreign press reactions in ibid.

16. Len Colodny and Robert Gettlin, *Silent Coup: The Removal of a President* (New York: St. Martin's Press, 1991).

17. Regan, *For the Record*, 35.

18. Ibid., 36.

19. Ronald Reagan, news conference, November 19, 1986.

20. H. W. Brands, *Reagan: The Life* (New York: Doubleday, 2015), 628–29.

21. Ibid., 630–31.

22. Wallison, *Ronald Reagan*, 195.

23. Reagan, *The Reagan Diaries*, November 21, 1986, 453.

24. Regan, *For the Record*, 37.

25. Ibid., 38.

26. Reagan, *The Reagan Diaries*, November 24, 1986, 453.

27. Robert McFarlane to Oliver North, 6 November, 1986, PROF Note, Culvahouse, Arthur B Files, "Iran/Arms Transaction = HEX Dump PROF Notes, Peter Wallison Files: PJW Classified Chrons, CFOA 1129)," RL.

28. Regan, *For the Record*, 38.

29. Regan, *For the Record*, 40.

30. Memorandum of Conversations, 10 December, 1988 (Regan, Baker, Wall[ison]), Culvahouse, Arthur B. Files, Iran/Arms Transition: Peter Wallison Files: PJW Classified Chrons, (CFOA 1127), RL.

31. Michael Kinsley, "The Case for Glee," *New Republic*, December 22, 1986; Greg Grandlin, "Still Dancing to Ollie's Tune," October 17, 2006,http://www.tomdispatch.com/blog/130406/; and Hayward, *Age of Reagan: Conservative Counterrevolution*, 532.

32. *Wall Street Journal*, November 13, 1986.

33. Regan, *For the Record*, 32. Don Regan, who had consistently urged Reagan to admit he made a mistake, stood faithfully by during the crisis and bore the brunt of press attacks. Peter Wallison, assistant to Regan and general counsel of the Treasury, made a spirited defense of his former boss, calling him probably "the most unfairly maligned person ever to hold the position" (Wallison, *Ronald Reagan*, 57–58).

34. Wallison, *Ronald Reagan*, 196.

35. Wallison claims that the discovery of North's activities was very nearly missed and was discovered only through a meeting he called on November 14 with all the counsels of all the agencies to "see if we could agree on a common set of legal theories" to support the administration's position. Arms shipments prior to August 1986 had to be reported to Congress if they exceeded a value of $14 million, and all shipments to "terrorist" states were prohibited unless Congress was notified in advance. The exception was the presidential "finding" prior to the shipment that had supposedly existed in January 1986, but none of those present had seen it. But even the finding had to be reported. But there was one shipment in September 1985, before a finding had been generated, and then Paul Thompson, the NSC's general counsel, noted that the first shipment was actually by Israel in August of 1985. So now there was no legal theory to support the first shipment.

In response to a series of demands from Reagan, Oliver North finally showed up with a single sheet of paper, a chronology of events from the initiative. "If Regan had not called for a review of the transcripts," Wallison wrote, "which brought North into the Roosevelt Room with a page from the chronology—neither Regan nor I would have known that a chronology existed." They did not know that Reagan had also received a copy of this false chronology. While counsels Chuck Cooper and Paul Thompson met with Wallison about the 1985 TOW missile sales to Iran, Abe Sofaer, the legal advisor for the State Department, called and asked about the Israeli shipment of Hawk missiles in November. Neither Cooper nor Thompson had been aware of the sale, and, upon further comparison of notes, they realized North had changed the date on his chronology and that Shultz and the president had been told of the Hawk shipment in November 1985. None of the dates seemed to jibe, and Cooper "probably reported this to Meese" and urged Meese to investigate. Wallison notes that had the meeting not been held at the time Sofaer called and asked about the Hawk sales, Poindexter likely would not have resigned and North would have continued his activities until he drew Reagan unwittingly into a full-blown Watergate-style scandal (Wallison, Ronald Reagan, 193–201).

36. Ronald Reagan, remarks to the press, November 25, 1986.
37. Edwin Meese, remarks to the press, November 25, 1986.
38. Nancy Reagan with William Novak, *My Turn: The Memoirs of Nancy Reagan* (New York: Random House, 1989), 274–75.
39. Reagan, *The Reagan Diaries*, December 17, 1986, 640.
40. Regan, *For the Record*, 57–59; and Brands, *Reagan*, 640.
41. Reagan, *The Reagan Diaries*, December 17, 1986, 640.
42. Brands, *Reagan: The Life*, 640–42; and Regan, *For the Record*, 69–71.
43. Wallison, *Ronald Reagan*, 158.
44. Regan, *For the Record*, 96–98.
45. Ibid., 97–98.
46. Ibid.
47. Brands, *Reagan*, 646.
48. John Tower, *The Tower Commission Report* (New York: Bantam Books, 1987), 29.
49. Reagan, *The Reagan Diaries*, August 11, 1985–September 1, 1985, 349–50.
50. Tower, *Tower Commission Report*, 81.
51. Reagan, *The Reagan Diaries*, February 26, 1987, 479; and Nancy Reagan, *My Turn*, 284.
52. Regan, *For the Record*, 373.
53. Ronald Reagan, address to the nation, March 4, 1987.
54. Ibid.
55. *Ronald Reagan: A Legacy Remembered*. Produced by the History Channel. United States, 2003. Documentary.
56. Hayward, *Age of Reagan: Conservative Counterrevolution*, 535.
57. Ibid., 543–45.
58. Reagan, *The Reagan Diaries*, July 10, 1987, 514.
59. Ibid., 516.
60. Hayward, *Age of Reagan: Conservative Counterrevolution*, 548.
61. *Senate Report of the Iran-Contra Investigative Report* (Washington, DC: Government Printing Office, 1987), 19.

CHAPTER 19

1. Ronald Reagan, *The Reagan Diaries*, ed. Douglas Brinkley, single-volume ed. (New York: HarperCollins, 2007), July 24, 1985, 345.
2. Ronald Reagan, remarks to employees of the Department of Health and Human Services, February 5, 1986.
3. Lou Cannon, *President Reagan: The Role of a Lifetime* (New York: Simon & Schuster, 1991), 814.
4. Ibid., 815. Despite Cannon's assertions, the scientific and medical facts of AIDS were still being learned in 1985–1987 and there were numerous scientists who even later still challenged the HIV explanation until further research was conducted. These would later be labeled "HIV/AIDS denialists" by the AIDS establishment (https://en.wikipedia.org/wiki/HIV/AIDS_denialism#The_HIV/AIDS_denialist_community).
5. Ronald Reagan remarks at the American Foundation for AIDS Research awards dinner, May 31, 1987.
6. Cannon, *President Reagan*, 819.
7. H. W. Brands, *Reagan: The Life* (New York: Doubleday, 2015), 661.
8. Ronald Reagan to Harold O. J. Brown, August 10, 1981, in *Reagan: A Life in Letters*, eds., Martin Anderson, Annelise Anderson, and Kiron Skinner (New York: Free Press, 2003), 552.
9. Ronald Reagan remarks on Robert Bork, July 1, 1987.
10. Steven F. Hayward, *The Age of Reagan: The Conservative Counterrevolution, 1980–1989* (New York: Three Rivers Press, 2009), 559.
11. Ibid., 560.
12. Donald Critchlow, *Phyllis Schlafley and Grassroots Conservatism: A Woman's Crusade* (Princeton: Princeton University Press, 2005).
13. See Richard Vigilante, "Who's Afraid of Robert Bork?" *National Review*, August 28, 1987, 25–30; Suzanne Garment, "The War Against Robert H. Bork," *Commentary* (January 1988): 17–26; and Ethan Bronner, *Battle for Justice: How the Bork Nomination Shook America* (New York: Union Square Press, 1989).
14. Hayward, *Age of Reagan: Conservative Counterrevolution*, 561.
15. Ibid., 563.
16. Reagan, *The Reagan Diaries*, July 1, 1987, 512.
17. "Second Thoughts on Bork," *National Review*, November 25, 1987.
18. Ronald Reagan to reporters, October 8, 1987.
19. Ronald Reagan remarks, October 29, 1987.
20. Annelena Lobb, "Looking Back at Black Monday: A Discussion with Richard Sylla," *Wall Street Journal*, October 15, 2007, https://www.wsj.com/articles/SB119212671947456234.
21. Mark Carlson, "A Brief History of the 1987 Stock Market Crash with a Discussion of the Federal Reserve Response," Federal Reserve Board, November 2006, 17.
22. Robert J. Shiller, "Investor Behavior in the October 1987 Stock Market Crash: Survey Evidence," National Bureau of Economic Research Working Paper No. 2446, November 1987, http://www.nber.org/papers/w2446.pdf.
23. Lobb, "Looking Back."
24. Hayward, *Age of Reagan: Conservative Counterrevolution*, 579. Someone should have told Galbraith that monetarism and supply-side were antithetical theories.

25. Ibid., 580.
26. Brands, *Reagan*, 265.
27. Dinesh D'Souza, *Ronald Reagan: How an Ordinary Man Became an Extraordinary Leader* (New York: Touchstone, 1997), 96–97.
28. Acting Secretary of Commerce to James C. Miller III, 15 April, 1988, in Crippen, Dan Files, Office of the Chief of Staff, Series 1; Subject File, Box 8, "Park Package(s)" (5), Reagan Library (RL).
29. Edwin Meese III, *With Reagan: The Inside Story* (Washington: Regnery, 1992), 74–5.
30. Edwin McDowell, "Reagan's Son Tells of Abuse as a Youth by a Man at Camp," *New York Times*, May 2, 1987, https://www.nytimes.com/1987/05/02/us/reagan-s-son-tells-of-abuse-as-a-youth-by-man-at-camp.html.
31. Michael Reagan, *Lessons My Father Taught Me* (West Palm Beach: Humanix Books, 2016), 160.
32. Scott Ross, "The Truth That Set Michael Reagan Free," Christian Broadcasting Network, n.d., http://www1.cbn.com/700club/truth-set-michael-reagan-free.
33. Michael Reagan, *Lessons My Father Taught Me*, 165.
34. Ronald Reagan, *An American Life* (New York: Pocket Books, 1990), 694–95.
35. Reagan, *The Reagan Diaries*, 543.
36. National Security Planning Group Meeting, NSPG 0165, 8 September, 1987, Executive Secretariat, NSC: Meeting File [Review of US Arms Control Positions], RL.
37. Ibid.
38. Ibid.
39. Ibid.
40. "Executive Order 12287 of January 28, 1981, Decontrol of Crude Oil and Refined Petroleum Products," https://www.presidency.ucsb.edu/documents/executive-order-12287-decontrol-crude-oil-and-refined-petroleum-products.
41. NSDD 87, "Comprehensive U.S. Energy Security Program (TS)," 30 March, 1983, National Security Decision Directives, Folder 81-90, RL, https://fas.org/irp/offdocs/nsdd/nsdd-87.pdf.
42. Daniel Yergin, *The Prize: The Epic Quest for Oil, Money & Power* (New York: Free Press, 2008), 696–736.
43. Ronald Reagan, handwritten note to Bud McFarlane, National Security Council, NSC 00097, 2 December, 1983 [Oil and Gas Export Controls, Libya, USSR], Executive Secretariat, NSC: Meeting File, Box 5, RL.
44. Peter Schweizer, *Victory* (New York: Atlantic Monthly Press, 1994), 255.
45. David C. Blee to the Deputy Secretary of Energy, 18 September, 1986, "Energy Security" (5), in Bledsoe, Ralph C. Files: Domestic Policy Council, Box 33, RL.
46. Nancy Risque to the President, 4 May, 1987, in Bledsoe, Ralph C. Files, 1986–1988, Domestic Policy Council, 310 "Emergency Management" (15), Energy Security, Box 33, RL.
47. Ibid.
48. Memorandum to the President from the Domestic Policy Council, "Energy Security," 27 April, 1987.
49. "Memo for the Economic Policy Council and the Domestic Policy Council RE: Energy Trends and National Security," 24 July, 1987, in Bledsoe, Ralph C. Files: Domestic Energy Policy, "Energy Security" (5), Box 33, RL.

50. See "U.S.-Canada Free Trade Agreement Energy Provisions: Negotiating History and Interpretive Notes," July 28, 1988, prepared by the U.S. negotiating team, document in author's possession. Special thanks to Frederick Cedoz.

51. NSPG 0168, 14 October, 1987, Executive Secretariat NSC: "NSPG Meeting File," [Shultz-Shevardnadze Meetings in Moscow], RL.

52. Ibid.

53. Ronald Reagan, address in Berlin, June 12, 1987.

54. Hayward, *Age of Reagan: Conservative Counterrevolution*, 593–94.

55. John F. Kennedy, "Ich bin ein Berliner"speech, June 26, 1961, http://www.let.rug.nl/usa/presidents/john-fitzgerald-kennedy/ich-bin-ein-berliner-speech-1963.php.

56. Mikhail Gorbachev, *Memoirs* (New York: Doubleday, 1996), 439.

57. Hayward, *Age of Reagan: Conservative Counterrevolution*, 594; and "U.S. Aide Urges E. Germany to Tear Down Berlin Wall," *Chicago Tribune*, October 13, 1988, 4.

58. William E. Odom, *The Collapse of the Soviet Military* (New Haven: Yale University Press, 1998), 132.

59. Ibid., 97.

60. NSPG 0165, RL.

61. Ibid., RL.

62. Gorbachev, *Memoirs*, 443–44.

63. Caspar Weinberger, *Fighting for Peace: Seven Critical Years in the Pentagon* (New York: Warner Books, 1990), 347.

64. George P. Shultz, *Turmoil and Triumph: My Years as Secretary of State* (New York: Charles Scribner's Sons, 1993), 1010.

65. US Department of State, "Treaty Between the United States of America and the Union of Soviet Socialist Republics on the Elimination of Their Intermediate-Range and Shorter-Range Missiles (INF Treaty)," December 8, 1987, https://www.state.gov/t/avc/trty/102360.htm.

66. Ronald Reagan remarks at the INF Treaty signing, December 8, 1987.

67. "Washington Summit Run-Up General Material," November 20, 1987, Racbox 20, Linhard, Robert Files, RL.

68. Haywood, *Age of Reagan: Conservative Counterrevolution*, 599.

69. Nancy Reagan with William Novak, *My Turn: The Memoirs of Nancy Reagan* (New York: Random House, 1987), 290.

70. Ibid., 293–94.

CHAPTER 20

1. Press conference by the president, May 17, 1988.

2. Nancy Reagan with William Novak, *My Turn: The Memoirs of Nancy Reagan* (New York: Random House, 1989), 38.

3. Lou Cannon, *Governor Reagan* (New York: Public Affairs, 2003), 172; and Ronald Reagan with Richard C. Hubler, *Where's the Rest of Me?* (New York: Dell, 1965), 283.

4. Steven F. Hayward, *The Age of Reagan: The Fall of the Old Liberal Order, 1964–1980* (New York: Three Rivers Press, 2001). Likewise, Craig Shirley, in *Reagan Rising: The Decisive Years, 1976–1980* (New York: Broadside Books, 2017), dedicates no serious discussion to the issue.

5. Paul Kengor, *God and Ronald Reagan* (New York: ReganBooks, 2004), 188.

6. Nancy Reagan, *My Turn*, 38.

7. Ibid.

8. Don Regan, *For the Record* (San Diego: Harcourt Brace Jovanovich, 1988), 3–4, 188.

9. Cannon, *President Reagan: The Role of a Lifetime* (New York: 1991), 585.

10. Ibid., 586.

11. H. W. Brands, *Reagan: The Life* (New York: Doubleday, 2015), 691.

12. Ronald Reagan remarks to the press, May 9, 1988 and May 17, 1988.

13. Pat Boone to Ronald Reagan, 4 June, 1988, in Bell, Marian Files, OA 17951, Box 1, Folder "Astrology" [Office of Public Liaison], Reagan Library (RL).

14. George Otis to Ronald Reagan, 5 May, 1927, in Bell, Marian Files, OA 17951, Box 1, Folder "Astrology" [Office of Public Liaison], RL; and Russell Chandler, "Petitions from Conservative Christians Urge the Reagans to Reject Astrology," *Los Angeles Times*, June 21, 1988, http://articles.latimes.com/1988-06-21/news/mn-4661_1_white-house.

15. "Reagans' Stargazing Concerns the Christian Right," *Atlanta Constitution*, May 5, 1988.

16. "Of Planets and the Presidency," *Newsweek*, May 16, 1988.

17. *Ronald Reagan: A Legacy Remembered.* Produced by the History Channel. United States, 2003. Documentary.

18. Ronald Reagan, *An American Life* (New York: Pocketbooks, 1990), 263.

19. Hayward, *The Age of Reagan: The Conservative Counterrevolution, 1980–1989* (New York: Three Rivers Press, 2009), 604. As Hayward notes, Reagan's frequent jokes and jibes at Gorbachev got to him, and he once told Reagan's aide to have the speechwriters stop putting them in. Hayward points out that as late as 1988, minutes of the Politburo contain references to Reagan's "Evil Empire" phrase, revealing that it gnawed at them.

20. George P. Shultz, *Turmoil and Triumph: My Years as Secretary of State* (New York: Charles Scribner's Sons, 1993), 1011.

21. Memorandum, National Security Council, 11 March, 1988, http://www.gwu.edu/~nsarchiv/NSAEBB/NSAEBB251/4.pdf.

22. Hayward, *Age of Reagan: Conservative Counterrevolution*, 605.

23. Shultz, *Turmoil and Triumph*, 1001.

24. Ibid., 1097.

25. Ibid., 1084.

26. National Security Planning Group Meeting, March 1988, NSPG 889014 [NSPG0176-"US Options for Arms Control Summit], Assistant to the President for National Security Affairs: Chron File, RL.

27. See Peter Schweizer's film *In the Face of Evil: Reagan's War in Word and Deed*, 2004.

28. Igor Korchilov, *Translating History: Thirty Years on the Front Lines of Diplomacy with a Top Russian Interpreter* (New York: Scribner, 1997), 155.

29. Memorandum of Conversation, 29 May, 1988, in 1988 U.S. Soviet Summit Memos May 26, 1988–June 3, 1988, (2), Racbox 9, Ledsky, Nelson C. Files, RL.

30. Ronald Reagan, remarks to Soviet dissidents at Spaso House, May 30, 1988.

31. Kengor, *God and Ronald Reagan*, 306.

32. Ronald Reagan speech at Moscow State University, May 31, 1988, http://www.digital-history.uh.edu/disp_textbook.cfm?smtID=3&psid=1234.

33. Brands, *Reagan*, 696.

34. Ronald Reagan, toasts at a state dinner, May 31, 1988.

35. Kengor, *God and Ronald Reagan*, 310.

36. It is worth noting that since the fall of communism, Russia has returned to its Christian roots and in many ways is, along with Poland, possibly the most Christian nation in Europe as measured by self-identification or attendance at religious services.

37. Hayward, *Age of Reagan: Conservative Counterrevolution*, 608.

38. Ibid., 611.

39. Ronald Reagan, address to the delegates of the Republican Convention, August 15, 1988.

40. Hayward, *Age of Reagan: Conservative Counterrevolution*, 615.

41. Bush latched onto issues such as the furlough and his opposition to having students recite the Pledge of Allegiance as indicators of his opponent's detachment from the values of ordinary Americans. Bill Clinton tried to educate him on how he was losing Middle America, but Dukakis only asked, "What does [the Pledge] have to do with being president?" Haywood, *Age of Reagan: Conservative Counterrevolution*, 619.

42. Kengor, *The Crusader: Ronald Reagan and the Fall of Communism* (New York: ReganBooks, 2006), 293.

43. Ronald Reagan, farewell address, January 11, 1989.

44. Ronald Reagan, *The Reagan Diaries*, ed. Douglas Brinkley, single-volume ed. (New York: Harper Collins, 2007), January 17, 1989, 691.

45. Craig Shirley, *Last Act: The Final Years and Emerging Legacy of Ronald Reagan* (New York: Nelson Books, 2015), 14.

CHAPTER 21

1. Craig Shirley, *Last Act: The Final Years and Emerging Legacy of Ronald Reagan* (New York: Nelson Books, 2015), 24.

2. Ibid., 34.

3. Ronald Reagan, remarks to administration officials on domestic policy, December 13, 1988.

4. Shirley, *Last Act*, 35.

5. Laurie Becklund, "Reagan's Fee Per Speech: A Cool $50,000, *Los Angeles Times*, January 28, 1989, http://articles.latimes.com/1989-01-28/local/me-1183_1_nancy-reagan. "One Has to 'Make a Living,' Bush Says of Big Reagan Fee," *Los Angeles Times*, November 8, 1989, http://articles.latimes.com/1989-11-08/news/mn-944_1_president-reagan.

6. Ronald Reagan, *The Reagan Diaries*, Douglas Brinkley, ed., single-volume ed. (New York: HarperCollins, 2007), 671.

7. Lee May, "North Trial Judge Refuses to Compel Reagan to Testify," *Los Angeles Times*, April 1, 1989, articles.latimes.com/1989-04-01/news/mn-786_1_president-reagan.

8. Robert Pear, "Reagan Is Injured in Fall Off Horse," *New York Times*, July 5, 1989, https://www.nytimes.com/1989/07/05/us/reagan-is-injured-in-fall-off-horse.html.

9. Nancy Reagan, *I Love You, Ronnie: The Letters of Ronald Reagan to Nancy Reagan* (New York: Random House, 2000), 180.

10. *New York Times*, September 18, 1990.

11. Ibid.

12. Ronald Reagan, address to the Republican Convention, August 18, 1992.

13. H. W. Brands, *Reagan: The Life* (New York: Doubleday, 2015), 723–25.

14. Lawrence Walsh, *Final Report of the Independent Counsel for Iran/Contra Matters* (Washington, DC: United States Court of Appeals, 1993); and "More on Iran-Contra," *New York Times*, January 19, 1994.

15. The Associated Press, "Reagan Criticizes Plan to Kill 'Star Wars,'" *New York Times*, May 16, 1993, https://www.nytimes.com/1993/05/16/us/reagan-criticizes-plan-to-kill-star-wars.html.

16. Shirley, *Last Act*, 49.

17. Bill O'Reilly and Martin Dugard, *Killing Reagan: The Violent Assault That Changed a Presidency* (New York: Henry Holt, 2015), 8. Of course, as part of their mantra, O'Reilly and Dugard had Reagan suffering from the defects of age and memory loss from the moment he got into office, repeatedly mentioning that he began to fade in the evening or wasn't as sharp after lunch. Yet as noted in an earlier chapter, Bill Verity, six years Reagan's junior, was stunned when he came to the Commerce Department at how full of energy Reagan was, to the point Verity asked him what his energy secret was, and Reagan had replied "bee pollen." Consider the absence of mainstream news comment when Barack Obama referred to the United States as having "fifty-seven states," or when he pronounced "corpsman" as "corpse-man"—or when President Bill Clinton, referring to the "candy bombers" of the Berlin airlift, called General Gail Halvorsen (a man) a woman pioneer in the U.S. Air Force. Such faux pas are committed all the time in office, by everyone, but only with Reagan was it automatically and retroactively associated with memory loss or Alzheimer's.

18. Ibid., 50.

19. Lawrence K. Altman, "The 40th President: The Doctor; A Warm Smile, a Vacant Stare, and One Last House Call," *New York Times*, June 8, 2004, https://www.nytimes.com/2004/06/08/us/40th-president-doctor-warm-smile-vacant-stare-one-last-house-call.html.

20. Shirley, *Last Act*, 143.

21. John R. Barletta and Rochelle Schweizer, *Riding with Reagan: From the White House to the Ranch* (New York: Kensington Press, 2005), 68.

22. Ibid., 213.

23. Memorandum by Marilyn Fisher, "Karl Mull's Diaries," September 26, 2014, Reagan Ranch Center, Santa Barbara, California.

24. Barletta, *Riding with Reagan*, 215.

25. Brands, *Reagan*, 114.

26. Shirley, *Last Act*, 77.

27. Ibid., 78–79.

28. Patti Davis, *The Long Goodbye* (New York: Knopf, 2011), 191–3.

29. Shirley, *Last Act*, 112.

30. Ibid.,186.

31. Ibid., 239.

32. Ibid., 247.

33. Margaret Thatcher, "Eulogy for President Reagan," Margaret Thatcher Foundation, June 11, 2004, https://www.margaretthatcher.org/document/110360.

34. George W. Bush, "President Bush Eulogizes Ronald Reagan," *Washington Post*, June 11, 2004.

35. Shirley, *Last Act*, 276–77.

36. Patti Davis, "The Gemstones of Our Years," *Newsweek*, June 14, 2004.
37. Shirley, *Last Act*, 271.
38. Michael Reagan, *Lessons My Father Taught Me* (West Palm Beach: Humanix Books, 2016), 191–92.

APPENDIX
1. Lou Cannon, *President Reagan: The Role of a Lifetime* (New York: Simon & Schuster, 1991), 837.
2. Joel Pollak and Larry Schweikart, *How Trump Won: The Inside Story of a Revolution* (Washington, DC: Regnery, 2017).